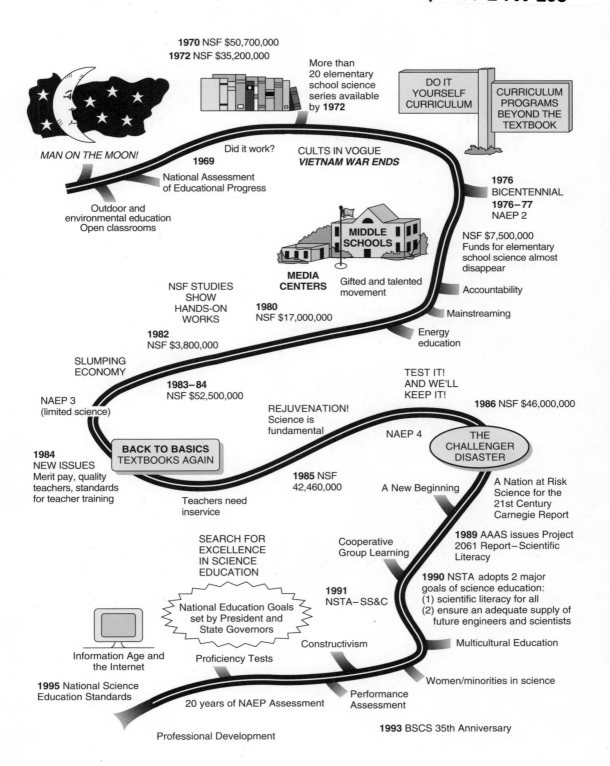

1970 NSF $50,700,000
1972 NSF $35,200,000

More than 20 elementary school science series available by 1972

DO IT YOURSELF CURRICULUM

CURRICULUM PROGRAMS BEYOND THE TEXTBOOK

MAN ON THE MOON!

Did it work?
1969
National Assessment of Educational Progress

CULTS IN VOGUE
VIETNAM WAR ENDS

1976
BICENTENNIAL
1976–77
NAEP 2

Outdoor and environmental education
Open classrooms

MIDDLE SCHOOLS

NSF $7,500,000
Funds for elementary school science almost disappear

MEDIA CENTERS

Gifted and talented movement

Accountability

NSF STUDIES SHOW HANDS-ON WORKS

1980
NSF $17,000,000

Mainstreaming

1982
NSF $3,800,000

Energy education

SLUMPING ECONOMY

1983–84
NSF $52,500,000

TEST IT! AND WE'LL KEEP IT!

NAEP 3 (limited science)

REJUVENATION!
Science is fundamental

1986 NSF $46,000,000

NAEP 4

THE CHALLENGER DISASTER

1984
NEW ISSUES
Merit pay, quality teachers, standards for teacher training

BACK TO BASICS
TEXTBOOKS AGAIN

1985 NSF 42,460,000

A New Beginning

A Nation at Risk
Science for the 21st Century
Carnegie Report

Teachers need inservice

1989 AAAS issues Project 2061 Report – Scientific Literacy

SEARCH FOR EXCELLENCE IN SCIENCE EDUCATION

Cooperative Group Learning

1990 NSTA adopts 2 major goals of science education:
(1) scientific literacy for all
(2) ensure an adequate supply of future engineers and scientists

National Education Goals set by President and State Governors

1991
NSTA – SS&C

Constructivism

Multicultural Education

Information Age and the Internet

Proficiency Tests

1995 National Science Education Standards

20 years of NAEP Assessment

Performance Assessment

Women/minorities in science

Professional Development

1993 BSCS 35th Anniversary

EIGHTH EDITION

Teaching Science Through Discovery

Arthur A. Carin

Professor Emeritus
Queens College

Merrill,
an imprint of Prentice Hall
Upper Saddle River, New Jersey   Columbus, Ohio

Library of Congress Cataloging-in-Publication Data

Carin, Arthur A.
  Teaching science through discovery/Arthur A. Cariin.—8th ed.
    p.   cm.
  Includes bibliiographical references and index.
  ISBN 0-13-234089-5
  1. Science—Study and teaching (Elementary)
  I. Title.
LB1585.C28
372.3'5044—dc20   96-27830
                                                CIP

Printed in the United States of America

10 9 8 7 6 5 4 3 2 1

ISBN: 0-13-234089-5

Prentice-Hall International (UK) Limited, *London*
Prentice-Hall of Australia Pty. Limited, *Sydney*
Prentice-Hall of Canada, Inc., *Toronto*
Prentice-Hall Hispanoamericana, S. A., *Mexico*
Prentice-Hall of India Private Limited, *New Delhi*
Prentice-Hall of Japan, Inc., *Tokyo*
Simon & Schuster Asia Pte. Ltd., *Singapore*
Editora Prentice-Hall do Brasil, Ltda., *Rio de Janeiro*

Editor: Bradley J. Potthoff
Developmental Editor: Linda Ashe Montgomery
Production Editor: Mary Harlan
Design Coordinator: Jill E. Bonar
Text Designer: Linda M. Robertson
Photo Researchers: Anthony Magnacca, Angela Jenkins
Cover photo: D. Young-Wolff MR/Photo Edit
Cover Designer: Proof Positive/Farrowlyne Assoc., Inc.
Production Manager: Deidra M. Schwartz
Illustrations: Rolin Graphics

This book was set in Galliard by Carlisle Communications, Ltd., and was printed and bound by R. R.
Donnelley & Sons Company. The cover was printed
by Phoenix Color Corp.

Photo credits: All photos copyrighted by the individuals or companies listed. Arthur A. Carin, pp. 79,
301; Scott Cunningham/Merrill/Prentice Hall, p. 55;
Larry Hamill Stock Photography, p. 19; Anne
Vega/Merrill/Prentice Hall, p. 204. All other photos
not listed above are © Anthony Magnacca/Merrill/
Prentice Hall.

PREFACE

The eighth edition of *Teaching Science Through Discovery* has been extensively revised not only to inform the reader of sweeping reforms in science education but also to provide some perspective and strategies to initiate these reforms in science classrooms. These strategies are interwoven into the text to introduce novice teachers to the specialized content and practical methodologies that better facilitate science teaching and learning in today's classrooms. At the same time, experienced teachers will recognize an increased emphasis on providing a learning environment that allows students to construct their own science concepts and develop critical thinking processes. Both pre-service and in-service teachers will find valuable the increased coverage on assessment and its place as a tool for planning for learning as well as evaluation.

Although several approaches to teaching and learning science and technology are described in this book, a greater emphasis is placed on a hands-on/minds-on, activity-based approach called *guided discovery teaching and learning*. Practical, classroom-tested activities and ideas are presented on planning, organizing, managing, and assessing an effective guided discovery science program for preschool, elementary, and middle or junior high classrooms. Included are step-by-step guidelines for creating dynamic science lessons and hands-on/minds-on experiences essential for cognitive growth.

New to the Eighth Edition

Charting a New Course opens each chapter. These features introduce teachers to concerns which the National Science Foundation recog-

nizes as areas in science classrooms where teachers can make a difference. They describe classroom events or opportunities that illustrate how effective teaching can help assure that all students become more scientifically and technologically literate. These features include:

- recognizing student misconceptions, and planning for hands-on/minds-on activities that address them
- encouraging more female students to recognize and develop their talents and abilities in scientific endeavors
- using authentic assessment opportunities including performance assessment activities
- using resources that promote the use of technology in the classroom to enhance science learning; some simulate science experiences that are not possible within science classrooms
- adapting instruction to meet the needs of exceptional students in the regular classroom
- finding ways to integrate curricula to make experiences relevant for children and enmeshing for them conceptual connections from one content discipline to another.

Included in the chapters are practical applications and strategies to meet the needs described in the *Charting a New Course* features.

- A thorough explanation of the differences between direct instruction, guided discovery, and constructivist teaching methodologies is included as well as a discussion on considerations for balancing the use of them.
- The Assessment chapter has been moved closer to the interior of the text to provide a

better integration with the planning of guided discovery and constructivist teaching lessons and an emphasis for ongoing assessment. The value and need for using a number of evaluation tools, and rubrics for scoring them, are included in this chapter.

■ Activities have been integrated within chapters so readers who take time to perform them can concretely sense how certain science concepts can be developed.

■ An emphasis is placed on the need for teachers to provide opportunities for learners to perform open-ended science activities, which are less structured activities that stress exploration rather than verification.

Companion textbooks include:

■ *Teaching Modern Science,* seventh edition, a paperback version of Part I of this text, and

■ *Guided Discovery Activities for Elementary School Science,* fourth edition, a paperback version of Part II of this text.

FROM THE AUTHOR

I am certain you will find this text a valuable resource as you become an even more competent, confident decision-maker. I strongly encourage you to adapt these strategies and apply these concepts in ways that are meaningful to both you and your students. It is my hope that it will empower you to feel confident to teach science to your students in your unique classroom situation. I wish you much success as you experience the joy of seeing your students construct and broaden their science knowledge and grow in their appreciation of this marvelous world.

While permission is granted to reproduce any part of the guided discovery activities that your students can use directly in the classroom, activities may not be further distributed or sold without written authorization from the author and the publisher.

ACKNOWLEDGMENTS

I wish to personally thank *all* of the personnel at Prentice Hall who worked together to bring this book to you, but especially the following: Jeffrey Johnston, Vice-President and Publisher of Merrill Education, and Brad Potthoff, Editor of Curriculum and Instruction, who each provided administrative and editorial guidance; Mary Harlan, who as Senior Production Editor used her expert experience in logistics and textbook "sense" to coordinate the work of my capable copyeditors, the artistic staff, the printers, and others who worked to produce this book; my copyeditors, Peg Gluntz (Part I) and Susan Snyder (Part II) who knitted together numerous details providing excellent suggestions that increased the readability of the text; and Anthony Magnacca who served as my photographer/photo researcher and took my word descriptions and converted them into choice visuals.

Linda Montgomery, my Developmental Editor, merits particular recognition. For over a year, Linda worked closely with me to organize, research, write, evaluate, and rewrite materials. She was there by voice-mail, e-mail, and snail-mail almost daily with ideas, encouragement, and professional guidance. Her wit, professional competence, uncanny experienced educational intuition, and keen sense of humor were greatly appreciated.

Many colleagues and other science educators magnanimously contributed ideas, data, materials, and time, but I am especially grateful to Richard W. Barnes, Bountiful, Utah; Rodger W. Bybee, Director, National Research Council; Marilyn Burns, Accept Education Collaborative, Memorial School, Medfield, MA; Kimi Dodds, teacher/educator at Blendon Junior High School, Westerville, OH; and Phyllis Marcuccio, Associate Executive Director of Publications of the National Science Teachers Association.

These reviewers supplied valuable contributions and insights and sincerely deserve special thanks: Joel E. Bass, Sam Houston State University; Carol Brewer, The University of Montana; Rosemarie Kolstad, East Texas State University; Richard H. Moyer, The University of Michigan–Dearborn; William A. Rieck, The University of Southwestern Louisiana; Leone E. Snyder, Northwestern College.

The encouragement I continually received from my wife and family urged me on to bring the latest science education innovations to teachers to stimulate and motivate their students. This was forcefully reinforced for me when my seven-year-old grandson, Andy, said, "I hope my teacher gets a copy of your book so we can do these fun science things." I want all of the Andys out there to enjoy the wonders that science can offer in their elementary/middle school classrooms. Hopefully this book will assist teachers to accomplish that.

CONTENTS

TEACHING MODERN SCIENCE   1

CHAPTER 1

Building a Foundation for Scientific
and Technological Literacy   2

Charting a New Course: Tapping Into New Resources   3
How Do You Define Science and Technology?   4
What Are Scientifically and Technologically Literate Citizens?   5
Science and Sciencing   5
Scientific Attitudes and Processes   6
What Kinds of Attitudes and Values Contribute to Good Sciencing?   14
Scientific Products   17
Investigating Phenomena Requires Asking Questions   19
Aspirations for Elementary/Middle Grade Sciencing   21
Common Components of National/State/Local Projects   21
Organizing Sciencing Goals Into Five Domains   24
Sciencing With an Emphasis on STS   24

ACTIVITY
Why Does Water Roll off
Some Things? A–19

ACTIVITY
What Is a Magnet? A–68

ACTIVITY
How Are Clouds and Fog
Formed? A–161

CHAPTER 2

Intellectual Development and Science Learning   36

Charting a New Course: Addressing Students' Misconceptions   37
The Impact of Piaget on Science Teaching/Learning   38
Behaviorists and Cognitivists: How Do They Define Learning?   39
The Importance of Prior Knowledge   41
Naive Theories and Misconceptions Affect Teaching/Learning   44
Physical, Logical-Mathematical, and Social Arbitrary Knowledge   46
Developmentally Appropriate Science Activities   49
Gagné's Learning Hierarchy   50
Practical Classroom Applications of Cognitive Research   50

ACTIVITY
How Can You Make Electricity
by Using Magnetism? A–78

ACTIVITY
What Is a Lever and How Can
You Use It? A–64

CHAPTER 3

The Teacher as Facilitator for Science Learning   60

Charting a New Course: Why More Girls Don't Do Science   61
No Best Method to Guide Learning in All Situations!   62
Direct, Explicit, or Exposition Instruction   63
Indirect Instruction and Guided Discovery Teaching   70
Guided Discovery Hands-On/Minds-On Teaching
    and Learning Methods   74

ACTIVITY
How Does the Rate of
Evaporation Affect Crystal
Size Formation? A–188

ACTIVITY
How Can Shadows Help You Tell Time? A–154

Applying Guided Discovery to Your Teaching   80
The Importance of Hands-On/Minds-On Activities in Guided Discovery   83

CHAPTER 4

Mastering the Art of Questioning and Listening   94

ACTIVITY
How Can We Find Air Pollutants in Our Environments? A–205

ACTIVITY
How Can You Make a Shadow Theater? A–85

Charting a New Course: Questions That Make a Difference   95
What Are the Purposes of Q/L Strategies?   97
Developing Problem-Solving Skills Using Q/L Strategies   104
Improving Your Guided Discovery Q/L Skills   107
Practical Classroom Q/L Applications   110
This Is Day #1 for Your Q/L Self-Improvement   114

CHAPTER 5

Assessing Science Teaching and Learning   120

ACTIVITY
What Do You Know About the Birds Around You? A–113

ACTIVITY
How Are Rocks Alike and Different and How Do We Use Rocks? A–178

Charting a New Course: Authentic Learning/Authentic Assessment   121
Assessment: A Continuous Teaching/Learning Process   122
Using Authentic Assessment in Your Science Teaching/Learning   127
Authentic Assessment: The Invitation   129
Authentic Assessment: The Exploration   133
Authentic Assessment: Discovery/Interpretation   141
Authentic Assessment: Explanations/Solutions   145
Authentic Assessment: Taking Action   148
Authentic Assessment: All Stages   150
Authentic Assessment: Applications   161

CHAPTER 6

Planning for a Supportive Science Classroom   168

ACTIVITY
What Are Plant Growth Stages and Parts? A–97

ACTIVITY
Where Did the Water Go? A–17

ACTIVITY
How Do Seed Pods Vary? A–94

Charting a New Course: Providing Different Kinds of Support   169
Constructivist Levels of Planning   170
Preparing and Using Guided Discovery Lessons   180
Less-Structured Guided Discovery Activities   184
Start Teaching Your Science Lesson Plans!   187
Organize Your Classroom Environment for Maximum Science Learning   187
Classroom Management in Guided Discovery Science   194
Classroom Applications of Management Techniques   197

CHAPTER 7

Selecting and Using Science Reform Projects, Programs, and Textbooks   204

ACTIVITY
How Does Your Body Cool Itself? A–120

Charting a New Course: A Clearinghouse of Resources   205
A Map of Science Reforms   207
Trends in Contemporary Science Reform Projects   207
Science Reform Project—Developed Commercial Program   209

ACTIVITY
What Is Thermal Energy or
Heat? A–28

Sample Lesson From Science for Life and Living: Integrating Science,
Technology, and Health   215
The Benefits of Reform Projects/Programs   218
"New Generation" Science Textbook Series/Packages   221
Applications of Science Reform Projects/Programs/Textbook Series to
Your Science Classroom   228

CHAPTER 8

ACTIVITY
What Is Air Pollution? A–203

ACTIVITY
What Makes You Breathe
Faster? A–125

ACTIVITY
What Makes a Drum Louder?
A–46

Integrating Science With the Whole Curriculum   234

Charting a New Course: Start With a Story   235
Integration of Science and Other Curricular Subjects
Around STS Themes   236
How Are Hands-On/Minds-On Science and Language
Learning Similar?   238
Science and Reading: A Natural Combination   242
Effective Use of Textbooks in Hands-On/Minds-On Science   245
Effective Use of Non-Textbook Science Printed Matter   248
Science and Social Studies   254
Integrating Science and Art   257
Integrating Science and Physical Activities   258
Integrating Science and Music   259
Integrating Science, Health, Physiology, and Nutrition   260
Integrating Science and Mathematics   261

CHAPTER 9

ACTIVITY
Learning About Magnets
A–213

ACTIVITY
Using Plants to Teach Visual
Sequencing A–221

Extending and Enriching Science Experiences for *All* Students   272

Charting a New Course: Creating Inclusive Environments   273
Extending and Enriching All Students' Science Learning   274
Special Needs Students Benefit From Hands-On/Minds-On Science   284
Science for Students With Specific Exceptionalities   287
Science for Students From Culturally Diverse Backgrounds   307

CHAPTER 10

ACTIVITY
How Can Solar Energy Be
Used? A–164

ACTIVITY
What Is the Greenhouse
Effect? A–161

Using Multimedia Technology Effectively   314

Charting a New Course: Making the Most of Multimedia   315
Multimedia Technology   316
How Can Multimedia Computers Enrich Science Teaching/
Learning?   318
What's the Latest Multimedia Technology for my Science Classroom?   326
Applications of Multimedia Technology to Your Classroom   335

GUIDED DISCOVERY ACTIVITIES   A–1

Using Guided Discovery Activities   A–3

Using Direct and Indirect Teaching in the Activities   A–4
Planning and Organizing Activities   A–5

Cooperative Learning: Vital to Guided Discovery Activities   A–6
Activity Preparation and Safety   A–10
Conducting Activities and Guiding Students   A–10
How Activities Are Organized   A–12
Guided Discovery Hands-On/Minds-On Activities Format   A–13
Format of the Less-Structured Guided Discovery Activities   A–16

SECTION 1   Physical Sciences and Technology   A–17

Matter and Energy   A–17
    Where Did the Water Go?   A–17
    How Can We Dry Clothes Faster?   A–18
    Why Does Water Roll Off Some Things?   A–19
    Why Does Water Appear to Disappear?   A–20
    What Are Water Molecules, and How Do They Affect
        Each Other?   A–22
Thermal Energy (Heat)   A–26
    What Makes Things Get Hotter?   A–26
    What Is Thermal Energy or Heat?   A–28
    How Is Heat Transmitted by Radiation, Convection,
        and Conduction?   A–31
    What Effect Does Heat Have on the States of Matter?   A–35
Air Pressure   A–36
    What Makes Balloons Grow Bigger and Move Farther?   A–36
    What's in Your Baggies? How Do You Know?   A–37
    How Can You Make a Kite and Get It to Fly?   A–38
    What Is Air?   A–39
    How Do the Effects of Moving Air Differ From the Effects
        of Nonmoving Air?   A–41
Sound Energy   A–46
    What Makes a Drum Louder?   A–46
    How Can You Make Sounds Less Noisy?   A–47
    What Is Sound, and How Is It Produced and Conducted?   A–48
    How Does the Length of an Air Column Affect Sound?   A–48
    How Do Solids and Liquids Conduct Sounds?   A–50
Simple Machines (Mechanics)   A–53
    How Can You Make Balls Roll Faster?   A–53
    How Do Wheels Help Toys Move?   A–54
    What Is an Inclined Plane, and How Can You Use It?   A–55
    What Is the Advantage of Using a Wheel and Axle?   A–56
    What Is a Screw, and How Is It Used?   A–60
    What Is a Movable Pulley, and How Can You Use It?   A–62
    What Is a Lever, and How Can You Use It?   A–64
Magnetic and Electrical Energies and Interactions   A–66
    What Can Magnets Do?   A–66
    What Are the Shapes and Names of Magnets?   A–67

What Is a Magnet?   A–68
What Is Static Electricity?   A–72
How Can You Make Electricity by Using Magnetism?   A–78
How Can You Make a Temporary (Electro) Magnet?   A–80
How Are Parallel and Series Circuits the Same and Different?   A–81
Light Energy, Shadows, Lenses, and Color   A–84
How Does Light Move and Pass Through Some Things?   A–84
How Can You Make a Shadow Theater?   A–85
What Does a Prism Do to White Light?   A–86
How Does Light Appear to Travel?   A–88

SECTION 2

Life Sciences and Technology   A–91

Plant Anatomy and Physiology   A–91
What Kinds of Things Can We Do With Plants?   A–91
How Can Some Plants Grow Without Seeds?   A–92
What Is Variation?   A–93
What Are Seeds and How Do They Grow?   A–94
What Are Plant Growth Stages and Parts?   A–97
How Is Sunlight Used by Growing Plants?   A–105
Animal Anatomy and Physiology   A–109
What Do Fish Need to Live?   A–109
What Are the Stages That Insects Go Through?   A–110
How Do Ants Live?   A–111
What Do You Know About the Birds Around You?   A–113
How Do Birds Differ From Mammals?   A–117
How Does a Lack of Oxygen Affect Animals?   A–118
Human Anatomy, Physiology, Nutrition, and Health   A–120
How Does Your Body Cool Itself?   A–120
How Big Are Your Lungs?   A–121
How Do Humans Breathe?   A–122
How Does Our Skin Protect Us?   A–128
Why Does Your Body Need Food for Growth and Health?   A–130
What Else Do We Need From Food, and How Can We Test
    for It?   A–132
How Can You See Which Soda Has More Sugar?   A–147
How Does Your Body Change and Use Starch in the
    Foods You Eat?   A–148

SECTION 3

Earth, Ecology, and Environmental Sciences and Technology   A–153

Astronomy (Earth in Space)   A–153
What Causes Shadows, and How Can They Be Changed?   A–153
How Can Shadows Help You Tell Time?   A–154
Why Is There Day and Night?   A–155

Why Does the Moon Shine?   A–156

Why Does It Appear That There Are Phases of the Moon?   A–158

Meteorology (Weather)   A–161

How Are Clouds and Fog Formed?   A–161

What Is the Greenhouse Effect?   A–161

How Can You Measure Temperature Changes?/What Is a
Thermometer?   A–162

How Can Solar Energy Be Used?   A–164

How Can You Measure Wind Direction and Speed?   A–166

How Can You Measure Air Pressure Changes?   A–171

How Can You Measure Humidity Changes?/What Is a
Hygrometer?   A–174

Geology (Earth's Changing Surface)   A–176

How Are Rocks Broken Up?   A–176

How Can You Build Stalactites and Stalagmites?   A–177

How Are Rocks Alike and Different, and How Do We
Use Rocks?   A–178

What Is a Fault, and How Does It Change the Earth's Surface?
A–181

How Are Crystals Formed?   A–186

Ecology and the Environment   A–191

How Clean Is the Air You Breathe?   A–191

Which Materials Break Down (Decompose) Easily?   A–192

How Does the Environment Affect Living Things?   A–193

How Do Animals and Humans Affect Their Water Environments?
(Water Pollution)   A–198

What Is Air Pollution, What Causes It, How Does It Affect
the Environment, and How Might It Be Prevented and
Reversed?   A–203

SECTION 4

Guided Discovery Science Activities for Students With Special Needs   A–212

Students With Blindness or Visual Impairments   A–213

Learning About Magnets   A–213

Identifying Objects in the Environment   A–214

Finding out About Body Position and Heart Rate   A–215

"Seeing" and Comparing Polluted Water   A–215

Students With Developmental Delays   A–216

Developing a Thermic Sense (Sense of Temperature)   A–216

Learning the Concept of Weight   A–217

Discriminating Among Tastes   A–218

Recognizing Common Odors   A–218

Students With Visual Perception Problems   A–219

Observing Properties of Leaves   A–219

Comparing Properties of Shells or Buttons and
Classifying Them   A–220
Using Plants to Teach Visual Sequencing   A–221
Learning Relative Position and Motion   A–221
Developing Visual Scrutiny and Analysis in an Outside-the-Classroom
Walk   A–222
Students With Emotional Disabilities   A–223
Learning About the Environment by Touching   A–223
Learning About the Environment by Listening and
Moving   A–224
Students With Deafness or Hearing Impairments   A–225

SECTION 5

Piagetian Types of Guided Discovery Activities   A–227

Class Inclusion: Do Children Know That Subclasses Are Included in a
Major Class?   A–228
Spatial Relations   A–228
One-to-One Correspondence   A–229
Coordinating Systems—Horizontal and Vertical   A–229
Conservation by Length   A–230
Conservation of Length   A–230
Conservation of Area   A–231
Ascending a Class Hierarchy   A–231
Spatial Relations   A–232
Constructing a Set Containing a Single Element   A–232
Ordering by Weight   A–233
Descending a Classification Hierarchy   A–233
Conservation of Weight   A–234
Conservation of Displacement Volume   A–234

APPENDIXES   AP–1

APPENDIX A   Fifty-Five Years of Elementary-School Science: A Guided Tour   AP–2

APPENDIX B   Science Supplies, Equipment, and Materials Obtainable
From Community Sources   AP–5

APPENDIX C   Selected Sources of Scientific Supplies, Models, Living Things, Kits,
Computers, and Collections   AP–7

APPENDIX D   Noncommercial Sources and Containers for Living Things   AP–9

APPENDIX E   Food Requirements for Various Animals   AP–11

APPENDIX F   Planning a Learning Center   AP–14

APPENDIX G   Selected Professional References for the Teacher or
                    School Library   AP–15

APPENDIX H   Professional Societies for Science Teachers and Supervisors   AP–17

APPENDIX I   Model for Problem Solving (Sample)   AP–18

APPENDIX J   Safety Suggestions for Hands-on/Minds-on Activities   AP–20

APPENDIX K   Constructing Storage Areas for Supplies and
                    Houses for Living Things   AP–21

**COMPUTER AND TELECOMMUNICATIONS
GLOSSARY   GL–1**

PIAGETIAN GLOSSARY   GL–4

INDEX   IN–1

TEACHING MODERN SCIENCE

CHAPTER 1

Building a Foundation for Scientific and Technological Literacy

It is the union of science, mathematics, and technology that forms the scientific endeavor and that makes it so successful. The study of science as an intellectual and social endeavor—the application of human intelligence to figuring out how the world works—should have a prominent place in any curriculum that has science literacy as one of its aims.[1]

TAPPING INTO NEW RESOURCES

A small boy greets retired engineer Bill Wisnawski at the classroom door with a big smile. "You're here! Great! Can we blow up the teacher again?"

Wisnawski smiles because he knows the boy doesn't mean his science teacher any harm: the child is just eager for more hands-on science. Wisnawski is one of the science resource agents (SRAs) who volunteer for Project RESEED (Retirees Enhancing Science Education through Experiments and Demonstrations). RESEED brings retired scientists and engineers into middle-school science classrooms to get students excited about learning science, especially physical science. RESEED, directed by Dr. Christos Zahopoulos, began in Boston in 1991 with six retirees; it was an outgrowth of other science education enhancement programs at Northeastern University.

The volunteer SRAs have spent their lives working with scientific principles, but before they work with the students, they complete a 12-week training program. During this program, the SRAs learn more about teaching at the middle-school level and become familiar with the 200 experiments and demonstrations that are available for them to use in classrooms. Each SRA volunteers at least one day a week in a science classroom, with many volunteering several days.

One day the hands-on science might involve "blowing up the teacher" by inserting straws into the four corners of an otherwise-sealed garbage bag. As students blow, the teacher, lying on the bag, rises several inches off the floor, demonstrating the power of hydraulic lift. Another time, the SRA might show the impact of atmospheric pressure by boiling water in a soda can, sealing the can, and watching it collapse on itself as the water inside cools and the steam condenses.

According to Zahopoulos, the engineers get as much out of the program as the students. Wisnawski, for example, reports that the 12-week training program "stirred in me a desire to get more involved and bring these things back into the classroom." SRA Bill Anderson says, "I've seen smiles like you wouldn't believe. That's why I do it." Anderson, an engineer who retired in 1990, now teaches 46 classes a month, even though he had never taught before becoming involved with RESEED.

Classroom teachers, who Zahopoulos says tend to be least prepared to teach physical sciences, welcome the RESEED volunteers. Rosemary Brandi, a teacher who has invited RESEED volunteers into her classroom, says that they "bring all that wonderful experience to the kids . . . like the wise grandfather a lot of kids wish they had."

And the students? On a questionnaire completed by 135 students, 90 percent said they learned a lot from the SRAs' visits, felt comfortable asking questions, and wanted the visits to continue. From an eighth grader: "We enjoyed learning; it was pretty cool."

In 1994, RESEED expanded beyond the Boston area by training a group of leader-volunteers for three weeks, full-time. These leaders then traveled throughout the New England area, training other retirees. As of the summer of 1995, RESEED boasted 14 training sites in New England, with 33 leaders and 150 SRAs. Although the SRAs are asked to volunteer for a year, about 80 percent return for a second year. Several are already in their third year.

Zahopoulos has had inquiries about RESEED from schools across the nation and plans to set up training sites outside New England as soon as possible. Even with just the New England sites, he projects adding 300 volunteers a year to the program and is trying to recruit more women to join those who already serve as leaders and SRAs. Zahopoulos calls the SRAs "an untapped resource for improving science education."

The Twenty-First century is almost upon us. An ever-expanding array of science and technology offers us better health, improved travel and communication, and exciting instructional and recreational devices. What implications do these have for *you* for helping *your* students construct intelligent understandings of themselves and the environments in which they live?

In the twenty-first century, this country will need increasing numbers of citizens with special training in science and technology. Perhaps only a small percentage of your students will choose to be scientists, engineers, physicians, or technicians, but *all* of them will need teachers who recognize a better way to teach science to understand a rapidly changing world. You can make the difference in each students' present and future encounters with science. What you choose to teach in science, the way you teach it, and how you arrange your classroom environment to stimulate your students to become scientific and technologically literate will be influenced by:

■ processes, attitudes, and products of science relevant to the everyday world of your elementary- and middle-grade students
■ research on how students can most effectively learn from being exposed to science and technology experiences
■ national, state, and locally directed reforms for scientific and technological literacy standards or guidelines
■ scientists' (and *your*) views of what constitutes science and technology

This chapter will open a dialogue on these four themes and subsequent chapters will elaborate them further. To begin, let's review what constitutes science and technology.

HOW DO *YOU* DEFINE SCIENCE AND TECHNOLOGY?

Write down several words that you would use to describe science and technology. Share your list of attributes with your professor, classmates, and/or colleagues. Do they emphasize the same things you do? Which additional attributes of science and technology do they suggest? As you read this chapter, see how your descriptions agree (or disagree) with the descriptions of science and technology presented here.

Science is an ongoing activity that can enrich the lives of children as well as adults. Youngsters of all ages are curious and enjoy observing and exploring the natural world. The earlier we encourage this curiosity, the better.

Not only is science enjoyable for children, but scientific/technological literacy is essential for modern life.[2] A strong case can be built for initiating scientific/technological literacy at the earliest grades. Science, with its methods for developing reliable knowledge and its applications in technology, is at the heart of modern civilization. The invention and discovery of new products and techniques are being made at an exponential rate. Yet even as we enjoy the benefits of science and technology, new demands are being made on society. Problems related to issues such as health care, energy, natural resources, environmental quality, and population dynamics increasingly demand our attention and our best thinking. As a teacher, you must prepare students for a world vastly different from the one you grew up in.

WHAT ARE SCIENTIFICALLY AND TECHNOLOGICALLY LITERATE CITIZENS?

Students and citizens who are scientifically *and* technologically literate should

- have an understanding of those aspects of science and technology that are meaningful to them at their present level of cognitive development
- find science and technology interesting and rewarding
- use their understanding of science and technology to enjoy the natural and social world in which they live[3]

There is evidence that the goals of scientific and technological literacy *can* be reached in schools. Here are 10 standards that have been achieved by students in exemplary schools by seventh grade:[4]

1. Exhibit effective consumer behavior by evaluating the quality of products, the accuracy of advertising, and personal needs for the product.
2. Use effective personal health practices.
3. Use new data and ideas in learning situations.
4. Recognize the effect of people on the environment and vice versa.
5. Recognize and accept ways in which each individual is unique.
6. Recognize that a solution to one problem often creates new problems.
7. Observe variations of individual interpretations of different data.
8. Recognize that science will provide neither magic solutions nor easy answers.

Hard work and scientific processes are required to re-solve—rather than solve—many problems.

9. Develop an understanding of information and concepts from a wide variety of topics selected from the life, Earth, and physical sciences.
10. Recognize the roles of people involved in scientific pursuits and the careers available in science and technology.

Obviously, human endeavors as complex, divergent, and encompassing as science and modern technology can barely be introduced in one chapter. Therefore, the balance of this chapter will be limited to (1) the spirit, structure, and beauty of science; (2) the attitudes that scientists value; (3) the processes of investigation they employ and; (4) the tested knowledge they construct.

The aim of this introductory chapter will be to focus on understanding science and technology from the standpoint of teaching and learning. Later in this chapter, suggestions are given for how you and your students might use these elements of science as you hunt for answers to questions relevant to your everyday lives.

SCIENCE AND SCIENCING

Science has been referred to as a human venture that involves continuing processes to discover order and recurring patterns in nature. Science should be viewed as a *verb*, which involves action, not as a noun or the name of a thing.

Science is *not* neat and tidy, but requires patience and perseverance. Scientists do not speak in terms of *absolute truths*. They support ideas but never prove things irrefutably; they formulate guesses (hypotheses) and test them relentlessly.

A primary goal of scientists is to construct knowledge of how our universe works, in order to explain, predict, and possibly control phenomena. This never-ending process has been termed

FIGURE 1–1

Interrelationships of scientific products, processes, and attitudes in investigating phenomena

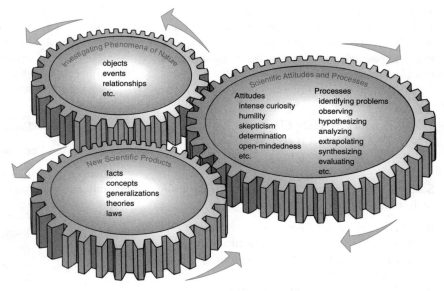

sciencing. When people are sciencing, they employ many processes to try to find answers to their questions. Let's explore these together.

How Are Scientific Attitudes and Processes, Products, and Investigations Interrelated?

Figure 1–1 illustrates the cyclical nature and interrelationship of three elements of sciencing:

- Scientific Attitudes and Processes
- Scientific Products
- Investigating Phenomena of Nature

These three elements are cyclical and interrelated. They are absolutely inseparable and affect each other. For expedience, they will be examined individually, starting with processes.

SCIENTIFIC ATTITUDES AND PROCESSES

Sciencing is not a linear, lock-step process, but is, rather, *cyclic*. The sequence may be started at any point but usually starts with an observed discrepancy, which Piaget referred to as "cognitive

disequilibrium." This discrepancy can be an encounter of something that does not fit in with previous knowledge or experience. To better visualize the sciencing cycle, look at Figure 1–2.

Scientists use a variety of empirical and analytic procedures in their efforts to clarify the marvelous mysteries of our universe; these procedures are called the **processes** of science. However, many people are not aware of the fact that we all use many of these processes without even realizing it (see Figure 1–3).

Examples of Everyday Sciencing Process Skills

Sciencing process skills have been called **lifelong learning skills**, as they can be used for daily living and for learning in school in *any* subject area. A paraphrase of a well-known proverb advises, "Give people fish and they eat for a day. Teach them how to fish and they eat for a lifetime."

In a national assessment, young learners did not always realize how useful science processes can be to them. Only 54% of seventh graders tested agreed with the statement, "Much of what you learn in science classes is useful in everyday life."[5] Help your students learn to use scientific

FIGURE 1–2

Sciencing cycle

Source: Adapted from Richard D. Kellough and Patricia L. Roberts, *A Resource Guide for Elementary School Teaching, Planning for Competence*, 3d Edition (Upper Saddle River, NJ: Merrill/ Prentice Hall, 1994), 460.

processes or inquiry skills to confront problems, and they can learn for a lifetime.

The effectiveness of developing everyday sciencing process skills in our students was summarized by Mechling and Oliver in this way:

Competence in using process skills provides children with the ability to apply knowledge, not only to science and other subjects in the classroom, but outside the classroom in their everyday lives as well. They are the same skills that will serve them as adults, when they measure their floor for a carpet, try to figure out why their automobile didn't start, or decide which presidential candidate to vote for. These are the thinking skills they will use when separating evidence from opinion while listening to someone's side of a story, or when looking for evidence and contradictions in written or spoken opinions. They are the science processes children will use as adults to separate inferences from evidence in a systematic way.[6]

A broad range of science processes or inquiry skills that are particularly appropriate for elementary/middle school students is summarized in Table 1–1. The processes are organized from the simplest (i.e., empirical, pragmatic, and using sensory/motor skills) to more complex (analytical or higher logic thinking). Each process is defined and an example is given for use with elementary/middle grades students. Some of these processes are described in more detail in the following sections.

Nancy Paulu and Margery Martin provide this summary of the processes appropriate for sciencing in your classroom:

- *observing* what happens
- trying to *make sense* of our observations
- using our new knowledge to *make predictions* about what might happen in the future
- *testing predictions* under controlled conditions to see if they are correct.[7]

Additionally, Paulu and Martin point out that science involves trial and error—trying, failing, and trying again. Science does not provide all the

---

We Are All Scientisits

Children and scientists have much in common. Naturally inquisitive, young children ask endless questions. They may spend half an hour watching a bug crawl on the floor. Children sort money, pictures, toys, shells, pasta shapes, and words. They experiment by pouring water into soil, mixing different colors of paints, or adding blocks to a tower until it falls. They draw conclusions about the way things work. They learn from and share information with others.

Scientists share with children curiosity about the world. They are trained to use a more systematic and sophisticated approach to inquiry than children do. They have developed the discipline to remain objective, to reserve judgment until they have the facts, and to recognize the limits of their knowledge. Nevertheless, the skills used in *doing* science are the same—whether you're a student or a scientist!

Science Process Skill	Children	Scientists
observe	look, touch, smell, taste, listen	microscope, X-rays, chromatography, seismograph
experiment	change something and watch what happens	change and control variables
collaborate	partners in classroom	colleagues around world
record	journal, score card	field notes, computer
measure	scale, ruler, stopwatch, measuring cup	computer analysis, calibrated apparatus
sort and classify	color, size, shape, weight	taxonomic key, relevant functional groupings
compare	fastest, largest, farthest	change over time, change in differing conditions
analyze	what happens most	statistical analysis
share information	class meeting; at recess, "Guess what I found out?"	scientific meetings, E-mail; over coffee, "Guess what I found out!"

FIGURE 1–3

We are all scientists

Source: Sharing Science: Linking Students with Scientists and Engineers. A Survival Guide for Teachers (Durham, NC: North Carolina Museum of Life and Science, 1993), p. 5.

answers; it requires us to be skeptical so that we can modify our models of the world or change them altogether as we make new discoveries.

Sciencing Requires Good Observation

Scientific observation is one process for gathering information. Using all of the senses or using instruments that extend the senses, it is the broadest and most essential process. Observing is an **empirical process** of sciencing; that is, it is based on practical experiences without regard to inference or theorizing. In one sense, sciencing begins with observations of the natural world. However, observation always takes place from a

Activity 1–1   HOW ARE SEEDS ALIKE AND DIFFERENT?

Obtain several seeds of at least two different kinds. Write down as many observations of the seeds as you can make. Compare your observations with those of another student.

framework of prior knowledge. *What* scientists or students look for in a situation and *how* they interpret what they see depend greatly on the relevant knowledge they bring to the situation, however naive and incomplete that knowledge might be. Observations, then, are colored by prior knowledge. Students must learn to distinguish carefully between their observations and their inferences.

Learning to be a good observer is a lifelong task. Under your guidance as a sensitive teacher or parent, students *can* develop observation skills. Activity 1–1 can be used to test your own observational skills or as an activity to help your students develop their skills of observation. Do this activity before reading further.

Now use the components of good scientific observation in Table 1–2 as a checklist to see how comprehensive your list of observations about the seeds is. Did you:

- follow a *plan* in observing?
- use all *appropriate senses,* and perhaps a magnifying glass to observe the seeds?
- raise any *questions* about the seeds?
- *measure* the length or circumference of the seeds, or perhaps weigh them?
- compare the seeds for *similarities and differences?*
- make any *changes* in the seeds? For example, did you soak one and split it apart to see what was inside it?
- choose to *communicate* your observations? How? Did you include any drawings, for example?

If you made any inferences in observing the seeds, were you careful to distinguish between your inferences and your observations, showing in some way that inferences are conclusions or opinions? For example, when describing the inside of the seed, did you say "I think this part is the embryonic root" or "I infer this part is food storage for the developing plant"?

The next section of the text can help you become more aware of the differences between observing and inferring. Now, go back to the activity, follow the checklist, and observe again. What are the values of observing in exploration and sciencing?

An Inference Goes Beyond Observing

Observations are statements about information that is available directly through the five senses; **inferences** are *interpretations* of these observations. In inferring we use experiences and knowledge that we already have or that we acquire to fill in gaps about observed events and information.

An **inference,** then, is a conclusion about observations that is based on prior knowledge and experiences. Inferences are made up of three interacting components:

- observations
- prior knowledge and experiences
- conclusions

It is useful to think of knowledge and experiences as being organized mentally into a *schema* (the plural is *schemas* or *schemata*). A **schema** is a mental framework, network, or construct of related details organized around a familiar event, theme, or process. When we observe a new situation that has elements

TABLE 1–1
Science processes or inquiry skills

Science Process or Inquiry Skill	Definition	Example
Manipulating Materials	Handling or treating materials and equipment skillfully and effectively	Arranging equipment and materials needed to conduct an investigation of the melting rate of ice, pouring liquids from one container to another, or carrying a balance or adjusting it for use.
Observing	Becoming aware of an object or event by using any of the senses (or extensions of the senses) to identify properties	Looking at a melting ice cube to determine its changing shape, feeling water from an ice cube to determine its slipperiness or coldness, or using a thermometer to determine the coldness of the water.
Classifying	Arranging or distributing objects, events, or information representing objects or events in classes according to some method or system	Taking objects such as buttons from a mixed collection and placing them in groups by color, number of holes, or shape; or arranging them in order according to size.
Measuring	Making quantitative observations by comparing to a conventional (or non-conventional) standard	Using a clock to count the number of seconds needed for an ice cube to melt, using a thermometer to determine the final temperature in degrees Celsius of the melted ice cube, or weighing ice cubes on a simple balance using paper clips as a standard.
Using Numbers	Applying mathematical rules or formulas to calculate quantities or determine relationships from basic measurements	Computing the average time for a 10-cubic-centimeter ice cube to melt.
Recording Data	Collecting bits of information about objects and events that illustrate a specific situation	Taking notes; making a list or outline; recording numbers on a chart or graph; tape recording; taking photographs; or writing numbers of results of observations and measurements in an investigation, such as recording the number of cubic centimeters of water formed as an ice cube melts over time.
Replicating	Performing acts that duplicate demonstrated symbols, patterns, or procedures	Operating a balance scale or using a thermometer following procedures previously demonstrated or modeled by another person.

Source: Modified from *Elementary Science Syllabus* (Albany, NY: The University of the State of New York, The State Education Department, Division of Program Development, 1985), 14–15. Used by permission.

Science Process or Inquiry Skill	Definition	Example
Identifying Variables	Recognizing the characteristics of objects or factors in events that are constant or change under different conditions	Listing or describing the factors that are thought to, or would, influence the rate at which an ice cube melts in air and in water, such as: original temperature of water and air, size of the ice cube, or volume of water and air.
Interpreting Data	Analyzing data that have been obtained and organized by determining apparent patterns or relationships in the data	Studying a graph, chart, or table of data collected about melting ice cubes and noting that smaller ice cubes melt faster than larger ones.
Predicting	Making a forecast of future events or conditions expected to exist	Stating "An ice cube whose weight is twice that of another ice cube will require twice the time to melt."
Formulating Hypotheses	Constructing a statement that is tentative and testable about what is thought likely to be true based on reasoning	Making a statement to be used as the basis for an experiment: "If one ice cube is placed in water and another placed in air at the same temperature, then the ice cube in water will melt faster."
Inferring	Making a conclusion based on reasoning to explain an observation	Stating that heat caused the melting of an ice cube that had been placed in water.
Generalizing	Drawing general conclusions from particulars	Making a summary statement following analysis of experimental results: "Ice melts faster in water than in air when both air and water are at the same temperature."
Creating Models	Displaying information by means of graphic illustrations or other multisensory representations	Drawing a graph or diagram, constructing a three-dimensional object, using a tape recording, constructing a chart or table, or producing a picture or photograph that illustrates information about the melting of ice cubes.
Making Decisions	Identifying alternatives and choosing a course of action from among the alternatives after basing the judgment for the selection on justifiable reasons	Identifying alternative ways to store ice cubes to avoid causing them to melt; analyzing the consequences of each alternative such as the cost, the effect on other people, or the effect on the environment; using justifiable reasons as the basis for making the choice;

TABLE 1–2
Components of good scientific observing

1. *Plan.* Use a plan to guide observations so you do not skip important things or repeat observations unnecessarily.

2. *Senses.* Use all appropriate senses as well as instruments that extend the senses in gathering extensive and clear information.

3. *Questions.* Be curious and keep an open mind while observing; be alert to discrepancies; raise questions that can lead to new observations and new information.

4. *Measurements.* Make measurements of important variables to supplement qualitative observations when it matters.

5. *Similarities and Differences.* Identify similarities and differences between the object and other comparable objects.

6. *Changes.* Observe natural changes occurring in the objects or system of interest; whenever appropriate, make deliberate alterations in a system and observe the responding changes.

7. *Communication.* Report your observations clearly, using verbal descriptions, charts, diagrams, drawings, and other methods as appropriate.

familiar from or similar to a previous situation, we call upon our schemata to expedite the interpretation of the new situation.

Schemata can be used to guide inferences about incomplete information. All of us have many schemata. In constructing inferences, we highlight particular cues in the observational data and search for matches between the cues and items in specific knowledge frames. The broader our range of knowledge and sensory experiences and the more carefully we observe and sift through our observations for relevant cues, the more powerful and accurate our inferences are likely to be. Schemata are addressed in more depth in Chapter 2. To better understand the process of inferring, consider Activity 1–2.

If you had appropriate prior knowledge and sensory observations, you might have inferred that the moisture on the glass came from water vapor in the air surrounding the glass. Younger students might infer that the moisture came from inside the glass, gradually seeping through its walls. Inferences in science need to be checked out through further investigation. What kinds of investigations might be carried out to help these students decide between these two differing inferences from the same observational data of the moisture on the glass of ice water? (Hint: They might put red food dye in the inside water and they could be guided to see that the water on the outside of the glass is clear.)

To construct an inference you always need some prior observations and knowledge. For example, the following facts, concepts, and principles are needed to support the first inference given, about the moisture on the glass of ice water:

- Air often contains water vapor.
- Water vapor comes from evaporated water.
- When warm moist air is cooled to a temperature called the dew point, water vapor from the air will condense onto available cool surfaces.

Research on human cognition suggests that students are much more likely to access and use relevant prior knowledge of a phenomenon (such as condensation) if it is based on the analysis of many similar everyday personal experiences, for instance, considerations about clouds, fog, dew, vapor trails, eyeglasses that fog up in winter, and so forth.

The Role of Variables

Learning to investigate and to communicate and interpret the results of investigations is an important goal of scientists, as well as sciencing in the elementary/middle grades. Investigating is a complex operation, consisting of many component steps. Working with variables is one impor-

Activity 1–2   WHY DOES AN ICED WATER GLASS "SWEAT"?

Moisture is often seen collected on the outside of a glass of ice water. Before reading on, make some inferences about where the moisture that formed on the glass came from.

tant component of investigating. A **variable** is a property of objects or events that can change and have differing amounts. The height and weight of a growing child, the time a candle can burn under a glass jar, and the amount of rainfall in a day are all examples of variables.

Three types of variables are important in scientific investigations:

- A **manipulated variable** (also called an *independent variable*) is a variable that the experimenter deliberately changes or manipulates in an investigation.
- A **responding variable** (also called a *dependent variable*) is a variable that changes in an investigation in response to changes in the manipulated variable.
- A **controlled variable** is variable that is deliberately kept constant or unchanged in an investigation in order not to confound the result.

An example of a simple controlled experiment for young students is germinating seeds on a wet sponge, as shown in Figure 1–4. This experiment establishes a cause–effect relationship between water and seed germination. It is very probable that seeds will germinate on the wet sponge in a few days, but not on the dry sponge. Students are helped to see some cause–effect relationship between water and seed germination if other conditions of temperature and light are constant and suitable. Thus:

- The presence or absence of water is the manipulated variable, the condition that is changed to test whether it affects germination.
- The unchanged variables, in this case temperature and light, are the controls. These variables are controlled and only water is manipulated to make the investigation an objective test of the effects of water on germination.

How would you conduct controlled experiments to see if light and temperature are needed for seed germination?

Generalizations about the manipulated variables may be discovered or constructed in investigations. A **generalization** is a broad conclusion drawn from a number of particular instances. An example of a generalization would be, "Water is needed for seed germination." As we discussed earlier, generalizations about relationships are sometimes called **principles.**

A **hypothesis** is a guess about a possible relationship in nature that might be confirmed through investigations. Hypotheses are used to guide experiments. They are often stated in a form such as "the greater the manipulated variable the greater (or less) the responding variable will be." An example would be, "The heavier a pendulum weight, the slower it will swing."

EXPERIMENT   CONTROL

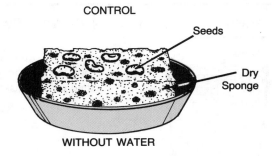

FIGURE 1–4
Controlled experiment in which the *manipulated* variable is water

(Surprisingly, a controlled investigation will show this hypothesis to be false.)

The notion of controlled experiments is an important tool in the search for replicable data and valid conclusions. It is extremely difficult to precisely control all variables at all times. Even slight changes in conditions may yield significant differences in findings. Scientists try to account for these slight changes and build sufficient degrees of accuracy and tolerance into the standards of their work.

WHAT KINDS OF ATTITUDES AND VALUES CONTRIBUTE TO GOOD SCIENCING?

Scientists—men and women trained in some field of science—study phenomena and events through observation, experimentation, and other empirical and analytical activities. Certain general attitudes, values, or propensities tend to characterize their work. Science education should cultivate these scientific attitudes and values. Important attitudes and values for students to learn and exhibit when they are sciencing include the following three from *Science for All Americans: Project 2061*.[8]

1. *Being Curious*. Scientists and children are driven by curiosity, an urge to know and understand the world.

2. *Insisting on Evidence*. Scientists insist on evidence to support conclusions and claims. Insisting on evidence means testing ideas rigorously and respecting the facts as they are accrued.

3. *Being Skeptical*. Scientists and students involved in sciencing must remain skeptical of their own conclusions and those of others. As evidence suggests different explanations of objects or events, scientists—and your students—must be willing to change their original explanations.

In addition, weigh the following attitudes and values and their implications for learners in your classroom:

4. *Accepting Ambiguity*. Scientists and students must be able to accept ambiguity. Scientific evidence seldom, if ever, proves something finally. Alternative viewpoints should be respected until shown to be incompatible with data.

5. *Being Cooperative*. Scientists today generally work and publish as a team. Being cooperative in raising and answering questions, analyzing data, and solving problems is another important attitude in the scientific enterprise in labs and in elementary/middle grade classrooms.

6. *Taking a Positive Approach to Failure*. Wrong turns and dead ends are a natural consequence of inquiry into the unknown.

Scientists and students must take a positive approach to failure and treat setbacks as temporary.[9]

Let's scrutinize a few of these attitudes and values in more depth, with emphasis on what this means for your students who are sciencing.

Curiosity: Fascination with the World Around Us

Human urges and needs are the forces that drive all of us to seek answers (some rational, some irrational) to questions about our world. These forces are the catalysts for the development of science. Young children enjoy discovering the texture, size, weight, color—even the taste—of sand at the seashore or in the sandbox simply because sand intrigues them. Similarly, scientists study the marvels of nature because they delight in them. This dynamic, almost compulsive, involvement of children and adults in searching for answers provides the fuel for investigation.

Here is an example of the total absorption of scientists in their work: "When he sits down at his computer in the morning, a physicist leaves the rest of us behind. When he comes back, he cannot explain where he has been, or what it is that he has been doing."[10]

The following description of the passion of finding something new in science says it well:

A discovery is like falling in love and reaching the top of a mountain after a hard climb all in one, an ecstasy induced not by drugs but by the revelation of a face of nature that no one has seen before and that often turns out to be more subtle and wonderful than anyone imagined.[11]

A thirst for knowing, properly nurtured in a positive learning environment, can assist students to become perpetual learners—constantly curious, continually seeking knowledge, and always inquiring. Your own curiosity can be the model for your students to follow. "He who would kindle others, must himself glow."

The world is full of wondrous things if we open our eyes and minds to them!

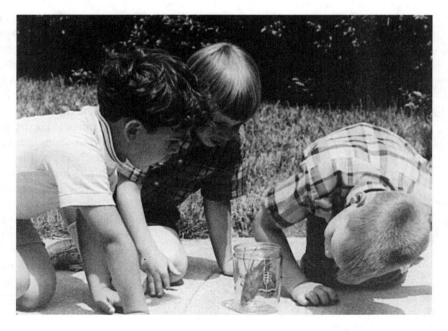

Group Cooperation Stimulates Creative Thinking

Endless numbers of men and women combine their talents and labors to inquire into the unknown through creative sciencing activities. National boundaries often become indistinct in the free interchange of research efforts, which we called the products of science. Teams of men and women of all races and all nationalities are an essential part of modern science and technology.

Group cooperation is so effective in generating new ideas, solving problems, and helping people learn from each other that industries worldwide are adopting cooperative group procedures in manufacturing. Japanese and American companies have adapted cooperative group learning techniques into what they call Quality Circles (QCs).[12] In **Quality Circles**, members from all levels of the company (president and other CEOs, foremen, hourly assembly-line workers, janitors, etc.) meet daily in small groups. Advantages claimed for QCs include the following:

- Improving the quality of work, products, and environment.
- Simplifying the employees' jobs.
- Cutting costs, eliminating product defects, and doing away with waste and expensive inventory stockpiles.

Learning to work cooperatively is such an important goal for students in science and all other subjects in elementary schools, that specific techniques are provided in Chapter 2, Chapter 4, and Chapter 6. Take a minute now (before your next class session) to form a cooperative learning group with one or more of your class members. Review together what you have learned about science teaching. Brain-storm about science teaching. Brain-storm ways to make your science methods course experience more valuable.

If At First You Don't Succeed . . .

Scientists tell us that the more they know, the more they discover how little they actually know. Scientific findings are just temporary stopping places on the continuum of research. In the process of investigating a problem, other unanswered questions often arise. At any given point scientists know that the results of their efforts—no matter how satisfying or frustrating—are incomplete because future work will doubtless reveal more about the subject. A failure in science, then, is not a dead end but a starting point.

Historical records are full of successes stemming from "failures." Dr. Paul Ehrlich, 1908 Nobel prize winner in medicine and physiology, developed Salvarsan for the treatment of syphilis after 605 "unsuccessful" experiments. In Polaroid's search for instant color pictures, chemist Howard Rogers spent 15 years experimenting with over 5,000 different chemical compounds before synthesizing a new molecule. "Failure" was never a barrier for Thomas Alva Edison. It is said that after more than 10,000 experiments to construct a battery had failed, Edison's response was, "I have not failed, just discovered ten thousand ways that won't work."

Burnett Cross says that the picture of scientists we often give to our students does not sufficiently proclaim them as persons just like us, who take wrong roads, have hunches that don't pan out, make errors and mistakes, and experience a "sometimes hostile behavior of apparatus." How they handle these roadblocks determines their progress. Scientists succeed in the long run because of daily, intelligent approaches to failures.[13] Have you ever failed at anything? How did your failure help you work to succeed at something else?

When sciencing, elementary/middle grade students should be guided to learn that the process of inquiry must necessarily result in occasional mistakes. Students often come to the inquiry process with naive conceptions about the world that lead to mistaken conclusions. The way you handle the mistakes and errors that come in hands-on/minds-on investigations is crucial in science teaching/learning. Pupils who

: their ideas are wrong may be reluc-
cipate in inquiry again. On the other
rect ideas left unchallenged can cause
nd interfere with the construction of
ledge. As a teacher, you will need to
ctful ways to nurture the inquiry
ile leading pupils to challenge wrong
to examine their consequences
rther investigations.

ng (that is, functioning like a scien-
s using the types of processes, atti-
d values identified earlier in this
nore consciously more of the time.
g these science attitudes and science
skills is an important task of elementary/middle
grade education.

Scientists and Students Construct Order and Knowledge

Hands-on/minds-on approaches to teaching
science are consistent with a philosophy of learning and instruction called **constructivism.**
According to the constructivist viewpoint, order
is not so much *discovered* as it is *invented.*
Scientists imaginatively *impose* order and predictability on the phenomena and events of the
world. As with many other human endeavors,
scientists *construct* this order based largely on
their own prior knowledge; that is, their own
active organization of facts, concepts, principles,
and models derived from previous studies. In the
constructivist viewpoint, knowledge is considered to be a dynamic, conceptual means to make
sense of experience, rather than a passive representation of an external world.

Constructivists stress that each person must
individually construct meanings of words and
ideas if they are to be truly useful. All of us—scientists and nonscientists alike—are strongly
influenced by other people through social interactions. But language *per se* cannot be the means
of transferring information. Knowledge acquired
from other people is useful in understanding the
world only to the extent that we make it meaningful for ourselves through thoughtful pro-

cesses. It is this meaningful knowledge that scientists and nonscientists use to cope with and
make sense of the environment.

The constructivist philosophy incorporates much of the work of psychologist Jean
Piaget and modern cognitive science. It implies
a hands-on/minds-on discovery approach to
teaching and learning science. Chapter 2 presents a fuller narrative of cognitive and constructivist contributions to understanding how
students learn, and their implications for teaching and learning science.

SCIENTIFIC PRODUCTS

In addition to experiencing the world in a hands-
on/minds-on way consistent with the descriptions of science and constructivism, it is
important for learners to discover and construct
their own scientific knowledge of the world.
Scientific knowledge, sometimes labeled the
products of science, has been accumulating for
centuries as the result of the empirical and analytic activities of scientists. Elementary/middle
grade sciencing also focuses on developing *scientific processes and attitudes, new scientific products,* and *investigating phenomena of nature.*
Figure 1–1 shows the relationships among these
three important components in elementary science. Refer to Figure 1–1 as you read the following sections.

Scientific knowledge or products generally
take the form of facts, concepts, principles, and
theories.

Scientific Facts Result from Tested Observations

Facts are products of the experimental activities
and processes in science. In contrast, concepts,
principles, theories, and laws are products of logical mental constructs.

Scientific facts are objectively confirmed
statements about things that really exist or
events that have actually occurred or been

observed. Examples of facts arrived at by many observations:

- It is a fact that water droplets bead up on wax paper but spread out on aluminum foil.
- Water drops take a spherical shape when they fall.
- When water is added drop by drop to a small plastic medicine cup, the water tends to mound up. Approximately 100 drops of water can be added to the full cup before it starts to flow over the edges of the cup. Even then, as many as 30 paper clips can be gently slid into the cup without the water overflowing.

Did you take for granted that the facts listed above were true? Why don't you take a moment and test them? How would you do that? Facts are the empirical data or products of our observations that we organize and attempt to explain. Facts begin to make sense only as they are placed into a larger framework of concepts, principles, theories, and laws.

Forming Scientific Concepts

In forming concepts, we are noting that even though items in a set may have many differences, they also have certain aspects that are similar. These similar aspects form the basis for grouping things together into concepts. Thus **scientific concepts** are mental organizations about the world that are based on similarities among objects, observations, or events. They are ideas generalized from analogous instances.

One example of a scientific concept concerns magnetic poles. Magnets come in an assortment of sizes, shapes, and colors. But in all magnets there are places called magnetic poles where the magnetic attraction for iron objects is greatest. All magnetic poles share the property of being the place of greatest attraction on a magnet. This is a scientific concept. Other scientific concepts encountered in elementary science include electric circuitry, heat, air, air pressure, length, weight, color, texture, planets, and plant cells.

The facts about water that we just described can be accounted for through the concept of surface tension, the skin-like effect of some liquids that is a result of the bonding of molecules.

What other scientific concepts can you think of that might form the basis of science activities for your students?

Scientific Principles Incorporate Related Concepts

Scientific principles are statements about the relationships among concepts. For example, "heated air expands" is a principle that relates the concepts of air, heat, and expansion in a causal way. This principle asserts that *if* air is heated *then* it will expand (unless otherwise constrained). Principles are analytical rather than empirical. They are inductive generalizations that are imaginatively based on a few examples. In forming principles, scientists (and students, too) go beyond limited observations and move to the conclusion that what was true in a few cases will likely be true in all similar cases. Scientists refer to principles as the best descriptions of objects and events they have at any given time. It is primarily because of their inductive nature that principles are thought of as tentative and subject to change as new observations are made.

Scientific Theories Provide Tentative Models

Scientific theories are broader networks of related facts, concepts, and principles. A theory is a type of model—a scientist's imaginative picture of how nature is put together. Like principles, theories are tentative generalizations and are subject to change as new evidence accumulates. For example:

- The geocentric theory of the universe was dominant 500 years ago, but today it is of only historic interest.
- The model of the atom as a tiny solar system with electrons orbiting a nucleus is useful to us in imagining the structure of nature, but

Hands-on/minds-on science experiences help students construct scientific concepts that are long-lasting.

chemists today have replaced it with quantum theory, which pictures electrons as cloud-like swarms of charges swirling about a nucleus.

■ The big bang theory of the origin of the universe, evolution as a theory of how life forms begin and change over time, and the theory of cells as basic life units of plants and animals are examples of scientific theories that best account for the evidence available today.

Replace the word *theory* in the previous sentence with the word *model* and you may better realize the tentative nature of scientific theories.[14]

Scientific theories facilitate the understanding, prediction, and sometimes the control of a wide variety of natural phenomena. For example,

meteorological theory enables scientists to *understand* how and why clouds and fog form. Meteorological theory also helps us determine what kinds of data to collect in order to *predict* when and where violent storms are likely to occur. Meteorological theory has already led to the production of rain through cloud seeding. Perhaps theoretical advances will someday lead to the *control* of potentially destructive hurricanes and tornadoes.

Scientific Laws Must Survive Intense Testing

Laws are particularly well established and widely accepted scientific theories or models, although they are still tentative. Laws have generally undergone more rigorous testing than scientific principles and theories, and are considered to be "durable"—at least as long as testing supports them. They are, however, still subject to change and refinement.

The **law of conservation of energy** says that in an interaction, energy is neither created nor destroyed, only changed from one form to another. In 1905, many years after the law of conservation of energy was first formulated, Einstein showed that energy could be created out of matter in special circumstances. When a little bit of matter is destroyed, a great deal of energy is created. This new discovery, which is expressed by Einstein's famous equation ($E = mc^2$), required that the law of conservation of energy be expanded. What other scientific laws do you know about?

INVESTIGATING PHENOMENA REQUIRES ASKING QUESTIONS

Sciencing must be guided by thoughtful questions—asked by both teachers and students. Paulu and Martin relate a story about Isidor I. Rabi, a Nobel prize winner in physics. A friend asked Rabi, "Why did you become a scientist, rather than a doctor or lawyer or businessman, like the other immigrant kids in your neighborhood?" Rabi responded:

My mother made me a scientist without ever intending it. Every other mother would ask her child after school: "Did you learn anything today?" But not my mother. She always asked me a different question. "Izzy," she would say, "did you ask a good question today?" That difference—asking good questions—made me become a scientist![15]

Young children exploring their sensory world and scientists working on deep intellectual problems ask many questions. Two types of questions are at the heart of scientific inquiry: "what" questions and "how and why" questions.

"What?" Questions Lead to Descriptions

"What" questions are at the empirical level. They generally ask for descriptions that lay the foundation for analytic work (e.g., "What did you see in the investigation?" "What changes took place in the plant?" "What bird is on that fence?" "What are the properties of this rock?").

"How and Why" Questions Seek Analysis

"How" and "why" questions are at an analytic level and require that one go beyond the information given (e.g., "Why did the balloon expand?" "How is heat or thermal energy conducted through a piece of iron?"). Answering such questions involves observing, inferring, generalizing, and using prior knowledge. Justifying answers to "why" and "how" questions may also involve identifying variables, formulating hypotheses, experimenting, and interpreting data.

"Why" questions may not have a final answer; each successive answer may lead to another, more fundamental, question. For example, a young child asks, "Daddy, why is grass green?" The father answers, "Because grass has chlorophyll," to which the child immediately asks,

"Well, why is chlorophyll green?" This could go on indefinitely because each question leads to more basic conceptional information.

Because questioning is the heart of scientific inquiry and the foundation of teaching/learning by hands-on/minds-on guided discovery, Chapter 4 is devoted to the specifics of questioning and listening techniques.

Sometimes Our Answers to Questions Are Nonscientific

Science is just one way of seeking and knowing about the world. There are many nonscience ways of answering questions that are completely appropriate under certain conditions.

Sometimes in our frustration or ignorance, we respond to "why" questions with answers that are not very scientific. We may give an **anthropomorphic** response. That is, we give human form or qualities to nonhuman things (The term *anthropomorphic* comes from the Greek *anthropos*, meaning *man*, and *morphos*, meaning *form*). An example of this might be how we sometimes ascribe human motives to computers with statements like, "The computer swallowed my last paragraph."

Occasionally, we may respond to questions that attribute end purpose, design, or will to nonhuman things. This is a **teleological** response, from the Greek word *teleos*, meaning *end*. "Water seeks its own level" is an example of a teleological explanation. It is the same as saying that water desires to be at some given level. Although a teleological approach may sometimes be useful as a model, it is more scientific to say that water moves because of the actions of forces upon it.

Scientists do not answer questions in anthropomorphic or teleological terms because these descriptions do not contribute to a better understanding of the phenomena. These answers are vague, untrue, and lead to dead ends. For example, if you are told a plant bends toward a light source because "it *likes* light," you have no need to find out how light stimulates plant hormones so cells grow more rapidly on one side of the plant, bending it toward the light source. The plant is *forced* to bend, it does not *choose* to bend (as far as we know at this time). Anthropomorphic and teleological answers may discourage efforts to look deeper at cause and effect.

ASPIRATIONS FOR ELEMENTARY/ MIDDLE GRADE SCIENCING

As we approach the twenty-first century, there is increased interest on the national, state, and local levels to develop teaching/learning standards to engage learners as early as possible in meaningful science experiences. What does this mean to you helping your students construct intelligent understandings of themselves and their environments?

Table 1–3 briefly describes a few current projects that may impact directly on the "whats and hows" of your science education program. Included are the name, address, and phone number of each project, along with its major emphasis. You are invited to contact each group for additional information. Other projects that are influencing science education will be explored in Chapter 7.

COMMON COMPONENTS OF NATIONAL/STATE/ LOCAL PROJECTS

Many of the following components appear in national/state/local projects' suggestions for science education. As you scan them, note their common elements and visualize how they will have a direct impact upon your selection of content and activities to teach your students.

1. National standards should be generated as guides for state and local educators in defining what all learners should know and be able to do.

2. Learners should be actively engaged in doing science, so they see science as on-going processes as well as interim products, with ways of formulating questions, techniques of inquiry, and rules of evidence.
3. A major goal is to assist all learners to become scientifically/technologically literate, regardless of gender, cultural background, or physical or mental impairment.
4. Learners should understand the natural world and their role in it.
5. After evaluating evidence they gain from multifaceted sources regarding personal, local, national, and global concerns, learners will think and act critically.
6. To ensure that learners develop deeper understandings of science, the amount of scientific factual knowledge (products) should be decreased.
7. Science educators must construct performance-based assessment systems to discern the degree to which learners have achieved the stated goals.

Concepts of science and technology presented in this chapter provide a framework for making decisions about what should guide us in elementary/middle grade sciencing. Schools are social institutions; broad social concerns and issues must be considered when developing goals. The nature and interests of students are especially important in planning these goals. The following statements of goals for elementary sciencing are adapted from the work of the National Center for Improving Science Education.[16] These goals are comprehensive and representative of the emphases of many different national and state organizations and local school districts.

1. *Curiosity.* Elementary science programs should nurture and sustain students' natural curiosity about the world.
   a. Allow students to explore the natural and technological world.
   b. Develop students' abilities to ask questions about the natural world.

TABLE 1–3

National science education and reform projects

Who	What
Benchmarks for Science Literacy Project 2061 American Association for the Advancement of Science (AAAS) Oxford University Press 1333 H St., NW Washington, DC 20005 (202)326-6666	■ a vehicle for teachers to use to design their own science curricula ■ statements of what all students should know or be able to do in science, mathematics, and technology by end of grades 2, 5, 8, and 12 ■ the nature of science, the scientific enterprise, historical perspectives, integrated disciplines, and themes ■ experiences with natural and social phenomena to which students should be exposed ■ episodes to encourage students to enjoy science
Science for All Americans American Association for the Advancement of Science (AAAS) Oxford University Press 1333 H St., NW Washington, DC 20005 (202)326-6666	■ students study interdisciplinary themes
The Content Core **Volume I, A Guide for Curriculum Designers**	■ the integration and coordination of the disciplines of science Grades 6–12, in which each year (for seven years) students study biology, chemistry, earth/space science, and physics ■ sequences topics developmentally; i.e., Grades 6–8 are presented descriptively and phenomenologically, progressing to more theoretical and analytical at later grades
Scope, Sequence, and Coordination, and Teacher Guides, NSTA, 1993 The National Science Teachers Association 1840 Wilson Blvd. Arlington, VA 22201-3000 (703)243-7177	■ content of the four disciplines in The Content Core is organized by three grade-level groups (6–8, 9–10, 11–12) and accompanied by narratives to encourage teachers to use innovative teaching procedures ■ coordination happens when teacher integrates one discipline with another ■ explicitly takes into account learners' prior knowledge and experiences as communicated in their preconceptions and metaphors ■ content (and the learning of it) is sequenced from concrete experience and descriptive expression to abstract symbolism and quantitative expression ■ concrete encounters with science phenomena *before* descriptive terminology is presented ■ integrate subjects outside science (e.g., music, art, history); practical applications using examples from technology; and challenges to solve personal and societal issues that have relevant, underlying scientific elements

Sources: Janet L. Gerking, "Editor's Corner," *The Science Teacher* 62, no. 1 (Jan. 1995), 6. Rodger W. Bybee, *Reforming Science Education* (New York: Teachers College Press, 1994). Rodger W. Bybee and G. DeBoer, "Research as Goals for the Science Curriculum" in D. Gabel (ed.) *Handbook of Research in Science Teaching and Learning* (Upper Saddle River, NJ: Merrill/Prentice Hall, 1994). Rodger W. Bybee and Audrey B. Champagne, "An Introduction to the National Science Education Standards: An Achievable Challenge for Science

Who	What
Goals 2000: Educate America Act Office of Educational Research and Improvement/FIRST United States Department of Education 555 New Jersey Ave., NW Room 522 Washington, DC 20208-5524 (202)219-1496	■ for the first time, the federal and state governments are committed by this law to national education-content standards in 13 content areas, including science ■ major aspirations for American students (by the year 2000) are to: (a) leave Grades 4,8,12 having demonstrated competency over subject matter in the 13 content areas, including science; (b) be first in the world in mathematics and science achievement; and (c) be literate and posses the knowledge and skills necessary to compete in a global economy. ■ makes funds available to develop comprehensive improvements to reform educational systems based on world-class standards and high expectations for all learners ■ teachers will have access to programs for the continued improvement of their professional skills needed to educate and prepare students for the twenty-first century
National Science Education Standards The National Research Council of the National Academy of Sciences 2101 Constitution Ave., NW Washington, DC 20418 (202)334-1399	■ all K–12 students will have (a) opportunities to attain high levels of scientific literacy; (b) sufficient time to achieve science knowledge with deep understanding of scientific concepts; and (c) experiences that assist them in learning that science is an engaging and active process. ■ standards for the professional development of science teachers will include learning science, learning to learn, learning to teach science, and developing professional development programs ■ methods of inquiry, rules of evidence, and ways of formulating questions reflect contemporary science practices ■ science education reform is systemic, and therefore the responsibility of all persons in the school community
New Standards Project Joint venture of the National Center on Education and the Economy and the Learning Research and Development Center at the University of Pittsburgh 700 Eleventh St., NW Suite 750 Washington, DC 20001 (202)783-3668	■ adopting a set of national education standards in mathematics, English language arts, science, and applied learning ■ developing a performance-based assessment system devised to measure learner performance against these national content standards ■ portfolios will be the primary assessment instrument ■ teachers will be trained in writing sample learner portfolios; these portfolio items will be field tested and student portfolios developed from them ■ teacher networking conferences and analysis sessions will study portfolio materials, construction, and scoring, to

Teachers, *The Science Teacher* 62, no. 1 (Jan. 1995), 40–45. Hans O. Andersen, "Teaching Toward 2000: Examining Science Education Reform," *The Science Teacher* 61, no. 6 (Sep. 1994), 49–53. Jack T. MacDonald, "Guest Editorial. Goals 2000: Educate America Act," *Technological Horizons in Education (T.H.E.)* 21, no. 10 (May 1994), 10. Gary G. Allen, "New Eisenhower Program Takes Shape: ESES Reauthorization Finally Signed Into Law," *NSTA Reports!* (Dec. 1994/Jan. 1995), 1, 20–21.

    c. Develop students' abilities to identify problems of human adaptation.

2. *Skills for Investigating.* Elementary/middle grade science programs should develop skills for investigating the natural world, solving problems, and making decisions.

    a. Enrich students' understanding of and ability to use processes of science.

    b. Advance students' understanding of and ability to use problem-solving and decision-making strategies.

3. *Knowledge.* Students' knowledge base in science and technology should be developed through elementary science programs.

    a. Guide students in acquiring relevant, useful content knowledge in science, technology, and health.

    b. Assist students in improving explanations of their world.

4. *Nature of Science, Technology, and Society.* Elementary/middle grade science programs should strive to develop students' understanding of and attitudes about the nature, limits, and possibilities of science and technology.

    a. Lead students to recognize and apply scientific attitudes and habits of mind.

    b. Increase students' understanding of science and technology as major human achievements.

    c. Help students to become more aware of interactions of science and technology with society.

    d. Assist students in using scientific and technological knowledge, attitudes, and skills in decision making.

ORGANIZING SCIENCING GOALS INTO FIVE DOMAINS

Alan J. McCormack and Robert E. Yager [17] propose these five categories or *domains* of sciencing, designed to help students become scientifically and technologically literate: knowing and understanding, exploring and discovering, imagining and creating, feeling and valuing, and using and applying.

These domains were organized by McCormack and Yager into a *taxonomy.* That is, each domain is arranged in a hierarchy, with each item in the domain ranked by its importance. Figure 1–5 presents the five domains with a description of what students may do or learn in each domain. McCormack and Yager say that too often science education is limited to the first two domains (knowing and understanding and exploring and discovering), which relate primarily to the products and processes of science. They contend that the other three domains must be included in these times of global environmental problems, complex social and political issues, and general concerns about the future. To address these concerns, the domain of imagining and creating emphasizes the creative dimension of using science for the benefit of people. The domain of feeling and valuing looks at human values, feelings, and decision-making skills. The domain of using and applying looks at how to use information gained from school science studies in everyday life. A science education program, especially one that is science/technology/society oriented, must focus on all of the interrelated five domains, but it should stress the vital importance of these domains: imagining and creating, feeling and valuing, and using and applying. It is in these domains that students use their acquired science knowledge and skills to clarify and strengthen their values and then apply and act upon them as responsible citizens. How can this be accomplished?

SCIENCING WITH AN EMPHASIS ON STS

As we've seen, science proposes *explanations* for observations about the natural world; technology proposes *solutions* for problems of human adaptation to the environment. Many scientists and other citizens are becoming increasingly concerned about the societal implications of science and technology.

Always, what is discovered through science and technology can be used for either the ben-

5. Using and Applying (applications and connections)
- sees instances of scientific concepts in everyday life
- applies learned science concepts and skills to real technological problems
- understands scientific and technological principles involved in household devices
- uses scientific processes in solving problems that occur in everyday life
- understands and evaluates mass media reports of scientific developments
- makes decisions related to personal health, nutrition, and lifestyles based on knowledge of scientific concepts rather than hearsay and emotions
- integrates science with other subjects

4. Feeling and Valuing (attitudinal)
- develops positive attitudes towards science, school, teachers, and self
- explores human emotions
- develops sensitivity to and respect for the feelings of other people
- expresses personal feelings in a constructive way
- makes decisions about personal values and social and environmental issues

3. Imagining and Creating (creative)
- visualizes or produces mental images
- combines objects and ideas in new ways
- produces alternate or unusual uses for objects
- solves problems and puzzles
- fantasizes
- pretends
- day dreams
- designs devices and machines
- produces unusual ideas

2. Exploring and Discovering (scientific processes)
- uses processes of science to learn how real scientists think and work (observe and describe, classify and organize, measure and chart, communicate, predict and infer, hypothesize, test hypotheses, identify and control variables, interpret data, and construct instruments, simple devices, and physical models)
- uses manipulative (psychomotor) skills as well as cognitive skills

1. Knowing and Understanding (scientific information)
- learns specific information (facts, concepts, theories, and laws)
- investigates knowledge of science's history and philosophy

FIGURE 1–5

The five domains of science education

Source: Modified for materials in Alan J. McCormack and Robert E. Yager, "A New Taxonomy of Science Education," *The Science Teacher* 56, no. 2 (Feb. 1989): 47–48.

efit or detriment of society. Increasingly, concerned people and scientists are trying to educate the public about problems such as population explosion, pollution, insecticide poisoning of the environment, AIDS, and drug and alcohol abuse. You must be prepared to help your students to learn *both* science and technology so they can see the impact of both on their everyday lives and on society. In modern life, science, technology, and society are inextricably entwined. That is why this text will use this combined word: science/technology/society (STS).

You can readily see the relationships between science, technology, and society—and their implications for your teaching—in Figure 1–6.

FIGURE 1–6

The relationship between science, technology, and society—and their connection to educational goals

Source: Susan Loucks-Horsley, et al., *Elementary School Science for the 90's* (Andover, MA: The NET-WORK, Inc., 1989), 30. Reproduced with permission of the National Center for Improving Science Education/The NET-WORK, Inc. Copyright © 1990.

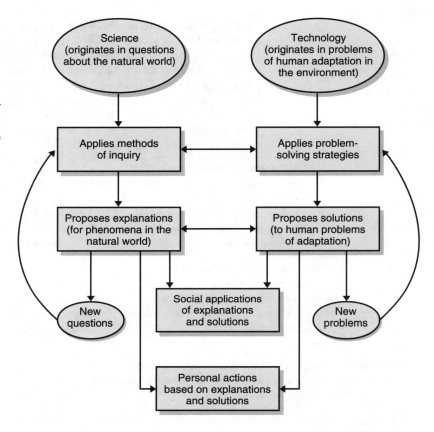

By linking science to technology to society, you facilitate students' learning in all three fields.

In your science teaching, *consciously* use STS themes. Help your students identify STS issues and problems that are relevant to *their* everyday lives and society in general. Here are some suggestions as you begin your search for ways to involve your students in exploring STS problems and issues.[18]

Emphasize Relevant STS Problems

Brandwein and Glass tell us that, "A primary purpose of science teaching is to address the most crucial problems of society. Problems . . . must become the focus of good teaching and thoughtful learning."[19] This goal of organizing learning in science around STS problems is reinforced by this recommendation adopted by the National Science Teachers Association's Board of Directors in January 1990: "Develop curricula that provide opportunities for all students and adults to study real-life, personal, and societal science and technology problems."[20]

From your own experiences with students, your community, and the national and international situations, you know there is no shortage of real-life personal and societal STS problems around which your students' learnings can be focused. Our lives are influenced by science and technology in areas such as communications, transportation, medicine, farming, manufacturing, space exploration, warfare, and politics. In the early grades your students are constantly in contact with and are curious about computers, TV and other electronic gadgets, how schools and their homes are heated and cooled, what happens to their garbage and toilet wastes, and how their bodies are changing. The National Assessment of Educational Progress (NAEP) results presented in Figure 1–7 show that 9-year-olds wanted to help solve serious environmental problems such as pollution, energy waste, disease, and food shortages, but that unfortunately, they had little experience with environmental issues in school and had taken few field trips related to the environment.

When your students investigate issues and problems that are real to them, they will not only learn the science and technology behind these issues and problems but also become aware of how this science and technology applies to machines, devices, and inventions. The "Self-Evaluation and Further Study" section at the end of this chapter, Chapter 7, and the Appendixes will assist you in identifying and using STS issues and problems.

Guiding Your Students to Be STS Decision Makers

You and your students make decisions every day about your own welfare and that of others, the environments in which you live, and, directly or indirectly, the world's environment. To assist your students in making wise decisions and acting on them, you must provide them with practice, skills, and guidance. Practice comes from actively involving your students in real-life problem solving/decision-making situations. Guidance means helping them develop skills in solving problems and making decisions and consciously avoiding telling them what and how to decide on alternatives. You must become familiar with ways of approaching problem solving/decision making and then learn how to guide your students. Here is a model to assist you.

Search, Solve, Create, Share, and Act

One model for developing STS student problem-solving skills is called "Search, Solve, Create,

	Yes
Use less electricity?	91
Spend a day helping clean up litter from a street, park, or road?	86
Use returnable bottles rather than "throw-away" bottles?	84
Walk and ride bicycles more often?	79
Separate trash (bottles, cans, paper, etc.) for recycling?	75
Use less heat in the winter to save fuel?	73
Drive or ride in a small economy car?	52

FIGURE 1–7

Percentages of 9-year-olds willing to perform various conservation activities

Source: Roger T. Johnson, "What Research Says," *Science and Children* (February 1981): 39–41.

Share, and Act."[21] The purpose is to conduct a search from what is known (prior knowledge) and extend that knowledge base through problem solving and application or action taking. Table 1–4 shows how the five phases work.

Integrate Problem Solving with All Content Areas

STS is one of the best examples of the trend to integrate student learning. The STS approach engages students in the active exploration of issues and problems they have identified and helps them make the important connection between human activities and science. Many educators support this and it has the endorsement of the American Association for the Advancement of Science in *Project 2061:*

Young children are veteran technology users by the time they enter school. They ride in automobiles, use household utilities, operate wagons and bikes, use garden tools, help with the cooking, operate the television set, and so on . . . . Activities should focus on problems and needs in and around the school

TABLE 1–4

STS problem-solving model

Phases	Procedures/Practices	Decision Making/Action Taking
Search. Select STS topics from community events relevant to learners' lives, topics in science textbooks, school/district/state science curriculum, hands-on/minds-on activities, field trips, TV/computer exposure, etc.	Students brainstorm to produce a list of initial ideas in question form for possible in-depth investigation. One or two questions are eventually selected as the search nucleus.	"How much food is wasted in our school's hot lunch program on a typical day?'"
Solve. Students apply previously learned processes, procedures, and information to seek solutions to the problems selected jointly with the teacher.	Describe and instruct students on how to use relevant research methodology such as descriptive, experimental, or correlational approaches to solving this STS problem.	Have students station themselves in the lunchroom at cans where food trays are emptied so samples of leftover food can be measured and recorded. Interviews can also be employed to discover which foods are uneaten and perhaps why.
Create. Collecting and analyzing data may be done through constructing and using line and bar graphs, dot charts, and other organizational procedures.	Students determine to use a graph to show the percentages of food wasted on a typical day.	A histogram could be constructed from the data above showing the kinds and amounts of specific foods wasted. (See Chapter 5 on Assessment for directions on constructing histograms and other graphs.)
Share. Students communicate findings and interact with their fellow students in a variety of ways.	Oral and written reports, posters, songs, videotapes, poetry and nonverbal projects can be used to communicate findings.	Students could videotape their fellow students emptying their food trays into waste receptacles. Food waste will be self-evident. Videotape could be viewed at total school assembly followed up by classroom discussions concerning food waste and how to cut down on it.
Act. STS problem solving is not complete until students act on their findings.	Individuals or groups of students might defend their points of view before the class or people in authority, write letters, or volunteer to do something to solve or alleviate the problem.	Students and their teachers could arrange a meeting with school teachers, district or school nutritionist, school lunchroom personnel, and administrators to show the results of their study and make recommendations for solving the food waste problem. Excess food could be donated to local soup kitchen.

that interest children and that are addressed feasibly and safely.[22]

By making STS problem solving part of your total classroom curriculum you reinforce and enrich science and technology and the other subject areas as well. This makes learning more meaningful for your students. Chapter 8 provides you with specific, practical, classroom activities and suggestions for integrating STS problem solving with all curricular areas.

Guiding Your Students in Problem Solving/Decision Making/Action Taking

Problem solving, decision making, and taking appropriate action are facilitated when students learn to work strategically. Figure 1–8 presents a

FIGURE 1–8

Model for problem solving/decision making/action taking

Source: Modified from *Elementary Science Syllabus* (Albany, NY: The University of the State of New York, The State Education Department, Division of Program Development, 1985), 8. Used by permission.

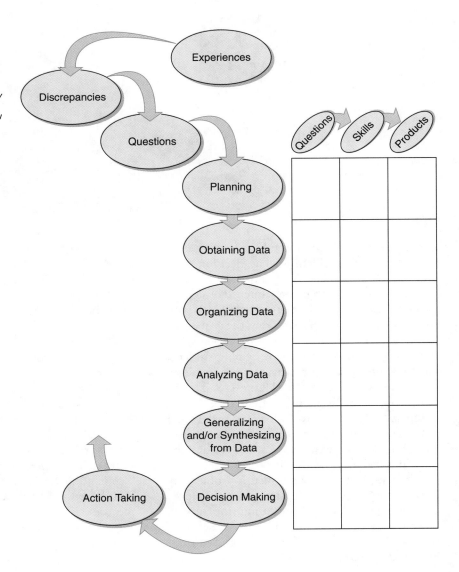

A histogram is one communication medium for data collection.

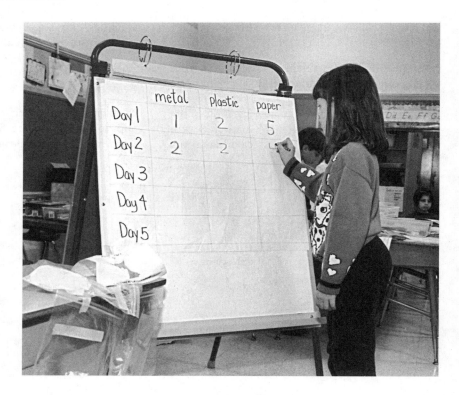

model that you will find useful for guiding your students in their problem solving, decision making, and action taking. You and your students should modify or change the sequence of steps as needed. Gear it to the developmental level of your students. Avoid slavishly following the sequence.

The problem-solving/decision-making/action-taking sequence begins by helping students identify a problem. To do this, use the sequence shown on the top left side of Figure 1–8. That is, assist your students in using their experiences, observations, and prior knowledge to make them aware of discrepancies in phenomena and events. This should lead them to raise questions, and the questions will help them define the problem.

Once students have identified a problem by constructing a precise question, they can proceed with problem solving using the model. Since the model is organized into a sequence of steps with specific tasks for each step, you can isolate each step for instruction. Once students

learn the tasks for each step, they will be able to use them, either consciously or automatically, to solve problems and take appropriate actions.

Shown at the top right of Figure 1–8 are the tasks for each step:

- *Questions.* The problem solver should construct precise questions that will help clarify the problem and the steps that must be taken to solve it. Students should view each precise question as a little piece of the problem to be solved.
- *Skills.* The problem solver can get answers to precise questions by applying appropriate skills or processes. Students should be taught to select and apply the best skills or processes for the specific task implied by the questions.
- *Products.* The problem solver creates tangible products by applying appropriate skills or processes to the specific tasks. For example, by applying the skill of recording data, the problem solver may create the tangible product of

a chart or graph. Tangible products contain answers to questions.

Next, let's explore the steps in the sequence.

Planning. Consider these focus questions in planning:

- What is the problem?
- What background information do I already have?
- What new information do I need?
- What procedure or sequence of actions do I need to follow?
- How will I know when I have solved the problem?

Students should be taught that when they construct a plan, they must always assume that the plan may have to be revised in light of new information.

Obtaining Data. Consider this focus question: What new information do I need? Obtaining data that is good quantitatively as well as qualitatively is essential to effective problem solving.

Organizing Data. The problem solver establishes some pattern of order or form for the data obtained. Consider this focus question: In what useful way(s) can the information be organized? Finding the best way to organize the data is very important in effective problem solving.

Analyzing Data. Consider the following focus questions in analyzing data: How do the data fit together? What patterns and relationships may be here? How can the data best be analyzed? Analysis of data must be careful and reasoned in effective problem solving.

Generalizing and/or Synthesizing From Data. Here the problem solver draws conclusions or creates alternative choices (potential solutions to the problem) to use in the next step—decision making. Consider the focus question: What can be drawn from the analyses of information? Sound alternative choices become the basis for informed decision making in effective problem solving.

Decision Making. In the decision-making step, a problem solver again uses a sequence of focus questions to arrive at a decision:

- Based upon the data and analysis, what decision(s) need to be made?
- What are some of the alternative choices and the rationale for each?
- What values are directly related to each choice, and how do they relate to it?
- Which choice(s) is(are) best?

The decision may lead directly to the solution of the problem; it may point to new directions in pursuit of the solution; or it may suggest new problems to be solved. In effective problem solving, the problem solver makes an informed decision by working from a rational base of data to make the best choice. Figure 1–9

FIGURE 1–9

STS and teaching/learning science

Source: Adapted from Carolyn Steele Graham, "STS in Middle/Junior High School Science: One State's Response," *Science Through Science Technology and Society Reporter* 2, no. 5 (Dec. 1986), 6.

shows how this is done in the middle grades with an STS focus.

Action Taking.   Decisions should lead students to action, and the action(s) freely chosen by the problem solver should address such questions as:

- What are some alternative actions and on what criteria shall they be selected?
- What might be consequences of each action taken?
- Who might be affected by each possible action and in what ways?

Although the problem-solving model is organized into a sequence of steps that have a logical progression, it is important that, in practice, problem solvers move back and forth among the steps as a problem is worked on.

As you go back over the three problem-solving models presented in this chapter, you should note that they *all* contain elements of the questions, skills, and products approaches described here. These models each lay a foundation for integrating the essential elements of science content, not the reverse. This concept describes the new challenge for science teaching today: To develop scientific, technologically literate students. We can't teach science as a separate subject, without relevant meaning to the everyday lives of students. If students discover facts, concepts, principles, theories, and laws for themselves, they can approach the future with confidence that they are problem solvers. Then they can create a better world.

SUMMARY

We live in a world brimming with diversity, yet it is orderly. The universe is not random. Human beings, endowed with innate curiosity, are driven to grasp the patterns of the universe and to discover the basic laws that produce the observed order. The activity of questioning and exploring the universe and finding and expressing its hidden order is called *science.*

Science offers all of us ways to understand, make predictions about, and adapt to our complex environment. Scientists' ways of studying the world include both empirical and analytic procedures. Science for children should model scientists' methods of investigation. This can be best achieved through a hands-on/minds-on approach.

At the empirical level of investigation, scientists/students take in information and organize it for analysis. Empirical processes of science include observation, classification, and measurement. At the analytic level, scientists/students interpret their findings by using processes such as hypothesizing, experimenting, inferring, and predicting. Numerous other scientific process skills are identified that can be used daily by all of us in our in-school and out-of-school problem solving. The products of empirical and analytic procedures in science are facts, concepts, principles, and theories. The products of science do not stand alone, but are connected to real-world evidence through science processes.

Science is intrinsically linked to technology and society. Science proposes explanations about the natural world, and technology proposes solutions for problems of human adaptations to the environment. The implications for developing an STS (Science/Technology/Society) focus for elementary and middle school students in science education therefore include: guiding students to search for STS connections in science investigations; finding real-life STS issues, questions, and problems to explore; and involving students in looking for answers to STS issues and making wise decisions.

The taxonomy of the five domains of science education offers a comprehensive view of STS education and suggests various STS problem-solving procedures. STS problem solving in the elementary and middle school grades should seek to integrate or correlate STS activities with all curricular disciplines.

Consistent with the descriptions of science, technology, society, and children developed in this chapter, the goals of science education are (1) to nurture and sustain children's curiosity about the world; (2) to help students develop and use process skills for investigation of the nat-ural world—solving problems, making decisions, and taking wise action; (3) to assist students in constructing and broadening their knowledge base and concept development in science and technology; (4) to facilitate students' under-standing of and positive attitudes toward the nature, limits, and possibilities of science and technology; (5) to guide students in identifying real-life problems of interest to them—propos-ing solutions, collecting data, and taking appro-priate actions.

SELF-ASSESSMENT AND ADDITIONAL STUDY

1. Without rereading the text, define the following *in your own words:*

   science   technology   sciencing
   scientific products, processes, and attitudes

   Now check your definitions against those in the text.
2. Keep a log of all your actions for several days. Which science processes did you use to conduct the activities and solve any problems that arose? Which nonscience processes did you use?
3. Record several facts, principles, and concepts associated with the theory of gravitation. (For example: *Fact*—all objects attract one another gravitationally; *principle*—gravitational forces are stronger for large objects; *concept*—mass.) Select a second theory and list facts, principles, and con-cepts associated with it.
4. Select two scientific or technological discoveries or inventions that have improved the earth's envi-ronment and/or improved the lives of people. In addition, list some positive and possible negative effects these technologies, discoveries, or inven-tions might have.
5. Using the following as an initial source, find real, everyday issues and problems that your students could use as the foci for an STS problem-solving investigation:
   - Nancy Kober, *What We Know About Science Teaching and Learning. EDTalk series* (Washington, DC: Council for Education Development and Research, 1993).
   - Leonard J. Waks, "The Responsibility Spiral: A Curriculum Framework for STS Education," *Theory Into Practice* 31, no. 1 (Winter 1992), 12–18.
   - Robert E. Yager, "Make a Difference with STS: Should We Toss out the Textbooks?" *The Science Teacher* 60, no. 2, (Feb. 1993), 45–48.
   - *Science Through Science, Technology, and Society (S-STS)* The Pennsylvania State University, 128 Willard Building, University Park, PA 16802. (Publishes *S-STS REPORTER* quar-terly, with the latest national STS activities and reviews of STS curriculum materials.)
   - *The Child's World: Presenting Technology to Children in the Primary and Junior Divisions* (Willowdale, Ontario, Canada: Metropolitan Toronto School Board, 1989).
   - R.W. Bybee, C.E. Buchwald, S. Heil, P.J. Kuerbis, C. Matsumoto, and J.D. McInerney, *Science and Technology Education for the Elementary Schools: Frameworks for Curri-culum and Education for the Elementary Years.* (Washington, DC: National Center for Impro-ving Science Education, 1989).
6. Conduct a discussion with your students to iden-tify everyday STS problems in their lives (e.g., consumer choices, health, nutrition, or local envi-ronmental issues). Record specific questions for which they want to find answers.
7. Conduct (with a student or students) an inter-view with a scientist, engineer, physician, com-puter expert, or other individual in your

community who uses science and technology in his or her career. Assist the student(s) in formulating interview questions, e.g., how and why the people chose their scientific or technological careers, who or what influenced them, what training they needed, what specifically they do, what are the positive and negative features of their work, and where is their field heading in the future.

8. Select a science program from your local school district, state education department, or any other source. Compare it to any of the national science education or reform projects on these criteria or others that you choose:

- What provisions are made for actively engaging learners in doing science and seeing science as on-going processes in their everyday lives?
- How are all learners assisted to become scientifically literate, regardless of gender, cultural background, or physical or mental challenges?
- What activities are presented to help learners understand their environments and their role in it?
- To what extent are performance-based assessment techniques used to determine the degree to which learners have achieved the stated goals?

9. Research and write a report on meeting the needs of a diverse student population including women, physically and mentally challenged students, and students from multicultural backgrounds in elementary/middle grade science. Start your research with these articles from *The Science Teacher* 62, no. 2 (Feb. 1995):

- Mary M. Atwater, "The Multicultural Science Classroom. Part I: Meeting the needs of a diverse student population," 21–23.
- Jennifer W. Harris, "Sheltered Instruction. Bridging the language gap in the science classroom," 24–27.
- Erica M. Brownstein and Thomas Destino, "Science Enrichment Outreach," 29–33.

10. Research a biography, autobiography, or article about the scientific or technological contributions of women, minority members, or persons with physical or mental challenges. You might start with one of the following:

- Thom Alcoze, et al., *Multiculturalism in Mathematics, Sciences, and Technology: Readings and Activities* (New York: Addison-Wesley Publications, 1993). Provides role models in science content areas.
- Marcia Myers Bonta, *Women in the Field* (Austin: Texas A&M University Press, 1991).
- Ivan Van Sertima, (ed.), *Blacks in Science* (New York: Transaction Books, 1990).
- S. Phyllis Stearner, *Able Scientists—Disabled Persons: Careers in the Sciences* (Clarendon Hills, IL: Foundation for Science and the Handicapped, Inc., 1990).
- Meg Wilson (ed.), *Options for Girls* (Arlington, VA: National Science Teachers Association, 1992).

Share your findings with your college classmates or school colleagues in whatever format suits you.

NOTES

1. American Association for the Advancement of Science, *Benchmarks for Science Literacy: Project 2061* (New York: Oxford University Press, 1993), 3.

2. For specific examples of scientific/technological literacy in everyday life see: Rodger W. Bybee, C. E. Buchwald, S. Heil, P. J. Kuerbis, C. Matsumoto, and J. D. McInerney, *Science and Technology Education for the Elementary Schools: Framework for Curriculum and Instruction* (Washington, DC: The National Center for Improving Education, 1989).

3. Bryan Nordstrum, "Advice from a Collegiate Colleague," *Science and Children,* 28, no. 8 (May 1991), 17.

4. Phyllis Huff et al., "Excellence in Elementary Education," in John E. Penick and Mitzi Bame, (eds.). *Focus on Excellence: Elementary Science Revisited*, 4, no. 3 (Arlington, VA: National Science Teachers Association, 1988), 7.

5. Ina V. S. Mullis and Lynn B. Jenkins, *The Science Report Card: Elements of Risk and Recovery* (Princeton, NJ: Educational Testing Service, 1988).

6. For excellent reporting on science processes, read Kenneth R. Mechling and Donna L. Oliver, *Handbook I: Science Teaches Basic Skills* (Arlington, VA: National Science Teachers Association, 1983), 8–12.

7. Nancy Paulu with Margery Martin, *Helping Your Child Learn Science* (Washington, DC: U.S. Department of Education, Office of Educational Research and Improvement, 1991), 5.

8. For a deeper look at scientific attitudes and values, see Chapter 12, "Habits of Mind" in American Association for the Advancement of Science, *Science For All Americans: Project 2061* (New York: Oxford University Press, 1990), 183–194.

9. A broader list of scientific attitudes and values for children to cultivate is given in Bybee et al., *op.cit.*, 5–52.

10. James Trefil, "Quantum Physics' World: Now You See It, Now You Don't, *Smithsonian*, (August 1987), 69.

11. M. F. Perutz, *Is Science Necessary?* (New York: Dutton, 1989).

12. "What Is TEI? Interview with Norman Bodek," *TEI: Total Employment Involvement* 1, no. 1 (May 1988), 4.

13. Horace Freeland Judson, *The Search for Solutions* (New York: Rinehart & Winston, 1980), 114.

14. Steven W. Gilbert, "Model Building and a Definition of Science," *Journal of Research in Science Teaching* 28, no. 1 (Feb. 1991), 73–79.

15. Nancy Paulu with Margery Martin, *Helping Your Child Learn Science* (Washington, DC: U.S. Department of Education, Office of Educational Research and Improvement, 1991), 5.

16. Rodger W. Bybee, C. E. Buchwald, S. Heil, P. J. Kuerbis, C. Matsumoto, and J. D. McInerney, *Science and Technology Education for the Elementary Schools: Framework for Curriculum and Instruction* (Washington, DC: The National Center for Improving Education, 1989).

17. Alan J. McCormack and Robert E. Yager, "A New Taxonomy of Science Education," *The Science Teacher* 56, no. 2 (Feb. 1989), 47–48.

18. The author is indebted to Susan Loucks-Horsley et al., *Elementary School Science for the 90's* (Andover, MA: The NETWORK, Inc., 1990), chapter 3, "Connect Science to Technology," 1990).

19. Paul W. Brandwein and Lynn W. Glass, "A Permanent Agenda for Science Teachers, Part II: What Is Good Teaching?" *The Science Teacher* 58, no. 4 (Apr. 1991), 37–38.

20. "Science Teachers Speak Out: The NSTA Lead Paper on Science and Technology Education for the 21st Century Adopted by the NSTA Board of Directors January 1990," *NSTA Reports*, (Apr./May 1990), 42.

21. Read the following for a fuller explanation: Edward L. Pizzini, Sandra A. Bell, and Daniel S. Shepardson, "Rethinking Thinking in the Science Classroom," *The Science Teacher* 55, no. 9 (Dec. 1988), 22–25.

22. American Association for the Advancement of Science, *Benchmarks for Science Literacy. Project 2061* (New York: Oxford University Press, 1993), 44.

CHAPTER 2

Intellectual Development and Science Learning

The substantial body of research on learning should be the basis for making instruction more effective. This research suggests that students learn by constructing their own meaning from experiences. A constructivist approach requires very different science curricula and methods of science instruction.[1]

ADDRESSING STUDENTS' MISCONCEPTIONS

When students come to science class, they have already formed many ideas about the world from their daily experiences. Frequently their ideas are incomplete or incorrect interpretations, not congruent with accepted scientific views. These misconceptions and naive theories reflect their special perspective as children. Below are two humorous examples from Paulu and Martin's[2] collection of sixth grade students' misconceptions:

- Fossils are bones that animals are through wearing.
- Some people can tell what time it is by looking at the sun, but I have never been able to make out the numbers.

William C. Philips,[3] an earth science teacher, also compiled a list of commonly held misconceptions in earth science from observations of his own students and research over a decade. Although Philips compiled his list by age levels, he cautions us to remember that those misconceptions held by adults may also be held by children and vice versa. Here is a small sampling of misconceptions about the atmosphere:

K–9

- Rain comes from holes in clouds.
- Rain occurs when clouds get scrambled and melt.
- God and angels cause thunder and lightning.
- Clouds are made of cotton, wool, or smoke.

College

- Frontal rain is caused by "cooling by contact" between fronts.

Adults

- The oxygen we breathe does not come from plants.
- One degree of temperature is smaller on the Celsius and Kelvin scales than on the Fahrenheit.

Research studies[4] show that learners' misconceptions must be changed *before* more accurate concepts and explanations can be learned. This is difficult, as research indicates that learners hold fast to misconceptions, even into adulthood. College students have even been known to ignore information presented in class when it is inconsistent with their prior convictions.[5] Further, research shows that when students' observations do not fit their predictions, they simply criticize the experiment. Also, students sometimes forget or choose not to use parts of the explanations that do not fit their own predictions. How then can you guide students into changing their scientific misconceptions and naive beliefs into new and more sophisticated scientific notions?

Addressing students' misconceptions is clearly a challenge, especially since daily experiences often reinforce misconceptions. If children are allowed to discuss their misconceptions and then to test them repeatedly, they are more likely to modify their beliefs and accomplish a conceptual change. However, this takes time. Just *telling* them the truth is quicker, but remember the conclusion of more than one researcher: "Classroom instruction in a topical area guarantees neither an understanding of the topic nor a reduction in misconceptions".[6]

Students are continuously affected by their environment and strive incessantly to interpret phenomena and events. Therefore, it is probable that your students will come to the classroom with existing ideas that make sense to them but which may be wrong from an accepted scientific perspective.[7] One of your most important responsibilities is to discover— and help modify—students' incomplete or incorrect interpretations (called **naive theories and misconceptions**). Changing naive theories and misconceptions and helping to build meaningful understandings about scientific concepts is quite difficult. To be successful you must first know how students learn. That is why this chapter is organized around the following questions:

- What is the nature of knowledge? How is knowledge acquired and organized into memory?
- What roles do prior knowledge, information processing skills, and metacognition play in the acquisition and use of knowledge?
- How do students' naive theories and misconceptions affect learning?
- What are the current findings and theories on learners' cognitive development, and what are the implications for your classroom teaching?

THE IMPACT OF PIAGET ON SCIENCE TEACHING/LEARNING

Let us start by examining the relevance of Piagetian, constructivist, and other cognitive theories to teaching and learning science.

Piaget's Cognitive Development Theory

Through some 60 years of research with children, Jean Piaget formulated a major theory of how children develop in their ways of knowing and solving problems. Science educators discovered Piaget's work around 1960. Piaget's view of knowledge as complex and hierarchically structured and of the learner as an active constructor of her own knowledge offered science educators a welcomed alternative to behaviorism and associationism that was in vogue at the time. Piaget's studies of children's thinking about a wide variety of phenomena, concepts, and principles of science proved to be a rich source of ideas for the design of science programs and instructional strategies. Piagetian theory was influential in virtually all elementary science curriculum development projects in the 1960s and remains prominent in science education research and practice today.

Although his findings about children have generally stood the test of time, cognitive psychologists today challenge some of Piaget's theoretical conclusions. Nevertheless, Piaget's work on children's thinking about natural phenomena and scientific concepts has heuristic value to science teachers.

At this point in your professional preparation, you probably have considerable knowledge of children's cognitive development; this is a cumulative result of your psychology, child development, and curriculum courses; of intelligently observing children; and perhaps of raising your own children. Therefore, the presentation here will focus on those aspects of Piaget's theory that are particularly applicable to science teaching.

Piaget's Developmental Stages Are Broad Benchmarks

Piaget has treated children's responses to the natural world in terms of four stages. Table 2–1 is a brief summary of research by Piaget and others of the four stages of cognitive development. He identified four main factors that influence cognitive development:

1. *Physical Maturation.* Biological growth of the central nervous system and other body parts.
2. *Physical Experiences.* Experiences with the physical world, including manipulation of material objects.
3. *Social Interaction.* Interactions with other people, including formal schooling.
4. *Equilibration.* A self-regulated learning process involving recognizing discrepancies between physical reality and personal ideas, and actively and persistently working to resolve the discrepancies through assimilation and accommodation.

The first three factors contributing to development are present in most other cognitive development theories. Equilibration is unique to Piaget's system and emphasizes the belief that individuals must actively construct their own meanings of the world. Equilibration is a self-regulated process involving curiosity, alertness, risk, effort, and persistence.

When using Piaget's stages in planning for your students, keep several considerations in mind:

- Even though the stage concept has been challenged by cognitive psychologists today, it is useful for elementary and middle grade science teaching because it gives teachers a *general* idea of the thinking patterns of pupils at different ages.
- The ages associated with each Piagetian stage are *only averages* and should be viewed as broad general benchmarks. Many children in a given age group may not have developed the characteristics indicated for that age.

- The stages are *hierarchical.* Each successive stage incorporates and builds on the preceding one. Thus, the sequence for passing through the four stages is always the same. No person skips a stage.
- When children reach each stage can *vary considerably* due to the factors influencing cognitive development. It is not unusual, for example, for children to be a year or more "behind" the average performance for their ages. Although they may be slower in cognitive development, this does not necessarily mean they will be cognitively inferior in later years to those who develop earlier.
- Many learners (including adults) have a tendency to *revert* to an earlier developmental stage when facing bewildering situations.

Look for ways Piaget's work has influenced science teaching in the following sections describing learning theories.

BEHAVIORISTS AND COGNITIVISTS: HOW DO THEY DEFINE LEARNING?

Two of the most popular approaches to learning used by teachers today are behaviorism and cognitivism. Prior to about 1975, the dominant approach to studying learning was **behaviorism**. Behavioral theories focus on the *external* aspects of learning, including external stimuli, behavioral responses of learners, and reinforcers that follow appropriate responses. Classroom discipline systems involving rewards and punishment are often based on behavioral theories. Behavioral theories also provide background for expository teaching approaches, in which teachers present information to be learned directly to learners. These approaches emphasize analyzing the material to be learned into small segments, writing behavioral objectives for each segment, presenting information to be learned very clearly and concisely, providing for a great deal of student practice, providing immediate

TABLE 2–1

Characteristics of thinking in Piaget's four stages of intellectual development

Sensorimotor (birth to 2 years)

The child

1. adapts to the external world through actions;
2. initially has no language or other means for labeling or representing objects and actions;
3. lacks representational means and does not "think" about the world;
4. by the end of the stage has developed rudimentary schemata for coordinating actions related to substance, space, time, and causality; and
5. begins to develop language for naming familiar things and actions.

Preoperational (2 to 7 years)

The child

1. develops extensive vocabulary;
2. makes judgments on the basis of perceptions, not conceptual considerations;
3. groups things based on familiar properties;
4. begins to develop extensive physical knowledge of the properties and behaviors of objects and organisms in the world;
5. does not think "reversibly";
6. does not think about parts and wholes simultaneously; and
7. takes a subjective, egocentric view of the world.

Concrete Operational (7 to 11 years)

The child

1. takes an objective view of the world, shifts reflectively from one aspect of a situation to another, and considers elements of a whole simultaneously rather than just successively;
2. begins to think operationally (i.e., groups elements into coherent wholes and considers elements and wholes reversibly);
3. uses operational thinking to form classes and series;
4. forms and uses relationships, including one-to-one correspondences, rules, simple scientific principles, and cause and effect relationships; and
5. conserves substance, liquid volume, length, area, and weight.

Formal Operational (11 to 14 + years)

The child

1. does higher-order thinking about the knowledge formed at the previous levels;
2. forms hypotheses, carries out controlled investigations, and relates evidence to theories;
3. deals with ratios, proportions, and probabilities; and
4. constructs and understands complex explanations involving deductive chains of logic.

Note: Children are unique, and Piaget's stages should be viewed only as broad, general benchmarks.

feedback on student responses, and providing for frequent review.[8] An expository teaching model called *direct instruction* is presented in Chapter 3.

Contrasting a behavioral approach is the **cognitive** perspective. Cognitive psychologists are concerned not only with the external, observable events of learning but also with what goes on inside the learner's head: how knowledge is acquired, organized, stored in memory, retrieved, and used in further learning and thinking. Look again at the chapter opening quotation, which emphasizes that in the cognitive view of learning, the learner must be an active constructor of knowledge rather than a passive recipient of information.

The next sections of this chapter focus on constructivist convictions that learning is linked to three related ideas:

1. prior knowledge
2. student learning styles
3. depth and understanding, rather than breadth of coverage and knowledge of vocabulary

To illustrate these points, selected contemporary cognitive theories about how students learn and think in science follow. These theories provide additional considerations for hands-on/minds-on guided discovery learning/teaching.

THE IMPORTANCE OF PRIOR KNOWLEDGE

Cognitive approaches to learning are centered on the nature and organization of knowledge and how it is acquired. What both students and scientists bring to their problem solving and learning experiences critically affects how they learn and build new knowledge. The acquisition of new knowledge always occurs in the context of, and is heavily influenced by, a pre-existing knowledge.

Look at Figure 2–1. What do you see? Study the figure before reading on. The same sensory data are available to all of us. You could probably reproduce an accurate sketch of the figure after studying it for a few seconds. The figure can be interpreted as a bear climbing up the other side of a tree. Do you see the figure differently after reading this interpretation? The bear is not inherent in the figure but is a result of your own perception of the lines, based on the ideas you bring to the picture.[9]

In a similar way, what a student is likely to see in a science investigation also depends on prior knowledge. In a research study, Champagne and Hornig[10] note that students who observed science demonstrations reported observations

FIGURE 2–1

What do you see in this figure? What you see depends on your prior experiences, knowledge, and assumptions.

Source: Norwood Russel Hanson, *Patterns of Discovery* (Cambridge, England: Cambridge University Press, 1965), 12–13. Reprinted with the permission of Cambridge University Press.

more closely aligned with their *existing* viewpoints than with what actually happened. Our prior knowledge and assumptions help us to make sense of new experiences and information.

What happens when new experiences and information do not make sense with what we already know or assume?

Schemata Help Organize and Store Past Experiences

Students are continuously affected by environment and incessantly strive to interpret these phenomena and events. They conceive interpretations that mollify them and permit them to function in everyday activities. Cognitive psychologists, including Jean Piaget, believe that associated experiences, information, and skills about a topic are organized in memory as networks or *schemata* (plural of *schema*). A **schema** is a cognitive framework in which we organize and store past experiences and knowledge.

When learners are faced with new experiences and information, a state of *disequilization* may

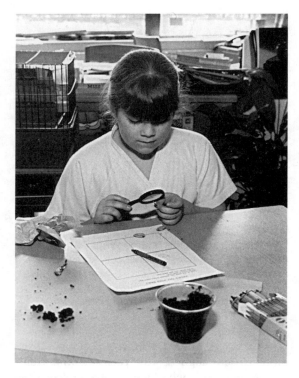

The prior knowledge students bring to their observations guides the inferences they make.

occur. That is, an inbalance develops when a learner is unsuccessful when trying to assimilate new experiences and information into existing schemata. Such learner discomfort prompts the need to expand a learner's basic knowledge.

Expanding the Knowledge Base. Because we are always encountering new experiences and ideas, knowledge is dynamic and in a constant state of flux. Growth of the knowledge base involves both the assimilation of new information to existing schemata and the accommodation or modification of existing schemata to better fit reality. Jean Piaget used the term *assimilation* for the learning process in which new information is incorporated into existing schemata without the need for major changes in the schemata. In assimilation, learners draw upon relevant schemata to assist them in orga-

nizing and making sense of new experiences. Current cognitive theorists have used the term *accretion* for the process of assimilating new knowledge into the knowledge base.

Piaget used the term *accommodation* to refer to the learning process in which existing schemata have to be altered to enable the schemata to better fit novel situations. Contemporary cognitive theorists have considerably elaborated Piaget's notion of accommodation, describing it in terms of creating, tuning, and restructuring schemata.[11]

Schema creation, the first type of accommodation, is the process of building new schemata to fit new information and ideas. For example, a student may have no schema to use in making sense of the term *first-class lever.* To understand the term the student would need to learn the following information:

- A lever is a bar that is free to turn on a pivot point called a fulcrum.
- A lever can be used to move a weight, called the resistance.
- The force exerted to move the weight is called the effort.
- For a first-class lever, the resistance is at one end of the bar, the effort is at the other end, and the fulcrum is in the middle, as shown in Figure 2–2.

In creating a schema, such information would have to be practiced, elaborated on, interrelated, and organized in the mind into a useful and coherent form.

Tuning, a second process involved in accommodation, is the modification and refinement of a schema as a result of using it in different situations. Shuell outlines these three learning mechanisms that are used as the basis for tuning:[12]

1. A schema is broadened in its range of application through its generalization to new situations. For example, students might be shown a variety of levers and asked to determine which of them are first-class levers; this is an example of tuning a schema. Students

FIGURE 2–2
For a first-class lever, the resistance is at one end of the bar, the effort is at the other, and the fulcrum is in the middle.

broaden their understanding of first-class levers as they struggle to generalize their concept to new situations.

2. Through a tuning process called **discrimination,** the range of applicability of a schema is refined by eliminating situations in which the knowledge would not apply. For instance, through recognizing that in some levers the fulcrum is not between the effort and the resistance, the students will further refine their schemata about first-class levers.

3. Schemata are strengthened through practice, that is, through their use in many varied situations.

Restructuring, the third process in accommodation, involves a more complete reorganization of an existing schema. For instance, suppose a student is required to construct a lever that can be used to move a larger weight by the use of a smaller effort. The knowledge incorporated in the first-class lever schema outlined previously is not sufficient to solve this task, which requires that the parts of a lever now be considered relationally. However, the student might restructure the schema by integrating it with knowledge gained from playground experiences with seesaws. Through playground experiences, students have learned to balance heavier students by having them sit closer to the fulcrum. Thus, the students might restructure their lever schema, reorganizing it around the general rule "the greater the resistance, the closer to the fulcrum it should be placed." The key to facilitating accommodation in teaching is to provide for the application of schemata in many different, challenging situations and to provide guidance and feedback to students as they work to apply and refine their existing knowledge.

In posing challenges to students, teachers must consider their levels of development. Some restructuring of schemata may call for higher-order thinking abilities that elementary students have not yet developed. Carrying the lever example a step further, suppose that a student is faced with the task of predicting where an 80-gram weight would need to be placed on a balance scale to balance a 40-gram weight. Generalizing from the seesaw schema, the student would have knowledge that the heavier weight would go closer to the center, but how much closer? According to Piaget, this task requires *proportional reasoning,* a type of formal operational thinking that develops in adolescence and beyond. The proportionality task, then, would not be developmentally appropriate for most elementary school students.

Use Schema Theory to Enhance Learning Opportunities

According to schema theory, information is organized in such a way that the activation of one piece of information in a schema tends to activate associated information in the schema. For instance, when a problem related to electricity is encountered, the whole electricity schema might be activated and made ready for potential use.

Schemata fulfill a number of functions in learning and problem solving. They help in the assimilation of new information, provide a basis for inferences that fill in gaps in incoming information, and help to direct searches of the environment for further needed information.

Instruction must attend to the development of schemata through allowing students time and opportunity to construct various links among information and procedures. Students should not be left totally on their own; teachers need to provide deliberate support for students in their construction of schemata. Support can be provided through questioning, supplying needed information, emphasizing connections, and suggesting alternative ways of looking at a situation.

NAIVE THEORIES AND MISCONCEPTIONS AFFECT TEACHING/LEARNING

Sometimes interpretations of information we have learned have been misconceived. This can be seen in the following widespread adult naive theory or misconception:

> *When people feel cold air when a door is opened to cold weather, they may respond by saying, "Close the door. You're letting the cold in."*

Adults who share this perception have not assimilated into their schema of heat that heat moves *from* a heat source (the warm air) *to* a heat sink (the cold outdoors). Howard Gardner explains that adults carry around explanations of the world that they develop in the first five years of life.[13] He believes these naive concepts persist because our early education does not provide opportunities to reexamine misconceptions acquired during early childhood.

Examples of Children's Naive Theories and Misconceptions

Table 2–2 lists some examples of discrepancies between students' naive theories and scientific explanations. Misconceptions and naive theories may persist even after students successfully complete traditional science courses. The problem is that naive theories are derived from prior experiences and have inherent validity. After all, stones do fall faster than leaves. Also, students may not experience things that contradict their naive theories, such as leaves and stones falling together in a vacuum. Naive theories are functional and allow students to function adequately in their everyday lives. They also represent a particularly tenacious type of prior knowledge that must be dealt with in teaching elementary and middle grade science.

Kathleen Roth describes an interesting example from her research and that of Charles Anderson and Edward Smith.[14] Students may not know the word *photosynthesis* but they have a lot of ideas about the concept—some of them false. For instance, they may have the misconception that plants get their food from soil through their roots. This naive explanation conflicts in critical ways with the scientific view that plants use sunlight to make food from carbon dioxide and water. But students have

TABLE 2–2
Naive theories versus scientific explanations

Science Topics	Naive Theories	Scientific Explanations
Heat and temperature	Temperatures change due to flow of heat into or out of objects.	Kinetic-molecular model describes heat as a form of energy of molecules.
Inheritance	Individuals acquire physical characteristics (fair-skinned parents darkened in tropics having dark-skinned children).	Only genetically determined traits are inheritable.
Motion of objects	Heavier objects fall faster than light ones.	Acceleration is proportionate to force.

arrived at their explanations through their own experience with plants (and perhaps with "plant food" that is mixed with the soil to "nourish" plants), and the explanation works for them. Personal theories are not easy to give up.

Meaningful learning in science often requires students to go through a difficult process of conceptual change. Roth suggests that for conceptual change to occur, students need to recognize that their own personal theories are in conflict with accepted scientific views. They need to be convinced that their own theories are inadequate, incomplete, or inconsistent with experimental evidence, and that the scientific explanations provide a more convincing and powerful alternative to their own notions. Roth believes that students need repeated opportunities to challenge the inconsistencies between their own ideas and scientific explanations, to reorganize their ways of thinking, to abandon or modify ideas that have served them well in everyday life, and to make appropriate links between their own ideas and scientific concepts. Providing a number of hands on/minds on guided discovery experiences gives students opportunities to explore science concepts and teachers the chance to address misconceptions.

Challenging Naive Theories and Misconceptions[15]

According to Pintrich, Marx, and Boyle,[16] the best way to eliminate naive theories and misconceptions is to expose them and confront them directly. These confrontations need to be more than mere teaching of science facts. They should be experience-based and supply students with motivational encouragement to change. Pintrich et al. summarized four conditions essential for changing student (and teacher) naive theories and misconceptions:

1. There must be enough *dissatisfaction* with present beliefs to abandon them.
2. New understandings must be *intelligible* to students and help them better understand the ideas.

3. New conceptions must be *plausible*, that is, they must be meaningfully related to students' existing knowledge organizations.
4. New frameworks must be *fruitful* to facilitate further study.

Here are a few possible strategies[17] for guiding students to revise their erroneous or naive beliefs and misconceptions:

- Help students learn correct information at a meaningful, rather than rote, level.
- Focus on an in-depth understanding of a few key ideas rather than covering many topics superficially.
- Show how new information contradicts the things students currently believe.
- Ask questions that challenge students' misconceptions.
- Give students corrective feedback about responses that reflect misunderstandings.
- Show students how the alternative explanation you present is more plausible and useful than their original misconception.

Additional ways of finding out about your students' misconceptions are addressed in Chapter 5, Assessing Science Teaching and Learning. These assessment techniques can help discover other student factors that affect learning and teaching (e.g., student learning styles). For further suggestions on changing naive theories and misconceptions see:

- Emmett L. Wright and Girish Govindarajan, "Discrepant Event Demonstrations: Motivating Students to Learn Science Concepts," *The Science Teacher* 62, no. 1 (Jan. 1995), 25–28.
- G. Robert Moore, "Revisiting Science Concepts: Projects That Span the Elementary School Years Can Lead to Broader Under-standing of Specific Concepts," *Science and Children* 32, no. 3 (Nov./Dec. 1994), 31–32, 60.
- Samuel J. Hausfather, "It's Time for a Conceptual Change: A Flexible Approach to Understanding," *Science and Children* 30, no. 3 (Nov./Dec. 1992), 22–23.

■ Bruce Watson and Richard Konicek, "Teaching for Conceptual Change: Confronting Experience," *Phi Delta Kappan* 71, no. 9 (May 1990), 680–685.

The biggest key is to allow considerable teaching/learning time to give students situations that reveal their naive beliefs so that they may be challenged.

PHYSICAL, LOGICAL–MATHEMATICAL, AND SOCIAL ARBITRARY KNOWLEDGE

Cognitive psychologists view knowledge as consisting of complex networks of information and skills. Much of the information in the knowledge base can be classified by constructivists into two crucial types of knowledge:

1. knowledge that is *not* constructed in the mind of the learner
2. knowledge that *is* constructed in the mind of the learner

Non-constructed (in learner's mind) knowledge is designated **social arbitrary knowledge,** which must be transmitted to learners by teachers and other external authorities via lectures, demonstrations, audiovisuals, textbooks, and other learner-passive means. Social arbitrary knowledge is also referred to as **declarative knowledge,** because facts, concepts, and principles are *declared* to others.

An example of declarative knowledge in science would be knowledge about light. Through science classes, students are expected to acquire factual knowledge about light; for example, that light appears to travel in straight lines; that light travels very fast; that the colors in the spectrum are red, orange, yellow, green, blue, and violet. Students must also know many terms related to light such as *transparent, translucent, opaque, lens, convex,* and *concave*.[18]

Chaillé and Britain[19] further divided constructed knowledge into **physical knowledge,** which is based on observation or experience, and

logical-mathematical knowledge, which is based on comparison or seriation of objects. Physical and logical-mathematical knowledges are also sometimes called **procedural knowledge,** because learners have to perform various physical and intellectual tasks with declarative knowledge (e.g., drawing conclusions, making generalizations). Procedural knowledge is knowledge that can be used in interpreting new situations, solving problems, thinking, and reasoning. In science, procedural knowledge is both needed in and constructed from such minds-on tasks as classifying minerals, inferring the cause of the morning dew, measuring the height of plants in an investigation, and predicting whether bulbs will light in a given circuit arrangement. In learning science, students should acquire both declarative knowledge (e.g., knowledge about reflection; knowledge about air pressure) and procedural knowledge (e.g., how to use knowledge about reflection to build a periscope; how to use air pressure concepts and principles to explain air pressure phenomena).

One criticism of elementary science teaching in the United States has been that teachers too often treat science primarily as declarative knowledge; that is, as a body of isolated facts, definitions of concepts, and statements of principles to be directly taught to the student. Although learning facts and definitions should be a part of science classes, science is much more than declarative knowledge about the world.

In summary then, constructivism

■ is inclusive of *all* sources of knowledge;
■ incorporates learners' experiences as essential bases for constructive learning, including hands-on/minds-on and teacher-directed instruction; and
■ provides a unifying concept of learning that may constitute the basis of a prototype for education that combines current concerns and future research.[20]

Constructivism is **not** an alternative learning/teaching model that may be used in place of other methods.

Meaningful Learning

Meaningful verbal learning is learning new information by relating it to previously learned information or experiences. This learning is more likely to happen when three conditions exist:

1. a meaningful learning set,
2. relevant prior knowledge, and
3. awareness that the knowledge is relevant.

David Ausubel, a proponent of meaningful learning, and other psychologists conclude that effective problem solving and schemata development are more apt to take place after students have mastered basic and supporting concepts, predominantly through a transmissive approach referred to as reception learning. They believe this happens through direct or expository teaching.

Ausubel recommends that teachers stress learning situations and illustrations familiar to students to foster assimilation of what is being learned with what they already know and to make learning more meaningful. He advises that students in primary grades work on as many hands-on activities as possible; however, he advocates increased use of such direct or expository teaching/learning as teacher demonstrations and explanations, concept mapping, and diagrams for students in higher grades. Ausubel advises against rote memorization by having teachers use what he calls **advance organizers**—ideas presented to students *before* new material is presented to mentally prepare them to assimilate new material into their previously constructed schemata. He postulates that the most important single factor influencing how you structure your advanced organizers is what your students already know.[21] Discovering (and eventually changing) your students' concepts and misconceptions can be accomplished by using concept mapping.

Concept Mapping and Building Concepts

The use of *concept maps* (sometimes called *concept webs* or *semantic webs*) is a teaching/learning technique that helps students form the interrelated knowledge and understandings that make up useful schemata. Concepts have been called classifications that strive to organize objects and events into progressively smaller units of categories. Scientific concepts are mental organizations about the world that are based on similarities among these objects and events (e.g., plants, water, electricity).[22] The concept map is a visual or graphic illustration of concepts with connections (called bridges) that show interrelationships.

In using concept maps, the teacher draws the framework on the chalkboard or transparency and explains that each of these three components is necessary for a good understanding of the concept:

1. What is it?
2. What is it like?
3. What are some examples?

Using information from prior experiences, hands-on investigations, texts, and other sources, the teacher and students complete as much of the framework as possible. The completed concept map is often referred to in subsequent investigations, reading, and discussion. The emphasis in instruction should be not only on understanding specific concepts but also on helping students learn how to use concept maps as a tool in developing concepts in general.

Using Information Processing for New Knowledge Acquisition

In acquiring new knowledge, information is received, encoded, transformed, and related to prior knowledge through the application of a variety of information-processing skills.

Attention. Processing of incoming information is strongly affected by attention. Under ordinary circumstances, learners can attend to only one information stream at a time. Competing stimuli vie for the learner's attention. Discovery learning activities are intrinsically interesting to students and naturally engage their attention. Further elaboration is presented in this and other chapters.

Encoding. Stimuli attended to must be encoded for further processing. Siegler[23] describes **encoding** as a process by which incoming information about objects and events is segmented and represented in memory. Information may be encoded in various forms: in terms of actions, images, words, or other symbols. The process of encoding plays a central role in learning. Situations that stimulate learning generally afford large amounts of information, only some of which is relevant. Learners do not usually attend to all possible features and relations within a situation, but they will likely encode a greater number of features and relations than they will use, even though they may initially fail to encode some features that are critical to learning or problem solving. How learners encode new stimuli depends on the nature and quality of their prior knowledge and whether they access that knowledge. Teachers can play an important role in facilitating encoding. The work of Siegler and others shows that when students,

including very young children, are helped to encode the necessary features of a situation, their problem-solving success increases dramatically.

Metacognition. You may be familiar with the notion of metacognition from your studies of the reading process. **Metacognition** refers to the use of strategies that enable us to control and regulate our cognitive efforts. According to Linda Baker,[24] a reading specialist, these strategies include planning what to do, implementing our plans, monitoring our efforts and checking the outcomes, assessing the effectiveness of our actions, remediating or adjusting any difficulties, and revising our learning and problem-solving approaches. Cognitive research indicates that learning can improve substantially when learners become more strategic in their approaches.

A goal of science instruction is that learners should develop autonomy or complete self-regulation of their own learning processes and

FIGURE 2–3

Self-regulation

Source: Modified from Charles R. Berman, *An Expanded View of the Learning Cycle: New Ideas About an Effective Teaching Strategy* (Washington, DC: Council for Elementary Science International, Jan. 1990), 3.

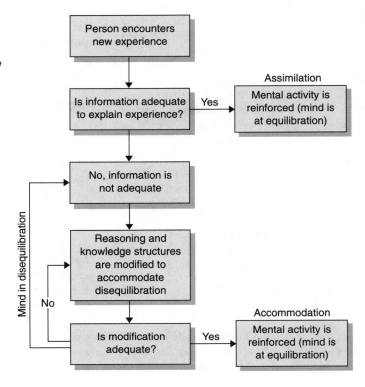

strategies. Figure 2–3 summarizes the self-regulation process, showing possible alternative routes to assimilation or accommodation.

DEVELOPMENTALLY APPROPRIATE SCIENCE ACTIVITIES

Here is a summary of teaching/learning activities that Piagetian and constructivist researchers agree are developmentally correct for the respective age ranges.

Kindergarten Through Grade 2

Kindergarten, first, and second grade children are most likely to think about the world preoperationally. The preoperational child can be characterized primarily as an explorer and intuitive thinker. To promote the development of thinking, knowledge, and cognitive structures during the preoperational period, teachers should take the following steps:

1. Provide children many opportunities to explore objects and events in the surrounding world.
2. Help children focus on the properties of objects; that is, on the characteristics that make one object like or different from other objects.
3. Teach the meanings of words in the context of activities; allow many opportunities for students to use language to describe objects and events.
4. Understand that using correct language and understanding a concept are not the same thing.
5. Provide for considerable practice on the things to be learned.
6. Help children learn to question their own ideas and those of others, to explore systematically, and to learn how to evaluate evidence.
7. Use social interaction, including cooperative learning, to provide the child with multiple viewpoints; children should exchange ideas honestly and argue among themselves about the merits of their ideas.
8. Help children look beyond salient characteristics of a situation to possible relationships; help children make connections between things; lead children to shift attention from one aspect of a situation to another and then to come back to the first thing; provide many opportunities for children to compare and contrast different objects and events.
9. Continually help children to see the parts of a situation or system in relation to the whole.

Grades 3 Through 5

Although learners at these grade levels are generally concrete operational, children in Grade 3 often show preoperational traits of thought. Fourth graders are beginning to observe more carefully, to collect and organize data, and to ask more profound questions about the "whys" of nature. To provide cognitive support to learners at these grade levels, teachers should help students with these tasks:

1. Gather complete information from a situation in a systematic way.
2. Be alert to problems, discrepancies, and conflicts in the perceived situation.
3. Analyze situations and problems into smaller parts.
4. Label objects, properties, and actions precisely so that they can be better remembered and discussed.
5. Identify variable factors that might enter into problem solutions.
6. Collect observational data or information for problem solutions into a table, chart, or some other organized form.
7. Use diagrams, working models, charts, graphs, and pictures as well as verbal language in expressing ideas.
8. Develop generalizations, draw many inferences, and make frequent predictions using observational information and prior knowledge.

Grades 6 Through 8

Many students in the sixth through eighth grades are not formal operational thinkers, but some are. However, there is a world of difference between them and their younger schoolmates. Students at this level tend to search for patterns in their physical and social environments, examining their own beliefs and those of others. They are aware of cause and effect, reciprocal relationships, and the influence of events on each other. Boys in this age group are interested in technology; the interest of girls in technology increases when some sort of social involvement with technology is evident; both sexes are very interested in animals.

The challenge for teachers of sixth through eighth grade students is to develop and implement a science program that will meet these criteria:

1. Introduce students to a wide variety of objects and events in the natural and man-made world.
2. Portray science as an unending quest to find hidden likenesses and order in a world filled with diversity.
3. Help students become familiar with styles of scientific thinking so that, as they grow, they can participate in science, use technology wisely, and analyze important social issues related to science and technology.
4. Help students—especially girls and minority youngsters—recognize science and technology as cooperative human endeavors open to everyone.
5. Supply ample opportunities for open inquiries that let students explore their own relevant, authentic questions.

GAGNÉ'S LEARNING HIERARCHY

Chapter 1 introduced you to the importance of students learning science process skills, such as observing, measuring, inferring, and investigating. Robert Gagné[25] has developed a learning hierarchy that emphasizes:

- structure and sequence (a hierarchy) in the learning of science processes (as well as other intellectual skills); i.e., a specific skill must be learned before higher-order skills can be undertaken.
- observable behavioral changes as the only criteria for inferring that learning has transpired.

Figure 2–4 shows Gagné's hierarchy of eight levels of learning, beginning with the *final* behavior to be learned (usually a complex, problem-solving skill) and working backward. For example, to do Level 8, you need to complete Level 7; to do Level 7, you need to complete Levels 6 and 5, and so on.

Prerequisite tasks are sequentially organized into a hierarchy of tasks, from simple to complex, described as behavioral objectives. Both content and skills are needed for mastery in science. In Gagné's approach, learning is assessed in terms of well-defined steps, moving from simple and concrete to more complex and abstract skills, concepts, and principles. *Science—A Process Approach,* an elementary school science program developed under the guidance of Gagné, uses this learning hierarchy theory.

PRACTICAL CLASSROOM APPLICATIONS OF COGNITIVE RESEARCH

John Dewey advocated that taking a theoretical perspective in your classroom can assist you to:

- make observations about learners that might otherwise escape you;
- interpret some facts that would otherwise be confused and misunderstood; and
- render instructional practices that are more intelligent, more flexible, and better adapted to deal effectively with concrete actions in the classroom.

In short, reading and integrating learning research can make teaching a true profession rather than just a technical activity.

Levels	Examples
8 Problem Solving	Finding ways to melt ice on sidewalk
7 Principle Learning	Relationship of a circle's circumference to its diameter
6 Concept Learning	Learn to call a block a *cube,* and apply the term to other cubes
5 Multiple Discrimination	Learning to distinguish between solid, liquids, and gases
4 Verbal Association	Rote memorization of sequences of numbers
3 Chaining (skill learning)	Winding up a toy to get it to move
2 Stimulus–Response Learning	Child repeats sounds and words of adults
1 Signal (conditioned response)	Pleasure at sight of pet

FIGURE 2–4

Gagné's Learning Hierarchy

Source: Modified from Richard D. Kellough, *Integrating Mathematics and Science for Kindergarten and Primary Children* (Upper Saddle River, NJ: Merrill/Prentice Hall, 1996), 14–15.

You can use your own understanding of Piagetian and other cognitive learning theories to begin to formulate your own approach to teaching. You can select from the viewpoints, suggestions, and applications that follow. No single method of teaching science has been found to be consistently best for the wide range of students, objectives, and classroom situations that you will encounter. Start by taking the information and teaching/learning activities that are suited to your unique educational classroom needs. Later, your can expand from this foundation.

Pay Attention to Your Students' Learning Styles

When teaching, look around the classroom and you will see that students not only look and dress differently and have different prior knowledge and misconceptions and naive theories, but they also react very differently to instruction. That is, they learn differently! Andy's answers burst out before your question is even finished. Paula reflects on possible answers for many seconds before timidly raising her hand. Jon doesn't respond at all and sits drawing pictures. Researchers call these varying ways of perceiving, interacting with, and responding to the learning environment **learning styles.** Learning styles are primarily habits—routes learners prefer to take when processing experiences and information.

Because students have different learning styles, you must provide for a variety of learning modalities:

- **tactile** (hands-on, involving bodily actions and manipulation of objects)
- **auditory** (using the ears)
- **visual** (employing sight)
- **cerebral** (involving the mind)
- **olfactory** (utilizing smell)

Dunn and Dunn tell us that when students are taught through modalities that complement their learning styles, they learn better and achieve higher test scores.[26]

Move Cautiously from the Concrete to the Abstract

Research supports moving students' thinking from concrete to more abstract levels. Table 2–3 provides guidelines to help you select appropriate concrete-to-abstract experiences for your students. Remember, providing a wide range of teaching/learning experiences accommodates students' different learning styles.

TABLE 2–3
Classroom activities for levels of abstract teaching/learning

	Levels	Descriptions	Classroom Examples
Most Abstract	6	Require children to establish relationships between or among entities	Read the words *plant* and *seed,* count out a specific number of seeds
	5	Complete task structured by adults	Color ditto picture of seeds, cut out teacher-drawn plants
	4	Use of pictures, diagrams, films, videotapes, teacher demonstrations	Teacher shows how to plant seeds, teacher reads books to children
	3	Use of 3-dimensional models	Sort artificial plants by size
	2	Activities that emerge from within child through art, music, and other forms of self-expression	Paint picture of garden, make up a song about seeds
Most Concrete	1	Active, multisensory experiences with real objects or places	Visit nursery to buy plants, plant seeds

Use a Variety of Teaching/Learning Activities

Researchers stress that students learn best through a variety of activities, since students in any given classroom are functioning on many different cognitive levels with diverse learning styles. Therefore, *all* of these activities should be used where appropriate to your students' developmental levels and learning styles:

> *telling; showing; reading to students of all ages; using textbooks, objects, diagrams, pictures, films, filmstrips, and videotapes; hands-on/minds-on guided and open discovery activities; computers and other electronic technology; and other teaching approaches with which you feel comfortable.*

This text presents a wide array of teaching activities. The direct, explicit step-by-step, or hierarchical instruction proposed by psychologists such as David Ausubel, Benjamin Bloom, Robert Gagné, Barak Rosenshine, and others should be selected when you want to teach specific skills in a sequential way. Their work and its applications to your classroom are discussed in Chapter 3.

Adopting Guided Discovery/Constructivist Strategies

Scientists and educators generally concur that, although science learning takes place in a variety of ways, one of the best ways is through an active approach that involves students in observing, measuring, predicting, inferring, investigating, and explaining the world in ways that parallel the methods of scientists. This textbook calls this approach **hands-on/minds-on guided discovery.** A hands-on/minds-on approach incorporates Piagetian/cognitive learning theories, students' learning styles and interests, and the goals of an active science education program. Such a teaching

TABLE 2–4

Constructivism and implications for a hands-on/minds-on guided discovery science/open inquiry teaching/learning approach

Teaching/Learning Activity	Constructivist Philosophy
Hands-on	Learners explore materials and events through their *senses* and learn by doing
Minds-on	Learners construct knowledge and relationships (schema) by *thinking* about what they are doing and learning from the manipulated materials and events
Guided Discovery	Teacher plans and organizes learning environment and provides experiences to *facilitate* and *guide* students' meaningful knowledge building and learning
Open Inquiry	Students *explore* questions of their own construction using a scientific way of knowing

strategy requires your careful planning and direction, so that students are guided to constructing schema and science concepts.

The hands-on/minds on guided discovery approach facilitates science learning and is consistent with a constructivist philosophy of learning and instruction. Remember, in the constructivist viewpoint, order is not "discovered" so much as it is "invented." Scientists imaginatively "impose" order and predictability on the phenomena and events of the world. Scientists construct this order based largely on their own prior knowledge; that is, their own active organization of facts, principles, concepts, and models derived from previous studies. From the constructivist perspective, knowledge is considered to be a dynamic, conceptual means to make sense of experiences, rather than a passive representation of the external world.

Constructivists stress that each person must individually construct ideas if they are to be truly useful. All of us—scientists and nonscientists alike—are strongly influenced by other people through social interactions. But language *per se* cannot be the means of transferring information. Knowledge acquired from other people is useful in understanding the world only to the extent that we make it meaningful for ourselves through thoughtful processes. It is this *meaningful* development of knowledge that scientists

and nonscientists use to cope with and make sense of the environment.

The constructivist philosophy incorporates the works of Jean Piaget, Lev Vygotsky, David Ausubel, Jerome Bruner, and Robert Gagné. See Table 2–4 for a more graphic description. Chapter 3 will provide specifics for setting in motion a hands-on/minds-on guided discovery approach.

Many constructivists also advocate *open inquiry,* in which students are encouraged to find answers to real life questions relevant to their lives. This is a very meaningful, powerful, and effective learning approach, especially if students have had practice with hands-on/minds guided discovery experiences. Many elementary and middle grade students are capable of successful open inquiries.

Select Fewer Science Topics and Study Them Longer

Learning is an active process of construction, relating new material and prior knowledge; it takes time and cannot be rushed. Therefore, your students should study fewer scientific topics, in depth, rather than superficially covering many topics. This view of topic selection has been referred to as "Less is more and longer is better."[27] Your science topics should be studied for several weeks or longer, to allow for many

54 TEACHING MODERN SCIENCE

opportunities for your students to ask *their* questions, conduct *their* inquiries, and then construct *their* own scientific concepts from *their* observations, data collection, and tests.

This long-range exposure gives your students time to construct their own meanings instead of cataloging isolated bits of information. You should emphasize *quality,* not *quantity,* of scientific ideas and understanding. Your classroom should be a rich learning environment that encourages depth in exploration and concept construction related to science, technology, and societal interactions of the two.

A perennial dilemma for teachers is deciding which concepts, topics, themes, or problems to select for students to study in depth. Scientific topics to be studied should:

- be of interest to students and relevant to their lives;
- be organized around scientific content and processes;
- include a focus on technological applications and societal implications;
- use materials readily available in school; and
- include scientific concepts modified to your own circumstances from many different sources.

Here are a few sources for you to consider when selecting and organizing themes, problems, concepts, attitudes, and skills (from whatever sources) for your science program:

AAAS Project 2061
American Association for the
 Advancement of Science
1333 H St., NW
Washington, DC 20005
Identifies six common themes that pervade science, mathematics, and technology: systems, models (including physical, conceptual, and mathematical), constancy (including stability and equilibrium, conservation, and symmetry), patterns of change (including trends, cycles, and chaos), evolution (including possibilities, rates, and interaction), and scale.

California State Department of Education
Publications
P.O. Box 271
Sacramento, CA 95802–0271
Identifies six major over-arching scientific themes: energy, evolution, patterns of change, stability, systems interactions, and scale and structure.

The National Center for Improving Science Education
A Partnership of the NETWORK, Inc. and Biological Sciences Curriculum Study (BSCS)
300 Brickstone Square, Suite 900
Andover, MA 01810
 OR
1920 L St. NW, Suite 202
Washington, DC 20036
Identifies nine major organizing concepts with STS focus: organizing, cause and effect, systems, scale, models, change, structure and function, discontinuous and continuous properties, and diversity.

NSTA Scope, Sequence, and Coordination (SSC) Project
National Science Teachers Association
840 Wilson Blvd.
Arlington, VA 22201-3000
Although the major work of this NSTA project is currently in secondary science education, elementary and middle school scientific concepts are also being identified.

Assess Your Students' Progress Frequently

Assessment is a vital part of teaching with a Piagetian, cognitivist, or constructivist approach: it shouldn't come only at the end of a study. By using a wide variety of assessment techniques at the beginning of, during, and at the conclusion of a science topic, you will get valuable information about your students that will help you plan appropriate learning experiences. Assessment will help you determine students' prior knowledge, misconceptions, and naive theories. You will discover what your students have learned in your

When you shift teaching roles from knowledge transmitter to learning facilitator, your students become active constructors of their own concepts and schemata.

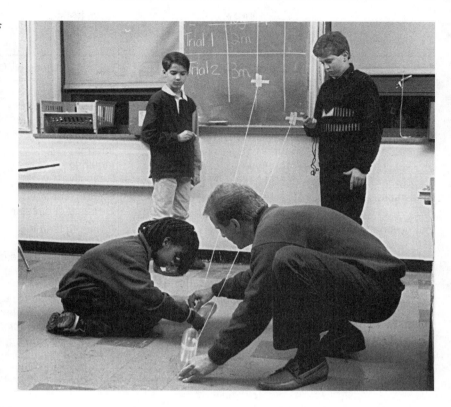

science lessons or what may yet need to be done. Assessment can also motivate students to better attend to any assigned materials. Assessment can help in finding out about students' interests, fears, and other relevant information. Chapter 5 presents formal and informal assessment techniques useful for effectively planning worthwhile science experiences for your unique students.

Prepare Yourself for A New Role

As you become more aware of the importance of your students' cognitive development, prior knowledge, misconceptions, learning styles, and need for hands-on/minds-on guided discovery experiences, you will find that your teaching style changes. Your teaching style includes your unique mannerisms, choices of teaching behaviors and strategies, and the ways you interact with and present information to students; these are determined by your personality, prior teaching experiences and

training, and familiarity with learning research. Your teaching style can be modified by deliberate changes in these three areas.

Your primary function will no longer be that of transmitter of information, knowledge, and concepts. You'll begin to recognize a need to shift away from the traditional roles of teacher as teller and students as receivers to roles of teacher as facilitator and students as actors and doers.

How Do "Traditional" and "Facilitating" Teaching Styles Differ? Table 2–5 presents aspects of differences between the traditional and facilitating teaching styles. Today's teachers must use aspects from *all* teaching styles because of the diversity of students in all classrooms. You must select and use whatever seems best for your students, regardless of the name given to the teaching function. This text strives to use such an eclectic approach with a strong emphasis on hands-on/minds-on guided discovery.

TABLE 2–5
A contrast of two teaching styles

Characteristic	Traditional Style	Hands-on/Minds-on Discovery Facilitating Style
Teacher	Autocratic	Democratic
	Curriculum-centered	Student-centered
	Direct	Indirect
	Dominative	Interactive
	Formal	Informal
	Informative	Inquiring
	Prescriptive	Reflective
Classroom	Teacher-centered	Student-centered
	Linear (seats facing front)	Grouped or circular
Instructional modes	Abstract learning	Concrete learning
	Teacher-centered discussion	Discussions
	Lectures	Peer and cross-age coaching
	Competitive learning	Cooperative learning
	Some problem solving	Problem solving
	Teacher demonstrations	Student inquiries
	From simple to complex	Starting with complex tasks and using instructional scaffolding and dialogue
	Transmission of information from teacher to students	Reciprocal teaching, using dialogue between teacher and students

Source: Modified from Richard D. Kellough, *A Resource Guide for Teaching: K–12* (Upper Saddle River, NJ: Merrill/Prentice Hall, 1994), 82.

As a facilitator of learning, you will be engaged more and more in teaching functions that require the following roles:

1. *Manage* the classroom environment and your students' learning.
2. Be a *model* of the attitudes, skills, and values (e.g., curiosity, empathy, and sensitivity) that you wish your students to develop.
3. *Present* learning options for individual students to consider, choices of goals for groups of students to pursue, and variety in activities for students to engage in.
4. *Observe* and *listen* to students for information that will assist you in providing the best possible learning environment.
5. *Ask questions* and *pose problems* to stimulate students to want to seek information and possible solutions.
6. Be a *learning strategist,* making wise decisions concerning when and how to use individual learning, cooperative groups, and competitive activities.
7. *Assess* your students' learning to determine their prior knowledge, how to motivate them for new studies, what they learn in the studies, and how to use all of this data to enrich further learning.
8. *Document* your students' learning.
9. *Coordinate* the "public relations" of your classroom by articulating progress to students, parents, and school administrators.
10. *Build and grow personally* and professionally in your own scientific/technological concepts and their interrelationships to your life and society.

Don't be overwhelmed by all of these teaching roles. Remember how terrifying it was to be separated from your mother for the first time in nursery school or kindergarten? Do you recall how anxious and apprehensive you were when you taught your first lesson to students? Take one step at a time. The rest of this book will supply you with additional practical resources to grow professionally, step-by-step. The benefits for both you and your students can be enjoyable and rewarding.

SUMMARY

An understanding of how students learn science is critical for guiding them in hands-on/minds-on science activities. Students' naive theories and misconceptions help teachers to know how students learn best. Naive theories and misconceptions are tenacious, even in the face of good instruction. Students must be guided to confront their own theories with evidence, justify their ideas, and modify them when necessary.

Two dominant approaches to learning theory are behaviorism and cognitivism. Behavioral approaches focus on the connections between the learning stimulus (S) and the learner's behavioral response (R). What is important in establishing S–R connections is clear presentations of stimuli, active learner responses, feedback and reinforcement to the learner from a teacher, and a great deal of practice by the learner. Direct instruction is a teaching model based on this theory. David Ausubel and other psychologists have concluded that effective problem solving and schemata development are more likely to occur after students have acquired supporting concepts, predominantly through reception learning.

Piaget's theory has been an important part of science education since the early 1960s. Although contemporary cognitive theorists have challenged portions of Piaget's theory, including his developmental stages, his work is important for teaching elementary science.

Piaget describes the child's thinking in terms of four stages. These four stages are useful as broad, general benchmarks in planning for teaching/learning in science. Cognitive learning theories are concerned with describing what goes on in the learner's brain during learning; that is, how knowledge is acquired, organized, stored in memory, and used in further learning and problem solving. It is helpful to classify knowledge as declarative knowledge (knowledge about something) or procedural knowledge (knowledge of how to do something). Acquiring declarative knowledge is important in science, but science teachers must guide students to develop procedural knowledge; that is, to be able to do something with what they know. Some theorists suggest that knowledge begins as declarative knowledge but becomes procedural as it is used in classifying, inferring, predicting, and generalizing. The prior knowledge and experience learners bring to new learning situations critically affect how they learn and build new knowledge.

According to cognitive theories, knowledge is organized in memory as schemata, networks of associated information and skills. The activation of one piece of information in a schema tends to activate other information in the schema. Schemata help learners assimilate new knowledge, fill in gaps in incoming information, and search for needed information. Assimilation is the process of fitting new information into an existing schema without having to distort the schema. Accommodation is the process of creating new schemata or adjusting existing ones to better fit reality. Assimilation and accommodation are important learning processes in Piaget's theory of intellectual development. Contemporary cognitive researchers have elaborated on the notion of accommodation, describing it in terms of the creation, tuning, and restructuring of schemata. The key to provoking accommodation in science teaching is to provide challenging situations in which the learner can apply existing knowledge.

A number of different teaching techniques and strategies were presented to help you become more comfortable with your new role as facilitator of learning rather than transmitter of information.

SELF-ASSESSMENT AND FURTHER STUDY

1. Describe prior concepts, naive theories, or misconceptions *you* had that were changed by being exposed to the ideas in this chapter. Try to analyze what made you alter your original views.
2. Research current books and article about learners' misconceptions and naive theories, then interview elementary school students (or your teaching or college associates) to discover their misconceptions or naive theories about a scientific concept of your choice.
3. Select a specific scientific/technological concept for a particular group of students and describe how you would teach it to them using concept maps, advance organizers, the learning cycle, and Gagné's learning hierarchies. What major differences would there be? Give reasons for selecting the approach you favor.
4. Using this chapter's introduction to learning styles, list different learning styles, the conditions under which each is most appropriate, and how they can be used successfully to guide the development of concept and skills in a science/technology area.
5. *Hands-on/minds-on* is the term coined to describe activities in which students mentally act upon (or think about) what is being physically manipulated through handling, observing, or testing. How effective is this type of activity for teaching/learning science/technology? To find out, start with these references:
   - David P. Butts and Helenmarie Hofman, "Hands-on, Brains-on: For Children, Their Words Following the Activity Complete the Concept." *Science and Children* 30, no. 5 (Feb. 1993), 15–16.
   - David P. Butts, Helenmarie Hofman, Margaret Anderson, "Is Direct Experience Enough? A Study of Young Children's Views of Sound," *Journal of Elementary Science Education* 6, no. 1 (Winter 1994).
6. Describe the similarities and differences in the learning theories of Jean Piaget, Robert Gagné, Jerome Bruner, Lev Vygotsky, and David Ausubel.
7. Become more familiar with the teacher role as facilitator of learning in a constructivist classroom. List specific ways you would incorporate this new role into *your* science/technology classroom.
8. Explain the role direct instruction or expository teaching plays in helping learners construct their own concepts.
9. Teachers struggle with deciding which concepts, topics, themes, or problems their students are to study. What are some of the variables and considerations that shape those decisions?

NOTES

1. Rodger W. Bybee, "Science Curriculum Reform in the United States," in Rodger W. Bybee and Joseph D. McInerney, Eds., *Redesigning the Science Curriculum: A Report on the Implications of Standards and Benchmarks for Science Education* (Colorado Springs, CO: Biological Sciences Curriculum Study, 1995), 18.
2. Nancy Paulu with Margaret Martin, *Helping Your Child Learn Science* (Washington, DC: US Department of Education, Office of Educational Research and Improvement, 1991).
3. William C. Philips, "Earth Science Misconceptions," *The Science Teacher* 58, no. 2 (Feb. 1991), 21–22.
4. W. C. Kyle and J. A. Shymansky, "Enhancing Learning Through Conceptual Change Teaching," *NARST News* 31 (Apr. 1989), 7–8; C. K. West, J. A. Farmer, and P. M. Wolff, *Instructional Design: Implications for Cognitive Science* (Englewood Cliffs, NJ: Prentice Hall, 1991).
5. D. Holt-Reynolds, "Personal History-based Beliefs as Relevant Prior Knowledge in Course

Work," *American Educational Research Journal* 29, 325–349.

6. Katharyn Ross and Thomas Shuell, "Children's Beliefs About Earthquakes," *Science Education* (Apr. 1993), 191–205.

7. For easy ideas on constructivism and its application to elementary school science education see: Mary Lewis Sivertsen, *State of the Art: Transforming Ideas for Teaching and Learning Science. A guide for elementary education* (Washington, DC: United States Department of Education, 1993).

8. For an expanded description of behavioral theory and explicit teaching see: Barak V. Rosenshine, "Synthesis of Research on Explicit Teaching," *Educational Leadership* 43, no. 7 (Apr. 1986), 60–69.

9. This example is adapted from Norwood Russel Hanson, *Patterns of Discovery* (Cambridge, England: Cambridge University Press, 1965), 12–13.

10. Audrey B. Champagne and Leopold E. Hornig, "Practical Applications of Theories about Learning," *Students and Science Learning* (Washington DC: American Association for the Advancement of Science, 1987).

11. Thomas J. Shuell, "Cognitive Conceptions in Learning," *Review of Educational Research* 56, no. 4 (Winter 1986), 411–436.

12. Shuell, *op. cit.,* 421.

13. Howard Gardner, *The Unschooled Mind* (New York: Basic Books, 1991).

14. Kathleen J. Roth, "Reading Science Texts for Conceptual Change," in Carol M. Santa and Donna E. Alvermann, Eds., *Science Learning: Processes and Applications* (1991), 48–63.

15. The author is indebted for considerable information about naive theories and misconceptions to Roger H. Bruning, Gregory J. Schraw, and Royce R. Ronning, *Cognitive Psychology and Instruction,* Second Edition (Upper Saddle River, NJ: Prentice Hall, 1995), 343–365.

16. P. R. Pintrich, R. W. Marx, and R. A. Boyle, "Beyond Cold Conceptual Change: The Role of Motivational Beliefs and Classroom Contextual Factors in the Process of Conceptual Change," *Review of Educational Research* 63, (1993), 167–199.

17. Jeanne Ellis Ormrod, *Educational Psychology: Principles and Applications* (Upper Saddle River, NJ: Merrill/Prentice Hall, 1995), 341.

18. Kathleen J. Roth, "Reading Science Texts for Conceptual Change," in Carol M. Santa and Donna E. Alvermann, Eds., *Science Learning Processes and Applications* (Newark DE: International Reading Association, 1991), 48–63.

19. C. Chaillé and L. Britain, *The Young Child as Scientist: A Constructivist Approach to Early Childhood Science Education* (New York: Harper Collins), 1991.

20. An expansion of these ideas is in: J. Preston Prather, "The Trend Toward Constructivist Learning," *Journal of Elementary Science Education* 5, no. 2 (Spring 1993), 52–70.

21. David P. Ausubel, *The Psychology of Meaningful Verbal Learning* (New York: Grune and Stratton, 1963), and *Educational Psychology: A Cognitive View* (New York: Holt, Rinehart and Winston, 1968).

22. These publications supply succinct details about concept mapping: Joseph D. Novack, "How Do We Learn Our Lesson? Taking Students through the Process," *The Science Teacher* 60, no. 3 (Mar. 1993), 50–56; P. A. Okebukola and J. J. Olugbemiro, "Cognitive Preference and Learning Mode as Determinants of Meaningful Learning Through Concept Mapping," *Science Education* 72, no. 4 (July 1988), 489–500.

23. Robert S. Siegler, *Children's Thinking* (Englewood Cliffs, NJ: Prentice Hall, 1986).

24. Linda Baker, "Metacogntion, Reading, and Science Education," in *Science Learning: Processes and Applications* (Newark, DE: International Reading Association, 1991), 2–13.

25. Robert M. Gagné, *The Conditions of Learning,* 2nd ed. (New York: Holt, Rinehart and Winston, 1970); Gagné, Leslie Briggs, and Walter Wager, *Principles of Instructional Design,* 3rd ed. (New York: Holt, Rinehart and Winston, 1988).

26. Kenneth Dunn and Rita Dunn, "Dispelling Outmoded Beliefs About Student Learning," *Educational Leadership* 44, no. 6 (1987), 55–62.

27. For further elaboration on science topic selection see: Dorothy L. Gabel, *Handbook of Research on Science Teaching and Learning* (New York: Macmillan and the National Science Teachers Association, 1994); Rodger W. Bybee and G. E. DeBoer, "Goals and the Science Curriculum," in *A Handbook of Research on Science Teaching* (Arlington, VA: National Science Teachers Association, 1994).

CHAPTER 3

The Teacher as Facilitator for Science Learning

Even hands-on instruction in which all children participate is not automatically "minds-on" instruction. For the activity to be effective, teachers must link it with specific science concepts and allow ample time for analysis, interpretation, and classroom discussion.[1]

WHY MORE GIRLS DON'T DO SCIENCE

As Karen faces her science class—and her supervising teacher—she is eager to seem well prepared. She has already arranged her materials on the table in front of her: a small and a large beaker, a container of water, and a small block of wood. She asks what she hopes will be a thought-provoking question: "Class, we've practiced ways of measuring the volume of an object directly. Look at these materials and tell me how you think we could use them to measure volume indirectly."

A few seconds drag by before Jared's hand shoots into the air. Beside him, Kim slowly raises her hand shoulder-high. Thank goodness, Karen tells herself. Jared should know how to do this. "Jared?"

"Well, I guess we could put the little beaker inside the big one. Then we could fill the little one up with the water." When he hesitates, Kim starts to raise her hand again.

"Go on, Jared," Karen urges. She doesn't want to cut him off.

"And then maybe we could put the block in the water and see how much spills out," he adds.

Karen feels her shoulder muscles relax, but she resists looking at her supervisor for his reaction. "Great, Jared! Then we could measure the overflow to find out the volume of the block. That's right!" She smiles at him. "Now, who will help me demonstrate how that works?"

Jared waves his hand eagerly. A row behind him, Craig stands up as he raises his hand. Kim seems to have lost interest, but Shelly taps one hand nervously on her desk and then raises it.

"Craig, why don't you help today?" Karen says. "You did such a good job a few days ago." Jared makes an exasperated noise while Shelly sighs and lets her hand drop.

Jared, Kim, Craig, Shelly, and the other students in this class are not only learning how to measure volume. They are also learning which students the teacher expects to have the "right" answer—and which ones she thinks are best able to help carry out demonstrations. In fact, research has established that teachers tend to call on boys as much as 80% more often than girls. Teachers also address boys by name more often and give them longer to answer. This bias is particularly evident in science classes, where one study found that 79% of the demonstrations were carried out by boys.

The problem is not just treating genders differently in the classroom. Girls also have less experience outside the classroom with tools and simple machinery, giving them less confidence in volunteering to help with demonstrations and carrying out lab experiments. One study found that while 51% of third grade boys had used a microscope, only 37% of the girls had. In eleventh grade, 49% of the boys had experience in using an electricity meter, but only 17% of the girls had.

The result of this and other factors is that boys outnumber girls three to one in the top 10% of science tests, and only 33% of scientists are women. Even if young women choose to enter fields other than science, they may not understand the science principles they need in order to be successful in those fields—unless we encourage their interest in science and make sure they have the knowledge they need. Teachers have to be alert not only to bias involving gender, but also their biases toward students from minority groups and to those with differing intellectual ability.

Our future scientists, both men and women, are sitting in elementary and middle school classrooms, waiting for us to light or feed the fires of their interest. As you read and study this chapter, think about strategies you can use to help avoid bias in your own science classroom.

Previous chapters have introduced you to important variables affecting how you guide your students' science learning: the processes and products of science; the interrelationships of science, technology, and society; how students learn and think best; and aims, goals, and objectives for teaching science. These variables are the *what* and the *why* of your science teaching. Now consider *how* you will transpose these ideas into optimal science learning conditions for your students.

NO BEST METHOD TO GUIDE LEARNING IN ALL SITUATIONS!

When you consider choosing any individual teaching activity, (e.g., your students' unique learning styles, your unique teaching style, your physical classroom environment, community and school administration priorities and pressures, and science teaching/learning resources available), you quickly see that there is no one way to teach science to all children. The best you can do is to base your professional judgment on research, knowledge of your students and school situation, and constant assessment of the results of your teaching methods. These teaching processes are analogous to coaching a sport.

Teacher as Coach

Early in your teaching career, you become aware that you can't just "stand up front and teach science." You must constantly make decisions in your role as the professional leader of the learning environment for your classroom. Teacher decision making has been compared to that of a coach calling the plays for a football team. Just as coaches read the opposition's defense, use their players' strengths, and employ this information to "hypothesize" the best play, you do the same with your classroom learning variables. You must select from the myriad of possible teaching/learning activities available to you.

In the football analogy, coaches have two or three main options that make up their plays: run, pass, or kick. You also have options in the "plays" you run, but the actions *you* initiate to guide your students down the field of learning are called *teaching methods*. They are your *how* to teach. Generally, you have two broad types of teacher/student transitions, or game plays: *direct* or *indirect teaching methods*. How do you decide which one to use in a particular situation? To answer that question, ask yourself: Would the desired outcome be better achieved through a straightforward transfer of information or through a learner-centered discovery-based method? *Both* direct and indirect teaching methods are needed.

Examples of Familiar Science Teaching Techniques

Some science educators have grouped direct and indirect teaching techniques into a **taxonomy** (classification) of three large groups of common teaching methods:

1. *Listening–Speaking.* **Auditory learning,** in which students learn by hearing.
2. *Reading–Writing.* **Visual learning,** in which students learn by seeing.
3. *Watching–Doing.* **Kinesthetic learning,** in which students learn by doing.

Table 3–1 presents such a taxonomy of common teaching techniques. As you study Table 3–1, you will see that teaching techniques involve several variables. Teaching methods *use* teaching/learning materials, but are distinct from the materials. For example, if you use a textbook, you could have your students use the text for such different tasks as reading to discover concepts, comparing textbook data with what they find in a hands-on/minds-on activity, or getting directions to make a chart or build a model. You might call your teaching technique by the name of the material used (e.g., textbook or chalkboard) because you are so familiar with it.

How well you use any teaching technique depends on how well you have developed or perfected your teaching skills. However, you can never predict or guarantee how effective any individual teaching method can be, because each student has a unique learning style and other classroom or environmental variables can affect teaching and learning. That is why you should plan for as wide a variety of teaching/learning techniques as you can. You will find that your teaching is enhanced when students use *all* of their senses rather than relying on only one. For example, you might show a film about insect metamorphosis and then give each student a vial of fruit fly eggs to hatch. To aid you in selecting such methods, Table 3–1 has a checkmark where a method can be used in more than one kind of learning experience.

Teacher Dominance: How Much and When?

The second column of Table 3–1 is titled *Amount of Teacher Dominance in Method,* with a scale showing high, medium, or low. The ratio of teacher dominance to amount of student participation is one of the most important variables in teaching methods.

Figure 3–1 is a continuum of teacher dominance/student passivity based on the teaching transactions in Table 3–1. On one extreme of this continuum is **direct instruction** (often called *explicit teaching* or *exposition*), where the teacher lectures, gives instructions, demonstrates, or leads a field trip. Teacher dominance is high, and students are relatively passive. On the other extreme is **indirect instruction** (often called *exploration, inquiry,* or *free discovery*), in which students are most active and the teacher acts as a facilitator for developing student processing skills and building concepts; teacher dominance is low. Between these two extremes is **guided discovery hands-on/minds-on instruction,** in which the teacher is an active facilitator and students are active as well.

You can apply one or all of these teaching methods in your science class as you deem appropriate. Here is a more detailed look at how direct learning facilitates student-owned learning.

DIRECT, EXPLICIT, OR EXPOSITION INSTRUCTION

Direct instruction (also called *explicit instruction* or *exposition*), as described in Chapter 2, is most effective for the transmission of *social knowledge* (scientific products). In this method, *you*—as teacher—are the doer; however, if this method of instruction is done correctly, students can be actively involved and gain the knowledge on which to build higher learning skills and concepts, as advocated by David Ausubel, Robert Gagné, and other information processing theorists.

TABLE 3–1

Taxonomy of common science teaching techniques

Nature of Transaction and Method	Amount of Teacher Dominance in Method			Usefulness of Method With Groups of Various Sizes (in numbers of students)				
	High	Medium	Low	1	5	10	15	30
Listening–Speaking Methods								
Lecture Method	*					*	*	*
✓ Giving Instructions	*			*	*	*	*	*
Recitation Method		*			*	*	*	*
✓ Drill Method		*		*	*	*	*	*
Review Method		*			*	*	*	*
✓ Questioning Method		*		*	*	*	*	*
Oral Exam Method		*		*	(Repeated with entire class)				
Discussion Method		*			*	*	*	*
Film Analysis Method			*			*	*	*
Debate Method			*				*	*
Oral Report Method			*		*	*	*	*
Brainstroming Method			*		*	*	*	*
Reading–Writing Methods								
Textbook Method	*			*	*	*	*	*
Workbook Method	*			*	*	*	*	*
Chalkboard Method	*					*	*	*
Bulletin Board Method	*							*
✓ Problem-Solving Method	*			*	*	*	*	*
Laboratory Report Method		*			*	*	*	*
✓ Team Learning Method			*	*	(Repeated with entire class)				
Peer Review Method			*	*	(Repeated with entire class)				
✓ Peer Tutoring Method			*	*	(Repeated with entire class)				
Programmed Instruction			*	*	*	*	*	
✓ Individualized Instruction			*	*	(Repeated with entire class)				
Note-Taking Method			*	*		*	*	*
Journal–Keeping Method			*	*	*	*	*	*
Watching–Doing Methods								
Demonstration Method	*				*	*	*	*
Field Trip Method	*							*
✓ Contract Method		*		*	(Repeated with entire class)				
Hands-On/Lab Method		*			*	*	*	*
✓ Inquiry Method		*		*	*	*	*	*
✓ Learning Center Method			*	*	(Repeated with entire class)				
Projects Method			*	*			*	
					(Repeated with entire class)				
Stimulation Method			*			*	*	*
Games Method			*	*	*	*	*	*
✓ Exploration-Discovery Method			*	*	*	*	*	*

Note: Checkmark (✓) indicates that the method is used in more than one kind of transaction: Listening–Speaking, Reading–Writing, and Watching–Doing.

Source: Rita Peterson et al., *Science and Society: A Source Book for Elementary and Junior High School Teachers* (Columbus, OH: Merrill, 1984), 121. Reprinted with permission of the author.

Teaching Strategy	Direct, explicit, or exposition	Guided discovery	Indirect, exploration or free discovery
Emphasis	Scientific products	Scientific products and processes	Scientific processes
Teacher Role	Active/dominant	Active/facilitator	Facilitator
Student Role	Passive or active	Active	Active

FIGURE 3–1

Dominance/passivity of science teaching/learning transactions

Research findings show that direct or expository instruction can be effective for certain types of learning when carefully planned and delivered.[2] For example, the learning of facts and simple concepts in science, or the mastery of specific procedures, can be effective when these factors facilitate students' learning from expository instruction: (a) connections to prior knowledge, (b) advance organizers, (c) organization, (d) visual aids, (e) processing time, (f) questions, and (g) summaries. See Table 3–2 for further elaboration.

Direct or expository teaching emphasizes the *products* of learning more centrally than the *processes* by which students learn. More complex learnings—such as learning to apply science concepts and principles, learning to plan investigations in science, and solving math problems—do not particularly lend themselves to direct instruction techniques.

In the specific and limited situations just mentioned, when teachers explain exactly what students are expected to learn, and clearly demonstrate the steps needed to accomplish a particular task, students learn more effectively.[3] These procedures are based on the assumption that knowing how to learn does not necessarily come naturally to all students. Direct instruction systematically guides students through specific learning steps, helping them to see both the purpose and result of each step. Therefore, ideally, students learn not only the lesson's content but also a method for learning that content, which may be applicable to other content learning. Barak Rosenshine tells us that almost twenty years of research on effective teaching has firmly established the effectiveness of systematic step-by-step direct or explicit instruction.[4]

When Is Direct Instruction Most Pertinent?

Piaget, constructivists, and other cognitive theorists say that of the three types of knowledge (social, physical, and logical–mathematical), only social knowledge can be taught directly by the teacher. In your science teaching, social knowledge would be the body of subject matter or scientific products: facts and concepts. These scientific products are usually presented to students after they have hands-on/minds-on

TABLE 3–2
Principles of expository instruction

Principle	Educational Implication	Example
▪ **Connections to prior knowledge** help students learn classroom material meaningfully.	We should remind students of something they already know and point out how a new idea is similar.	When introducing new vocabulary on molecules, relate to smallest part in body—the cell.
▪ An **advance organizer** helps students develop an overall organizational scheme for the material.	We should introduce a new unit by describing the major ideas and concepts to be discussed and showing how they are interrelated.	When beginning a unit on mountains, we can briefly describe the four types we will be talking about—volcanic, dome, fold, and block mountains.
▪ An **organized presentation** of material helps students make appropriate interconnections among ideas.	We should present related ideas within the same lesson and at the same time.	If we want students to notice leaf structure similarities, present many leaves with similar characteristics.
▪ **Visual aids** help students encode material visually as well as verbally.	We can illustrate new material through pictures, diagrams, maps, models, and demonstrations.	When describing world fault areas, show them on a large map.
▪ Providing **processing time** gives students a chance to encode and elaborate on information.	We should pace our presentation slowly enough so that students can mentally process each idea.	We can intersperse lecture material with hands-on activities illustrating the principles we present.
▪ **Questions** during and after expository instruction promote elaboration and help students monitor their comprehension.	We can ask lower-level and higher-level questions during a lecture or after a reading assignment.	Before students color a wheel with primary colors to produce white light, ask: "Why is it important to clean the brush after finishing with each separate color?"
▪ **Summaries** help students review and organize material and identify main ideas.	After a lecture or reading assignment, we should summarize the key points of the lesson.	At the end of a unit on clouds, we can summarize the characteristics of the four types we've talked about—cumulus, cirrus, stratus, and cumulonimbus.

Source: Modified from Jeanne Ellis Ormrod, *Educational Psychology: Principles and Applications* (Englewood Cliffs, NJ: Merrill/Prentice Hall, 1995), 436.

experiences with the science areas, or are guided to the products in books, videos, computers, or films. You can readily see that direct or explicit instruction is most useful for teaching a body of content or knowledge or well-defined performance skills. It has been found to be most effective with young learners, slower learners, students with language difficulties, or all students when the content is too difficult or hierarchical.

Here is a brief summary of research on direct instruction showing the situations when its use is most effective:

1. For disseminating information to students not available in any other form.

When doing a demonstration (a direct instruction technique), describe each step, encouraging students to identify the purpose and predict the result of the activity.

2. To stimulate interest or motivate students.
3. To learn mastery of facts, rules, or procedures necessary for later learning.
4. To give an introduction to an indirect learning activity.
5. For efficiency, or when control is vital.

Some of the direct instructional strategies you might pick for teaching facts and simple concepts in science are

- telling,
- demonstrating using scientific apparatus,
- carrying on a discussion,
- reading to children,
- showing a film, filmstrip, slides, or TV presentation, and
- having a resource person present something.

Let's examine the direct instructional approaches of Ausubel, Rosenshine, and Bloom.

Ausubel's Advance Organizer

A hands-on/minds-on guided discovery approach to science teaching is critically important and is the approach most emphasized in this text. However, expository or direct teaching methods are still useful for teaching prior information as a pre-cursor for hands-on/minds-on activities. The problem when teaching by direct, expository methods is how to make the new information truly meaningful. Remember reading in Chapter 2 about David Ausubel, an educational psychologist. Ausubel emphasizes that information presented in an expository way through lecture, text, or some form of media is meaningfully learned only when it relates to prior knowledge.[5] Ausubel recommends the use of advance organizers to facilitate meaningful expository learning.

You may recall that an **advance organizer** is an abstract, general introduction to a new body of information or subject matter content to be learned and is presented early in instruction to provide a framework for assimilating new ideas. What you may not yet know is that in developing advance organizers, the new subject matter, whether from textbooks or teachers, should be assembled, organized, and sequenced in ways that can be made meaningful to students. Advance organizers should be drawn from the main principles and supporting concepts and facts to be learned. The use of teacher demonstrations, diagrams, pictures, and graphic organizers (e.g., schema or concept maps) are especially recommended to be used as advance organizers in the intermediate, upper elementary grades, and middle school grades. Many textbook programs are consistent with these ideas.

Rosenshine's Direct Teaching Approach

Barak Rosenshine, in summarizing research studies on effective teaching, divided direct or explicit instruction into these six teaching functions:

1. Daily review.
2. Presentation of new materials.
3. Conducting guided practice.
4. Providing feedback and corrections.
5. Conducting independent practice.
6. Weekly and monthly reviews.

Six teaching functions aid student learning of explicit, well-structured information and skills such as mathematical procedures, science facts and concepts, grammatical rules, and vocabulary.

1. Each day, start the lesson by correcting the previous night's homework and reviewing what students have recently been taught.

2. Tell students the goals of today's lesson. Then present new information a little at a time, modeling procedures, giving clear examples, and checking often to make sure students understand.

3. Allow students to practice using the new information under the teacher's direction; ask many questions that give students abundant opportunities to correctly repeat or explain the procedure or concept that has just been taught. Student participation should be active until all students are able to respond correctly.

4. During guided practice, give students a great deal of feedback. When students answer incorrectly, reteach the lesson if necessary. When students answer correctly, explain why the answer was right. It is important that feedback be immediate and thorough.

5. Next, allow students to practice using the new information on their own. The teacher should be available to give short answers to students' questions, and students should be permitted to help each other.

6. At the beginning of each week, the teacher should review the previous week's lesson and at the end of the month review what students have learned during the last four weeks. It is important that students not be allowed to forget past lessons once they have moved on to new material.

These steps may be less important and are not sufficient for less well-defined topics, such as writing a term paper, a research report, or analyzing literature.

FIGURE 3–2

Rosenshine's direct or explicit teaching functions

Source: Barak V. Rosenshine, "Synthesis of Research on Explicit Teaching," *Educational Leadership,* 43, no. 7 (April 1986), 68. Reprinted with permission of the Association for Supervision and Curriculum Development. Copyright © 1986 by ASCD. All rights Reserved.

In Figure 3–2, Rosenshine outlines how to use these six direct or explicit instruction components successfully in your classroom.

Here is a condensation of Rosenshine's direct instruction steps:

- Precisely state lesson goals for students.
- Focus on one thought at a time before beginning another.
- Teach in small steps, checking for understanding before going to next step.
- Give step-by-step directions.
- Organize material so one point is mastered before the next is given.
- Avoid digressions.

Kellough's General Principles for Direct Instruction

The following principles are advocated by Richard Kellough, whether your direct instruction is formal or informal:

1. Start your presentation with an **advance mental organizer,** an introduction that helps students mentally prepare for study by
   - helping them make connections with material already learned (**comparative organizer**).
   - providing them with a conceptual arrangement of what is to be learned (**expository organizer**).

   An advance mental organizer can be a brief statement about your main topic, a conceptual map of the topic, or a discrepant event.
2. Plan your presentation to have a beginning, an end, and a logical order, and reinforce with such visuals as writing unfamiliar terms on the board, using graphs, charts, photos, or audio-visuals.
3. Pace your presentation to be lively but not too fast, with these cautions:
   - Be brisk, but occasionally slow down to change pace and to check for student comprehension.
   - Allow students time to take notes and ask questions.

- Prepare a flexible time plan, but remember your 15-minute planned presentation will take longer when students are very interested and participate fully.
4. Encourage active student participation to enhance learning by asking thought-provoking questions, eliciting student comments and questions, or developing a conceptual outline for students to fill in during your presentation.
5. Design a clear ending, followed by another activity during the same or next class period that secures the learning.

In conclusion, Kellough advocates that you[6]

- plan a clear and captivating beginning,
- design an engrossing lesson body, and
- conclude with a firm and meaningful closure.

Bloom's Mastery Learning

Another direct instruction approach that utilizes many of these techniques is **mastery learning.** This method was developed by Benjamin Bloom and his associates.[7] Similar approaches are the Fred Keller Plan or the Personalized System of Instruction (PSI),[8] Rita and Stuart Johnson's Self-Instructional Package (SIP), and Madeline Hunter's Instructional Theory Into Practice (ITIP) and Program for Effective Teaching (PET).[9]

In Bloom's mastery learning, students must effectively learn one lesson before progressing to the next one. This teaching technique has these characteristics:

1. Subject matter is broken into small, discrete units or lessons.
2. Lessons are planned in a logical sequence, so that basic concepts and procedures are learned first and later lessons build on them.
3. The teacher teaches the whole class, actively involving students and reinforcing their contributions frequently.
4. Before moving on to the next lesson or unit, students must demonstrate mastery of content by taking tests.

5. At the end of a teaching unit (ranging from 2 or 8 weeks), the teacher gives a "formative test" to ascertain needs for *corrective, remedial,* or *supportive teaching*. This test is not for grading, but to assess what students have not learned.
6. Common errors are identified from test results.
7. Unlearned materials are retaught in new ways.
8. Students work cooperatively in groups of two or three for 20 to 30 minutes to help one another on items missed previously. If no one in the group can help, they call on the teacher.
9. Workbook exercises, text readings, films, videotapes, and computer assignments are assigned for students who need additional help.
10. An evaluation test is given to students as a final step.

When using direct or explicit instruction, you should know that students seem to work better when the teacher circulates around the room during instruction. It was found that short contacts with students (averaging 30 seconds or less) are effective for monitoring and supervising their work. Students also achieve more in direct or explicit instruction when they help each other in cooperative settings during seatwork. Slower students are also helped more in cooperative classroom environments when fellow students explain the content in language they understand. Teachers can help slower students in direct or explicit instruction by giving them more review, guided practice, and independent practice than faster students.

Summary of Direct Instruction Benefits

In using direct or explicit instruction, you initially take full responsibility for presenting content or a specific skill, and then gradually guide students to greater independence. Research has consistently shown that student achievement in content and skills improves when teachers instruct systematically, along the lines recommended by Rosenshine and Bloom. Helping your students with more complex learning (e.g., applying science concepts and principles, planning science investigations, or solving problems) requires more indirect instruction strategies.

INDIRECT INSTRUCTION AND GUIDED DISCOVERY TEACHING

Indirect instruction focuses on engaging students in exploration, inquiry, or discovery and is based on these premises:

- Questions and problems precede answers in the learning process.
- Students must process information mentally to achieve meaningful understanding.
- Students must be actively involved in the learning.

Researchers[10] say indirect instruction has a better chance of success when

1. concepts, patterns, and abstractions are primary goals,
2. higher thinking skills are to be developed,
3. students participate to achieve the objectives,
4. problem solving is the main goal, and
5. it is necessary for long-term retention.

Two additional factors are crucial for successful guided discovery learning:

- Prerequisite knowledge
- Structured experiences

Reexamine Figure 3–1 and notice that exploration or free discovery strategies are at one extreme of the teaching strategy continuum; these strategies allow students to develop their abilities to manipulate and process information from a variety of sources—academic, social, and experiential. In free discovery or inquiry, students identify their *own* problems, generate their *own* hypotheses or possible solutions, test these hypotheses in the light of available data, and attempt to apply their *own* conclusions to new

Even young learners can benefit from open-inquiry activities and make predictions about what might happen.

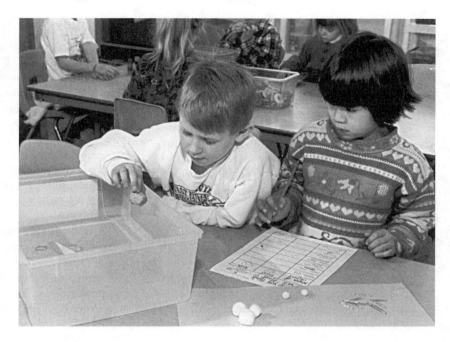

data, new problems, or new situations. Free discovery or inquiry focuses on *how* students process data (processes) rather than *what* they process (products).[11]

Educators David A. Welton and John T. Mallan have summarized free discovery or inquiry this way: "In an educational context, inquiry is both a noun and a verb—both an act and a process . . . inquiry is a learning process, a way in which students and adults can go about solving problems or processing information."[12]

Note: It is unlikely that elementary and middle school teachers will encounter large numbers of students who can engage independently in this very advanced mental strategy called inquiry or free discovery. Piaget's evidence about children's development (presented in Chapter 2) indicates that such students are rare. Yet, free discovery or inquiry processing is an important goal of science teaching. Teachers are reporting that students, even in lower elementary grades, are perfectly capable of open-ended inquiry learning. The key seems to be that as young students ask interesting questions, much open inquiry can

take place if teachers allow them to simply "mess around" with various concepts. Students do not have to be "mature," merely curious.

You can combine some free discovery or inquiry processes with direct or exposition teaching methods. This will result in hands-on/minds-on guided discovery, which is very appropriate for elementary and middle school students.

Learning Cycles Constructed Around Reliable Cognitive Research

Your teaching techniques should parallel the methods scientists/technologists use for solving their professional problems. Your instruction should be organized in a pattern that coordinates the most current cognitive development research with scientific/technological/societal (STS) teaching/learning theory. As pointed out in previous chapters, many science educators recommend instructional models congruent with constructivist learning theory. In these instructional models, teachers select activities that encourage students to construct their own understandings of concepts by

- beginning with the knowledge, skills, misconceptions, and naive theories students bring to the new classroom experience (*prior knowledge*)
- providing students with motivating experiences to test new ideas against their own previous ideas, thus supporting or questioning their thinking (*common experiences*)
- introducing students to new, specific information (e.g., terms, definitions, other language) to see how they apply to students' prior knowledge (*invent language*)
- engaging students in additional experiences that challenge, refute, or extend their own ideas (*clarifying experiences*) and
- guiding students to question, discuss, argue, conclude, and construct a new or revised concept understanding (*concept construction and understanding*).

Various instructional models attempt to meet these learning criteria. Here is an introduction to some of them.

The Karplus and Thier SCIS Cycle

Robert Karplus and Herbert Thier, co-developers of the Science Curriculum Improvement Study (SCIS), have devised a three-step learning cycle modeled after what Piaget and other cognitive theorists said were optimal conditions for learning and concept construction. Research on the learning cycle shows that students understand science better and are more likely to apply what they learn if they are given not only the opportunity and time to explore natural phenomena directly but also the chance to interact with a knowledgeable teacher who can provide relevant instruction and feedback related to their questions.[13] In this approach to learning, teachers act as facilitators, guides, and informers.

Karplus and Thier labeled their three stages *exploration, invention,* and *discovery.*[14] Figure 3–3 shows the three stages of the SCIS learning cycle. (Figure 3–3 also shows the names Charles R. Barman gave the last two stages: *concept introduction* and *concept application.*) Notice how the three stages in Figure 3–3 correspond to Piagetian and other cognitive learning theories and

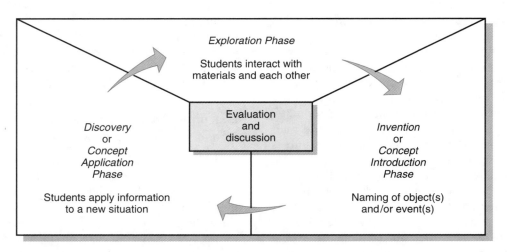

FIGURE 3–3

The Karplus and Thier learning cycle

Source: Modified from Charles R. Barman, "An Expanded View of the Learning Cycle: New Ideas About an Effective Teaching Strategy." Monograph and Occasional Paper Series, no. 4 (Washington, DC: Council for Elementary Science International, 1990), 5.

teacher/student roles. In the learning cycle, three concept formation factors (physical knowledge, social knowledge, and self-regulation) interact.

Exploration. Students' physical experiences and social interaction help them build mental images (physical knowledge). In this phase, students are allowed to spontaneously handle and freely explore materials, leading to questions and tentative ideas. Prior knowledge relevant to the problem is accessed and used in the initial organization of new ideas. The teacher plays an indirect role as observer, question poser, and assistant to students. Students actively manipulate materials.

Invention or Concept Introduction. Students interact with and communicate new ideas to teacher and peers to assimilate or accommodate specific ideas (social knowledge). In this phase, the teacher "invents" or imparts concepts, principles, or relationships that relate directly to the exploration phase, generally through expository (i.e., direct instruction) methods. This structure allows students to incorporate the prior exploratory experiences and leads to the third phase, discovery. In the invention stage, the teacher has a traditional role: gathering information about students from the exploration stage and introducing terminology and other information. Students participate mentally and socially.

Discovery or Concept Application. Students' physical experiences and social interactions with new ideas in new situations are applied in problem-solving situations (self-regulation). In this phase, students try out their newly learned ideas by transferring them to new situations, thereby strengthening and reinforcing the mental structure. The teacher poses new situations or problems for possible solution using information from previous stages. The students are active.

Note: At the invention phase, students are guided in forming new, powerful ideas and linking them with prior knowledge. This phase is described in more detail in Chapter 8. At the invention phase, students' incorrect notions or misconceptions should be squarely confronted. Students need repeated opportunities to realize that there may be problems with their spontaneous ideas and to modify those ideas under the guidance of a teacher. In the discovery phase, the newly formed ideas are elaborated and strengthened through application in new situations.

The SCIS learning cycle has been modified and used in many science programs over the years. Several current instructional models, although differing somewhat, have been built on the foundations of the SCIS model. Here are a few of these models with sources for additional information.

- *Personal Construct Model*
  L. H. T. West and A. L. Pines, Eds., *Cognitive Structure and Conceptual Change* (Orlando, FL: Academic Press, 1985).
- *Neurologically Oriented Model*
  J. Levy, "The Evidence Strongly Disputes the Idea That Students Learn with Only One Side of the Brain," *Educational Leadership* 40 (1982), 66–71.
- *Science, Technology, and Health Model* (Colorado Springs, CO: Biological Sciences Curriculum Study, 1991).
- *Descriptive, Empirical-Inductive, and Hypothetical-Deductive Models*
  A. E. Lawson, "A Better Way to Teach Biology," *American Biology Teacher* 50, no. 5 (1988), 266–278.
- *General Learning Cycle Reference*
  J. W. Renner and E. A. Marek, *The Learning Cycle and Elementary School Science* (Portsmouth, NH: Heinemann, 1988).

Constructivist-Oriented Teaching/Learning Model

One current constructivist-oriented learning model deserves a longer look. It appears in the research literature under several different names, but can be recognized as either the Constructivist Learning Model (CLM)[15] or the Constructivist-Oriented Instructional Model to Guide Learning (The Teaching Model).[16]

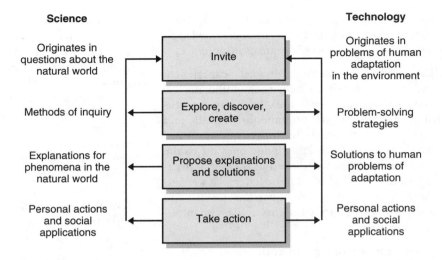

FIGURE 3–4
Constructivist-oriented instructional model to guide science learning

Science

Originates in questions about the natural world

Methods of inquiry

Explanations for phenomena in the natural world

Personal actions and social applications

Invite

Explore, discover, create

Propose explanations and solutions

Take action

Technology

Originates in problems of human adaptation in the environment

Problem-solving strategies

Solutions to human problems of adaptation

Personal actions and social applications

In the last section, we discussed the philosophy underlying the constructivist teaching/learning model. This philosophy is depicted graphically in Figure 3–4, in which students

1. accept an invitation to learn;
2. explore, discover, and create;
3. propose explanations and solutions; and
4. take action on what they learned.

Note that this fourth step is an STS modification of the original SCIS learning cycle.

The four-step format is based on the ways practicing science/technology professionals learn and apply new skills and information within their fields, as well as how students construct their science concepts. Figure 3–4 highlights these science and technology approaches. Although the model is sequential, the arrows and loops display the complex nature of problem solving. This model is cyclical and dynamic, which means that "although single lessons or units of study may have a beginning (invitation) and an end (taking action), any new knowledge or skills will inevitably lead to new invitations, and therefore, a continuation of the cycle."[17]

Figure 3–5 goes into greater detail of the four stages, emphasizing examples of teaching applicable to both science and technology. By using both Figures 3–4 and 3–5, you can see how well the four stages of the teaching model correlate with constructivists' criteria for students building their own concepts. Notice also the similarities between the SCIS Learning Cycle and the updated Constructivist-Oriented Instructional Model with its STS emphasis. The SCIS Learning Cycle and the Constructivist-Oriented Instructional Model can be adapted to your current science teaching; the next section gives specific details of how to do this.

GUIDED DISCOVERY HANDS-ON/MINDS-ON TEACHING AND LEARNING METHODS

Guided discovery hands-on/minds-on teaching and learning methods blend teacher-centered and student-centered techniques. Figure 3–6 illustrates the relationships that may exist between teacher dominance and what Piaget and other constructivists call **mental readiness** to internalize concepts, that is, students' ages or mental development, the relationships between their prior knowledge and science concepts construction, and their ability to engage in discovery learning, either free or guided. Because students can internalize only those concepts for

Teaching Examples for Science	Stages in the Teaching Model	Teaching Examples for Technology
	Invitation	
Observe the natural world		Observe the human-made world
Ask questions about the natural world		Recognize a human problem
State possible hypotheses		Identify possible solutions
	Explorations, Discoveries, Creations	
Engage in focused play		Brainstorm possible alternatives
Look for information		Experiment with materials
Observe specific phenomena		Design a model
Collect and organize data		Employ problem-solving strategies
Select appropriate resources		Discuss solutions with others
Design and conduct experiments		Identify risks and consequences
Engage in debate with teachers and peers		Evaluate choices
Define parameters of an investigation		Analyze data
	Proposing Explanations and Solutions	
Communicate information and ideas		Construct and explain a model
Construct a new explanation		Constructively review a solution
Evaluation by peers		Express multiple answers/solutions
Determine appropriate closure		Integrate a solution with existing knowledge and experiences
	Taking Action	
Apply knowledge and skills		Make decisions
Share information and ideas		Transfer knowledge and skills
Ask new questions		Develop products and promote ideas
	New Invitation	

FIGURE 3–5

Detailed functions of the constructivist-oriented instructional model

Note: Although this figure has two distinct columns, a review of teaching examples clearly shows that science and technology are intertwined; many of the examples could easily be placed in both columns. Communicating information and ideas, for example, is as much a part of science as it is a part of technology.

which they are mentally ready, the younger the students, the more you must present experiences for them to gain new information (prior knowledge) and guide them to build their own concepts. The older the student, the less you present, and the more they will initiate work with you as a facilitator, resource person, encourager, and guide.

This text emphasizes guided discovery for these important reasons:

1. More of us are familiar and comfortable with expository teaching, probably because it was used almost exclusively in our own education. In 1993, a national survey interviewed 6000 science and mathematics educators throughout the United States. Figure 3–7 shows that the largest proportion of science class time (38%) devoted to lecture/discussion, only 23% of science class time was devoted to hands-on laboratory work. If we want our students to be

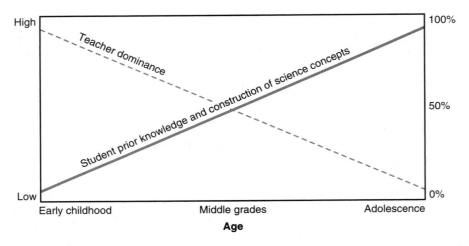

FIGURE 3–6
Teacher dominance and student learning variables

scientifically/technologically literate and able to solve problems, they must actively participate at their appropriate level in science activities with your assistance and guidance.

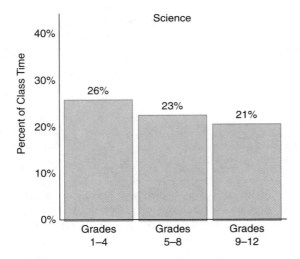

FIGURE 3–7
Percent of Science Class Time Devoted to Hands-on/Manipulative Activities by Grade Range

Source: Modified from Iris R. Weiss et al., *A Profile of Science and Mathematics Education in the United States: 1993* (Chapel Hill, NC: Horizon Research, Inc., 1994), 15.

2. Guided discovery is especially important with young children, because they *need* concrete learning experiences. Opportunities for them to manipulate materials may lead to free discovery or more open inquiry in adolescence and adulthood.
3. Guided discovery teaching will broaden your repertoire of teaching methods to meet the diverse backgrounds, learning styles, and levels of development of the students you teach.

Guided Discovery Advantages

Jerome Bruner, instrumental in leading the movement toward discovery teaching, outlined four reasons for using this approach:

1. Intellectual potency.
2. Intrinsic rather than extrinsic motives.
3. Learning the heuristics of discovery.
4. Conservation of memory.

Intellectual Potency. By **intellectual potency,** Bruner means that an individual learns and develops his or her mind only by using it. He emphasizes that the only way people learn discovery techniques is by having opportunities to discover them by themselves. Through guided discovery, a student slowly learns how to organize and carry out investigations independently. The greatest payoffs of the guided discovery approach are that it aids memory retention and is easily applied to new situations. Something a student discovers independently is more likely to be remembered, while concepts he or she is told can be quickly forgotten. Robert Glaser, in summarizing research on teaching and thinking, concluded that knowledge acquired in problem-solving contexts is more likely to be applicable to new situations.[18] Research also found that discovery learning is preferable for fostering problem solving, creativity, and independent learning.[19]

Guiding Students to Intrinsic Motivation. Learning may occur in response to some reward; students may also be motivated to learn to avoid failure. These two types of motivation may become a pattern in which students seek cues about how to conform to what is expected of them. The students in your class may spend the first few days finding out what it is you want, so they can please you. David Reisman, a sociologist, uses the term *outer-directedness* to explain that students do things for us as teachers. They want to elicit our praise and avoid our wrath. This works against our goals in science education by making the student dependent on an authority for rewards, motivation, and constant direction.

Conversely, guided discovery helps students become more autonomous, self-directed, and responsible for their own learning. Your students will become more self-motivated when they learn by discovering something themselves, rather than by hearing about it. They learn to carry out their activities with autonomy and become inner-directed. For students who are inner-directed, the reward is the discovery itself. Students learn to manipulate their environment more actively. They achieve gratification from coping with problems. Bruner believes that, as a consequence of succeeding at discovery, the student receives a satisfying intellectual thrill—an intrinsic or self-satisfying reward. Teachers often give extrinsic rewards (*A*'s, for example), but if

they want students to learn for the fun of it, they have to devise instructional systems that offer students intrinsic satisfaction.

Intrinsic rewards are personal, vary widely from person to person, and are directly connected to obvious external incentives.

Research has shown that extrinsic motivation is more efficient in terms of the relative amount of time spent in learning the task, skill, or knowledge. But information learned by intrinsic motivation is retained longer.[20]

With discovery-oriented teaching, you are more likely to provide a nonpunitive, stimulating atmosphere where students engage in learning because it is fun, interesting, and self-rewarding. Your job, then, is to act as a facilitator and provide your students with an environment responsive to their needs. Try to eradicate your view of the teacher as a dispenser of information and rewards. Give your students an opportunity to try things without fear of your (external) rewards or punishment.

The Heuristics of Discovery and Metacognition. As John Dewey said, "We learn by doing and reflecting on what we do." A great deal of evidence shows that learning is not a passive process. Jerome Bruner put it this way, "The student is not a bench-bound listener, but should be actively involved in the learning process."[21]

The student must be actively involved in learning. Sometimes people misinterpret this concept and limit activity to manual or manipulative activities. Students can be actively involved by listening, speaking, reading, seeing, and thinking *if* their minds are acting on what is being learned. Your job is to find ways to get the learner actively involved in whatever activities are presented. Piaget said that no learning occurs without action. It is only through the exercise of problem solving that your students will learn the **heuristics of discovery,** that is, learn how to learn. The more they are involved in solving problems, the more likely they are to learn to generalize what they have learned into a style of discovery that serves them best.

Heuristics is similar to the process of metacognition. *Meta* is derived from the Greek and means "after, amidst, and over and above." In the case of our thinking process, metacognition goes beyond thinking, to thinking *about* thinking.[22] Metacognition, then, focuses on the mental skills and processes used within a specific problem situation. Sternberg and Frensch[23] describe **metacomponential skills and processes** as metacognitive skills used in finding and delineating problems: planning what to do in seeking solution(s) to the problem, implementing the plan, and monitoring and assessing actions.

Knowing the *that, how,* and *when* of learning is crucial to reflective metacognition and heuristic discovery. Put another way, "Knowledge about when to use strategies is a particularly critical form of metacognition."[24] Your job as teacher is to assist students in learning how to do this. One important way is to guide them in processing new information.

Guiding Students in Their Information Processing. The human mind has often been compared to an extremely complicated computer; the biggest problem of this human computer is not the storage but the retrieval of data. Psychologists and learning researchers believe the key to retrieval is organization—knowing *what* information to find and *how* to get it. Research indicates that any organization of information that reduces the complexity of material by putting it in a pattern the *learner* has constructed will make that material easier to retrieve. Material that is organized in terms of the learner's own interests and uniqueness has the best chance of being accessible in memory. You probably can think of something you learned by setting up a system that worked for you. Do you remember high school or college science classes where your teacher tried to help you remember something by association? The best kind of system is one a person invents personally, but we still should show our students how other people remember and structure things. The very attitudes and activities that characterize discovering things for oneself also seem to make material readily retrievable in the learner's memory. Psychologists call this **transfer of training.**

There is little evidence that learning one subject will enhance mastery in another subject. Teachers once believed that it would, and they taught Latin to train the mind, make the learner more logical, and improve the understanding of English grammar. However, it just didn't work that way. For the transfer of training to be most effective, two factors must be at work.

1. Positive transfer of training will take place if there is a similarity between subjects. The closer the similarity of the subjects, the better the chance of a transfer of training.
2. Positive transfer of training will take place if the knowledge, concepts, principles, or techniques learned in the first situation can be usefully applied to the second situation.

Therefore, if you want your students to be problem solvers, learn by discovery, and do things for themselves, you must give them practice in these very things. The more your students solve problems with your guidance, the greater will be the chances that transfer of training will find its way into new situations. To find out more about transfer of learning, read David Perkins and Gavriel Salomon, "Teaching for Transfer," *Educational Leadership, 46,* no. 1 (1988), 21–31.

Guiding Students to Lifelong Learning

Guided discovery hands-on/minds-on teaching/learning tries to assist students in learning to learn, that is, to acquire knowledge and construct concepts that are uniquely their own because they discovered them themselves. Guided discovery is not restricted to finding something entirely new to the world such as an invention (television) or theory (heliocentric view of the universe). It is a matter of internally rearranging data so students can go beyond the mere facts to form concepts *new to them*. Guided discovery lets students find their own meanings, organization, and structure of ideas.

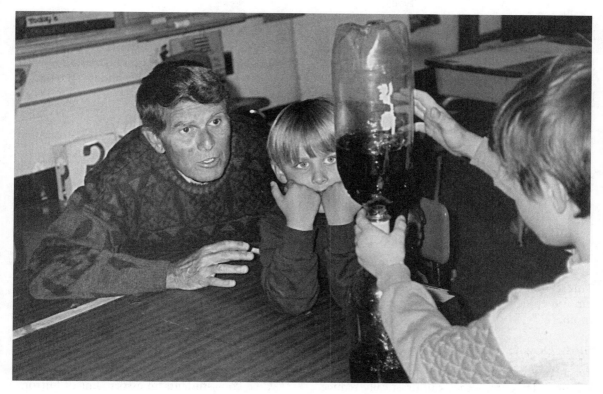

Teachers play an important role in guiding students' processing of information.

Research Confirms Discovery Learning Is Effective. Although research is continuing, evidence suggests that discovery learning is effective. Students exposed to inquiry-oriented, process-approach science perform better on measures of general science achievement, process skills, analytical skills, and related skills such as language arts and mathematics.[25]

One of the best studies of discovery teaching was a three-year longitudinal investigation to see what differences (if any) this type of teaching made on the students' learning behaviors. Investigators at Carnegie–Mellon University found that a discovery-oriented social studies curriculum increased the students' abilities to inquire about human affairs significantly more than a program using nondiscovery materials. This study was impor-

tant, since it showed that discovery teaching over a three-year period actually made individuals better learners.[26] The implications for science teaching are numerous.

In another study, T. E. Allen found that discipline problems from troublemakers were significantly reduced in science classrooms where the teachers were nondirective and nonauthoritarian and where student opportunity to select and explore alternatives was increased.[27]

Edmund Amidon and Ned A. Flanders found that highly anxious students functioned better in student-centered classrooms in which there was less structure and teachers gave fewer directions.[28]

When affective learning is considered, discovery learning promotes more positive attitudes toward teachers and schoolwork than traditional teaching techniques. In other words, students like school better and this affects their learning.[29]

In summary, studies show that students prefer a discovery process approach over a more traditional textbook-oriented science program, causing them to

1. find science exciting and interesting;
2. wish they had more science;
3. feel science is useful in their everyday lives;
4. have feelings of success; and
5. have a more positive view of science and scientists than non-SCIS students.[30]

APPLYING GUIDED DISCOVERY TO YOUR TEACHING

This section will explore some practical ways you can use guided discovery teaching in your classroom.

Slow Down, You Teach Too Fast!

Teachers sometimes try to rush or short-circuit learning. They think they can drastically reduce the time it takes for students to learn something. However, students need adequate time to think, reason, and gain insights into scientific concepts, principles, and skills. It takes time for students to act on things in their minds for meaningful learning. The learning process may seem meaningful to teachers, but unless it becomes meaningful to the learner, it is all for naught.

Piaget and others believed that no true learning can occur unless students have time to assimilate and accommodate what they encounter in their environments. Unless this happens, you and your students are involved in what Piaget called **pseudolearning**—parroting an explanation without a real change in mental awareness about a subject. Mary Budd Rowe addresses this need for the teacher to slow down to allow student learning to adequately occur.[31]

In Figure 3–8, you can review the many advantages you will have by increasing the number of guided discovery activities in your science teaching. Although no instructional model is perfect, the shortcomings of guided discovery teaching are far outweighed by its advantages, particularly helping students to learn how to learn and construct their own concepts and understandings.[32]

How Much Guidance in Guided Discovery?

Guided discovery teaching is *not* a *laissez-faire* approach. You need to provide enough structure to ensure that students use their minds to discover science concepts and principles. You should have broad objectives in mind, and your classroom activities should guide students toward these objectives. However, some of the time you have to refrain from telling students what you want them to learn or they will merely memorize.

You have to present a variety of activities, so students can build storehouses of sensory experiences and prior knowledge from which verbal (and eventually written) words and symbols are "invented" by the teacher. Here is an example of how this can easily be done at the preschool or primary level.

Give your students an assortment of buttons and ask them to group them any way they want. Your purpose is to *guide* them to discover the buttons' characteristics or properties. This stage is called *exploration* in the SCIS Learning Cycle or *invitation and exploration* in the Constructivist Model.

Without telling students that buttons can be grouped according to their color, shape, texture, size, or material, ask, "What do all of Alice's buttons have in common?" or "What is alike in all of the buttons Harry grouped together?" Then say something like, "When you put the buttons together by their color, shape, or how they feel, scientists say you are grouping by *properties.*" This is the SCIS *invention stage,* where the teacher communicates words for the sensory experience.

Now give students a variety of seeds and ask, "How can we group these seeds by their properties?" This gives students an opportunity to *apply* what they learned in the exploration and invention stages to new situations (this is

Grouping objects is one kind of sensory experience that asks students to classify matter by discovering like properties.

Expository or Telling About Science	Guided Discovery Science
Teacher covers MORE but less is retained	Teacher covers less but MORE is retained and transferred

Teacher Orientation	Student Orientation
View students as a reservoir of knowledge, subject-centered. Teachers have covering compulsion. The more they cover, the better they think they are.	More holistic view of the learner, student-centered. Teachers more interested in cognitive and creative growth. Teach for the development of multi-talents in helping students develop their self-concepts.

FIGURE 3–8

Attributes of expository and guided discovery teaching/learning

Source: Modified from Harold H. Jaus, "Activity-Oriented Science: Is It Really Good?" Reproduced with permission by *Science and Children* (April 1977). Copyrighted by the National Science Teachers Association, 1840 Wilson Blvd., Arlington, VA 22201–3000.

the *discovery stage* in SCIS terminology or the *taking action* stage in the Constructivist Model). By being involved in all these activities, students slowly build in their mind what Piaget called physical knowledge.

Ruth S. Charney describes the fact that more guidance is needed in guided discovery with very young children or children not familiar with this approach:

Guided discovery is the process that I use to structure these first introductions to materials, routines, and areas of the classroom. The guided discovery protects children from the assault of a classroom that is too full of materials and choices at first, and it provides deliberate teaching of work habits and social habits, skills and concepts. It is an opportunity to model, to role-play, and to represent a variety of outcomes. Our guided discoveries prompt and excite children to play, to explore, to communicate, and to cooperate.[33]

"Inventing" New Words for Students' Concepts

Words are the verbal labels you must use to focus your students' attention clearly and explicitly on the conceptual ideas they have been investigating. In your guided discovery science program, you have supplied multisensory, hands-on/minds-on activities for your students. After they have experienced exploratory manipulative activities, you "invent" words and terms for what they have been doing. Constructivists say teachers "invent" words to assist learners to construct and understand scientific concepts and principles. To do so, follow these guidelines:

1. Group your students near you so they can all see anything you demonstrate, hear your questions, and communicate with each other.
2. Carefully plan and interestingly remind the students of an activity they have done themselves before this lesson.
3. During the activity, introduce the label (word) for the concept you want to develop. For instance, if you show a large magnet lifting a toy truck you could say: "When the magnet lifts the truck, we say it is evidence of *interaction* (new "invented" word) between the magnet and the truck." Write the word *interaction* on the chalkboard at this point. This gives visual as well as oral introduction of the new word to students. This repeats an activity your students have already done, but adds a new word for the concept.

4. Now perform a new activity using interaction. For instance, pour vinegar over baking soda and ask, "What do we call what is happening to the vinegar and baking soda?" (The bubbles are evidence of *interaction*.)
5. Ask your students about the similarities and differences in the two demonstrations. You are trying to stress that something happens between the objects—magnet and truck, vinegar and soda.
6. Ask your students to focus on the changes in both demonstrations and show them how we interpret this as evidence of interaction between objects.
7. To reinforce—and to see which students understand—the concept of evidence of interaction, ask, "Give us an example where you have seen evidence of interaction between objects."
8. Focus the students' attention on examples given to clarify interaction.
9. As a follow-up, have students cut pictures out of magazines at home of evidences of interaction.
10. The next day, make a bulletin board from the students' magazine pictures using the words *evidence of interaction* often as reinforcement.

Encourage Students to Use Operational Definitions

Science educators use the term ***operational definition*** to describe the inventing of science words growing out of your students' activities. Operational definitions use *actions* to describe what is happening, such as evidences of interaction. Note, however, as Piaget suggested, that the invention of terms must come *after* the learners have actually handled various materials. Otherwise students will be learning by rote. Numerous follow-up activities are needed to reinforce the concept presented with a variety of new situations containing the same concept, that is, evidence of interaction in the environment.

Guiding/Encouraging All Students to Discover Science

At the onset of this chapter, in *Charting a New Course,* you read about gender bias inadvertently practiced in a science classroom. As you have studied different learning theories, and guided discovery in particular, have you thought about practices you might employ to avoid introducing bias in your own science classroom? Look at the list of strategies below. How do these fit into a guided discovery approach?

- Pay attention to how often you call on children of both genders. Call all children by name, and give both genders equal time and encouragement to answer.
- Allow all students time to think about their answers before you call on anyone—even if the boys are waving their hands.
- Provide time for girls to manipulate and experiment with science tools and equipment, without boys' "help."
- Introduce activities that involve working together rather than competing, as girls tend to learn better in cooperative groups. Consider setting up single-sex groups.

The publications listed below can also help you become more aware of gender bias so you can avoid it in your classroom.

- *How Schools Shortchange Girls,* a report from the American Association of University Women (AAUW), 1992). Call 800-225-9998 to order.
- *Lifting the Barriers: 600 Strategies That Really Work to Increase Girls' Participation in Science, Mathematics, and Computers* (Jo Sanders Publications, 1994). Call 212-642-2672 for a copy.

- *The Scientist Within You: Experiments and Biographies of Distinguished Women in Science,* featuring hands-on activities relating to the research of women scientists (ACI Publishing, 1994). Call 800-935-7323.

THE IMPORTANCE OF HANDS-ON/MINDS-ON ACTIVITIES IN GUIDED DISCOVERY

All of the new promising curriculum projects, national science standards studies, and innovative science textbooks unanimously endorse the necessity for laboratory-type (manipulative) experiences for teaching and learning science. This is succinctly put in one sentence by James Rutherford:

Hands-on learning activities used appropriately can transform science learning by engaging the student in the process of science.[34]

For the elementary school science program this means hands-on experiences emphasizing the science process skills of observing, measuring, recording, classifying, interpreting data, inferring, predicting, investigating, and making models. Hands-on experiences, if properly guided by the teacher, can provide practice in thinking and reasoning. Darrell Phillips summarizes the place of hands-on activities in guided discovery learning.

The individual's construction of the tools of thought (i.e., Piaget's operations and operational structures) are abstracted from actions on objects. In essence, without action on objects there can be no abstraction, operations, or structures. Teaching science as a reading lesson, a "cookbook" lab, or an exercise in memorization inhibits the development of reasoning. . . . Teachers must offer *sciencing* (active exploration and discovery of relationships) as opposed to school *science* (passive mimicking and memorization).[35]

Elementary and middle school students are in a formative stage of mental development, which requires actions on objects for the development of reasoning. What you must supply during these vital growth years is a variety of hands-on/minds-on activities in which your students manipulate objects, are guided to see relationships, and draw conclusions.

By asking yourself the questions below and evaluating activities ahead of time, you can make wise decisions in picking, planning, and conducting the best hands-on/minds-on guided discovery activities.

Relative to students' prior knowledge or current learning experiences, does the hands-on/minds-on guided discovery activity

1. provide meaningful, accurate science learning?
2. warrant the time it takes?
3. justify the money it may cost?
4. subject students to potential dangers?
5. fit into learners' cognitive developmental levels and interests?
6. have an easy-to-follow, teacher-friendly format?
7. work?

One of the best ways to judge an activity is to *try it yourself first*! Then you will see whether it satisfies the seven criteria for selecting activities.[36]

Format for Guided Discovery Hands-on/Minds-on Science Lessons

The format for the guided discovery hands-on/minds-on approach should address all or most of these ten questions:

1. What age range might benefit from this activity?
2. What questions or problems might be investigated?
3. What scientific/technological concepts might students be exposed to, discover, or construct in this activity?
4. What must *I* know? Where do I find it?
5. What concepts, naive theories and misconceptions do students have on this topic? How will I find out?
6. What science processes are involved?
7. What will I need for guiding this activity?
8. What will we communicate or discuss?
9. What actions will students take, individually or in groups?
10. How will students use or apply what they construct or discover to their everyday lives and/or science/society/technology relationship?

Chapter 6 provides specific suggestions for using this activity format.

As you scrutinize the guided discovery hands-on/minds-on format, compare it to the Constructivist-Oriented Instructional Model in Figure 3–4. As Figure 3–9 shows, the two have overlapping characteristics. As teacher, you have great latitude in deciding how to use the two models in your particular teaching/learning environment.

Constructivist-Oriented Model Stages	Guided Discovery Hands-On/Minds-On Format
Invitation	What scientific/technological topics might students be exposed to in this activity? What questions or problems might students investigate?
Explorations, Discoveries	What science processes are involved? What will students do individually or in groups?
Proposing Explanations and Solutions	What scientific concepts might students discover or construct? What will we communicate or discuss?
Taking Action	How will students use or apply what they construct or discover?

FIGURE 3–9

Correlation between constructivist-oriented model and the guided discovery hands-on/minds-on activity format

Use Less-Structured Guided Activities

If you and your students have not had experience in learning through discovery, you may initially need more structure initially in your lessons. But after you have both gained some experience in how to carry out discovery investigations, you will be more comfortable with an even freer discovery or open inquiry approach. At that point you will probably want to use less-structured discovery activities.

Less-structured activities differ from guided discovery in that you only motivate or initiate the problem and then invite your students to suggest (through questions) ways they can predict, observe, explore, or work out procedures for resolving it. In less-structured guided discovery, either you or your students may pose a problem. You provide the materials or the setting for resolving it, and give your students a lot of freedom to solve the problem(s).

How could you use them? Activity 3–1 is a minimally structured "Quickie Starter" discovery activity that illustrates how you (and the students themselves) can unearth students' misconceptions about sink and float.

In summary, less-structured activities like Quickie Starters extend opportunities for more open and creative student explorations while assisting you in discovering students' naive theories or misconceptions. Here are some other problems that might involve students in less-structured guided discovery activities and, at the same time, identify students' naive theories or misconceptions.

Primary Level—Mainly Exploratory

What do you notice about fish in our aquarium?
What did you find out about the butterflies?
In what ways could you group these different things?
What living things do you see in the pond, on the edge of the pond, several steps back from the pond?
What did you find out about leaves?

How are these rocks different?
What things do the magnets do and what do they attract?
What can you do with these objects?

Upper Elementary/Middle School— Devising and Carrying Out Experiments

How would you determine the effects of DDT on water snails?
What effect might temperature have on the sprouting of seeds?
What are all the ways you can get the light bulb to light using the wire and batteries in the trays on the science table?
What types of things stimulate the worms?
What affects the swing of pendulums?
What is the fastest way to get beans to sprout?
How could you determine whether this water is polluted?

Encourage your students to attack similar problems on their own or in small groups. Set yourself up as a resource person. Give only enough aid to ensure that the students do not become overly frustrated, experience undue failure, and give up. The assistance you give should be in the form of questions to guide students' thinking about possible investigative procedures. Ask the students questions that help them sense the direction for solving a problem rather than tell them what to do. For example, when students are studying what affects the movements of earthworms, you might ask, "What effect do you think light might have on the movements of earthworms? How could you find that out?" Questions like these, asked at the right time, may stimulate the students to become more involved in their creative investigation. Contrast this approach with that of a teacher who says, "Study earthworms and find out their characteristics and what things affect them." Such a statement might limit students' investigation to the physical appearance of worms, robbing them of opportunities for thought and creativity in their approaches.

Activity 3–1   QUICKIE STARTER: OPEN-ENDED ACTIVITY

WILL RAISINS SINK OR FLOAT IN SODA POP?

Materials

Enough of the following for 3–4 students to work together: clear carbonated soda pop, raisins, clear plastic cup, paper and pencils where appropriate

Opening Questions

Predicting

What do you think might happen to the raisins if we put them into the soda pop? (for younger students, you might ask a more specific question like:

Predicting

Will the raisins sink or float?)

Exposing Beliefs

Have students individually write their predictions and explain why they think it will happen that way. Invite students to share their predictions and explanations with their group members. Have them pick someone to share this data with the whole class.

Confronting Beliefs

Invite students to take turns placing raisins in soda pop in cup and recording their individual observations on paper.

Ask
Based on what you observed, what (if any) changes would you make in your predictions?

Ask

Accommodating Concept

Based on your observations, what can you say to explain what happened to the raisins in the soda pop?

When teaching elementary/middle students, consider asking these questions to stimulate "messing around" in less structured activities:

If you were the teacher of this class and you were going to select the most exciting things to investigate this term, what would they be?

What are some problems related to our community that you would like to study?

Now that you have studied, for example, salts, algae, light, heat, pollution, animal behaviors, and so on, what problems can you list that you would like to investigate individually or in teams?

After finishing this experiment, what other experiments can you think of, and which of them would you like to do?

When you see problems in the community (e.g., pollution), or when you discover some problem related to science that you would like to discuss, bring it to our attention in class.

What kind of science fiction story would you like to write?

Are *You* Ready for Constructivist-Oriented Science Activities?

Although the question asks if you are ready for teaching science with a constructivist or guided discovery hands-on/minds-on approach, you probably are involved in some aspects of it already. Robert Yager has devised a scale for analyzing the degree to which constructivist learning is already happening. Where are you in Yager's self-check device in Figure 3–10? Where do you want to be a week, a month, or a year from now? How will you get there? The remaining chapters will assist you in achieving your goals.

SUMMARY

No one method of teaching science is best for all students, all the time, under all circumstances. A taxonomy of common teaching methods, including a wide range of possible teaching methods, can be organized around these teacher/student transactions:

- Listening–Speaking (auditory or hearing learning).
- Reading–Writing (visual or sight learning).
- Watching–Doing (kinesthetic or muscular learning).

The amount of teacher dominance in these common teaching methods can vary. The three points on a teacher dominance continuum are Direct Teaching or Expository (telling) on one extreme, Indirect Teaching or Free Discovery or Inquiry on the other extreme, and Guided Discovery between the two.

Teaching methods should be organized in a pattern that coordinates the most recent cognitive development research with STS teaching and learning. Various instructional models are presented to meet these learning criteria, and two were examined in detail: the Karplus and Thier SCIS Learning Cycle and Barman's Constructivist-Oriented Instructional Model.

Guided discovery incorporates the best of what is known about science processes and products: how students learn best at the elementary and middle school levels; the aims, goals, and objectives of science education; and the relationships between science, technology, and society.

Discovery is the process by which learners use their minds in logical and mathematical ways to organize and internalize concepts and principles of the world. The learner is guided to learn to learn, which is called heuristics or metacognition. John Dewey fostered the idea of learning by doing and then reflecting on what was done. The research of Jean Piaget, Jerome Bruner, and others renewed interest in discovery learning.

Teacher	Identifies the Issue/Topic	Student
No	Issue is Seen as Relevant	Yes
Teacher	Asks the Questions	Student
Teacher	Identifies Written and Human Resources	Student
Teacher	Locates Written Resources	Student
Teacher	Contacts Needed Human Resources	Student
Teacher	Plans Investigation and Activities	Student
No	Varied Evaluation Techniques Used	Yes
No	Students Practice Self-Evaluation	Yes
No	Concepts and Skills Applied to New Situations	Yes
No	Students Take Action(s)	Yes
No	Science Concepts and Principles Emerge Because They are Needed	Yes
No	Extensions of Learning Outside the School in Evidence	Yes

FIGURE 3–10

A scale for analyzing the degree to which constructivist learning is occurring

Source: Robert E. Yager, "The Constructivist Learning Model," *The Science Teacher, 58,* no. 6 (September 1991), 56.

Advantages of guided discovery learning are that the students learn how to learn; learning becomes self-rewarding, self-motivational, and, thus, more easily transferable; rote learning is minimized; and learners become more responsible for their own learning.

Guided discovery activities may have four elements: invitation to learn, exploration and discoveries, proposing explanations and solutions, and taking action. According to Piaget, hands-on/minds-on experiences are extremely important at the elementary and middle school levels because of operational structures. They are also important because students need to react to objects and phenomena to develop reasoning.

The amount of structure you supply depends on your students' level of development and experiences with sciencing. Guided discovery teaching requires more structure than free discovery or inquiry. You provide the problems, materials, and equipment, but you encourage your students to work out the procedures for solving the problems themselves. The format for guided discovery lessons was introduced along with how it correlates with the Constructivist Instructional model stages.

In less-structured discovery activities, *you* pose the problems and provide the materials or setting; students have a lot of freedom in solving the problems. You function mainly as a resource person or facilitator and give only enough aid to keep your students moving toward the solutions.

In free discovery or inquiry activities, *students* identify what they would like to study as well as how they will go about answering their questions, solving their problem(s), and taking actions.

SELF-ASSESSMENT AND FURTHER STUDY

1. Choose a science topic for a specific grade level and plan a science activity for each of the categories in Table 3–1 (i.e., listening–speaking, reading–writing, and watching–doing). Vary the amount of teacher dominance in your activities.

2. How would you find out what your students' science concepts, naive theories, and/or misconceptions are in a particular science topic? Devise an activity or activities that would help you find out about their misconceptions. How might you go about guiding their misconception changes? You might start your search with these publications:

   - R. Driver and E. Scanlon, "Conceptual change in science." *Journal of Computer Assisted Learning, 5,* 25–36
   - Janice Koch, "Face to face with science misconceptions." *Science and Children, 30,* no. 6, March 1993, 39–40
   - Joseph Stevans, "Developmental patterns in students' understanding of physics concepts." in S. Glynn, R. Yeany, and B. Britton (Eds.), *The Psychology of Learning Science* (Hillsdale, NJ: Lawrence Erlbaum, Publishers, 1991)

   - Bruce Watson and Richard Konicek, "Teaching for conceptual change: confronting children's experiences," *Phi Delta Kappan,* May 1990, 680–85.

3. Develop a series of guided discovery hands-on/minds-on activities for any science area to fit each phase of the Karplus/Thier SCIS Learning Cycle or Barman's Learning Cycle. To assist you, investigate:

   - E. Marek and S. Methven, "Effects of the learning cycle upon student and classroom teacher performance," *Journal of Research in Science Teaching, 28,* 1991, 41–53.

4. Hands-on/minds-on guided discovery is more than manipulation of materials. Use the following to prepare a paper about what is essential for effective learning in this mode.

   - David P. Butts, Helen Marie Hofman, and Margaret Anderson, "Is direct experience enough? A study of young children's views of sound," *Journal of Elementary Science Education, 6,* no. 1, Winter 1994, 1–6.
   - _____, "Is hands-on experience enough? A study of young children's views of sinking and

floating objects," *Journal of Elementary Science Education, 5,* no. 1, Winter 1993, 50–64.

5. Why is guided discovery learning more transferable and longer lasting than exposition or learning by rote? Use these resources and/or any others you feel document your case:
   - Jeanne Ellis Ormrod, *Educational Psychology: Principles and Applications* (Englewood Cliffs, NJ: Merrill/Prentice Hall, 1995), 375–86
   - David Perkins, "Selecting Fertile Themes for Integrated Learning," in Heidi Jacobs (Ed.), *Interdisciplinary Curriculum: Design and Implementation* (Alexandria, VA: The Association for Supervision and Curriculum Development, 1989).

6. Describe, in your own words, what Robert Sternberg means by metacomponential skills and processes and how they affect learning. Supply specific examples applicable to any group of students with which you are working.

7. Identify a science problem interesting to a particular group of students. Prepare a series of less-structured activities, like the Quickie Starters in this text, that encourage them to "mess about." Keep a diary of their initial concepts, naive theories and misconceptions, and conclusions.

8. Many current innovative science education projects contend that teaching less is better. Explain what this means and give reasons why you agree or disagree.

9. Science educators have expressed concern that many science teaching terms lack clarity. Explore sources and find functional definitions of these commonly used science education terms: *teaching, learning, instructional strategies, lecture, inquiry, discussion, discovery, hands-on/minds-on activities,* and *instructional tools.*

10. Are there any questions you have about material in this chapter? How might you find answers to your questions?

11. Recall the teacher or teachers who had the greatest impact on you and your thinking. What personal characteristics and teaching attributes did they posses that impressed you?

NOTES

1. Nancy Kober, *EDTALK: What We Know About Science Teaching and Learning* (Washington, DC: Council for Educational Development and Research, 1993), 37.

2. A. J. Corkill, "Advance organizers: Facilitators of recall," *Educational Psychology Review, 4,* no. 4, 1992, 33–67. W. G. Holliday and G. Benson, " Enhancing learning using questions, adjunct to science charts," *Journal of Research in Science Teaching, 28,* no. 6, 1991, 523–535. W. R. Robinson and M. Niaz, "Performance based on instruction by lecture or by interaction and its relationship to cognitive variables," *International Journal of Science Education, 13,* no. 2, 1991, 203–215.

3. *What Works: Research About Teaching and Learning* (Washington, DC: United States Department of Education, 1986).

4. I am indebted to the following authoritative article on direct or explicit instruction, and highly recommend it for elaboration on the points presented in this section of the chapter: Barak V. Rosenshine, "Synthesis of Research on Explicit Teaching," *Educational Leadership, 43,* no. 7 (1986), 60–69.

5. As reported in Anthony Lawson et al., "Hypothetico-Deductive Reasoning Skill and Concept Acquisition: Testing a Constructivist Hypothesis," *Journal of Research in Science Teaching, 28,* no. 10, (1991), 953–970.

6. Modified from Richard D. Kellough, *A Resource Guide for Teaching: K–12* (Englewood Cliffs, NJ: Merrill/Prentice Hall, 1994), 325–326.

7. For greater detail about mastery learning examine Paul Chance, "Master of Mastery," *Psychology Today,* (April 1987), 43–46.

8. F. S. Keller, "Goodbye Teacher," *Journal of Applied Behavior Analysis, 1,* 1968, 79–89.

9. For a description of Madeline Hunter's programs and analysis of controversy surrounding them scrutinize: Madeline Hunter, *Mastery Teaching* (El Segundo, CA: Instructional Dynamics, Inc., 1982). Robert E. Slavin, "PET and the Pendulum: Faddism in Education and How to Stop It," *Phi Delta Kappan, 70,* no. 2, October

1991, 28–34. Noreen B. Garman and Helen M. Hazi, "Teachers Ask: Is There Life After Madeline Hunter?" *Phi Delta Kappan, 69,* no. 9, May 1988, 669–672. Garrett K. Mandeville and Janelle L. Rivers, "The South Carolina PET Study: Teachers' Perceptions and Student Achievement," *Elementary School Journal, 91,* no. 4, March 1991, 377–401.

10. R. E. Mayer, *Educational Psychology: A Cognitive Approach* (Boston: Little, Brown, 1987). J. A. Shymansky, L. V. Hedges, and G. Woodworth, "A reassessment of the effects of inquiry-based science curricula of the 60's on student performance," *Journal of Research in Science Teaching, 27,* 127–144.

11. For expansion of differences between inquiry and discovery peruse Frank X. Sutman, "Define Your Terms," *Science and Children, 32,* no. 4, January 1995, 33–34. For specific examples of four types of inquiry, see Donald C. Orlich, "Science Inquiry in the Commonplace," *Science and Children, 26,* no. 6 (March 1989), 22–24.

12. David A. Welton and John T. Mallan, *Children and Their World: Strategies for Teaching Social Studies,* 2nd ed. (Hopewell, NJ: n.p. 1981), 182.

13. Charles R. Barman and M. Kotar, "The Learning Cycle," *Science and Children, 26,* no. 7, 30–32. A. E. Lawson, M. R. Abraham, and J. W. Renner, *A Theory of Instruction: Using The Learning Cycle to Teach Science Concepts and Thinking Skills* (Monograph) (Washington, D.C.: National Association of Research in Science Teaching, 1989). J. W. Renner and E. Marek, *The Learning Cycle and Elementary School Science Teaching* (Portsmouth, NH: Heinemann, 1988).

14. For a fuller explanation of the SCIS Learning Cycle see Robert Karplus and Herbert Thier, *SCIS Teacher's Handbook* (Berkeley, CA: Science Curriculum Improvement Study, University of California, 1974).

15. Robert E. Yager, "The Constructivist Learning Model," *The Science Teacher, 58,* no. 6 (September 1991), 52–57.

16. Susan Loucks-Horsley et al., "Use a Constructivist-Oriented Instructional Model to Guide Learning," in *Elementary School Science for the 90's* (Andover, MA: The National Center for Improving Science Education, A partnership of the NETWORK, Inc. and The Biological Sciences Curriculum Study, 1990), 58–72.

17. Rodger W. Bybee, chair, et al., *Science and Technology Education for the Elementary Years: Frameworks for Curriculum and Instruction* (Colorado Springs, CO: The National Center for Improving Science Education. A partnership of the NETWORK, Inc. and The Biological Sciences Curriculum Study, 1989), 79.

18. Robert Glaser, "Education and Thinking: The Role of Knowledge," *American Psychologist, 39,* (1989), 93–104.

19. J. A. Shymansky, L. V. Hedges, and G. Woodworth, "A reassessment of the effects of inquiry-based science curricula of the 60's on student performance," *Journal of Research in Science Teaching, 27,* no. 127 (1990), 127–144.

20. N. L. Gage and David C. Berliner, *Educational Psychology,* 4th ed. (Boston, MA: Houghton Mifflin, 1988), Chapter 15.

21. Jerome S. Bruner, "The Art of Discovery," *Harvard Educational Review, 31,* no. 1 (1961), 21–32.

22. To deepen your understanding of metacognition, these sources present the latest research: Arthur Costa and Larry Lowery, *Techniques for Teaching Thinking* (Pacific Grove, CA: Midwest Publications, 1989). Arthur Hyde and Marilyn Bizar, *Thinking in Context* (White Plains, NY: Longman, 1989). Robert Swartz and David Perkins, *Teaching Thinking—Issues and Approaches* (Pacific Grove, CA: Midwest Publications, 1989).

23. R. J. Sternberg and P. A. Frensch, "Mechanisms of transfer" in D. K. Detterman and R. J. Sternberg (Eds.), *Transfer on trial: Intelligence, cognition, and instruction* (Norwood, NJ: Ablex, 1993).

24. Michael Pressley et al., "What Is Good Strategy Use and Why Is It Hard to Teach? An Optimistic Appraisal Associated with Strategy Instruction." Paper presented at the Annual Meeting of the American Educational Research Association, Washington, DC, April 1987.

25. James A. Shymansky, William C. Kyle, Jr., and Jennifer M. Alpert, "How Effective Were Hands-on Science Programs of Yesterday?" *Science and Children, 20,* no. 3 (1982), 14–15. James A. Shymansky, "The Effects of New Science Curricula on Student Performance," *Journal of Research in Teaching, 20* (1983), 387–404.

26. John M. Good, John U. Forley, and Edwin Fenton, "Developing Inquiry Skills with an Experimental Social Studies Curriculum," *The*

Journal of Educational Research, 63, no. 1 (September 1969), 35.

27. T. E. Allen, "A Study of the Behaviors of Two Groups of Disruptive Children When Taught with Contrasting Strategies: Directive vs. Nondirective Teaching," (Ph.D. diss., The Florida State University, 1976).

28. Edmund Amidon and N. A. Flanders, "The Effects of Direct and Indirect Teacher Influence on Dependent-Prone Students Learning Geometry," in Edmund Amidon and John B. Hough (Eds.), *Interaction Analysis: Theory, Research, and Application* (Reading, MA: Addison-Wesley, 1967), 210–216.

29. R. M. Giaconia and L. V. Hedges, "Identifying features of effective open education," *Review of Educational Research, 55,* 1982, 579–602.

30. William C. Kyle, Jr., et al., "What Research Says: Science Through Discovery: Students Love It," *Science and Children, 23,* no. 2 (October 1985), 39–41. William C. Kyle, Jr., R. J. Bonnstetter, and T. Gadsen, Jr., "An analysis of elementary students' and teachers' attitudes toward science in process-approach vs. traditional science classes. *Journal of Research in Science Teaching, 25* (1986) 103–120. William C. Kyle, Jr., et al., "What Research Says . . . About Hands-on Science, *Science and Children, 25,* no. 7 (April 1988), 39–40, 52.

31. Mary Budd Rowe, "Wait Time—Slowing Down May Be a Way of Speeding Up," *American Educator II,* (Spring, 1987), 1.

32. For an insight into possible shortcomings of teaching science by inquiry, see Kathleen J. Roth, "Science Education: It's Not Enough to 'Do' or 'Relate,'" *American Educator, 13,* no. 4 (Winter, 1989), 16–22, 46–47.

33. Ruth S. Charney, "Guided Discovery: Teaching the Freedom to Explore," *A Newsletter for Teachers, 3,* no. 1 (Spring 1991), 1–3.

34. F. James Rutherford, "Hands-on: A Means to an End." *Project 2061 Today 3,* no. 1 (Washington, DC: American Association for the Advancement of Science).

35. Darrell G. Phillips, "The Importance of Laboratory (Hands-On) Experiences in Science in the Elementary School: A Research Prospective," in "Science Activities Are Central to Science Education in the Elementary School," Robert E. Yager et al., *Science and Children, 19,* no. 2 (October 1981), 43. Reproduced with permission from *Science and Children,* (October 1981). Copyright by the National Science Teachers Association, 1840 Wilson Blvd., Arlington, VA 22201–3000.

36. For a fuller description of how to select activities along with examples read: Betsy Feldkamp-Price, Peter Rillero, and Erica Brownstein, "A Teachers' Guide to Choosing the Best Hands-on Activities. Avoid the trial-and-error approach with this seven point system," *Science and Children, 31,* no. 6, March 1994, 16–19.

CHAPTER 4

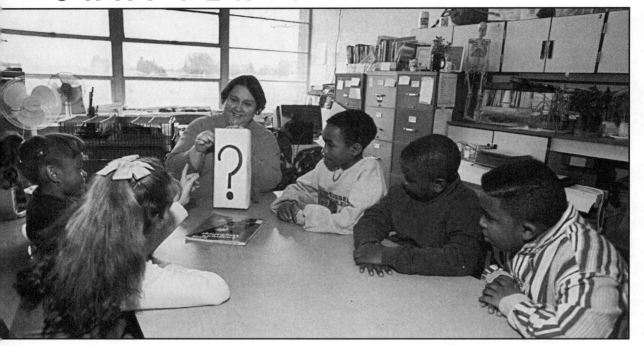

Mastering the Art of Questioning and Listening

In a science classroom that encourages students to construct understanding through scientific inquiry, questioning plays different roles during distinct phases of the learning process. An initial question posed by the teacher or raised by a student—Why are there waves in the ocean?—can set learning in motion and induce the class to conduct an experiment. . . . In the investigation stage, additional questions from the teacher and classmates—What would happen if you changed this?—help students see different routes to a solution and propose subsequent explorations and new hypotheses. When students are ready to propose explanations, questions help clarify, justify, and in some cases alter thinking. Did anything you discover surprise you? . . . A concluding round of questions— Where could you get more information on this topic?—can stimulate students to act on what they have learned.[1]

QUESTIONS THAT MAKE A DIFFERENCE

Questioning can not only help us determine what students know, but enable them to learn more. Questioning is basic to the guided discovery or constructivist approach. What kinds of questions should we ask students? Let's eavesdrop on three science classrooms, all of which are studying photosynthesis, and examine the kinds of questioning that occur.

Teacher 1 asks, "And what do we call those little round disks you saw under the microscope?"

Gary raises his hand and answers at the same time. "Chloroplasts! Or maybe chlorophyll?"

"You were right the first time, Gary," Teacher 1 says. "They're chloroplasts. The green part in them is called chlorophyll. What does chlorophyll collect from the sun?"

"Light energy?" Jason asks.

"Right, Jason," Teacher 1 assures him. "The chlorophyll collects light energy and turns it into. . . .who knows?"

Teacher 1 is training these students to offer the "right" answers. In fact, the rising inflection in both Gary's and Jason's voice shows that they are fishing for that elusive right answer. But how much thinking is occurring in this classroom? These are recall and labelling questions, which fall at the lowest level of thinking.

A few students are answering all the questions, quickly and without reflection, hoping to be right. Many of the other students, especially some of the girls, would like a little more time to think about their answers. In fact, they may know a great deal about this topic, but they aren't being given an opportunity to demonstrate their knowledge. Let's go to the next classroom.

Teacher 2 asks, "How does a plant produce food?" Several students raise their hands, but Teacher 2 has taught them not to blurt out their answers. He waits three more seconds, trying the patience of several children, before calling on a girl who has been looking at him steadily. "Carly?"

"They get food from dirt!" Carly announces. "The food comes up the roots . . . . "

Teacher 2 interrupts so the other students won't think her answer is correct. "Is Carly right?" he asks the class.

"No!" Julian almost shouts. "Plants make food with their leaves. They need sunlight. Everybody knows that!"

Teacher 2 ignores Julian's last comment and asks, "Class, is Julian correct? What is a way we could design an experiment that would test his hypothesis?"

The class is quiet, trying to process Teacher 2's last question. Earlier in this exchange, Teacher 2 wisely encouraged more participation in the discussion by allowing time for students to think. However, they better not be wrong when they answer! It may be quite a while before Carly risks answering another question in this class. Teacher 2 might have let her finish. Then he might have invited other students to enter the discussion by asking, "Who agrees or disagrees with Carly's answer?" (He would say "Carly's answer," not "Carly," so students could disagree with her answer, not with her as a person.)

With his last two questions, Teacher 2 is trying to encourage students to apply the scientific method, but he needs to ask one question at a time and simplify his language. Let's see how the third science class is doing.

Teacher 3 asks the class, "What can you tell us about how a plant produces food? I'll give you 30 seconds to think about it." She then pointedly watches the clock as students sit and think or scribble notes to themselves. Finally, she announces, "Time's up. What do you know about how a plant produces food?" A sea of hands spring up. "Shawna?"

"I know that the chloroplasts we saw with the microscopes help the plant make food," she says.

"That's a good start, Shawna. How do the chloroplasts help?" When Shawna shrugs her shoulders, Teacher 3 asks her, "Well, what if we put the plant in a dark room? Could the chloroplasts still help?"

All around her come whispers of "I know, I know," but now Shawna's eyes light up. "Light! They need sunlight. The chloroplasts use sunlight to make food for the plant. They couldn't do that in the dark!"

Teacher 3 smiles and turns to the rest of the class. "Now, what else do you know about how a plant produces its food?"

Teacher 3 asks questions that encourage students to structure their own concepts, basic to the guided discovery approach. She asked a question with a narrower focus to help Shawna flesh out her answer. Her hint was designed to keep Shawna "in the game" when Shawna was ready to drop out. As an alternative, Teacher 3 might have asked the class, "Who can add to Shawna's answer?"

The other students are eager to share what they know because they are confident that Teacher 3 will respect their answers, even the incorrect ones. She will also help them salvage a bit of truth when they're off base.

Learning effective questioning techniques takes some practice, but the guidance in this chapter will give you a head start!

The essence of an active hands-on/minds-on guided discovery science classroom is good questioning and listening. Intrinsic in this belief is the conviction that any discussion of questioning, listening, and teaching should consider the following guidelines:

■ Listening skills and strategies should always be combined with questioning. Therefore, this chapter will refer to the process as **questioning/listening** or **Q/L.**

■ Both teacher and student Q/L skills and strategies are important and need to be developed.

Q/L skills and strategies are comparable to batteries in cars or hearts in humans; they are the energy and push behind any movement, or learning. If you practice the ideas in this chapter, you will see improvement in your Q/L skills and strategies. As a bonus, you can even modify your own personal behavior, becoming less manipulative and more sensitive and facilitative in your social and professional life.

Let's start by looking at students and Q/L strategies. Consider these questions:

1. What are the purposes Q/L serves in a constructivist-oriented or hands-on/minds-on guided discovery science program?
2. How is Q/L used for guiding students to higher levels of thinking?
3. What are some Q/L strategies for making your classroom a more effective hands-on/minds-on guided discovery, problem-solving learning environment?

Following the presentation of research findings and proven classroom Q/L strategies that answer these three questions, a section called "Practical Q/L Applications for Your Classroom" will answer the question, "What can you do *now* to enrich your teaching Q/L strategies?"

WHAT ARE THE PURPOSES OF Q/L STRATEGIES?

In a successful constructivist-oriented science program, students pose their own questions and work together to find answers. They spend more time asking their own questions than responding to ours. In such a classroom, beginning activities are planned to stimulate student questions that motivate them to want to learn the answers. Teachers arrange their classroom learning environment to encourage student-generated questions. Many of the students' questions arise from their own sensory experiences and observations during the hands-on/minds-on activities to which we expose them. The "I wonder what will happen if . . . ?" questions they raise are the "sense of wonder" questions of Rachel Carson. As students collect more prior knowledge and build more concepts, they raise even more questions and search even harder for new informa-

tion. Chaillé and Britain have organized the "sense of wonder" questions of young children into three main groups:

How can I make it move?
How can I make it change?
How does it fit or how do I fit?[2]

Students' Nonverbal Questions

Most of the questions teachers and students ask are verbal, but sometimes words are not used or even necessary. For instance, when a student reaches for a magnet to separate iron filings from a mixture of iron filings and sand, it is not necessary for her to verbalize, "I wonder if the magnet will pick up the iron filings?" The student's selection of a possible solution *is* the nonverbal question the student has raised in her mind. Many nonverbal questions are raised during such sensory science experiences.

Every time students use a nonverbal question or ask a verbal question, they supply us with data about how they are thinking, processing information, and constructing concepts and schemata. Sometimes their questions ask for obvious details, showing that they may be experiencing difficulty with important concepts. Other times, student questions may reveal misconceptions, naive theories, and other difficulties in relating prior knowledge and concepts.

Sometimes, teacher nonverbal questioning (asking a question without using words) is the best Q/L strategy to assist floundering students. You have probably done this many times without realizing it. For instance, when my grandson, Andy, was unsuccessfully trying to reach something on the top of his bookcase, sliding a step-stool toward him nonverbally said, "Do you think this will assist you in getting to the top?" Andy was able to see the step-stool, consider its use, and use it, all without words. Think of all the situations where you might strategically place a helpful item within the student's grasp. The result of good questioning should be that students are encouraged to think things out independently, rather than relying on the teacher's verbal answers and solutions to their problems. Here are several other strategies for fostering independence through thoughtful questioning.

Returning Questions to Students for Improved Learning

When students ask you questions or request assistance by responding with a good question, try to challenge their thinking processes instead of giving them the answer. If students ask, "What can we use to separate iron filings from the sand/iron filings mixture?" you might respond with, "Look in the basket. Can any of those items (magnets, screening, or sandpaper) help you separate the iron filings?" Psychiatrists use this technique of turning patients' questions back to them to encourage them to reason out their problems for themselves.

When there is a classroom conflict, a safety problem, or an unusual mess as a result of an activity, questions can be used (after danger or problems are resolved) to turn the situation into a learning opportunity. Your questions should help students to

■ look back at the situation for an understanding by asking
What could have caused . . . ?
How did you feel when . . . was happening?
■ hypothesize solutions to the problem and avoid or minimize future occurrences by asking
Next time, how can we . . . ?
What are other ways we could . . . ?

These kinds of questions help students learn from adverse situations without casting blame or causing guilt.

Q/L Strategies for Better Student-Centered Discussions

Students need encouragement to formulate their own questions as well as to respond to your questions. How you structure your classroom for questioning/answering will strongly influence how students respond and participate in class discussions.

There are two general patterns of class discussion, or students responding to questions. One is the **ping-pong pattern,** illustrated in Figure 4–1.

Lowest-Level Student Responding and Thinking

Highest-Level Student Responding and Thinking

FIGURE 4–1

Patterns of teacher/student discussions

Student-to-student interactive activities provide opportunities for students to ask questions of one another and set up rich discussions.

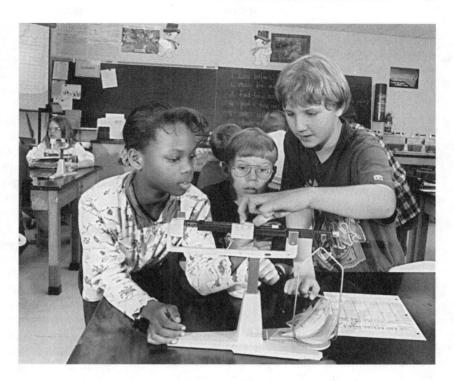

A teacher using this approach says something, a student responds, and the teacher says something else. Class discussions follow a teacher-to-student-to-teacher pattern. Most of the interaction takes place between the teacher and one student at a time. At best, it is a low level of thinking and responding.

In a guided discovery environment, discussions are more like a **basketball pattern.** The teacher says something, then a student–student–student–teacher–student interaction occurs. Instead of merely passing the ball back to the teacher, students are encouraged to pass the ball directly to each other.

Teachers who direct basketball–type discussions pause between question-asking and answer-getting to stimulate as many different student respondents as possible. When students respond, the teacher usually says little but looks around the class to see if other students might want to respond.

These teachers perform different roles than teachers who use ping-pong discussions. They serve as traffic directors of the discussion, pointing to whoever might speak so not more than one student is talking at a time. These teachers do not interject their thoughts until the students have finished their remarks. As a consequence, these teachers are more student-centered than ping-pong discussion instructors. Some questions teachers might ask to direct and keep discussion moving in basketball-type discussions are:

Who agrees or disagrees with Terry's ideas?
What can anyone add to Selma's report?
What questions are still unanswered?

Emphasis is placed on guiding students to be better question answerers and participants in verbal exchanges. Many times this also includes helping them develop their own questioning techniques.

Encouraging Students' Own Questions

Some elementary and middle school teachers use oral or written classroom or homework assignments to encourage development of students' own questions. Students are asked to write down (or present orally) any questions they are curious about as they work with science materials or complete their readings. Students are told that the questions should be ones that interest them but are still unanswered by them. If students experience difficulty with this at the beginning, the teacher might suggest the following kinds of questions to "prime the pump" for forming questions:

Who knows about . . . that I'm curious about?
What might happen if . . . ?
What does it mean if . . . ?
Where do you think I could find out about . . . ?

Small-group discussions can follow the sharing of these questions and suggest possible ways of finding answers.

However this questioning is done, students must be motivated to identify questions of interest to *them* for the initiation of concept building. It is then the leader's job to most effectively deal with their questions.

Q/L Teaching Strategies

Q/L teaching strategies play a major role in hands-on/minds-on guided discovery science teaching. Questioning is utilized in so many teaching functions that it is vital for you to be skillful in its use. You must be able to suit the type and format of each question to the purpose(s) you want to accomplish.

Some of the purposes questions might serve are to

1. impart directions,
   "Jon, could you please give out the science materials?"
2. review and reinforce classroom policies,
   "Jill, will you please read our classroom rule to the class about what we must do to clean up after our experiments?"
3. recover student attention,
   "Sally, would you please stop talking and help Lee with the feeding of the hamsters?"
4. discern student interests,
   "Who would prefer to work on finding videos of space travel?"
5. maintain classroom control,
   "Class, we're rather noisy. Why must we whisper when working in small groups?"
6. encourage students in discussions and cooperative group activities,
   "I know you all know a lot about magnets. Who would like to start discussing what a magnet is and what it does?"
7. expose students' prior knowledge, naive theories, and misconceptions,
   "You want to study about animals. Who knows how animals are different from plants?"
8. encourage students to explore further,
   "What are some other things we might investigate in our study of our environment?"
9. foster student problem-solving and real life application skills.
   "In which electronic equipment in your home are electromagnets and switches used?"[3]

Questioning Is Job #1: Finding Out What Students Know or Don't Know

To help your students build and strengthen their scientific concepts and schemata, you must be aware of their prior knowledge, concepts, misconceptions, naive theories, levels of thinking, and schemata at the start of any study. One way to assess students' knowledge is to question them and then listen sensitively to their responses. Questioning that asks for information is one of the easiest types of questioning. Here are some ways to find out what your students know.

Cognitive Levels of Thinking. There are many ways to classify questions. Several of these are presented in Chapter 5. Figure 4–2 presents three levels of questioning that have been used successfully by many teachers. As you study Figure 4–2, focus your attention on these important aspects of questioning:

3. Highest Level (Application/Evaluation)
- Questions encourage: intuitive, creative, hypothetical thinking, imagination, value system exposure, and judgement making
- Key words/behaviors: apply principle, build model, evaluate, extrapolate, forecast, generalize, hypothesize, imagine, judge

2. Intermediate Level (Processing Information)
- Questions encourage: cause and effect relationships, data analysis
- Key words/behaviors: analyze, classify, compare, contrast, explain, group, infer, synthesize, make an analogy.

1. Lowest Level (Gathering and Recalling Information)
- Questions encourage: finding student concepts, naive theories, misconceptions, feelings, stored experiences
- Key words/behaviors: name, observe, recall, describe, identify, count, list, match, select

FIGURE 4–2

Three levels of questioning and thinking

Source: Modified from Arthur L. Costa, *The Enabling Behaviors* (Orangevale, CA: Search Models, Unlimited, 1989), 7–9.

- There are different levels of student thinking inherent in the three question levels.
- Each level of questioning has key words or behaviors that use scientific processes, (e.g., observe, classify, compare, etc.) to increase the incidence of higher thinking levels.
- Question levels parallel cognitive learning levels.
  1. lowest level—data input stage
  2. intermediate level—data processing stage
  3. highest level—data output stage

"The terms *higher level* and *lower level* have nothing to do with the worthwhileness of the questions themselves. Whether a question is "good" or "bad" depends on its purpose, how it is stated, and its suitability for the students to whom it is directed."[4] Only *you* can decide which type of question is best suited for your purposes, when to use the various levels of questions, and how to structure questions to shift your students' thinking to higher levels. How can you start making these decisions? It's always best to start at the lowest levels of questioning.

Lowest Level of Questioning. One of the simplest ways to classify questions is as closed (convergent) or open (divergent). If you are looking for students' specific concepts or prior knowledge of objects and cause-and-effect relations, you would pick **closed,** or **convergent,** questions. They are called closed-ended questions because they focus on a single answer (i.e., they converge on one point) and may be thought of schematically as:

QUESTION > **ANSWER**

Open, or **divergent,** questions encourage a broader and deeper range of diverse responses and are often referred to as open-ended questions. They look like this:

QUESTION < **ANSWER**
ANSWER
ANSWER

Convergent and divergent questions differ in the type of thinking they stimulate in students. Both are useful in your science teaching.

Uses for Closed or Convergent Questions. In a hands-on/minds-on guided discovery science program it is generally desirable to start with convergent questions and move toward more divergent ones later on. Convergent questions serve many purposes.

In Figure 4–3, we see an insect walking on water and a needle floating on water. The student is presented with a discrepant event, an event in which there is an inconsistency between what can reasonably be expected to happen in a given situation and what is happening. You can use convergent questions to guide the learner and assess what he sees, knows, or feels about a discrepant event.

Convergent questions can direct the learner's attention to specific objects, phenomena, or events. They can also sharpen the student's recall or memory faculties. In addition, convergent questions help you assess students' observational and recall skills and allow you to adjust your teaching to present ideas again, present new ideas, or go back to less complicated ideas. The questions accompanying Figure 4–3 do this.

Although a balance between convergent and divergent questioning is desirable, studies have shown that approximately 70 to 80% of the questions asked by teachers require only simple recall answers.[5] Convergent questions are necessary to provide students with the skills and concepts they need to move to higher levels of learning where they can benefit from divergent or open-ended questioning.

Using Divergent Questions to Promote Higher Level Thinking. Here are some divergent (open-ended) questions you might ask about the two dishes in Figure 4–3. Notice that they are broader questions and ask for higher levels of thinking.

Divergent Questions	Purpose
What can you say about these pictures?	drawing inference
Under what conditions could this be possible?	hypothesizing
How could you illustrate the scientific principles involved in this riddle?	organizing data/ experimentation
What causes the needle and the insect to "float"?	hypothesizing
Under what conditions would both the needle and the insect sink?	hypothesizing
How could you set up an experiment to show the above?	organizing data/ experimentation

Today's complex science/technology/society problems often require more than one solution. Divergent thinking is a particularly important skill. How you question can stimulate divergent thinking. Open or divergent questions will broaden and deepen your students' responses and spur them to think creatively and critically. Divergent questions stimulate students to become better observers and organizers of the objects and events you present. Your questions can guide students in discovering things for themselves, help them to see interrelationships, and make hypotheses or draw conclusions.[6]

When opening a lesson, it is much more stimulating to start with any of the open-ended questions just suggested than to ask, "Does surface tension affect how an object floats?" The latter question asks students to guess what is in your head; the former allows them the freedom to use their minds.

Figure 4–4 shows that even a slight increase in the percentage of divergent questions yields a large increase in divergent productivity by students; that is, a larger number of students respond, and their responses are more thoughtful and exhibit higher levels of thinking. These types of responses, in turn, stimulate further discussion among the students.

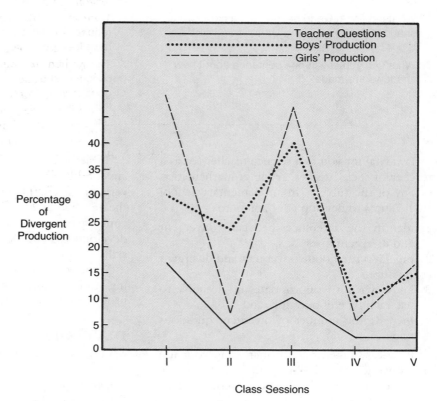

Convergent Question	**Purpose**
What objects are in the riddle picture?	observation
Describe what is happening in dish 1.	description
Name the object in dish 2.	observation/recall
Which dish has the insect?	observation/recall
How are dishes 1 and 2 alike?	observation/comparison
How are dishes 1 and 2 different?	observation/comparison

FIGURE 4–3

Pictorial riddle using closed (convergent questions)

FIGURE 4–4

Divergent teacher questions stimulate divergent student responses

Source: Arthur Carin and Robert B. Sund, *Creative Questioning and Sensitive Listening Techniques—A Self-Concept Approach* (Columbus, OH: Merrill Publishing Company, 1978), 215.

TABLE 4–1

A guided discovery discussion using both convergent and divergent questions

Teacher Asks:	Analysis
1. What can you tell about shadows?	1. This is an excellent question because it allows for several *(divergent)* responses. There is no right or wrong answer, and the teacher is able to find out what the students know about the topic before introducing the rest of the lesson.
2. What ways can you make shadows?	2. This is another *divergent* question because it still allows for several answers while focusing the students' thoughts on the topic.
3. How could we find out if your ideas are correct? Determine if your idea is correct.	3. The teacher asks the students to consider some ways to proceed with an experiment and then lets them explore.
4. What did you find out about shadows?	4. This is also a relatively *divergent* question since it allows the students to share several of their observations and conclusions.
5. How could we make a super giant shadow here at school?	5. This again is a *divergent* question that allows for a lot of creative input by students.
6. What did you have to do to make a big shadow?	6. This is a relatively *convergent* question that requires the students to focus on what they have learned related to producing shadows.
7. What can you say in one sentence about how shadows are made?	7. This requires the students to construct mental concepts about what they have learned. It is a good *culminating* question because it helps them summarize their learning experiences.

It is vital for you as a science teacher (or as a teacher of social studies, reading, mathematics, or any of the subjects in an elementary school curriculum) to develop your ability to

1. identify the differences between convergent and divergent questions,
2. quickly write good convergent and divergent questions,
3. know when it is appropriate and desirable to use each type of question, and
4. increase the number of divergent questions you use.

Practical suggestions for increasing your use of convergent and divergent questions are presented later in the chapter in the section "Practical Classroom Q/L Applications."

Table 4–1 analyzes a guided discovery discussion about shadows as an example of convergent/divergent questioning. Notice how the teacher uses a variety of questions, both convergent and divergent, to guide students in developing higher level thinking concepts and skills.

What are some other Q/L strategies for raising students' levels of thinking and developing problem-solving skills?

DEVELOPING PROBLEM-SOLVING SKILLS USING Q/L STRATEGIES

Scientific processes are the backbone of a problem-solving science program for elementary and middle school students. The same scientific processes scientists use to find answers to their problems can be used by students, on their own maturation levels and for their own relevant problems. The development of such problem-solving skills is a vital part of your science program. One way you may accomplish this goal is to structure your questions around the crucial scientific problem-solving thinking processes.

Simple questions, intelligently thought out and strategically used, can do much to guide students in problem-solving situations. For instance, in helping students design an investigation to solve a problem, you could ask:

How would you determine the effects of pollution on the trees on our school grounds?

Or, to encourage students to measure and record, ask:

How much has the plant grown since we started the experiment?

Gear Questions to Science Processes Appropriate for Your Students

Piaget and other cognitive researchers have pointed out that significant differences exist between the thought processes of primary students and those in the middle and upper grades. You must adjust your questioning accordingly.

Primary/Lower Elementary (Ages 5 to 10). Primary and lower elementary teachers, as well as all teachers whose students function on lower levels of thinking, should devote a great deal of attention to asking appropriate questions based on the following science processes.

1. Observing.
2. Grouping and simple classification; for example, multiple classification, class inclusion.
3. Measuring.
4. Using numbers; for example, counting leaves and animals.

5. Placing objects in series or ordering them; for example, from small to large, short to tall, or light to heavy.
6. Making inferences.
7. Indicating time and space relations.
8. Conserving substance, length, number, and area.
9. Reversibility.
10. Values.
11. Interpersonal relations, such as learning to see things from other people's perspectives.
12. Predicting.
13. Making one-to-one correspondences.

Upper Elementary and Middle Grades (Age 11 and Beyond). Students in the upper elementary and middle grades may be asked questions related to any of the above skills when appropriate. Similarly, teachers may use the following with younger students who are cognitively ready.

1. Formulating hypotheses.
2. Learning to control a variable, such as growing one plant in light and one in the dark.
3. Designing relatively sophisticated experiments.
4. Interpreting data from experiments.
5. Understanding the conservation of weight and volume.
6. Making operational definitions.
7. Constructing models (theories about natural phenomena), such as molecules. (This probably should be limited to Grades 6 to 8 or students in Grades 1 to 6 who are cognitively ready to effectively use this process.)

Table 4–2 gives samples of possible questions derived from these scientific problem-solving processes.

In evaluating appropriateness of the scientific process questions you create, determine whether your students are cognitively able to answer them. In many cases, this may be difficult. Test your questions in your classroom and note your students' responses through *sensitive listening,*

TABLE 4–2

Questions derived from scientific problem-solving processes

Scientific Problem-Solving Processes	Sample Questions
1. Classifying	How would you group these buttons?
2. Assuming	Using what you know about sinking and floating, what can you assume about the relationship between weight and floating?
3. Predicting, hypothesizing (making good guesses)	What do you think will happen if more salt is added to the oceans each year?
4. Inferring, interpreting data, or making conclusions	What conclusions can you make from the experiment information?
5. Measuring	How much has the plant grown?
6. Designing an investigation to solve a problem	How would you determine the effects of pollution on curb trees in our town?
7. Observing	What do you observe about these animals?
8. Graphing	How would you graph your findings?
9. Reducing experimental error	How many measurements should be made in order to report accurate data?
10. Evaluating	If you had only one heart to transplant for five patients, which type of person would you give it to and why?
11. Analyzing	Based on the things we've done with magnets, what do you think causes short circuits and fires in our electrical systems at home?
12. Time and space relations	Is this the same distance as that is?
13. Values	How can we keep our classroom environment "user friendly"?
14. Making one-to-one correspondence	For every one in this row, how many are there in that row?

then adapt your questions accordingly. But don't stop at the "right" answer!

Keep Creative Problem-Solving Juices Flowing[7]

When you ask questions to stimulate problem-solving process thinking in your students, don't stop the discussion when you get a "correct" answer; to do so prevents your students from probing even more deeply into the questions you have posed. Elicit other responses. You can return to the "right" answer later and discuss it. When you do return to the correct answer, tell your students that their answers are good and indicate a lot of good thinking. Say that you

would like to talk about one thing they said, however, and continue the discussion. Handling questions and answers this way shows your students that you prize their **thinking first** and the content second, that you value thinking over mere memorization and recall of isolated facts.

Encourage your students to think beyond their initial responses to your questions. Use follow-up questions, or **probes,** to elicit more complete answers with questions like these:

What else do you remember about . . . ?
    (recall/memory)
What other information can you give to . . . ?
    (comprehension)
How else might you . . . ? (reflection)

Probing questions stimulate greater comprehension and problem-solving processes. Use a lot of "what if" questions:

What if you changed the size, shape, color of . . . ?
What if you added or took something away from . . . ?
What if you were going to begin a better . . . what would you do?
What if different materials were used, what would happen?

Ask future-oriented questions.

What will you look like in the future?
What things do you think will happen to our town in the future?
What would happen if we were to plant more trees around our school or in our park?
What kind of energy will you use in the future?

Use more "How-would-you" questions.

How would you design an investigation to find out about . . . ?
How would you improve the experiment?
How would you make something to . . . ?
How would you do it better?

Q/L Encourages Problem-Solving and Stimulates Exploration[8]

Occasions arise in a hands-on/minds-on guided discovery problem-solving science program when the teacher may notice interest waning or students in need of encouragement and direction. At these times, a well-directed question can stimulate students very effectively. For instance, if a student is stuck or giving up in frustration, you might ask, "What might happen if you . . . ?" By asking that question, you are not telling the student what to do but are raising a possibility to be considered. If the student is still unable to see what should be done, you could ask a more limited or direct question such as, *"How could you use this magnet to show . . . ?"* Start with the broadest, most open-ended question before moving to a more focused or directed one. The criterion for selecting your questions should be:

Will my question(s) alleviate students' frustrations and move them along with a minimum of my intrusion?

Often, you are better off not asking questions and letting students work things out for themselves. Other times, a well-timed question is helpful. Remember, only you can decide whether your question will advance the discussion, inhibit students, or divert them from pursuing the solution to their problem.

IMPROVING YOUR GUIDED DISCOVERY Q/L SKILLS

Slow Down to Speed Up Thinking

Elementary and middle school teachers often feel pressured by the clock to cover everything in the six hours that students are in the classroom. So it is no surprise teachers try to rush through many of the things they do, even question and answer times. Mary Budd Rowe found that most teachers usually wait less than a second for a response after asking a question! These very brief intervals, or **wait-times,** result in rote, verbatim memory recall, usually of textbook or teacher-made information. This is the lowest level of thinking and learning.[9]

What differences in student responses do you think were found in longer teacher wait-times? Rowe found that teachers who waited three seconds or longer got greater speculation, conversation, and argument than those teachers with shorter wait-times. She also found that when teachers are trained to wait an average of more than three seconds before responding, the following positive student behaviors happen:

1. The length of student response increases by 400 to 800%.
2. The number of unsolicited but appropriate responses increases.
3. Failure to respond decreases.
4. Confidence increases.

5. The number of questions asked by students increases.
6. Slow students contribute 1.5 to 37% more.
7. The variety of types of responses increases. There is more reacting to each other, structuring of procedures, and soliciting.
8. Speculative thinking increases by as much as 700%.
9. Discipline problems decrease.
10. Achievement improves in cognitively complex items on written tests.[10]

Rowe also found that teachers trained to prolong wait-time changed their classroom behavior in the following ways:

1. They exhibited more flexible types of responses.
2. The number and kinds of teacher questions changed.
3. Teacher expectations for student performance were modified. (Teachers were less likely to expect only the brighter students to reply and viewed their class as having fewer academically slow students.)
4. Teachers changed the direction of discussion from teacher-dominated to teacher–student discussion.

Come Up for a Breath

Halt-time is related to wait-time in that an instructor halts and waits for students to think, but the students do not answer questions. When teachers explain something that is relatively complex, they present some information and then stop, so students have time to see what the teachers have done and to think about it. The teachers then continue and may repeat this behavior several times. While stopping, they visually check the class to see whether the students are with them. If they obtain positive indications that the students are following the explanation, they continue. If the students are not following, teachers may have to ask more specific questions or retrace the work. Effective public speakers often demonstrate this technique. They make a state-ment, pause a few seconds for listeners to digest it, and then continue to the next point.

Halt-Time and Wait-Time and Cultural/Ethnic Differences

Wait-times and halt-times are especially meaningful for teachers who have students from different cultural backgrounds. All students need time to think about the questions we ask and how they will respond to them, but non-English speaking students need **translation wait-time.** In some cultures, especially in Native American cultures, a lengthy pause between question and response shows respect. Consider this Northern Cheyenne declaration:

> *Even if I had a quick answer to your question, I would never answer immediately. That would be saying that your question was not worth thinking about.[11]*

Students from many minority groups are more likely to take part in class discussions and answer questions when given more time to respond. One noteable exception are some native Hawaiian students who actually have a preference for **negative wait-time,** where they often interrupt classmates (or even the teacher) who have not finished speaking. Although many of us would consider these interruptions as rudeness, these students see it as a sign of personal involvement in the community culture.[12]

By the year 2000, one-third of U.S. public school students will be members of ethnic minorities.[13] You must discover ways in which your ethnic and cultural students are unique and adapt your teaching techniques to maximize their learning.

Use Rewards Cautiously

Teachers traditionally have thought that giving positive verbal rewards facilitates class discussion. But in fact, research[14] indicates that rewarding students may cause *less* student involvement. When teachers change their modes of response over several weeks so as not to give positive verbal rewards, the class participation begins to change. Not only do more students interact, but a greater number of less academically able students participate. Those students who are reward seekers may initially become somewhat disoriented because they are not receiving their usual rewards, but after two or three weeks they, too, adapt to the new teacher behavior and become more autonomous.

Students apparently perceive subtle teacher behavior that suggests favoritism and a lack of fairness in the interaction process, preventing true democratic discourse. Teachers might find it helpful to make audio or video tapes of their class discussions to evaluate how their expectations interfere with the discussion process. They should count how many praise words they use and determine which students receive them the most. Praise inappropriately used, particularly with minority students, has been found to give students an unrealistic and distorted impression of their ability, which often causes problems when the students are advanced or try to enter college.[15]

Remember, We All Need Strokes!

The point of not giving rewards is to spark more speculative and critical thinking among your students and to encourage more involvement during group discussions. However, it is helpful to recognize the achievement of students during individual work or for performing certain types of basic skills well, especially if you make a point to recognize each student for specific things he or she has done well.[16]

Teachers who try to look for good in every student and who inform them specifically and privately about these things are effective. They also are more likely to enjoy their teaching. It is possible to look for something good to say to each individual, for example, when they come into class or in private discussions. As Abraham Maslow indicated in his theory of human needs, we all need to be recognized as valuable persons so our self-concepts continue to grow positively.[17]

Use Cooperative Learning to Improve Classroom Discussions

Small-group learning, or **cooperative learning,** where members are assigned and rotate roles, provides students with excellent opportunities to verbalize what they know, believe, or feel and to consider the multiple viewpoints of their fellow group members. These groups offer a chance for students to test their understandings against the understandings of other group members on a face-to-face basis. How different this is from traditional "ping-pong" class discussions (especially in college classes), where all you see are the backs of your fellow classmates' heads.

For activities like problem solving, divergent thinking, and hands-on/minds-on guided discovery, cooperative learning is much more effective than total class discussions.[18] By working collaboratively on a group problem, students are able to interact positively and noncompetitively. Their discussions become a sharing of ideas and materials as they work toward solutions of their problems. They support each other as they take risks and contribute to the group effort. The diversity of views of the students enriches the discussions and assists individual students in constructing their concepts.[19] Many shy or slower thinking students are encouraged to contribute and participate in this nonthreatening, supportive group environment. Group cooperative learning offers teachers a strategy for breaking the ping-pong pattern common in total class discussion.

Practical suggestions for organizing and using cooperative learning in your classroom are given in Chapter 6.

Close Your Mouth and Open Your Ears

"Nothing new ever entered the mind through an open mouth."[20] If teachers and students spent more time listening to each other, they both would improve their questioning skills and respond more intelligently to each other. Research has shown that people who listen well are able to relate to what the speaker is saying, understand the reasoning behind what is being said, and are better able to participate thoughtfully in discussions.[21] The implication of this for teachers is clear. Listening carefully and sensitively—not only to the answer but to the thinking behind the answer—provides you with much more information about your students. Students may have difficulty listening to fellow students and need practice in how to listen effectively. Karen Mahr, a first grade teacher, used this role-playing technique to focus on listening skills with her class.[22] She coached several fifth graders on what each of their roles would be when they acted out a poor small-group discussion. In the discussion that followed the role-playing, the first graders concluded that the fifth graders were not listening to each other. Because the first graders were now conscious of the importance of listening to each other's contribution, they had better small-group discussions in the future. Like anything else, good listening skills are learned best by students who construct the concepts for themselves.

Be a Model of Sensitive Listening Techniques

Krishnamurti, an Indian philosopher, once said that Americans do not truly listen because they are always judging, composing their thoughts, or preparing salvos for reacting during the time a speaker is discoursing. A person who truly listens in an open, accepting, nonjudgmental way probably is a rarity.

The way teachers perceive their roles is undoubtedly related to their listening skills—or each of them. If you see your function as being mainly to develop or achieve some subject matter concept or principle, you naturally will focus on its achievement. However, if you perceive your role as helping students develop cognitively and construct their own concepts, you will tend to focus on the student first and on the content

second. Listen intently to what students have to say, and formulate questions and responses only when they have finished, to help them make discoveries and use their thought processes. There is no substitute for a teacher who is primarily interested in people and really listens to them.

Teachers should listen—not analyze, evaluate, or judge—until the student has completed the response to a question. Unfortunately, some teachers start to dissect what students say before they have had a chance to finish. Many students' ideas are good, but they suffer from poor verbalization. If you wait until students finish their answers before reacting, you will grasp their ideas better and be more likely to convey in nonverbal ways that you are sincerely interested in their ideas.

Guiding Your Students to Become Better Listeners

Students often do not learn and achieve as well as they could because they have not developed their listening skills. As a model of a good listener, you can help your students become better listeners. The following section contains practical suggestions to help you improve your—and your students'—listening skills. At first you may have to consciously use these suggestions, but with time and practice they will become a pattern of your normal conversational behavior.

PRACTICAL CLASSROOM Q/L APPLICATIONS

Here are practical, classroom-tested suggestions for improving your Q/L strategies that can be put into practice immediately. Included in each subsection are actual questions you might ask as you begin to work on improving your Q/L strategies.[23] Select those that fit your particular needs or modify them as needed. As you become more familiar and confident with them, you will be able to construct and use many of your own questions.

How Can You Write and Use Better Convergent/Divergent Questions?

Because they are the most frequently used type of questions, you should learn to write and ask better convergent/divergent questions. Here are some practical guidelines.

1. Avoid or minimize yes or no questions.
2. Look at the words that start your questions: they often dictate the style of the answer.
3. Questions that begin with the words *do, did, are, is, can, will, would,* and *should,* require a *yes* or *no* response.
4. If *yes* or *no* questions must be used, you should make them more divergent by adding: *"Why? How do you know? How might we find out? What makes you think so? What gives you that idea?"* (e.g., *"Is baking powder a producer of gas? How might I set up an experiment to test my idea?"*)
5. Look for questions that ask students to discover conditions that could change objects or events, such as, *"What can you do to the magnets to make them stronger?"* or *"What ways can you make the lights burn brighter with the wire, switch, and dry cell?"*
6. Ask students questions that require them to discover and compare things (e.g., *"In what places do we find mold in summer?"* or *"Using these objects and the bowl of water, which objects do you think will sink and which will float?"*).
7. Use convergent questions to focus children's attention on specifics.
8. Use more divergent questions. You will be pleased with the resultant higher level of responses.

Eliminate Multiple Questions. Avoid using multiple questions without giving students opportunities to respond. Multiple questions usually preclude wait-time. For example, *"What causes do you think might have contributed to this situation? Which of these were important?"* These questions are not bad, but when teachers run them together, they hinder the thinking processes of their students.

Avoid Overreactions. Avoid overreacting to student responses. For example, *"That is terrific—fantastic thinking, George. Wow, what an answer!"* This type of reaction may act as a constricting force because other students may think their ideas will not be so highly valued if you respond with less enthusiasm to them.

Break Limited Thinking. Sometimes students become fixed on one aspect of a problem. Teachers then have to devise questions that will break the students out of their limited perceptual field. They might do this by asking the following questions:

What other factors might be contributing to . . . ?
What other information are we given in this . . . ?
What other interpretations are possible?
What alternatives are there?
What other things or ways are . . . ?

Ask Students to Clarify Their Ideas. A student may sometimes give a prolonged reply that is not easily understood by the other members of the class. The teacher may help to clarify this reply and move the discussion along by suggesting,

You said it was similar. Similar in what respect?
Please give an example to show where this is occurring.
What other examples are there?
What do you mean when you say . . . ?

Help Students Avoid Overgeneralizations. Students (and many adults) tend to overgeneralize. When your students make overgeneralizations, sensitively focus class attention on these by asking questions such as,

You mean that is true for all . . . ?
What in your investigations indicated that this was true for all . . . ?
Where and under what conditions would this be true?
How could we check to see if that is true for all situations?

Ask Your Students to Summarize. Asking students to summarize is particularly useful when

Your sensitivity, reflective in the questions you ask and in your behavior, can affect how and what students learn.

the concepts involved are abstract or vague, when the student reply has been lengthy, or when some investigations have taken a great deal of time. You might ask,

Briefly, please summarize what you have just said.
Tell us in your own words what we have learned.
What were the main ideas discussed today?
What is the main point of what you are saying?

Expand and Deepen Student Thinking. Often, you need to act as a stimulus to keep the discussion going. This can be done by having students refocus, summarize, and consider alternatives, other forces, and factors that might move the discussion to a higher level. This may be done in the following ways:

I see you have come up with an answer. How did you obtain it?
What evidence do you have that it is correct?
You said that this animal behaved in this manner. Why do you think that?
What effect do you think, for example, polluting the stream will have?

Consider Emotional Overtones in Your Questions and Demeanor. Because of students' diverse backgrounds and cultural differences, some questions—and how you ask them—may have emotional overtones. In discussions where this is the case, you must be particularly sensitive to phrase questions so that they do not inhibit the rational responses of the students. For example, a boy who was bitten by a snake may become emotional if you ask questions about snakes.

With some Native American and other ethnic students, you may want to avoid eye contact, as a student who looks an adult in the eye is showing disrespect. American teachers often call upon specific students and carry on a dialogue while the rest of the class listens. For some students from different cultures this common procedure can cause confusion and may even alienate them from other members of their culture. For example, some Native Hawaiian students respond willingly as a group to teacher questions, but often remain silent when individually called upon. It is thought that one-on-one interactions with teachers or other adults remind them of scoldings from parents.[24]

Some Native American students are also averse to responding when called upon in class. It may be that they perceive the traditional classroom, where teachers control all activities and interactions with one student as classmates look on, as very different from their community social events, where there are no clear leaders and no clear separation between performers and audience. These students usually perform better one-on-one with the teacher or in cooperative settings with small groups of classmates.[25]

You must know your students well so that your manner of questioning and presentation does not conflict with their cultural backgrounds.

Carefully Paraphrase What Students Say. When you do not understand what a student has said, you can paraphrase her statement to make the point clearer, for example, *"I hear you say that. . . . Am I correct?"* You can also use this strategy when you think other students may not have heard the student's comments. Do not paraphrase each student's responses, as it tends to make their presentation less important.

Do Not Upstage Students. Students are the ones who need to develop their minds. To do this, they must practice speaking, formulating their own questions, constructing their ideas and concepts, and sharing their ideas with their classmates. The teacher cannot do it for them.

Remember—students learn by constructing their own schemata.

Use Appropriate Nonverbal Signals. Show your students you are concerned and that you are listening by

1. maintaining eye contact, if appropriate to individual students' backgrounds;
2. holding a concerned posture, for example, with your body turned toward the student;
3. smiling appropriately because the student is expressing himself or herself;
4. nodding to indicate understanding to the student; and
5. using gestures.

Develop Teacher Silent-Time. **Teacher silent-time** is similar to wait-time, except that silent-time is the time taken after a student has finished speaking before you reply or move on to the next teaching item. Silent-time prevents you from cutting off a student's statements and allows others to interject their ideas without your interference. Calm silence also indicates to the student and the class a trust in their abilities to think and make significant statements.

Many teachers, like radio announcers, fear silence and in fact call it "dead time." Silence can be such a pleasant break in many classrooms.

Look for Students Who Want to Talk. Look for indications that students want to say something. Be sensitive to students who may want to contribute to class discussion. Especially look for students who are

1. waving their arms;
2. rising up in their seats;
3. making eye contact with you;
4. glancing meaningfully at you or the speaker;
5. pressing their lips together as if they are going to say something; and
6. mumbling.

When these signs occur, invite participation (e.g., *"Jon, is there something you would like to say?"*).

Invite Students to Publicly Affirm Their Values. During the time students are in school, they develop values for life. Teachers need to help them construct their own values without imposing or moralizing. The following questions will help students focus and clarify their values.

What valuable things have you learned today?
In what ways have you been successful today, this week, this year?
What makes you feel great about what we have been doing in science?
What makes you feel bad?
What do you think about, for example, what science does for society, pollution, or health?
How do you feel about this part of your work?
How did you come to this opinion?
What other conclusions could you have reached?
How do you think the other person sees the problem?
How do most people feel about that?
What have you done about, for example, keeping our environment clean?

Be sensitive to the cultural mismatch between home and school values, so students are not embarrassed or overly conflicted by cultural/ethnic differences. For more information about possible student home/school cultural/ethnic differences and their implications for your teaching, see

- B. T. Bowman, "Educating language-minority children: Challenges and opportunities," *Phi Delta Kappan, 71,* 1989, 118–120.
- C. R. Harris, "Identifying and serving the gifted new immigrant," *Teaching Exceptional Children, 23,* no.4, 1991, 26–30.
- P. Phelan, A. L. Davidson, and H. T. Cao, "Students' multiple worlds: Negotiating the boundaries of family, peer, and school cultures," *Anthropology and Education Quarterly, 22,* 1991, 224–250.

THIS IS DAY #1 FOR YOUR Q/L SELF-IMPROVEMENT

Research indicates that teachers who focus upon improving their Q/L techniques are able to construct and effectively use significantly better questions than those who do not.[26] Your task is to modify your questioning behavior, not only in teaching science but also in other areas. To help your students learn how to ask good questions, show them that you aren't afraid to say, "I don't know the answer. But together we can find out."[27] Good Q/L skills will enhance learning and human development by you and your students.

SUMMARY

The foundation of hands-on/minds-on guided discovery teaching/learning is good questioning and listening (Q/L) skills and strategies for both students and teachers. Students must be encouraged and shown ways to ask themselves questions as they engage in sensory and cognitive activities. Emphasis must shift from teacher domination during question and answer sessions to student-centered questioning and responding.

Teachers use Q/L strategies for many purposes: one important one is to assess what your students know and don't know in order to facilitate the best learning conditions. Suggestions were given for using convergent and divergent questions for this purpose and for stimulating students' thinking. Higher level questions are used for developing students' problem-solving skills. Scientific processes can provide the structure to guide students' problem solving. Scientific process questions appropriate to a wide age-range were presented, as were ways to motivate and keep students' creative problem-solving "juices" flowing. Verbal and nonverbal questioning was discussed, along with how to turn questioning back to students for them to structure their own concepts and schemata.

Q/L strategies for better student-centered discussions focused on the effective uses of patterns of peer interaction (ping-pong vs. basketball), wait-time, rewards, and cooperative learning groups. Sensitive listening techniques for both students and teachers must be learned, and examples of how to achieve this were explored. Emphasis was placed upon teachers becoming aware of, and sensitive to, students' cultural/ethnic mismatch between home and school.

The "Practical Classroom Q/L Applications" section is a resource of specific Q/L strategies for immediate classroom adaptation, including topics such as writing and using better convergent and divergent questions; avoiding multiple questions, overreaction, and overgeneralization; asking students how to summarize, amplify, and pursue thinking; improving listening skills of students and teachers; and asking a variety of questions for particular purposes.

Research indicates that teachers trained in questioning and listening techniques change their questioning and listening behavior in the classroom, asking more sensitive, creative, and science process questions.

Specific suggestions for improving your Q/L skill presented in this chapter were

1. Talk less, but ask more.
2. Use some classification system to analyze your questions, as a basis for improving them.
3. Use more divergent questions.
4. Avoid asking questions that can be answered by *yes* or *no*.
5. Try to ask more questions that stimulate students to use higher level thinking.
6. Evaluate your questions for the scientific processes your students should be using in your hands-on/minds-on guided discovery activities.
7. Ask more questions to discover student talents.
8. Don't stop a discussion with the "right" answer.
9. Increase your wait-time and halt-time to at least three seconds.
10. Lead more student–student–student basketball-type discussions and cooperative learning groups.
11. Avoid or minimize rewards during a discussion.
12. Look for something good to say to individuals in private discussions.
13. Avoid asking multiple questions.
14. Avoid overreaction.
15. Ask students to clarify those parts of their presentations that are vague or incorrect.
16. Guard against student and teacher overgeneralizations.
17. Ask students to summarize.
18. Develop your own and your students' sensitive listening techniques.
19. Develop silent-time for you and your students.
20. Ask questions appropriate to the Piagetian level(s) of your students.
21. For guiding students to greater creativity and high level thinking:
    a. Ask many *what-if* questions.
    b. Ask future-oriented questions.
    c. Use more how-would-you questions.
22. Be more aware of, and sensitive to, the questions you select for your multicultural/ethnic students.

SELF-ASSESSMENT AND FURTHER STUDY

1. Look at the nine teacher questions in Table 4–3. Rate them according to whether you think they stimulate high or low levels of student thinking. Explain why. Now write your answers to these questions about Table 4–3.
   - Which three questions are the *best* to ask? Why?
   - Which questions require the student to *evaluate* something?
   - Which questions allow only a *few* responses?
   - Which questions encourage *many* respon-ses?
   - Which questions require the student to mainly *observe?*
   - Which questions require the students to formu-late *operational definitions?*
   - Which questions require the student to mainly *classify?*
   - Which questions require the student to demon-strate *experimental* procedure?
   - Which questions require the student to *hypothesize?*
   - How would you group or *classify* most of the questions?
   - What could you add to the low thinking level questions to make them higher level thinking questions?

2. Work on guiding your students to listen more to each other. For example, occasionally have them paraphrase what has been said. Also, invite them to play "add on," where one student says something about a topic and another student adds to it with her ideas. Keep a log of what you do, ask, or respond to, as well as students' contributions.

3. Ask someone to make an audio or video recording of a pictorial riddle or guided discovery activity-based discussion that you lead. Using the tape, do the following evaluations:
   a. Check every time you ask a question that is con-vergent (*yes* or *no* type).
   b. Determine your average wait-time and halt-time.

TABLE 4–3
Categorizing questions on stimulating levels of students' thinking

Teacher Questions	Stimulates Children's Thinking	
	High Level	Low Level
1. Which tree is taller?		
2. Does the heat of the candle affect the air in the jar?		
3. What do you think will happen if you add cold coffee to the water with the brine shrimp?		
4. If you were going to design an experiment to show, for example, the effects of cigarette smoke on an animal or plant, what would you do?		
5. How would you group these objects?		
6. Can you tell which of these metals was influenced by the magnet?		
7. What did you notice about how the flies in the jar behaved when half of it was covered with black paper?		
8. Which of these things are metals and which are not?		
9. What do you conclude from the experiment?		

c. Categorize your questions as to whether they encourage low, intermediate, or high level thinking.

d. Determine what areas of questioning you need to improve.

4. Prepare a science lesson for a group of elementary/middle students or your colleagues in a college class. Try to lead a basketball-type discussion. Evaluate how well you did. Use a cassette recorder to determine how many students you get to interact before you respond.

5. Select a science topic (e.g., air pressure, magnets, etc.) and write questions that elicit scientific processes.

6. When you question your students, you must be concerned about how students from different cultures/ethnic groups might respond to particular types of questions. Find out which cultural/ethnic groups are represented in your class and ascertain any mismatch between their home and school values, beliefs, or other aspects that should be considered when using Q/L strategies.

List your informational sources and describe how you collected your data about your students' cultural/ethnic backgrounds.

NOTES

1. Nancy Kober, *EDTALK: What We Know About Science Teaching and Learning* (Washington, DC: Council for Educational Development and Research, 1993), 44.

2. Christine Chaillé and Lory Britain, *The Young Child As Scientist: A Constructivist Approach to Early Childhood Science Education* (New York: HarperCollins, 1991), 63.

3. The author is indebted to the information in: Richard D. Kellough, *A Resource Guide for Teaching: K-12,* Chapter 10: "Strategies for Teaching: Questioning" (NY: Macmillan Publishing Co., 1994), 299–323.

4. John Jarolimek and Clifford D. Foster, Sr., *Teaching and Learning in the Elementary School,* 5th ed., Chapter 9: "Using Questions to Guide Children's Learning" (Englewood Cliffs, NJ: Merrill/Prentice Hall, 1993), 227–241.

5. Joseph P. Riley, "The Effect of Teachers' Wait Time and Knowledge Comprehension Questioning on Science Achievement," *Journal of Research in Science Teaching* 23, no. 45 (Apr. 1986), 335–342. Selma Wasserman "Asking the Right Questions: The Essence of Teaching," *Fastback* 343 (Bloomington, IN: Phi Delta Kappa Educational Foundation, 1992).

6. For additional examples of divergent questions and the teacher's role in using them, see Mary Jo Puckett Cliatt and Jean M. Shaw, "Open Questions, Open Answers," *Science and Children, 23,* no. 3 (November/ December 1985): 14–16 and Steven W. Gilbert, "Systematic Question-ing," *The Science Teacher, 59,* no.9 (December 1992), 41–46.

7. To help you select the right questions to guide your students to not only producing the "right" answers but also developing the skills to learn for themselves, see Patricia E. Blosser, *How to Ask the Right Questions* (Arlington, VA: National Science Teachers Association, 1991).

8. For excellent treatment of this topic for early childhood education students, see Christine Chaillé and Lory Britain, *The Young Child as Scientist,* 66–67; for older students, see, W. W. Wilen, *Questioning Skills for Teachers,* 3rd ed., (Washington, DC: National Education Association, 1991).

9. Mary Budd Rowe, "Wait-Time: Slowing Down May Be a Way of Speeding Up," *American Educator, 11,* no. 1 (Spring 1987): 38–47.

10. Rowe, ibid, 38–47.

11. H. Gilliland, "Discovering and emphasizing the positive aspects of the culture," in H. Gilliland and J. Reyhner (Eds.), *Teaching the Native American* (Dubuque, IA: Kendall/Hunt, 1988), 27.

12. R. G. Tharp, "Psychocultural variables and constants: Effects on teaching and learning in schools," *American Psychologist, 44,* 1989, 349–359.

13. J. A. Banks, *Ethnicity, class and cognitive styles: Research and teaching implications.* Paper

presented at the American Educational Research Association, Washington, DC, April 1987.

14. K. O. McGraw, "The Detrimental Effects of Reward on Performance: A Literature Review and a Prediction Model," in M. A. Pepper and D. Green, Eds., *The Hidden Costs of Reward: New Perspectives on the Psychology of Human Motivation* (Hillsdale, NJ: Erlbaum, 1978); and S. Graham, "A review of attribution theory in achievement contexts," *Educational Psychology Review, 3,* 1991, 5–39.

15. D. W. Johnson and R. T. Johnson, *Learning Together and Alone: Cooperative, Competitive, and Individualistic Learning* (2d ed.) (Englewood Cliffs, NJ: Prentice-Hall, 1987).

16. E. L. Deci and R. M. Ryan, "The Support of Autonomy and the Control of Behavior," *Journal of Personality and Social Psychology* 53, 1024–1037; and M. R. Lepper and M. Hodell, "Intrinsic Motivation in the Classroom," in C. Ames and R. Ames (Eds.), *Research on Motivation in Education, Vol. 3. Goals and Cognitions* (San Diego, CA: Academic Press, 1989).

17. Abraham H. Maslow, *Motivation and Personality* (3rd ed.) (NY: Harper and Row, 1987).

18. David W. Johnson and Roger T. Johnson, *Learning Together and Alone: Cooperation, Competition, and Individualization* (Englewood Cliffs, NJ: Prentice-Hall, 1987); and R. E. Slavin, *Cooperative Learning: Theory, Research, and Practice* (Englewood Cliffs, NJ: Prentice-Hall, 1990).

19. An excellent classroom resource based on the cooperative learning works of Johnson and Johnson in Dee Dishon and Pat W. O'Leary, *A Guidebook for Cooperative Learning* (Holmes Beach, FL: Learning Publications, 1984).

20. Andrew Wolvin and Carol Coakley, *Listening,* 2nd ed. (Dubuque, IA: Wm. C. Brown, 1985), 15.

21. J. T. Dillon, *Questioning and Teaching: A Manual of Practice* (NY: Teachers College Press, 1988).

22. Karen Mahr, "Mr. Detective, Can You Help Solve This Problem?" Unpublished manuscript, Montclair State College, NJ, 1989.

23. For a greater variety and specification of practical Q/L suggestions, you are urged to see Arthur Carin and Robert B. Sund, *Creative Questioning and Sensitive Listening Techniques: A Self-Concept Approach,* 2nd ed. (Columbus, OH: Merrill, 1978).

24. K. H. Au, "Participation Structures in a Reading Lesson to Hawaiian Children: Analysis of a Culturally Appropriate Instructional Event." *Anthropology and Education Quarterly, 11,* 91–115.

25. J. A. Vasquez, "Teaching to the Distinctive Traits of Minority Students," *The Clearing House, 63,* 1990, 299–304.

26. L. R. DeTure, "Acquisition of Wait-Time: Training Techniques and Related Teaching Behaviors, Modeling Protocols" (Paper presented at the annual meeting of the National Science Teachers Association, Cincinnati, OH, April 1985).

27. For an excellent one-page summary of the importance of teachers admitting not knowing the answers and how to handle it, see Robert E. Yager, "Wanted: More Questions, Fewer Answers," *Science and Children, 25,* no. 1 (September 1987): 22.

CHAPTER 5

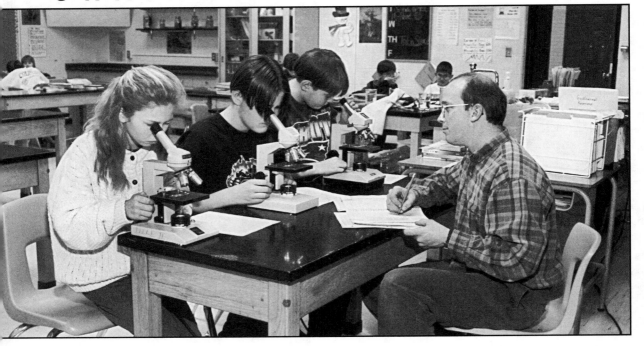

Assessing Science Teaching and Learning

Teaching and assessment are mirror images of one another. Assessment guides instruction, and instruction guides assessment. . . . Assessment should be a continuous process involving listening, observing, and asking questions to promote intellectual growth.[1]

AUTHENTIC LEARNING/AUTHENTIC ASSESSMENT

- Students observe as a classmate picks up metal shavings with a magnet. Then they each draw a line down the middle of a page in their science logs. On one side, they write everything they know about what they just saw; on the other side, they list questions and things they would like to know about the magnet and its powers. Small groups pool their knowledge and questions before sharing them with the class.
- A student ponders a written question: "You have just found a rock in the park. How will you determine whether it is sedimentary, igneous, or metamorphic?"
- Angela practices reading the script she and Arnold wrote for their television weather report. Arnold watches carefully and then suggests, "I think we need another chart to show how the cold front moved toward the coast last night."

What do all of these students have in common? They are all being assessed to determine their mastery of concepts the teacher is about to introduce (in the first two examples) or of skills and content they have already explored (in the remaining examples). The variety of approaches reflects assessment as an ongoing process that measures students' conceptual development and process skills, not just their knowledge of terms and facts.

Assessment has many forms, facets, and gray areas that can require much teacher time for scoring, tracking, recording, and so on. To meet the need for assessment that is effective and relevant, but easy to administer, researchers across the nation have been working to develop approaches that will help teachers find out what students already know, what they are learning, and what they have learned.

For example, a project called the California Learning Assessment System (CLAS) has been field-testing new assessments that support that state's educational goals in science and focus on "big ideas," not isolated facts. These new assessments include performance tasks and portfolios, along with enhanced, open-ended, and justified multiple-choice questions. Students respond by writing, drawing, manipulating data, and/or applying science knowledge to solve problems. Holistic scoring guides (rubrics) are provided for the performance tasks and most multiple-choice questions. For the portfolios, teachers score students in several categories, such as evidence of science applied outside the classroom.

During the field-testing of the CLAS performance assessments, students rotate through a series of stations. At each station, they are given materials and asked to perform experiments and solve problems within a specified period of time. Nearly all teachers involved in this field-testing have felt that these assessments provided students with an intriguing learning experience and offered feedback the teachers had not received through traditional testing. Plus, students did not seem to feel the anxiety that often accompanies paper-and-pencil testing.

The enthusiastic response by both students and teachers to CLAS's field-testing seems to indicate that updated assessment methods encourage more meaningful science learning—learning that students can and do use in their everyday lives.

As you reread the opening quotation, it quickly becomes apparent that current assessment functions, procedures, and techniques are changing to correspond to the new approaches to science teaching and learning. During this assessment transition, you will need newer and more relevant assessment techniques, and you'll need to utilize current techniques in more creative ways. This transition compels us to continually focus on five principal reasons for sound assessment as a crucial part of instruction:

1. Our classrooms define for students the outcomes we value—they define the truly important *achievement targets*.
2. Classroom assessments provide the *basis of information* for student, parent, teacher, principal, and community decision making.
3. Assessment *motivates students* to try—or not try.
4. They *screen students* in or out of programs, giving them access to the special services they may need.
5. Classroom assessments provide at least part of the basis for *teacher and principal evaluation*.[2]

This chapter will focus on these assessment guidelines and on their applications to teaching science with a hands-on/minds-on guided discovery approach:

1. Assessment as a continuous tool for planning, guiding, and enriching science learning/teaching in your classroom.
2. Assessment techniques for monitoring outcomes of authentic student learning and your teaching and program improvement.
3. Assessment as communication of the importance and progress of science to your students, administrators, school boards, parents, and the public.

ASSESSMENT: A CONTINUOUS TEACHING/LEARNING PROCESS

Productive assessment does not just happen by chance. It must be well thought out, executed, and redone daily (even minute-by-minute) from your first to your last day of school. To do this effectively, you have to go back to your goals in hands-on/minds-on guided discovery science teaching, which could be organized around these three questions:

1. *What* will I teach (content, processes, STS problem-solving skills, attitudes and values)?
2. *How* will I teach it (physical and intellectual environment, teaching methods, student activities, and science materials and equipment)?
3. *How well* have I taught? (What have my students learned? What must be retaught? How will I grade them?)

In realistic terms, you use assessment each time you engage in *any* teaching function with your students. As indicated in the previous chapter, every question you ask is an assessment probe to find out more about your students, what they do and don't know, how they are reacting to your teaching, and what on-the-spot and future teaching modifications you must make. Let's explore the latest reforms in assessment and how they are impacting science learning and teaching.

A Rose by Any Other Name . . .

The current plethora of science teaching techniques and assessment procedures reforms is like a tortoise and hare competition. Science teaching improvement has sprinted ahead while assessment has dawdled. We are ready now to close the disparity between what we attempt to teach and what we try to assess. When we have done so, we will know more precisely the extent to which our science teaching has resulted in student learning—because students will be able to demonstrate the science content and processes they have acquired.[3]

In this transformed view, assessment is the servant, not the master, of curriculum. A new bond has been forged making science teaching/learning and assessment inseparable. Assessment must be more closely affiliated with the purposes of science hands-on/minds-on guided discovery teaching.[4]

Higher order science thinking skills and processes can be assessed—and students can learn through these assessment procedures—when assessments necessitate *thought,* not mere recall. These *alternative assessment approaches,* using techniques more compatible with science teaching goals than more traditional or conventional testing, appear in the literature under such terms as *authentic assessment, alternative assessment, performance-based assessment, embedded assessment, portfolio assessment, targeted assessment,* etc.[5]

For alternative assessment to be effective, students must be offered a wide range of options for communicating what they know; demonstrating their ideas; quantifying their results; making written, oral, and/or visual presentations of their findings and hypotheses; and raising new questions about what they are learning. Two alternative assessments meet these criteria:

performance and authentic. Although *performance* and *authentic assessment* are occasionally used synonymously, there are differences.

Performance assessment generally refers to the type of student response being assessed, whereas **authentic assessment** refers to the assessment situation.[6] Authentic assessment is a broad procedure that *includes* performance or demonstration of complex cognitive behaviors. "Although not all performance assessments are authentic, assessments that are authentic are most assuredly performance assessments."[7] "To the extent that these assessments are set in the real world, they may be authentic as well as performance-based."[8] In this text, I will use the term *authentic assessment* to describe the belief that "the performance test of any skill or the application of newly learned knowledge should always take place in a context as close to the 'real thing' as classroom conditions will allow."[9] See Table 5–1 for general examples of authentic assessment techniques. Specific

TABLE 5–1

General authentic assessment techniques

Students may perform these authentic assessment activities involving complex behaviors not easily assessed by traditional paper–pencil tests.

plan and conduct an experiment	graph data
write a story, composition, or poem	construct a concept map
give an oral report	research information in library
design and make a videotape	complete an art project
construct a scientific model	draw a chart or diagram
program a computer	give photo or slide presentation
tutor a classmate	compose a song
keep a science journal	write science questions
interview a scientist	record long-term plant growth
guide classmates on local trip	care for/keep records of animal
correspond with a scientific author	organize a healthy luncheon

Students can collect samples of the above items over a long time for inclusion in a portfolio.

Source: Modified from Jeanne Ellis Ormrod, *Educational Psychology: Principles and Applications* (Englewood Cliffs, NJ: Merrill/Prentice Hall, 1995), 606.

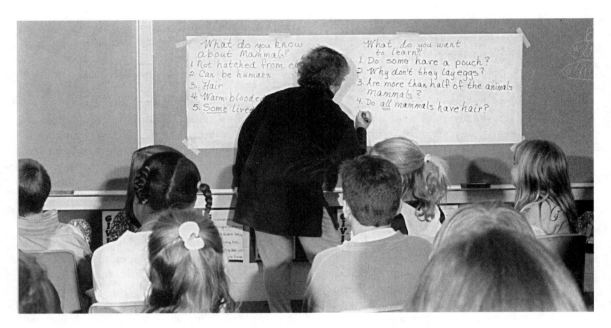

Creating a K-W-L chart can assist you in discovering your students' prior knowledge of a science topic and then assessing what they have learned when a study is complete. [K-What Do You Want to Know?, W-What Do You Want to Learn?, L-What Did You Learn?]

authentic assessment techniques will be covered in the rest of this chapter.

How Are Measurement and Assessment Connected?

Although the terms *measurement/evaluation* and *assessment* are related, they are not synonymous. **Measurement/evaluation** usually involves collecting information about your students through tests, checklists, and worksheets. Very often, measurement involves a score, grade, or other numerical reading.

Assessment is a broader concept that involves your professional judgment, based on a variety of data such as measurement, your feelings and observations, student performance, and other information you gather from the learning environment. Assessment is not merely a device you use at the end of a science lesson or unit of study.

Instead, you need to use assessment minute by minute throughout all of your teaching. You can accomplish much assessment by judicious and effective informal questioning and sensitive listening, as discussed in Chapter 4. Continuous assessment will help you quickly spot science areas your students have been exposed to previously, prior knowledge, misconceptions, and naive theories. It will also help you learn how students construct concepts.

It has been said that measurement is a descriptive activity (usually involving numbers), whereas assessment involves judgment. To deepen your understanding of the differences between measurement and assessment scrutinize:

■ Sabra Price and George E. Hein, "Scoring Active Assessments: Setting Clear Criteria and Adapting Them to Your Students Are the Keys to Scoring Classroom Performance,"

Science and Children, 32, no. 2, October 1994, 26–29.

■ Robert E. MacDonald, *A Handbook of Basic Skills and Strategies for Beginning Teachers: Facing the Challenge of Teaching in Today's Schools* (New York: Longman, 1991), 190–193.

This analogy may help you understand the differences between assessment and measurement/evaluation:

Assessment documents the course of learning and teaching; i.e., how you get to some end point.

Measurement/evaluation is only about the end point;, e.g., score, grade, or mark.

Measurement (in terms of numerical scoring, marking, and grading) is discussed at the end of this chapter.

Let's look now at the kinds of assessment approaches you will need in your hands-on/minds-on guided discovery teaching/learning.

Broad Assessment Approaches

Three broad types of assessment strategies will help you carry out your assessment objectives: diagnostic, formative, and summative.

Diagnostic assessment is useful *before* you start teaching material to discover what your students know and don't know about the topic to be explored, their misconceptions, and partial or naive theories.

You will use **formative assessment** *during* your teaching to discover what your students are learning (or not learning) and to supply you with feedback to modify your lesson plans and teaching methods where needed.

Summative assessment is used *after* you have taught the material to assess how much students have learned or not learned, assign grades in a measurement mode, share data with students and parents, and make judgments with students about what next teaching/learning steps are appropriate.

Formative and summative assessment procedures may also be diagnostic: through them we may learn where there are student weaknesses and what must be retaught.

At various times in your science teaching, you will need to use all three of these assessment strategies. Table 5–2 summarizes when, why, and how each type of assessment can be used in your teaching. Further elaboration of specific uses and techniques in the three assessment strategies will be given later in this chapter.

TABLE 5–2

Authentic assessment strategies

	Diagnostic	Formative	Summative
When?	*Before* teaching	*During* teaching	*After* teaching
Why?	Assess student needs and prior knowledge. Find out how much students know. Match 1 and 2 with teaching methods.	Provide immediate feedback to guide students to complete tasks. Modify teaching of concepts.	Use primarily for assigning grades. Assess how much students have learned before moving on to next topic. Report to parents, administrators, community.
How?	Three broad categories of evaluation techniques: Paper and pencil tests Student projects and written reports Teacher observations and student performance tasks		

Diagnostic Assessment Is Vital in Constructivist Classrooms

Assessment procedures can supply you with much diagnostic data about individual students in your class. Such procedures can help you identify a student's science strengths, weaknesses, prior knowledge, partial and naive theories, skills, and interests. This information will also indicate how well students work alone or in groups, with your direct assistance or on their own, with a variety of devices (computers, filmstrips, films, and audiotapes), or by reading. By using informal questioning, a hands-on/minds-on authentic test, or a paper and pencil device for assessment *before* you start your teaching, you can determine what specific experiences will best encourage students' science progress. Diagnostic data will help you to adjust the teaching/learning environment to your students' individual differences.

Once the learning is under way, it becomes your responsibility to find out how well students are doing with the learning activities you have prescribed as a result of your diagnosis.

Research has shown that you can increase science content achievement by using diagnostic assessments that correspond closely to your learning objectives. Studies also show that if you follow your diagnostic assessment with reteaching and student restudying, you will bring about significant increases in achievement, even among students who have low aptitudes.[10]

Assessment techniques give you insights into how well your students are learning the scientific content and process skills you planned for them through diagnostic devices. By skillfully using these achievement data with your students, increased interest and motivation can be provided by

1. making students active partners in the teaching/learning act rather than passive absorbers of information,
2. inviting students to set realistic and obtainable goals and providing information to both you and them concerning their progress toward these goals,
3. showing students that progress has been made, no matter how small, to help them

Portfolios help make students' work and progress concrete and understandable to parents.

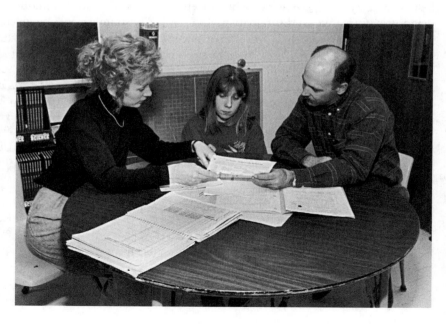

attain satisfaction and a desire to continue learning,

4. guiding students to become increasingly self-directed as they put into perspective where they were, are, and should be in the future, and
5. showing students that an adult really cares about their progress.

Assessment Data Communicates With the Public

Assessment can provide you with the raw data you need to report to parents, school administration and boards, and the community at large. Good communication between you and your students' parents helps supply the best possible learning experiences for your students. By having good assessment procedures and solid information on which to make interpretations to your community, you are better able to handle questions and criticisms of your science program intelligently. You will be better equipped to communicate your objectives and achievements in the science program with such information. Through adequate science assessment, administrators will be provided with valid information to make their judgments and recommendations to school boards of education. Administrators need such data to support your efforts. With millions of dollars and countless hours being spent on science programs, communities deserve to know the effectiveness of the programs they support. The back-to-basics movement in some communities means, unfortunately, an across-the-board de-emphasis of science education from kindergarten through high school. Some school systems have cut science programs to transfer additional funds into more politically acceptable areas of education, such as reading and language arts.

Our science objectives and assessment techniques—and our communication of them to the public—must be specific, in concrete, unambiguous terms. Keep in mind the words of Isaac Asimov, speaking before the annual convention of the National Science Teachers Association in 1977: "Science must fight to maintain its honor. We must reach out to the public. We must be proselytizers."

USING AUTHENTIC ASSESSMENT IN YOUR SCIENCE TEACHING/LEARNING

The rest of this chapter will provide specific practical suggestions for implementing authentic assessment in your science teaching/learning and specific directions on how to construct and effectively use them; as you study these, please use the following as guidelines:

1. A wide range of authentic science assessment techniques, instruments, and procedures are necessary to understand and display what each student has learned.
2. Materials and scientific processes of authentic assessment are to be so developed and used that they are integral to, not apart from, the other learning processes in a course.
3. Authentic assessment procedures are most effective when students and teachers work together in their development and implementation. Authentic assessment should provide students and teachers with opportunities to summarize and interpret what they have accomplished. It should not be restricted to securing data for marks and grading.
4. Planning, judging, and revising procedures for authentic assessment are most effectively accomplished when students and teachers work together to improve their quality.
5. Quality of thinking, development of competencies in criticism and assessment, and reflection on and integration of learning will take priority over moving on to new subject areas whenever these alternatives are in contention for class time.[11]

FIGURE 5–1

The seven principles of sound assessment: A critical blend

Source: Richard J. Stiggins, *Student-Centered Classroom Assessment* (Englewood Cliffs, NJ: Merrill/Prentice Hall, 1994), 10.

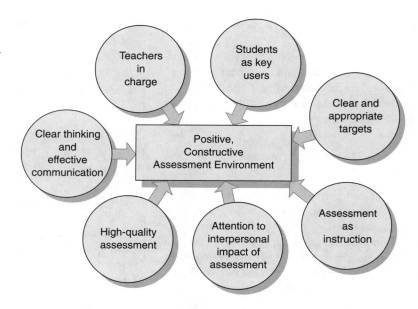

Figure 5–1 graphically summarizes seven inter-related principles of sound assessment.

Here are realistic classroom-tested techniques for implementing these guidelines in authentic assessment of your hands-on/minds-on guided discovery science teaching/learning.

Organizing Authentic Assessment Around the Constructivist Learning Cycle[12]

The constructivist-oriented instructional model in Chapter 3 presented examples of scientific processes with an STS focus that can form the basis for your hands-on/minds-on guided discovery science program. It will be used here as the base around which authentic assessment can be integrated. Figure 5–2 shows how specific authentic assessment techniques can be employed within each learning cycle stage to target students' scientific content and process skills. You will notice that assessment is integrated in every teaching/learning task. In the following sections, a sample of an authentic assessment device will be elaborated

in only one learning cycle stage, even though it may be used in several stages. The core category, All Stages Assessment, displays broad techniques that are applicable for all stages of the learning cycle.

Only when you have resolved what your purposes and targets are for a particular classroom assessment can you pick, develop, and administer a proper assessment technique. Figure 5–3 shows this process as a jigsaw puzzle: only pieces that belong together will fit properly.

Some authentic assessment devices are simple and easily used, while others are time-consuming and multifaceted. The devices selected here are presented as sparks to ignite your interest in trying authentic assessment techniques in your hands-on/minds-on guided discovery science teaching/learning. This chapter also provides references to assist you in getting additional information about authentic assessment techniques. At the end of the chapter, there is discussion about scoring student performance and its relationship to grading and marks. Now, on to authentic assessment and the constructivist learning cycle.

FIGURE 5–2

Organizing authentic assessment around learning cycle stages

Source: Modified from K–8 Alaska Science Consortium, *The Great Northern Science Book* (Fairbanks, AK: University of Alaska, 1992), 1.

AUTHENTIC ASSESSMENT: THE INVITATION

In the invitation stage, authentic assessment is primarily information gathering for both student and teacher. The teacher discovers students' prior knowledge, naive and partial theories, and concept level (schema) for the selected science topic. This can operate as the baseline to which student growth can be compared. Students gather information about a new science topic and can be guided to build upon what they

FIGURE 5–3

How do the authentic assessment pieces fit together?

Source: Richard J. Stiggins, *Student-Centered Classroom Assessment* (Englewood Cliffs, NJ: Merrill/Prentice Hall, 1994), 83.

know. These invitation stage techniques assess students' preconceptions:

- Discrepant Events
- Student Materials Manipulation/Teacher Question
- Concept Mapping
- Data Capture Assessment

Discrepant Events

Present a **discrepant** event—an event that is atypical, unusual, or in which there is an inconsistency between what can reasonably be expected to happen and what is depicted as happening. Discrepant events can be done through a teacher guided demonstration using science materials or, if that is impractical or inefficient in terms of time commitment and resources, through a pictorial riddle. You and your students can create pictorial riddles by:

- Selecting a scientific concept or principle to be learned or discussed.

- Drawing a picture, using an illustration, or utilizing existing photos that demonstrates a scientific concept, process, or situation.
- Formulating convergent and divergent process-oriented questions to stimulate students' thinking about the subject, unveiling their preconceptions of the science topic, and setting the intellectual stage for further scientific investigations.
- Discussing and recording responses.

A divergent event can be either teacher/student conducted or a pictorial riddle. In Figure 5–4, two cubes of identical size are in containers of liquid; one is floating and one is sinking. This confronts students with a discrepant event. Use convergent questions initially to guide learners' observations and to assess what they see, feel, or know about the elements of the event. These questions:

1. direct the learners' attention to specific objects or elements of the event.
2. sharpen students' recall or memory schema.

Dish 1   Dish 2

FIGURE 5–4
Pictorial riddle

3. help you evaluate students' observational and recall skills.
4. allow you to adjust your teaching to present ideas again, present new ideas, or regress to less complicated ideas.

You might ask:

Convergent Questions	Scientific Processes
What objects are in the event?	observation/recall
What is happening in Dish 1?	description/ communication
What has happened to the object in Dish 2?	observation/recall
Which dish has a floating object? a sinking one?	observation/recall
How are Dish 1 and Dish 2 alike?	observation/ comparison
How are Dish 1 and Dish 2 different?	observation/ comparison

To broaden and deepen your students' responses and involve them in creative and critical thinking, ask divergent questions. Many of these questions guide students in discovering things for themselves, help them to see interrelationships, and make hypotheses or draw conclusions from data.

Here are some divergent questions you might ask about the two dishes in Figure 5–4.

Divergent Questions	Scientific Processes
What can you say about these two pictures?	drawing inference
Under what conditions could this be possible?	hypothesizing
How could you go about showing the scientific principles involved in this event?	organizing data/ designing experiment
What might cause one cube to float and one to sink?	hypothesizing
Under what conditions might both cubes sink or float?	hypothesizing
How would you set up an experiment to show your answer to the above question?	organizing data/ designing experiment
In what situations have you seen similar happenings?	application to new situation

Student Materials Manipulation/ Teacher Questions

Science materials can be set out on tables and individuals or groups of students can be guided with minimal instructions to "mess about" or experiment in a hands-on activity. Teacher/student discussion can follow and be supplemented by a pictorial assessment. For example, you can set the working conditions by saying something like *"Try each object in water to see what happens to it. What do we call it if an object falls to the bottom of the water (sinks) or stays on top of the water (floats)?"* If students don't know, you can invent (give word for concept) term for students. Then groups of students experiment with objects and put objects in boxes labelled "sink" or "float." Discussion can follow and you can assess levels of knowledge the students possess. Figure 5–5 shows examples of Piagetian concrete operations your students may exhibit with floating

FIGURE 5–5
Examples of Piagetian concrete operations with floating and sinking

Operation	Activity or Observation
Classifying	Floating versus sinking Heavy versus light Large versus small
Identifying variables and serially ordering them	Weight Volume
Placing two sets of variables in correspondence	Large and heavy Small and heavy Large and light Small and light

and sinking. You can then follow up with a pictorial assessment like the one in Figure 5–6.

Concept Mapping

A **concept map** is a diagram of the concepts of a science unit (usually shown as circles) and the interrelationships between them (usually drawn as lines connecting two or more concepts). Here are some benefits for using concept mapping in the invitation stage of the learning cycle:

Student Benefits

■ Students organize materials better—focusing on how concepts relate to one another—when they construct their own concept maps.

■ Students are more likely to observe how new concepts are related to their prior knowledge; therefore,

■ Learning the material becomes more meaningful and schema development is facilitated; therefore,

■ Students can encode this material verbally and visually in long-term memory.

Teacher Benefits

■ The organizational plan of a lesson becomes clearer to teachers when they construct their own concept map for that lesson.

■ This leads to an improved view of how to sequence the ideas in their lesson.

■ By examining students' concept maps, teachers discover their concept understandings and misconceptions.[13]

Test each object in the water.
Circle the word *floats* if your object floats in water.
Circle the word *sinks* if your object sinks in water.

rock — floats / sinks	scallop shell — floats / sinks
button — floats / sinks	bean — floats / sinks
piece of metal — floats / sinks	piece of wood — floats / sinks

Test each object in the water.
Circle the word *floats* if your object floats in water.
Circle the word *sinks* if your object sinks in water.

rubber band — floats / sinks	crayon — floats / sinks
plastic spaghetti — floats / sinks	paper clip — floats / sinks
sugar cube — floats / sinks	bottle cap — floats / sinks

FIGURE 5–6
Pictorial assessment of knowledge of classification

Source: Science Curriculum Improvement Study (SCIS3), *Material Objects Student Guide,* Section 5, Chapter 18 (Hudson, NH: Delta Education, Inc., 1992), 14.

Teachers can assess students' growth by having them complete a concept map at the end of a lesson/unit for comparison with initial understanding of material. This is a powerful tool for showing progress.

Figure 5–7 shows a science concept map for classifying animals. It can be used as an advance organizer and for making connections between various animal types. Notice how body covering labels are connected.

Data Capture (Observing/ Communicating Skills) Assessment

Figure 5–8 shows a data capture assessment that provides teachers with knowledge of students' observing and communicating skills. It is suitable for use with students from K–8, depending upon their prior experiences and levels of cognition. It may be adapted for a variety of science topics observation guide sheets.

AUTHENTIC ASSESSMENT: THE EXPLORATION

The goal of these authentic assessments is to unearth students' science processing skills. Most of the assessments employ hands-on/minds-on activities and include:

- Hands-on Practical Assessment
- Student Observation Journals
- Scientific Processes Observation Checklist

Hands-on Practical Assessment

During the 1980s, data were collected in the United States and sixteen other countries from students in Grades 5 and 9 on a series of practical

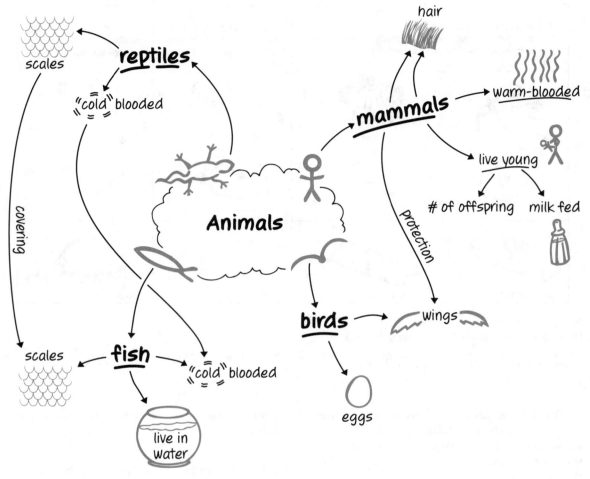

FIGURE 5–7
Animal concept map

Source: Hal Hemmerich, Wendy Lim, Kanwal Neel, *Prime Time! Strategies for Lifelong Learning in Mathematics and Science in the Middle and High School* (Portsmouth, NH: Heinemann, 1994), 56.

hands-on tests. The research was published in 1988 by the International Association for the Evaluation of Educational Achievement (IEA) and is titled "Second International Science Study" (SISS).[14]

Six hands-on tasks were developed to assess students' skills in three broad categories: investigating, performing, and reasoning. Table 5–3 shows the specific skills included in these three categories.

These tests used science content and equipment common to each grade from physics, chemistry, and biology. A person (other than the teacher involved) administered specific oral directions. Equipment and materials were set out at six stations, with a different hands-on situation at each station. Students were asked to manipulate equipment and materials, observe, reason, record data in test booklets, and interpret data. For each task, questions and pictures

TABLE 5–3

Process skills categories assessment

Skill		Comments
Performing	To include:	observing, measuring, and manipulating.
Investigating (problem solving)	To include:	planning and design of experiments.
Reasoning	To include:	interpreting data, formulating generalizations, and building and revising models.

Source: Willard J. Jacobson and Rodney L. Doran, *Science Achievement in the United States and Sixteen Countries: A Report to the Public* (New York: Columbia University, 1988), 68.

FIGURE 5–8

Data capture assessment

Source: "Leaves: An Investigation" and "Leaves Data Capture Sheet" in TCM771 Science Assessment (Westminster, CA: Teacher Created Materials, Inc., 1994), 67–68.

Leaves: An Investigation

Relevant Skills

Observing/Communicating

Knowledge Base

Is familiar with the function of the five senses

Setting Up the Investigation

This investigation would be appropriate at any time of the year except winter in most parts of the northern hemisphere. (It would be interesting to investigate leaves in the fall and then repeat the investigation in the spring to compare the differences in the leaves that could be observed.)

- Bring in branches from trees and bushes with different kinds of leaves and display them around the classroom, allowing students to become familiar with them and discuss them.

- If possible, take a nature walk and allow students to collect leaves.

- Tell students they will be investigating leaves and then sharing what they find out.

- Encourage students to discuss the leaves that people eat or use for flavoring, but caution them that they will not be able to taste the leaves during this investigation, since some leaves could be dangerous to eat.

- Have each child choose two leaves to observe. Give them the "Leaves Data Capture Sheet" to complete. Allow plenty of time.

FIGURE 5–8
continued

Leaves Data Capture Sheet

Name _____ Date _____

Lay one leaf in each box. If your leaves are too big, draw them.

Leaf #1

Leaf #2

Look at Leaf #1.
What do you see?
_____

_____

Look at Leaf #2.
What do you see?
_____

_____

Listen to Leaf #1.
What do you hear?
_____

_____

Listen to Leaf #2.
What do you hear?
_____

_____

Put your nose near Leaf #1.
What do you smell?
_____

_____

Put your nose near Leaf #2.
What do you smell?
_____

_____

Rub your finger over Leaf #1.
What do you feel?
_____

_____

Rub your finger over Leaf #2.
What do you feel?
_____

_____

---

of equipment are presented in the student test booklets.

Figure 5–9 is a sample from the student test booklet for a hands-on task where students are asked to describe and explain color change of bromothymol solution (from blue to yellow) after they blow through the straw. Students were given 45 minutes to perform and manipulate equipment, record their observations, and interpret their results in their student test booklets. After a brief rest, they repeated the procedure for the second half of the hands-on tests. Standardized

FIGURE 5–9

SISS hands-on processes assessment

Source: "International Science Study," Grade 5 A, Booklet 2, page 2 in Willard J. Jacobson and Rodney L. Doran, *Science Achievement in the United States and Sixteen Countries: A Report to the Public* (New York: Columbia University, 1988).

International Science Study

Lab Exercises, Set 5A, page 2

Experiment 1

Before you are two containers.
One contains a blue liquid.
Place the straw in the stopper of the container that has no liquid in it, and blow into the straw for about one minute.

1. What change has taken place?

_____

_____

_____

2. What is an explanation for this change?

_____

_____

_____

_____

equipment and a detailed scoring guide were used to assess students.

Survey your science program to see where you can use these suggestions to develop assessment devices suited to your immediate needs. When you do, you will need methods of recording students' responses and resulting products.

Student Observation Journals

Student observation journals are a chronicle that students can keep as they engage in hands-on/minds-on activities. The journals can take many forms and give teachers an assessment of students' scientific processes. A few that will be examined here are student science dictionaries, science logs, record pages, and observational diaries and journals.

Student Science Dictionaries. As students are exposed to sensory experiences and the subse-quent "inventing" by you of words and terms for science concepts, you can help them make up-to-date **science dictionaries.** As a science topic is investigated, hands-on/minds-on activities done, and new terms introduced, a "class science dictionary" can be made and displayed by your students in your science center or on a corner of the bulletin board. Using large primer paper, you and/or your students can keep a running list of science words and their meanings for the science concepts studied. For younger students, include a picture instead of (or in addition to) the definition, as in Figure 5–10.

Interest older students in keeping an individual science dictionary in which they can record new science words growing out of their hands-on/minds-on activities, and research the origins of interesting science words. You can "invent" the term *etymology*—the origin and development of words. You can also read

FIGURE 5–10
Science dictionary with pictures

Things in our Aquarium

Elodea - <u>water plants</u>: elodea

duckweed

eelgrass

<u>water animals</u>: female guppy

male guppy

daphnia

snail

FIGURE 5–11
Class science sensory experience chart of field trip observations

Our Trip to the Park		
Things We Saw	**Things We Heard**	**Things We Smelled**
Sally: Branches moving in wind	Birds singing	
Greg: Little bugs crawling		Fresh air
Tom: A bird's nest	An airplane	Flowers
Amy: Yellow flowers in grass	Dog barking	
Jon: Squirrel running	Twigs snapping	Dirt (soil)
Jill: Water drops on grass	Our class laughing	Wet grass

to students about interesting words such as *sandwich,* which was named for a gambler (the Earl of Sandwich) too busy to leave his gaming table to eat his roast.

To become familiar with the etymology of words, see Wilfred John Funk's *Word Origins and Their Romantic Stories* for general words. For scientific word origins and development, see one of Isaac Asimov's specialized dictionaries, such as *Words of Science and the History Behind Them.* Have your students keep a science words etymology dictionary and have them share it with each other and other classes.

Student Science Experience Charts. Keeping records is as important to science as breathing is to people. It is through records that we compare and analyze scientific experimentation. Students need to do this, too. Through their own record keeping, your students will build scientific schema and expand their scientific vocabulary.

The first records your students keep may contain a minimum of words but lots of pictures. For example, one record may be a small group or total class experience chart, in which students record on primer paper things they observed after a field trip walk around the park near your school. The experience chart may look like the one shown in Figure 5–11.

Teacher-Guided and Student-Generated Science Record Pages. Record keeping for older students can include brief descriptions of what they did, observed, and thought, in addition to specific evidences of the number of objects they observed, counted, etc. At first, you may want to use a group activity such as the experience chart described above. As your students learn how to give brief descriptions of what they did in groups, they are ready to start their own individual record keeping. You can design a page such as the one shown in Figure 5–12, on which your students record their sink or float experimentation. Figure 5–12 offers students three focused

assignments: *write* description of what they did, *draw* a picture of the activity, and *record observations* in chart supplies. Once students become familiar with this strategy, encourage them to devise their own observation format.

Student Science Logs. Collecting, recording, sharing, and reading their science record books, science logs, and science lab reports (or any other name given by you) give students much practice in observing and recording their observations. Another record-keeping experience for your students is the science log.

You and your students can make your own science minibooks or logs. They can be class collections of student reports, computer-generated materials, logs, or other written works illustrated

You have been working with things that sink or float. What did you do to find out which objects sink or float? Draw a picture.

We put objects in the bowl of water. If the object floated, we put it in box with label Float. If it sank, we put it in box Sink. Then we tried all the objects in the Float box to check if they all floated. We did the same with the objects in the Sink box.

What did you find about which objects sink or float? Record your observations on the chart below.

OBJECT	MADE OF	SINK	FLOAT
PENNY	METAL	X	
PENCIL	MOSTLY WOOD		X

FIGURE 5–12

Hands-on/minds-on science record page

with students' drawings or instant photos. Individuals or small groups of students could also make their own science logs.

To begin, select a size that appeals to you and the students. The size may be dictated by the materials available (e.g., the paper used in most schools is $8\frac{1}{2}$" $\times$ 11"). Have the students put in their science logs things they have studied and found for a particular science topic, field trip, and so on. These might include experiments or other activities, observational records, drawings, magazine pictures, and handwritten or typed science content.

Have your students add front and back covers, illustrate them, laminate and bind them together, or put in a binder. They can share their science logs with each other. Some schools have even set up a special section in their libraries for student science logs. This is an excellent opportunity to integrate and assess science with reading, writing,

art, mathematics, and other subjects. Figure 5–13 shows how science log covers can be made attractive.[15]

Scientific Processes
Observation Checklist

The assessment of scientific processes in practical or hands-on/minds-on activities can be structured or formalized to guide teacher observations. An example of this is shown in Activity 5–1, on pp. 142–143.

The oral instructions, hints, and prompts furnished in Activity 5–1 were standardized, allowing for comparisons among behaviors and responses of different students. This checklist is valuable because it shows how to construct an assessment checklist that uses content (the behavior of mealworms) as the vehicle to gather data on the skills and processes used by students

FIGURE 5–13
Student science log minibooks, grades K–12

in scientific investigation or problem-solving. Which of *your* hands-on/minds-on activities lend themselves to this type of assessment?

AUTHENTIC ASSESSMENT: DISCOVERY/INTERPRETATION

In this stage, teachers highlight an individual student's degree of conceptual change and observe concrete and verbal models of his conceptual knowledge. Students exhibit these behaviors and knowledge by creating such products as:

■ oral/written pictorial interpretations of situations,
■ essay interpretations of data, and
■ graphing of data.

These are the most authentic documents to use for assessing in this stage.

Oral/Written Pictorial Interpretations

Teachers can gain insights into their students' ability to interpret data by using assessments that ask them to respond to pictorial situations. Look for more than mere observations—hidden meanings, underlying patterns, and explanatory schema that bring coherence to the students' observations. The assessment is intended to determine students' ability to communicate the trends and sequences of the pictorial situation.

Show a science pictorial situation, then give directions for how to respond to the questions. This can be done orally for younger students or those with limited reading skills, and in written form for others. Figure 5–14 shows how this can be done.

Essay Interpretations of Data

In the discovery/interpretation stage, the student discovers relationships among facts, generalizations, definitions, values, and skills. Essay assessment is one way to assess interpretation skills. Like all assessing devices, the essay has disadvantages as well as advantages.

1. Essays show how well the student is able to organize and present ideas, but scoring may be subjective without firm answers unless you have a clear scoring rubric.
2. Essays show varying degrees of correctness, since there is often not just one right or wrong answer, but scoring requires excessive time.
3. Essays assess abilities to analyze problems using pertinent information and to arrive at generalizations or conclusions, but scoring is influenced by spelling, handwriting, sentence structure, and other extraneous items.
4. Essays assess deeper meanings, reasoning, and interrelationships rather than isolated bits of factual materials, but questions may be either ambiguous or obvious unless you carefully construct them.

To offset the disadvantages of the essay test, you must carefully construct each essay question. Word the question so pupils will be limited, as much as possible, to the concepts being tested. For instance, for upper elementary or middle school level, it is better to use an item like this:

If you moved to Greenland, how would the days and nights differ from where you live now? How would the seasons differ?

than an item like this:

Discuss the differences between the places in the world in relation to their days and nights throughout the seasons.

The second question is much too broad and does not give your pupils a good idea of what you expect.

With a fourth grade student, you might ask this question for an essay assessment on the same topic.

How is your life affected by the shorter daylight hours in winter? How do you think animals in your area are affected?

You will be able to overcome or minimize subjectivity in scoring essay questions by preparing a

Activity 5–1

Students are introduced to mealworms and directed to find out mealworms' food preferences using this equipment: 20 mealworms in a container, empty container, hand lens, 4 tubes filled with bran, mashed banana, sugar, and sawdust, 30 cm ruler, spoon, stop-clock, deep-sided tray (approximately 40 × 25 cm) lined with white paper, and a large drawing of a mealworm. A student record page can be set up as shown for observational notes and results.

Teacher/observer may provide a cue, prompt, or question if students are stuck and cannot continue, or if teacher seeks students' thinking or reason for some action, for example: "One way you can try is to make a mark in the middle of the paper. Take some of each food and place it at the same distance from the mark and then put some mealworms on the mark."[16]

If cues are given, the teacher/observer records it on the Laboratory Student Behavior Checklist along with observed student behaviors. NOTE: The Laboratory Student Behavior Checklist lists problem-solving skills for the observer to focus upon. If cues or prompts are given, the

Example of student record page for mealworms activity

Source: Elizabeth Meng and Rodney L. Doran, *Improving Instruction and Learning Through Evaluation: Elementary School Science* (Columbus, OH: ERIC Clearinghouse for Science, Mathematics, and Environmental Education, 1993), 93.

Mealworms

Find out if the mealworms prefer some of these foods to others. If they do, which ones do they prefer?

a) Put down here any notes and results as you go along:

b) Write down here what you found about the foods the mealworms prefer:

observer should make a record of them and students should not be given credit for them on the checklist. The checklist spotlights specific behaviors to look for as students progress toward finding answers to the question. Emphasis is placed on observable behaviors and low student inferences, such as: "Puts almost equal quantities of food."

Uses hand lens correctly

Hint given

Deliberately provides mealworm with choice; i.e., at least 2 foods at once

Employs an effective strategy such as:
  (i)   uses 6 or more mealworms if all 4 food compared at once
  (ii)   compares foods in all possible pairs with 1 mealworm
  (iii)   tries at least 4 mealworms with one food at a time

Attempts to provide equal quantities of different foods

Puts approximately equal quantities of food

Attempts to release mealworms at equal distance from all foods *or* arranges mealworms to be randomly distributed around food

Arranges to release mealworms from points equidistant from foods, *or* places mealworms randomly around foods

Arranges for all mealworms to have same time to choose (i.e., puts them all down together or uses a clock)

Uses clock to time definite events

Allows about 4–7 minutes for mealworms to make choice (not necessarily timed)

Examines behavior carefully (to see if food is being eaten)

Counts mealworms near each pile after a certain time (or notes which food the mealworm is on for strategy (ii) above)

Makes notes at (a) (however brief)

Records details such as time of choice and numbers near each food

Can read stop clock correctly (to nearest second)

Makes a record of finding at (b) without prompting

Results at (a) and (b) consistent with evidence (even if only rough)

Results based on and consistent with quantitative evidence

Laboratory student behavior checklist

Source: Elizabeth Meng and Rodney L. Doran, *Improving Instruction and Learning Through Evaluation: Elementary School Science* (Columbus. OH: ERIC Clearinghouse for Science, Mathematics, and Environmental Education, 1993), 124.

FIGURE 5–14

Pictorial interpretation assessment

Source: SCIS 3, *Materials Object Student Manual,* Section 5, Chapter 18, (Hudson, NH: Delta Education, Inc., 1992).

Teacher shows pictures and says to children:

What differences do you see in these 3 pictures?
Which do you think will happen first? Second? Last?
Why do you think the snowman is changing?

scoring guide beforehand and scoring each question separately. If a list of the important ideas you expect is made before scoring, there is less chance for indecision while scoring.

You should be flexible and open-minded in setting up the important ideas you will accept as answers for an essay. There may be valid student ideas that you have not considered. Explain your scoring to your students so they can benefit from the assessment and use it for a further learning experience.

Two examples of essays to assess your students' ability to interpret scientific concepts into their own words might be:

In the Cartesian diver you made, how does the medicine dropper that went up and down as you squeezed the plastic bottle compare to a submarine submerging and surfacing?

Contrast the "scientific" explanations of the universe of people who supported the heliocentric point of view as opposed to the geocentric one.

Graphing From Data

Many activities and assessment devices in science involve using graphs or pictorial and tabular display. The ability to make and interpret graphs from raw data collected by students is an advanced and complex series of skills that is stressed in elementary science programs. Therefore, devices for assessing graphing skills must be carefully selected. Chapter 8 will examine the uses of graphing in your hands-on/minds-on science classes in more depth.

The difficulty of graphing skills may vary depending on how much is already done for the student and how much the student must do. Here are levels of graphing difficulty:

- lowest—only need to record data on the graph
- middle—less assistance in constructing the graph
- upper—must construct graph from raw data

Figure 5–15 is an example of an assessment device that requires the upper level of graphing skills. For excellent descriptions and examples of graphing assessment see:

- Elizabeth Meng and Ronald L. Doran, *Improving Instruction and Learning Through Evaluation: Elementary School Science* (Columbus, OH: ERIC Clearinghouse for Science, Mathematics, and Environmental Education, 1993), 29–31, 138–144.

Suggestions for scoring graphs will be explored in "Authentic Assessment: All Stages," later in this chapter.

Our class planted bean seeds, watered them as needed, observed them, staked them on sticks, and measured their growth each Friday afternoon. Here are the average heights when we started measuring (when plant had grown above ground) and for six weeks after:

        0 week ....10 cm
        1 week ....15 cm
        2 weeks ....25 cm
        3 weeks ....50 cm
        4 weeks ....60 cm
        5 weeks ....70 cm
        6 weeks ....75 cm

Draw any kind of graph you want (one of those we studied or any other kind you might want) to show how our beans grew over time.

FIGURE 5–15
Assessing graphing skills—upper level of difficulty

AUTHENTIC ASSESSMENT: EXPLANATIONS/SOLUTIONS

In this stage, teachers use assessment to uncover students' skills in analyzing, planning, and explaining/communicating aspects of their hands-on/minds-on experiences beyond mere observation and recall. Assessment devices that can aid in this endeavor include:

- enhanced and justified multiple-choice answers/solutions,

- assessment of student planning skills, and
- communication assessment.

Multiple-Choice Answers/Solutions

Multiple-choice tests are one of the most frequently used ways to assess students' understanding of scientific principles and concepts. They have these practical advantages for teachers:

- A wide range of scientific skills and knowledge can be tested in a short time.
- They are easy to construct, administer, and score.
- They can be used to assess all levels of learning, from knowledge to analysis, evaluation, and application.
- They provide a lower probability of correct guesses than true–false tests.[17]

However, multiple-choice assessment also has disadvantages:

- It does not usually provide teachers with knowledge about how the student arrived at the answer (i.e., concept constructs).
- Higher-level assessment items may be difficult and time-consuming to write.
- Generally, students are not asked to generate information in their own words.
- Reading, concentration levels, and format may be inappropriate for younger students.
- It may be difficult or impossible to use in some STS problem-solving situations or process skills areas.[18]

You will probably use multiple-choice frequently in your assessment program. To be sure multiple-choice assessments (your own or commercially made ones) assess what you really want, keep these things in mind:

1. Multiple-choice questions have three parts:
   a. *Stem:* presents the task to your students
   b. *Distractors:* incorrect responses
   c. *Correct response*
2. Be sure your stem
   a. asks a direct question or poses a problem in a simple and clearly worded manner.

b. avoids use of confusing negatives.

3. Check your distractors to
   a. see if you have one correct response.
   b. keep your responses (both distractors and correct response) to four. More responses are unwieldy, and fewer make it almost a true or false test.
   c. avoid the phrases *all of the above* or *none of the above,* because these responses may confuse some students.
   d. ensure that the relative length of the choices does not provide a clue to the correct response.
   e. make all distractors plausible.

4. In your correct response
   a. distribute the order randomly, so there isn't a discernable pattern (e.g., favoring the first or last answer).
   b. make sure there is clearly only one correct response.
   c. avoid verbal clues like *never* and *all* and avoid repeating words used in the stem.[19]

There are two types of multiple-choice assessments that require students to reflect upon higher level scientific principles and concepts rather than merely observing and recalling factual details: enhanced and justified.

Enhanced Multiple Choice. Enhanced multiple-choice questions occur in clusters that provide the context and setting for students, as in Figure 5–16.

Justified Multiple Choice. In justified multiple-choice questions, students first mark the best answer and then explain in several sentences why they chose that answer, as in Figure 5–17.

Discussion about scoring multiple-choice items is included in the "Authentic Assessment: All Stages" section of this chapter.

Assessing Students' Planning Skills

To assess planning skills, we must ask students to move beyond "cookbook experiences" where everything is planned out for them. They must be asked to devise other ways of investigating by questions such as,

We just finished studying about static electricity and ways of producing and controlling it. Use that information to explain why you get a "shock" when you slide across the plastic seatcovers in your parents' car. How could you prevent the shock?

Planning skills can also be assessed by asking students to set up problem-solving procedures, for example,

We are on a class picnic and field day. As the bus stops at the park, three volunteers go to find us a good picnic spot. They all come back excited about their finds for the spot. What questions would you ask them to decide which spot to pick? Give the reasons you picked your particular questions.

FIGURE 5–16
Enhanced multiple-choice assessment

Teacher: Look carefully at the big picture. Now look at these pictures (indicating Row A). Which of these shows the most likely way that the wood came to be in two pieces?

FIGURE 5–17

Justified multiple-choice assessment

Directions

Three candles, exactly the same size, were put in different boxes like those in the drawing below, and were lit at the same time. Then the boxes were closed.

Large closed box

Medium closed box

Small closed box

Candle 1   Candle 2   Candle 3

Circle the letter that shows the order in which the candle flames most likely will go out.

A.   1, 2, 3   C.   3, 1, 2
B.   2, 3, 1   D.   3, 2, 1

Explain (in two or three sentences) why you think the answer you selected is correct.

In each example, the last sentence delves into students' thinking and encourages communication.

Communication Assessment

A very important skill in science is the ability to communicate data to others. This ability to put information gathered into coherent communication statements can be assessed using a variety of techniques. You might structure this type of question:

We have just come back from a trip to our city's water purification plant. For homework tonight, write your answers to these questions so we can discuss them tomorrow.

- *I agree with the water commissioner that big industries in our town are polluting our waters because . . .*
- *I disagree with the water commissioner that little can be done to correct the pollution because . . .*

Older students could address local situations thus:

Housing developments on wetlands should not be permitted because . . .
A request to build an atomic power plant outside the city should not be granted because . . .

What are some topics of interest to you, your students, and the community that might lend themselves to this type of assessment?

AUTHENTIC ASSESSMENT: TAKING ACTION

Students use previously acquired knowledge and comprehension skills to solve problems in situations that are new or different from those to which they were exposed. In the taking action stage of assessment, we are asking whether students understand a particular idea well enough to apply it in another context. Some of the products students generate could include:

- story applications,
- creative drama,
- product creation,
- student artwork
- model building, and
- student demonstrations.

Story Applications

At the conclusion of scientific studies, teachers might ask the following story completion questions to see how well students have learned and can apply relevant concepts.

> *Now that we have studied heat and thermal energy for some time, see if you can apply your understandings to these new situations:*
> *a. According to your understanding of energy source and energy sink, why is this common statement inaccurate: "Close the door; you're letting in the cold."*
> *b. How would you correct Statement A to make it accurate?*
> *c. Using the ideas in Items A and B, how would you account for a person getting a bad burn if he or she touches dry ice?*

Here is another example of an item to assess your students' application skills after studying human physiology:

> *If you were in a stalled elevator, which action(s) would be best for you to take until you were rescued? Explain your choice in terms of ideas you learned in our study of the human body.*

> *a. take deep breaths*
> *b. sit on the floor*
> *c. stand quietly*
> *d. move periodically from corner to corner*

What story application can you devise for the science topic you are currently studying?

Creative Drama

Creative drama can incorporate role-playing, pantomime, movement, improvisation, and oral and written communication in the form of scripts, advertising billboards, or audio and video presentations. Teachers often recognize creative drama as an effective assessment vehicle. Creative drama permits teachers to scrutinize meanings students have constructed during and at the conclusion of the learning process. Any misconceptions observed as students act out a concept can be pointed out and students can be guided to correct them.

Here is an example of assessment criteria or a scoring rubric used to evaluate a creative drama of a plant's life cycle.

- *Minimal achievement:* The student correctly acts out the stages of the plant's life cycle, but does not indicate how the plant moves from one stage to the next or highlight the function of flowers in the production of new seeds.
- *Moderate Achievement:* The student correctly acts out the stages of the plant's life cycle and indicates some understanding, through actions, of how the plant moves from one stage to the next. For example, the child demonstrates that the root is the first part to emerge from the seed or acts out the bud opening into a flower.
- *Excellent Achievement:* The student acts out all the stages of the plant's life cycle and shows, through action, clear understanding of how the plant moves from one stage to the next. For example, a student demonstrates that a plant needs moisture and warmth prior to germination or dramatizes a flower being pollinated before the formation of a fruit."[20]

To help ensure fair, consistent, and unbiased judgment of student work, criteria for evaluation should be determined in advance.

Product Creation

Student products at the termination of a science study may uncover much about student thinking. Teacher and students should work out expectations of what the projects will encompass *before* students start their projects. Primary grade students usually make something as part of their science learning, such as in this study of plants and plant growth.

> *Students collect seeds and class discussion leads to planting them. Conditions necessary to start the seed growing (germination) are arrived at and planting begins. Plant growth is dependent upon a number of variables and students try out various conditions to maximize plant growth. Product assessments for this topic include teacher observations, the state of the plants at conclusion of study, students' oral and written observations, non-numerical bar charts or graphs using paper strips cut weekly to plant size, etc.*

Product assessments provide the teacher with insight into how well students have learned, recorded, and put their knowledge into practical use in growing healthy plants.

Middle and upper elementary students may engage in this product assessment activity by designing a plant to survive and thrive in a given environment, after studying plant parts, growth patterns and variables, habitats, interrelationships of plants and the elements of their environment, and adaptation.

"Inventing a Plant" Assessment Activity.[21]

1. After studying plant concepts, ask students to describe problems plants have surviving in such environments as the arctic, desert, ocean, tropics, etc.
2. Distribute arts and crafts materials (e.g., toothpicks, glue, leaves, twigs, soft thin wire, scissors, small pieces of styrofoam, clay lumps, all kinds of paper, tape, colored plastic film, etc.).
3. Ask students to build a model of a plant—using the materials listed above or any other materials they feel are pertinent—that can survive under one of these conditions:

   Shield itself under extreme heat
   Reach water 40 centimeters down
   Withstand strong winds
   Live on pond surface
   Withstand fire
   Compete with other plants for light
   Live in rapid stream or river
   Store water
   Catch insects
   Withstand cold

4. When models are completed, have students explain how their invented plants adapted to the condition they chose.
5. A real-life follow-up could be to:

   Find real plants in the community for any of the conditions listed above.
   Determine what plant adaptations and specific local plants they might look for if they were to pick plants for their homes and school (inside and outside), their town or city, or a parkway or freeway.

Student Artwork

Students' artwork (drawings, paintings, crayon and/or chalk rubbings, picture collections for students with handicaps or less creative ability) frequently uncovers much more than artistic ability. You will begin to see how idiosyncratic artwork can be even when students all work on the same assignment. For instance, a total class could engage in this artwork product assessment activity, called "Adopt a Tree."

> *Select a specific tree on or near your school grounds. Have each student scrutinize that tree monthly throughout the year, making a drawing of their observations each time. Students should keep these drawings in their*

Encouraging more detail in the work of students who are naturally artistic can enhance their understanding of science concepts.

portfolios (which will be discussed in detail in the section that follows). Often, teachers have students share their drawings with each other and discuss any changes they have observed. By perusing these drawings, you may acquire insight into students' progress in observation skills, drawing, and communication of their thought processes. Some criteria or questions that could assist you in assessing the artwork are:

■ *How well did the student represent the general shape and proportions of the tree?*

■ *What details were included (e.g., leaves, buds, trunk texture, flowers if any, etc.)?*

■ *How accurate is use of color (for tree bark, leaves, flowers if any, etc.)?*

■ *Which elements (if any) of the tree's environment are included?*

■ *How are seasonal changes depicted in the drawings?*

Be sensitive to your individual students and their artistic skill levels: some may draw what is easiest for them instead of what they are observ-ing. Questioning them allows you to get a broader picture of what they are trying to say than merely evaluating the drawing.

Model Building

Models—physical representations that illustrate natural phenomena—are excellent student products for assessment. Students are required to research relevant information, discover what kind of models lend themselves to illustrating the scientific concept(s) to be shown, collect needed scientific supplies and equipment, plan and build the model, and explain it to the class and teacher. Students have successfully accomplished these things for models of the solar system, geological structures, physiological systems of the human body, diode crystal radios, Cartesian divers, and so forth.

What model building assessments would lend themselves to your unique science studies and students?

Student Demonstrations

Students can divulge much of what they know about scientific concepts and interrelationships among these concepts through planning, manipulating, and demonstrating these concepts using scientific supplies and equipment. These student demonstrations may be given to their own classmates and teacher, other classes, their parents, or other persons. Demonstrations may be by individual students or by groups. Demonstrations might include showing how electrical circuits work, building a volcano, or exhibiting static electricity in everyday situations.

What student demonstrations might lend themselves to your classroom and students?

AUTHENTIC ASSESSMENT: ALL STAGES

Teachers use a wide range of assessment procedures to evaluate students' progress in science and to communicate to students their achievement and growth. Portfolios, cooperative group performance, teacher anecdotal records, and checklists require different techniques, but in all, teachers find rubrics or scoring assessments to be very valuable.

Portfolios[22]

A device that has gained popularity for more authentic assessment of students' science achievement, knowledge, and concept construction, as well as for positive attitude development, is the student portfolio. Besides being valuable for *teacher* data, portfolios can also be used by *students* to keep abreast of their scientific learning development. But what is a portfolio, how is it organized, and how can it be effectively used in your science assessment?

Portfolios are containers (folders, boxes, crates, or other containers) into which students and teachers place student products or other evidences of their skills in science, such as written assignments, logs, group work, tests, homework, projects, models, drawings, and other creative expressions. These samples should present evidence of growth in scientific content knowledge, concept construction, processes, skills, and attitudes.[23]

Portfolio item selections should be *positive* (e.g., what students did correctly) rather than *negative* (student mistakes). Either the teacher (for younger students) or the student can catalog items with an index or table of contents listing each item, its date, descriptions of each assignment, and any other pertinent information.

The purpose of the portfolio usually determines the type of container selected and items to be included. Students can customize their own portfolios. By having students pick the items *they* want to include, there is strong learner ego involvement, leading to greater self-learning and self-assessment. Having students pick items for inclusion in their portfolio prompts them to make a greater commitment and feel more ownership about their work. Students may be guided to choose among the following samples of work (or others of their own choice) to be included in their science portfolios:

science observations	book reviews
journals	data collection
projects	writing samples
research reports	tests
computer work	photographs
graphs	trip evaluations
drawings	dramatics
models	

Students and teachers must work together to establish selection and assessment criteria for portfolio items. Part of that assessment should be students' self-assessment of their portfolios. This makes students more active learners as they develop their own internal criteria for selecting and assessing each portfolio item. Figure 5–18 is an example of a self-assessment portfolio checklist.

Portfolios are also excellent tools for teachers to use to assess their own professional development and may include such items as

- certification of student performances on forms or checklists that summarize their skills, projects, and explorations
- anecdotal records of observations of individual students
- student–teacher–parent conference reports
- science unit/lesson plans
- professional journal articles
- samples of students' work

Teacher portfolios provide a permanent record of insights into students' thinking processes and products. They can help clarify what students value and use in the classroom learning environment, and provide an important supplement to paper and pencil assessments for areas that do not readily lend themselves to easy assessment. Portfolios also provide evidence of achievement beyond factual knowledge and allow for different learning styles of students.

FIGURE 5–18

Portfolio item self-assessment

Source: Modified from *The Great Northern Science Book* (Fairbanks, AK: K–8 Alaska Science Consortium, University of Alaska Fairbanks, Spring 1992), 30.

Name _____

Portfolio item _____

Date _____

Worked alone_____   **Worked with** _____

Answer only those questions that fit this portfolio item.

■ Why did you pick this item? _____

_____

■ What did you learn from working on this item? _____

_____

■ If you had more time with this item, what else would you do? _____

_____

■ What problems did you have while working on this item? _____

_____ How did you solve them? _____

_____

■ What area(s) of interest would you like to explore that resulted from

working on this item? _____

For assistance in setting up *your* portfolios, see references in the endnotes and

■ J. L. Herman, P. R. Aschbacher, and L. Winters, *A Practical Guide to Alternative Assessment* (Alexandria, VA: Association for Supervision and Curriculum Development, 1992).
■ B. C. Hill and C. Ruptic, *Practical Aspects of Authentic Assessment: Putting the Pieces Together* (Norwood, MA: Christopher-Gordon Publishers, 1994).
■ J. Jasmine, *Portfolios and Other Assessments* (Westminster, CA: Teacher-Created Materials, 1993).

Ways of systematizing and scoring portfolios will be examined later in the chapter.

Cooperative Group Performance

In cooperative learning, students work with their classmates to accomplish group goals and to assist each other in learning. See Chapter 6 for an extended review of cooperative learning groups' advantages, team formation, job assignments and functions, and applications for your classroom. This section will address itself to three techniques for recording student responses during cooperative group learning for assessment purposes:

■ Audio/video tape recordings of discussions and question-and-answer sessions
■ Anecdotal record keeping
■ Checklists

Electronic technology today offers teachers user friendly, almost foolproof, devices to assist you in recording students' performances. Either you or students trained in their use can do the actual recording. Audio and video tape recordings provide the simplest means of assessing your students' accuracy in observations of objects and events. The tape recordings can be used even if you teach in a nursery, preschool, or kindergarten. Audio recorders are relatively inexpensive, easy enough for even young children to operate, and durable. You can pre-record practical science situations and questions. Students can then listen to the tape, stop where instructed, and perform the required tasks using materials you supply. Or try taping assessment questions for students who might have difficulty reading them. This is especially useful for presenting materials to students who are blind or visually challenged. If you have such students in your class, record your questions and have the students respond to the questions by recording their answers or working with a classmate.

Occasionally, you may want to tape class discussions so you and your class can evaluate them. This can lead to *your* self-evaluation, perhaps consisting of these questions you have about your questioning techniques (as discussed in Chapter 4).

■ What cognitive processes and operations did I try to develop?
■ How much time was involved in teacher talk compared with student talk?
■ If I were to conduct this discussion again, how would I modify my behavior?

■ How many of my questions did *I* answer?
■ In how many situations did I not give sufficient wait-time after a question?
■ What types of reasoning questions did I use?

Beginning with a short segment of one of your class discussions (about 15 minutes would be sufficient), you might concentrate on how you open or structure the lesson. In subsequent recordings, you could focus on student responses or other aspects of the class discussion.

Teacher's Anecdotal Records

Teachers have always observed their students and made mental notes about their learning progress. The **anecdotal record** procedure merely requires written notes so they can be analyzed over time; they are a simple way to informally assess your students' accuracy about objects and events. Anecdotal record-keeping is in keeping with the emphasis you teach in science: that people should write their observations down, because humans forget things and may not remember when they need the data. Your records can be brief notations of student observations, reactions to hands-on/minds-on activities, and scientific questions raised by students. An anecdotal record can also be kept for an individual student (as in Figure 5–19) with short, concise entries at the end of each school day. These forms can be part of your portfolio.

Date	Learning Activity	Observation/Student Reaction

FIGURE 5–19

Individual student anecdotal record form

Checklists

Checklists are lists of student behaviors and/or skills to which observers simply respond *yes* or *no*. The check shows only whether the behavior/skill was observed, no effort is made on a checklist to assess *how well* the skill was performed. Checklists are effortless, quick, and handy. They help keep teacher observations focused. In making your own checklist, consider these items:

1. Do an analysis of what tasks are necessary for achieving a particular learning goal. Because this is a time consuming operation, you might refer to your science textbook teacher's manual scope and sequence chart, your school district or state science curriculum, or commercial science programs.
2. Once behaviors/skills are identified, choose how often you will observe and record on the checklist.
3. Your checklist should have sufficient spaces to conform to the observation frequency you've determined.
4. Keep a separate record for each student. Review it with students periodically to assess their progress in specific skills.

A sample of a checklist to observe students' skills in using a microscope is shown in Figure 5–20.

Rubrics

You may be wondering how you can find the time necessary for scoring, corollating, storing, tracking, and communicating the information harvested from your hands-on/minds-on authentic assessment tools. But authentic assessment must center on scientific knowledge, processes, and skills that cannot be effectively assessed by quick and easy methods such as multiple choice tests.

Data collected from authentic assessment activities has limited value if it is not "teacher-friendly." Observed student behavior must be **quantified** (translated into a usable numerical scale) or **qualified** (put into categories). Thus, it is essential that you have a system for coping with authentic assessment data. This system is called a **scoring guide** or **rubric**. In effect, it's a a simplified storage system.

What Is a Rubric?[24] *Rubric* is derived from the Latin word for red. The term was originally

Behavior/Skills	Date	Yes	No	Date	Yes	No	Date	Yes	No
Is careful in handling microscope									
Cleans lenses properly									
Focuses instrument properly									
Prepares slides correctly									
Arranges mirror for correct amount of light									

Student's Name _____

FIGURE 5–20
Checklist for observing microscope skills

applied to religious service directions—noted in red—in the margins of prayer books.

In science authentic assessment, a rubric is a set of criteria students see before they start an activity. A rubric spells out what features the teacher expects to see in each student response, and assigns these features to points along a scale. Students know exactly what is expected in order to get a particular score, because they examine the criteria before doing the activity. In summary, authentic assessment rubrics

1. take time to develop,
2. require teachers to identify specific science instructional goals,
3. let students know what is expected,
4. assist in teacher planning, and
5. facilitate communicating district's curriculum to public.

Authentic assessment is often criticized as being too subjective, but when rubrics are used, consistent scoring can be obtained. Figure 5–21 depicts the place rubrics have in the assessment cycle. The authentic assessment cycle can be thought of as having three W's and an H.

- **What** to assess?
- **Which** levels are assessed?
- To **Whom** is assessment communicated?
- **How** to assess?

Figure 5–21 also gives insight into the basic elements necessary for preparing or writing a rubric.

Rubric Writing. Teachers do not have to continually reinvent the wheel. This is true with writing rubrics to use with your authentic assessments. Research *rubric* or *assessment scoring* in the indexes of professional journals and you will find many helpful references. You might start with:

- California Learning Assessment System, California Department of Education, Sacramento, CA 94244;
- Professional Guide Series, Teacher-Created Materials, Inc., 6421 Industry Way, Westminster,CA;
- *A Practical Guide to Alternative Assessment, Update Magazine,* and *Student Outcomes: Performance Assessment Using the Dimensions of Learning Model,* ASCD, 1250 N. Pitt St., Alexandria, VA 22314; and
- Educational Resources Information Center (ERIC) Clearinghouses (throughout the United States). ERIC indexes education journals. Its *Current Index to Journals in Education* can be found on computer online search services or on CD-ROM at many libraries.

As the use of authentic assessment expands, scoring rubrics are being used in more and more classrooms. Criteria for good science projects are being shared among teachers, so teachers do not always have to do things alone. What things make up a good rubric?

FIGURE 5–21

Authentic assessment cycle

Source: Modified from Margaret Jorgensen, *Assessing Habits of Mind: Performance-Based Assessment in Science and Mathematics* (Columbus, OH: ERIC Clearinghouse for Science, Mathematics, and Environmental Education, 1994), 55.

Content standards
What to assess?

Assessment design and implementation
How to assess?

Scoring/rubric based on performance standards
Which levels to assess?

Reporting scores and performance standards
To whom communicated?

What Is It You're Trying to Asess? To produce a rubric, you must precisely state your assessment purpose(s), so that you can determine the specific details needed for the rubric. You need to generate precise delineations of what you expect your students to do. You must resolve what type(s) of learning you value and what skills, products, and behaviors you propose to observe. The purpose(s) of the assessment could be

1. to identify which students have mastered an explicit instructional unit, or
2. to find student diagnostic information.

In the first type of assessment, only two conclusions are possible: mastery and nonmastery. This is called *holistic scoring;* the teacher makes a single, overall judgment of the student's responsive quality. When looking at diagnostic information, many variations in performance are possible. In this case, *analytic* scoring is used: the teacher scores each performance on different, specific task elements, and the overall performance is the combination of the elements.

Which type of scoring rubric you pick depends on its intended use. The more precisely you can state your purpose, the better able you will be to construct a scoring guide or rubric. You may already have such purposes spelled out in your local or state science curriculum guides, or in your science textbook or innovative program. Once your purpose(s) are decided, your next step is to set up standards for your rubric.

Setting Your Assessment Standards. A rubric can use the same standards as assessment scoring. For example:

In looking at a child's transplanted seedling, the criteria might include *depth of planting* or *whether the seed is still alive;* in looking at a drawing of a mealworm, one criterion might be *inclusion of particular body parts;* and in judging a student's graph of an experiment, one criterion might be *whether the axes have been labeled correctly.*[25]

Standards can embrace science content/knowledge, processes, skills, actions, and feelings and attitudes. Include your students in establishing standards and scoring themselves, as there are benefits for both of you.

Let's examine how standards and scoring guides or rubrics are entwined.

Authentic Assessment Categories. There are no absolute, universal standards for assessing students's science activities. There isn't sufficient research to calculate what is an "appropriate" or "superior" five-year-old observation, or how well a ten-year-old might be expected to use a microscope. You will need to develop your own rubrics, starting with choosing which science areas to assess and then assigning levels of proficiency for each area.

There are four major categories of authentic assessment in science:

1. Using scientific knowledge or demonstrating conceptual understanding of major science connections and relationships.
2. Using science concepts, generalizations, and processes to solve problems and display conceptual comprehension.
3. Completing written reports and a variety of projects that supply results of your own problem-solving investigations, and concurrently applying specific results and concepts to a solution of related problems.
4. Communicating and displaying scientific attitudes in an assortment of practices that reveal understanding of science/technology/society issues.

After categories of science performance to be assessed are identified, levels of proficiency are determined for each of these categories.

How Can Performance Levels Be Scored? A review of the latest rubric scoring practices shows that a four-point rubric is the most frequently used because it is

- easy to write (descriptors are identified for an average response) and
- easy to grade (distinctions between the three scores are very distinct).

The number of points you pick for your rubric should be based on the needs of your class and your observations of what your students are actually doing in science activities.

Names of proficiency levels vary but basically there are these student levels:

- *Level 3, Advanced, Outstanding, Clear/Dynamic:* performance demonstrated thorough understanding.
- *Level 2, Proficient, Good, Acceptable/Adequate:* a complete and accurate understanding.
- *Level 1, Basic, Attempted, Inadequate:* partial proficiency, demonstrated incomplete understanding, or severe misconceptions.
- *Level 0:* Student did not do the task, complete the assignment, or show comprehension of the activity.

An example of general or generic levels of authentic assessment for the four major categories of science performance mentioned previously that may be used can be seen in Table 5–4.

TABLE 5–4
Authentic assessment rubric levels for major scientific categories

---

Knowing Science Information

1. Responds only in terms of specific examples experienced in class or presented in instructional materials.
2. Responds in terms of generalizations of these experiences but is unable to show relationships or to go beyond that which was experienced.
3. Demonstrates thorough understanding by applying information in a new context or by explaining relationships, implications, or consequences.

Using Science Concepts and Generalizations

1. Rarely connects previous learning with new situations in which it could be applied unless told what skill or idea is relevant.
2. Uses previous experiences in new situations once the relationship between the new and previous situation has been pointed out.
3. Works out what earlier learning could be applied in a new context by using relationships between one situation and another.

Doing Written Reports and Projects

1. What he writes or says is disorganized and difficult to follow; takes time to understand information in books or verbal directions.
2. Seems to have a clear idea of what he wants to express but does not always find the word to put it precisely or concisely; prefers to seek information orally than to use books.
3. Expresses himself clearly, using words appropriately and economically and at a level which can be understood by whomever receives the message; expands his knowledge through reading.

Experimenting/Investigating

1. Is unable to progress from one point to another in a practical investigation or inquiry without help, failing to grasp the overall plan.
2. Tries things out somewhat unsystematically unless the various steps in a practical inquiry are planned out for him, in which case he uses materials and collects results satisfactorily.
3. Has a clear idea of the reason for the various steps in an investigation; can work through them systematically, making reasonable decisions with only occasional guidance.

Source: Elizabeth Meng and Rodney L. Doran, *Improving Instruction and Learning Through Evaluation: Elementary School Science* (Columbus, OH: ERIC Clearinghouse for Science, Mathematics, and Environmental Education, 1993), 162–163.

FIGURE 5–22

Rubric for plants unit
authentic assessment

Source: Sabra Price and George
E. Hein, "Scoring Active
Assessments: Setting Clear
Criteria and Adapting Them To
Your Students Are the Key to
Scoring Classroom Performance,"
in *Science and Children* 32, no. 2
(Oct. 1994), 29.

Sample Scoring System

Question One. Students are asked to measure the height of two
seedings and to record their results.

Scoring Rubric for Question One

0 = The student either did not record results or reported measurements that were inaccurate by more than a certain percentage
determined by the teacher.

1 = The student did not record results, but did report approximate
measurements. The teacher needs to determine the meaning of
"approximate." This will depend on such things as the markings
on students' rulers and students' classroom experiences.

2 = The student recorded approximate measurements.

3 = The student recorded accurate measurements. The teacher
needs to determine the meaning of "accurate."

Question Two. Students are tasked to explain their recorded
measurements to their teacher.

Scoring Rubric for Question Two

0 = The student provided either no explanation or one that makes no
sense to the teacher or is unrelated to any unit activities.

1 = The student's explanation related to unit activities but did not
explain the growth pattern.

2 = The student provided an explanation for the growth pattern.

3 = The student gave more than one reasonable explanation for the
growth pattern.

Figure 5–22 shows how authentic assessment using a rubric can be applied to a science unit involving students observing pairs of growing plants and answering questions about them. Because the rubric is detailed, teachers will need to adapt it to their particular situations.

An assessment rubric for a hands-on/minds-on activity is given in Figure 5–23. The scientific process of identification by sense of touch is assessed by students touching (without using eyes) and calculating which object is rubber. Prior to beginning, the teacher tells them there are five objects in the box. The scoring rubric is:

■ one point for correctly identifying rubber, and

■ one point for each property identified (must be one which could distinguish rubber from the other materials) to a maximum of two points

This rubric lends itself to many variations (e.g., identifying all five materials and properties, substituting liquids, or tasting common foods). What additional tests can you invent and what rubric would you use?

It is impossible to supply a rubric for every authentic assessment technique introduced in this chapter. Selected samples have been given and extensive references are provided for you to research, construct, try out, and refine with your students rubrics for *your* authentic assessment.

Assessment Guide for a Sensory Activity

Material given to pupils:

Squares of material on inner surface

Numbers on outer surface of box

Folded edge to conceal materials

Space

Question Page

Inside the box behind each number there is a thin square which may be made of:

>   glass
>   metal
>   wood
>   leather
>   rubber

Put your fingers in the box and feel the squares.

(a) Decide which is *rubber.* Write below the number that is in front of the one you think is rubber:

(b) How did you decide it was this one?

_____

_____

_____

_____

Comment

The tester showed the pupils how to put their fingers into the box through the space and touch the squares of material on the inside of the numbered surface. The tester than presented the question in the following words:

For this question you use your fingertips to feel the surfaces inside the box behind the numbers, like this. Stuck on the inside there are thin squares of five different things: glass, metal, wood, leather, and rubber. By feeling them only (don't try to peek!) decide which one is rubber. When you have decided, put down the number which is in front of the one you think is rubber. Then write down at (b) how you decided it was this one.

Marking scheme

(a) 5   1 mark
(b) One mark for each acceptable
    property to a maximum of   2 marks
    Examples of acceptable properties:
>   smooth
>   soft/squashy
>   spongy/bouncy
>   can press into it
To be acceptable the property must be one which could distinguish rubber from the other materials.

FIGURE 5–23

Rubric for hands-on/minds-on authentic assessment

Source: Elizabeth Meng and Rodney L. Doran, *Improving Instruction and Learning Through Evaluation: Elementary School Science* (Columbus, OH: ERIC Clearinghouse for Science, Mathematics, and Environmental Education, 1993), 146.

Storage and Retrieval of Rubric Data. Since teachers began scoring and grading students' work, there has been a need for ways to productively store the data that is collected. Most teachers keep folders or portfolios of students' tests, work samples, health records, and other pertinent information. Though it would be superb to assess every skill of every student on every hands-on/minds-on science activity, time and other teaching constraints make this most unlikely.

A practical compromise is a system that assists teachers in assembling student skills and performance assessments by using a sampling system. A Sampling Assessment Rubric Chart is seen in Figure 5–24. For each hands-on/minds-on activity, the teacher selects skills appropriate to that specific task. Those skills become the focus for specific observations or assessments. A rubric for performance levels is determined by the teacher beforehand using a three-point system, with 3 as the highest level. Where a number score does not appear, it indicates the student did not conduct any activity that required that performance skill on that day, or the teacher did not observe the student performing the skill. A chart like this can be put on the computer to save the teacher time in organizing assessment data. Visual records, such as video recordings or photographs, can supplement the

Student Name: John Lidstone			Science Unit: Earth/Environmental	
Activity Assessed	Date	Observation/ Record Data	Manipulative Skills	Data Interpretation
1	9-18-96	3	3	
2	10-19-96	2	2	2
3	11-27-96		3	
4	12-10-96	3		3
5	01-08-97	2	3	
6	02-02-97			3
7	03-20-97	3		
8	04-21-97		3	2
9	05-15-97	3	3	
10	06-06-97			3

FIGURE 5–24

Hands-on/minds-on skills sample rubric record

Source: Modified from Elizabeth Meng and Ronald L. Doran, *Improving Instruction and Learning Through Evaluation: Elementary School Science* (Columbus, OH: ERIC Clearinghouse for Science, Mathematics, and Environmental Education, 1993), 164.

skills assessment chart. The overall assessment is balanced and significant because data are collected over a period of time.

The development of authentic assessments is worthwhile for both you and your students. Give it a try!

AUTHENTIC ASSESSMENT APPLICATIONS

Teaching a science lesson or unit requires thorough planning, skillful execution, and careful, constant review and modification. Here is a suggested format to use to assess your science teaching:

1. Develop an assessment plan based on your goals and objectives for teaching science. Identify your objectives clearly. Avoid objectives that are vague, nebulous, or too broad. Whenever possible, write your objectives in specific, observable terms. Emphasize objectives you can phrase in human behavior. Good objectives are specific, capable of being observed (and therefore assessed), and varied.
2. Identify and stress the specific scientific skills, knowledge, and processes you will emphasize during your science teaching.
3. Choose appropriate assessment techniques (hands-on/minds-on, oral, written, pictorial, etc.). Table 5–5 shows how to match your

TABLE 5–5

Matching authentic assessments to science teaching goals

	Authentic Assessment Procedures		
	Oral	Written	Performance
Instructional Strategy: Individual	A student can be called on in class to give a brief summary of basic information discussed in class that day. A student can be asked to critique an experiment conducted by a fellow classmate or critique a published study.	A student can be asked to write a review of a science program shown on television. A student can be asked to write a brief report of research he/she conducted.	A student can take responsibility for studying an experiment and presenting a demonstration of it to the class.
Instructional Strategy: Group	Students can collaborate on presenting a summary of the key concepts studied in a unit. Students can conduct a roundtable discussion of an important topic.	Students can collaborate on producing a bibliography of important books or articles.	Students can share the responsibility for preparing and presenting an experiment or discussion on an interesting topic to the class or school.
Instructional Strategy: Class	A class might conduct an assembly on a topic of interest or concern to the entire school.	A class might keep a log of their science experiments and provide written comments and critiques of each other's work.	A class might dramatize an important event in the history of science.

teaching strategies (individual, small group, or total class) to your assessment procedures. Oral, written, and performance tasks are the assessment devices used to assess students' science processes, knowledge, skills, and attitudes.

4. Select and use a variety of assessment techniques. Avoid overdependency on any one type of evaluating device. Include a wide range of tests and other assessment devices such as:
   Essay
   Enhanced and justified multiple-choice
   Pictorial assessments
   Situational assessments
   Performance or motor skills assessment
   Checklist/rating scale
   Student self-assessment
   Student observations
   Students explain actions
   Listen to student discussions

5. Gather and record authentic assessment data to identify the performance and cognitive levels of your students. Make your assessment techniques assess what you taught and want learned. Assess only those things that your students were exposed to or can reasonably be expected to project. Assess often, and have your students participate in the results. If you assess your students continually, you can lessen their anxiety about assessment, especially if the results are used for instruction instead of punishment. You should stress that assessment is merely one step along the path to learning, not the end of the journey.

6. Analyze the assessment data. Continually assess your assessment. Scrutinize your assessment often and revise your assessment techniques as a result of your students' responses to them.

7. Study the implications of your assessment data analysis for future teaching. Your assessment should show what you value in science teaching. Your students will follow your lead. If you stress memorization or recall in your assessment, they will memorize. If process, problem solving, and higher cognitive levels of thinking are important to you, make certain your assessment reflects these criteria.

8. Involve your students in your assessment. Invite your students' comments on your assessments and even have them try making up their own. Suggest that they make self-assessments, such as that shown in Figure 5–25.

9. Continue your own self-assessment. Teachers today must be committed to improving the learning of all students. You probably believe "students do not fail to learn; they can only assimilate what their minds are ready to learn." Therefore, do not blame the students or yourself if not all of them do well on some form of assessment. Use the situation to look more closely at your students. At the same time, look more introspectively at your own teaching to examine the impact of your goals, methods of teaching, and assessment techniques. Such self-assessment will also make you more effective with students who are physically or mentally challenged, or who have culturally diverse backgrounds. Assessment will help you grow as a person and a teacher. It will help you see the individual differences of your students with clearer and more sensitive vision. Learning to use assessment effectively will help you become a better teacher, and it is clearly worth the effort.

Mark a B below for what you knew before-about the science topics we studied. Mark an A for what you knew after the study.

Science Topics

volcanoes	1	②	3	④	5
		B		A	
floods	①	2	3	④	5
	B			A	
weather	1	2	③	4	⑤
				B	A

1 = knew little
5 = knew a lot

FIGURE 5–25

Self-assessment device

SUMMARY

Assessment in science education is undergoing an exciting transition. Newer and more relevant assessment techniques are needed for conducting guided discovery hands-on/minds-on STS problem-solving science programs. This has given rise to many different assessment terms; the term used in this text is authentic assessment.

In constructivist teaching/learning, assessment is a continual process: for planning, guiding, and enriching students' science learning; for communication with students, school administrators, parents, and the public; for monitoring outcomes of your science program; and as an influence on science curriculum and teaching.

Seven principles form the foundation for assessment; they critically affect the *what, how,* and *how well* of your science teaching/learning. Three general kinds of assessment were outlined: *diagnostic* (before starting teaching), *formative* (during teaching), and *summative* (after teaching). The purposes and effective uses of each kind of assessment were examined.

Our study of authentic assessment was organized around the five constructivist learning cycles introduced in Chapter 3: Invitation, Exploration, Discovery, Explanation/Solution, and Taking Action. Specific assessment examples were given for each stage, and additional techniques applicable to all stages were offered. Discrepant events, concept mapping, hands-on/minds-on practicals, graphing, model building, and projects all were suggested as possible techniques for authentic assessment. Special attention was given to two assessment techniques and their unique contributions to all aspects of authentic assessment: *portfolios* and *rubrics.*

Rubrics—authentic assessment scoring guides—have vital functions in assessment. They are a tool to assign value to a given assessment. Samples of rubrics or scoring guides are appearing in the literature and teachers are beginning to adapt these to their teaching situations as well as write their own rubrics. Keep these things in mind:

■ Set clear assessment standards to interpret the specifics of your students' work.
■ Determine levels of rubric scoring—often on a four-point scale—that are applicable to the unique scientific processes, skills, content, and attitudes you are teaching.

Examples of generic and particular rubrics were displayed.

The issue of storage, retrieval, and subsequent usage of authentic assessment data was faced and a sampling assessment rubric chart was offered as one way of handling this dilemma.

SELF-ASSESSMENT AND FURTHER STUDY

1. Pick several hands-on/minds-on science activities in which students handle simple science equipment and materials. Construct authentic assessment devices, teacher checklists, and rubrics to record, score, and rate their scientific processes and psychomotor skills. Use the prototypes of assessment devices presented in this chapter and these references:

- R. J. Marzano, D. L. Pickering, and J. McTighe, *Performance Assessment Using the Dimensions of Learning* (Aurora, CO: Mid-Continent Regional Educational Laboratory, 1993).
- E. Quellmalz, "Developing criteria for performance assessments: The missing link," *Applied Measurements in Education, 4,* no. 4, 319–332.

2. Performance assessments are based on observations and judgments. List six examples of instances outside your school setting where this mode of assessment enters your lifestyle; e.g., sports activities, hobbies, or work place. Identify specific skills that are inherent in each situation and the levels of performance you would assign for a rubric of each.

3. Arrange your class for setting up and maintaining student portfolios using suggestions and references in this chapter. To begin, ask your students to put in their portfolio two samples of their work that *they* are most proud of:
   - how they learned something new;
   - where they solved a problem;
   - something they "invented" (unusual or different);
   - evidence of growth in scientific knowledge; or
   - anything *they* feel is important to include.

4. Make a list of authentic assessments that focus on scientific processes or skills and products.

5. Work with a group of students to devise ways of cooperatively assessing your teaching and their learning. Have your students prepare a variety of assessment techniques (such as the pictorial type), administer and score them, and share the results with their peers. When they have completed this work, assess the assessment with your students.

6. Prepare a practical hands-on/minds-on authentic assessment at the conclusion of a science study. Use the SISS Science Process Laboratory Skills Test introduced in this chapter as a starting point. Write a simply worded problem with a drawing or photo of the actual equipment that students will handle during the test. Arrange equipment and materials on tables. Give succinct directions and have students manipulate equipment and record their observations and analysis in test booklets. Review students' responses with them and produce a rubric collaboratively. For assistance see:
   - Darling–Hammond, Einbender, Frelow, *Authentic Assessment in Practice: A Collection of Portfolios, Performance Tasks, Exhibitions and Documentation* (New York, NY: National Center for Restructuring Education, Schools, and Teaching, Teachers College, Columbia University, 1993).
   - Janet Brown and Richard Shavelson, "New Ways to Measure What Students Know and Can Do," *Instructor,* March 1994.

7. Explain why you agree or disagree with this statement: Performance assessments are too loaded with potential bias due to evaluator subjectivity to justify the deliberation they are getting.

8. What is your opinion of linking authentic assessment to the constructivist learning cycle? Document your reasons based upon students' learning, the goals of science education, and your views of what is effective assessment. Include research sources, perhaps beginning with:
   - G. W. Bracey, "Assessing the New Assessments," *Principal, 72,* no. 3, January 1993, 34–36.
   - B. R. Worthern, "Critical Issues That Will Determine the Future of Alternative Assessment," *Phi Delta Kappan, 74,* no. 6, February 1993, 444–454.

9. Why is it risky to use true–false or completion test items for assessing student science learning and then using these results for calculating grades? Explain under what conditions such test items could be legitimately used in assessment.

10. Videotape a science activity where small groups of students are involved in hands-on/minds-on operations. Then analyze your students' scientific processes, behaviors, and reactions and prepare a rubric (including levels of performance) based on your analysis. Check the following for suggestions:
    - Ronald L. Doran et. al., "Authentic Assessment: An Instrument for Consistency," *The Science Teacher, 60,* no. 6, September 1993, 37–41.
    - G. J. Pallrand, "Multi-Media Assessment: Evaluating your Students' Thinking Skills," *The Science Teacher, 60,* no. 6, September 1993, 42–45.

NOTES

1. Gerald William Foster and William Anton Heiting, "Embedded Assessment: This Method Not Only Helps Teachers to Evaluate Students But Also Guides Instruction," *Science and Children, 32,* no. 2, October 1994, 30.
2. Richard J. Stiggins, *Student-Centered Classroom Assessment* (Englewood Cliffs; NJ: Merrill/Prentice Hall, 1994), viii.
3. Anne Grall Reichel, "Performance Assessment: Five Practical Approaches: *Science and Children, 32,* no. 2, October 1994, 21.
4. Mary Lewis Sivertsen, *State of the Art: Transforming Ideas for Teaching and Learning Science. A Guide for Elementary Science Education* (Washington, DC: U. S. Department of Education, Office of Educational Research and Improvement (Sep. 1993) 11.
5. For further details read: Elizabeth Meng and Rodney L. Doran, *Improving Instruction and Learning Through Evaluation: Elementary School Science* (Columbus, OH: ERIC Clearinghouse for Science, Mathematics, and Environmental Education, 1993; and John Jarolimek and Clifford D. Foster, Sr., *Teaching and Learning in the Elementary School,* 5th ed. Chapter 13, "Assessment and Evaluation of Student Performance" (Englewood Cliffs, NJ: Merrill/Prentice Hall, 1993).
6. Richard D. Kellough et al, *Integrating Mathematics and Science for Kindergarten and Primary Children* (Englewood Cliffs, NJ: Merrill/Prentice-Hall, 1996), 121.
7. Kellough, ibid., 120.
8. Margaret Jorgensen, *Assessing Habits of Mind: Performance-based Assessment in Science and Mathematics* (Columbus, OH: ERIC Clearinghouse for Science, Mathematics, and Environmental Education, 1994), 15.
9. John Jarolimek and Clifford D. Foster, Sr., *Teaching and Learning in the Elementary School,* 5th ed. Chapter 13, "Assessment and Evaluation of Student Performance" (Englewood Cliffs, NJ: Merrill/Prentice-Hall, 1993).
10. J. L. Herman, "What research tells us about good assessment," *Educational Leadership, 49.* no. 8, May 1992, 74–78; and L. A. Shepard, "Psycho-metrician' Beliefs About Learning," *Educational Researcher, 20,* no. 7, October 1991, 2–16.
11. Senta A. Raizen et al., *Assessment in Elementary School Science Education* (Andover, MA: The National Center for Improving Science Education, a partnership of the NETWORK, Inc. and The Biological Sciences Curriculum Study, Colorado Springs, CO, 1989), 45–74.
12 The author acknowledges invaluable contributions from *Science and Children, 32,* no. 2, October 1994, 1–72.; Richard J. Stiggins, *Student-Centered Classroom Assessment* (Englewood Cliffs, NJ: Merrill/Prentice-Hall, 1993); and especially Alaska Science Consortium, *The Great Northern Science Book* (Fairbanks, AK: University of Alaska, Spring 1992), 1–36.
13. Joseph D. Novak and D. Musondra, "A Twelve-year Longitudinal Study of Science Concept Learning," *American Educational Research Journal, 28,* 1991, 117–153.
14. For an excellent summary of the SISS and other international science surveys see Rodney L. Doran, "What Research Says ... About Assessment," *Science and Children, 27,* no. 8 (May 1990), 26–27.
15. For assistance with making science logs or mini-books see Charlotte King, "Making First-Class Books," *Science and Children, 28,* no. 3 (November/December 1990): 40–41 and J. Baskwill and P. Whitman, *A Guide to Classroom Publishing* (New York: Scholastic, 1986).
16. Elizabeth Meng and Rodney L. Doran, *Improving Instruction and Learning Through Evaluation: Elementary School Science* (Columbus, OH: ERIC Clearinghouse for Science, Mathematics, and Environmental Education, 1993), 91–92, 123–125.
17. For greater detail on multiple-choice testing see Janice K. Johnson, ". . . Or None of the Above: What Do Your Multiple-Choice Questions Really Measure?" *The Science Teacher, 56,* no. 4 (April 1989), 57–61.
18. For additional suggestions on multiple-choice (and other kinds) testing improvement, read Chapter 10, "Evaluating and Grading Student Performance," in Robert E. MacDonald, *A*

Handbook of Basic Skills and Strategies for Beginning Teachers: Facing the Challenge of Teaching in Today's Schools (New York: Longman, 1991), 189–211.

19. See the clearly written, comprehensive coverage of multiple-choice test improvement in Jacqueline Shick, "Textbook Tests: The Right Formula?" *The Science Teacher, 57,* no. 6 (September 1990), 33–39.

20. Anne Grall Reichel, "Performance Assessment: Five Practical Approaches," *Science and Children, 32,* no. 2, October 1994, 24.

21. For additional directions and assistance with this activity see "Invent a Plant.Bio Key: Arts and Crafts Simulation Adaptation," developed by Outdoor Biology Instructional Strategies (Berkeley, CA: University of California, 1979), 1–6, and published by Delta Education, Nashua, NH.

22. The author is appreciative of the comprehensive description of the purposes, development, and uses of portfolio assessment in science education for and with students in the entire assessment issue of *Science and Children, 32,* no. 2, October 1994. Also, Concetta Doti Ryan, "Portfolio Assessment Chapter," in *Professional Guide to Authentic Assessment* (Westminster, CA: Teacher-Created Materials, Inc. 1994), 7–20; and Mary Hamm and Dennis Adams, "Portfolio Assessment: It's Not Just for Artists Anymore," *The Science Teacher, 58,* no. 5 (May 1991), 18–24.

23. Lehman W. Barnes and Marianne B. Barnes, "Assessment, Practically Speaking. How can we measure hands-on science skills?" *Science and Children* 28, no. 6 (March 1991), 14–15.

24. Recognition is due to the following for ideas that influenced the structure of this section: Margaret Jorgensen, "How Can Scoring Rubrics Communicate Complex Information? in *Assessing Habits of Mind: Performance-Based Assessment in Science and Mathematics* (Columbus, OH: ERIC Clearinghouse for Science, Mathematics, and Environmental Education, 1994), 47–58; Elizabeth Meng and Rodney L. Doran, "Using the information gathered," in Elizabeth Meng and Rodney L. Doran, *Improving Instruction and Learning Through Evaluation: Elementary School Science* (Columbus, OH: ERIC Clearinghouse for Science, Mathematics, and Environmental Education, 1993), 136–166; and Sabra Price and George E. Hein, "Scoring Active Assessment: Setting Clear Criteria and Adapting Them to Your Students as the Keys to Scoring Classroom Performances," *Science and Children, 32,* no. 2, October 1994, 26–29.

25. Sabra Price and George E. Hein, "Scoring Active Assessment: Setting Clear Criteria and Adapting Them to Your Students as the Keys to Scoring Classroom Performance," *Science and Children, 32,* no. 2, October 1994, 27.

Planning for a Supportive Science Classroom

If we want children to live fully today and at the same time be prepared to live fully throughout their entire lives, then their learning cannot be left up to chance encounters with the environment. The adults who care for, guide, and teach children will want to have clear goals and objectives for children's learning.[1]

PROVIDING DIFFERENT KINDS OF SUPPORT

"As the number of students increases in a school, they all have less elbow room and less space of their own," science teacher Ron Jones observes. "In this classroom, students know where their space is, which equipment is theirs, and what they're responsible for. They have more space and more ownership of that space."

The physical arrangement of the classroom is an important part of the experience Jones has designed for his students. He has set up a centralized lecture area, although he does very little "lecturing." Lab tables line three walls of the room. Each lab area has two drawers of equipment, one with slides and other materials for working with microscopes and one with beakers and test tubes for chemistry activities. Each lab area also is assigned one of the microscopes that are kept in a nearby cabinet. In addition, Jones has trays of equipment that he gets out when a class needs them for what he calls "cut and paste": scissors, glue, markers, and so on.

Jones' classroom organization is not really the key to his success, not the reason why former students have written him notes that say "The only reason I came to school each day was because of science." Students like his science class, Jones knows, because they want to "do science, not read about it."

"I try to teach less, but do it better," he reports. He points out that science knowledge is increasing so fast that no one can teach it all. "After you're taught content for a while, you can see the heart of the subject matter," he says. "You can pick out the fundamentals and teach those clearly. The students can figure out the rest on their own."

Jones begins most classes with a 10 to 15 minute introduction of a science concept that he has selected from any of three textbooks he uses as resources. Students take notes in special notebooks they set aside for science class. Then they have the rest of the period to work with partners on lab activities that enable them to experiment with that day's concept and learn more about it through a hands-on inquiry approach.

Jones has adapted these lab activities from activity ideas he found in textbooks, making any changes necessary so the activities match the concepts he has introduced and meet the students' needs. Some activities take more than one class period, but students work at their own pace. They know what they are expected to learn and produce and when everything is due. "I give them the information and then let them go. That way, they have more responsibility for what they do and learn," Jones says.

Jones, who teaches seminars in developing a nurturing environment in the classroom, says he begins each year by getting to know his students. As they move into the subject area, he tends to answer their questions with more questions. This technique often frustrates them at first, he reports, but after only two weeks, they are ready to move directly from his introduction of a concept into a lab activity with their partners. He is always ready to make changes and shows his students he cares whether they understand the concepts. "Students work better with people they like and people who like them," he says.

Jones has accumulated his knowledge of science, students, and teaching during sixteen years in the classroom and seven years of working part-time as a teacher and part-time in his school district's personnel office, interviewing potential teachers and coordinating their hiring. This is the first year he will be back in the classroom full-time, and he is clearly excited. To him, teaching science is "like working with your twenty-four best friends."

It can take years to develop Ron Jones' level of comfort with students and with teaching science. Some school systems and districts offer new teachers a head start by pairing them with experienced teachers who serve as mentors or master teachers. These mentors are available to help beginning teachers handle classroom management; to guide them in choosing textbook lessons, activities, and labs; and to show them how to modify activities to meet their students' needs. School or district in-service sessions can also allow teachers to share new approaches and explain ways they have adapted activities.

If your district does not offer this kind of support, you might suggest it, along with a "hands-on" learning day that involves teachers in making science discoveries, just like students.

In previous chapters you learned that science is a dynamic human activity made up of products, processes, STS problem-solving skills, and attitudes that are closely interrelated. Also, you discovered that people are environmental investigators from birth (and even before birth, we are discovering), using all their senses to observe, sample, experience, and construct concepts about everything around them. In addition, you saw how science teaching is concerned with developing scientifically/technologically literate citizens who understand how science, technology, and society influence one another and are able to use this knowledge in their everyday decision making. The *why* and *what* in your science teaching is concerned with these science attributes, how students develop and learn, how science/technology/society are interrelated, and how scientifically/technologically literate citizens are developed.

In Chapter 3, you investigated *how* these aspects of science education are effectively achieved by using the learning cycle in a guided discovery hands-on/minds-on teaching/learning approach. This chapter will focus on helping you put this all into action with suggestions for

- selecting science goals and objectives meaningful for your students,
- planning the best learning experiences for your students to successfully accomplish their goals,
- arranging a rich learning science classroom environment, and
- managing and guiding student learning.

Only you can supply the *when* and *where*. To start, let's look at the levels of planning needed to become a successful science classroom manager.

CONSTRUCTIVIST LEVELS OF PLANNING

If you trust that students learn every day of their lives, construct their own knowledge, and that most effective learning is integrated and whole, you will agree that planning for teaching is more complicated than getting pre-made lesson plans from a commercial source outside your classroom. In Chapter 2, we saw that constructivists assert that students must initiate much of their own learning. Students construct their own knowledge and comprehension; therefore, it holds true that no one can teach anything to anyone else. However, constructivists do believe that:

1. Students should not be left alone to construct their own knowledge.
2. Teachers should identify goals to guide students' learning.
3. Teachers need to structure the learning environment and schedule ample time for students to explore and experiment within that environment.
4. Effective teachers plan learning experiences around students' interests and needs, framed to assist students to achieve the goals.
5. Teachers should modify their teaching based upon observations of their students in the learning environment.
6. Teachers are the decision makers. They decide *what* and *how* students will learn, basing their decisions on knowledge of their students, the subject matter, and the community.

To select, prepare, and provide meaningful science learning activities for your students, you must plan on a long-range and short-range basis. Your students' achievement of science understandings, processes, skills, and attitudes depends on how well you spell out these long-term, daily, individual lesson expectations. To accomplish this, teacher planning usually takes place on three interrelated levels:

1. *Your Aims: Entire School Year.* Broad science education aims from national science groups, state education department, school district, school, textbook, or other sources.
2. *Your Goals: General.* Interdisciplinary thematic teaching unit.
3. *Your Objectives: Specific.* Individual lessons or learning activities incorporating students' interests and needs.

Each of these three levels of planning plays a part in successful student learning.

Let's look now at the function that aims, goals, and objectives can play in your science teaching: what they are, where you can find them, and how you can personalize their use for your particular science teaching/learning needs.

Aim for High Aspirations for Science Teaching/Learning

Aims are the highest expectations or general purposes you have for yourself, your students, your school, and your community, usually for the entire school year. They often are broad and philosophical, and may include such science education principles as these from The National Science Education Standards Project:

- All students, regardless of gender, cultural or ethnic background, physical or learning disabilities, future aspirations, or interest and motivation in science should have the opportunity to attain high levels of scientific literacy.
- The science that all students are expected to learn is defined so that students have sufficient time to develop a deep understanding of essential scientific ideas rather than superficial acquaintance with many isolated facts. All students can attain science knowledge with understanding.
- Science in school will reflect the intellectual tradition—modes of inquiry, rules of evidence, and ways of formulating questions—that characterizes the practice of contemporary science.[2]

How you respond to these broad principles and others like them shapes how you view science teaching. They are your philosophy of science teaching, or your aims, and were discussed in Chapter 1. The aims you subscribe to shape what you value in science teaching and influence every one of your teaching acts.

The aims of science programs in elementary and middle schools should correlate with other curricular areas and be part of a planned and coordinated K–12 curriculum. Generally, where such a K–12 curriculum exists, a syllabus is provided to teachers for planning purposes. Is one available to you?

Because aims are so broad, some may take more time to achieve than the years you have students in your elementary or middle school. This was evidenced in Chapter 1 by the broad "ten standards" or aims that scientifically/technologically literate students should achieve in exemplary elementary/middle schools by the seventh grade.

You may find aims for your science teaching in publications from national science teacher organizations such as NSTA and AAAS, your state education department, your school or local school board, or a science textbook. Chapter 1 listed some of these sources. They can provide you with a general direction for your science teaching. After that beginning, you will need to gear your planning specifically to your philosophy, the philosophy of the school and community where you teach, and the needs, interests, and abilities of the students you have in your classroom. More specific goals and objectives will help you meet these criteria.

Interdisciplinary Thematic Units: Your More Specific Goals

Your interdisciplinary thematic unit goals should answer this question:

> *What specific attainable outcomes do I want my students to accomplish by the end of this year?*

Notice that interdisciplinary thematic unit goals have these characteristics that make them distinct from aims:

1. Although interdisciplinary thematic unit goals are somewhat long-range, they have a shorter, definitive time frame, or *target date,* for being accomplished.
2. Thematic unit goals are more specific than aims.
3. Students can accomplish these goals within their developmental levels.
4. Interdisciplinary thematic unit goals may originate with local schools and teachers or on the national or state levels.

5. These goals may be stated in terms of what is expected of the teacher, or what is expected of the students.
6. Because they are more specific, goals can be assessed, making local schools and individual teachers more accountable for specific learnings by predetermined target times.

How May Goals Help Me in My Science Teaching? Since you probably teach many subjects besides science, you may well ask, "How can I use goals in my teaching?" Every time you select anything for your students to learn, you are setting goals that give direction to your teaching and help you plan to accomplish your goals. Having goals also helps you to assess or measure the extent to which your students have achieved these goals. Identifying goals for your science teaching and student learning does not restrict you in revising your teaching, nor does it curb students' spontaneity and interests. Instead, goals act like a compass to guide you: furnishing the direction for choosing teaching/learning activities, suggesting student/teacher interactions, and helping you clarify and communicate what you are doing in your science program.

Goals help you articulate your science program to your students (so they know what is expected of them), to their parents, and to your colleagues and school administrators. In addition, written goals help a substitute teacher prepare good science lessons should you be absent. When someone visits your classroom (e.g., a parent or the principal) to observe your science lessons, well-planned goals show them where you're going.

Some teachers send goal statements home to parents when they seek materials or assistance:

> *One of the goals I have for your children this year is to plan, shop for, cook, serve, and clean up several meals, using what they've learned about good nutrition and consumer education. Below is a schedule of times when we could use your help and also some items we may need. If you are able to help, please support us by signing up. Thank you.*

In addition, you will often be asked to give a presentation at meet-the-teacher night or open-school night. Good goal statements will enhance your performance and show parents that you have carefully considered the things to which their children will be exposed.

Now you are ready to organize these broad goals into very specific ways to help your students achieve these goals. Teaching/learning interdisciplinary thematic science units will help you do this.

Organizing Goals Into Teachable Interdisciplinary Thematic Units.

After you identify the aims and goals for your class, your next task is organizing your goals into units of teachable size. Exciting science learning for your students relates to and originates from your broader science teaching aims and goals and your students' needs, interests, and intellectual development levels. Science interdisciplinary thematic units can help you provide this kind of learning for your students. Chapter 8 will supply specific ways in which disciplines from the whole science curriculum can be integrated.

Interdisciplinary thematic science units are organized around an interdisciplinary science theme, question, or central problem, rather than a single-subject topic. Thematic units expedite students' abilities to connect disciplines and unite school learning with their real-life experiences. They focus learning activities around large blocks of time and may take from several days to several weeks to complete. From a constructivist point of view, the topic to be studied should interest students and arise from a problem relevant to their lives. Units contain broad goals, as well as a wide range of detailed strategies and activities for students to learn the anticipated scientific content, processes, problem-solving skills, and attitudes. Interdisciplinary thematic units can be prepared and taught by one teacher, but may be a product of a team of teachers. In either case, interdisciplinary thematic science units offer opportunities for

- students to learn concepts as parts of an integrated whole in a particular science content area, rather than isolated informational bits and pieces,
- groups of students to build a sense of community over a period of time, by working together around a common concern, and
- students to see science concepts as relevant to their daily lives.

Actual unit formats vary; however, Figure 6–1 shows an example of an interdisciplinary thematic science unit on measuring from a state science curriculum guide. It contains these common interdisciplinary thematic science unit elements:

- *Theme, Topic, or Title.* States a focusing question ("Which Is More?").
- *Theme or Problem Overview.* Provides the setting or context for the problem ("Problem Overview").
- *Suggested Approach.* Provides an overview of the teaching/learning procedures and activities you might use to conduct the unit.
- *Materials.* Lists materials needed for the entire unit in quantities per student and per class.
- *Syllabus Emphasis.* Indicates the cross-reference of each activity to the science processes/ skills/science attitudes/content sections of the syllabus.
- *Suggested Schedule.* Lists specific program activities in the recommended sequence for instruction. Times shown are approximate amounts of weekly class time needed to complete activities.
- *More Ideas.* Lists other interdisciplinary activities from the whole elementary curriculum that can be used at the teacher's discretion to extend the unit, enrich the unit, or reinforce learning outcomes.

Built into this and every science interdisciplinary thematic unit is continuous assessment to help you monitor and modify the suggested unit plans as they actually unfold in your particular classroom. This is vital if your unit plan is to

PROBLEM OVERVIEW

A child is often confronted with problems that have to do with making comparisons. Determining which distance is longer or shorter, which object is heavier or lighter, or which container is larger or smaller in capacity are only a few of the many instances that occur in presenting the problem. The activities in this unit identify situations in which the student cannot easily resolve comparisons unless measurements are made. Each situation poses a different kind of measuring problem that will expose the student to objects and events with distinctive properties, provide an opportunity for the student to develop the skill of measuring, and help the student develop scientific attitudes toward investigations.

SUGGESTED APPROACH

This unit is flexible in many aspects. The total amount of time to be devoted to the unit or to individual activities can be adjusted in accordance with the teacher's judgment of student interest and readiness. Comparison activities can be deleted or changed in sequence according to the results of the preliminary brainstorming activity.

Some of the activities in the unit may provide students with new experiences to reinforce learning acquired earlier.

Some activities may serve as an introductory experience for more formal instruction at a later time. Care must be taken to keep the emphasis of each activity at the appropriate level for the students at this point in their development.

The unit has a strong connection to mathematics, providing many opportunities to develop other specific skills and understandings listed in the mathematics syllabus.

MATERIALS

(per student, unless otherwise indicated)

Paper squares, approximately 5 cm square or $2\frac{1}{8}$ inches square—100

Double-pan balance materials: support pans (pie plates), balance arm, etc. (one for two to four students)

Tongue depressors or ice cream sticks

Ruler (cm scale)

String 1–2 meters

Paper tape, 1–2 meters

Thermometer (one per two students)

Medicine cup

Kitchen measuring cup

Paper cups, 8 oz.

Sponges, mops (available for class)

Pails, small (one for two to four students)

Geoboards (four per class)

Small washers (one bag per class)

Colored rubber bands (four sets per class)

Balance board and fulcrum (one for two to four students)

Large washers (one bag per class)

Ice cubes, uniform size

Paper clips (one box per class)

Plasticine (one package per class)

Objects from home such as toys

Containers of various sizes: cereal boxes, plastic cans, tubs, bottles, etc.

Wrapping paper, brown (one roll per class)

Clock (wall type with sweep second hand)— one for class

FIGURE 6–1

Sample interdisciplinary thematic unit format

#	Activity Title	Week 1	Week 2	Week 3	Week 4	Week 5	Week 6	Emphasis
1	Brainstorming Which is More?	▨						Classifying/Communicating Information A-2.24 Contributions, others I-C Objects, events, properties
2	Measuring Distance		▨					Measuring/Manipulating Ideas A-1.31 Concepts, terms, techniques I-C-1.3 Object properties, amount of space
3	Measuring Temperature			▨				Measuring/Manipulating Ideas A-2.21 Safety I-C-1.5 Object properties, surrounding conditions
4	Measuring Capacity				▨			Measuring/Manipulating Ideas A-2.22 Use of resources I-C-1.3 Object properties, amount of space
5	Measuring Surface					▨		Measuring, Using Numbers/Manipulating Ideas B-1.2 Resourcefulness, innovativeness I-C Objects, events, properties
6	Measuring Weight					▨	▨	Manipulating, Measuring/Communicating Information B-1.2 resourcefulness, innovativeness I-C-1 Object properties, material condition I-D-3.1 Uniform balance beam
7	Measuring Time						▨	Manipulating, Measuring/Communicating Information A-2.25 Truthful reporting I-C-2.2 Event, duration of time

MORE IDEAS

1. Make cutouts of hands, feet, or head profile. Use very small squares to determine the amount of surface.
2. Determine which is the shortest route from home to school.
3. Determine which is colder, warmer, or the same temperature: indoors-outdoors; one person's hand or another's hand; oral temperatures (done by nurse).
4. Determine which is heavier: one sheet of paper or a penny; one sugar cube and a glass of water or the sugar cube dissolved in the glass of water; a slice of bread or the slice of bread toasted; two slices of bread or 1 hard-boiled egg.
5. Determine volume change in popcorn when cooked. ($\frac{1}{4}$ liter uncooked equals what volume cooked? Compare brands.)
6. Determine which takes longer: cold water to freeze or hot water to freeze; a large diameter candle to burn a fixed length or a small diameter candle to burn the same length.
7. Determine equals in a student's own body dimensions: handspan, distance between ears, head size (circumference), arm length (nose to fingertips), foot size, knee height, step or pace, arm span, waist, length of nose, width of smile. It is important for you to take into special consideration possible differences in a student's measurements due to a handicapping condition.

Source: Supplement to the Science Syllabus, Level 1 (Ages 4 through 7) (Albany, NY: The University of the State of New York, The State Education Department, 1986), 30–31.

respond to the unique learning pace and styles of you and your students.

Here is an abridged bibliography to start adding to your knowledge about interdisciplinary thematic units:

- N. J. Gerhrke, "Explorations of Teachers' Development of Integrative Curriculum," *Journal of Curriculum and Supervision, 6,* no. 2, Winter 1991, 107–117.
- H. H. Jacobs et al., *Interdisciplinary Curriculum: Design and Implementation* (Alexandria, VA: Association for Supervision and Curriculum Development, 1989).
- John Jarolimek and Clifford D. Foster, Sr., *Teaching and Learning in the Elementary School,* 5th ed. (Englewood Cliffs, NJ: Merrill/Prentice Hall, 1993), 149–152.
- B. New, "The Integrated Early Childhood Curriculum: New Interpretations Based on Research and Practice," in C. Seefeldt (Ed.), *The Early Childhood Curriculum: A Review of Current Research* (New York: Teachers College Press, 1993), 286–325.
- W. M. Roth, "Bridging the Gap Between School and Real Life: Toward an Integration of Science, Mathematics and Technology in the Context of Authentic Practice," *School Science and Mathematics, 92,* no. 6, October 1992, 307–317.
- S. Willis, "Interdisciplinary Learning: Movement to Link the Disciplines Gains Momentum," in *Curriculum Update* (Alexandria, VA: Association for Supervision and Curriculum Development, November 1992).

Translating Interdisciplinary Thematic Units Into Your Specific Objectives and Lesson Plans. After studying Figure 6–1, surveying the above resources, and preparing your own unit, it is time to break the learning activities into manageable pieces for each day's teaching. Daily lesson plans help you to do this.

Visualize lesson planning the same way you do vacation planning, as shown in Table 6–1. Short-range vacation planning uses state and local maps to plan daily trips, just as lesson planning uses specific learning behaviors. In both cases, assessment is used—to plan next-day's travel or the next teaching lesson. Daily lesson plans help you select and use specific objectives in your science program, but these objectives must be flexible enough that you can adjust them according to your students' enthusiasm and curiosity. Table 6–2 gives an analogy between the fields of medicine and teaching using aims, goals, and objectives. You can see from this table that after the broad aim (originated in both cases by outside authorities), physicians and teachers use their professional training and sharpened observational skills to diagnose (set goals) and prescribe actions (state objectives).

Tailoring Lesson Plans for Interdisciplinary Thematic Science Units. This section focuses on how to make and use science lesson plans

TABLE 6–1

Similarities between lesson planning and vacation planning

Time Frame	Lesson Planning	Vacation Planning
Long-range	Select aims, goals, and objectives; establish interdisciplinary thematic units in large time blocks	Decide on cross-country drive; select states to visit; agree upon time to spend for trip
Short-range	Make daily lesson plan with specific behaviors; assessment helps plan next lesson	Use state and local maps to plan daily trip; next day's destination planned from current day

for interdisciplinary thematic science units with an emphasis on actively (physically and mentally) involving your students in hands-on/minds-on activities. This doesn't mean that every lesson you teach in science must have students handle or manipulate science materials. Rather, it means your lessons should include all the teaching/learning modes mentioned in Chapter 2: listening–speaking, reading–writing, and watching–doing.

Figure 6–2 illustrates the range of teaching/learning experiences available in a study of tidal pools, from the most direct (see, hear, smell, touch, taste) to the most abstract (mostly listening). Each experience has potential for individual lesson plans for teaching/learning.

This text emphasizes activity-based science lesson plans, because constructivist research shows that students learn science best by doing. Activity-based science lessons are sometimes referred to as *laboratory, hands-on/minds-on, doing,* or *guided discovery lessons. Hands-on/minds-on guided discovery lessons,* as used in this text, designates active physical and/or mental participation by the learner. Other types of science lessons were presented in earlier chapters.

Preparing hands-on/minds-on guided discovery science lesson plans takes practice. You cannot learn to write science lesson plans just by reading about them, any more than you could learn to play tennis by just watching. You must actually prepare several lessons. You must translate your aims and goals into manageable daily teachable objectives. To do this, you need to describe specific objectives—for your students to achieve each day or each lesson—that lead to your selected broad aims and goals. Objectives are usually stated in performance (behavioral) terminology as specific actions that each student is expected to be able to do as a consequence of a particular teaching/learning experience. Chapter 5 stressed the necessity for specificity in objectives, so that teachers know when their students have successfully achieved the stated objectives. These performance objectives are known by names such as *competency-based, performance-based,* or *outcome-based teaching/learning.*[3]

The following kinds of objectives are possible:

- *Instructional or Teaching Objectives.* Stated in terms of *teacher behavior,* these objectives answer the question, "What will the teacher do to help students achieve the kinds of behavior the students should exhibit?"
- *Behavioral or Performance Objectives.* Stated in terms of what *students* do to achieve the desired

TABLE 6–2
Medicine/teaching similarities

Medicine	Teaching
Aim: Care and cure of patients (Source: Hippocratic Oath)	**Aim:** Develop scientifically/technologically literate citizens (Source: Project Synthesis)
Diagnose: Identify single illness or disease (Source: doctor using training, patient symptoms, judgment)	**Goal:** Use information and values to make rational decisions and evaluate the personal consequences (Source: textbook, teacher judgment)
Prescribe: Specific medicine or other medical protocol (Source: training, pharmaceutical company information, judgment)	**Objective:** Rank and select alternatives on basis of most positive effect for those concerned (Source: teacher-written objective based on teacher judgment)

Abstract

Verbal Experiences

Teacher talk, written words; engaging one sense; the most abstract symbolization; students are physically inactive.
Examples
1. Listening to the teacher talk about tide pools.
2. Listening to a student report on the Grand Canyon.

Visual Experiences

Still pictures, diagrams, charts; engaging one sense; typically symbolic; students are physically inactive.
Examples
1. Viewing slides of tide pools.
2. Viewing drawings and photographs of the Grand Canyon.

Vicarious Experiences

Laser video-disc programs, computer programs, video programs; engaging more than one sense; students are indirectly "doing," possibly some limited physical activity.
Examples
1. Interacting with a computer program about wave action and life in tide pools.
2. Viewing and listening to a video program on the Grand Canyon.

Simulated Experiences

Role-playing, experiments, simulations, mock-ups, working models; all or nearly all senses are engaged; activity often integrates disciplines and is closest to the real thing.
Examples
1. Building a working model of a tide pool.
2. Building a working model of the Grand Canyon.

Direct Experiences

Students are actually doing what is being learned; true inquiry; all senses are engaged; activity usually integrates disciplines.
Examples
1. Visiting a tide pool.
2. Visiting the Grand Canyon.

Concrete

FIGURE 6–2

The Learning Experiences Ladder

Source: Richard D. Kellough, Arthur A. Carin, Carol Seefeldt, Nina Barbour, and Randall J. Souviney, *Integrating Mathematics and Science for Kindergarten and Primary Children* (Englewood Cliffs, NJ: Merrill/Prentice Hall, 1996), 169.

behavior, these objectives answer the question, "What will students be able to do after completing the learning activity?" Table 6–3 shows the differences between instructional or teaching objectives and student behavioral or performance objectives. Preparing instructional objectives is a vital teaching skill.

Preparing Behavioral/Performance Objectives. When writing student behavioral/performance objectives for your lessons, you should compose them in action terms, recognizing that you will never anticipate all learning that may occur. Also recognize that not all that is learned can be translated into behavioral terms, especially before it happens. That is why, many times your teaching will be pointed to concurrent learning of multiple objectives.

Ask yourself this question as you approach writing behavioral/performance objectives:

What observable action(s) will students perform that will demonstrate the objective has been achieved?

The action part of the objective is often referred to as the **terminal behavior** or **measurable performance.**

There are four components to consider as you write objectives in your lesson plans. Richard D. Kellough refers to them as "The ABCDs of Writing Objectives."[4]

Audience: student, for whom objective is aimed: "The student will be able to . . . ." or "You will be able to. . . ."

Behavior: measurable action verbs: *do, identify, write, choose, explain, recite,* etc.

Conditions: setting in which behavior will be demonstrated by student and observed by teacher: "The student will care for her plant at school for two weeks and maintain a daily written log of her activities."

Degree of expected performance: assesses student learning.

Let's see how these objectives are used in lesson planning.

Alter Ready-Made Lessons to Fit Your Teaching Needs. Do not let commercially prepared materials prevent you from designing your own lessons. Remember, if you use something you modified or made, you probably will do a much better job of teaching than if you follow someone else's lessons. *Never* follow any lessons like recipes, even the classroom-tested ones in this text! Always vary each lesson and adapt it in any way that you think will make it better. By so doing, you will continually increase your understanding of, appreciation for, and commitment

TABLE 6–3

Differences between teacher and student objectives

Teacher Instruction/Teaching Objectives	Student Behavioral/Performance Objectives
Teach respect for plants and animals.	Students will handle, care for, and be responsible for plants and animals in the classroom under supervision.
Present concepts of magnetism.	Students, after using a variety of magnets, will state that like poles repel and unlike poles attract.
Instruct how to measure temperature.	After being instructed, students will be able to read temperature differences from hot to cold among a range of substances.

Activity 6–1   SAMPLE SCIENCE HANDS-ON/MINDS-ON DISCOVERY LESSON

How Does the Length of the Vibrating Body Affect Sound? (3–6)

What Concepts Might Students Discover or Construct?	Bodies in vibration make a sound. The longer the vibrating body, the lower the tone.

What Will I Need?

Balsa wood strip 12 inches long   3 tacks or nails
10 straight pins   Rubber band
Piece of wood approximately   Hammer
    6 × 6 inches × 1 inch

What Will We Discuss?   *What do you think would happen if you vibrated pins set to different depths in a strip of balsa wood?*
Would you get the same sound from each of the pins?
If you think that different pins will give off different tones, which one would give off the highest tone?

PROCESSES   **Part 1**

What Will Students Do?   1. Obtain a balsa strip and set pins in it to varying depths. (See the diagram below.)

Observing   2. Determine if each vibrating pin gives off the same tone.
Inferring   *What relationship is there between pin length and tone?*
Hypothesizing   *Would nails stuck in balsa wood give the same results as pins?*

to hands-on/minds-on guided discovery learning. Keep your creative potential alive, and write or modify all of the science lessons you use.

PREPARING AND USING GUIDED DISCOVERY SCIENCE LESSONS

Before formulating discovery lessons of your own, look over published guided discovery science lessons. If possible, teach some of them to your students. Do not use them verbatim, but modify them to suit your own creativity and teaching style. They are valuable resources to use in con-

structing a science curriculum or for enriching a program. I know from working with thousands of teachers over the years that they can quickly learn to teach guided discovery by microteaching (teaching short, mini-lessons about 10 minutes in length) several kinds of lessons. Once you know how to use and give guided discovery lessons of this type, it is relatively easy to construct similar lessons of your own.

A Sample Hands-on/Minds-on Guided Discovery Lesson

Activity 6–1 shows a sample hands-on/minds-on guided discovery science lesson. Notice that

Part II

What Will Students Do?	1. Look at the diagram below.
Hypothesizing	*Where would you pluck the rubber band to get the highest note?*

Hypothesizing	*Where would you pluck the rubber band to get the lowest note?*
	2. Obtain three tacks or nails, a rubber band, and a piece of wood. Pound the tacks or nails into the wood block as shown in the diagram. Place the rubber band around the tacks or nails.
	3. Pluck the rubber band to see if your hypothesis was correct.
Comparing	4. *How do the results of Part I compare with the results of Part II?*
How Will Children Use or Apply What They Discover?	1. *What would happen if you plucked rubber bands having the same length but different thicknesses?*
	2. *What would happen to a tone if the vibrating length of the rubber band were kept the same, but different amounts of tension were applied?*
	3. *How does sound travel from the rubber band to your ears?*
Where Do I Find It?	1. Melvin Berger, *The Science of Music* (NY: Crowell, 1989).
	2. Etta Kaner, *Sound Science* (Menlo Park, CA: Addison-Wesley, 1989).

certain activities are mainly for teachers and others are essentially for students. Under the section called *Processes* on the left side of the lesson plan, are action verbs that guide children's performance. These are performance objectives.

Review Activity 6–1 carefully; study the format and the nature of the questions to gain a good understanding of how to make your own guided discovery science lessons. Notice that the hands-on/minds-on guided discovery lesson plan format is very similar to a cognitive instructional lesson model adapted from the works of Daniel Neale,[5] Charles W. Anderson,[6] and others. Both of these cognitive instruc-

tional model lesson formats provide an instructional framework for planning such things as the learning cycle, advance organizers, concept maps, hands-on/minds-on activities, and direct instruction. The model consists of ten segments:

1. *Introduction.* Make preliminary comments on lesson goals, content, or activities. This segment is intended to establish focus and to engage the learners.
2. *Review.* Discuss previous relevant lessons, and help make appropriate prior knowledge ready for use.

3. *Overview.* Provide an overview of new information or problems; develop advance organizers; elicit students' ideas; brainstorm; discuss; clarify. This segment initiates the accommodation (i.e., creation, tuning, or restructuring) of schemata needed in understanding the phenomena being investigated.

4. *Investigations/Activities.* In hands-on/minds-on activities, students manipulate materials to test their ideas; teacher demonstrations that involve the students may also be appropriate. This segment incorporates the exploration phase of the learning cycle. A wide range of investigative activities are appropriate here. Some teacher guidance in the form of suggestions, hints, questions, and information is appropriate.

5. *Representation.* Students represent results of activities through actions, drawings, charts, tables, measurements, words, and concept maps. The key here is developing powerful means of communication; language arts methods of instruction (e.g., writing in journals and webbing) are appropriate here.

6. *Discussions.* Activity results are presented and discussed. The teacher may use questioning strategies here (What did you see or do? Why do you think it happened? What is your evidence?). The teacher particularly notes the use of naive theories and misconceptions, vague and incomplete notions, and blocks to learning that appear to be developmental in nature.

7. *Invention.* New concepts, principles, procedures, or explanations are taught at developmentally appropriate levels through brief direct instruction presentations. Task analysis and sequencing are important. Reading in the text may be useful here. Concept maps may also be used. The focus is not on memorizing but on constructing new knowledge and on meaningful accommodation of existing knowledge that can be used in thinking and problem solving. In this segment students' misconceptions must be confronted with developmentally appropriate scientific knowledge.

8. *Application.* Newly constructed knowledge must be tried out in new situations. This may require repeating segments 4, 5, 6, and 7.

9. *Summary/Closure.* Findings, conceptualizations, explanations, and conclusions are summarized and linked to other lessons.

10. *Assessment.* To discover the degree to which students have accomplished objectives and to supply indicators of your next step for lesson planning, some sort of assessment must be made.

Writing Your Own Guided Discovery Lesson Plans

The following list gives you steps for creating your own hands-on/minds-on guided discovery science lessons. In following these procedures, you will not only be able to make better lessons but will also be able to modify and improve almost any science activities. In writing your own lessons, be sure to refer to Chapter 4, "Mastering the Art of Questioning and Listening."

1. Decide what scientific/technological concepts or principles you want to teach and state the problem in the form of a question.

2. In determining an appropriate grade level, indicate a range of grades for each lesson.

3. List the specific scientific/technological content concepts you want your students to discover.

4. Leave space for a list of materials but do not fill in this section until you have completed writing the activity section.

5. Write questions (especially divergent) that will set the stage of the lesson.

6. Consult science source books, science curriculums, or elementary science texts, or look around you for ideas to use. This part of the lesson is given to the students in writing if they are able to read or orally if they cannot.

   a. Design the activities so the students will be involved in hands-on/minds-on activities and science processes.

b. After roughly outlining the activity, write the first step of the activity sheet, in which you tell the students to collect the materials they will need.

c. Ask how they would use the equipment to find an answer to the problem.

d. Write a question asking what they think will happen if a certain procedure of investigation is used (hypothesize).

e. Tell the students to perform the procedure and observe what happens to test their hypotheses.

f. Ask the students to record what they observe. Strive to have them use mathematics in measuring and graphing where possible.

g. Ask them to interpret or make inferences about the data they collected.

7. Reread your statements and compare them with these scientific thinking processes: comparing, summarizing, criticizing, assuming, imagining, making decisions (evaluation of what to do), and applying. (See Chapter 2.) List one of these appropriate processes in the left margin by each of the questions you have asked. Compare your lesson with the list of scientific processes and determine how it can be modified to include more processes. This will assist you in assessing how sophisticated your lesson is and what it requires students to do cognitively. Review the Piagetian and constructivist operations described in Chapter 2.

8. Ask divergent, open-ended questions to determine how students can use and apply what they discovered.

9. Finish listing the materials you will need for the lesson.

10. Include any source content you need to know.

Using Open-Ended Questions in Your Science Lesson Plans

One of the most important considerations in your lesson planning should be preparing quality questions. Here are some questions to include in lesson planning.

1. *Experimental Factors or Variables.* In any experimental situation, **variables,** or factors, are being tested. The question, "What effect does water have on the sprouting of seeds?" is asking: What does the variable—water—have to do with the sprouting of seeds?

   Look at the problem of sprouting seeds again and think of three open-ended questions that suggest further investigation. You should have little difficulty doing this. All you have to do is ask yourself what might influence the sprouting of seeds. You may think of factors such as light, temperature, pH (acidity), and seed population (the number of seeds present). The following list shows some variables that may be involved in experimental conditions. You probably will think of many others. Use this list or prepare one yourself to guide you in writing open-ended questions:
   - Temperature.
   - Light.
   - Sound.
   - Water or humidity.
   - Food or presence of minerals.
   - pH—alkalinity or acidity.
   - Air or other gases or lack of them (space flight conditioning).
   - Pressure.
   - Type of motion.
   - Fields—gravitational, magnetic, electrical.
   - Friction.
   - Force.
   - Population density.

2. *Qualitative Questions.* Several of the factors or variables listed here may vary in qualitative ways. For example, a student may have done an activity to find out whether light is needed for photosynthesis in leaves. The student does not know, however, whether all wave lengths of light are necessary. The teacher may then ask the following qualitative questions about light in the open-ended questions section of the lesson:

What colors of light do you think are necessary for photosynthesis to take place?
How will different colors of light speed up or slow down photosynthesis?

The students may then cover plants with different colored cellophane to find answers to these questions.

3. *Quantitative Metrical Questions.* All of the factors in this list may also involve quantitative questions. For example, "How much light is necessary for photosynthesis to take place?" "How do different intensities of light affect photosynthesis?"

Look at the list of factors again and design qualitative and quantitative questions for the various factors that affect the sprouting of seeds. If you can accomplish this task, you will have little difficulty writing open-ended questions to accompany your own activity exercises.

LESS-STRUCTURED GUIDED DISCOVERY ACTIVITIES

As discussed in Chapters 2 and 3, less-structured guided discovery activities offer students a chance to find out—through their own ingenuity—as much as possible about some phenomenon. They also offer teachers opportunities to observe students' naive scientific theories and misconceptions.

The teacher may provide the problem and materials and then allow time and freedom for the students to "mess about." For example, the teacher may give students many different things

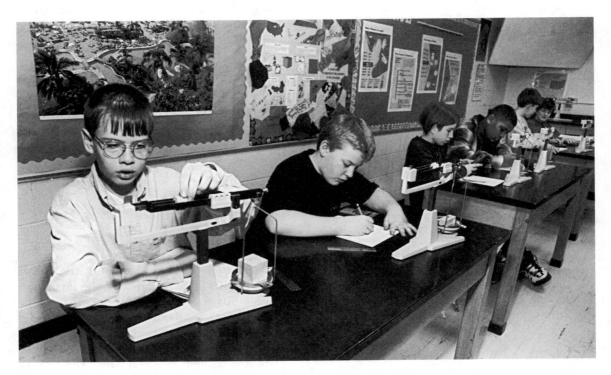

Open-ended or less-structured guided discovery activities stimulate students' thinking.

that roll on inclined planes or ask them to observe as many things as possible. The teacher may also provide metric sticks, hand lenses, flashlights, lemon juice, forceps, and jars to serve as aquaria for the students to use in studying organisms. After allowing the students to investigate for some time, the teacher will collect the animals or equipment and discuss what was discovered. This activity may be followed by more structured assignments, such as writing and reading about their discoveries or doing experiments related to them.

Less-structured hands-on/minds-on guided discovery experiences with physical objects are particularly important for students because these activities allow them to develop physical and logical knowledge, such as the realization that things can be classified, conserved, and ordered in different ways. Less-structured lessons, then, have relevance for *all* grades. The sophistication of student involvement depends largely on experience, cognitive development, and the motivations of the children. An example of a less-structured guided discovery lesson is shown in Activity 6–2.

Guiding Students to Greater Learning Autonomy

The purpose of less-structured discovery activities is not merely to teach science concepts. More importantly, such activities provide experiences where students can work alone or in groups to gain physical, social, and logical-mathematical knowledge. They are designed to allow students a great deal of autonomy, so they may become more self-directed and creative persons. Piaget and other constructivists believed that students construct knowledge only through their *own* physical and mental actions on objects. The purpose of less-structured discovery activities is not necessarily to advance students from one cognitive level to another (though the activities undoubtedly will contribute to this), but to help students, on their individual cognitive levels, learn to generate questions and solve problems themselves. If teachers always tell students what to do, the students will never learn to be responsible for their own learning, or to develop their own creativity and social competence.

Less-structured activities often focus on the learner performing various types of actions on objects: pushing, sliding, rolling, floating, swinging, dropping, attaching/gluing/clipping, listening to sounds, mashing, or stirring. The role of the teacher is to present the materials to the learner and ask divergent questions, for example, "What can you do or make with these objects?" and then allow a lot of time for the learner to investigate. Teachers should withdraw and interject with questions only when they see the students are losing interest. When they do ask a question, they might have the students focus on some action. For example, "What do you think would happen if you were to mash it, place it in water, and so on?"

Review the lesson illustrated in Activity 6–2 once more and create some activities of your own. All you need to do is collect some objects—for example, clothespins, cloth, juice cans, toothpicks, rubber bands—and think of different actions your students might perform using these things. You might use the following criteria for selecting less-structured guided discovery activities:

1. The student must be able to produce the movement by his or her own action.
2. The student must be able to vary the action.
3. The reaction of the object must be observable.
4. The reaction of the object must be immediate.

Some movements of objects fascinate children and others do not. The reason this difference occurs can be partially explained by how well the movements meet the criteria just listed. Although these criteria may appear at first to apply only to preschool children, they have relevance for other levels as well. For example, video games that meet these criteria have found vast acceptance among older children and adults. For

Activity 6–2   LESS-STRUCTURED GUIDED DISCOVERY LESSON

What Do Feathers Do? (K–4)

Materials

Bring several different feathers into class. Give them to the students; also provide trays of water.

Opening Questions

What can you find out about these feathers?
What can you do with feathers?

Allow a lot of time for the children to "mess around" with the feathers. Later ask questions such as

What did you find out about your feathers?
What did you do with them?
What do they do?
How do they do it?
How do they vary in shape?
In what other ways are they different?
Which feathers would be the best to have for flying? Why?
Which would be the best to keep a bird warm? Why?
Which would act as a raincoat?
How could we make a wing from feathers?

Some Possible Activities

You might suggest, if the students don't think of it themselves, what would happen if they poured water over wing feathers. Do the same with the down feathers and note what happens.

You might also bring to class a down-filled parka or gloves and let the children place their hands inside to feel how warm they become. Invite the children to drop various types of feathers and note how they float and how lightweight they are. Discuss how birds need strong wings but how they must be lightweight so they don't have to work so hard in flying. Set up a place in your room where children can pin feathers they collect. Talk about how Native Americans used feathers. Talk about how the children's grandparents or great-grandparents used feathers.

more about electronic and/or computer-assisted instruction, see Chapter 10.

START TEACHING YOUR SCIENCE LESSON PLANS!

Elementary and middle school teachers who do a great deal of planning are better classroom managers than those who do not.[7] Now that you have prepared your interdisciplinary thematic units and daily lesson plans, you are ready to put your plans into action by becoming the best classroom manager you can be. This means you must become as proficient as possible in dealing with all of the important elements of designing and managing shown in Figure 6–3. Here are some suggestions to start you on the road to becoming a top classroom manager.

Teacher of science will design and manage a learning environment that provides students with the time, space, and resources needed for learning science. In doing this, they:

- structure the time available so that students are able to engage in extended investigations,
- generate a setting for student work that is flexible and supportive of science inquiry,
- ensure a safe working environment,
- make the science equipment, materials, print, and technological resources accessible to students,
- identify and use resources outside the school, and
- engage students in designing the environment.

FIGURE 6–3

Designing and managing a supportive science learning environment

Source: National Science Education Standards: Discussion Summary (Washington, DC: National Research Council of the National Committee on Science Education Standards and Assessment, September 12, 1994), 6.

ORGANIZE YOUR CLASSROOM ENVIRONMENT FOR MAXIMUM SCIENCE LEARNING

Your elementary classroom must encompass the entire elementary curriculum of math, social studies, reading and language arts, music, art, and other disciplines. Timing and the physical arrangement of teaching materials must be flexible and, in most cases, serve more than one purpose or subject area. Let's start with how flexible schedules can help make your classroom management more effective.

Build Specific but Flexible Science Times Into Your Weekly Plans

John Goodlad said, "The amount of time spent on a given subject is a powerful factor in learning."[8] Table 6–4 shows the minimum amount of time most national teaching groups say should be scheduled for science.

Traditionally, science is scheduled into 25- to 40-minute daily segments, but there are advantages for scheduling two or three 60- to 90-minute time slots weekly when using an interdisciplinary thematic unit approach:

1. It usually takes five minutes or more—to organize, get supplies and materials, and

TABLE 6–4

Suggested weekly schedule for classroom science instruction

Grades	% Weekly Teaching Schedule	Actual Teaching Schedule (Hours per Week)
K–2	5	1.5
3–4	5–10	1.5–3
5–6	10	3

Source: Rodger W. Bybee and Joseph D. McInerney (Eds.), *Redesigning the Science Curriculum: A Report on the Implications of Standards and Benchmarks for Science Education* (Colorado Springs: Biological Sciences Curriculum Study, 1995).

distribute them—to start your students on the science activity. The same time is spent at the end of the lesson for clean-up, returning supplies, and concluding the activity. Because preparation time and clean-up remain constant, scheduling two or three lessons a week saves you a great deal of time.

2. You have fewer preparations.
3. You have more flexibility for different levels and interests of your students: some students can manipulate materials while others read, think, or interact with you and other students.

Arranging for the Physical Science Learning Environment

Hands-on/minds-on guided discovery science teaching necessitates that the following science areas be established in your self-contained classroom:

1. Activity area.
2. Temporary or portable science areas.
3. Material storage areas.
4. Equipment storage areas.
5. Student work storage.
6. Small item storage (e.g., shoe boxes).
7. Space and suitable containers for living things.
8. Discovery learning centers.
9. Research and reading materials center.
10. Total class teaching area—teacher-directed learning area.
11. Electronic equipment area (e.g., audiovisual, computer, TV, etc.).

Figure 6–4 shows how these science areas might be arranged in a self-contained classroom for elementary grades. Note the following areas:

- Total class or large-group teacher-directed learning area.
- Skills reinforcement areas.
- Student choice areas (e.g., art, library, and individual activities).
- Subject matter centers (science, social studies, math, etc.).

- "Special" areas (e.g., listening and writing areas).
- Flexible areas that can change as needs change.

Note especially that the classroom appeals to students' interests, and that each area serves learning needs. Teachers of students in upper elementary or middle school (or in schools that departmentalize science) can modify this classroom setup. You will find invaluable sources for this purpose in:

- Johanna Kasin Lemlech, *Curriculum and Instructional Methods for the Elementary and Middle School,* 3d ed. (Englewood Cliffs, NJ: Merrill/Prentice Hall, 1994).
- Diana W. Rigden, *School Restructuring: Designing Schools for Better Student Learning* (New York: Council for Aid to Education, 1990).
- Robert E. Slavin, (ed.), *School and Classroom Organization* (Hillsdale, NJ: Lawrence Erbaum Associates, 1989).

The following sections discuss some of the specific areas shown in Figure 6–4.

Science Activity Area. Your elementary school classroom probably contains movable furniture. In Figure 6–4, the center of the room houses the movable desks, tables, and chairs. The wall space areas provide storage for stationary science equipment and facilities. Science facilities should be grouped as much as possible in one general area of your room. The science equipment, supplies, and other materials you need should be readily available for making, assembling, experimenting, and demonstrating.

For active pupil participation in the guided discovery hands-on/minds-on science program, you must supply adequate space for all students to work. Even if your classroom is small and crowded, experiments, demonstrations, and construction activities can be performed. For instance, the space next to and beneath window sills and countertops can be used for work areas.

FIGURE 6–4
Self-contained classroom stressing active student involvement

If your classroom has flat-top desks, you can move them together to make larger work areas. You will find it helpful to get at least one large table in your classroom for doing hands-on/minds-on activities. Try to get tables that are water- and acid-resistant. Otherwise, use fiberboard or laminated plastic to cover your desks and tables. If burners will be used, the best tops are stone or composition stone. If you do not have permanent science work areas, you can cover desks and tables with tempered fiberboard.

Science Activity Area Storage. When you plan your work areas, plan for storage of certain equipment and materials:

1. Science supplies.
2. Science apparatus and equipment.
3. Consumable science items.
4. Chemicals.
5. Charts.
6. Models.
7. Electronic equipment and supplies.
8. Handtools.
9. Living things (plants and animals).
10. Unfinished student work.

Your classroom has unused space that you can use for storage. Consider using the spaces beneath window ledges, countertops, sinks, above and around heating units (radiators), and even under student desks. You can purchase excellent commercially made cabinets that fit any of these spaces, or your students or your custodian and you can construct them. With some creativity, you and your students can arrange these cabinets in a variety of ways. Sources of science cabinets, shelving, and other laboratory storage furniture are listed in Appendix C.

With a guided discovery activities science program, you will constantly need to store many small items. Small boxes provide space for collecting, organizing, and storing small, readily available materials for particular science areas. Appendix K illustrates how to construct and store shoe boxes for small science items.

Investigate the suggestions for making your classroom user friendly in Ronald E. Converse and William C. Wright, "Suggestions for Constructing or Renovating Science Laboratory Facilities," in Gerry M. Madrazo, Jr. and LaMoine L. Moltz, *Sourcebook for Science Supervisors,* Fourth Edition, (Arlington, VA: National Science Teachers Association and the National Science Supervisors Association, 1993).

Caring for Living Things. Encourage your students to bring small animals (including insects) and plants into your classroom. To be well prepared, have these kinds of containers always available:

- Insect cages.
- Small animal cages.
- Aquariums.
- Terrariums.

See Appendix K for information on constructing and using these houses for living things.

Suggestions for caring for plants and animals and for setting up different kinds of terrariums can be obtained from Biological Supply House, Inc., 8200 South Hoyne Avenue, Chicago, IL 60620. Useful leaflets are available free by writing on school stationery to Turtox Service Leaflets, NSTA Publications, 1742 Connecticut Avenue, N.W., Washington, DC 20009. Especially helpful are No. 10, *The School Terrarium,* and No. 25, *Feeding Aquarium and Terrarium Animals.* Send $1.50 to the same source for how-to-do-it pamphlets, especially *How to Care for Living Things in the Classroom,* by Grace K. Pratt (Stock No. PB 38/4).

Food and other requirements for a variety of water and land animals are presented in Appendix E.

Keeping Animals in Classroom for 24 Hours. Although it is recommended that animals be studied and not removed from their natural habitat, students' curiosity occasionally motivates them to remove certain animals from their environment and bring them into your classroom. Here are some directions to help the students adopt a humane attitude toward the living things they are observing.

John J. Dommers of the Humane Society of the United States recommends we adopt a 24-hour rule to best serve the interests of the animals and children: Small animals, such as insects, turtles, frogs, and salamanders, may be kept for a period not exceeding 24 hours, if the habitat in which they were found is simulated as closely as possible in captivity. Students should observe the animals but not handle them. They should research information about identification, characteristics, feeding habits, and values. The animals should then be released unharmed where they were found.

Discovery Science Classroom Learning Centers. In classrooms where students actively engage in hands-on/minds-on activities, learning centers are essential. Learning centers are created and directed by the teacher. They motivate, support, guide, and reinforce students' learning. Learning centers will better enable you to meet individual needs, provide students with self-directed learning, and encourage their responsibility. There should be learning centers for all content areas.

Set aside at least one area of your classroom as a discovery science learning center. This center should contain collections, direction or activity sheets, activities, and materials that meet these criteria:

1. Present new science materials.
2. Reinforce previously learned science materials.
3. Develop a scientific skill.
4. Drill on specific science information.
5. Develop other science interests and creativity.
6. Make efficient use of limited class time.
7. Encourage students to work independently.[9]

Science learning centers allow teachers to design supplemental science curricula which closely match the developmental levels of their students. Tasks at the center can range from hands-on activities to written and research assignments.[10] Learning centers are places where one or more students may work apart from your regular, ongoing science activities. Students are relatively free to explore, discover, experiment, or just tinker.

Figure 6–5 offers a view of a typical elementary or middle school classroom using learning centers. The different learning centers are separated by dividers such as movable screens, workbenches, display or bulletin board space, bookcases, planters, tables, or shelves. There should be enough tables, chairs, and appropriate, easily obtainable materials for all of your students. See Appendix F for directions on how to construct a learning center.

Types of Science Learning Centers. There are many types of science learning centers, including (a) directed discovery learning centers, (b) science process centers, and (c) open learning centers.

The **directed discovery learning center** focuses on specific science concepts. For this type of center, place materials in shoe boxes with a series of guiding discovery questions, such as, "Using the materials in this box, how would you show that light appears to travel in a straight line?" Directed learning centers may be set up with one theme or separate problems.

A **science processes learning center** focuses on developing science processes, such as observing, predicting, and measuring. Using collections of materials and discovery guidance questions, you could ask your students to measure the items in a box in both metric and standard measurements.

The last and most creative type of center is an **open learning center.** You supply many random materials, not according to any one theme or science area. Give your class minimum direction. For example, use the direction, "Invent something with the materials in this box."

Format for Planning Your Learning Centers. All three types of learning centers should be based on the following format for planning a learning center.

Specific Objectives for Center. The purpose of a learning center should be clear to both the teacher and student, and stated as an action performance objective (e.g., "At this center you will examine some seeds. You will compare sizes, weights, volumes, and shapes of the seeds.").

Consider Your Students' Maturation Levels. The center must be appropriate for the students who will be using it. The backgrounds and experiences, the cognitive level of operation, the socioeconomic level, the maturity level and level of independence, and the psychomotor level must be defined and used as the basis for

Four learning centers back-to-back.
Children move from 1 to 2 to 3 to 4.

FIGURE 6–5
Learning centers in self-contained classroom

planning the activities and expected learning outcomes from the center.

Clearly Define Scientific Concepts, Processes, and Skills to be Developed. A clear statement of the scientific concepts, processes, and skills to be developed by the students using the center is necessary if the center is to be a true teaching/learning situation. If these criteria are not met, centers break down into busy work.

State Expected Learning Outcomes. These statements can be in the form of performance or behavioral objectives. A concise statement of what the student is expected to learn as a result of using the center can also serve as a guideline for assessing student success.

Select Appropriate Activities and Methods. Activities and methods must be carefully selected to harmonize with the criteria mentioned above. The activities must serve the purpose of the center and be appropriate to the students using it. They must be designed to assist the student in reaching the expected learnings. The directions must be clearly within the ability of the student and presented so that the student can follow them independently. The materials must be readily available.

Make Assessments. Use the performance objectives for the center as a base to determine whether the student has attained the expected learning, concepts, and skills stated.

Implement Changes as Needed. Student performance will provide insight into how each center can be improved to meet the needs of the students it serves, the curriculum, and the objectives and goals stated for the center. The center and its materials may also need periodic servicing.

Science Learning Just Outside Your Classroom. Every school—whether in an urban, suburban, or rural area—has areas just outside the classroom that are excellent laboratories for extending the science program into the local environment. The school yard, a vacant lot, a community park, or the school itself provides almost endless opportunities for students to examine soil composition; make measurements of everyday weather phenomena; hone observation skills looking for shapes and patterns in their local environment; or investigate playground puddles, melting snow, common local plants and animals, weeds, grasses, and many other things.

Outdoor science extends the classroom walls. Students enlarge their science studies by taking nature walks, doing data collection and scientific analysis in the "real world," and feeling that science is not something relegated to a schoolroom. Even the most concrete-covered urban environment is rich in science possibilities. Here are a few just-outside-the-classroom science activities:

- Adopt a tree, bush, or plant on the school grounds or neighborhood, observe and record observations bimonthly, and share ideas with other classes and/or community by way of a "Neighborhood Environment Newspaper."
- With help from a high school biology teacher, agricultural extension division personnel, or local resident animal expert, identify a local endangered species. Have these people work with your class to design a project to save that species from extinction.
- Cultivate a native ecosystem on your school grounds. Enlist the assistance of your school principal, a local gardener, your school custodian, and interested parents, and high school teachers and students. Follow these ideas suggested by Jerry Trust in *The Science Teacher* (December 1991):

  1. Get approval from your school district and principal to construct a habitat, preferably on your school site.
  2. Locate a landscape architect or knowledgeable gardener (using PTA, school newspaper, or flier sent home to parents), have him/her draw up a *plant habitat plan* with you, and review the plan with a plant habitat committee (comprising you, your school principal, school custodian, parents, and others you feel are necessary).

3. Establish a *time line* with the committee such as:
   a. September: Final approval of plant habitat plan
   b. October/November: Custodians, students, parents prepare site by pulling weeds, removing grass, turning soil.
   c. December–March: Collect donations of cash and/or plants, tools, materials donations from local florists/gardeners, businesses (especially fast food restaurants), PTA; have cake sale to raise money; send flier home for parental contributions; get materials ready for next stage. Many grants are available for these projects. Seek help from your local or state governments and from these two excellent grant sources: *Directory of Research Grants* (generally available in your school administrative offices or local library); U.S. Fish and Wildlife Service, Office of Management Authority, (703)358–2104.; and the Science Linkages in the Community (SLIC) Institute at the American Association for the Advancement of Science, (800)351–7542.
   d. March–June: you, your students, and adult helpers start the pleasurable part— constructing your habitat—by starting ground work, planting, watering and maintenance, and student committees.

The objective of all the planning is to develop science activities that will enable your students to construct greater knowledge and appreciation for their immediate environment. Such activities might include:

Objective: Students will observe, record, and explain the interrelationships between plants, animals, and insects in their school site habitat.

Activities: Students will visit the site often to observe what happens to plants, animals, and insects when people do not use insecticides, *chemical plant killers, and fertilizers, or mow, or tamper with nature in any other way.*

For further information on establishing a native plant ecosystem see:

■ Jerry Trust, "A habitat-forming experience: Cultivating a native plant ecosystem," *The Science Teacher, 58,* no. 9, December 1991, 22–27.

These publications offer other good suggestions for outdoor science:

■ *Outdoor Study Techniques,* Outdoor Biology Instructional Strategies (OBIS), Delta Education, Inc., Box 915, Hudson, NH 03051.
■ Margaret Collis and Doug Kincaid, *Out Of Doors, Learning Through Science* (London, England: Macdonald, 1982).
■ Council for Science International, *Outdoors Areas as Learning Laboratories: CESI Sourcebook* (Columbus, OH: ERIC Clearinghouse for Science, Mathematics, and Environmental Education, 1979).

Urban teachers will find the following monthly publication helpful; it has science activities designed for them (e.g., "Uncovering Roaches," "Sneaker Science," and "Welcome to City Science"):

■ *City Science Newsletter,* City College R 6/207, 138th St. & Convent Ave., New York, NY 10031.

CLASSROOM MANAGEMENT IN GUIDED DISCOVERY SCIENCE

The *physical environment* you've created in your classroom is enhanced by interest centers, attractive and informative bulletin boards, posters, and other visual displays. But it is just as important for your students to have a positive, supportive *learning environment*. Your science program should allow them to draw on each other's discoveries and communicate their ideas to each other. Science is a participation activity;

if its social aspects are to be fully realized, students must have guided activities involving interaction with each other.

The physical arrangements of the classroom can advance or hinder this interaction. Reexamine Figures 6–4 and 6–5. Rows are not straight, and desks do not face all in one direction so that the students see only the backs of the heads in front of them. This arrangement promotes the development of active, involved students.

In a well-planned classroom, traffic patterns allow students to move about the room quickly and quietly. Easy access to materials facilitates cooperation rather than competition. Changes can be made by students and teacher as needed to maximize interaction. Providing clean-up items and trash receptacles around the room— rather than in one corner—improves opportunities for cooperation with minimum conflict.

Physical arrangement of your classroom is very important, but the heart and soul of your science teaching is classroom management. *Classroom management* may be used in a variety of ways; however, as used in this text, **classroom management** is organizing and keeping a classroom environment that is favorable to learning and achievement. It's a broad concept that includes such aspects as

- *control:* the process of controlling student behavior in a classroom, and
- *discipline:* responding to and reducing inappropriate student behaviors.[11]

Even if you have a well-thought out science program, a carefully prepared classroom, and adequate supplies, faulty classroom management can wreck your teaching. Table 6–5 compares classroom management, control, and discipline to the practice of medicine.

Prevention: Anticipating Problems Before They Occur

An ounce of prevention is worth a pound of cure in your science teaching. Thinking and planning can help you spot many, though never all, potential trouble areas. Here are some things to keep in mind for *preventing* problems in classroom management, control, or discipline.[12]

Phase A: Teacher/Student Preparations
- Identify what you want students to learn and relate it to the cognitive level of your students.
- Pick appropriate activities for your students to learn.
- Collect supplies and equipment you and the students will need.

TABLE 6–5

Similarities between classroom management and medical practice

Condition	Medical Practice	Science Classroom Management
1. Prevention	check-ups, good nutrition, exercise, sleep	preassessment/diagnosis; teacher/student preparation; teacher observation; student grouping; preactivity discussion; material distribution; teacher/student interactions *(classroom management)*
2. First-aid treatment	stopping bleeding, bandaging	separating and quieting problem students; halting disruptive activity *(classroom control)*
3. Long-term treatment	vitamin supplements, chemotherapy, limb in cast	individual skills improvement; teacher/student/parent conferences; student removal *(classroom discipline)*

- Plan the room arrangement and other logistics for the activity.
- Organize the class into working teams.
- Organize science materials before starting activities. The distribution of materials and transition from one activity to another can make or break your science lesson.[13]

Phase B: Pre-Activity Teacher/Student Discussions

- Use verbal and visual directions—pointing, using arrows, and asking questions—to help direct and focus attention on what will be done when students are working in their groups. Be very specific.
- Guide students to identify the problem being investigated, design the experiment, determine data-collecting and record-keeping techniques, and decide what and how equipment and supplies will be used.
- Give students time to discuss, explain what will be done, and exchange ideas. It is important for students to internalize what will be done and to form working relationships with other students. Research has shown that:
   a. highly anxious students do better if the teacher is less directive;
   b. students with low anxiety levels respond better to stronger direction from the teacher;
   c. average and low ability students benefit more from greater structure in teacher presentations and materials; and
   d. above average students learn better when they have more latitude to imagine, interpret, and rapidly manipulate symbols.

Gear your pre-activity discussion to the individual anxiety needs of the specific groups with which you are working.[14]

- By effectively using open-ended questions, you can guide students toward the goals you have for the activity.
- Establish a reason in students' minds for doing the activity. List on the board the reasons for conducting the activity, and write down how supplies and equipment will be distributed and collected.
- Remember that science supplies and materials should be assembled at the distribution and collection stations *before* the lesson begins.

Phase C: Distribution and Collection of Science Materials

- Review with the groups what they will do, what they need, and how they will proceed before having them go for supplies. Make sure each group knows exactly what to get. Then assign one group at a time to go to the supply stations and get the needed items.
- Establish a realistic time limit for supply gathering and collection.
- Always check to see that each group has all necessary science supplies.

Phase D: Doing the Activity

- With all the groups in their places with their supplies, review once more what each group will be doing. Sometimes it helps to check by asking the students who have the most difficulty, so that you can be sure all students understand the directions.
- For students unaccustomed to group work, try assigning a number to each task. Giving each student a numbered task ensures total group participation.

First-Aid Approaches to Management, Control, and Discipline

As your students begin their group work, you perform a wide range of tasks to keep the groups working effectively.

- Move about the room. Do not plant yourself in the front of the room, but move quietly to each group.
- If students are bogged down, ask questions to guide them and move them back on the tasks to be done.

- Encourage communication among the students in each group.
- Assess the noise level and see if it's appropriate for the specific activity. If it's too noisy, you might try these solutions:
  1. Establish beforehand a signal calling for quiet (e.g., putting lights out for a moment, ringing a bell, raising a hand in the air). When everyone quiets down, remind the class that it is too loud. Ask the students to quiet down.
  2. Move to the offenders and quietly remind them to lower their voices.
  3. Conclude the lesson if you are unable to quiet the class. Do this only as a last resort.
- Praise students who are working well instead of criticizing those who are not working well. Be specific with your praise so students know exactly the behavior you are praising, such as, "Notice how quietly Ann's group is discussing what effect the length of the pendulum cord has on its swings," or "Class, Jon's really helping by going around and showing each group how to wire the bell."
- Temporarily remove from their groups students who cause problems and ask them to watch groups that are working well together. In a few minutes you might say, "Jason, I know you want to work with your group, so when you're ready, quietly go back to them and see if you can now work quietly and share your materials properly."
- Be enthusiastic!
- Show respect for students by speaking politely and listening to each student in an unhurried manner.
- Do not add to class noise by shouting above students' voices. Calm and quiet the students with a firm but soft voice.

Long-Term Approaches to Classroom Management, Control, and Discipline

Assess your group lessons to see if you need to address any of these obstacles:

- Some students may be too immature for group work. You may have to work with them individually while the rest of the class works in groups.
- Additional total class or small-group instruction may be necessary for those students who need science concepts/skills improvement before they are able to fully benefit from group work.
- Review, sharing of information, and discussions are necessary to follow up students' work.
- Make sure that all students understand the conclusions and generalizations.
- Build time into each lesson for students to clean, disassemble, and return to collection stations all supplies and equipment used. This responsibility teaches students that teachers are not servants or maintenance people.
- After each lesson, abstract a minimum set of working rules from the students to be used for future work, such as, "Make certain you know what you must do," or "Find out what materials you will have to use in the lesson."
- If there is a chronic offender in your class, you might
  1. talk with the student;
  2. try to determine her or his interests;
  3. ask for the student's perceptions of the problem and schedule a student–parent–teacher conference to see what can be done; and
  4. if necessary, invite the principal, school psychologist, social worker, or other professional to attend.

CLASSROOM APPLICATIONS OF MANAGEMENT TECHNIQUES

Although no classroom management system is foolproof or a substitute for an alert and intelligent teacher, Table 6–6 summarizes classroom management techniques that can help in your hands-on/minds-on guided discovery science teaching/learning activities. Combine the ideas

TABLE 6–6
Whole class/small group/individual learning

Environmental Factor	Whole-class I: Students Listen to Teacher	Whole-class II: Students Work Independently	Small Groups	Individual
Example teaching methods	Giving class directions; discussion; demonstrations; science review drills	Worksheets; short quizzes; reinforcement sheets; problem-solving puzzles	Role-playing; lab activity groups; manipulative investigations; field trips; simulations and games	Learning centers; science/math fair projects; individualized homework or task cards
Cooperative vs competitive instruction	Competitive	Mostly competitive unless using peer teaching strategy	Most cooperative class arrangement	Neither
Use of manipulative materials	Most difficult arrangement to use manipulatives. Students are most passive in their learning	Can be done in this arrangement, but is limited to simple exercises such as mystery boxes or puzzle pieces	Easy to use manipulatives. Students are highly active in their learning	Easiest to use manipulative materials. Most active learning takes place
Content coverage, selection, and individualization	The most content can be covered and is selected by the teacher. Retention is generally low	Good content coverage, but opportunity to individualize is limited	Less content covered because more time is needed in small group activities. More individualized instruction can take place	Less content covered in traditional "textbook sense," but students' content selection is high and so is retention level
Student values and decision making	Student preferences not explored or considered to a high degree	More student choice is permitted	Best opportunity to conduct affective activities such as simulations on topics like the environment	Best opportunity to encourage student decision-making skills
Creativity and problem solving	Not conducive to actual problem-solving process other than as an excellent way to present problems to be solved by the class in other arrangements	Can be conducive through the use of "brainteaser" types of problems. It is hard to determine, however, the difficulty level of problems presented to the whole class	Best opportunity for problem solving and creative activity, since students benefit from listening to the solutions of others in the group	Very good arrangement to encourage problem solving and creativity, especially for those students who work well alone.

Source: Modified from Stan Rachaelson, "Rethink and Regroup." Reproduced with permission by *Science Scope, 14,* no. 2 (October 1990): 39. Copyright © 1990 by the National Science Teachers Association, 1840 Wilson Blvd., Arlington, VA 22201-3000.

in Table 6–6 with the following summary of classroom management, control, and discipline suggestions, and you will probably have a successful activity-oriented science program.

Simple, Clear Work Rules and Directions

1. Establish with students a minimum set of rules and working directions that primarily cover fairness and courtesy behaviors. Wherever possible, give students a reason for the rule, e.g., "We will ask that only one team come up at a time to the science supply station so we can avoid bumping into each other and spilling things. Understand?" Post the rules on a chart.
2. Determine an appropriate attention and quieting signal to which students can automatically respond.
3. Set up and review often the system for distributing and collecting science supplies and equipment, as well as clean-up procedures.

Classroom Management/Control Maintenance and Reinforcement

1. Develop a repertoire of praise and reinforcement for students working cooperatively. These articles give specifics in this area:
   - Elizabeth B. Baron, "Discipline Strategies for Teachers," *Fastback 344* (Bloomington, IN: Phi Delta Kappa Educational Foundation, 1992).
   - S. Black, "In praise of judicious praise," *Executive Editor, 14,* no. 10, October 1992, 24–27.
   - Jack Blendinger, et al., "Win–Win Discipline," *Fastback 353* (Bloomington, IN: Phi Delta Kappa Educational Foundation, 1993).
   - S. W. Soled, "What affects student performance? Creating an atmosphere for achievement," *The Science Teacher, 61,* no. 1, January 1994, 34–37.

2. Present concise understandable directions for each activity. Assess often to see if all students know exactly what to do.
3. Demonstrate what is expected, as well as any new idea or procedure.

Handling Discipline Problems and Emergencies

1. Prepare contingency plans for disruptive situations, e.g., spilling of science supplies, explosive student behavior (fighting and pushing), or unexpected science occurrence (hamster gives birth). Remember—if anything *can* go wrong, it *will!*
2. Consider beforehand the pros and cons of various methods discipline, such as removing a student from the situation or physically restraining him, so you can use them effectively if necessary. Consider routinizing procedures for handling improper actions so students understand beforehand the reasons for and consequences of bad behavior. If it fits within your school/district policy, you might review the following policy with students and then display it in the classroom:
   - **First offense:** warning addressed to student by name in clear, calm voice.
   - **Second offense:** student given 10-minute time-out in an isolated part of the classroom, another teacher's classroom, or school office. Never use learning centers.
   - **Third offense:** 15 minute time-out in isolation.
   - **Fourth offense:** phone call to student's parents or guardian.
   - **Fifth offense:** conference with student, parent or guardian, school principal, and/or school psychologist or counselor.[15]
3. If you feel the lesson is getting away from you, don't hesitate to end it. Assess what went wrong and plan the next lesson to eliminate the problem.

SUMMARY

You must adequately provide for these four aspects of your teaching to put a hands-on/minds-on guided science discovery teaching program into effect in your classroom:

1. Long- and short-range planning
2. Physical classroom environment
3. Student interaction
4. Classroom management: control or discipline

Exhilarating science lessons do not happen by chance. Begin your planning by deciding on your long-range goals (aims) for the whole year. Find out what your students know and then start putting your broad goals into an interdisciplinary thematic science unit format. This will help you in writing individual guided discovery lesson plans.

Broad unit goals must be translated into specific observable performance/behavioral objectives for preparing individual lesson plans. In writing lesson plans, include all types of teaching and learning methods including listening–speaking, reading–writing, and watching–doing. Emphasis is placed on hands-on/minds-on guided discovery activity-based lessons because research shows that students learn science best this way. Resources help teachers use this approach. However, you still need to know how to construct guided discovery lessons on your own. Lessons tailored to your own class are more appropriate than commercially prepared ones. Suggestions and sample lessons were presented to assist you with guided discovery lessons and less-structured lessons.

Once you learn how to construct guided discovery science lessons, you will be able to write them—as well as less-structured lessons—because you will know the nature of the process.

Most science in the elementary school is taught in self-contained classrooms. This chapter suggests various physical arrangements of the classroom, including storage for materials, small items, and living things.

Discovery learning centers allow your students to explore, discover, and experiment in less-structured situations. This chapter describes how to construct and use learning centers as well as the environment outside the classroom.

Student interaction is just as critical as the physical arrangement of the room, since science is a participation activity. Teachers must arrange and utilize furniture in flexible and creative ways.

Classroom management—control or discipline—can make or break your science teaching. Classroom management was compared to medicine in that both feature prevention, first-aid, and long-term treatment. Specific practical classroom examples of classroom management, control, and discipline were highlighted.

SELF-ASSESSMENT AND FURTHER STUDY

1. Using your science textbook, school or school district science syllabus, or commercially prepared program, select a topic or problem and plan an interdisciplinary thematic science unit for a particular class of students. You might start with these publications:
   - *Integrating the Curriculum* series, especially "Adventures in Science," "Math: Integrated Activities for Young Children," and "Integrating Aerospace Science into the Curriculum K–12," Delta Education, P. O. Box 3000, Nashua, NH 03061–3000.
   - National Science Resources Center, Smithsonian Institution/National Academy of Sciences, Integrated Science and Technology for Children (STC) units (Carolina Biological Supply Company, 2700 York Rd., Burlington, NC 27215, (800)334–5551).

- Nancy N. Stahl and Robert J. Stahl, *Society and Science: Decision-Making Episodes for Exploring Society, Science, and Technology,* 1995 (National Science Teachers Association, 1840 Wilson Blvd., Arlington, VA 22201)
- Professional Guide Integrated Thematic Units, Thematic Units, Interdisciplinary Units, (Teacher-Created Materials, P. O. Box 1040, Huntington Beach, CA 92647)

2. On graph paper, draw a floor plan for your hands-on/minds-on science classroom. Arrange the room to include these areas: activity, equipment and supplies storage, living things storage, discovery learning center, research and library center, conference center, computer/audiovisual/electronic equipment center.

3. List reasons why it is important to prevent control or discipline problems before they arise. Outline at least five preventative management steps you can employ now to reduce or avoid conflicts in your hands-on/minds-on activities.

4. Using the information in this chapter and in Appendix K, construct with your students several containers to house insects, small animals, or birds and/or build several of the storage areas or shoe box collections. You and your students can obtain free materials from a local grocery, fast-food chain, or other source.

5. With your class, cooperatively plan and develop a discovery science learning center around a single topic of science.

6. Select a guided discovery hands-on/minds-on science activity and write a plan for classroom management using prevention, first-aid, and long-term treatment. Be specific.

7. Prepare a list of positive reinforcement statements to encourage and reinforce cooperation among your students. Start your research with

- P. Chance, "Sticking up for Rewards," *Phi Delta Kappan, 74,* no. 10, (June 1993), 787–790.
- R. Merrett and K. Wheldall, "Teachers' Use of Praise and Reprimands to Boys and Girls," *Educational Review, 44,* no. 1, (September 1992), 73–79.

8. Explain why you agree or disagree with this statement: "90% of classroom control or discipline problems are caused by teachers themselves."

9. Give at least five reasons why it is more effective in hands-on/minds-on science to use larger science blocks of time less frequently each week (2 to 3 days) than smaller blocks of time more frequently (3 to 5 days)?

10. Some teachers make mountains out of molehills. Describe:
    - some "minor misbehavior" and why you think it is best ignored, and
    - behavior problems that can be dealt with simply and quickly.

11. Distributing, using, collecting, and cleaning up of science materials, as well as the transition from one activity to another, can make or break a well-planned lesson. How can these procedures be handled smoothly?

12. Survey your school site or nearby vacant lot or park as a potential for setting up a native plant ecosystem habitat. Prepare a site plan and design for the habitat with a local landscape architect, gardener, or high school biology teacher. Using resources suggested in this chapter, plan a year's activities for your students' planning, collecting materials, building, and maintaining the habitat. What science learnings are applicable to your habitat?

NOTES

1. Richard D. Kellough, Arthur A. Carin, Carol Seefeldt, Nina Barbour, and Randall J. Souviney, *Integrating Mathematics and Science for Kindergarten and Primary Children* (Englewood Cliffs, NJ: Merrill/Prentice-Hall, 1996), 47.

2. *National Science Education Standards: Discussion Summary* (Washington, DC: National Research Council of the National Committee on Science Education Standards and Assessment, Sept. 12, 1994), 2.

3. For additional information on performance or outcome-based teaching/learning see: John M. Kudlas, "Implications of OBE: what you should know about outcome-based education," *The Science Teacher, 61,* no. 5, May 1994, 32–35; and the outcome-based education issue of *Educational Leadership, 51,* no. 6, March 1994.

4. For greater detail, see Chapter 4, "Lesson Planning" in Richard D. Kellough, Arthur A. Carin, Carol Seefeldt, Nina Barbour, and Randall J. Souviney, *Integrating Mathematics and Science for Kindergarten and Primary Children* (Englewood Cliffs, NJ: Merrill/Prentice-Hall, 1996), 73–116.

5. Daniel C. Neale, "Primary Teachers' Current Practices and Needed Expertise in Science Lessons," presented at the annual Meeting of the National Association for Research in Science Teaching, Washington, DC (April 1987).

6. Charles W. Anderson, "Strategic Teaching in Science," in B. F. Jones et al., (Eds.), *Strategic Teaching and Learning: Cognitive Instruction in the Content Areas* (Alexandria, VA: Association for Supervision and Curriculum Development, and Elmhurst, IL: North Central Regional Educational Laboratory, 1987), 73–91.

7. L. A. Froyen, *Classroom Management: The Reflective Teacher–Leader,* second edition (Englewood Cliffs, NJ: Merrill/Prentice Hall, 1993).

8. John I. Goodlad, *A Place Called School: Prospects for the Future* (New York: McGraw-Hill, 1983).

9. For additional specifics on science learning centers, see Kathleen A. O'Sullivan, "Creating a Learning Center," *Science and Children, 24,* no. 6 (March 1984), 15–17.

10. Donald C. Orlich et al., "Science Learning Centers: An Aid to Instruction," *Science and Children, 20,* no. 1 (September 1982), 18–19.

11. For greater insight into definitions and inter-relationships between classroom management, control, and discipline, see: John Jarolimek and Clifford D. Foster, Sr., *Teaching and Learning in the Elementary School,* fifth edition, Chapter 4, "Classroom Management and Student Discipline," (Englewood Cliffs, NJ: Merrill/Prentice Hall, 1993), 103–132; Richard D. Kellough, *A Resource Guide for Teaching K–12,* Chapter 4, "Establishing and Maintaining an Effective and Safe Classroom Learning Environment," (Englewood Cliffs, NJ: Merrill/Prentice Hall, 1994), 125–179; and Jeanne Ellis Ormrod, *Educational Psychology: Principles and Applications,* Chapter 12, "Classroom Management and Discipline," (Englewood Cliffs, NJ: Merrill/Prentice Hall, 1995), 516–554.

12. These publications provide excellent ideas on classroom management, control, and discipline in hands-on/minds-on science: Robert E. MacDonald, *A Handbook of Basic Skills and Strategies for Beginning Teachers: Facing the Challenge of Teaching in Today's Schools,* Chapter 9, "Staying on Top of Classroom Management," (NY: Longman Publishing Group, 1991), 168–185. Ray Petty, "Discipline in Your Classroom. Teachers Forum: Immediate, Firm, and Consistent," *The Science Teacher, 55,* no. 2 (February 1988), 34–35. Susan O. Spellman, "Mission Possible: Teaching Hands-On Science to Disruptive Students," *Science and Children, 26,* no. 4 (January 1989), 15.

13. Carol Seefeldt and Nita Barbour, *Early Childhood Education,* third edition (Englewood Cliffs, NJ: Merrill/Prentice Hall, 1994), 282.

14. Structure and student anxiety in learning are discussed in W. Doyle, "Classroom management techniques," in O. C. Moldes (Ed.), *Student Discipline Strategies: Research and Practice* (Albany, NY: State University of New York Press, 1990); C. L. Spaulding, *Motivation in the Classroom* (New York: McGraw-Hill, 1992); and E. A. Wynne, "Improving pupil discipline character," in O. C. Moles (Ed.), *Student Discipline Strategies: Research and Practice* (Albany, NY: State University of New York Press, 1990).

15. Elizabeth B. Baron, "Discipline Strategies for Teachers," *Fastback, 344* (Bloomington, IN: Phi Delta Kappa Educational Foundation, 1992).

CHAPTER 7

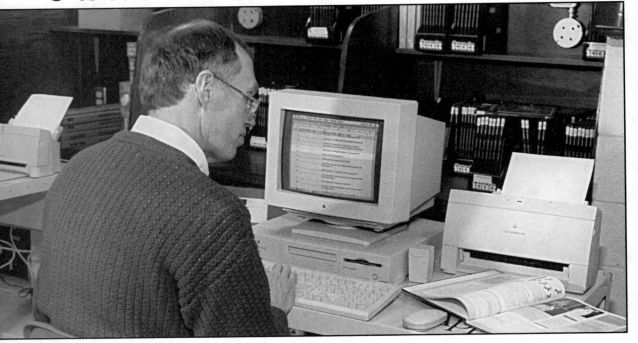

Selecting and Using Science Reform Projects, Programs, and Textbooks

If achieving scientific literacy is the goal and leaders in the science education community understand the various aspects of scientific literacy, then it seems important to have a map of the territory so you know your location, means of movement, and the direction and difficulties of travel. But for many, the contemporary reform of science education presents a confusing array of maps, destinations, directions, i.e., reports, goals, and standards, all being discussed at national, state, and local levels.[1]

A CLEARINGHOUSE OF RESOURCES

Few science programs can offer everything you need or want, although they certainly try. Thousands of supplementary programs and resources are available, some free or nearly free, but how can you find out about them?

A number of magazines review new commercially produced materials, including *Science and Children, The Science Teacher, Technology Connection,* and *Multimedia Schools.* In addition, the Eisenhower National Clearinghouse for Mathematics and Science Education (ENC), founded in 1992, offers an online computer catalog of federal, commercial, and teacher-produced curriculum resources. This catalog can be accessed at no charge and is also available on CD-ROM at no cost.[2] For example, if you wanted a video on food chains for your fourth grade class, you could search the ENC catalog by food chains (subject), by fourth grade (level), or by video (format).

The ENC catalog offers extensive information about available resources, including reviews and prices. In some cases, you will be able to download software and/or lesson plans. You can also locate information and materials related to national standards, including exemplary materials. An online discussion group enables you to ask other teachers whether they like materials you are considering for your classroom.

In addition to reviewing curriculum materials, the ENC lists federally funded national and regional resources for students and/or teachers. The ENC now publishes nine *Directories of Federal Resources,* soon to be combined into one volume. These directories describe nationwide educational programs and services offered by sixteen government agencies, such as:

- Ag in the Classroom (career information and other programs in the agricultural sciences from the U.S. Department of Agriculture)
- Project WILD (training and materials in environmental sciences, sponsored by the U.S. Department of Natural Resources)
- NASA Educational Workshops for Elementary School Teachers (seminars by NASA scientists, including materials that help teachers incorporate aerospace topics into the curriculum)
- Hands-on Universe (offers astrophysics research tools and technologies, sponsored by the U.S. Department of Energy)
- National Diffusion Network (oversees the classroom introduction of 70 proven programs in math, science, and technology, including teacher training and activities for students, sponsored by the U.S. Department of Education)
- International Science Fair (world's largest fair, sponsored by the U.S. Department of Transportation, Federal Aviation Administration)
- Cargo for Conservation (wildlife education program sponsored by the U.S. Fish and Wildlife Service)
- The GLOBE Program (involves students in monitoring the environment; lead agency: National Oceanic Atmospheric Association)

■ Heritage Education Program (focuses on archaeology, history, and paleontology for schools, U.S. Department of Natural Resources Bureau of Land Management)

ENC directories also describe unique regional resources, such as:

■ Sapelo Island National Estuarine Research Reserve in Georgia, which offers archaeological and natural history tours for school groups.
■ Indiana Dunes National Lakeshore, which has guided walks and teacher guides about lakeshore ecology.
■ Great Lakes Environmental Research Laboratory in Michigan, which provides tours and discussions of lake problems.
■ Lawrence Livermore National Laboratory in California, which sponsors teacher workshops, research apprenticeships, student internships, and other programs.
■ Kaloko–Honokohau National Historical Park in Hawaii, which offers programs on geology, anthropology, biology, and history within the park.

If you cannot visit one of these sites, the ENC catalog will help you locate information that you could purchase or sometimes download at no cost. For example, if you live in New England, students could learn about Maine's Great Bay estuary through the *Great Bay Living Lab,* a resource manual for teachers and students that provides information and activities. If you live in the Midwest, you might want to use *Waves on the Great Lakes,* teacher/student guides that include activities and investigations. If you live in the Northwest, you might consult *Northwest Women in Science: Women Making a Difference,* a book that includes 250 interviews with women from this region.

Peg Hanley, Outreach Specialist at ENC in Columbus, Ohio, reports that all of the clearinghouse's services were designed with teachers in mind. "We make an extra effort to meet the needs of elementary teachers," she says, "because they often receive the least preparation in science. . . . Anywhere teachers are, they can get to the Eisenhower National Clearinghouse, even if it's just a phone call."

Cognitive tools are important in helping children construct their understandings. You will be delighted to know that there is a large variety of useful and effective educational materials, aids, and resources from which to draw as you plan your instructional experiences for science and mathematics learning.[3]

This chapter's opening quote challenges you to see where science education has been and where science reforms are. The quotation above alludes to the many usable practical programs, teaching/learning ideas, and materials available to use in your classroom.

This chapter will introduce you to a few of the many innovative science reform projects/programs that are available. Sources are provided in this chapter and in the National Science Teachers Association annual supplement of science education suppliers. These 130-page supplements to the February issues of *Science and Children, Science Scope,* and *The Science Teacher* contain sources for science equipment/supplies, educational services, computer software, media producers, and publishers of textbooks, programs and resource materials, and tradebooks.

In addition, this chapter will inquire into how science reform projects influence textbooks, programs, and other teaching/learning materials for your science classroom. Specific non-electronic science teaching aids (textbooks and other printed materials, charts, posters, bulletin boards, etc.) will be introduced in Chapter 8. Electronic aids, such as videos, computers, and projectors,. will be examined in Chapter 10.

Science reform projects/programs/textbooks greatly influence what and how you will teach. Many schools rely solely or partially on science programs and/or textbook series as the foundation for their elementary school science syllabi or curriculums. In fact, 90 percent of all classroom activity is regulated by textbooks.[4] There is much that is valuable and useful in textbooks. Teachers must be able to select wisely from among the many possible projects/programs/textbook series.

A MAP OF SCIENCE REFORMS

Let's start building a knowledge base of past and present science reforms. Rodger W. Bybee suggests a simple framework for classifying contemporary reforms.[5] These science education reform terms are used in his framework and were introduced in previous chapters:

- *Purpose:* Universal goal statements of what science education should achieve. These are abstract and apply to all aspects of science education; e.g., achieving scientific literacy; lack of concrete statements of scientific literacy, and how to adapt to various factions of the science education community.
- *Policies:* Concrete translations of purposes, e.g., district syllabi for K–12 science, state frameworks, and national standards and benchmarks.
- *Programs:* Actual curriculum materials, textbooks, and courseware based on the policies unique to grade levels and disciplines; may be developed by national organizations (e.g., BSCS) and marketed commercially, or developed by states or school districts.
- *Practices:* Specific science teaching actions in schools including personal teacher/students' interactions, etc.

Table 7–1 shows the scope of science reform. After reviewing Table 7–1 you see how long it takes to form national standards, develop a new program, implement it, and get it into classrooms in school systems. Literally, a million people and upwards of a decade are necessary to fully implement a reform.

TRENDS IN CONTEMPORARY SCIENCE REFORM PROJECTS

Appendix A lists specific science reforms that have taken place over almost 60 years. A summary of the evolution of elementary school science education reforms can be seen in Table 7–2. As you scrutinize the science reform projects of the 1990s in Table 7–2, notice these trends:

- Science programs employ a more humanistic approach using examples from the student's life to emphasize and correlate the science concepts introduced.
- Science programs increasingly show the direct relationship of people's lives and conditions to the processes and concepts of scientific investigations.
- More emphasis is placed on relating the science programs to environmental and ecological issues.
- Values and the social aspects of science and technology are integrated into the science curriculum.
- Science is being more broadly integrated with the other curricular areas—language arts, social studies, and mathematics.
- Science programs are making wider use of flexible techniques and individualization of instruction because more special needs and

TABLE 7-1

Scope of science reform

	Time	Scale	Space	Duration	Materials	Agreement
Perspectives	For actual change to occur	Number of individuals involved	Scope and location of the change activity '	Once change has occurred	Actual products of the activity	Difficulty reaching agreement among participants
Purpose -Reforming goals -Establishing priorities for goals -Providing justification for goals	*1–2 Years* To publish document	*Hundreds* Philosophers and educators who write about aims and goals of education	*National/ Global* Publications and reports are disseminated widely	*Year* New problems emerge and new goals and priorities are proposed	*Articles/ Reports* Relatively short publications, reports, and articles	*Easy* Small number of reviewers and referees
Policy -Establishing design criteria for programs -Identifying criteria for instruction -Developing frameworks for curriculum and instruction	*3–4 Years* To develop frameworks, legislation	*Thousands* Policy analysts, legislators, supervisors, and reviewers	*National/ State* Policies focus on specific areas	*Several Years* Once in place, policies are not easily changed	*Book/ Monograph* Longer statements of rationale, content, and other aspects of reform	*Difficult* Political negotiations, trade-offs, and revisions
Program -Developing materials or adopting a program -Implement the program	*3–6 Years* To develop a complete educational program	*Tens of Thousands* Developers, field-test teachers, students, textbook publishers, software developers	*Local/School* Adoption committees	*Decades* Once developed or adopted, programs last for extended periods	*Books/ Courseware* Usually several books for students and teachers	*Very Difficult* Many factions, barriers, and requirements
Practices -Changing teaching strategies -Adapting materials to unique needs of schools and students	*7–10 Years* To complete implementation and staff development	*Millions* School personnel, public	*Classrooms* Individual teachers	*Several Decades* Individual teaching practices often last a professional lifetime	*Complete System* Books plus materials, equipment and support	*Extraordinarily Difficult* Unique needs, practices, and beliefs of individuals, schools, and communities

Source: Rodger W. Bybee, "The Contemporary Reform of Science Education," in *Issues in Science Education* (Arlington, VA: National Sciences Teachers Association, 1996).

TABLE 7–2

The evolution of science education reforms

Period	Science Education Priorities	Period	Science Education Priorities
1850s	Memorization of facts for religious explanations Descriptions and memorizations in object teaching Structured curriculum based upon formal scientific classification and terminology Methodology and utilitarianism of science curriculums based upon sequence of major science principles and their applications	1980s	Individualized science for all children: handicapped, gifted, normal More emphasis on human values, ecology, and the government Science, technology and society emphasis
		1990s	Integration of STS science activities with mathematics and all other subject areas
1950s	Textbook series and state adoptions Textbook series scope and sequence School's science content and methods of teaching	1900s– 2000s	Stress on problem solving of relevant everyday, real-life personal, society, and STS issues Encouraging students to seek alternative solutions in problem solving and to take action Concern for environmental and ecological problems and solutions Emphasis on fewer, broader thematic science topics in depth, rather than more areas superficially Using cooperative learning groups to enhance science concept and group skills learning
1960s	Curriculums influenced by funded national science projects Expanded teacher training in science		
1970s	Teaching science as processes and products: discovery and inquiry approach; conceptual schemes		

gifted students are being mainstreamed or included in the elementary school classroom.

■ More programs are using cooperative learning groups to develop skills for problem solving.

The number of science education reform projects is sizable and it would be unmanageable to attempt to list them all. Table 7–3 contains a sampling of major elementary science curriculum projects.

Many science education projects originate under grants from governmental and/or private sources. If successful, many projects become commercial programs including hardware and software, booklets, and science materials—almost everything teachers need for a whole program. Here is an example of such a project-developed commercial program.

SCIENCE REFORM PROJECT— DEVELOPED COMMERCIAL PROGRAM

Project Name: Science for Life and Living: Integrating Science, Technology, and Health

Project Developer: Biological Science Curriculum Study (BSCS). This is a nonprofit educational research and development organization affiliated with Colorado College, 830 North Tejon Street, Colorado Springs, CO 80903, (719)578-1136. The project was supported in part by the National Science Foundation.

Commercial Developer: Kendall/Hunt Publishing Company, 4050 Westmark Dr., P.O. Box 1840, Dubuque, Iowa 52004-1840, (800)288-0810.

TABLE 7–3

Contemporary elementary science project-developed programs

Name	Grades	Address	Characteristics
OBIS	K–8	Delta Education P.O. Box 915 Hudson, NH 03051-0915	*Outdoor Biology Instructional Stra-tegies:* Developed at the Lawrence Hall of Science (University of California, Berkeley), this program of four outdoor activity packets is designed to give children hands-on experiences in different ecological environments. Packets can stand alone or be used in sequence or with other programs.
STC	1–6	Carolina Biological Supply Co. 2700 York Rd. Burlington, NC 27215	*Science and Technology for Children:* This program consists of units of hands-on instruction that integrate science and mathematics with other disciplines. A primary focus of program developers is to interest more females and minority children in science.
SAPA	K–6	Delta Education, Inc. P.O. Box 915 Hudson, NH 03051-0915	*Science—A Process Approach:* These two similar and highly structured programs are process oriented and module based. Developed around se-
SAPA II		Ginn and Company 191 Spring Street Lexington, MA 02173	quenced behavioral objectives. SAPA II provides more flexibility for teacher use. Contains a sequence of 105 modules that are not grade specific.
SAVI/SELPH (Designed for disabled students)	2–10	Center for Multisensory Learning Lawrence Hall of Science University of California Berkeley, CA 94720	*Science Activities for the Visually Impaired/Science Enrichment Learning for the Physically Handi-capped:* Teacher activity guides in nine modules, student equipment kits.
SCIS	K–6	Delta Education P.O. Box 915 Hudson, NH 03051-0915	*Science Curriculum Improvement Study:* Originally developed by a team at the University of California, Berkeley, there have been several generations of SCIS
SCIIS 3	K–6	Delta Education P.O. Box 915 Hudson, NH 03051-0915	developed, with the most recent being SCIS 3. The SCIS programs are built around a hierarchy of science concepts.
SCIS 3	K–6	Delta Education P.O. Box 915 Hudson, NH 03051-0915	Science process skills are integrated into the materials-centered programs, which use an inductive instructional approach and a three-phase learning cycle: (1) student exploration, (2) teacher explanation of concepts, and (3) student application of the old with new.

Source: Richard D. Kellough, *Integrating Mathematics and Science for Kindergarten and Primary Children* (Englewood Cliffs, NJ: Merrill/Prentice Hall, 1996), 396–397.

Name	Grades	Address	Characteristics
USMES	K–8	ERIC, Ohio State University 1200 Chambers Rd Columbus, OH 43212	*Unified Sciences and Mathematics for Elementary School:* Interdisciplinary units build around science, math, social sciences, and language arts, using a problem-solving approach. Twenty-six units are available. Can be coordinated with the regular curriculum.
Windows on Science	1–6	Optical Data Corp. 30 Technology Dr. Warren, NJ 07059	Primary, earth, life, and physical science videodisc program.
AIMS	K–10	AIMS Educational Foundation P.O. Box 8120 Fresno, CA 93747	*Activities for Integrating Math and Science Project:* Integration of math skills with science processes into a series of enjoyable investigatory activities; accompanying teacher booklets.
BSCS	K–6	BSCS 830 N. Tejon St., Suite 405 Colorado Springs, CO 80903–4720	*Biological Science Curriculum Study:* Name of project, "Science for Living: Integrating Science, Technology, and Health." Integrated curriculum designed to relate what children know with their exploration and evaluation of new knowledge. Designed around concepts and skills for each grade level: order and organization (grade 1); change and measurement (grade 2); patterns and prediction (grade 3); systems and analysis (grade 4); transformation and investigation (grade 5); balance and decisions (grade 6). Each investigatory lesson has five sequenced phases: engagement, exploration, explanation, elaboration, and evaluation.
ESS	K–6	Delta Education P.O. Box 915 Hudson, NH 03051–0915	*Elementary Science Study:* A program of 56 nonsequential, open-ended exploratory activities that are not grade-level specific. Student worksheets, booklets, and teacher's guides. Most units are accompanied by kits of materials. Films and film loops also available. Although designed for regular students, ESS units have been shown to be useful in teaching science to children who have language deficiencies, learning difficulties, or other learning disadvantages.

TABLE 7–3
continued

Name	Grades	Address	Characteristics
FOSS	3–6	Center for Multi-Sensory Learning, Lawrence Hall of Science University of California Berkeley, CA 94720 Also available from: Encyclopedia Britannica Educational Corp. 310 S. Michigan Ave., 6th Floor Chicago, IL 60604–9839	*Full Option Science System:* Designed for both regular and special education students, 12 modules with lab kits are available. Lessons are in earth, life, and physical sciences with extension activities in language, computer, and math. Can be integrated with textbook programs and state frameworks.
GEMS	1–10	Lawrence Hall of Science University of California Berkeley, CA 94720	*Great Explorations in Math and Science:* Developed at the Lawrence Hall of Science, this is a series of more than 30 teacher's guides for activities using easily obtained materials.
IUES	K–6	Educational Development Center 55 Chapel St. Newton, MA 02160	*Improving Urban Elementary Science:* Developed by EDC, which also developed ESS, this program contains 24 open-ended, activity-based modules that are self-contained or can be used with other programs. Designed with urban children in mind, it integrates science with other areas of the curriculum and with children's experiences.
NGKN	4–6	Technical Education Resource Center (TERC) 1696 Massachussetts Ave. Cambridge, MA 02138	*National Geographic Kids Network:* Six week-long units, each problem centered; computer networked with scientists.

Source: Richard D. Kellough, *Integrating Mathematics and Science for Kindergarten and Primary Children* (Englewood Cliffs, NJ: Merrill/Prentice Hall, 1996), 396–397.

Major goal: To have students learn about science, technology, and health because they need to make informed choices in their daily lives and as future citizens.[6] Many of the science reform trends listed in the previous section have found their way into this program.

Features

1. At each level of the program one major concept and one major skill that integrate science, technology, and health are introduced to help students make meaningful connections between the three study areas.

2. Cooperative learning is an integral part of the series and built into each lesson to promote student learning and help teachers with classroom management. Much time is spent on developing teachers' knowledge of team and social skills and how to organize and conduct the cooperative learning team jobs (e.g., communicator, manager, tracker, checker, and coach).

3. The instructional model that frames the learning experiences is based on constructivist learning theory with these five E's:
*E*ngage the learner with an event or question.
*E*xplore the concept, skill, or behavior through hands-on activities so students acquire a common set of experiences.
*E*xplain the concept, skill, or behavior and define terms.
*E*laborate the concept, skill, or behavior by applying what has been learned in unique situations.
*E*valuate students' understanding of the concept and their intention to use the skills or behaviors.

4. Major concepts and skills that connect the hands-on activities in science, technology, and health include the following:

Levels	Major Concept	Major Skills
1	Order	Organization
2	Change	Measurement
3	Patterns	Prediction
4	Systems	Analysis
5	Energy	Investigation
6	Balance	Decisions

5. Students are encouraged to participate physically and mentally and share responsibility for their learning and improvement in problem solving, critical thinking, decision making, and taking action.

6. Hands-on materials not readily available in classroom or students' homes are included in the program.

7. An implementation guide assists teachers and other school personnel in using the project successfully.

8. The components of the program are:
a. *Teacher's Guides* contain an Introduction to the Curriculum, including the philosophy of the program, the instructional model, assessment, tips for managing activity-based science, safety, equity issues, cooperative learning, etc.

b. Unit overviews detail the concepts and skills included in each unit, the flow of lessons in the unit, the outcomes students should achieve, necessary advance preparations, required materials, and tips for structuring and managing cooperative learning.

c. Teacher pages for each lesson give stage of the instructional model, lesson number and title, overview of lesson, expected student outcomes and indicators of student achievement, background information, lesson extensions, and suggested resources for the classroom.

d. Numbered blackline masters (pages that can be duplicated for students prior to starting lessons) are matched to particular lessons.

e. An *Enrichment Through Children's Literature* appendix lists trade books reviewed and recommended by scientists, science educators, early childhood educators, and media specialists.

f. The *Student Guides* are structured differently than traditional elementary school science textbooks. They incorporate these attributes:
   - procedural text, so students can follow directions independent of the teacher
   - the team task, team jobs, and team skills necessary for cooperative learning
   - expository text
   - tables, charts, and diagrams
   - poems, short stories, and cartoons
   - articles from children's magazines
   - writing opportunities, recording in journals, creative writing, and displaying data in graphic form

Pages from the student text are reduced in the teacher's guide to put all teacher information in one place.

9. The series is a complete program that provides a full year of instruction.

10. As the program scope and sequence (Table 7–4) shows, there are four units at each level. Although there is some flexibility in

TABLE 7–4
Science for Life and Living scope and sequence chart

	Science	Technology	Health
K Awareness of Myself and My World			
1 Order and Organization			
Introduction to Order and Organization	Objects and Properties	Materials and Structures	Safety and Security
2 Change and Measurement			
Introduction to Change and Measurement	Comparison and Evidence	Tools and Machines	Wellness and Personal Care
3 Patterns and Prediction			
Introduction to Patterns and Prediction	Records and Data	Construction and Testing	Nutrition and Dental Care
4 Systems and Analysis			
Introduction to Systems and Analysis	Interactions and Variables	Problems and Solutions	Self and Substances
5 Energy and Investigation			
Introduction to Energy and Investigation	Energy Chains and Food Chains	Design and Efficiency	Fitness and Protection
6 Balance and Decisions			
Introduction to Balance and Decisions	Ecosystems and Resources	Constraints and Trade-Offs	Communication and Conflict

Source: *K–6 Science for Life and Living: Science, Technology, and Health. An Inside Look at the New BSCS Elementary Curriculum* (Dubuque, IA: Kendall/Hunt, 1992), 13.

the placement of units (particularly Units 3 and 4), it is recommended you teach the lesson within each unit sequentially because:

a. Lessons proceed through the stages of the series' four-point learning cycle. Students should move through the model from engagement to evaluation stage.

b. One major concept and one major skill connect the series' units.

11. It is recommended that teachers should allow the following approximate times if they teach science an average of three times a week:

a. Introductory unit takes about three or four weeks to teach.

b. Remaining three units (one each in science, technology, and health) each require about eight weeks of instruction.

c. The following chart displays the recommended amount of time per class session at each level.

Level	Minutes per class session
K	20
1	20–25
2	20–30
3	30–40
4	30–40
5	45–50
6	45–60

SAMPLE LESSON FROM SCIENCE FOR LIFE AND LIVING: INTEGRATING SCIENCE, TECHNOLOGY, AND HEALTH

The excerpts that follow are from the Level 2 teacher's edition of *Science for Life and Living: Integrating Science, Technology, and Health.* These excerpts illustrate the features of the teacher's edition, including student pages.

To begin, examine Table 7–5, the Expanded Scope and Sequence for Level 2 of the series. The major concept, *change,* the major skill, *measurement,* and the lesson selected are from Unit 2: **"Comparison and Evidence: Change and Measurement in Science."** Lesson 8 is from the *Explore* stage of the 5 *E*'s learning cycle and is called "Strange Stuff." The teacher's objective, written in student performances, is:

Students will share a common experience that deals with multiple changes. Working in teams, they will add water to dry granules of a polymer and observe the resulting changes. They will also measure volumes to solve a problem.

The lesson outcomes (also in observable student performance objectives) are:

1. Students should understand that objects can change in several ways. They will show their

understanding by describing changes in size, color, shape, and feel of pieces of polymer when the polymer is wet.
2. Students should be able to measure and solve a problem. They will show their ability by:
- *measuring the volume of polymer granules that have absorbed water, and*
- *finding out how much water another team added to its granules.*

The lesson is introduced to students in the Student Guide using an alien being who comes to Earth, can change her size and color, and has all sorts of surprises in her pockets. One of these surprises is some strange stuff, and students are asked: "What properties does it have?" They are cautioned never to taste anything unknown as they are finding out. They are given a team task:

Observe the strange stuff. Talk about what you observe with your teammates. Find out how the strange stuff looks, feels, smells, and sounds. Make a team record of your observations.

A series of "Do It" activities follows. The teacher's awareness of her students' prior knowledge, manipulation and social skills, and other relevant learning environment factors determine how many activities are completed and how quickly.

Lesson Activity 1: Observing Changes

Pages 51–54 of the series' *Student Guide* (in Figure 7–1) show how students in different cooperative learning groups will conduct experiments to observe what happens to the strange stuff when water is added to it.

TEAM TASK
Add water to the strange stuff. Find out what happens.

TABLE 7–5
Science for Life and Living: Expanded scope and sequence, Level 2

Major Concept: Change	Major Skill: Measurement	Unit 2: Comparison and Evidence: Change and Measurement in Science
Change is a process in which objects and events become, or are made to become, different. Learning to understand, predict, quantify, and control such changes is basic to education in science, technology, and health. Concepts relevant to learning about change include change over time, reversible change, and irreversible change.	*Measurements* is a procedure by which people assign a quantitative value to some characteristic of an object or an event. Measurement contributes to accurate descriptions, and is vital for conveying scientific information. By measuring, students can quantify the properties of objects or of events at different times, compare the measurements, and determine what changes have occurred.	*Comparison* is defined as the act of observing and noting the similarities and differences among several objects or events. Only through comparison can one recognize whether an object or event has, or has not, changed. During this unit, students will make quantitative comparisons of the length of shadows, the height of plants, and the volume of popcorn. *Evidence* is defined as the data or information on which an explanation is based. Evidence also includes facts or signs that help one come to a conclusion. In this unit, students use direct observations—what they see, hear, smell, feel, or measure— as evidence for their decisions or conclusions about change. **Students will be able to:** 1. understand that objects can change in several ways, some of which are reversible and some irreversible; 2. provide evidence to support a statement that something has changed; 3. understand that comparisons of both observations and measurements can provide evidence of a change; 4. be able to compare measurements and decide whether a change has occurred; 5. realize that evidence of a change can come from written or oral information provided by other people; and 6. listen when others talk.

Source: K–6 Science for Life and Living: Science, Technology, and Health: An Inside Look at the New BSCS Elementary Curriculum (Dubuque, IA: Kendall/Hunt, 1992), 40–41.

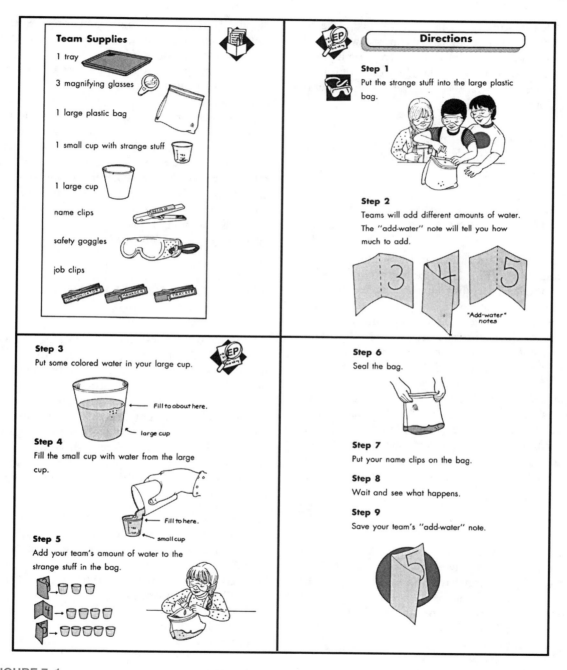

FIGURE 7–1

Changes in strange stuff

Source: K–6 Science for Life and Living: Science, Technology, and Health: An Inside Look at the New BSCS Elementary Curriculum (Dubuque, IA: Kendall/Hunt, 1992), 54–55.

Closely observe the box labeled "Team Supplies". Safety goggles are almost always used to protect the eyes, especially when using liquids. Notice the clothes pin label—Communicator, Manager, and Tracker—for the three cooperative learning team jobs.

Lesson Activity 2: Measuring and Problem Solving

> ### TEAM TASK
> *Find out how much water another team added to its strange stuff.*

Directions are simple and well illustrated for students who may lack reading skills. Students are told that different teams have added different amounts of water to their strange stuff. They are reminded that they added a specific amount of water to their strange stuff and are now asked: "Can you find how much water another team added to its strange stuff?"

Figure 7–2 shows pages 56–58, which guide the measuring and problem-solving activity. Students are asked how they will solve the problem and plan and conduct experiments to try out their hunches. Step 6 has students sharing their findings with other groups to see if their experiments obtained correct responses to the original questions.

Extending the Science Concepts

The series "invents" vocabulary and definitions so that students may enlarge upon the knowledge they've constructed as a result of the activities. This is part of the 5 *E*'s learning cycle and is in the section of the *Student's Guide* called "Read About It." A sample of the information about polymers and their uses is given in Figure 7–3.

Another feature of the program is the "Think About It" section in *Student's Guide*. It poses thought-provoking questions for more hypothe-

sizing, planning, observing, comparing, experimenting, and measuring. Figure 7–4 indicates how this is done for polymers.

Although project-developed programs are well planned, well written, and have excellent activities and materials for a year's science hands-on/minds-on program, they may not be applicable to all classroom situations. Student backgrounds, skills, and social skills, district science goals, finances, and other factors all play a role in whether such a program can be adapted in a school. However, ideas can be gathered from such programs for use in your science activities. What else can you glean from the project-developed programs available today?

THE BENEFITS OF REFORM PROJECTS/PROGRAMS

According to the research, students in science reform project/programs stressing science/technology/society (STS) outperformed those in traditional, textbook-based classrooms.

One extensive study was conducted in Iowa. Twelve teachers taught one section of students with STS strategies and another with a regular textbook. Pre/post tests were given to both sections at the semester's start and finish. Figure 7–5 shows the results of those tests and demonstrates that STS:

- does *not* result in greater concept proficiency (however, some say STS strategies result in more long-term learning due to direct experiences).
- leads to improvement (at 0.01 statistic level) in all other domains:
  1. process skills
  2. student attitudes
  3. creative skills
  4. questioning skills
  5. hypothesizing
  6. prediction
  7. application.[7]

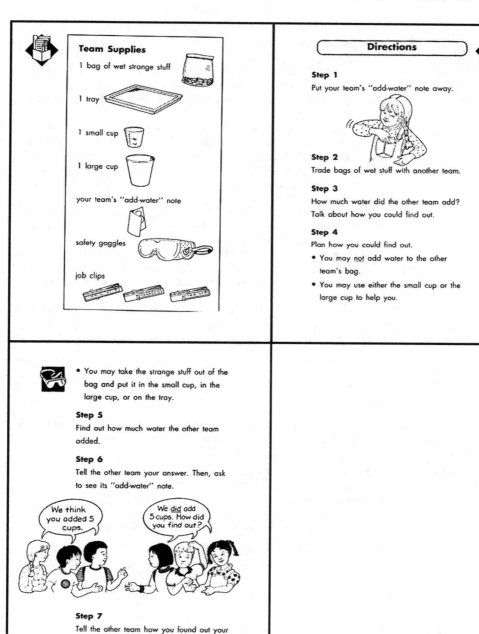

FIGURE 7–2

How much water?

Source: K–6 Science for Life and Living: Science, Technology, and Health: An Inside Look at the New BSCS Elementary Curriculum (Dubuque, IA: Kendall/Hunt, 1992), 55–56.

FIGURE 7–3

Read about it

Source: K–6 Science for Life and Living: Science, Technology, and Health: An Inside Look at the New BSCS Elementary Curriculum (Dubuque, IA: Kendall/Hunt, 1992), 56.

What Is the Strange Stuff?

The strange stuff is a material called *polymer*. Some polymers are found in nature, and other polymers are made by people, You have been finding out about one kind of polymer by adding water to it. Do you know you have been using objects made of other kinds of polymers, too?

Some polymers are called plastics, like the tray, cups, and bag. But there are many other kinds of polymers. For example, your eraser is a polymer, and so is the elastic in your underwear. Each kind of polymer has special properties that make it useful. People make things out of the kind of polymer that has the properties they need. What special properties does the elastic have?

The polymer that you called "strange stuff" has special properties, too. One property is the way the pieces soak up water. Some people call this polymer a "water-grabber."

People use this water-grabber polymer to help plants grow. They add the polymer to the soil. The polymer soaks up water and holds it until the plants need it. Then, the plant's roots absorb the water from the polymer.

Forest rangers use the water-grabber polymer when they plant new trees after a fire. They put the polymer in the holes they dig for the trees. Then, they water the trees. The polymer stores some of the water

FIGURE 7–4

Think about it

Source: K–6 Science for Life and Living: Science, Technology, and Health: An Inside Look at the New BSCS Elementary Curriculum (Dubuque, IA: Kendall/Hunt, 1992), 57.

Finding out about this kind of polymer might help you think of more interesting questions. Here are some questions to think about:

1. Can you use this polymer more than one time?
2. Will wet polymer change back to dry polymer?
3. How long does it take wet polymer to dry out?
4. How does wet polymer look when it dries out?
5. Does this polymer dry out when it is in the dirt?
6. How long can you keep wet polymer in the sealed bag?

How can you find out these things?

STS students develop more attributes that harmonize with contemporary elementary school science goals: STS students exhibit traits of scientifically literate citizens.

Research has shown that students in other science reform project/programs, too, scored higher on tests of science processes, attitudes, concept application, reading, and arithmetic skills than students in comparable textbook-based programs.

Regardless of what kind of science program you have, you can benefit from reform projects/programs. See what you can adapt for your particular classroom and students.

FIGURE 7–5

Comparison of student growth in five assessment areas for those enrolled in textbook and STS sections

Source: Robert E. Yager, "Make a Difference With STS: Should We Toss Out the Textbooks?" *The Science Teacher, 60,* no. 2, (February 1993) 46.

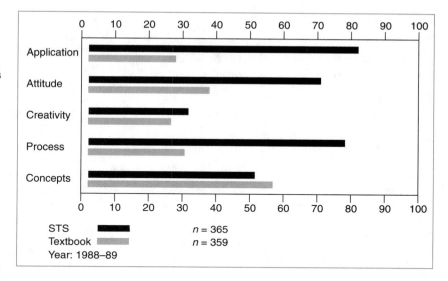

"NEW GENERATION" SCIENCE TEXTBOOK SERIES/PACKAGES

Contemporary textbook authors and publishers have been influenced by earlier funded science reform projects. They have incorporated many of the better points of these projects into their textbooks and textbook series, resulting in high-quality textbooks for elementary school teachers and students. Among the more visible science textbook improvements resulting from science reform projects are:

1. Publishers have made a greater effort to improve the accuracy of scientific information.
2. A hands on/minds-on discovery, or laboratory-centered approach is more common in recent textbooks. Today's texts put greater emphasis on question-and-answer techniques than previous elementary science textbooks did.
3. Authors are beginning to develop styles of writing that convey the fascination and intellectual excitement inherent in science disciplines.

4. An emphasis on science processes is appearing more frequently in current textbooks, including manipulative activities.
5. Several of the publishers are including kits of materials to carry out the experimental activities included in their texts.
6. Limited opportunities are beginning to appear in texts for developing scientific attitudes, creative skills, and critical thinking.
7. The format of modern textbooks is much more inviting than that of previous texts; there are more pictures of scientific phenomena. Film loops, films, videos, CD-ROMs, computer software, etc. are available to supplement the books.
8. Publishers are offering comprehensive interdisciplinary, thematic science units rather than providing the numerous isolated lessons as in the past.

Macmillan/McGraw-Hill Science

The Macmillan/McGraw-Hill science series is an example of the influence of science reform projects. How many of the textbook reform items mentioned above can you find in this science textbook series?

Science Reform Project Developer: The series is based on the work of these major projects:

- Project 2061, an ongoing venture of the American Association for the Advancement of Science (AAAS)
- The Science Education Standards Committee of the National Research Council
- The Scope, Sequence and Coordination of Secondary School Science Project, sponsored by the National Science Teachers Association (NSTA)

The philosophy of this textbook series is that "all students can learn anything they put their minds to, hearts in, and hands on." It is an activity-based series in which students construct science concepts and solve problems through inquiry and exploration.[8]

The foundation for the series is based on the following contemporary trends in science education:

1. *Scientific Literacy for All.* Science learning should be accessible to all students regardless of background, future aspiration, or interest.
2. *Activity-Based Learning.* Learning is an active process resulting from hands-on/minds-on explorations in which learners construct their own knowledge. Assessment procedures should be varied and reflect learning approaches and application.
3. *Integrated Organization.* There should be a connection among aspects of content, as well as a development of concepts around major themes. Science should be seen in tandem with technology, society, and personal experience. There should be integration of science with math and other subjects.
4. *Flexible Design.* Curriculum should be flexible. Content should promote in-depth study of fewer key concepts rather than superficial coverage of many topics.

5. *Science Processes and Skills.* Scientific ways of thinking (e.g., questioning), problem solving, and critical thinking should be an integral part of science learning.

The series has these attributes:

- A four-step lesson cycle built from a constructivist point of view, similar to the 5 *E*'s of the *Science for Life and Living: Science, Technology, and Health program.*
  1. *Engage* students in a motivating learning activity to focus their thinking on the concept, find out what they know, and set up the problem to be explored.
  2. *Explore* a question or problem by hands-on activities, critical thinking, problem solving, and decision making, as students begin to construct their own understandings of the concept.
  3. *Develop* additional activities, aided by links to other curriculum areas, and introduce vocabulary so students can construct explanations of the concepts they have explored.
  4. *Extend/Apply* students' new understandings to real-world examples as part of technology, society, and personal experience.
- Three types of activities make science exciting:
  1. hands-on explorations to help students to construct concepts,
  2. building one concept on another to develop deeper understandings, and
  3. minds-on activities to spark students' critical thinking about science phenomena.
- Assessment is made easy by performance assessment, portfolio assessment, and tests that reflect the learning approaches. Together, these assessments ensure the teacher's understanding of each student's knowledge of science.
- Additional activities and approaches meet student individual needs, enabling *all* students to have equal opportunities to learn and succeed; e.g., students acquiring English, students with different learning modalities, and students with multicultural perspectives.

- The series has an integrated organization: exploring major science issues of today, linking science concepts to other curricular areas (e.g., math, literature, social studies, health, reading/language arts, art, and music), and interconnecting science disciplines.
- The teacher's anthology, with the literature to literacy activities, lists other good books to read, and hands-on activities that explore science with reading/language arts all help integrate science and literature.
- Figure 7–6 shows the series' curriculum overview chart that permits teachers to build their own science curriculum and teach it in any sequence that is appropriate to their classroom situation.

Observe these aspects of flexible design, which promote in-depth study of fewer key concepts rather than superficial coverage of many concepts:

1. You can personalize your curriculum to meet the needs of your students by looking at the suggested grade level and then choosing from among 42 stand-alone, self-contained units and three human body units.
2. Key concepts revolve around these seven major themes so students experience and make sense of the connections in science:

Systems and Interactions	Energy
Scale and Structure	Evolution
Stability	Models
Patterns of Change	

3. Life, earth, and physical sciences are presented in real-world settings. The 45 units are in blocks that list the unit title, major theme, and science content. Color dots next to each unit title indicate a life, earth, or physical science emphasis.

Components and Resources of Series. The series encompasses an extensive array of components and resources flexibly packaged in a unit box, as an individual unit package, or as individual components. To see how the components are coordinated in the series, let's walk through a single lesson in the series.

Mix It, Beat It, Bake It, Eat It! In the teachers' planning guide, teachers are given a one-page condensed outline of each lesson, including:

1. Theme
2. Learner outcomes
3. Science vocabulary
4. Misconceptions
5. Background

Figure 7–7 displays the teacher's planning guide with lesson cycle segment, suggested pacing, hands-on activities (title, objectives, materials needed), and resources (audio tapes, trade books, videodiscs, activity cards). The lesson, **"If You Put It Together, Can You Take It Apart?,"** recommended for Grade 4, is:

- in the "Explore" learning cycle segment
- suggested for one day
- in Student Book pages 64–69
- in Activity Log pages 29–30

Student Books. On pages 62 and 63 of the Student Book, students are introduced to the "Explore" part of the lesson. The activity will investigate how mixtures can be separated by their physical properties. Notice that the suggested activities and questions in Figure 7–8 guide the students in the investigation.

Students record the results of their investigations on the Activity Log (student book pages 29 and 30), as shown in Figure 7–9.

Assessment Options. Suggestions are offered for assessing student results (Figure 7–9). Activity Log pages can be included in student portfolios, along with a review of *Fun With Physics,* a short story about a change in the chemical state of matter, and a dialogue about why oxygen cannot be easily separated from hydrogen in water. Transparencies included in the series help students identify and describe chemical changes.

FIGURE 7–6

Macmillan/McGraw-Hill science series curriculum overview

Source: Teacher's Planning Guide, Macmillan/McGraw-Hill Science Series (New York: Macmillan/McGraw-Hill, 1995), T8–T9. Reprinted with permission of Macmillan/McGraw-Hill.

Lesson Cycle Segment	Suggested Pacing	Hands-on Activities				Resources
		Title	Objectives	Materials Needed (per activity group)		
ENGAGE Student pp. 60–61	1 day	none	none	none		**Audio Tape** **Concept Summary and Glossary Masters**
EXPLORE Student pp. 62–63 *Activity Log* pp. 29–30	1 day	If You Put It Together, Can You Take It Apart?	• **Experiment** to examine two methods of separating mixtures. • **Hypothesize** and **experiment** to test the applicability of using these methods to separate other mixtures.	• Warm water • Table salt • Sand • Four 9-oz. clear plastic cups • Straw* • 2 filters (coffee filters will do)* • Spoon		**Audio Tape**
DEVELOP Student pp. 64–69 *Activity Log* pp. 31–32	3 days	A Different Use for Lemon Juice	• **Observe** a change in matter and **infer** that a chemical change took place.	• Lemon juice • A penny • Dropper* • Tissue		**Audio Tape** **Family Science Master:** *Kitchen Scavenger Hunt* **Teacher's Anthology:** *The Wonderful Wizard of Oz* **Trade Book:** *Sugaring Time* **Videodisc:** *Properties of Matter* **Activity Card:** *Fire!*
		Can Wool Rust?	• **Predict** which pieces of steel wool will rust. • **Experiment** to determine which piece of steel wool will rust. • **Observe** changes in pieces of wool. • **Infer** from findings what conditions cause rust. • **Hypothesize** about possible ways to prevent rust.	• 3 pieces of steel wool without soap* • Water • Cooking oil • 3 cups • Marker		
EXTEND/APPLY Student pp. 70–71	1 day	none	none	none		**Audio Tape** **Activity Card:** *Mix It Up*

FIGURE 7–7

Macmillan/McGraw-Hill science series, lesson 5 planning guide

Source: Teacher's Planning Guide: Properties of Matter, Macmillan/McGraw-Hill Science Series (New York: Macmillan/McGraw-Hill, 1995), 60a

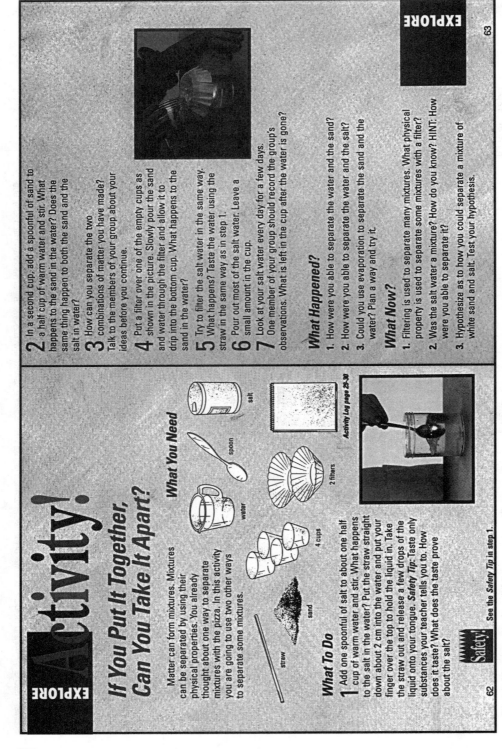

FIGURE 7–8

Macmillan/McGraw-Hill Science Series Student book "Explore" activity: "If You Put It Together, Can You Take It Apart?"

Source: Teacher's Planning Guide: Properties of Matter, Macmillan/McGraw-Hill Science Series (New York: Macmillan/McGraw-Hill 1995), 62–63. Reprinted with the permission of Macmillan/McGraw-Hill.

On **Activity Log** page 29, students record the results of their investigations into separating mixtures.

 Assessing Student Results

Students should conclude that the methods used in the activity should work for separating other types of mixtures.

ctivity!

If You Put It Together, Can You Take It Apart?

What to Do

What happens to the salt when you stir it into the water?
Students should note salt can no longer be seen.

How does the water taste? What does the taste prove about the salt?
Water tastes salty.

What happens to the sand that you stir into the water?
Sand doesn't "disappear" the way the salt did.

Write your group's ideas for separating the combinations of salt and water and sand and water that you have made.
Answers will vary.

What was left in the cup that contained salt water after a few days?

Salt.

29   Use with Student Edition pages 62–63.

Explore continued

What Happened?

1. How were you able to separate the water and the sand?
The water and sand were separated by filtration. The filter caught and held the particles of sand.

2. How were you able to separate the water and the salt?
The water and salt were separated by evaporation. As the water evaporated, the salt was left behind.

3. Do you think that you could use evaporation to separate the sand and the water? Plan a way and try it.
Yes, you could separate the sand from the water by evaporation, but filtration works faster.

What Now?

1. Filtering is used to separate many mixtures. What physical property is used to separate some mixtures with a filter?
The physical property of size is used to separate some mixtures with a filter.

2. Was the salt water a mixture? How do you know? (HINT: How were you able to separate it?)
Salt water is a mixture. The salt and water can be separated by physical means.

3. Hypothesize as to how you could separate a mixture of white sand and salt. Test your hypothesis.
White sand and salt could be separated by dissolving the salt in water and filtering out the sand. The salt could then be recovered by evaporating the water.

30   Use with Student Edition pages 62–63.

On **Activity Log** page 30, students record their answers to What Happened? and What Now?.

 Assessing Student Results

Performance Assessment
Ask students to discuss what would happen during the experiment if flour were substituted for the table salt. (The flour and water would form a paste, which would be difficult to separate.)

FIGURE 7–9

Macmillan/McGraw-Hill science series, Student activity log

Source: Teacher's Planning Guide: Properties of Matter, Macmillan/McGraw-Hill Science Series (New York: Macmillan/McGraw-Hill 1995), 62–63. Reprinted with the permission of Macmillan/McGraw-Hill.

APPLICATIONS OF SCIENCE REFORM PROJECTS/PROGRAMS/ TEXTBOOK SERIES TO YOUR SCIENCE CLASSROOM

You may be asking, "All of this research, innovation, and experimentation is great, but what does it have to do with me? I'm a classroom teacher, not a science education researcher." These innovative programs have a lot to do with *any* elementary school teacher who includes science in the curriculum.

More educational ideas and materials are being produced today than ever before. What used to take 30 years to accomplish—from the development of a new educational idea to actual classroom implementation—now occurs very rapidly. Because of the rapid pace of current scientific and technological advances, we must all be more committed to professional growth (including self-improvement and pre-service and inservice training) than ever before in history.

Teacher education courses must present the new science education projects/programs/textbook series to all prospective teachers. It is less expensive and more effective to do this before teachers enter the profession than to "retrain" teachers through in-service education. Pre-service science education courses must include factual materials about hands-on activities and the most recent science education projects.

Elementary school teachers (and administrators) currently in service will have to study these projects in depth before committing themselves to any specific program or incorporating parts of innovative science programs into their existing science curriculum or textbook program. How can this be done?

Reaching Out for Data About Science Reform Projects/Program/Series

In order to use parts or all of innovative science projects in your classroom, you must become knowledgeable about what projects/programs/series are available. Here are some ways to accomplish that.

Assemble a Science Reform Project/Program/Series Portfolio. Create a science reform project/program/series portfolio in your school with assistance from the school or community librarian. To begin, get and read these excellent resources from cover to cover:

- *Science for Children: Resources for Teachers,* (1988). This guide (developed by the National Science Resources Center) lists hundreds of recommended materials and resources for teaching science to students. It includes information on curriculum materials, science activity and teaching books, students' and teacher magazines, past and present elementary science reform projects, professional organizations and associations, science publishers, and materials suppliers. The publisher is National Academy Press, 2101 Constitution Ave, NW, Washington, DC 20418.

- *Science Education Programs That Work: A Collection of Proven Exemplary Educational Programs and Practices in the National Diffusion Network* (October 1990). This inexpensive ($1.75), short (24 pages) booklet is produced by the National Diffusion Network (NDN), a federally funded system that makes exemplary educational programs available for adoption by schools. NDN provides dissemination funds to exemplary programs, called Developer Demonstrator Projects or Dissemination Process Projects. NDN helps local schools improve their science teaching at little or no cost by (a) providing teacher inservice training, (b) in-school follow-up assistance, and (c) access to a regional network of adopters of similar projects. Besides giving data on 15 innovative science programs available now, this booklet lists a State and Private School Facilitator for every state. The person can arrange for your school to start improving your science teaching. State facilitators are supported by NDN grants, so there is no cost to you for their

In your search for science reform materials look for innovative technology that will facilitate science teaching and learning. The technology shown here allows the teacher to place a slide on the microscope for the whole class to view it at once by video.

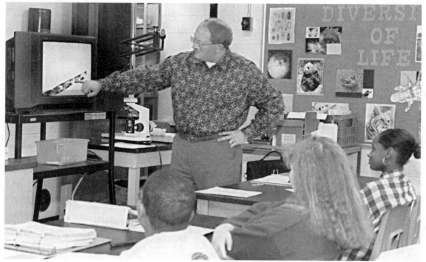

services. For more information, contact your state facilitator or the U.S. Department of Education, Recognition Division, 555 New Jersey Avenue, NW, Washington, DC 20208-5645. Phone: (202)219-2134.

- *Science Education Programs That Work,* PIP 90-846, U.S. Government Printing Office, Superintendent of Documents, Washington, DC 20402-9329.

Request Local Colleges to Teach About Science Reform Projects/Programs/Textbooks. If you are teaching, take a course in innovative science reform projects/programs/ textbooks for the elementary schools. If one is not currently offered by your local college, request one. The course you take should involve a hands-on approach. You should actually do the science activities the same way students will;

merely talking about the projects is not enough. Specifically ask how these projects/program/textbooks can be modified if you do not use the total program.

Send for Supplementary Information. A group of teachers in your school or school district could send for information about science reform projects from the sources listed in this chapter. List the things you want to investigate; consider the following questions:

1. How do the units cover the elements of science/technology and learning espoused by your school or school district?
2. Are there many varied activities for students to obtain information and develop attitudes?
3. How are the concepts appropriate for the interests and abilities of your particular students?
4. In what ways do the concepts challenge the students?
5. How does the project provide for systematic development of concepts, skills, and attitudes?
6. How do the teacher's guides provide sufficient science and pedagogical information for you to guide the students to discover the goals of the program?
7. What provisions are made should you wish to use selected units rather than the entire program?

Contact Distributors of Projects/Programs/Textbook Series. Distributors usually arrange for a consultant to speak to you about your interests and concerns about the program without any commitment. Prepare a list of questions ahead of time. Many state education departments also provide such a consultant.

Communicate With Distributor When You Choose a Specific Program. The distributor will usually set up a series of free inservice workshops for all teachers using the program. Consultants giving workshops are often former classroom teachers or college professors trained in the new science project/program/textbook series.

Experiment With Materials Yourself. Become familiar with the materials, science concepts, and teaching strategies during the workshops. Try the activities yourself! If you feel comfortable with the activities, you can be a good guide for your students.

Make Certain You Have All the Materials Needed. Contemporary science projects/programs/textbooks depend on materials, student activity record sheets, and assessment sheets. Be sure the program offers the materials you need, or that they can be easily obtained from local sources.

Share Your Successes and Failures. Communicate with your fellow teachers and the consultant or distributor about which programs are effective and which are not. Constant self-evaluation and sharing of ideas will help you achieve the goals of the project.

If you become involved in teaching any of the new science reform projects/programs, you will be part of a new and exciting venture. You have a new and very important role in developing the science curriculum. Remember, you are the only member of the program evaluation team (which includes professional scientists, child psychologists, curriculum writers, classroom teachers, and so on) setting up a new science program who knows *your* students. You are on the firing line, testing the value of any new science program *with students.*

Many of the decisions about new science reform project/programs rest with you. You must be well informed about current science projects and texts, so you can select, carry out, and evaluate science education in elementary and middle school. The unique contributions and potential power of elementary and middle school teachers are summarized in this statement of Hubert H. Humphrey, former school teacher and vice-president of the United States:

Experimenting with activity materials yourself, before using them with students, will help you know if you have all the necessary material and if the activity works well.

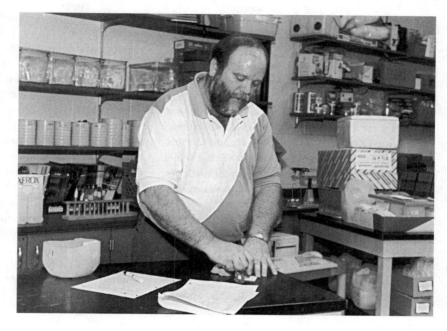

What you really need is a little teaching power. Who knows better what ought to go in a classroom? Who knows better about the kind of teaching tools that work? Who knows better about young people than those who work with them and live with them? Who knows better what the purposes of education are than a trained teacher?

SUMMARY

Radical changes have occurred in elementary school science curriculums over the past 100 years, reflecting a century of unprecedented social, economic, scientific, and technological transformations. Changes in science programs are born out of the needs and interests of a particular time in history. From the 1950s to the 1980s, science programs reflected intense interest in science as both process and product using the discovery approach and conceptual schemes.

During the 1990s, new aspects were added to science education as a result of changing global perspectives and greater knowledge of how students learn: Science/Technology/Society approach to solving real-life problems, encouraging hands-on student activity, studying fewer thematic science topics in greater depth, and using cooperative learning groups.

Experimentation, innovation, and reform in elementary school science were accelerated by massive grants of money from federal, state, and local governments, as well as private foundations such as the Ford Foundation and the National Science Foundation. Table 7–1 showed the scope of contemporary science reform using a matrix of time, scale, space, duration, materials, and agreement. It takes a long time to frame national standards, develop new projects/programs/textbook series, and actually implement them in elementary school classrooms.

Table 7–3 highlighted some of the major science reform projects, and resources were given for additional information on these and other projects. Trends and contributions of science reform projects were cited, along with how they impact upon today's science in the elementary schools. An important trend in science today is the wider use of teaching/learning activities for all students, especially the mainstreaming or inclusion of special needs students, inner-city students, women, and students with diverse cultural backgrounds. Chapter 9 will investigate methods and resources for helping these students learn—and use—science/technology/society concepts and skills.

Successful science reform projects often become commercial science programs and/or textbook series. Usually, they can be used as total science programs (packaged with everything necessary to implement them), as separate units (materials optional), or as individual lessons.

To illustrate, two examples of science reform project-developed ventures that were acquired by commercial companies were examined in detail: *Science for Life and Living: Integrating Science, Technology, and Health,* and *Macmillan McGraw-Hill Science.* Note: The reform project-developed programs presented here are *not* necessarily endorsed by this author.

Teachers in school districts that are contemplating or have adopted reform-developed science programs or textbook series must become familiar with them, and this chapter suggests how to do that. As teacher, you are the key to whether new science programs and textbook series succeed or fail.

SELF-ASSESSMENT AND FURTHER STUDY

1. You have been asked by your principal or supervisor to pick a reform-developed program to use in your science teaching.
   a. What criteria would you use to pick one?
   b. How would you collect data to make your choice?
   c. Which innovative project-developed science program would you pick? List the reasons for your selection.
   d. How would you assess your teaching and your students' learning in the selected program?

2. Designate an innovative science reform project from the list in Table 7–3 or other source (e.g., AIMS, FOSS, IUESS, OBIS, or STC) and compare it either to a local or state school science curriculum or to a major science textbook series. How are they different? similar? Which do you prefer? Why?

3. Identify a science reform project and give examples of how it attempts or does not attempt to present these trends in science education:
   a. Humanistic approach relating concepts to students' lives
   b. Environmental and ecological orientation
   c. Values and social aspects of science
   d. Integration of other subject areas with science
   e. Individualization of teaching/learning strategies
   f. Science/Technology/Society approach
   g. Cooperative learning groups
   h. More in-depth coverage of fewer science topics
   i. Problem solving of real-life situations leading to action
   j. Inclusion of learning activities for women, mainstreamed students with special needs, inner-city students, and culturally diverse students.

4. Choose a science unit, or one or more lessons, from any science reform project-developed program or textbook series that fits into a science topic you are currently teaching or plan to teach. Formulate a plan to show how you can integrate it into your teaching. If not currently teaching your own class, prepare to teach such a unit or lessons to a group of students.

5. Contact a science reform projects or the commercial producer of a science programs or textbook series. Volunteer to be a teacher user/evaluator. Transcribe your participation experiences in a diary.

NOTES

1. Rodger W. Bybee, Chapter 1, "The Contemporary Reform of Science Education," in *Issues in Science Education* (Arlington VA: National Science Teachers Association, 1996).

2. The phone number for a modem is (800) 362-4448. Set your telecommunications software to VT100 terminal emulation, 8 data bits, no parity, 1 stop bit, and full duplex. After you are connected, press *Return* or *Enter* once to bring up a screen. You can also access ENC's online services through the world wide web (WWW). If you don't have access to a computer with a modem, call ENC at (800) 621-5785 for more information.

3. Richard D. Kellough (ed.), *Integrating Mathematics and Science for Kindergarten and Primary Children* (Englewood Cliffs, NJ: Merrill/Prentice Hall, 1996), 155.

4. J. Starr, "The Great Textbook War." in H. Holtz, I. Marcus, J. Dougherty, J. Michaels, and R. Peduzzi (Eds.), *Education and the American Dream: Conservatives, Liberals and Radicals Debate the Future of Education* (Grandy, MA: Bergin and Garvey, 1989), 106.

5. Much of the discussion concerning contemporary science education reform has been influenced by Rodger W. Bybee, Chapter 1, "The Contemporary Reform of Science Education," in *Issues in Science Education* (Arlington, VA: National Science Teachers Association, 1996).

6. The descriptions of *Science for Life and Living: Integrating Science, Technology, and Health* appear in *Inside Look, Science for Life and Living: An Inside Look at the New BSCS Elementary Curricu-lum* (Dubuque, IA: Kendall/Hunt, 1992), 1–73.

7. This excellent article contributed much to the coverage in this section: Robert E. Yager, "Make a difference with STS: Should we toss out the textbooks?", *The Science Teacher, 60,* no.2, February 1993, 45–48.

8. Most of the materials about the Macmillan/McGraw-Hill Science Series come from: *Properties of Matter, Teacher's Planning Guide, Macmillan/McGraw-Hill Science Series* (New York: Macmillan/McGraw-Hill School Publishing Co., 1995), T2–T12.

CHAPTER 8

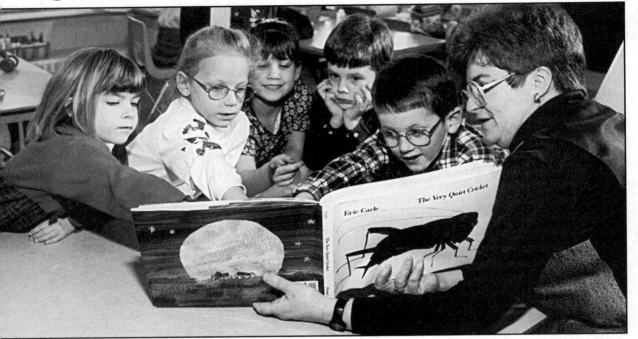

Integrating Science With the Whole Curriculum

As we carefully read the research on integration of subject matter, we learn that advocates of an integrated curriculum do not promote "mush," but rather strive to provide an environment where students are involved in using all of the disciplines in a relevant, meaningful way and where each discipline is an integral part of the whole. I bring this to your attention so that good elementary science is not sacrificed or neglected when you are writing and/or planning units of integrated instruction.[1]

START WITH A STORY

In one corner of the classroom, the science group is making a mural of an ocean food chain. "It always ends with a big fish," Keith points out. "Let's use a whale shark, like in the story."

Lee shakes her head vigorously. "Don't you remember? Whale sharks take a short-cut in the food chain. They eat those little planktons. To make a lo-o-o-ng food chain, we need some pictures of really big fish that eat smaller fish."

As the science group migrates to the class library to do some research, the social studies group is examining the ocean currents they have drawn on a map of the world. "Now I see why Columbus landed so far south," Rosa tells her group. "Look at these currents! I bet they took him right to the Caribbean! Wait 'til the class sees this!"

In the middle of the classroom, the math group is constructing a circle graph showing the relative numbers of plankton, fish, and mammals in the ocean. "Let's make the mammals' slice wider," Sarah says. "I can barely see it now. Anyway, mammals are way bigger than those little plankton. Especially whales."

"We're showing the number of things in each group, not their size," Raymond reminded her. "We have to show that the ocean is full of kajillions of plankton and just a few mammals, even if the mammals are lots, lots bigger."

Over by the windows, Bryant has a question for his language arts group. "Should we put a comma after the 'dear' part? Is this going to be a friendly letter?"

"I think it's a business letter," Candice says. "We're writing to a big company, right? So it must be a business letter."

"Let's start by telling the company that we won't drink any more soda until they stop putting the cans in those plastic rings," Phil suggests. "And we can send them that newspaper picture we found—the one with the turtle all tangled up in the rings."

How did these students get so involved in their tasks? They began with a common experience—reading *The Magic School Bus on the Ocean Floor* by Joanna Cole [Scholastic, 1992], one of a series of tradebooks. With the help of the media specialist, the teacher also gathered related trade and reference books, videos, computer programs, and even poetry about the ocean. Then she asked students to choose from a range of group projects that relate the ocean theme to several subject areas. Besides the groups already mentioned, a music group is gathering songs about the ocean, and other students are working with a parent volunteer to plan a tasting party with food from the ocean.

The *Magic School Bus* books are informational storybooks: they entertain students with an exciting adventure while they saturate them with science concepts and facts. Because the books combine fact and fantasy, they also challenge students to distinguish between the two. (Can ocean animals really speak? What would actually happen if a school bus drove into the ocean?)

Research has indicated that after reading an informational storybook, elementary students stayed on the topic longer, interacted more with their peers concerning the topic, and formed hypotheses twice as often about the causes or results of events described in the book. These children were also more likely to explore related topics than they were after reading a fictional storybook or a nonfictional information book.[2] The *Magic School Bus* approach has been so well received by students that some districts have turned old school buses into reading, creative writing, and general learning centers.

Older students who read books such as Issac Asimov's *Fantastic Voyage* or Jules Verne's *An Antarctic Mystery* are often eager to test their hypotheses related to events in the stories. In the same way, the book and movie of *Jurassic Park* challenge students to discover what is—and is not—possible.

Curricular integration is becoming a universal educational goal. These resources may stimulate your own ideas about ways to marry science with other subject areas.

There are more pressures on teachers today than ever before. There is a "back-to-basics" movement and a diminished emphasis on science teaching in elementary schools by both the public and the funding agencies. You must be efficient and judicious in planning your restricted class time to "fit science in" and still help your students develop skills in all the other self-contained classroom subjects. One excellent way to do this is to integrate science with other subjects around a central STS theme.

INTEGRATION OF SCIENCE AND OTHER CURRICULAR SUBJECTS AROUND STS THEMES

As science competes for time in the school day, researchers, educators, and scientists are examining new ways to integrate science with other curricular subjects without watering down science. **Integration** means connecting science to other curricular subjects (e.g., mathematics, social studies, and art). **Interdisciplinary science** coordinates disciplines within science (astronomy, geology, physics, etc.).

Researchers assert that:

- integrated learning activities are more feasible and appealing for elementary schools because they require fewer scheduling changes and can be done by one teacher.[3]

- when science is integrated with other subjects, especially around a central STS theme, both science and the other subjects are learned more effectively.[4]
- the integration of science with other disciplines has potential for improving both the quantity and quality of science instruction and learning.[5]

Blend Science and Other Curricular Subjects Around Central STS Themes

Themed studies are successful because they help students:

- become responsible, self-disciplined independent learners who cooperate with classmates
- gain self-confidence and self-esteem as they become motivated to learn and succeed at applying what they are learning,
- understand and remember better when they listen, talk, read, write, and "do" to explore what they are learning,
- reinforce their language learning, and
- learn best by active involvement, collaborative projects, and interaction with classmates, teachers, and their world.

Therefore, as you select a science area for your students to investigate, select an STS theme and weave other subjects into your unit. Figure 8–1 shows how a middle grade teacher integrated science and other subjects in a study of insects.[6] All

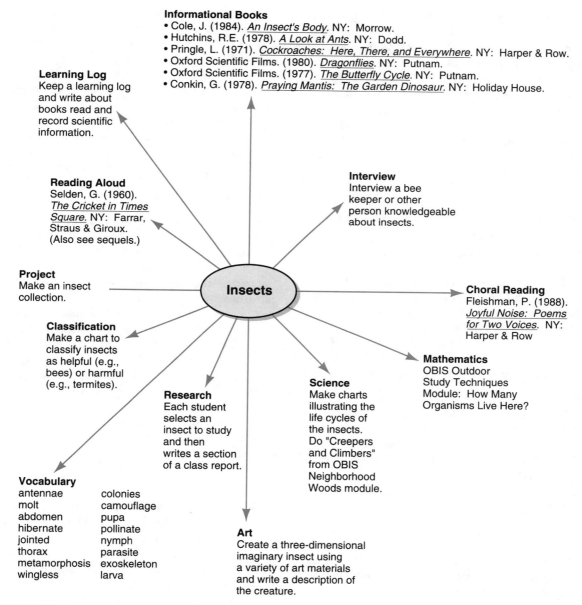

Informational Books
- Cole, J. (1984). *An Insect's Body*. NY: Morrow.
- Hutchins, R.E. (1978). *A Look at Ants*. NY: Dodd.
- Pringle, L. (1971). *Cockroaches: Here, There, and Everywhere*. NY: Harper & Row.
- Oxford Scientific Films. (1980). *Dragonflies*. NY: Putnam.
- Oxford Scientific Films. (1977). *The Butterfly Cycle*. NY: Putnam.
- Conkin, G. (1978). *Praying Mantis: The Garden Dinosaur*. NY: Holiday House.

Learning Log
Keep a learning log and write about books read and record scientific information.

Reading Aloud
Selden, G. (1960). *The Cricket in Times Square*. NY: Farrar, Straus & Giroux. (Also see sequels.)

Project
Make an insect collection.

Classification
Make a chart to classify insects as helpful (e.g., bees) or harmful (e.g., termites).

Vocabulary

antennae	colonies
molt	camouflage
abdomen	pupa
hibernate	pollinate
jointed	nymph
thorax	parasite
metamorphosis	exoskeleton
wingless	larva

Research
Each student selects an insect to study and then writes a section of a class report.

Art
Create a three-dimensional imaginary insect using a variety of art materials and write a description of the creature.

Science
Make charts illustrating the life cycles of the insects. Do "Creepers and Climbers" from OBIS Neighborhood Woods module.

Insects

Interview
Interview a bee keeper or other person knowledgeable about insects.

Choral Reading
Fleishman, P. (1988). *Joyful Noise: Poems for Two Voices*. NY: Harper & Row

Mathematics
OBIS Outdoor Study Techniques Module: How Many Organisms Live Here?

FIGURE 8–1

Thematic cluster of curricular subject matter on insects

Source: Modified from Gail E. Tompkins and Kenneth Hoskisson, *Language Arts: Content and Teaching Strategies,* 3d ed. (Englewood Cliffs, NJ: Merrill/Prentice Hall, 1994), 545. Used by permission.

of the activities extend students' learning about insects, while giving direct experiences with a wide variety of subject matter and skills. Such an integrated lesson speaks to the broad range of learn-ing levels and styles of students. You can easily adapt and use this model in your own class-room.

To help you integrate science with other curricular subjects in your STS thematic units, let's investigate each subject's potential for integration.

HOW ARE HANDS-ON/MINDS-ON SCIENCE AND LANGUAGE LEARNING SIMILAR?

Researchers have found recurring themes in cognitive and linguistic development. Language development and hands-on/minds-on science emphasize the same intellectual skills, and both are concerned with thinking processes.[7] Facil-itating language development contains the same teaching/learning elements as sciencing:

■ Invent vocabulary that is related to topics being studied and look for and correct students' misconceptions of word meanings.
■ Provide students with opportunities to practice receptive language skills (listening and reading).
■ Supply many practice episodes in expressive language (writing and speaking).[8]

Let's investigate how science and receptive and expressive language can be integrated. Language learning will be examined from two teaching/learning perspectives: science/listening/reading, and science/talking/writing.

Language Learning: Science/Listening/Reading

Advocates of whole-language learning validly stress that the assorted elements of the language arts are closely interrelated and thoroughly enmeshed in the total elementary school curriculum. In fact, 90% or more of school teaching/learning takes place by means of language! As you know, good teaching/learning relies on quality communication. Therefore, language arts should not be taught in isolated classroom settings. Reading, writing, speaking, and listening occur in all curricular areas and should not be separated from content and substance. Whole-language teaching/learning is a more natural way for students to learn and use language skills in their everyday lives.[9] Early language development starts with listening.

Listening and Science. Science and language are both process-oriented; that is, both integrate and use all related language abilities and skills, and both use all or most of the five senses. Listening—the ability to listen to others, to empathize with and understand their point of view, and to accurately listen to words and environmental sounds—is, like science, considered to be one of the highest forms of intelligent behavior. Scientists regularly congregate to share their research, to explore their findings and views, and to broaden their positions by listening to the concepts and responses. Listening is like observation in that students must be precise about what they hear and see in order to collect accurate data.

Here are some ways you might assist your students to become better listeners.

1. For younger children, play listening games:
   a. *Locate the Ringing Bell.* Have students close their eyes and point to the direction of the sound of a bell. Then have students cover one ear to develop the concept that we usually need two ears to tell which direction a sound is coming from.
   b. *Identifying Sounds.* Record individual students' voices and have students identify them. Record familiar sounds (e.g., toilet flushing, bird chirping, airplane, bus, telephone, dog barking) and have students name the source of the sounds.

c. *Play Finger Games.* "Simon Says" requires correct listening. If the teacher says, "hands on head" without first saying "Simon says," and students put their hands on their heads, they are not "good science listeners."

2. For older students provide more advanced listening activities:

a. Find a place where you can sit quietly (e.g., a park, the front of your house or apartment, or a mall). Listen to the sounds you hear. Describe the sounds in a notebook. Describe not what is making the sound, but how the sound sounds, (e.g., high or low, loud or soft). Share your sound descriptions with your classmates to see if they can guess what you heard.

b. Have students bring in their favorite CDs. Play a five-second section and have students identify what the song is and who is performing it.

c. Try this three-part science experiment, then explain how the sounds you heard differed:

• With your back turned, stand next to your partner. Have your partner strike a tuning fork on the heel of his shoe and hold the fork 10 cm from your ear. Listen carefully to the sound.

• Now put your head down on your desk and have your partner strike the tuning fork again and put the handle 20 cm from your ear. Listen carefully to the sound.

• Put a full, unopened 2 liter soda bottle on the edge of your desk. Put your ear against the soda bottle. Have your partner strike the tuning fork and gently touch the handle to the soda bottle. Listen carefully to the sound.

There are infinite opportunities for you to engage your students in listening experiences. Listening skills are useful for building other language skills, especially reading. This publication

(a)

(b)

(c)

Listening to audio tapes about science-related topics integrates the development of science conceptual knowledge and communication skills.

contains useful listening activities: Deanna D. Winn, "Developing Listening Skills as Part of the Curriculum," *The Reading Teacher 42,* no. 2, Nov. 1988, 144–146.

Reading and Science. Reading is another skill built into a guided discovery approach to science. Hands-on/minds-on activities require students to define problems, locate information, organize information into graphic form, evaluate findings, and draw conclusions. In short, this type of science curriculum demands a myriad of skills concomitant with a well-developed reading program.[10]

You are currently teaching reading in your science program whether you realize it or not. For instance, when you help your students develop scientific processes, you are also helping them develop reading processes.[11]

Table 8–1 gives examples of problem-solving skills in science and corresponding reading skills. For instance, when students are observing in science, they are also learning to discriminate shapes, sounds, syllables, and accents for reading. Predicting, classifying, and interpreting are skills essential to scientific thinking *and* reading.

Science and reading are both concerned with processes and content. Content can be thought of as subject matter. Processes consist of reading and other scientific skills necessary to acquire and apply content. This is consistent with constructivist learning theory.

Remember, your students had to be able to recognize relationships between sounds and symbols before they could learn to read. They had to be able to distinguish between vowels and consonants, and they had to learn the sounds of letters, letter blends, and syllables. Only then could they begin to build a reserve of sight words. Once students have mastered a basic reading vocabulary, they can start to build comprehension skills: reading for the main idea, following directions, and solving problems. You can see the parallel between these reading skills and science skills.

Evidence suggests that early experience with science helps students with language and logic development. Several studies have found that young children's experiences with natural phenomena in active science programs improved reading readiness and reading skills.[12]

TABLE 8–1

Skills/processes essential to both hands-on/minds-on science and reading

Examples of Problem-Solving Skills in Science	Corresponding Reading Skills
Observing	Discriminating shapes Discriminating sounds Discriminating syllables and accents
Identifying	Recognizing letters Recognizing words Recognizing common prefixes Recognizing common suffixes Recognizing common base words Naming objects, events, and people
Describing	Isolating important characteristics Enumerating characteristics Using appropriate terminology Using synonyms
Classifying	Comparing characteristics Contrasting characteristics Ordering, sequencing Arranging ideas Considering multiple factors
Designing investigations	Asking questions Looking for potential relationships Following organized procedures Reviewing prior studies Developing outlines
Collecting data	Taking notes Surveying reference materials Using several parts of a book Recording data in an orderly fashion Developing precision and accuracy
Interpreting data	Recognizing cause and effect relationships Organizing facts Summarizing new information Varying rate of reading Inductive and deductive thinking
Communicating results	Using graphic aids Logically arranging information Sequencing ideas Knowledge of technical vocabulary Illuminating significant factors Describing with clarity
Formulating conclusions	Generalizing Analyzing critically Evaluating information Recognizing main ideas and concepts Establishing relationships Applying information to other situations

Source: Glenda S. Carter and Ronald D. Simpson, "Science and Reading: A Basic Duo," *The Science Teacher, 45,* no. 3, March 1978, 20.

SCIENCE AND READING: A NATURAL COMBINATION

What can you do *today* in your science program to enhance your students' reading abilities and, at the same time, enrich your science teaching? What can you do to wed your science program and your reading program? What are you currently doing with reading in your science program that should be enlarged and expanded?

Using Printed Science Materials With Nonreaders

One of the best things to do with nonreaders is *read to them*. Investigations on the effects of reading aloud to students regularly showed significant increases in vocabulary, knowledge of word meanings, visual decoding, motor decoding, and reading comprehension achievement. Two important elements in improving reading performance are the regularity of reading to students and the length of time the reading aloud is done. It was found that *daily* reading aloud was the most effective frequency and 10 minutes per session was the most effective length. Younger children may benefit more from being read to than older children. Reading aloud to young children increases their interest in reading. After being read to, young children are more eager to read for themselves the books that have been read aloud to them. Librarians found science was the second most popular category of books. The most popular category was fiction—and some of that was in science fields or science fiction.

Do not limit your reading aloud to younger children. Reading aloud to students who are in the lower ranges of reading achievement in any grade produces reading growth. When fourth graders heard taped readings of stories, those at the lower extremes of reading achievement showed the greatest growth in comprehension and total reading scores.

Many companies (e.g., Listening Library) produce audio cassettes packaged with print books. This helps today's children, many of whom have not developed inner picture-making skills because of overexposure to television and computers. Many children's TV shows (e.g., "Sesame Street") read to children while simultaneously showing them the printed book.[13]

We all can find times in our hands-on/minds-on discovery science programs when it would be useful and appropriate to read aloud to our students.

Besides providing students with experience using another sense (hearing), this chance to listen helps them see that words in books are merely spoken words in written form. This in turn helps students begin to see a relationship between spoken and written language. How can *you* do more reading aloud in your science activities?

Inventing Words for Students' Constructed Knowledge

Words are the verbal labels that focus students' attention clearly and explicitly on the conceptual ideas they have been investigating. In your guided discovery science program, you have supplied multisensory, hands-on/minds-on activities for your students. After they have experienced exploratory manipulative activities, you "invent" words to assist learners in constructing and understanding scientific concepts and principles. To do so, follow these simple guidelines.

1. Group your students near you so they can all see anything you demonstrate or put on the writing board, can hear your questions, and are able to communicate with each other.
2. Carefully plan and introduce an activity the students have done themselves before this lesson.
3. During the activity, introduce the label (word or words) for the concept you want to develop. For instance, if you show roots growing down from seeds in a glass holder, you could say: "When the roots of your plants grow down toward the Earth, it is evidence of *geotropism* (new "invented" word). *Geo* means Earth and *tropism* is a natural tendency to react in a definite way to stimuli, in this

FIGURE 8–2
"Evidence of Geotropism" bulletin board

case, gravity." Write *geotropism* on the writing board at this point. (This gives visual as well as oral introduction of the new word to students.) This repeats an activity your students have already done or observed, but adds a new word for the concept.

4. Now suggest a new activity using geotropism. For instance you might say, "How do you think geotropism will affect the roots if we turn the seed holders on their sides for a few days?"

5. Ask your students for responses. You are trying to get them to see that the roots will start growing down.

6. Have students place their seed holders on their sides for a few days and keep records of their observations.

7. Use your students' records to make a bulletin board entitled something like, "Evidence of Geotropism," as in Figure 8–2.

Using Operational Definitions to Invent Science Words

Science educators use the term **operational definition** to describe the invention of science words that occurs as a result of hands-on/minds-on activities. Operational definitions use *actions* to describe what is happening. Piaget and other constructivists caution that the invention of terms must come *after* learners have actually handled various materials and observed reactions. Otherwise, you will be teaching by rote. Numerous follow-up activities are needed to reinforce a concept or operational definition. For instance, a pebble or rock can be placed between the root and the Earth to show that the root is forced around the rock by geotropism.

Visual displays are very important in science and the language arts. Writing boards, flannel or felt boards, and bulletin boards will be covered here. More detail can be found in: Richard D. Kellough (ed.), *Integrating Mathematics and Science for Kindergarten and Primary Children* (Englewood Cliffs, NJ: Merrill/Prentice Hall, 1996), 160–167.

Writing Boards. It would be almost impossible to conduct a science program without a writing board. Slate blackboards used to be in fashion. Today, plywood chalkboards, magnetic backing plywood, or white or colored multi-purpose boards are more popular because of these advantages:

■ You write and draw on them with special marking pens, eliminating allergy-irritating, computer-clogging chalk dust.
■ They can double as projection screens.
■ Colored transparency figures stick to them and can be removed easily.
■ Ferrous items will adhere to them if the boards have magnetic backing.
■ Special electronic whiteboards can transfer images written on them to any connected computer monitor and be stored as a computer file.

Regardless of the type of writing board you have, here are some suggestions for using it effectively in your science program.

1. Use a "Billy the Kid" approach in writing on the board—never fully turn your back to your class!
2. Be certain every student can see what you put on the board.
3. Begin each day and each lesson with a clean board, except for announcements that must be there, and clean board at end of lesson.
4. Start writing on board's top left, use your best manuscript printing or cursive, make your writing large enough for every student to see, and highlight your writing by using colored chalk or marking pens. If your writing tends to slant up or down, consider drawing light pencil lines on the writing board.
5. Write material on the board before class begins and cover it, or put it on transparencies for projection on board, if you have large quantities of material. Resist writing too much.
6. Write only key words and simple diagrams when you use the writing board to complement hands-on/minds-on invention lessons or teacher-conducted demonstrations.

Flannel/Felt Boards. Flannel or felt boards are inexpensive, easy for teachers and students to make, lend themselves to illustrating science concepts, and are fun to make and use. Children's literature authorities underscore the importance of letting students use them to practice organizing and sharing concepts with their classmates.

Flannel/felt boards are excellent props around which students can organize their thoughts. Through them, students can gain confidence in speaking to their classmates and you. They are also valuable for helping student audiences focus and build listening skills. Once students see their teacher make and use flannel boards, they are impatient to make their own.

Here are some other advantages of using a flannel/felt board in your science teaching.

1. *You* are totally responsible for making, presenting, and moving board pieces.
2. Students are stimulated to take part by moving pieces and discussing what they are doing.
3. Students can plan and construct their own boards (individually or in small groups) and cut pieces to illustrate some science process or concept. They may use their board in a presentation to their classmates.
4. Students can follow your lesson and place board pieces on their individual flannel/felt boards at their tables or desks.
5. Groups of students may be assigned to plan, construct, and present to classmates a thematic science board of their choice. You could call it "The Science Board of the Month."

Richard D. Kellough recommends we think of a flannel/felt board's many uses as *T.O.P.S.*: Thematic use; Object variety; Planning, Presenting, and Plotting; and Student use.[14]

Thematic use. Science themes lend themselves to flannel/felt boards. Flannel/felt cutouts can be made by teachers and students or commercial ready-made sets can be purchased and adapted for such themes as:

- Plant cycle sequence with figures to show seed, germinated seed with root, plant with stem, plant with stem and leaves, plant with stem, leaves, and flowers, and plant with stem, leaves, flowers, and seeds.
- Insects' life cycles with individual parts.
- Water cycle.
- Bar graphs to show heights of plants grown in class.
- The solar system with all its parts.
- Display of magazine pictures of space travel.

Object variety. Variety is almost limitless for the types of materials that may be used for the backing or cut-out pieces. Consider felt, flannel, sandpaper, Pellon (found in fabric or hobby shops), published matter (like magazines, catalogs, discarded science textbooks, student workbooks) backed with material that adheres to flannel or felt, Velcro, or magnets (if a cookie sheet is put under the flannel).

Planning, Presenting, and Plotting. Plan to use objects that are familiar to your students from previous activities with the same science content and processes. *Present* your science board lesson logically and sequentially, at a level that is suitable for your students. *Plot* your presentation to invent new words, present new data, extend previously learned concepts, or introduce an innovative approach to a topic (e.g., mountain formation by folding) not covered adequately in textbook.

Student use. Students can quickly and easily assemble their own individual flannel/felt board by pasting a 9" × 12" piece of flannel or felt on one side of a manila folder and standing it on edge. Students can keep their flannel board pieces in their folders. Using their individual boards, students can

- Follow along with you as you present a lesson,
- Develop their own stories and flannel/felt cutouts, and
- Share their flannel/felt boards with the class.

Bulletin Boards Almost every classroom has a bulletin board. Science topics are especially adaptable to bulletin board displays. With very little money and effort, you and your students can create appealing and educationally useful bulletin boards by, as Richard W. Kellough says, "Making a C.A.S.E. for bulletin boards."[15] Kellough's C.A.S.E. stands for these criteria:

Colorful constructions and captions.
Attractive arrangements.
Simple and student prepared.
Enrichments and extensions to connect learning.

See Kellough for specific directions and practical suggestions for using the C.A.S.E. approach for your bulletin boards. Then select a science topic and plan and construct the most attractive and stimulating bulletin board you can.

EFFECTIVE USE OF TEXTBOOKS IN HANDS-ON/MINDS-ON SCIENCE

Textbooks are by far the predominant instructional material in science education. The vast majority of science teachers use published textbooks to determine the topics they cover (or don't cover), to organize lessons, to assign homework, and to provide test questions and problems.[16] The science textbooks you use may have been selected by state or local textbook adoption committees. Your challenge is to learn to use textbooks to ensure the best science learning experiences for your students.

Even in a hands-on/minds-on guided discovery and process-oriented program, textbooks are of value, especially if you use them judiciously. Help your students to see reading as a process to enrich their first-hand experimentation. Text-books are a resource of reliable and tested facts, concepts, and principles. Instead of reinventing the wheel at every step of your investigations about the universe, you can use reading to find and share other people's information and to check your own findings for validity.

See these references for more ways you can use science textbooks to enrich and expand your students' scientific explorations:

- M. P. Driscoll, "How Does the Textbook Contribute to Learning in the Middle School Science Class?," *Contemporary Educational Psychology, 19,* no. 1, 1994, 79–100
- B. R. Gifford, "The Textbook of the 21st Century," *Syllabus, 19,* 15–16
- C. Hynd et al., "Promoting Conceptual Change with Science Texts and Discussions," *Journal of Reading, 34,* no. 8, May 1991, 596–601.

Can Your Students Read Your Science Textbooks?

Using Piagetian measures for cognitive levels, the cloze method for determining reading level, or other methods, select textbooks that your students can read. Here's how to use the cloze method:

- Select several passages of 400–415 words in length from whatever printed materials you are using.
- Delete every eighth word in a passage except for words in first and last sentences, numbers, and proper names. Try to delete about 50 words.
- Duplicate the sections with blank spaces replacing the deleted words and distribute to your students.

- Have students read the passages and fill in the blanks with the most appropriate words they can think of.
- Collect papers and score them by

  1. Counting all student-supplied words that are exactly the same as the words in the original passage, and
  2. Dividing the number of *correct* responses by number possible.
     Those students who score better than 50% can read the book quite well.
     Those students who score better than 40% can read at the instructional level.
     Those students who score below 40% will probably find the book hard to read.

Try to get texts with a variety of levels, so you can individualize assignments. When investigating a science topic, list pages in each of the levels where your students can find information about that topic. Allow your students to select the level of their choice or suggest particular pages to specific students. Most science textbook series have a wide range of reading levels for each science topic from one grade to the next; consult with a sales representative for the publisher. Also check this reference for help with student textbook readability:

- R. H. Barba et al., "User-Friendly Text: Keys to Readability and Comprehension," *The Science Teacher, 60,* no. 5, May 1993, 15–17.

Arrange Your Class for Reading in Science

Group your students in any way that facilitates using books. Sometimes it is practical to group students homogeneously if you are working on skills and only a small group of your students needs help. Other times, you may find that you can use heterogeneous groupings. Try pairing students who have trouble reading with better readers who are more cognitively advanced. Or consider forming groups of four to six students with varying levels of reading abilities. Let them read and discuss assignments cooperatively.

Individualize Textbook Assignments

So that each of your students will get the maximum benefit from science textbooks, incorporate some or all of these individualization techniques into your classroom.

If you have poor or immature readers and/or disadvantaged or at-risk students in your class, reading to them may be useful. By listening to you as they follow their textbook, they hear words at the same time they are learning to decode and thus learn to read independently. To be most effective, try reading to and with your students under the following conditions:

- Have students put other work away.
- Pick a special listening place, such as on a rug or the lawn under a tree in warm weather, so your students can sit or lie down.
- Read with expression and enthusiasm, so the students can see the relationships between written and spoken language.
- Stop occasionally and ask questions. Invite questions, too. Be careful, though, that the kinds of questions and their frequency do not detract from the reading, but whet your students' interest.
- Stop occasionally and ask the students to read the next portion to themselves to find a particular answer to your question or to prepare to read to the class if they want to.
- Ask for a volunteer to read to the class only after the students have had an opportunity to read and prepare first.

Avoid asking poor readers to read to a group anything they are seeing for the first time and have not prepared. Sometimes it is valuable to record sections of your textbook for poor readers to use either with or in place of the text. Commercially prepared cassette and picture science programs for the elementary level, such as those by Coronet Films, are also available. They provide oral reinforcement and assistance and help with word recognition and concept development. Your better readers can get practice with oral reading by making the cassettes for you. Supplement reading assignments for poor readers with other learning activities such as films, filmstrips, tradebooks, and field trips.

You can enrich the textbook assignments for your advanced readers by trying these approaches:

- Improve your reading assignments. All your reading assignments should include these three elements:
  1. *Content.* Specifically indicate what you expect your students to get from reading the text: facts, interpretations, or conclusions.
  2. *Motivation.* Relate the assignment to ongoing work and previous materials; demonstrate its relevance.
  3. *Skills.* Indicate how an assignment should be read, for instance, what type of recall is expected.

Guide your students to learn to locate and organize information from their textbooks. Teach them reading skills and enhance comprehension and retention of science concepts in written materials. Help them become familiar with reading/study tools, such as those listed in Table 8–2.

- Teach E. B. Kelly's *PQRST* technique for studying:
  1. *P*review to identify the main idea.
  2. Ask *Q*uestions to which you expect to find answers.
  3. *R*ead the material very carefully, especially for specific details.
  4. *S*tate the main idea of the material.
  5. *T*est yourself by answering the questions you proposed earlier.[17]
     - Stimulate students to explore diverse sources for science content that will update material in their textbook.
     - Motivate students to be vigilant for errors in their textbooks such as facts, typographical errors, and imbalances and discrepancies in the handling of women, special needs people, and minorities.

TABLE 8–2
Reading/study skills in science

Locating Information in Text
1. Tables of contents
2. Indexes
3. Appendices
4. Glossaries
5. Footnotes
6. Bibliographies
7. Chapter headings
8. Unit titles
9. Keys
10. Cross-references

Using Reference Books
1. Encyclopedia
2. Dictionaries
3. Atlases
4. Almanacs
5. Periodical indexes
6. Library card catalogs

Selecting Information
1. Recognizing main ideas
2. Differentiating between relevant and irrelevant ideas

3. Differentiating between supporting and non-supporting ideas
4. Noting important details

Organizing Information
1. Note-taking
2. Outlining
3. Summarizing information

Using Graphic Aids
1. Maps
2. Illustrations
3. Graphs
4. Tables
5. Cartoons
6. Charts

Following Directions

Developing Reading Flexibility
1. Scanning for specific information
2. Skimming for general ideas
3. Slow, careful reading and rereading for detailed mastery

• Inspire students to write to the authors and publishers of books with errors, to enrich their writing skills, sharpen their comprehension, and build their egos. Corresponding with humans who happened to be authors will help them see that authors are humans who make mistakes. This is a very worthwhile activity and students love it.

Currently, 22 states adopt science textbooks. In these states, only the approved science texts may be used in schools. California, Texas, Utah, and West Virginia allow adoptions of videodisc-based programs, such as Optical Data's *Windows on Science,* as alternatives to traditional textbooks. "The textbook of the twenty-first century may be an interactive device that offers text, sound, and video."[18]

EFFECTIVE USE OF NON-TEXTBOOK SCIENCE PRINTED MATTER

Studies recommend that teachers use their textbooks as references instead of curriculum guides. You should also use non-textbook printed materials in your hands-on/minds-on science program to enrich both your science and reading processes and content. Some effective uses include the following:

1. Children's literature
   a. Tradebooks or informational books
   b. Science minibooks and logs
   c. Fiction/science fiction
2. Student or teacher-made reading materials
   a. Creative writing
   b. Science magazines
   c. Other written communications

All kinds of literature supply enrichment science learning experiences. Your students' literature and science programs complement each other.

Children's Literature in Integrated Hands-on/Minds-on Science

Fusing science with children's literature is currently very popular, especially when science is integrated with other curricular subjects in the elementary school. Children's literature encompasses library books, tradebooks, informational books, and fiction books, but *not* basic textbooks. These references provide insights into the role of literature and science in an integrated science program:

■ W. Saul et al., *Science Workshop: A Whole Language Approach* (Portsmouth, NH: Heinemann Educational Books, 1993).

Tradebooks on science topics provide opportunities for students to find more in-depth or different information than textbook space allows.

■ C. Butzow, *Science Through Children's Literature: An Integrated Approach* (Englewood, CO: Libraries Unlimited, 1989).

Tradebooks got their name because they are sold through trade outlets such as bookstores. They may be fiction or nonfiction, and they offer many opportunities for integrating literature with your science program. Usually, tradebooks limit themselves to one topic, such as weather, rocks, or trees.

Used in conjunction with your hands-on/minds-on science program and/or your science textbook series, tradebooks provide these important aspects of learning for your students:

■ Because some students learn best through reading or reinforcing what they have previously learned, tradebooks help meet the individual learning styles of your students.
■ Students learn to research and to cross-check data from many different sources.
■ Students are given opportunities to work independently at their own pace, reading materials geared to their individual reading levels.
■ Trade books give students in-depth information on the subject being investigated.
■ For students who have difficulty with reading, tradebooks can be especially helpful by increasing motivation and involvement.
■ Many recently published books contain information on timely subjects students hear and see on radio or TV or in newspapers.
■ Informational books provide students with opportunities to experience the excitement of new discoveries.
■ Tradebooks encourage self-reliance, because one enjoyable discovery can motivate students to make further investigations.
■ Critical reading and thinking skills can be developed by comparing books on the same subject to evaluate objectivity, qualifications, and accuracy of authors.
■ Informational books stretch students' minds by informing them about values, beliefs, and lifestyles of others, as well as introducing them to new words and technical terms.

To see how to put tradebooks or informational books to work for you, see:

- Donna E. Norton, *Through the Eyes of a Child: An Introduction to Children's Literature,* 4th ed., Chapter 12, "Nonfiction: Biographies and Informational Books" (Englewood Cliffs, NJ: Merrill/Prentice Hall, 1995), 645–713).
- Patricia R. Crook and Barbara A. Lehman, "On Track With Trade Books: Try Direct Instruction With Trade Books for Teaching Science Content With Flair," *Science and Children, 27,* no. 6 (March 1990): 22–23.
- Seymour Simon, "Behold the World! Using Science Tradebooks in the Classroom," *Science and Children, 19,* no. 6 (March 1982): 5–7.

Ask your school or local librarian to suggest tradebooks for the topics you want to investigate. Many outstanding science tradebooks have been published in the last ten years. Book lists and book reviews abound to help you select. These resources can get you started:

- *Appraisal: Children's Science Books.* Children's Science Book Review Committee, Harvard Graduate School of Education, Cambridge, MA. Issued three times a year.
- *Bulletin of the Center for Children's Books.* University of Chicago Press, Chicago, IL. Issued monthly.
- "Outstanding Science Tradebooks for Children." *Science and Children* magazine (jointly with Children's Book Council), National Science Teachers Association, 1840 Wilson Blvd., Arlington, VA 22201-3000. Appears annually in the March issue of *Science and Children*.
- *Science Books: A Quarterly Review.* American Association for the Advancement of Science, 1776 Massachusetts Ave., NW, Washington, DC 20036. Issued quarterly.

Here are some criteria to help you select effective nonfiction science tradebooks. Such books should

1. have accurate facts,
2. eliminate stereotypes,
3. have illustrations that clarify the text,
4. encourage analytical thinking,
5. organize material to help understanding, and
6. stimulate interest by the writing style.[19]

Should fiction science tradebooks be selected and used differently?

How to Use Fictional Tradebooks Effectively

Advocates assert that children's fiction and picture tradebooks can augment elementary science concept teaching/learning. However, others maintain children's literature's *fictional* components may actually interfere with learning science concepts, confuse students, or produce misconceptions. What is your opinion? To broaden your perspective, read these concise articles:

- Deborah A. Mayer, "How Can We Best Use Children's Literature in Teaching Science Concepts?," *Science and Children, 32,* no. 6, March 1995, 16–19, 43.
- Joan McMath and Margaret King, "Open Books, Open Minds," *Science and Children, 30,* no. 5, February 1993, 33–36.
- Myra Zarnowski, "Learning about Fictionalized Biographies: A Reading and Writing Approach," *The Reading Teacher, 42,* no. 2, Nov. 1988, 136–142.

The judicious selection and use of fictional tradebooks can improve your students' construction of science concepts. The primary consideration is picking tradebooks that fit into your science topics and do not unintentionally foster science misconceptions or negatively influence attitudes about science/technology/society issues.

Figure 8–3 is an uncomplicated, easy-to-use checklist that can be helpful in choosing fictional tradebooks for use in your science program. The questions on the checklist provide a guide for assessing the effectiveness of a fictional tradebook

FIGURE 8–3

Checklist for assessing fictional tradebooks for use in teaching/learning science concepts

Source: "How Can We Best Use Children's Literature in Teaching Science Concepts?", *Science and Children, 32,* no. 6, March 1995, 18.

Checklist for Choosing Children's Literature to Teach Science

Title:
Author:
Publisher:
Date:

Is the science concept recognizable?

yes _____ no

Is the story factual?

yes   moderately   not at all

Is fact discernible from fiction?

yes   possibly   no

How many misrepresentations does the book contain?

a few   some   many

Are the illustrations accurate?

realistic   representative   inaccurate

Are characters portrayed with gender equity?

yes   not applicable   no

Are animals portrayed naturally?

yes   not applicable   no

Is the passage of time referenced adequately?

yes   not applicable   no

Does the story promote a positive attitude toward science and technology?

yes _____ no

Will children read or listen to this book?

read _____ listen to

for your students. Notice that "good fiction tradebooks" focused around science topics are identified by responses circled in the left column. The more positive marks, the better the book. Conversely, more right-hand responses indicate the book is not conducive for teaching the science concepts you desire. A *no* response to the question "Is the science concept recognizable?" probably means the tradebook is not a good science source for your purposes.

Figure 8–3 does *not* try to quantify the worth of individual tradebooks as good science resources, but only suggests some attributes for making informed decisions. You may decide to use a fictional science tradebook that has some flaws by using only part of the book, or by bringing the flawed part to the attention of your students.

You may add questions of your own to the checklist, e.g., What is the approximate reading level of the book? Older or more advanced students can be guided to use this checklist or a checklist of their own to assess the fictional science tradebooks they read and share the results with their classmates.

Teacher/Student Made Science Books

Would you like to increase the number of printed science materials available to your students by 25 or even 100? Would you like to make the printed science materials you currently have more attractive to your students? Would you like to recycle old science textbooks to enhance your discovery science program? If the answer to any or all of these questions is positive, you should become familiar with the construction and use of minibooks

Minibooks are small, usually single-topic books that are teacher- or student-made. Minibooks are just like tradebooks. They are made by assembling as many and as wide a variety of reading-level science books as you can get. The books you pick for making minibooks should be those that can be separated into parts and cut up.

Using a single-edged razor blade, slit the paper near the binding within the front and back covers. Separate each chapter (or part of a chapter) into specific science topics. You or your students can make cardboard or oaktag front and back covers. Staple them together and have the students illustrate the covers with drawings, magazine pictures, or other materials. If an outdated science textbook originally had 8 units of approximately 50 pages each, you will now have 8 separate books of 50 pages each! A 50-page unit on "Plants and Food for the World" can be further divided into separate minibooks on topics such as kinds of leaves, plants that eat animals, how leaves make sugar, and how leaves change color.

What are you waiting for? Get started with your students on making hundreds of interesting and useful classroom-made tradebooks.

Students Write Their Own Science Tradebooks!

Another way to increase science books in your classroom and library is to have your students write them! According to Richard J. Reif and Kristin Rauch, "making books is a creative and enjoyable way to integrate science with other subjects, to extend learning, and to make science relevant to children's lives."[20] They suggest you and your students start by surveying your school or local library or media center to decide what type of book(s) to write. The choices might include:

1. Alphabet books
   - Focusing on broad topics like plants, animals, insects, etc. Students highlight the subject in words from A–Z. A picture of an animal can appear on a page along with text about it. Sample text for the *T* page of animal alphabet book might say: "The biggest *Turtle*, or *Tortoise*, is the Galapogos *Tortoise*. They can grow to 5 feet long and 2½ feet tall, weigh up to 500 pounds, and live up to 100 years!"
   - Focusing on specific topics, like machines, biography of a woman scientist, forces and energy, etc. Sample text for the *W* page of the machines alphabet book might say: "An inclined plane used to push things apart is called a *Wedge*. A doorstop works as a *Wedge*."
2. Specific science-related theme books such as changes in matter, earth's ecosystems, properties of matter, etc.
3. Student-generated science-question books such as, "Why is it hotter in summer even though the Earth is closer to the sun in winter in the Northern Hemisphere?," or "Why do all our plants by the window grow toward the window?"

4. Class science-related books growing out of neighborhood field trips, museums, hospitals, or local scientific laboratory.

Consider some of these suggestions for assisting students in making their own books.

1. Have students pick their own topic, research it, and write a draft for the text.
2. If students are making alphabet books, have small groups brainstorm to increase their vocabularies with such a challenge: "List as many words you can think of on (*selected topic*). If you have a computer with a thesaurus, demonstrate its use and have students use it to broaden their word bases.
3. To begin, select a size that appeals to you and the students. The size may be dictated by the materials you have available to you, for example, the size of paper (8½" × 11") used in most schools.
4. Discuss how students might illustrate their books by:
   a. concocting their own artwork using crayons, colored pencils, markers, paint, etc.
   b. making collages from magazine articles, art supplies (colored papers, cloth, string, etc.), and photographs.
   c. using computer-generated illustrations from drawing programs or clip-art software.
5. Compile text, artwork and illustrated covers.
6. Bind books by punching three holes in edge of covers and using rings to hold books together. Some school library/media centers have provisions for binding your books with glue or plastic bindings.

Completed books can be shared with classmates, with other classes, at school book fairs, or with parents or guardians.

The condensed suggestions for helping your students make their own books can be augmented by these references:

- G. Chapman and P. Robson, *Making Books* (Brookfield, CT: Millbrook, 1992).
- P. R. Crook and B. A. Lehman, "On Track with Trade Books," *Science and Children, 27,* no. 6, 1990, 22–23.
- R. Freedman, *Connections: Science by Writing* (Paradise, CA: Serin House Publishers, Project SEAS, 1990).
- Charlette King, "Making First-Class Books," *Science and Children, 28,* no. 3, 1990, 40–41.
- G. Kydd, "Wrap Up with a Write Up," *Science and Children, 27,* no. 7, 1990, 28–29.

Other Writing Activities in Science

There are many other opportunities in an integrated activity-based science program to enrich and enlarge students' science and communication skills through written and oral activities, such as creative writing and creating science magazines.

Creative Writing and Science

Combining science and creative writing can benefit your science program and encourage students' imaginations to soar. One of your goals in science education is to get students to think not only vertically (logically, analytically, precisely), but also laterally and more holistically. **Lateral thinking,** according to Edward deBono of Cambridge University in England, moves sideways from established or ingrained ways of looking at problems to novel and unusual approaches. Lateral thinking is not looking for the best answer, only for a variety of alternatives. From this perspective, you can see that what deBono calls lateral thinking is what we are most familiar with as **creativity.**

Creative writing can stimulate lateral thinking or creative, holistic thinking using science language. Encourage your students to write their own fiction, implementing the science concepts learned in your discovery science program. Combining scientific knowledge with creative writing allows the students to reinforce concepts and develop their creative and critical thinking skills. They also are motivated to check scientific facts, look for additional data if needed, develop research skills, practice science vocabulary in meaningful new situations, and increase their oral and written language skills.

H. Kay Reid and Glenn McGlathery have suggested 33 science creative writing themes that are adaptable to any grade level in an elementary or middle school. Here are three of these science themes:

- *Just-So* (Rudyard Kipling's stories). Explain how the monkey got a long tail or the leopard its spots; any other animal characteristic basic to protection, motion, or eating can be used.
- *Trash Machine*. Collect pieces of litter and design your machine. How does it work and how does it help us?
- *Haiku*. Write a poem about nature. The haiku form has three lines: five syllables are in the first and third lines, seven syllables are in the second. The following poem is a haiku:

Fall brings new colors
Bright orange, yellow, and brown
Marking summer's end

—*Laurie McGlathery*[21]

Don't forget to stimulate your students' creative thinking abilities by asking divergent, thought-provoking questions like these:

Why do you think a particular character behaved in a certain way?
What are some other ways the character could have handled the problem?
What might happen if . . . ?
Suppose you substitute a different animal (or anything with different attributes). How would this alter the situation?

Students Create Science Magazines

Another way to use creative writing in science is to arouse your students' interest in planning and making science magazines. Some school districts encourage this on a district-wide basis. You can gain much insight into how the Halifax County–Bedford School District's students and teachers developed its biannual science magazine,

Science Stew, in Surjit Verna, "The story of *Science Stew,*" *Science and Children, 31,* no. 4, 1994, 26–27. You can use their experience to customize a science magazine for your school or classroom. Here are some ideas for you to consider.

- A combination of student and teacher ideas should be used, with the primary focus on students' work, augmented by teacher tips and suggestions.
- Allow your students to name their magazine.
- If the magazine is to be school-wide, get student and teacher volunteers to serve as an editorial committee. If the magazine is to be produced by an individual classroom, work with a small committee for planning but involve *all* students whenever possible.
- To begin, elicit contributions on a predetermined topic of interest to your students.
- Student-submitted articles are read by the editorial committee, which selects articles for the next issue. Whenever possible, use all articles submitted, even though some may need additional guidance and work.
- Make certain that the students' names are prominently displayed on every article used.
- Students who have articles published in your magazine should be recognized in the presence of their peers, in writing by the editorial committee and by you.

There are so many cognitive benefits from a science magazine, but never forget the ego enhancement. We all love to have our names in print!

SCIENCE AND SOCIAL STUDIES

Many decisions concerning societal problems require a basic understanding of science, technology, and society (STS). Thus, science and social studies are clearly interrelated, and have a mutual, specific mandate: the development of an informed population of scientifically/technologically literate citizens. What are some ways you can incorporate the best of social studies into your science program without diminishing either the science or the social studies?

Integrating Science and Social Studies

Integrating social studies with science is a natural way your students learn. In life, the learning we do is usually multidisciplinary, unlike elementary school learning, which separates knowledge into subject areas like reading, social studies, mathematics, and science. Social studies/science integration can also have these advantages for the teacher and learner:

- Students can use concepts and processes learned in science in other curricular areas, especially the social studies.
- Other subject areas can be used to reinforce science skills.
- Both science and social studies are often taught through a problem-solving approach.
- Science and social studies share two common categories of learning, namely concepts and processes.

Process skills for science include classifying, formulating hypotheses, generalizing, identifying variables, inferring, interpreting data, making decisions, measuring, observing, predicting, and recording data. Social studies process skills include problem solving, communicating, map and globe reading and interpretation, time and chronology usage, data evaluation, and chart/graph/table interpretation. Notice that the social studies process skills are similar to the science process skills. These similarities are easily included in the recommendations of the National Council for the Social Studies (NCSS) task force on scope and sequence in Table 8–3.

You can find common ground for science and social studies where science and technology affect human concerns and issues. Where this happens, you can identify central societal themes for your science studies.

Integrate Science and Social Studies Around Societal/Technological Themes

Another method for integrating science skills and processes with social studies involves planning your science around societal/technological themes instead of narrow science topics. Some of these STS themes might include:

- Energy and its everyday applications, such as heating/cooling, transportation, sources (for instance, oil and its geopolitical ramifications), alternative sources (solar, wind, and geothermal).

TABLE 8–3

Recommendations of the NCSS Task Force on Scope and Sequence

Kindergarten	Awareness of Self in a Social Setting
Grade 1	The Individual in Primary Social Groups: Understanding School and Family Life
Grade 2	Meeting Basic Needs in Nearby Social Groups: The Neighborhood
Grade 3	Sharing Earth-Space with Others: The Community
Grade 4	Human Life in Varied Environments: The Region
Grade 5	People of the Americas: The United States and Its Close Neighbors
Grade 6	People and Cultures: The Eastern Hemisphere
Grade 7	A Changing World of Many Nations: A Global View
Grade 8	Building a Strong and Free Nation: The United States

Source: Modified from National Council for the Social Studies, *Social Studies Curriculum Planning Resources* (Dubuque, IA: Kendall Hunt, 1990), 25.

- Industrial production and its adverse effects on communities (air, water, and noise pollution).
- Physical environmental influences on the settlement and development of cities.
- Weather/climate influences on people, their histories, and agriculture.

Here are some ways that STS theme studies can enhance students' learning of science and social studies:

- In studying heat and heat transmittal, students could investigate how their school is heated, insulated, and cooled by having the custodian show them the heating/cooling systems and tracing the movement of heat in the building.
- Students' bicycles, roller skates, and other toys could be examined when you are studying machines, gears, and mechanical advantage. All could be tied to manufacturing.
- Radio, television, and electronic games could be used to study light and sound in communication.
- As students study plants or animals, you might introduce them to population concepts and the problems associated with overpopulation.
- In a science unit on weather and climate, you might help children see the interrelationship between geographical areas and how pollution in one area could cause acid rain or other pollutants to fall on people thousands of miles away.
- Insect studies lend themselves to exploring ways of ridding urban areas of rodents, roaches, and other disease-carrying animals.

The Cider Mill School in Wilton, Connecticut, generated a study of its schoolyard and surrounding vicinity with the history, physical features, and ecosystem management of their community.

Here is how you can do the same thing:

1. With your students, analyze your school grounds and community resources for topics, ideas, and concepts of science and social studies curricula that:
   a. are closely tied to social studies and science curricula;
   b. lend themselves to both outdoors and indoors;
   c. are directly connected to your local environment;
   d. show the connections between science and social studies;
   e. relate to current environmental issues
2. Designate indoor and outdoor activities that will help your students learn the concepts identified above.
3. Enlist parent volunteers to map the community, supply the community's historical and geological history and current status, and bring in relevant newspapers, magazines, books, and videotapes for you and your students.
4. For the science portion of the unit, guide learners with such outdoor activities as field trips, interviewing older residents, visiting local museums, etc. Indoor activities could include building model watersheds, constructing models of glaciers (frozen water in milk cartons) designing flannel/felt boards of the water cycle, etc.
5. For the social studies part of the unit, have volunteer-led community walks to introduce human history into the geophysical studies: native Americans' roles in the community's history; environmental impact of colonists and modern populations, etc.
6. Share your unit with other classes, students' parents and guardians, and the community at large through student-produced writing, newspaper articles, school meetings, etc.

For more information, see:

Lois R. Stanley, "A River Runs Through Science Learning: Tap Community Resources to Create an Integrated Science and Social Studies Unit," *Science and Children, 32,* no. 4, 1995, 12–15, 58.

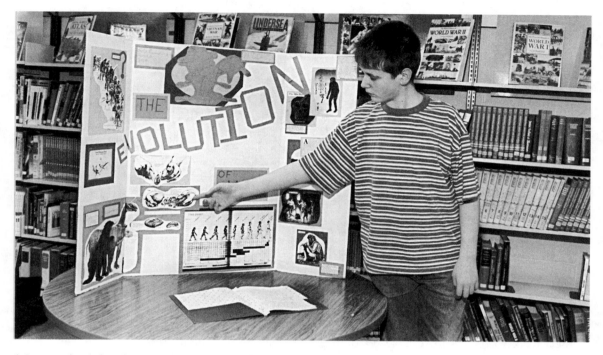

Science and social studies are naturally integrated not only through STS themes but also through historical strands, including anthropology.

INTEGRATING SCIENCE AND ART

As we have seen, art and science can be integrated by using bulletin and flannel/felt boards, projecting objects, posters, and drawings, making and illustrating student books and magazines, etc. Here are some additional ways to get students involved in the integration of art with science.

- While studying light, cover the ends of flashlights with different colored cellophane, using several layers to produce strong colors. Darken the room and have students experiment with various colors.
- In discussions about the properties of matter, give each student several different kinds of textured papers, such as sandpaper, watercolor paper, or oatmeal paper. Have students draw or scribble with crayons to discover the different textures.
- Mobiles are excellent ways to show the solar system or weather elements.
- Puppets of all kinds (paper bag, hand, or tennis ball) allow children to engage in artistic and fantasy extensions of science (see Figure 8–4).
- Making objects with clay or other malleable substances permits children to produce three-dimensional representations of mental images.
- Working with wood and tools (saws, hammers, drills, or screwdrivers) shows students how machines make work easier.
- Have students make crystal art: Make a saturated solution of water and Epsom salt, make crayon drawings, then coat the drawings with the Epsom salt solution and let them dry.

FIGURE 8–4
Puppets stimulate creative
science thinking

■ Make magnetic art by putting iron filings or steel wool fragments in sealable plastic bags and have students fabricate designs through the plastic.

To increase your repetoire of science/art activities read:

■ S. Criswell, *Nature Through Science and Art* (New York: McGraw-Hill, 1994).
■ Jean Shaw and Sally Blake, "Helpful Hints: The Art of Science," *Science and Children, 31,* no. 3, 1993, 43.
■ K. Tolley, *The Art and Science Connection* (Menlo Park, CA: Addison Wesley).

INTEGRATING SCIENCE AND PHYSICAL ACTIVITIES

It is often difficult to approach theoretical concepts with elementary or middle school students, especially those in the primary grades. It is difficult to help these students see the how and why of physical occurrences; activities like games, dances, and role-playing can help us explain physical occurrences. Story-dances, in which students role-play familiar physical phenomena, have these advantages for science learning:

1. Dances that tell a story have an ancient and universal appeal that helps to motivate students.
2. Students involved in physical activity are not as easily bored as those listening passively.
3. Sufficient roles can be included so that the whole class can have a part. Nobody has to sit and watch; students with disabilities can also participate.
4. Each dance is short, usually less than five minutes. Time is available for two or three repetitions with a chance for trading roles.
5. No stage equipment is required—only a roll of masking tape or some chalk to outline objects on the floor.[22]

Dances can help children "see" invisible particles in such areas as matter, energy, and motion in melting ice, boiling water, electricity, atoms, and subatomic particles. By acting like the microscopic particles, children can act out such concepts as molecules slowing down or speeding up or the movement of electrons. They can visualize what happens in expansion and contraction of metals due to heat or cold by moving closer together or farther apart, as shown in Figure 8–5.

Help students conceptualize invisible particle theories by using more physical movement. However, in relating physical activities to science, consider the appropriateness of the cognitive level. For example, the concept of particles and their relationships is too abstract for preoperational or early concrete operational students.

INTEGRATING SCIENCE AND MUSIC

Investigating vibrating bodies presents opportunities to show that science and music are interrelated. Your students can make simple musical instruments from drinking straws, rubber bands, and soda bottles. Then these science concepts can be used to observe how "real" musical instruments work. Have the students discover how the length and thickness of piano strings determine the pitch (high or low) of the sounds produced. Ask your students or band members from upper grades to bring their musical instruments to class. Encourage them to

■ demonstrate how the musical instrument works,

■ classify the instruments by how the sound is produced (You may have to introduce *sustained vibration* through continuous excitation and *damped vibration* through single excitation), and

■ point out the *excitor* (what causes the vibration).

Students could construct a chart showing instrument, type of vibration, how vibration is initiated, and the excitor. Your students can be helped to see that plucked instruments produce damped vibrations, while bowed and wind instruments produce sustained vibrations. Your class will be fascinated by the roles that valves, air column lengths, strings, and reeds play in producing sound.

Use folk music and popular songs as often as they fit naturally into your science studies. Many popular musical groups sing about people, the environment, pollution, and other societal issues. Analyze the lyrics and see how they relate to science, technology, and society. The words of "Home on the Range," for instance, can be used as you discuss variables of weather changes.

COLD—particles close together

HOT—particles further apart

FIGURE 8–5

Physical activity involving molecular concepts

Contrast this to "Dakota Land," about drought in the West, and discuss with your students the different effects of weather on people.

Teachers have found that setting science curriculum topics to music stimulates students' interest.

1. Pick facts or concepts students are learning and use these for your lyrics.
2. Start with an easy tune most students know, e.g., "Mary had a little lamb."
3. Give a handout of lyrics or project them on a writing board.
4. Introduce the song by singing it to the class.
5. Delegate single verses to groups of students and have the whole class sing choruses together.
6. Have students write their own science songs.

Sharon Clark describes the process in "Helpful Hints: Singing Science," *Science and Children, 31,* no. 3, 1993, 43.

Encourage older students to bring records or audiotapes and videotapes to class for the science topics you investigate, such as whales (recordings of their sounds), birds, or insects. In addition to helping students learn science concepts, music offers students emotional experiences not limited to an intellectual level. Music truly is an international and cross-cultural experience. Use more of it in your science classroom, and you and your students will enjoy learning a great deal.[23]

INTEGRATING SCIENCE, HEALTH, PHYSIOLOGY, AND NUTRITION

Your elementary or middle school students are very interested in their bodies, including food and nutrition, height and weight, exercise and sports, disease, body parts and systems, and genetics. In the past, elementary and middle grade teachers lectured, scolded, scared, and preached about science and health to their students. They used to put long lists of *don'ts* on the board such as:

- Don't drink coffee.
- Don't eat sugar.
- Don't use drugs.
- Don't drink alcohol.

Research does support the negative effects on health of these items, but this negative approach has not succeeded in improving children's health. What does?

Positive Science/Health/Nutrition Teaching Makes an Impact

The content of science/health/nutrition should include topics that interest children. However, your most important concern should be to teach science/health/nutrition concepts in ways that *positively* affect your students' health and health habits. To do this, educators agree that science/health/nutrition should be taught by involving students with science processes and teaching them to think and use decision-making skills applicable to their own health. Your teaching should focus on students developing responsibility for their own health through discovery activities. They can learn how their bodies function, what they can do, and how they can improve or change the way their bodies perform. Two programs can give you specifics on how to do this. See Chapter 7 for information about *Science for Life and Living: Integrating Science, Technology, and Health* from the Biological Sciences Curriculum Study (BSCS) and *Health Activities Project (HAP)*.

Here are some science/health/nutrition activities that use science processes to make health a "get-up-and-find-out-about-yourself" subject. Students can use a hands-on/ minds-on approach to these activities:

- Count and record pulse rates before and after exercise.
- Compare reaction times to sight, sound, and touch stimuli.
- Formulate and test hypotheses concerning factors that affect lung volume.

- Predict, measure, and record external body temperatures at various locations on students bodies.
- Design investigations to observe the effects of exercise regimens on muscular strength.
- Simulate nutritional choices and predict effects on their bodies.
- Devise experiments to test peripheral vision.
- Collect and analyze data on local and regional sources of environmental pollution.[24]

Teaching science/health/nutrition in a hands-on/minds-on activity-oriented way can make it interesting, relevant, and more likely to be absorbed into students' lifestyles. Positive attitudes and health habits grow out of relating science/health/nutrition to students' everyday lives. Try it, and it may even impact positively on *your* health habits.

INTEGRATING SCIENCE AND MATHEMATICS

Science and mathematics are integrally related. Many elementary and middle school science activities have a number of mathematical implications. Let's investigate some now.

Science/Mathematics Develop Cognitive Skills

Piagetian or constructivist operations are required for learners to achieve well in science and mathematics. Some of the operations basic to these disciplines are:

- conservation of substance,
- conservation of length,
- conservation of number,
- one-to-one correspondence,
- ordering,
- seriating, and
- classifying.

Students who do not do these operations well—and this includes many children aged 7 to 8—have trouble reading and solving mathematical and scientific problems. They are still *prelogical* (unable to do logic) and *prenumerical* (unable to do things with numbers) in their development. Many science and math curricula involve students in Piagetian and constructivist activities to help them develop operational competencies.

Research on Science Projects and Math Learning

Science and math curricula in the primary grades necessarily have some duplication, because students on the preoperational level need to experience operational concepts, such as conservation, over and over in order to develop their cognitive abilities. These competencies are not only fundamental to science and math but to all subjects that require thinking. For example, Donald Strafford and John Renner found that the Science Curriculum Improvement Study (SCIS) caused significant gains in conservation of length, number, and other abilities in the first grade.[25]

Science/Mathematics and Problem Solving

Research has also shown that science can be useful for teaching students to solve problems. Research shows that using real-world science/mathematical problems, instead of contrived made-up problems, can enrich and expand the problem-solving skills of your students.[26]

Science and mathematics are important because they help students develop not only mental operations but also a greater willingness to solve problems. This willingness to solve problems is critical for students learning both science and mathematics. Mary Budd Rowe showed this was especially important for disadvantaged children. "Without science experiences, disadvantaged children tend to be frightened and frustrated by simple problems. Their problem-coping skills simply do not

The need to solve problems in science by applying mathematical processes makes the integration of these disciplines an essential science teaching/learning goal.

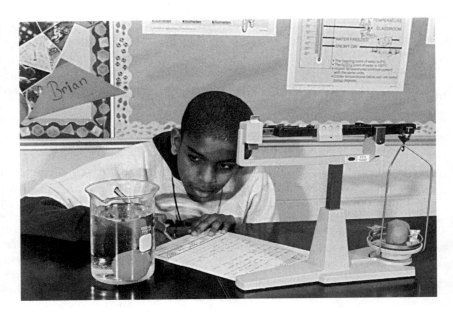

develop satisfactorily. With it, they usually learn strategies for attacking problems."[27]

Elementary science teachers who integrate science and mathematics agree that the primary value of this integration lies in helping their students solve real-life problems. The carry-over of these problem-solving skills to your students' everyday lives is high.[28]

Science/Mathematics and the Metric System (SI)

Although the movement to adopt the metric system in our country seems to have lost its momentum, the country is becoming more metric. The metric system, now termed the International System of Measurement (SI), is used by all other English-speaking countries in the world. It is used exclusively in all scientific work. The pressure to change to SI has already affected machine tools, packaging (especially liquor), and temperature. Competition with the rest of the world will continue to accelerate the use of SI in business, science, and government. Students will have to know both systems during this transition period. You will have to teach both. The Metric Information Office of the National Bureau of Standards has published a paper to help individuals compare the two systems (See Figure 8–6.)

Making Conversions to Metric Measures. The metric system is convenient because conversion factors within the system are powers of ten. For example, in measuring and adding the length of objects together, the metric system is often easier to use than the English system. It is easier to add 4.5 cm and 2.4 cm than to add 1¾ and 1⅜ inches. Also, because the metric system has smaller units (millimeters), it is easier to measure exactly.

With the national concern about changing to the SI system, many states are insisting that greater attention be given to using metric measures. Many science curriculum projects and texts use only metric units.

Teachers often think the SI system is difficult; they are familiar with the English system and have problems converting from it to the metric form. However, students do not have difficulty learning the metric measures. Since they do not yet have good concepts of the English system,

FIGURE 8–6

Comparing measurement systems

Source: From the Metric Information Office of the National Bureau of Standards.

the SI system is as easy for them to learn as the English system. Do not stress converting from the metric to the English system. When a student measures something 2.54 cm long, accept that as a description of its length. Do not ask how many inches it is. Students' concepts of a unit of length will be just as good without knowing the equivalent in the English system.

A somewhat amusing article on student activities using metric is found in Cherly Eagles, "Mad for Metric Measure," *Science and Children, 31,* no. 4, 23–25, 59.

Using Graphs and Tables in Science Mathematics

Graphs and tables are vital in your science/mathematics teaching. When you teach students how to make and interpret graphs and tables, they learn to use mathematical data and communicate their scientific findings by:

1. Putting data obtained from their science observations into a form that other people can understand and
2. Understanding their own data when they reexamine it.

Learning to use graphs and tables enables students to make predictions from collected data, to see relationships between variables in the science/mathematical activities performed, to hypothesize about possible changes in their obtained data, and to draw conclusions and inferences from data.[29]

The following are some ways to introduce graphs and tables in your science/mathematics teaching.

Histograms or Line Plots. A *histogram* (also called *line plot*) is one of the simplest types of graphs and can be used as an introduction to graphs. You can construct a histogram by having your students place on the graph a gummed, colored dot that corresponds to or stands for the color of leaves collected in autumn, for example. For a line plot, an *X* may be used to represent each leaf. The left side, or *vertical axis,* shows the number of leaves. The bottom line, or *horizontal axis,* shows leaf color (see Figure 8–7). Students stack gummed dots of the appropriate color at the appropriate number: four orange, six red, three yellow, and two purple leaves have been collected.

Histograms or line plots introduce students to graphing and using symbols to represent the actual item. They help students classify data. Then you can help them think about and discuss data differences.[30]

Variations of histograms or line plots are referred to as *picture graphs, pictographs, pictograms,* or *pictorial graphs.* Pictures can also be used to label axes, which is most advantageous for younger children or for introducing graphs to some older students.

Bar Graphs. *Bar graphs* (also referred to as *bar charts*) vividly show differences in data collected. They are usually used to compare different

FIGURE 8–7
Histogram of fall leaves

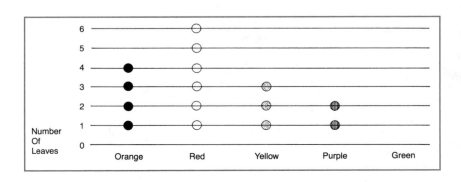

groups. Bar graphs can be horizontal or vertical. They are relatively easy to understand and can be introduced to students in Grades K through 12 because the graphs can be nonnumerical. Data presented in picture graphs easily lend themselves to bar graphs. Converting a picture graph to a bar graph is a logical progression, for students move naturally from semiconcrete representations of data to more abstract forms.

A good extension of this activity would be for all of your students to record their own growth and to predict how tall they will be next year. A big-as-life graph may be made by placing masking tape on the floor to form grids, and having students place objects within the grids, e.g., shoes grouped according to how they stay on: slip-on, laced, Velcro-attached, or buckled. Then, bar graphs can be made of the data.

More examples of bar graph activities may be found in Susan Pearlman and Kathleen Pericak–Spector, "Graph that Data!," *Science and Children, 32,* no. 4 (Jan. 1995), 35–37.

Line-Segment Graphs. *Line-segment graphs* (also called *broken-line graphs*) are more advanced than bar graphs, and students in Grades 3 to 6 can learn to make and interpret them. With line-segment graphs, your students can graphically show numerical data that are continuous or fluctuate. Line-segment graphs represent changes in quantities over a period of time.

Two perpendicular lines, the horizontal and the vertical axes, serve as the reference lines. For example, if students are line graphing plant growth as in Figure 8–8, the vertical axis shows plant height (in millimeters) and the horizontal axis shows days after planting. Direct students to "Measure your plant from the soil to the top each day. Place an *X* on the graph to show the height each day." See Activity 8–1.

You will have to show the students on the chalkboard how to put an *X* where the vertical and horizontal axes intersect, as well as how to connect points with lines. After a few days of measuring

FIGURE 8–8
Line graph of plant growth

Activity 8–1   QUICKIE STARTER: OPEN-ENDED ACTIVITY

In using bar graphs for recording and analyzing plant growth, your students could cut strips of paper to measure the height of the plant. Use one strip to represent each day's growth.[31] After collecting strips for five days, help your students develop prediction skills by asking, "How tall do you think your plant will be in two days? Mark your strip (or your bar graph) to represent your prediction. In two days, we will compare your prediction strip with your measurement strip to see how accurate your prediction is."

and posting on the line graph, have students predict where they think their plant height will be after 10 or 15 days by placing a red *X* at the point where the 10 or 15 days line intersects.

Frances Curcio has aptly summarized why elementary and middle school teachers must include graphing in their science teaching:

Elementary school children should be actively involved in collecting 'real-world' data to construct their own simple graphs. They should be encouraged to verbalize the relationships and patterns observed among the collected data (e.g., larger than, twice as big as, continuously increasing). In this way, the application of mathematics to the real world might enhance students' concept development and build and expand the relevant mathematics schemata they need to comprehend the implicit mathematical relationships expressed in graphs.[32]

For additional ideas on graphing in science/mathematics (including other graphing techniques such as *circle graphs, line plots, stem-and-leaf plots,* and *box-plots*), see:

- J. R. Lehman, "Concrete Graphs Build Solid Skills," *Science and Children,* 27, no. 8, 1990, 28–29.
- Antonia Stone, "When Is a Graph Worth Ten Thousand Words?" *Hands-On!* (TERC, 1969 Massachusetts Ave., Cambridge, MA 02138, Spring 1988), 16–18.

- Susan Jo Russell, "Who Found the Most Shells? (Who Cares?)" *Elementary Mathematician* (1988), 4, 9.
- Kristine L. Eng, "Real Graphs, Real Fun, Real Learning," *Learning, 88,* no. 17, Oct. 1988, 58–62.
- Susan Jo Russell and Susan N. Friel, "Collecting and Analyzing Real Data in the Elementary School Classroom," in Paul R. Trafton, (ed.), *New Directions for Elementary School Mathematics, 1989 Yearbook of the National Council of Teachers of Mathematics* (Reston, VA: The National Council of Teachers of Mathematics, 1989), 134–148.

Examples of Science/ Mathematics Integration

Many opportunities exist for integrating science and mathematics. Here are a few:

- *Mathematics through science experiences.* Students explore how much water is needed to seed germination. Quantitative evidence requires mathematics. Students plant seeds, decide on various amounts of water needed, and measure water each time plants are watered.
- *Mathematics with science to show relationships.* Students measure their height and arm span to see if there are any relationships.
- *Mathematics with science in interpolation.* Here are data that students collect in weighing a hamster 7 and 14 days after its birth: seventh day, 10 grams; fourteenth day, 20 grams. Students are asked to interpolate the point at which the hamster weighed 15 grams. Line or bar graphs could be intro-

duced also. Usually hamsters come in multiple births, so students will need help in calculating average weight gain.
- *Mathematics with science in extrapolation.* While investigating the effects of plant hormone on pea seed growth, students dip some seeds in water and some in hormone solution. Every 24 hours for 5 days they measure seed growth and plot points on a graph to show growth. After examining the data, students are asked to extrapolate (go beyond) and predict the plant heights on the seventh day.
- *Mathematics with science in problem solving.* Students investigate a variety of materials to see which are better insulators. The problem-solving processes used will include (a) the kind of investigation selected, (b) procedural steps, (c) measurement tools, (d) data recording, or (e) conclusions reached.
- *Mathematics with scientific objectivity.* In investigating reaction times of first, second, and third graders, student researchers discover that they need a "language" to communicate what they are doing. They use exact numbers instead of *some* or *group* for the number of children tested and reaction times. Exact data allow the children to duplicate their tests to check their accuracy.
- *Mathematics with science and the metric system.* Students measure temperature each morning in Celsius and place data on a large class graph.[33]

There are many more opportunities for you to integrate mathematics into your science program; the possibilities are limited only by your imagination.

SUMMARY

Students' learning in both science and other subjects is enhanced when science is properly integrated around interdisciplinary STS themes in an unforced and natural way.

Hands-on/minds-on activity science programs expand and enrich the language development of students. Receptive language (listening and reading) and activity science require the same intellectual skills. Through active involvement with physical objects, students learn the cognitive processes (such as class inclusion, conservation, and ordering) required to improve reading in science better than they learn them through reading alone. One of the best techniques is to frequently read to nonreaders to encourage the development of reading skills and positive attitudes toward reading. This develops good listening skills. Specific science/listening activities were introduced to assist with this development.

Specific techniques for broadening and deepening vocabulary for science reading have been presented, such as "inventing" new science words for students, using printed materials with nonreaders, and formulating operational definitions. Suggestions were provided for making and using writing, bulletin, and flannel boards as tools for enriching both science and language. Practical activities were offered for effectively using science textbooks in an integrated science program in your classroom.

Techniques were explored for productively using other non-textbook reading in your science program such as children's literature (tradebooks, minibooks, fiction/science fiction), student-made science magazines, and creative writing.

Classroom-tested activities were also given for integrating science with social studies around science/technology/society themes, physical activities, music, and health.

Mathematics and science are integrally related and have contributed to each other through the ages. Because mathematics and science are wedded in the investigation of natural phenomena, many of the educational objectives of these two disciplines overlap. When scientists collect data, they do so in quantitative ways. Mathematics aids the scientist in collecting objective data, revealing relationships, suggesting problem-solving techniques, and replicating experiments. As a scientist works, mathematics and science are often both involved in the inquiry process, requiring many mental inductive and deductive operations.

Science curriculum projects and the more recently published elementary science texts include more investigations using quantitative approaches. All of these curriculums emphasize the use of the metric (SI) system, because scientists use the metric system in their work. Ways to use the metric system were presented.

Using graphs and tables is vital in the teaching of science. Examples were given of how to construct and use histograms, bar, and line-segment graphs.

Science is a legitimate subject of itself, and should not be diluted or diminished when combined with any other subject matter. If the full impact of your science program cannot be realized by integration, then don't integrate it.

SELF-ASSESSMENT AND FURTHER STUDY

1. The selection of nonfiction tradebooks or informational books to integrate in your science teaching/learning must be given considerable thought. Use the following articles to help you pick books for the science topic your class is investigating: In *Science and Children,* see "Resource Reviews" and "Outstanding Science Trade Books for Children." (An annotated bibliography is prepared annually in the March edition.)

2. If you are using a science textbook as all or part of your science program, choose hands-on/minds-on activities that supplement what is in the text. Plan and introduce these to your students.

3. Help students identify the parts of nonfiction tradebooks that will help them use these informational books in their science studies. Choose one part (e.g., table of contents, index, glossary, or additional readings) and prepare a lesson that

increases your students' understanding of that part of the book.

4. After completing a field trip, a visit to a museum, or a tour through a water purification plant, guide your students in writing an experience chart of the event on primer paper. Illustrate it with your students' drawings or photos. Use the students' exact words whenever possible.

5. Together with your students and the school or community librarian, gather old or discarded science textbooks and tradebooks, and help your students make minibooks on science topics you will study this year.

6. Select an informational book that encourages students to perform an experiment to understand a scientific principle. Perform the activity and evaluate it with such questions as, "Are the directions clear and appropriate for the level for which it is intended?" "What modifications (if any) would you recommend?" "As a result of doing this activity, did you (and will students) better understand the scientific principles involved?"

7. Launch a school-wide science magazine committee composed of students, parents or guardians if possible, and your fellow teachers. Using information in this chapter, have the committee plan and put together a science magazine that will interest your students.

8. Fiction and science fiction books are valuable resources for science studies. Consult with your school and/or community librarian for a list of books that fit into a science topic for your students. Using the checklist in Figure 8–4 select those you feel are appropriate. To assist you, see:
   - Donna E. Norton, *Through the Eyes of a Child: An Introduction to Children's Literature,* 4th ed., Chapter 12, "Nonfiction: Biographies and Informational Books" (Englewood Cliffs, NJ: Merrill/Prentice Hall, 1995), 645–713.
   - Seymour Simon, "Behold the World! Using Science Tradebooks in the Classroom," *Science and Children, 19,* no. 6, Mar. 1982, 5–7
   - Patricia R. Crook and Barbara A. Lehman, "On Track With Trade Books: Try Direct Instruction With Trade Books for Teaching Science Content With Flair," *Science and Children, 27,* no. 6, Mar. 1990, 22–23.

9. Help your students make their own science flannel/felt boards. Have each student, or groups of three, prepare the flannel/felt cutout pieces and describe the science topic they will present to their classmates.

10. Expository and descriptive writing are essential skills for students to develop in hands-on/minds-on elementary science activities. Using these references, plan lessons to guide students in expanding their writing skills:
    - M. Hill, "Writing Summaries Promotes Thinking Across the Curriculum—But Why Are They so Difficult to Write?", *Journal of Reading, 34,* no. 7, Apr. 1991, 536–539.
    - National Writing Project, 5627 Tolman Hall, University of California–Berkeley, Berkeley, CA 94720.
    - *Writing to Learn,* Council for Basic Education, 725 15th St., N W, Washington, DC 20005.

11. Devise art activities that naturally lend themselves to science topics your students are studying.

12. Plan dance-plays to help students visualize topics they will explore this year.

13. Prepare some metric activities for the grade level you teach.

14. Describe how Piagetian operations are integrated in science and mathematics.

15. Construct a histogram, bar graph, or line-segment graph with your students. Try to use real-life situations from suggestions in this chapter and suggested references.

16. Select a science/technology/society theme and plan integrating activities using all curricular subjects, especially the social studies.

17. Have your students bring in their musical instruments and integrate them into your science program.

18. Plan an activity-based health study in your science program.

19. Listening skills are intregal parts of both science and the language arts. Prepare a lesson for introducing and expanding your students' listening skills, and research how listening to books can help. For additional information on listening to books see:
    - "Audiocassettes for Kids," *EPIEgram, 16,* no. 4, 1989, 4–5.

NOTES

1. Joan Braunagel McShane, "Editor's Note: Integrate with Integrity," *Science and Children, 31,* no. 7, Apr. 1994, 4.

2. D. J. Leal, "The power of literary peer-group discussions: How children collaboratively negotiate meaning," *The Reading Teacher, 47* (2), 1993, 114–120.

3. Nancy Kober, *EDTALK: What We Know About Science Teaching and Learning* (Washington, DC: Council for Educational Development and Research, 1993), 46.

4. R. Gamberg et al., *Learning and Loving it: Theme Studies in the Classroom* (Portsmouth, NH: Heinemann, 1988); and C. C. Pappas, B. Z. Kiefer, and L. S. Levstik, *An Integrated Language Perspective in the Elementary School: Theory into Action* (New York: Longman, 1990).

5. Thomas R. Koballa, Jr. and Lowell J. Bethel, "Integration of Science and Other Subjects," in David Holdzkom and Pamela B. Lutz, (eds.), *Research Within Reach: Science Education. A Research-Guided Response to the Concerns of Educators* (Charleston, WV: Appalachia Educational Laboratory, Inc., 1985).

6. The author is indebted to and highly recommends the coverage of themes and integration of subject matter in Gail E. Tompkins and Kenneth Hoskisson, *Language Arts: Content and Teaching Strategies,* 3rd ed. (Englewood Cliffs, NJ: Merrill/Prentice Hall, 1994).

7. "Science and Talking," "Science and Writing," and "Science and Reading": in J. Scott (ed.), *Science and Language Links: Classroom Implications* (Portsmouth, NH: Heinemann Educational Books, Inc., 1993).

8. For an expansion of this topic read: Chapter 2, "Cognitive and Linguistic Development" in Jeanne Ellis Ormrod, *Educational Psychology: Principles and Applications* (Englewood Cliffs, NJ: Merrill/Prentice Hall, 1995), 28–76.

9. Patricia A. Robbins, "Implementing Whole Language: Bridging Children and Books," *Educational Leadership, 47,* March 1990, 50–54.

10. Gail E. Tompkins and Kenneth Hoskisson, *Language Arts: Content and Teaching Strategies,* 3rd ed. (Englewood Cliffs, NJ: Merrill/Prentice Hall, 1994), 521.

11. Kenneth R. Mechling and Donna L. Oliver, *Handbook I: Science Teaches Basic Skills* (Washington, DC: National Science Teachers Association, 1983).

12. For an excellent review of research in science teaching and reading, read Ruth T. Welman, "Science: A Basic for Language and Reading Development," in Mary Budd Rose, (ed.) *What Research Says to the Science Teacher,* vol. 1 (Washington, DC: National Science Teachers Association, 1978), 1–12.

13. For additional information on listening to books see "Audiocassettes for Kids," *EPIEgram, 16,* no. 4 (1989), 4–5.

14. Richard D. Kellough et al. (eds.), *Integrating Mathematics and Science For Kindergarten and Primary Children* ((Englewood Cliffs, NJ: Merrill/Prentice Hall, 1996), 163–166.

15. Richard D. Kellough et al. (eds.), *Integrating Mathematics and Science For Kindergarten and Primary Children* ((Englewood Cliffs, NJ: Merrill/Prentice Hall, 1996) 161–163.

16. Nancy Kober, EDTALK: *What We Know about Science Teaching and Learning* (Washington, DC: Council for Educational Development and Research, 1993), 52.

17. E. B. Kelly, "Memory Enhancement for Educators" *Fastback 365* (Bloomington, IN: Phi Delta Kappa Educational Foundation, 1994).

18. B. R. Gifford, "The Textbook of the 21st Century," *Syllabus, 19,* 1991, 15.

19. National Science Teachers Association, "Outstanding Science Tradebooks for Children in 1985." *Science and Children, 23,* no. 6, Mar. 1986, 26.

20. An excellent description of how to guide students' making of science minibooks is found in: Richard J. Reif and Kristin Rauch, "Science in Their Own Words: A Library Filled with Science Books Students Wrote Themselves Becomes their Favorite Retreat," *Science and Children, 31,* no. 4, Jan. 1994, 31–32.

21. H. Kay Reid and Glenn McGlathery, "Science and Creative Writing." Reproduced with permission by *Science and Children,* 14, no. 4, Jan. 1977, 19–20. Copyright 1977 by the National Science Teachers Association, 1742 Connecticut Ave., N W, Washington, D.C. 20009.

22. For an expanded discussion on the use of physical activity in elementary and middle school science, see James H. Humphrey and Joy N. Humphrey, *Developing Elementary School Science Concepts Through Active Games* (Springfield, IL: Charles C. Thomas Publisher, 1991) and Lloyd D. Remington, "Let's Get Physical in Science," *Science and Children, 19,* no. 7, Apr. 1982, 13–15.

23. For excellent examples of how to use science and music, you are urged to read Kathleen M. Bayless and Marjorie E. Ramsey, *Music: A Way of Life for the Young Child,* 4th ed. (Englewood Cliffs, NJ: Merrill/Prentice Hall, 1991).

24. For additional information, see David J. Anspaugh and Gene Ezell, *Teaching Today's Health,* 3rd ed. (New York: Macmillan, 1990.)

25. Donald G. Strafford and John W. Renner, "Development of Conservation Reasoning Through Experience" in *Research and Learning with the Piaget Model* (Norman, OK: University of Oklahoma Press, 1976), 34–55.

26. Howard Goldberg and Philip Wagreich, "Focus on Integrating Science and Math: For a Real Lesson in Science, Students Should Conduct an Experiment Involving Quantitative Variables," *Science and Children, 26,* no. 5, Feb. 1989, 22–24.

27. Mary Budd Rowe, "Help Is Denied to Those in Need," *Science and Children* (March 1975), 25.

28. National Council of Teachers of Mathematics, *Curriculum and Evaluation Standards for School Mathematics* (Reston, VA: The Council, 1989); and Douglas Cruikshank and Linda Jensen Sheffield, *Teaching Mathematics to Elementary School Children: A Foundation For the Future* ((Englewood Cliffs, NJ: Merrill/Prentice Hall, 1988).

29. For outstanding coverage of graphing and its uses in elementary and middle school curriculums, especially science and mathematics, you must add this source to your professional library: Frances R. Curcio, *Developing Graph Comprehension: Elementary and Middle School Activities* (Reston, VA: The National Council of Teachers of Mathematics, Inc., 1989).

30. For further elaboration on this technique see James M. Landwehr and Ann E. Watkins, *Exploring Data: Quantitative Literacy Series* (Palo Alto, CA: Dale Seymour Publications, 1986).

31. For a fuller description of this activity, see *Supplement to the Elementary Science Syllabus, Level I (Ages 4 through 7)* (Albany, NY: The University of the State of New York, State Education Department, 1986), 65–66.

32. Frances R. Curcio, "Comprehension of Mathematical Relationships Expressed in Graphs," *Journal for Research in Mathematics Education, 18,* no. 5, Nov. 1987, 382–393.

33. The author acknowledges ideas in Kenneth R. Mechling and Donna L. Oliver, *Handbook I: Science Teaches Basic Skills* (Washington, DC: National Science Teachers Association, 1983), 24–26.

CHAPTER 9

Extending and Enriching Science Experiences for *All* Students

Our world is rapidly changing and expanding. As a result, the face of today's classroom is also changing. No longer do students come from relatively common backgrounds. Many are recent arrivals from other countries and do not speak English fluently. Increasingly, many children in large cities are raised in other countries, urban settings that are significantly different and separate from the national mainstream. The challenge for teachers is to include and support these students, supplying them with learning experiences that help validate their ability to participate and succeed in learning.[1]

CREATING INCLUSIVE ENVIRONMENTS

How do real teachers adapt their lessons for students with special needs?

Teaching Concepts

Karen Heck is a regular second-grade classroom teacher, but several developmentally handicapped (DH) children join her class during science lessons. "These kids have a very short attention span for listening to stories or even watching filmstrips," she says, "but they love hands-on activities and will pay attention much longer for those.

"I begin hands-on activities by pairing the special students with the other kids. Then I give the class clear, one-step directions. I also use the desks of the special kids when I do the demonstrations for the whole class. That way, the special kids are close up and can see and touch the equipment. Then I ask them to show the other students how to do it."

Second-grade teacher Marie Kenzie also has DH students come into her classroom for science. "Paper-and-pencil tasks tend to be difficult for these kids," she reports, "but you can change the task so it still works for them." Marie often has students dictate answers or responses instead of writing them. Sometimes she cuts apart worksheets and creates pages for her special students that include just the activities that are within their capabilities. After the pages are photocopied, they look much like the ones for the other students. With this approach, the children with special needs do not feel uncomfortably different.

Monica Freado, a special education teacher in a middle school, helps classroom teachers modify their approach for students with special needs. Although her students are older than Karen's and Marie's, Monica follows the same principles. "Everything has to be hands-on. Teachers need to apply all the learning modalities: touch, sight—all of them. You can't just stand there and lecture, because many of these kids can't take notes quickly enough to keep up. Some of them can't listen and take notes at the same time, so teachers need to make their lessons less talking and more doing."

Monica points out that more time for manipulation means some lessons will take two days instead of one. Students' physical limitations, such as cerebral palsy, might interfere with hands-on activities, but they are less of a problem, Monica says, if a teacher pairs students. Then the partner can help the student with special needs handle test tubes and so on. "All kids learn. These kids just learn in different ways," Monica says. "Teachers need to be creative."

Managing Behavior

Learning problems can be accompanied by behavior problems. Karen stresses the need to build a good rapport with the primary teacher for mainstreamed students. Often these teachers have set up a system to encourage appropriate classroom behavior. They need to know if the children are being cooperative or disruptive. "You're part of a team that's working with these kids, so you need to communicate with the other members," Karen points out.

Marie sets up a behavior chart that includes all the students in her class. Behavior goals may range from a regular student remembering to wear her glasses to a student with special needs remembering to raise his hand instead of yelling out. "That way, everyone has a goal and can earn stickers on the chart."

Assessing Progress

"You need to have different expectations for these kids than for the rest of the class," says Karen. "They won't learn the same things, but they will learn some things. The special education teacher at our school helps me remember that and be realistic."

"When you work with kids with special needs, you need to keep an open mind and use what works," Marie notes. That might mean an oral test instead of the paper-and-pencil version. Marie often checks with her special kids during lessons to make sure they are understanding the concepts involved.

"When these kids are successful, it means even more because learning was more difficult for them," Marie says. "My regular students learn a lot from having kids with special needs in the classroom. They see what these kids can do, instead of just what they can't do. And the special kids now have friends at school they can talk to at recess and during lunch. They feel more like they're a part of the school community. Now that I think about it, having them here makes us all feel more like a community."

All students are unique. They come to your classroom with a wide range of learning abilities and styles, diverse cultural backgrounds, and physical, social, and emotional differences. Some will have a limited proficiency using the English language and all will have had different sensory experiences and prior knowledge. What implications do students' differences have for how you teach science to your students? How can you provide worthwhile science learning activities for every student?

This chapter shares strategies that will enable you to individualize your science teaching. In addition, suggestions are given for making you more multiculturally aware, so that you may provide science experiences compatible with your students' backgrounds. This will also provide you with ways to promote multicultural understanding in your students. Let's look first at what's involved in making science teaching more individualized for *all* your students.

EXTENDING AND ENRICHING ALL STUDENTS' SCIENCE LEARNING

Enriching science teaching/learning and making it more available for your students requires more than methods of teaching. It requires a philosophy of addressing each student's unique needs or special circumstances. All aspects of each student's uniqueness—learning abilities and styles; cultural background; and physical, social, and emotional differences—are accommodated in individualized science teaching/learning. You recognize the unique way each of your students learn, and modify your teaching to recognize their differences and needs. This approach is commonly called **regular education initiative (REI)**.

Where Do You Start?

You can immediately use the following six elements of individualization with all your students:

1. Present a wide variety of instructional materials and activities.
2. Select different media for different students.
3. Give your students the option of working on different topics or activities.
4. Wherever practical, have students design their own activities.
5. Increase your interaction with individuals or small groups and decrease time spent on total class presentations.
6. Spend less time checking materials, assignments, or grading.[2]

Investigate ways of accomplishing the above. For example, organize a cadre of responsible students to carry out certain duties related to facilitating cooperative learning.

These elements of individualization can be easily incorporated into your science program right now! For instance, most science textbooks or programs can be easily adapted for individualizing. You will find many suggestions in the teachers' guides that accompany your science programs and textbooks. Some teachers get different level science textbooks within their adapted series, for students with varying reading and science background status. Some curricula have been specifically designed for easy individualization.

The classroom-tested suggestions that follow offer specific, pragmatic, and either free or very inexpensive ideas for incorporating individualization into your science teaching. Following these suggestions will be additional teaching ideas for individualizing your science teaching for your students with special needs.

Practical Suggestions for Extending and Enriching Science Learning

You can use these suggestions to extend and enrich science learning for all your students, regardless of your teaching situation—self-contained classroom, team teaching, departmental, or systems approach. This list is not exhaustive; alert teachers will adapt and vary these ideas for their unique classrooms, as well as discover new ones. Do not be afraid to try any procedure that you think will provide broader and richer science experiences for your students. Encourage your students to be constantly alert to things *they* could be doing in science.

Initiate an Enrichment Center for Your Science-Oriented Students. An enrichment center offers optional, free-time (before school, lunch hour, after school, etc.) recreational science activities, similar to the kinds of activities students get in intramural sports, band, art or photography club, and dramatics. Ideally, an entire room will be provided for the enrichment center, but it can function in a corner of a classroom, library, multimedia or audiovisual room, or any other room. See Chapter 6 for practical suggestions on setting up such a center.

Enrichment centers can be stocked with challenging ideas and materials for conducting simple and safe self-directed activities. Alan McCormack suggests that 100 or more challenges should be available on posters or "challenge cards." Students should be free to choose any one that interests them and try to solve it. Usually they have two options once a challenge is selected.

1. Solve it completely on their own, with simple equipment and science supplies in the center, from home, or from the teacher.
2. Request a solution card and the corresponding box of materials that go with it. The solution cards have instructions for doing an experiment or using a method to solve the challenge, but, of course, not a specific answer. Divergent questions are used on the solution cards to stimulate the student's thinking without giving cookbook answers.

These two options let students choose the amount of structure suitable for them at that particular time. Next time it may be a different selection. See Chapter 6 and Appendix K for ideas on shoebox collections of science materials to accompany each challenge card. Invite parents to serve as volunteer assistants in the enrichment center, or encourage students to make their own shoebox collections and challenge cards.

Motivate Students to Improve Their School Environment. Some ways students can be encouraged to participate in the improvement of their school environment include:

- organizing and participating in a general cleanup of grounds;
- making a survey of needed improvements and possible remedies for playground and school ground problems, such as worn paths where students cut across grass, eroding slopes, dust-bowl play areas, and so on;
- taking responsibility for improving one of the problem areas given in the previous item;
- writing letters to agencies for help, such as ecology groups and county agricultural agents; and
- reclaiming eroded areas by planting bushes, trees, or ground cover.

As a result of the activities above, students could be inspired to set up a rock garden; bird house, feeder, and bath; or other outdoor beautification projects on their school grounds. Assist your students in collecting information about what is needed and why to set up, maintain, and continue their selected project. Parents/guardians/grandparents and other community volunteers can assist you with this and other science extension activities.

Advocate Student-conducted Community Surveys. Students can be encouraged to survey people and places in their community as possible resources for their science studies. Fast-food establishments are logical places to start surveying.

Make a portfolio of the kinds of science topics you teach and the places and persons who might contribute to each, and update it often (see Table 9–1). Some teachers duplicate a brief letter for students to use when surveying, which tells community persons the science topics your students will investigate, some items they might supply gratis, the names and phone numbers of contact persons should follow-up be necessary, and asks them to act as volunteers or consultants. You'll be amazed how cooperative business and community people are and you can quickly get a long list of potential helpers in your science teaching.

Organize Volunteers to Help Extend Student Learning. How many times have you wished for another pair or two of hands to help with your science teaching? One way is to recruit parents/guardians/grandparents, retired teachers, undergraduate college students, scientists and engineers, or anyone else as volunteer science aids. To be most effective, it is best to organize a volunteer program, perhaps around these four components:

1. *Recruiting.* Send out an S.O.S. about your hands-on/minds-on science program and needs through take home handouts, sign-up sheets at open house and parent/teacher conferences, personal telephone calls, and school principal's newsletter. If parents cannot volunteer as classroom aides on a regular basis, encourage them to help by collecting needed materials, chaperoning community trips, or making science kits.
2. *Defining volunteer roles.* Specify the day and time they will volunteer each week or month. Precisely define the roles and limitations of a classroom volunteer, e.g.,
   - Prepare materials that students will use in the hands-on/minds-on activities.
   - Contribute an extra pair of hands to the teacher and students.
   - Support the teacher during the activity by working directly with students who need assistance, e.g., reading stories to small groups, helping students clean up after an activity, writing down younger students' verbatim dictation, or assisting with the construction of a science bulletin board.
3. *Orienting volunteers.* Usually two- or three-hour orientation sessions are adequate to acquaint volunteers with your hands-on/minds-on science philosophy and techniques.

TABLE 9–1
Community science people/materials/places

Biological Sciences	Chemistry	Earth Sciences	Physics
Biology department (local college)	All kinds of factories	Abandoned quarry	Airport
Farm	Chemistry department (local college)	Field	Astronomical observatory
Fish hatchery	Drugstore	Geology department (local college)	Electronics factory
Food processing plant	Electroplating shop	Museum	Gas station
Greenhouse	Oil refinery	Seashore	Physics department (local college)
Hospital	Plastics industry	Stream	Power dam or electricity generator plant
House excavation	Water purification plant	Weather station	Radio station
Park	Chemical engineer	Astronomer	Television station
Pharmaceutical lab	Chemist	Geologist	Telephone exchange
Vacant lot	Druggist	Mining engineer	Newspaper printing plant
Dentist	Photographer	Pilot or navigator	Architect
Druggist	Fast-food restaurants	Weather forecaster	Builder
Farmer	Medical technician	Construction crews	Automobile mechanic
Florist		Utility workers	Electrician
Laboratory technician		Nature preserve rangers	Electronics engineers
Nurse			
Pet shop owner			
Physician			

Let them try the activities themselves. Tell them what happens in a typical science activity and how they might be helpful. Be very specific about how you want them to serve in your classroom and which things they are *not* expected to do (e.g., discipline students, teach science classes). Discuss any concerns they have.

4. *Maintaining communication between teacher and volunteers.* Plan a few minutes before or after school, during breaks, or at lunch to discuss the day's activity and to ask for any questions from volunteers. School and home science follow-up activities can be examined to extend your students' science learning. Perhaps even a Family Science Night can be planned by you and the volunteers.

You will find more time to do hands-on/minds-on science with the help of adult volunteers. These resources can help you in identifying and using volunteers in your science teaching:

- Susan Pearlman and Kathleen Pericak–Spector, "Helping Hands From Home: Parent Volunteers Make Active Science More Manageable," *Science and Children, 29,* no. 7, Apr. 1992, 12–14.
- National Retired Teachers Association and the American Association for Retired People, 601 E St., NW, Washington, DC 20049.
- Science-By-Mail Scientist Mentor Program, Museum of Science, Science Park, Boston, MA 02114, (800)729-3300.
- *Sharing Science With Children Series:* "A Guide for Parents," "A Survival Guide for Scientists and Engineers," and "A Guide for Teachers," FREE from Georgiana M. Searles, North Carolina Museum of Life and Science, P.O. Box 15190, Durham, NC 27704.

Cross-Age Tutoring. Another group of potential volunteers is students. Older, more mature students or students with strong science orientation can be easily instructed to be cross-age tutors for younger children. Students might bring in and discuss raising their pets, give slide or videotaped talks of their recent trips, show and explain how their musical instruments work, or actually teach a lesson. Some schools have a cadre of *cadet teachers*—older students who teach younger children.

Here is a summary of how this was done in one school, with sixth graders teaching a lesson on plant parts to first graders:

1. Teacher taught the sixth graders the learning cycle.
2. Teacher and the sixth grade tutors prepared materials and practiced the lesson together.
3. Sixth graders taught the plant part lesson to the first graders with the first grade teacher in the room to assist and handle class management and discipline.
   a. *Exploration.* After each pair of first graders collected three weed samples from their school grounds, a sixth grader asks them, "What can you tell about the plants we are looking at?" If little or no response, she asks a more direct question, "How is this part different from that part?" First graders examine their weeds with hand lenses. Tutor suggests recording the data, and writes down the exact words the first graders say.
   b. *Concept Introduction and Invention.* After the above activity, the tutor introduces the terms *stem, leaf,* and *root* and writes them on the writing board.
   c. *Concept Application.* The tutor has first graders test their understanding of these new concepts by identifying parts on their own plants. Pictures are drawn of their weed plants and a bulletin board with parts labelled by the tutor is made.
4. Sixth-grade tutor returns to her classroom elated because the first graders shout, "When will you come back and work in science with us?"

Student tutors gain by strengthening and deepening their science knowledge, for as **you** know, "If you want to learn something, teach it!" To find out more about cross-age tutoring, see:

- Walter S. Smith and Cindy Burrichter, "Look Who's Teaching Science Today! Cross-Age Tutoring Makes the Grade," *Science and Teaching, 30,* no. 7, 1993, 20–23.

Explore Community Resources to Extend Science Learning. Informal science education opportunities are abundant. Family and other adults can have a great impact on students' science learning. Families and the community can stimulate students' science interests both in school and out through informal science activities. Suggest that your students—together with their parents, guardians, or grandparents—explore science in places from A to Z!

Airports, Aquariums, Beekeepers, Botanical gardens, Buildings under construction, Chemical plants, Dairies, Electrical generating plants, Farm, Flower shows, Forests, Gardens, Gravel pits, Greenhouses, Hardware stores, Health clinics, Industrial plants, Junk yards, Kitchen in school, Lumber yards, Mines, Museums, Nature centers, Newspaper plants, Observatories, Optical labs, Parks, Planetariums, Playgrounds, Quarries, Recycling centers, Science centers, Sewage treatment plants, Shorelines, Television stations, Utility companies, Vending machine companies, Vegetable gardens, Water purification plants, Weather stations, Wildlife sanctuaries, X-ray departments in hospitals, Yards, and Zoos.[3]

Many of these locations feature hands-on exhibits, offer science programs and activities for all ages, and serve as an educational resource for their communities. Parents should be included in the planning by meetings or by notes sent home to them. They could accompany their children and guide their learning if requested or necessary.

You and/or your students could contact these out-of-school resources to see what special science programs are scheduled. Your students might attend these out-of-pocket school programs individually, in small groups, or with their parents. Work cooperatively with your students and the resources to prepare a self-directed guide so your students do not wander through them aimlessly. Some places even offer an audiotape that guides visitors from exhibit to exhibit. A letter to parents may get their cooperation in the project and extend school/home/community ties. Excellent sources for family activities that influence informal science learning are:

- *The Informal Science Review,* published bi-monthly, P. O. Box 43228, Washington, DC 20015, tel/fax (202)364-8841.
- Anne T. Henderson and Nancy Berla, *The Family Is Critical to Student Achievement* (Washington, DC: National Council for Citizens in Education, 1994).
- Project Prism, National Urban League, Inc., 500 East 62nd St., New York, NY 10021, (800-TO-PRISM).
- *Playtime Is Science: Implementing a Parent/Child Activity Program,* Educational Equity Concepts, 114 East 32nd St., New York, NY 10016, (212)725-1803.

Students and Teachers Can Make Their Own Science Kits. Encourage individuals or small groups of students to explore and use science kits (such as those from Elementary Science Study) during leisure or free time, science time, or at home, if you think they are mature enough. If your school system does not have sufficient funds to purchase science kits, obtain some of the ESS teacher's guides. You can select individual science units or lessons and find the materials locally at little expense. These ESS units have been particularly popular:

Tangrams	Behavior of Mealworms
Tracks	Mirror Cards
Mystery Powders	Bones
Batteries and Bulbs	Drops, Streams, and
Attribute Games	Containers

See Chapter 7 for the distributor of ESS units and other resources for individualization ideas and materials.

Use TV Shows to Extend Science Learning. You and your students can get television listings and teacher's guides from your local commercial and educational television stations or by writing directly to one of the following major national television networks:

- American Broadcasting Company, Inc. (ABC), 1330 Avenue of the Americas, New York, NY 10019.
- Columbia Broadcasting System, Inc. (CBS), 51 East 52nd street, New York, NY 10019.
- National Broadcasting Company (NBC), RCA Building, 30 Rockefeller Plaza, New York, NY 10020.
- Your local Public Broadcasting System (PBS).

Make and distribute to students and their parents a list of science shows pertinent to what you are studying, as shown in Figure 9–1.

Suggest that your students view programs of interest to them, or assign specific programs and ask students to report to the class. You may want to prepare a worksheet with specific questions to guide your students' viewing. Ask your students to add to your list by checking TV programs for science-related topics.

Surprise Science Boxes: A Fun Way to Learn Science. Set up surprise science boxes and encourage your students to work with them. Surprise science boxes are popular with students, especially with students who have learning difficulties. Periodically you can display a labeled box. On the front of the box you can print a statement of its content in riddle form such as

I am hard.
I can push some things without your seeing me push them.
I can pull some things without your seeing me pull them.
I am made of iron and nickel.
What is my name?

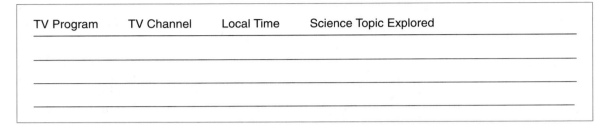

TV Program	TV Channel	Local Time	Science Topic Explored

FIGURE 9–1
Format for listing suggested science shows

FIGURE 9–2
Science discovery bulletin board

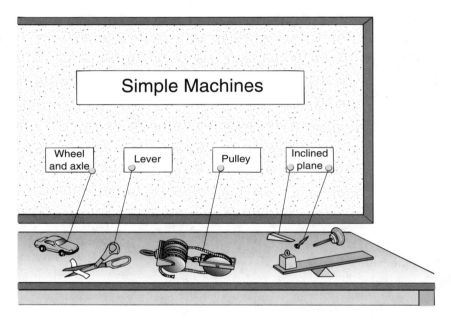

One use of the surprise box is to introduce a new area of study. Some teachers put a different surprise science box out daily for use by individual students when they complete all their assigned work. Students can also make their own surprise science boxes and share them with their classmates. For excellent suggestions on additional surprise science boxes see:

- Eddie L. Whitfield and Eva D. Samples, "Small Box Science: Independent Learning Exercises for Younger Children," *Science and Children, 18,* no. 7, Apr. 1981, 9.

Bulletin Boards Enrich Science Learning. Have your students, individually or in small groups, pick a scientific topic, collect science materials from magazines and newspapers, and set up a science bulletin board. By changing bulletin boards every week, you can give all your students an opportunity to participate in making one. Students are interested in the bulletin boards because they participated in planning and constructing them, and the boards are not displayed long enough to get stale.

Another variation of the bulletin board is the science discovery bulletin board. The science

Encouraging students to begin a collection of rocks, shells, or other science-related categories can promote in-depth studies for any kind of learner.

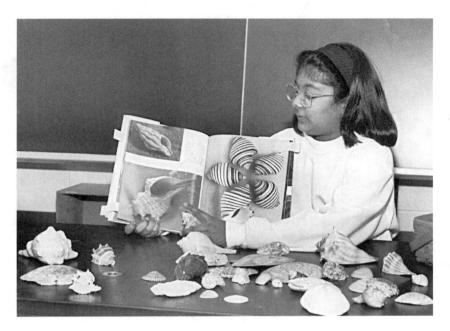

discovery bulletin board has pieces of string going from the board to objects on a nearby table. Students print what they think the object is on small cards, along with their names. They pin the cards to the bulletin board at the end of the string. After several students have had a chance to pin their cards on the board, the teacher discusses their answers. For example, a science discovery bulletin board on simple machines might show an inclined plane, a pulley, a lever, a screw, and a wheel and axle, as in Figure 9–2. Science discovery bulletin boards can be used to introduce or review an area of science.

Evaluating Other Viewpoints in Science Panel Discussions. Several students can form a panel discussion on a science/technology/society theme, such as the problems and value to society of space exploration. Students can organize the panel discussion themselves or you can guide them with questions like the following as the focus:

What provisions would you need to take to the moon? Mars? Antarctica? Mohave Desert?

What types of research or studies do you think should be carried out when you get there? How do you see society benefiting from scientific space exploration?

If you tape the panel discussion, ask your students to assess their own contributions and those of their classmates.

Biographies Show Scientists as Human Beings. Help your students recognize the human orientation of science by providing them with a wide variety of biographies of scientists. Select books on as broad a reading level as possible. Several students may work together to put on a play or other dramatic presentation showing particular parts of their scientist's life. Include biographies of minority group scientists such as women, blacks, Hispanics, and Asians, as well as people with physical impairments.

Welcome Students' Collections and Hobbies. Provide a table or bookcase for your students to display their collections of rocks, leaves,

FIGURE 9–3
Pictorial riddle

How Does a Lever Work?
(Grades 5–8)

What do you notice about this picture?
What are all the ways this is possible?

Teacher's Note: There are over 100 possible explanations: The board is nailed in place. The big individual has just pushed up. He is filled with air, pillows, etc. He only appears larger since the board is rotating and he is closer to you. This is in outer space. The board is not made of the same material on each side of the pivot point or fulcrum, etc. How many more can you add?

bird nests, insects, coins, etc.. Encourage your students to explain their collections with signs, oral reports, or an audio- or videotape for classmates to play, listen to, and watch by themselves.

Pictorial Riddles Whet Students' Science Appetites. Pictorial riddles are similar to challenge cards. They use a picture format and are usually mounted on 5″ × 8″ index cards or on larger oaktag. Here's how to make pictorial riddles.

1. Select some scientific concept or principle to be learned or discussed. Alternatively, present a discrepant event.
2. Draw a picture, use an illustration, or use a photograph that shows the scientific con-

cept, process, or discrepant situation. (See Figure 9–3.)
3. Devise a series of divergent process-oriented questions related to the picture which will help students gain insights into what principles are involved.

As students become more accustomed to this technique, you can ask them to create their own pictorial riddles to share with their classmates.

Activity Cards and Task Cards. You and/or your students can design activity and task cards like the one in Figure 9–4. The activity card asks students to write a story about what they see happening and share their story with their

FIGURE 9–4

Activity and task card for upper elementary and middle school grades

For an Activity Card
Write a short story about what you see happening in this picture. Then share your story with the rest of the class.

For a Task Card
Write a short story about what you see happening in this picture. After you're finished, go back and underline what you *observed* with a *red* pen. Then underline what you *inferred* with a *black* pen. Then share your story with the rest of the class.

classmates. The task card goes a little further. After writing their story, they are asked to review the picture and

- underline what they *observed* with a red pen, and
- underline what they *inferred* with a black pen.

These cards can be placed in a learning center or other place where they are available to your students. Encourage them to make as many as possible for their learning experiences and for you to build up a repertoire for your class to use.

Start a Science/Technology/Society Club and Magazine. The club can meet before or after school, during free time during the day, at lunchtime, or on Saturdays. Perhaps a parent can serve as a guide or adult leader. Students from this club may also function as cadet science

teachers or science helpers. Many schools find these students are excellent resources for teachers throughout the school.

Extend the Science/Technology/Society Club with a weekly or monthly school science newspaper. Students from kindergarten on up love to contribute art, pictorial riddles, brain teasers, or book or TV reviews. News of which class has rock collections, pets, insects, plays, or dioramas can be inserted so the entire school may share the science activities. See the specific details of how to plan and put together a science magazine in Chapter 7.

Microcomputers Expand Science Learning. If at all possible, integrate microcomputers into your science teaching and learning. For practical applications of computers and other electronic technology in your science program, see Chapter 10.

SPECIAL NEEDS STUDENTS BENEFIT FROM HANDS-ON/MINDS-ON SCIENCE[4]

All of the science extension and enrichment activities we've discussed are appropriate for all students, but some may have to be adjusted for your special needs students.

Educators and the public are very much involved in providing *all* students with an education appropriate to their physical, mental, social, and emotional abilities. In particular, there is a great emphasis on educating students who have needs that other students do not. There are some students who have a limited ability to model and learn science incidentally from their environment—because of physical, mental, or social impairment; limited prior sensory knowledge and/or experiences; or language difficulties. These students are at risk of being experientially deprived, because they are unable to learn from the world around them.

Special needs students are in *every* classroom of *every* school, including yours. They require teaching strategies and approaches designed to meet their individual special needs.

Laws That Affect How Special Needs Students Will Be Taught

Federal laws directly affect what and how you teach science in your classroom. One law—**Public Law (PL) 94-142,** now called the **Individuals with Disabilities Education Act (IDEA)**—and its amendments direct that all students have a right to a full free public education *with the least restrictive environment.* This means that schools are required to educate students with disabilities with nondisabled students to the maximum extent appropriate for the students with disabilities.

A second law, the **Americans with Disabilities Act (ADA)** (42 U.S.C. Secs. 12101–12313) prohibits discrimination because of disability.

IDEA and ADA are different in three important ways:

1. IDEA benefits people with disabilities only between birth and twenty-one, while ADA benefits all people with disabilities regardless of age.
2. IDEA only benefits people in school, but ADA benefits all people with regard to a wide range of public and private services, not just education.
3. IDEA provides money to state and local educational agencies to assist in the education of students with disabilities. ADA prohibits discrimination, but does not provide money to assist anyone to comply with it.

These two laws, however, work together. IDEA helps state and local educational agencies create services to educate students with disabilities. ADA protects these students against discrimination when they are not in school.[5]

As elementary school teachers, you must be concerned with how IDEA impacts on our students and our teaching. The current trend is for students identified as special needs to be integrated into the regular classroom for the *entire day,* as well as in the life of the neighborhood school. This is called **inclusion.** Inclusion begins with the premise that general education classrooms should be structured so that all students belong from the very outset and so that student diversity is celebrated. Superior summaries of the case for inclusion are found in:

- John L. Goodlad and Thomas C. Lovitt, (Eds), *Integrating General and Special Education,* (Englewood Cliffs, NJ: Merrill/Prentice Hall, 1993).
- C. L. Salisbury, M. M. Palombaro, and P. M. Hollowood, "On the Nature and Change of an Inclusive Elementary School," *The Journal of the Association for Persons with Severe Handicaps, 18,* no. 2, 1993.

Educators recognize that not all students learn science in the same way. Viewed from that perspective, PL 94-142 guarantees education for all students. This was reinforced by the NSTA Position Statement on Laboratory Science for Preschool/Elementary Level with this suggestion:

Children at all developmental levels benefit from science experiences. Appropriate hands-on experiences must be provided for children with special needs who are unable to participate in classroom activities.[6]

How Does Inclusion Affect Your Science Teaching?

It is very possible that you currently are, or very soon will be, in an inclusion school. You may already have students with a wide range of needs in your class. Here are two questions you should consider as you plan for the inclusion of special needs students in your science class:

1. What values and principles shall I adopt in helping special needs students learn science to the maximum extent they are capable?
2. What are general and specific teaching/learning modifications that will assist special needs students in my science program?

Your Values Affect How and What You Teach Special Needs Students

Don't feel you face an insurmountable task with regard to inclusion of special needs students. Research has shown that you can create positive visions of what is possible when you combine state-of-the-art practices with a positive values system.

Figure 9–5 lists six values that can nurture a positive vision and be a powerful force in your hands-on/minds-on science activities for special needs students. A physician once said, "My colleagues sometime lose sight that our duty is to treat *people* and not symptoms!" That sometimes happens with teachers when teaching special needs students. Like nondisability students, disability students have many untapped capabilities; contribute positively to their families, friends, classmates, and the community; and have strengths that we can identify, highlight, and build upon.

Be very guarded about labels that are put on your students. Get as much information as you can to give you a *Human Profile,* not just a special needs category or name of a disability.

FIGURE 9–5

Six values guiding inclusion of special needs students

Source: From *Exceptional Lives: Special Education in Today's Schools* by A. Turnbull, H. R. Turnbull, M. Shank, and D. Leal, (Englewood Cliffs, NJ: Merrill/Prentice Hall, 1995), 17. Reprinted by permission.

- *Great Expectations.* Students have many capabilities that have not been tapped. We can develop new visions of what is possible. These visions can become realities. We need new perspectives of what life can be as well as support for fulfilling these dreams.
- *Positive Contributions.* Individuals with disabilities contribute positively to their families, schools, friends, and communities. We need to develop greater opportunities for these contributions.
- *Inherent Strengths.* Students and families have many natural capacities. They need greater opportunities for educational programs to identify, highlight, and build upon their strengths.
- *Choices.* Students and families can direct their own lives. Enabling them to act on their own preferences allows them self-determination.
- *Relationships.* Connections are crucial to quality of life. Students and families need to connect to each other and to educators and friends in the community.
- *Full Citizenship.* Less able does not mean less worthy. Students with exceptionalities and their families are entitled to full participation in American life.

What Kinds of Special Students Might Be in Your Classroom?

What categories do schools use to classify students according to their differences? The federal special education law distinguishes students according to disability categories. These categories are listed in Table 9–2 with corresponding numbers and percentages of students in each, according to 1990–1991 school year data. An analysis of Table 9–2 shows that three-fourths of all students with disabilities fall into two categories: specific learning disabilities or speech and language impairments. If you combine these two categories with the categories of mental retardation and serious emotional disturbances, you account for almost 95% of all students with disabilities.

You probably have students in your class who are identified as special by federal laws. If so, you have unique teaching challenges. Therefore, this chapter emphasizes the need for individualizing your science teaching for *all* your students.

Humanity's beauty is in the diversity of its skills, abilities, and talents. Your students have the potential for manifesting their talents. One

reward of teaching is the satisfaction you will receive from helping *all* your students develop their talents. Together, let's explore how you can successfully develop your skills to accomplish this.

Practical Techniques for Providing a Supportive Special Needs Learning Environment

Here are some pragmatic teaching/learning techniques that are easy to put into use, right this minute, to make your classroom special-needs friendly.

- Consider including special needs students in regular class activities to the extent they are capable.
- Set a wide range of competence goals for your class, including special needs students.
- Assess the abilities of *all* your students, including special needs students, and realistically consider how each student's abilities affect his capacity to do science.
- Locate and/or adapt science materials for the particular needs of your students. Start with: The National Information Clearinghouse for

TABLE 9–2

Exceptionality categories and incidence

Disability	Number	Percent
Specific learning disabilities	2,117,087	50.5
Speech or language impairments	979,207	23.4
Mental retardation	500,877	12.0
Serious emotional disturbance	356,050	8.5
Multiple disabilities	80,272	1.9
Hearing impairments	42,317	1.0
Orthopedic impairments	43,763	1.0
Other health impairments	52,027	1.2
Visual impairments	17,783	0.4
Deaf-blindness	794	0.0
All conditions	4,191,177	100.0

Source: "To assure the free appropriate public education for all children with disabilities: Fourteenth annual report to Congress on the implementation of the Individuals with Disabilities Act" (Washington, DC: U.S. Department of Education, 1992).

Handicapped Children and Youth, P.O. Box 1492, Washington, DC 20013–1492, (800)999–5599.

■ Secure a broad range of science experiences to meet the needs of all your special children. Contact: ERIC Clearinghouse on Disabilities and Gifted Education, Council for Exceptional Children, 1920 Association Drive, Reston, VA 22091.

■ Use cooperative learning groups that include special needs students.

■ Encourage help and friendship between disabled and nondisabled students.

The Roles and Importance of Help and Friendships for Special Needs Students

Friendships are common among students, especially elementary school students who rely on friendships for companionship and emotional support. These friendships can be positive or negative influences. In an inclusion classroom you must be aware of the differences between helpers and friends.

In many classrooms, peers (usually girls) interact with severe disability classmates by getting materials for them and generally treating them in a parenting way. They often say they are "working with" a disability classmate. But as Van der Klift and Kunc have articulated, working with someone and being a friend are different types of activities.

Clearly, there is nothing wrong with help; friends often help each other. However, it is essential to acknowledge that help is *not* and cannot be the basis of friendship. . . . Friendship is about choice and chemistry and cannot be readily defined, much less forced. This is precisely its magic. . . . However, teachers and others do have some influence over the nature of proximity. Thus, to create and foster an environment in which it is possible for friendship to emerge might be a reasonable goal.[7]

The implications for your classroom are:

1. Present information on disabilities to children, parents, and other teachers, especially those with whom the disabled students come in contact.

2. Implement approaches that emphasize students learning together, e.g., CLGs.

3. Teach nondisabled students to be peer tutors and/or partners.

4. Teach social interaction skills to all students, with or without disabilities.

For additional coverage on help and friendship read:

■ Angel Novak, Ed., *Friendship and Community Connections Between People With and Without Developmental Disabilities* (Baltimore, MD: Brookes, 1993).

General Considerations for Expediting Science Learning for Special Needs Students

The previous teaching ideas can be used by all of your students, but some of them need modification for students with special needs. You will also need to modify your physical classroom environment, methods and materials of teaching, concepts, and assessment procedures for these students. In some cases, you may have to provide alternative activities entirely.

Table 9–3 gives general suggestions for teaching science to students with a variety of differences—physical, social, and cognitive. As you study it, you will see ways you can adapt your science teaching to meet the needs of your students with differences. The following sections give more specific suggestions that you can use in your classroom to assist students with special needs.

SCIENCE FOR STUDENTS WITH SPECIFIC EXCEPTIONALITIES

Science Experiences for Students With Visual Impairments

You will probably have visually impaired students in your classroom at some time. These include

TABLE 9–3

Science teaching/learning adaptations for special needs students

Disability	Physical Environment	Materials Modification	Methods Modification	Content Modification	Assessment Techniques
Visual Impairment	Materials kept in predictable place Students seated near activity Sighted guide to aid in giving directions Well-lighted work area	Large-print or Braille reading materials Taped lessons Sighted tutor to read directions or guide movements Training with equipment prior to use Braille writer, slate & stylus, Braille typewriter, or largeprint typewriter	Hands-on activities—use of other senses to observe More verbal description and use of touch Contact with real objects	None	More verbal evaluation, or Braille or large-print materials Aid in writing responses Assistance with manipulation of materials
Hearing Impairment	Students seated near activity so they can hear better and lipread if necessary Students seated away from distracting noises	Captioned films, filmstrips Visual text to accompany tapes Model or repetition of directions	Hands-on experience to develop concept Visual aids to accompany lectures List of new vocabulary before verbal presentation Eye contact before speaking Clear enunciation Contact with real objects Repetition of instructions and verbal presentation as necessary	None	None
Health Impairment	Removal of things that could aggravate health condition (e.g., no sugar for diabetics; no plant pollen for allergic child)	None	None	None	None
Physical Impairment	Adequate space for movement Desk and table height adjusted for wheelchairs Seats near exits whenever possible for safety Barrier-free access	Training with equipment prior to use Peer to help with manipulation of materials Mechanical aids for manipulation of materials as necessary	Contact with real objects	None	Assistance with manipulation of materials Aid in writing responses

Disability	Physical Environment	Materials Modification	Methods Modification	Content Modification	Assessment Techniques
Behavior Disorders	Students seated away from distracting noises	Training with equipment prior to use	Motivation Immediate reinforcement Cueing of relevant details Short activities Eye contact and priority seating for discussions Social praise	None	None
Cultural Differences	None	Concrete, relevant materials	Contact with real objects Cooperative learning	None	None
Limited English Proficiency	None	Modified reading material	Cooperative learning Concrete activities	None	Oral tests or modified for language
Gifted	None	More advanced reading material	Less repetition More emphasis on problem solving	More advanced concepts, such as universals & abstractions Emphasis on processes and synthesis & evaluation levels	More emphasis on organization and application of information
Learning Disabilities	Students seated away from distracting noises	Concrete, relevant materials	Immediate feedback Short activities Cueing of relevant details Social praise Pairing of an object and its symbol Eye contact and priority seating for discussion Multisensory activities	None	Oral tests or modified reading level Aid in writing responses Structure and frequent progress checks on projects

TABLE 9–3

continued

Disability	Physical Environment	Materials Modification	Methods Modification	Content Modification	Assessment Techniques
Mental Retardation (and slow learners)	Students seated away from distracting noises	Low reading level materials Training with equipment prior to use Concrete, relevant, tangible materials	Social praise Eye contact and priority seating for discussion Short activities Repetition Active involvement Practice in a variety of settings Contact with real objects Immediate feedback Pairing of an object with its symbol Adaptations of reading material Cueing of relevant details Mastery learning	Emphasis on knowledge of specifics Emphasis on concrete and relevant experiences	Structure and frequent progress checks on projects Oral tests or modified reading level materials Aid in writing responses More objective format

any students who need special aids and/or instruction to read ordinary print (low vision), students who must read using Braille (functionally blind), and those who do not receive meaningful input through the visual sense (totally blind). Braille may be used by both totally blind students and partially sighted students.

It is very important for the visually impaired to be well oriented with the laboratory equipment and classroom activity arrangements. When appropriate, students should prepare Braille labels and affix them to the scientific equipment; Braille grades can be affixed to papers and quizzes.

The Lawrence Hall of Science of the University of California at Berkeley has produced a program for mainstreaming special needs students—SAVI/SELPH. Two separate programs SAVI (Science Activities for the Visually Impaired) and SELPH (Science Enrichment for Learners with Physical Handi-

caps) were combined and reworked into a single program, mostly for upper elementary school and beyond, with several of its nine modules adapted for primary grade students.

SAVI/SELPH consists of sets of activity folios, with sections on overview, background, purpose, materials, anticipating (what to do before starting), doing the activity, and follow up. Figure 9–6 is an example of how the program developers provided metric measurement activities for visually impaired students. For information about SAVI/SELPH, Adapting Science Materials for the Blind (ASMB), Full Option Science System (FOSS), and other science programs for special needs students, contact the Center for Multisensory Learning, Lawrence Hall of Science, University of California, Berkeley, CA 94720.

To modify your present science program for visually impaired students, try these classroom-tested approaches:

SCIENCE EDUCATION IN THE BALANCE

During the past spring and fall, SAVI answered the cry for metric measurement activities for visually impaired students with the SAVI **Measurement Module.** The six hands-on activities contained in this module introduce youngsters to standard units of metric measurement.

To develop the concept of *mass,* we needed a measuring tool that would be suitable for use by the visually impaired. We finally decided to use a balance instead of a spring scale or other device and this decision resulted in some unexpected dividends for the project.

We looked at a lot of balances before we made the decision and even built a few of our own. Finally, we chose a simple, vacuum-formed model that is commercially available at a reasonable price. Then, we went to work on it!

First, we cut the bottoms of the two balance pans so that a paper or plastic cup could be dropped securely into the hole and then removed easily. Then, we added a tactile balance indicator. These slight modifications made it possible for blind students to determine weight to an accuracy of one gram!

The removable cup was the breakthrough we needed to make accurate weighing easy for visually impaired students. Both the weights (20g, 10g, 5g, 1g plastic pieces) and the objects or substances to be weighed automatically center in the cups, thus eliminating discrepancies due to the position of objects in the cups. An object, substance, or liquid can be removed from the balance—cup and *all;* a new cup can then be inserted and a new material weighed. There's no more trouble "getting all the powder out," or "transferring the beans"; the objects stay in the cups.

The students use the balances to verify that 50 ml of water (measured with a modified SAVI syringe) weigh 50g, thereby establishing the relationship between volume and mass.

Since its introduction, the SAVI balance has crept into other modules. The forthcoming **Kitchen Interactions Module** will feature an activity that focuses on the concept of *density.* Density is defined operationally using the SAVI balance: equal volumes of two different liquids are compared on the balance and the heavier one is identified as the denser liquid.

FIGURE 9–6

Science activity for the visually impaired

Source: Reprinted by permission of The Center for Multisensory Learning, Lawrence Hall of Science, University of California, Berkeley, CA 94720.

- Keep expectations high but realistic for all levels of visually impaired students.
- Pair a sighted student and a visually impaired student as partners in such science activities as safety in handling equipment, fire, and chemicals; observing chemical changes; and reading thermometers.

- Use tactile/kinesthetic approaches, such as different-textured sandpaper on rulers or other measuring devices or knotted string for measuring. A good source for adapted materials is the American Printing House for the Blind, 1839 Frankfort Avenue, P. O. Box 6085, Louisville, KY 40206–0085.

Activity 9–1   QUICKIE STARTER: OPEN-ENDED ACTIVITY

> Place on a table in front of the student five objects with which a visually impaired student is familiar, such as a pencil, a Braille book, a shoe, comb, and spoon. You might ask: Here are five objects that you use a lot. After you identify all of them, choose two objects you use in school.

- Use verbal directions, including recorded instructions, to tell the student what you are doing as you explain the procedures to be used.
- Expect the student to use his or her remaining sight often, unless directed otherwise.
- Be patient and encouraging about any spills and broken equipment.
- Provide as wide a range of multisensory, concrete activities as possible. See Activity Box 9–1.

To find additional science activities for the visually impaired, see the following sources:

- S. A. Curry, "A Model Assessment Program," *Journal of Visual Impairment and Blindness,* *87,* no. 6, 1993, 190–193.
- D. Fazzi, et al., "Social Focus: Developing Socioemotional, Play, and Self-Help Skills in Young Blind and Visually Impaired Children," in R. L. Pogrund and J. S. Lampert (Eds.), *Early Focus: Working with Young Blind and Visually Impaired Children and their Families* (New York: American Foundation for the Blind, 1992), 50–69.
- K. Heydt et al., *Perkins Activity and Resource Guide* (2 volumes) (Watertown, MA: Perkins School for the Blind, 1992).
- N. Levack, *Low Vision: A Resource Guide With Adaptations for Students With Visual Impairments* (Austin, TX: Texas School for the Blind, 1991).
- R. Pogrund et al., *TAPS: Teaching Age-Appropriate Purposeful Skills: An Orientation and Mobility Curriculum for Students With Visual Impairments* (Austin, TX: Texas

School for the Blind and Visually Impaired, 1993).
- K. L. Tapp, J. G. Wilhelm, and L. J. Loveless, *A Guide to Curriculum Planning for Visually Impaired Students* (Madison, WI: Wisconsin Department of Public Instruction, 1991).

These associations can provide you with suggestions on inclusion of students with visual impairments into your science program:

- American Council of the Blind (ACB), 1155 Fifteenth St., NW, Suite 720, Washington, DC 20005.
- American Foundation for the Blind (AFB), 15 West Sixteenth St., New York, NY 10011
- The Lighthouse for the Blind and Visually Impaired, 1155 Mission Street, San Francisco, CA 94103.
- Association for Education and Rehabilitation of the Blind and Visually Impaired (AER), 206 North Washington St., Suite 320, Alexandria, VA 22314.
- National Federation of the Blind (NFB), 1800 Johnson St., Baltimore, MD 21230.

Science Teaching for Students Who Are Deaf

Students who are deaf range in their hearing ability from partial hearing (hearing aid used) to total deafness.

There is no consensus about how to refer to people with hearing impairment, but the people-first approach—"Persons who are deaf"—will be used in this section. To gain greater insights into this approach, see: I. K. Jordan, "Language and

Change: Viewpoints on Deafness," *A Deaf American's Monograph, 42,* 1992, 69–71.

Sign language, lip reading, and reading facial movements help these students with oral communication. However, one of the major problems of persons who are deaf is language development. As people who are deaf mature, there are increasing gaps in vocabulary, concept formation, and the ability to understand and produce complex sentences; both language and intellectual development may be neglected.

Hands-on/minds-on science activities can provide a variety of learning experiences that may enhance both language and cognitive growth. Here are some science teaching suggestions for implementing these types of activities in your classroom.

Use Science Hands-on/Minds-on Activities to Develop Vocabulary. Hands-on/minds-on activities can help show students differences in the meanings of words. Begin with shape words (such as *circle, square,* or *triangle*) and provide cutouts of the shapes for students to identify. Introduce other words related to objects, such as color, size, and texture. Also, use objects in the students' environment to enhance concept and language development. Stress handling the objects during language/concept development. This process follows the constructivist learning cycle where the learner manipulates materials and then the teacher introduces or invents words for the scientific concepts.

Use Multimedia for Concept Development. Introduce or explain concepts using pictures, drawings, models, films, filmstrips, or videotapes. Screen all materials first to see if they are appropriate for your students who are deaf, and to decide what modifications you must make. Older students who can read can be given written materials before they view the film for orientation to new concepts. Keep written language a grade or more below that of your average class level, because the reading skills of people who are deaf may develop more slowly.

Assist Students Who Are Deaf With Language Development.

1. Encourage students who are deaf to participate in all verbal activities using whatever speech they have.
2. If they are working with a professional to develop speech, give your science vocabulary to the professional to work on proper pronunciation and understanding.
3. Assist students who are deaf with using mime, drawings, written communication, and demonstrations when communicating with their non-deaf classmates.
4. During oral work, always check the student's hearing aid for proper functioning, volume, and battery operation.
5. When you speak, always position yourself so that your face is well lit and the student is not looking into a bright light. Also, try to maintain direct eye contact with the student.
6. Use an overhead projector rather than a writing board so your face is in view for students. The light from the projector on your face is beneficial for speech reading.
7. Speak at a normal volume, speed, and tone when addressing students who are deaf. They will understand you better than if you shout or use exaggerated speech patterns.
8. Avoid speaking *for* students who are deaf, so that they may practice their own speech.
9. Seat students who are deaf as close to the activity as practical and away from distracting noises, so they can hear better and lip-read if necessary.
10. Seat students who are deaf near competent hearing classmates who can alert them to the intercom and fire alarm, help them follow directions, and generally assist in any way they can.
11. Provide a swivel chair, if possible, to let the student more easily follow group discussions.

Have High Expectations for Students Who Are Deaf. Encourage students who are deaf to participate in the same activities as their peers.

However, use the following modifications when hearing is the primary sense used to learn the concepts, and change auditory observations to visual ones:

- Use a light in a circuit instead of a buzzer.
- Substitute a "probe box" for a "mystery box."
- Have students feel vibrations rather than listen to pitch.
- Show vibrations of strings and tuning forks in water waves and sand movements.
- Make language cards to be used as students who are deaf engage in the activities. These help students identify with and relate to the activity and concepts. Use diagrams and pictures to enrich the cards.
- Encourage students who are deaf to verbalize as much as possible to practice relating their experiences, observations, discoveries, and interpretations.
- Whenever practical, pair students who are deaf with students who can hear.

Use Current Technology to Bolster Learning. You or someone in your school could investigate the use of a teletypewriter (TTY), in which a message is printed for the person who is deaf as the person on the other end of the line speaks. The person who is deaf "hears" by reading a printout. For information, see

- O. Sacks, *Seeing Voices: A Journey into the World of the Deaf* (New York: Harper Collins, 1989).

Computer technology has great potential for teaching science to all children, with special applications for those who are deaf. The Wicat Company of Orem, Utah, has developed a computer Integrated Learning System (ILS) to assist students who are deaf. The ILS program consists of a file server with 28 learning stations that have substituted "phonic ears" for the regular headphones or small speakers. These phonic ears provide controls for volume, tone, and filtering that can be adjusted for each student. Each station has an extra headphone jack to allow teachers to listen in and sign to students who need help. For additional information, see:

- "Hearing Impaired Kids to Benefit from ILS," *Technological Horizons in Education (T-H-E) Journal, 10,* no. 2, Feb. 1991, 14.

Chapter 10 has more on technology and education for all students.

Suggestions for Your Professional Growth Regarding Students Who Are Deaf. Keep abreast of research about teaching students who are deaf. These resources offer practical applications of modifications for students who are deaf in your science classroom:

- E. Dolnick, "Deafness as Culture," *The Atlantic Monthly, 272,* no. 3, 1993, 37–53.
- B. Luetke–Stahlman and J. Luckner, *Effectively Educating Students With Hearing Impairments* (White Plains, NY: Longman, 1991).
- T. Regan, "Cultural Considerations in the Education of Deaf Children," in D. Moores and K. P. Meadow-Orlans (Eds.), *Educational and Developmental Aspects of Deafness* (Washington, DC: Gallaudet University Press, 1992), 73–84).
- S. J. Salend, *Effective Mainstreaming: Creating Inclusive Classrooms* (2nd ed.) (Englewood Cliffs, NJ: Merrill/Prentice Hall, 1994).

In addition, here are associations that can supply suggestions for maximizing learning for students who are deaf:

- Alexander Graham Bell Association for the Deaf, 3417 Volta Place NW, Washington, DC 20007, (202)237–5220.
- Gallaudet University Bookstore and the National Information Center on Deafness, 800 Florida Avenue NE, Washington, DC 20002.
- National Association of the Deaf, 814 Thayer Avenue, Silver Spring, MD 20910.
- National Technical Institute for the Deaf (NTID), One Lomb Memorial Drive, Rochester, New York 14623.

Science Teaching for Students With Orthopedic Impairments

Students with orthopedic impairments can have a variety of physical differences, such as large muscle dysfunctions (causing mobility or balance problems) and/or small muscle malfunctions (causing loss of coordination, dexterity, hand strength, or erratic muscular spasms). Students with these handicaps may need crutches, braces, wheelchairs, walkers, or other devices.

For many physically impaired students, the greatest obstacles are attitudinal and architectural barriers. Generally, these students do not have intellectual handicaps. If you are to be effective in helping them learn as well as they can, you must understand the nature of their handicapping conditions and the parameters of their physical capabilities. Often, a little ingenuity on your part will enable orthopedically impaired students to be active learners in your science class. Here are some ways to begin.

Meeting the Physical Needs of the Orthopedically Impaired. Be aware of the ways you can modify your classroom environment:

1. Provide adequate space for movement by wheelchair, walker, crutches, and other devices.
2. Ensure barrier-free movement by clearing aisles and keeping traffic lanes uncluttered.
3. Ensure safety by placing seats or wheelchairs near exits wherever possible.
4. Be sure desk and table heights are appropriate for wheelchairs. Use trays to hold materials for science activities.
5. Provide plastic bags or buckets that can be carried over the shoulder by students who use canes or walkers, so they can carry simple science materials.
6. Make outdoor areas accessible to wheelchairs or canes. Alternatively, wheel impaired students in a wagon or carry them.
7. Provide book holders or book scanners if students cannot hold books or turn pages. Students who have impaired hand coordina-

tion may need pencil holders, tape recorders, or electric typewriters.

Meeting the Learning Needs of the Orthopedically Impaired. Modify your teaching/learning activities to accommodate students with physical impairments. Some suggestions include the following:

- At the beginning of the school year, send a letter home to all parents about your science teaching goals. Mention the impairments of the students in your classroom, and refer to your pairing of impaired and non-impaired students. Explain the experiences you plan for all students.
- Plan to pair students as often as possible, stressing to your class that we all have some type or degree of impairment.
- In pairing students, expect impaired students to do as much for themselves as they can.
- Try to capitalize on physically impaired students' well-developed sensory channels when you present science lessons.
- Look for adaptations and modifications for manipulations in hands-on/minds-on science activities, such as the following:
  - In a lesson on interaction of materials with a magnet, tape a magnet to the arm or hand of a student with no or limited limb control. This will enable the student to feel and see which objects interact.
  - Students can be wheeled around in a circle by their non-impaired classmates to take the paths of planets in a lesson on the revolution of Earth around the sun.
- Position yourself so your demonstrations and other teaching methods are visible, especially for students unable to move their heads. Avoid pacing or moving around the room while teaching if it could hinder students' ability to learn.

Maintain Realistic High Expectations for the Orthopedically Impaired. Encourage students with physical impairments to participate as fully as they can. Encourage them to think of ways you can modify your teaching so they will be able to engage in the activities.

Develop Positive Attitudes Toward the Orthopedically Impaired. Help your class accept the impaired. Plan lessons on individual differences. Have your non-impaired students try to get through a day as "impaired" by tying their fingers together or by staying in a chair.

Supply Multisensory Experiences. Encourage all your students to roll and slide to feel the forces of nature that affect us in our environment. Do this outdoors in the grass or on sand, or in the gym or playroom on mats. With parental permission and assistance, take physically impaired students out of wheelchairs or remove or unlock their braces, so they can participate, too. Multisensory experiences of this type are much more meaningful for the physically impaired than reading about environmental forces.

The Use of Technology. Make computers and other technology available to students with physical impairments. Computers can be excellent learning devices for the physically impaired, depending on how much of a physical and communication problem they have. If physically impaired learners can type on a computer keyboard, they can use the computer with special software. A control switch can be installed so that students with muscular problems can operate the computer. See Chapter 10 for additional information on the use of computers with the physically impaired student.

Check Professional Literature for Other Ideas for Working With Students With Physical Impairments. These references will supply many practical suggestions for modifying your classroom and for teaching science to physically impaired students.

- J. L. Bigge, *Teaching Individuals With Physical and Multiple Disabilities* (3rd ed.) (Englewood Cliffs, NJ: Merrill/Prentice Hall, 1991).

- R. A. Neely and P. A. Neeley, "The Relationship Between Powered Mobility and Early Learning in Young Children With Physical Disabilities," *Infant-Toddler Intervention, 3,* no. 2, 1993, 85–91.
- E. C. Keller, Jr., "Strategies for Teaching Science to the Physically Handicapped," *AAAS Abstracts* (Washington, DC: American Association for the Advancement of Science, 1982).
- Herbert D. Thier, "Independence for the Physically Disabled Through Science and Technology, *Education Horizons 62* (Fall 1983): 28–29.

Several sources that offer assistance with ideas for your students with impairments include the following organizations:

- Science for the Handicapped Association, Science Center, Moorhead State University, Moorhead, MN 56563.
- National Science Teachers Association, 1840 Wilson Boulevard., Arlington, VA 22201-3000.
- ERIC Clearinghouse on Handicapped and Gifted Children, 1920 Association Drive, Reston, VA 22091.

Science for Students With Varied Cognitive Differences

The students in your classroom will come to you with a variety of cognitive abilities. For some students, there will be a discrepancy between their perceived intellectual ability and their level of performance. Educationally, these students are often grouped as having learning disabilities.

Students with learning disabilities commonly have normal or above normal intelligence. However, they usually do not achieve in the same age or grade level in one or more of the basic academic skill areas such as reading, written language, or math and other important areas of learning such as memory or metacognition.[8]

Students with learning disabilities are a very heterogeneous group, since they often have overlapping problems. This makes it very difficult to classify their learning discrepancies and prescribe learning activities for them. Refer to Table 9–3 for ideas that could be used to meet the individual needs of students with learning disabilities.

Of greater cognitive discrepancy are students with intellectual impairments labeled in the past as *mentally retarded*. Definitions vary widely for the severity of mental retardation. The American Association on Mental Deficiency (AAMD) uses this definition: "*Mental retardation* refers to subaverage general intellectual functioning which originates during the developmental period and is associated with impairment in adaptive behavior."

Currently, many noted persons in the field, however, propose that the term *mental retardation* be abandoned because it has negative connotations and because it does not relate to education. They generally suggest the alternative term **general learning impairments.** While the latter term helps us develop a more positive definition of mental retardation, the major professional organizations actively serving the retarded advocate the use of the AAMD term, *mental retardation*.

Educators often classify retardation according to these levels of severity: *mildly retarded* (referred to as "educable mentally retarded"), *moderately retarded* ("trainable mentally retarded"), and *severely retarded*. Research at Colorado State College and Florida State University has found that moderately retarded students can learn some basic concepts. Mildly retarded students, in addition, can learn to predict, compare, group or classify, control a variable (with help), outline a simple investigation, measure, observe, communicate, and interpret simple data.

Mildly retarded students can be effectively educated in a regular self-contained elementary school classroom with individualized instruction and the help of specialists such as a resource teacher. Moderately retarded students generally need a highly specialized program and are commonly placed in self-contained classes with students with the same learning disabilities.

Most likely you will at some time have students who are mildly retarded. These students often have difficulty focusing on one aspect of an activity at a time. Therefore, it is best to limit your goals for each lesson. If you want to discuss the students' findings at the conclusion of a lesson, collect all materials from the students *before* starting the discussion, since these students are easily distracted by the materials before them and will not pay attention to the discussion.

Meeting the Needs of Students With General Learning Impairments

Here are some practical suggestions for meeting special needs of students with general learning disabilities in your regular classroom science program.

- Emphasize concrete, meaningful content. It is vital for these students that you use examples from the students' environment, such as colors of a school bus, grass, or their clothing when talking about colors.
- Reinforce mastery of new materials through repetition and use of multimedia. For instance, after working with students on germinating seeds, reinforce their new learning by reading a story, showing a filmstrip, or listening to a tape.
- Teach information sequenced from the easy to the difficult. If these students are to learn to cut paper strips to measure the growth of their plants, start them cutting short straight lines, then move into cutting longer straight lines, then teach how to make two-dimensional cuts.
- Increase attention initially by highlighting relevant dimensions and minimizing unnecessary stimuli. For example, darken the room and present materials about magnets on an overhead or opaque projector.
- Secure commercially prepared materials. The Biological Sciences Curriculum Study (BSCS) has designed and field-tested activity-centered science curricula for mildly retarded children. They offer two commercial programs: *Me*

Now, for elementary-age children, and *Me and My Environment,* for older children. Materials include filmstrips, models, film loops, teacher's guides, 35 mm daylight projection slides, test booklets, student worksheets, charts and picture cards, and scientific equipment. BSCS is planning a similar type of curriculum for the primary level.

■ Use ESS units for special education. Thirty-one ESS units have been identified as appropriate for students who have learning difficulties. A guide has been designed for use by teachers of mildly retarded students, but other teachers will find it valuable. If interested, you may send for a copy through the nearest ESS distribution center. Ask for David W. Ball, *ESS Special Education Teacher's Guide* (St. Louis, MO: Webster/McGraw-Hill, 1978). Units selected for special education are divided into three categories: perceptual, psychomotor, and other appropriate units. They follow the same sequence:

1. Description of audience (that is, type of child, grade range, and so on)
2. Overview of unit description and what it can do for the child
3. Specification of objectives
4. Ways of getting started for unit initiation
5. Keeping it going
6. Other classroom tips
7. Evaluation checklist
8. Time required
9. Ordering information

If you work with exceptional children, you will find this new guide extremely helpful.

■ When using films or videotapes, point out the important parts in advance. Show small segments of the films and conduct only brief discussions afterwards, because of the short attention spans of students with cognitive differences.

■ Help science contribute to the student's ability to function in everyday society. Therefore, consider such science topics as health (including drugs, tobacco, and alcohol), human body, plants and animals, and high-interest topics (such as space travel and dinosaurs).

■ Use positive reinforcement. Offer praise *immediately following* successful learning by students with cognitive differences.

Review the literature for more ideas for the student with cognitive differences.

■ C. D. Mercer, *Students With Learning Disabilities* (4th ed.) (Englewood Cliffs, NJ: Merrill/Prentice Hall, 1992).
■ C. D. Mercer and A. R. Mercer, *Teaching Students With Learning Problems* (4th ed.) (Englewood Cliffs, NJ: Merrill/Prentice Hall, 1993).
■ B. Y. L. Wong, "The Relevance of Metacognition to Learning Disabilities," in B. Y. L. Wong (Ed.), *Learning About Learning Disabilities* (San Diego, CA: Academic Press, 1991), 231–258.
■ N. Zigmond and J. Baker, "Mainstream Experiences for Learning Disabled Students: Project MELD Preliminary report," *Exceptional Children, 57,* no. 2, 1990, 176–185.

These organizations will add to your professional growth on general learning disability students:

■ Adults and Children with Learning and Developmental Disabilities, 265 Post Avenue, Westbury, NY 11590. (516)334–4210
■ Learning Disabilities Association, 4156 Library Road, Pittsburgh, PA 15234. (412)341–1515.
■ National Center for Learning Disabilities, 99 Park Avenue, New York 10016. (212)-687–7211
■ Orton Dyslexia Society, 724 York Road, Baltimore, MD 21204. (301)269–0232

Science for Gifted/Talented Students

Although not impaired, some other students provide a different kind of challenge for teachers. They may have unusual skills, interests, talents, attitudes, or motivations. Often these students are identified as **gifted or talented.**

FIGURE 9–7

Unexpected characteristics of gifted and creative students

Source: M. Friedel, *Characteristics of Gifted/Creative Children* (Warwick, RI: National Foundation for Gifted and Creative Children, 1993).

- Exhibit high sensitivity
- Have excessive amounts of energy
- Bore easily and may appear to have short attention spans
- Require emotionally stable and secure adults around them
- Resist authority if it is not democratically oriented
- Have preferred ways of learning, particularly in reading and mathematics
- Become easily frustrated because they have big ideas but lack the resources or people to assist in carrying these tasks to fruition
- Learn from explorations and resist rote memory or just being a listener
- Cannot sit still unless absorbed in something highly interesting
- Are very compassionate and have many fears, such as fears of death and loss of loved ones
- May give up and develop permanent learning blocks if they experience failure early

A recent federal report, *National Excellence: A Case for Developing America's Talent* (Washington, DC: U.S. Department of Education, 1993), deleted the word *gifted* and substituted **outstandingly talented** and **exceptionally talented**. Although the controversy continues on which words to use, there is agreement that the descriptor *gifted* more accurately reflects the broad range of abilities displayed by these students. One of the key changes in emphasis with the gifted is to include more than one category of giftedness.

Defining gifted/talented usually reflects what we as teachers (as purveyors of our society/culture) value. We observe, identify, and value those students who stand out from the others in science because of the way they usually, but not always,

- speak well and have large and varied vocabularies,
- display longer attention spans,
- are extremely curious,
- possess excellent academic skills, especially reading,
- comprehend and follow directions very well,
- seek out activities and hobbies in science areas,

- enjoy puzzles and games of an open-ended type (e.g., Rubik's cube or electronic games and computers), and
- are more interested in broad concepts and issues than other students.[9]

There is often a flip-side to students who are highly gifted or talented: They may also demonstrate attributes not usually associated with giftedness, such as those characteristics listed in Figure 9–7.

As a teacher, you quickly see that there is no typical gifted student, but most have general intellect, specific academic ability, creative and productive thinking, leadership ability, and visual and performing arts. These students love to participate in many activities previously mentioned in this chapter. In addition, you can challenge their intellects by providing them with meaningful enrichment activities. The following suggestions may prove useful.

Fear Not: Learn With and From Your Gifted/Talented Students. Most elementary and middle school teachers have not majored in science and, therefore, may find that some of their gifted/talented students know more about certain areas of science than they do.

Not feeling totally competent with science should not stop you from having gifted/talented students do more advanced work than the rest of the class.

Students enjoy seeing their teachers get excited about the results of students' work. In addition, this approach tends to break down the traditional view of teacher as giver of knowledge. Become a teacher/facilitator/arranger of the gifted/talented student's learning environment, an adult questioner, and a constant positive critic. Keep this perspective when you feel inadequate in science: for all their knowledge, gifted/talented students are still elementary or middle school students socially, emotionally, and physically. They need your mature adult guidance and professional training in education and psychology. Remember, these students need and want democratically oriented and emotionally stable adults around them for guidance. That's you!

Gifted/Talented Students Need Challenges. Encourage your gifted/talented students to engage in, and perhaps design or originate, more open-ended hands-on/minds-on activities. These students should be challenged to do simple, *unstructured* experiments to find answers that are not easily available from texts or encyclopedias. These experiments do not have step-by-step procedures or predetermined results worked out in advance.

Keep these things in mind while guiding gifted/talented students through unstructured experimentation:

■ Start by working with the entire class or a group. Later, when routines are established, individuals may explore on their own.

■ Keep the experimentation within the limits of time, talents, and available apparatus. Explore these limitations before suggesting problems.

■ Be alert to the open-endedness of this type of experimentation. Frequently, questions will arise such as, "Suppose we vary the experiment in this way, what will happen?"

■ Do not assume that the gifted/talented student will have a sustained interest in the problem. You must continually check on progress.

Broaden Gifted/Talented Students' Perspectives. Gifted/talented students should be encouraged to use science in all curricular areas. Mathematics is the language of science, and gifted/talented students should be encouraged to use it as much as possible. They should be as much involved with *how much* or *what relationships exist between* as they are in answering *how, what,* and *why.* Whenever possible, ask students to quantify their findings, and encourage them to use graphing in their communications to other students and you.

Gifted students especially are drawn to electronic learning devices. See Chapter 10 for ways to use electronic learning devices like microcomputers, television, and video recorders in your science teaching. Art, music, physical movement, language arts, and social studies are all areas that gifted/talented students should be encouraged to integrate with their science activities. For ideas of how to do this, see:

■ Joy Kataoka and James R. Patton, "Teaching Exceptional Learners: An Integrated Approach," *Science and Children, 27,* no. 1 (September 1989), 48–50.

■ C. M. Callahan, "Science" in R. H. Swassing, (Ed.), *Teaching Gifted Children and Adolescents* (Columbus, OH: Merrill, 1985).

Roles of Parents in Gifted/Talented Learning. Coordinate home and school learning with gifted/talented students' parents. Encourage parents of gifted/talented students to obtain books, magazines, and science kits and materials and to discuss science with their children. Often, desirable scientific learning situations arise when a family takes a vacation. Stress the importance of the parents buying or borrowing from the library supplemental booklets such as *How and Why Wonder Books* and the *Golden Books.* Explain the desirability of motivating and supplying intellectual fuel

Meaningful learning experiences can be fostered by identifying conceptual links between the special interests of gifted/talented students and science and technology.

for the gifted/talented child. Encourage the parents of gifted/talented students to give their children many leadership opportunities.

Encourage parents of your gifted/talented students to seek out television programs that stimulate and enrich children's science interests (e.g., *Nova, Jacques Cousteau, 3-2-1 Contact*). Science videos can be borrowed from many public libraries or rented to be viewed and discussed at home. Gifted/talented students can share these with you and their classmates in school through written or oral presentations.

Gifted/Talented Students Often Have Leadership Qualities. Provide leadership experiences for gifted/talented students. Ask gifted/talented students to be science assistants to help with preparing materials, dispense and collect equipment and supplies, collect information about experiments, and assist less able classmates. Often, peer teaching/learning is more effective than learning from teacher–pupil exchanges. Students who are gifted/talented in science may also create teaching models related to the science units being studied, such as

weather instruments, electrical devices, atomic or solar systems, or scale models of local environmental or ecological systems.

As mentioned in previous chapters, cooperative learning groups are excellent ways for gifted/talented students to work collaboratively with their classmates. They can share their abilities and talents as well as develop group skills. This can help overcome the possible concern that gifted/talented students become elitists or loners.

Making Inclusion of Gifted/Talented Students Most Effective. Make gifted/talented students in your classroom feel welcome and accepted. Previously, gifted/talented students were accelerated to higher or special pull-out classes. Currently, greater emphasis is placed on inclusion, incorporating changes in science content and activities to introduce higher levels of abstract thinking and independent thinking and problem-solving skills. Your challenge is to help your gifted/talented students modify, adapt, and learn how to discover new skills and concepts for themselves.

Most highly motivated, bright students need little encouragement. For those who do, try these suggestions.

1. Provide recognition for their efforts, but be wary of gifted students with "know-it-all" tendencies. Encourage cooperative efforts.
2. Provide extra credit for novel ideas or products. An example would be a class challenge box, where students write questions they think are difficult and then allow gifted/talented students to work in small groups to find answers to these.
3. Stress positive comments in all teacher–pupil exchanges.
4. Offer special privileges for specified performances, but avoid putting the gifted/talented on a pedestal.
5. Permit high-achieving students to act as teacher by giving them responsibility for leading a class discussion or performing a hands-on/minds-on activity.
6. Encourage student-initiated projects and activities for those who have completed assignments.
7. Make arrangements for high-achieving students to take selected subjects in higher grades.
8. Introduce elementary and middle grade students to research methods.
9. Teach debating skills and encourage students to sponsor and participate in debates on topics of their choice.
10. Have high-achieving math students create mathematical puzzles.
11. Encourage students to write scripts for TV and radio programs and participate in the programs.
12. Have students present a synopsis of a magazine or newspaper article to their classmates in a way that is interesting and understandable.
13. Have a "crazy idea session," where only unusual notions can be discussed.
14. Let them conduct a brainstorming session.
15. Let them express themselves in art forms such as drawings, creative writing, and role playing.
16. Have them dramatize their readings.
17. Have a great books seminar to introduce students to the classics.
18. Help them organize and publish a classroom or school science magazine.

Expand Gifted/Talented Students' Learning Into Their Communities. Provide out-of-classroom opportunities for gifted/talented students. It is very difficult, if not impossible, to provide information and activities to your gifted students in all their areas of interests in the classroom. These out-of-classroom ideas may be helpful to you.

■ Make library services available. If the school library is inadequate, take them on regular trips, if possible, to a public library. Arrange to secure hard-to-get materials from state or university libraries.
■ Try to guide the students to the research sources they need. Refer them to encyclopedias, dictionaries, and other reference sources.
■ Develop a catalog of other resources that students can use, possibly containing addresses of agencies providing free and inexpensive materials or local community resources.
■ Form science interest clubs with gifted/talented students as officers.
■ Identify community people who are available to work with individual gifted/talented students in a mentor program. Help those who are knowledgeable in their fields but do not know how to manage or teach students.

Stimulate Your Gifted/Talented Students by the Way You Teach. Your teaching methods can encourage gifted/talented students. In our society, students' thinking is often trained to focus on *the right* answer, which sometimes discourages gifted/talented students from taking risks in academic situations. They may be confused or feel threatened with failure when they are faced with tasks in which there are either no clear answers or a variety of correct answers. Try some of these techniques to encourage them:

1. Use a questioning technique rather than giving information.
2. Use hypothetical questions beginning with "What if . . . ?"
3. Ask students to develop open-ended situations where no one answer is correct.
4. In subjects such as arithmetic, where specific answers are required, encourage students to estimate their answers.
5. Have students check your written work for errors; let them see that all adults are fallible.
6. Instead of information, emphasize concepts, principles, relationships, and generalizations.
7. Provide opportunities and assignments which rely on independent reading and research.
8. Have students give reports on their individual research and experimentation; this helps them acquire a sense of sharing their knowledge.
9. Provide foreign language materials—books, periodicals, recordings, newspapers—for young gifted/talented students.
10. Ask gifted/talented students what science things *they* would like to do!

Investigate Professional Literature for Additional Ideas. Use these resources for additional ideas for the gifted/talented:

- J. Piirto, *Talented Children and Adults: Their Development and Education* (Englewood Cliffs, NJ: Merrill/Prentice Hall, 1994).
- B. Davison, "Kids Development Corporation," *Gifted Child Today, 16,* no. 2, 1993, 2–6.
- M. D. McKay, "No One Wants to Be a Bad Teacher," *Gifted Child Today, 16,* no. 3, 1993, 40–41.
- B. Kerr, "Educating Gifted Girls," in N. Coangelo and G. A. Davis (Eds.), *Handbook of Gifted Education* (Boston, MA: Allyn and Bacon, 1991).

- "Giftedness" in J. R. Patton, J. M. Blackbourn, and K. Fad, *Exceptional Individuals in Focus,* 6th ed. (Englewood Cliffs, NJ: Merrill/Prentice Hall, 1996).
- S. Winebrenner, *Teaching Gifted Kids in the Regular Classroom* (Minneapolis: Free Spirit, 1992).

Contact these organizations for further assistance with gifted/talented students:

- Association for the Gifted (TAG), 2216 Main Street, Cedar Falls, IA 50613. (319)266–0205.
- Gifted Children's Information Office, 12657 Fee Fee Road, St. Louis, MO 63146.
- National Association for Gifted Children, 1155 Fifteenth Street, NW, Suite 10002, Washington, DC, 20005.

Science for Students With Emotional/Behavioral Disorders[10]

Despite your best efforts, you may have students who exhibit disruptive or asocial behaviors in your classroom. Chapter 6 covered typical classroom disciplinary problems. IDEA defines **seriously emotionally disturbed students** as students with emotional disorders taking place over a long time who have a substantial negative effect on other students' classroom performance. Fortunately, only a small percentage of students are so identified. But some behaviors are so severe that regular classroom inclusion may be inappropriate.

Substantial variation exists from state to state in defining emotional and behavioral problems. Table 9–4 shows some of the terms that might refer to this exceptionality.

Labels often get in the way of seeing all these students as flesh and blood. Descriptive words for students in this group might be *aggressive, antisocial, disruptive, hyperactive;* but when you know a particular student, you could add *smart, good soccer player, lively, helpful, creative, tenacious,* and *daring.* Picture the student(s) in your class exhibiting these characteristics. What words would *you* use to describe them?

TABLE 9–4

Possible combinations of emotional/behavioral/social/personal terms

A	B
Emotionally	Disturbed
Behaviorally	Disordered
Socially	Maladjusted
Personal	Handicapped
	Conflicted
	Impaired

Source: James M. Kauffman, *Characteristics of Emotional and Behavioral Disorders of Children and Youth,* 5th ed. (Englewood Cliffs, NJ: Merrill/Prentice Hall, 1993).

Another term used by teachers to refer to students who act out, become aggressive, and commit antisocial acts is *conduct disorder.* How can you handle conduct disorder students?

Facilitating a Safe and Supportive Classroom

Your classroom must be a safe and supportive place for all students, where everyone is warmly received and accepted in spite of blemishes, warts, or physical, mental, or emotional/social disorders. *No one* has the right to disrupt classroom learning or endanger the safety of others. Violations of that cannot be accepted and must be handled expeditiously in the most constructive manner. In the way in which you treat conduct disorder, you must serve as a model. Your students must see that your rejection of students' undesirable behavior is *not* rejection of them as worthwhile people. Consider these items for structuring your unique supportive classroom:

1. Each day, warmly acknowledge each student individually as she enters in the morning, leaves at the end of the day, as you pass her in the hallway, or other appropriate times. Show her you have a sincere interest in her well-being. Similarly, show your concern when students appear upset, troubled, or overly stressed; this can be done by extending a sympathetic and supportive ear to students who want to share ideas, feelings, or frustrations, and perhaps even tactfully sharing parallel aspects of your own life.

2. Use the "shoes test" for students with conduct disorders. Stand in the conduct disorder student's shoes, take his perspective and ask yourself, "If I were Juan, what might trigger my acting out behavior, and what would be the most successful way to help me learn alternate responses?"

3. Be very alert to physiological factors and how they may influence the behavior of students with conduct disorder: sickness/allergies, side effects of medication, fatigue, hunger or thirst, increased stimulation due to missing the bus, a fight with classmate or parent/guardian, disrupted routine, etc.

4. Check often each day for these classroom elements that could be a catalyst for conduct disorder, especially for students most likely to act out asocially: excessive noise level, uncomfortable temperature, over- or understimulation, poor seating arrangements, constant classroom disruptions, etc.

5. Check your teaching methods often to avoid these curriculum components:
   - Unclear directions for successful activity completion
   - Few permissible opportunities to communicate
   - Activities that students dislike, are too difficult, or take too long

6. Encourage each student to work at his or her level. Keep all students to high realistic standards, and convey your confidence that they can achieve success.

7. Develop cooperative learning skills.

8. Use humor often, but appropriately and reasonably, to create a fun learning environment and to alleviate tension.

9. Intermittently during the day, as needed, engage students in a few minutes of guided physical activities (e.g., Simon Says, simple classroom calisthenics.) This helps alleviate tension.

10. Where age-/maturity-appropriate, involve students in all aspects of their learning.
11. Consistently reward positive behaviors and individual successes, no matter how small the achievement.

Can You Unintentionally Trigger Student Conduct Disorders?

Regrettably, some student conduct disorders are inadvertently caused by teachers, especially in students prone to behavioral problems. Try to avoid:

■ Scolding, criticizing, and nagging. This does nothing but upset recipients and incite resentment from classmates toward the teacher.
■ Yelling, screaming, and excessive loud talk. This causes already anxious and edgy students to be even more agitated.
■ Using group punishments for every instance of misbehavior. This breeds hostility and loss of respect for the teacher and may set the class against the student who caused the group punishment, triggering further asocial behavior.
■ Premature judgments that may lead to reprimanding the wrong student. This lowers the teacher's stature and effectiveness.
■ Humiliating and cruel punishment. This sort of punishment is ineffective and symptomatic of teacher loss of control.
■ Competition between students by comparing them. Don't tell students how much better they can do, and don't give up (or even appear to give up) on any student.

What Are Structured Approaches to Changing Misconduct?

In spite of everything, there are times when students' behavior difficulties require more than careful supervision and the modification of your classroom environment and teaching methods. Consider using more structured approaches to behavioral change, such as behavior modification, level systems, and a token-economy strategy. These are only some of the possibilities.

Behavior Modification. To work successfully with conduct disorder students, you need to view their deficit of appropriate social behaviors just as you would academic deficits—skills that need to be taught. Don't condone inappropriate behaviors; teach alternative, appropriate ways to interact. Many conduct disorder students can learn "correct" social behaviors just as they learn "correct" academic behaviors. One way to teach "correct" behavior is to use behaviorist principles.

When behaviorists' principles are systematically applied to classroom practices and therapeutic settings, it is called **behavioral modification.** Hundreds of research studies reveal that behavioral modification improves not only classroom behaviors, but academic performances. See especially, Jeanne Ellis Ormrod, *Human Learning: Theories, Principles, and Educational Applications* (2nd ed.) (Englewood Cliffs, NJ: Merrill/Prentice Hall, 1995).

Behavioral modification is often effective when other techniques are not, because (1) students know exactly what is expected of them, (2) through the gradual process of shaping, students attempt to learn new behaviors only when they are truly ready to acquire them, and (3) students find learning new behaviors usually leads to success.

These four steps are routinely used in behavioral modification:

1. Identify problem behavior to be modified.
2. Log behavior with regard to how often and under what conditions it occurs.
3. Determine the type of positive reward or reinforcer to use: manipulative (computer games, interactive videos, games); visuals (videos, CD-ROMS, films, photos); physical (extra gym/recess privileges, dance); social (praise, attention, status); tactile (art time); edibles (food and drink); auditory (music tapes/CDs); and others selected by students. Positive (or negative) reinforcers can vary.
4. Reinforce desired behavior(s) with a reward or positive reinforcer.

For specifics on behavioral modification and two other management techniques, read: Ennio Cipani, *Disruptive Behavior: Three Techniques to Use in Your Classroom* (Reston, VA: The Council for Exceptional Children, 1993).

A Levels System for Behavior Management. A **levels system** is an approach to total class behavior management used often in self-contained classrooms where there are many students with conduct disorders. Students advance through a hierarchy of academic, behavioral, and social guidelines and privileges. At each level, students are required to handle a new set of guidelines and privileges.

An example is the **Group-Oriented Adapted Levels System** (GOALS), a total class behavior management system devised to teach fundamental peer-interaction skills while furnishing effective classroom management. These four steps are recommended for successful GOALS operation.

- Develop group identity (e.g., Smart Owls, Science Buffs) to afford students an opportunity to initiate their cooperative identity.
- Generate classroom rules and expectations jointly with students at brief meetings during the first three weeks of school. Agree upon at least three major rules, such as help the group, follow directions, and use good classroom manners. From these major rules, specify classroom expectations, such as for good classroom manners, don't push or hit people, don't talk loud, and don't make fun of classmates. Standard point losses are set once classroom rules and expectations are agreed upon; for example, hitting, 5 points; pushing, 4 points; making fun of classmates, 3 points. Accepted rules are posted prominently in classroom and reviewed often.
- Use peer positives (positive comments made to an individual), helpful hints (suggestions or advice given to the group), and peer cueing (advice given at time of a problem situation) daily. Teach students (by model–lead–test methods) to use specific positives, helpful hints, and cues with their peers.
- Hold group meetings at beginning and end of each school day to give students the opportunity to give and receive positives, helpful hints, and cues. The meeting also amplifies group cohesiveness.

The major component of GOALS is earning (or losing) daily points based on the classroom rules and expectations. A maximum of 100 points can be earned by each student daily. Students self-monitor point losses on sheets taped to their desks. Bonus points can be earned to reinforce appropriate behavior. All points earned by individuals and the group are totaled and posted in classroom. A three-level system may look like this:

Top level (90–100 points earned): free time in preferred activities, additional computer time, etc.
Middle level (80–89 points earned): lunch in classroom, science activities before or after school, etc.
Bottom level (less than 80 points earned): free time must be spent at seat, no time at videorecorder, etc.

For more itemized data, see P. M. Barbetta, "GOALS: A Group-Oriented Levels System for Children With Behavior Disorders," *Academic Therapy, 25,* no. 46, 1990, 645–46.

Token Economy System. Another way to use rewards or reinforcers for behavior modification is the **token-economy** system. In this system, students earn tokens (such as play money, poker chips, or tickets) or symbols (such as stars, check marks, funny face stickers) for agreed-upon appropriate behaviors. Tokens can be traded for something of value, such as additional computer or CD-ROM time, games, or other extra privileges.

To assist you in adapting these behavioral modification techniques to your classroom, see:

- *Working with Behavioral Disorders Mini Library,* 9 volumes (Reston, VA: Council for Exceptional Children, 1991).
- Ennio Cipani, *Non-Compliance: Four Strategies That Work* (Reston, VA: The Council for Exceptional Children, 1993).
- Sylvia Rockwell, *Tough to Reach, Tough to Teach: Students With Behavior Problems* (Reston, VA: The Council for Exceptional Children, 1993).
- E. A. Wynne, "Improving Pupil Discipline and Character," in O. C. Moles (ed.), *Student Discipline Strategies: Research and Practice* (Albany, NY: State University of New York Press, 1990).

SCIENCE FOR STUDENTS FROM CULTURALLY DIVERSE BACKGROUNDS

Our nation's motto is *"e pluribus unum,"* "out of many, one." Schools today are rich in student diversity. Meeting the needs of a diverse group of students in our classrooms has become an important issue in education.

NSTA Multicultural Position Paper

The National Science Teachers Association recognizes and appreciates the strength and beauty of cultural pluralism. NSTA is committed to work with other professional organizations, institutions, and agencies to seek the resources required to ensure effective science teaching for culturally diverse learners. In its 1991 *Position Statement on Multicultural Science Education,* NSTA asserts that:

- Culturally diverse children must have access to quality science education experiences that enhance success and provide the knowledge and opportunities required for them to become successful participants in our democratic society;

- Curricular content and instructional strategies selected for use with culturally diverse children must reflect, as well as incorporate, this diversity;
- Science teachers must be knowledgeable about children's learning styles and instructional preferences, which may be culturally related;
- Science teachers have the responsibility to expose culturally diverse children to career opportunities in science, technology, and engineering.[11]

How Does the NSTA Position Paper Affect You?

As you read the NSTA *Position Paper on Multicultural Science Education,* consider these implications for your science classroom:

1. You must employ as wide a range of content and teaching strategies as possible to meet the learning needs and interests of students with different cultural backgrounds.
2. You must become knowledgeable about the learning styles of your diverse cultural students and how their cultures aid or hinder their science learning.
3. You must build on and broaden the prior knowledge your multicultural students bring to your classroom.

Multicultural students prompt teachers to ask, "How do I ensure that *all* my students, including the multicultural, have opportunities for learning success?" Statistics reveal that some multicultural students are considered to be at-risk students, that is, they have a high probability of failure to acquire the minimum academic skills necessary for success in the adult world. Many others graduate without basic skills, Which students are most likely to be at risk?

At-Risk Students

Some at-risk students have special needs, e.g., learning disabilities, emotional or behavioral problems, and so on. Others may be students:

1. whose cultural background doesn't easily mesh with the dominant culture of the school.
2. from homes where academic success is neither encouraged nor supported.
3. whose home environments do not supply tactual/kinesthetic experiences in early childhood.

At-risk students come from all socioeconomic levels, but students especially likely to leave school prior to high school graduation are:

- the poor
- students from single-parent families
- boys
- African–Americans
- Hispanics or Latinos
- Native Americans
- students from families where little or no English is spoken and whose own knowledge of English is very limited

Benefits of Hands-on/Minds-on Science for Multicultural Students

Hands-on/minds-on science programs, with their emphasis on actual manipulation of concrete materials, are especially relevant to the needs, interests, and expectations of multicultural students. These kinds of activities are especially valuable for multicultural students who are probably wrestling with the development of a new language, customs, friendships, and living environment. The constructivist learning cycle (which builds on sensory experiences, introduces vocabulary based on those concrete experiences, then applies this new vocabulary to other situations) is a natural for multicultural students.

Your job is to provide appropriate constructivist learning cycle activities that will help your students feel comfortable with two cultures. Your modified hands-on/minds-on science activities will help the students span the gap between their past experiences and language and their immediate environment.

Limited-English-Proficient Students and Hands-on/Minds-on Science

Limited-English-proficient (LEP) students face a range of challenges in learning science, including having to learn a new language concurrently with mastering demanding new science subject matter and being placed in a science class where no one, including the teacher, understands their native language. Many are recent immigrants who received little or no formal schooling in their homelands. Others are U.S. citizens whose culture differs from that of the school. They may have had scant exposure to science in the home. Science has a unique vocabulary, which LEP students are unlikely to have faced in other contexts.

Here are some general strategies you can use to help improve the English of multicultural students who are limited English proficient (LEP), even when all your teaching is conducted in English.

1. Because many LEP students learn to read English before they learn to speak it, use the writing board more than you otherwise might.
2. Save class time by preparing, on large sheets of paper, lists of vocabulary you will introduce during the lesson or assign for homework. Tape these sheets to the wall in full view of all students. Point to each word when you say it and talk about it.
3. Always print (upper- and lower-case) legibly. Most writing that newcomers encounter out of school is in print.
4. Display prominently in the classroom any written regulations or procedures that students are to follow every day. Each time you remind students of one of these regulations, point to the chart and read the words aloud.
5. When you give directions, give them one at a time, step-by-step: "Do *A* first. Next, do *B*. Then *C*."
6. When students do not understand what you've said, rephrase using different words and simpler sentences.

7. Let an English-speaking student repeat instructions for the class when repetition is necessary. This will be useful for all students, and LEP students will benefit from hearing the sentences spoken in a different voice and accent.

8. Review important points from previous lessons and list them on the writing board as you do so.

9. Summarize what has been taught so far at frequent intervals. Print the key points on the board, or refer to a wall chart.

10. Beginning with the upper elementary grades, require all class members to keep notebooks written in English.

Figure 9–8 gives tips for implementing hands-on/minds-on science with LEP students. This method of teaching science and English to LEP students—with minimum dependency on language, concentration on concept development, and non-language cues and prompts—has been called *sheltered instruction.*

Perhaps the best way to help LEP students is to view these students as an asset in science classrooms. LEP students can contribute language enrichment for native English-speaking students and abundant occasions for cross-cultural teaching/learning.

Further sources for teaching English and science to multicultural students through hands-on/minds-on science are:

■ Mary M. Atwater, "Multicultural Science Education. Assumptions and Alternative

---

Simplify the output
- Slower speech rate
- Clear enunciation
- Controlled vocabulary
- Controlled sentence length
- Use of cognates
- Limited use of idioms

Use contextual clues
- Gestures
- Facial expressions
- Act out meaning
- Props
- Graphs
- Realia
- Overheads
- Maps
- Manipulatives
- Visuals

Check frequently for understanding
- Confirmation checks
- Comprehension checks
- Clarification requests
- Repetitions
- Expansions
- Vocabulary emphasis
- Variety of question types

Design appropriate lessons
- Appropriate to English fluency
- Listening and speaking activities precede reading and writing activities
- Reading assignments include pre-reading, during reading, post-reading activities
- Writing activities preceded by pre-writing
- Cooperative activities and grouping
- Topical rather than grammatical emphasis
- Hands-on activities
- Use of various modalities

FIGURE 9–8

Teaching suggestions for implementing hands-on/minds-on science for LEP students

Source: Jennifer W. Harris, "Sheltered Instruction: Bridging the Language Gap in the Science Classroom," *The Science Teacher* 62, no. 2 (February 1995), 26. Reprinted with permission from NSTA Publications, copyright © 1995 from *The Science Teacher,* National Science Teachers Association, 1840 Wilson Boulevard, Arlington, VA 22201–3000.

Views," *The Science Teacher, 60,* no. 3, Mar. 1993, 33–37.

■ —————, "Multicultural Science Education, Part I: Meeting the Needs of a Diverse Student Population," *The Science Teacher, 62,* no. 2, Feb. 1995, 21–23.

■ —————, "Multicultural Science Classroom, Part II: Assisting All Students With Science Acquisition," *The Science Teacher, 62,* no. 4, Apr. 1995, 42–45.

■ —————, "Multicultural Science Classroom, Part III: Preparing Science Teachers to Meet the Challenges of Multicultural Education," *The Science Teacher, 62,* no. 5, May 1995, 26–29.

■ James A. Banks, *Multiethnic Education: Theory and Practice* (Boston, MA: Allyn and Bacon, 1994).

■ "Educating for Diversity and Contemporary Issues: Urban Schools," *Educational Leadership, 51,* no. 8, May 1994, 1–111.

■ Jennifer W. Harris, "Sheltered Instruction: Bridging the Language Gap in the Science Classroom," *The Science Teacher, 62,* no. 2, Feb. 1995, 24–27.

Becoming an Effective Multicultural Science Learning Facilitator

In a sense, *all* students are culturally diverse, because each family is unique and has its own cultural identity. Here are some ways to adapt your science teaching to maximize the learning of all students, while fostering a multicultural environment in your science classroom.

■ Find techniques for fostering collaboration, such as cooperative learning groups.

■ Capitalize on the broad cultural diversity within your classroom and have your students share their heritages through luncheons of their native foods, dances, or songs.

■ Provide a reasonable, caring, and supportive interpersonal environment for all students.

■ Work to improve home/school relations with the cooperation and collaboration of parents.

■ Foster a classroom atmosphere that has success as the expected norm for every student.

SUMMARY

The individualization of teaching/learning is not new; it was the main system in one-room schoolhouses for hundreds of years. Current research has shown that learning achievement in individualized science teaching classrooms is as high as, or higher than, in traditional classes, especially for underachieving and at-risk students. Individualization also leads to greater interest, better attendance, more enjoyment by students, and a more positive attitude toward teaching and schools by teachers and parents.

Most elementary and middle school science teaching can easily be individualized. Consider the following general, practical, classroom-tested suggestions to individualize your science teaching:

1. Enrichment centers.
2. Challenge and solution cards.
3. School grounds and other out-of-doors activities.
4. Visits to museums, parks, and other cultural centers.
5. Students teaching students.
6. Cooperative learning groups.
7. Science kits.
8. Television.
9. Surprise science boxes.
10. Student bulletin boards.
11. Student panel talks.
12. Student progress files.
13. Museums.

14. Science discovery charts.
15. Science trade-book reports.
16. Scientist biographies.
17. Student displays.
18. Pictorial riddles.
19. Science clubs.
20. School or classroom newspapers.

Detailed directions were also introduced for how to organize and utilize a Volunteer Science Classroom Aides Corps and a Student Cross-Age Tutoring Corps to assist you with individualizing your science teaching.

Two laws have direct impact upon your science teaching: Public Law 94-142, the Individuals with Disabilities Act (IDEA), mandates that individuals from birth to age 21 have the right to a full free public education in the least restrictive environment. This has led to the current trend of inclusion, which means that all students, including those with a wide range of disabilities, including physical, social, and cognitive, are in regular classrooms for the entire school day. The Americans with Disabilities Act (ADA), 42 U.S.C. Secs. 12101–12313, is a civil rights bill that guarantees people of all ages a wide range of public and private services, whether they are in school or not.

Practical teaching/learning techniques were presented for providing for the needs of students who may be visually, hearing, or physically impaired. Additionally, special science curricula and teaching methods have been presented for the mildly retarded and visually and hearing impaired. Ideas were also discussed for students with emotional/behavioral disorders.

Gifted/talented students present different kinds of challenges for teachers. Ideas were given on how to enrich your science teaching to meet their needs. These students have unusual talents and motivations in science and can benefit from doing relatively unstructured experiments, exploring enrichment activities with their parents and in their communities, and being given leadership roles in class.

The National Science Teachers Association position paper recognizes and appreciates the strength and beauty of cultural pluralism and advocates an adequate science education for culturally diverse students. This challenges all science teachers to employ a wide range of content and teaching methods to meet the learning needs and interests of students with different cultural backgrounds, some of whom are more likely to be at-risk than the general population. Hands-on/minds-on science teaching/learning activities have many benefits for multicultural students, especially limited-English-proficient students. Strategies for adapting hands-on/minds-on activities were highlighted. Classroom-tested teaching/learning techniques were given for adapting your science teaching to maximizing science learning for all students, while fostering a multicultural classroom environment.

SELF-ASSESSMENT AND FURTHER STUDY

1. Make a floor plan for a classroom. Arrange the furniture for the effective inclusion of special needs students, e.g., visually impaired, physically impaired, hearing impaired.
2. Plan, and carry out with a class, sensitizing lesson(s), in which students take on the role of someone with special needs by working with a partner and selecting one of these things to do for the full day: being blindfolded, wearing earplugs, sitting in chair or wheelchair, having fingers tied together, etc. Have students discuss and/or write about the problems they had, the way others treated them, and what they felt would have helped them.
3. Pick a thematic science unit you will teach this year. Devise individualizing activities to integrate your science content and other subject matter, suited to the range of interest and abilities in your classroom.

4. Construct, on your own or with a group of students, some challenge cards and surprise science boxes. Look at science resource books or texts to get ideas. Use the appendices for possible sources of science-related materials.

5. Organize your class (or total school if you can get administration and colleagues assistance) to produce a science magazine.

6. Start a parent/guardian/grandparent/retirees Science Volunteer Corps in your school. Begin with your class, then expand gradually. Include school administration and colleagues.

7. Select one or more gifted/talented students. Prescribe a series of in-school or out-of-school activities for these students that will enrich the science topics you are studying with your class.

8. Select science themes to explore with multicultural students. Use real-life problems from their immediate environments that are relevant to their lives. Prepare a science teaching unit incorporating as many cultural aspects as possible, especially language, customs, and foods.

9. Identify several students who exhibit conduct disorders. Using the "shoes test," identify what triggers their misbehavior. Select a method that would be appropriate, frame a plan to change the behavior, and devise an assessment plan.

10. Determine which students in your class are most at risk. Investigate their backgrounds (academic, social, physical, family, emotional) and try to discover why they are at risk. Speak to school and/or community service people for assistance in helping them achieve academically, socially, and emotionally.

NOTES

1. Maria Alicia Lopez–Freeman, "Invited Papers," *The Science Teacher, 62,* no. 2, 1995, 10.

2. The author acknowledges James A. Shymansky, "Rating Your Individualized Program," *Science and Children, 17,* no. 5, Feb. 1980, 33.

3. *Sharing Science Series—A Guide for Parents* (Durham, NC: North Carolina Museum of Life and Science, n.d.), 1–8.

4. This section draws heavily on Ann P. Turnbull et al., *Exceptional Lives: Special Education in Today's Schools* (Englewood Cliffs, NJ: Merrill/Prentice Hall, 1995). You are urged to read it for intelligent insights into the education of special needs students.

5. H. Rutherford Turnbull III, *The Law and Children With Disabilities* (4th ed.) (Denver, CO: Love, 1994).

6. "An NSTA Position Statement: Laboratory Science, Adopted by the NSTA Board of Directors in January, 1990," *NSTA Reports!* (October/November 1991): 15.

7. E. Van der Klift and N. Kunc, *Epilogue: Beyond Benevolence—Friendship and the Politics of Help,"* In J. Thousand, R. Villa, and A. Nevin (Eds.), *Creativity and Collaborative Learning"*

A Practical Guide to Empowering Students and Teachers (Baltimore, MD: Brookes, 1994), 391–402.

8. Ann P. Turnbull et al., *Exceptional Lives: Special Education in Today's Schools* (Englewood Cliffs, NJ: Merrill/Prentice Hall, 1995).

9. Barbara Clark, *Growing Up Gifted: Developing the Potential of Children at Home and at School,* 4th ed. (Englewood Cliffs, NJ: Merrill/Prentice Hall, 1992).

10. These references were extremely helpful in the preparation of this section: Richard D. Kellough, *A Resource Guide for Teaching: K–12* (Englewood Cliffs, NJ: Merrill/Prentice Hall, 1994), 157–180; Jeanne Ellis Ormrod, *Educational Psychology: Principles and Applications* (Englewood Cliffs, NJ: Merrill/Prentice Hall, 1995), 198–200, 229–302, 517–554; Ann P. Turnbull et al., *Exceptional Lives: Special Educatoin in Today's Schools* (Englewood Cliffs, NJ: Merrill/Prentice Hall, 1995), 186–235, 326–364.

11. "An NSTA Position Statement: Multicultural Science Education," *NSTA Reports!* (October/November 1991): 7. Reprinted with permission of the NSTA.

CHAPTER 10

Using Multimedia Technology Effectively

Technology—when used wisely—is an enabler, motivating students to achieve, to excel, to think, and to learn. Study after study documents the effectiveness of multimedia technology, teasing reluctant learners into the content of the material, sometimes with astonishing results. . . . When technology becomes an end in itself, it becomes the dark side of the moon.[1]

MAKING THE MOST OF MULTIMEDIA

Mi and her three teammates watch the monitor closely as the lost space probe sends back images of the planet where it has crashed. They can see craters, so they know the planet is terrestrial, but which one is it?

"Temperatures here range from very mild to −135° Celsius," the probe informs them.

Mi, the meteorology expert on the team, quickly searches her data to learn more about the weather on the terrestrial planets. "Only Earth and Mars have mild weather," she tells her teammates, "and only Mars has temperatures as low as −135° C. The probe must be on Mars!"

Angelo is the geology expert for this mission; Cassie, the astronomer; and Gerald, the space historian. After listening to information from the probe in their areas and consulting their own expert data, they concur: the lost probe crashed on Mars.

"I'm going to check it out," Cassie says. She clicks the mouse on the Mars symbol on the screen to test her team's hypothesis. The screen confirms their educated guess: the probe is on Mars!

"But," Gerald says, "where on Mars?" The team has four possible locations on Mars to check out. The monitor now shows the problem sitting on the planet's surface.

"Let's check the probe's elevation detector first." Angelo clicks the mouse on the probe's detector, and the probe informs them that its location is 4 km deep.

Angelo quickly searches through his data on the geology of the four possible locations. "It must be either Valles Marineris or Argyre Basin," he tells his teammates. "The other two locations aren't that deep. Let's try rock analysis." He clicks on the rock analysis label on the probe. The probe tells the team that it senses violent activity with Mars' crust.

"It has to be Valles Marineris!" Angelo tells them. "That's where there's folding and faulting of the surface due to Marsquakes!"

These students seem to have completely forgotten they're in science class. They're working cooperatively, serving as experts on their teams, extracting information from the booklets included with this program, and sharing what they learn with each other. They are determined to complete their mission in space, one of several chosen by their teacher.

What student—or teacher—could resist an activity like this? "The Great Solar System Rescue" by Tom Snyder Productions is one of a number of new computer-based programs that includes not only absorbing simulations but lessons plans and worksheets that encourage students to make other predictions, experiment, and test their hypotheses. This particular package combines computer graphics with footage from real space probes; it also offers a section on ancient skywatchers, adding a multicultural perspective. (The cost is less than you might expect, although you must have a laserdisc player and monitor available.)

Recent advances in computer technology certainly have much to offer science teachers. However, if you've looked through a recent catalog of educational computer products, it's easy to feel overwhelmed. All of the products sound exciting, but what would you expect from a catalog of advertisements?

Fortunately, help is available. A number of magazines review new computer-based materials, including *Science and Children, The Science Teacher, Technology Connection,* and *Multimedia Schools.* In addition, the Eisenhower National Clearinghouse for Mathematics and Science Education (ENC) offers an online catalog of curriculum resources that includes extensive information about available resources, plus prices.

In some cases, you will be able to download free software or programs. You can also join an online discussion group to find out what other teachers think of the programs or materials you are considering for your classroom. Some descriptions list schools where materials have been field tested or reviewed.

You might also contact your state department of education to determine whether it has established sites where teachers and librarians can evaluate and try out new materials. In addition, some software companies offer previews of their products and encourage teachers to return products that don't meet their needs. Whatever technology is available to you, be sure to explore the programs and packages that can help you and your students take advantage of the computer age.

How do you move you and your students into the Information Age? In what ways will you learn and teach your students to use the tools of the Information Age? The opening quotation and these two questions put multimedia technology into perspective and enable you to see how they can be used in the most effective way. This chapter will help you incorporate multimedia into a hands-on/minds-on science program in your classroom.

MULTIMEDIA TECHNOLOGY

Your life is inundated with multimedia technology; you use or come in contact with it everyday. **Multimedia technology** is electronic products that use numerous media (e.g., printed text, graphics, animation, audio, sound) to deliver information. Common examples are the computer, TV, VCR, cellular telephone, projectors, and combinations of all of them. Often, these electronic products are also interactive, allowing the user to choose from a variety of information options. Let's see how they can be used to enrich your classroom by starting with computers.

Computers, Computers Everywhere

Think of a typical day and you will quickly see which multimedia technologies directly influence your life. Computers will probably appear often in your day's routine in these four guises:

1. *Mainframe computers.* Giants that probably prepare your phone bill, handle your transactions at the 24-hour ATM banking stations, or process your college registration.
2. *Minicomputers.* Intermediate size, generally found in offices and businesses. They read bar codes at the grocery and automatically print each item on the register tape with prices, date, and time. Your paycheck may be produced on one.
3. *Microcomputers.* Smaller computers, used most frequently at home or school for

personal uses, such as word processing, record keeping, playing computer games, learning activities, and collecting and analyzing data. Microcomputers are frequently called *personal computers* or *PCs*. They are becoming so powerful they are replacing minicomputers for many applications.

4. *Laptops.* Battery-operated portable computers. These book-sized computers are for people who want or need a computer while they travel or are not at a source of electrical power.

In this chapter, the word *computer* refers primarily to the microcomputers that are used in classrooms. Which activities in your typical day involve computers? See how your school compares to these statistics of technology availability in schools:

- photocopiers: 97%
- television: 95%
- VCRs: 98%
- computers in school: 88% (but only 66% in classroom)
- modem: 43% in high-income schools, 30% in low-income schools
- fax machine: 28%
- Internet access: 50%
- home computers: 72%
- instructional laser discs or videodiscs: 27%
- hypermedia or multimedia software: 23%

For additional information, see:

- Sheila Heaviside, *Advanced Telecommunications in U.S. Public Elementary and Secondary Schools, 1995* (Washington, DC: U.S. Department of Education, Office of Educational Research and Improvement, Feb. 1996).
- *National Education Association Communications Survey: Report of the Findings* (Princeton, NJ: Princeton Survey Research Associates, June 2, 1993)

You either have, or shortly will have, computers in your elementary school. If you are to use this new technology effectively in your science teaching, you must become computer literate.

How to Develop Your Computing Literacy Skills

You probably have heard the term *computer literacy,* which generally refers to knowledge of computers and their components and how to use them for particular purposes. Some have expanded this definition beyond just machines and use the term *computing literacy* to include using computers as machines, tools, and creative instruments. Under this definition, you as a teacher using computers must learn and eventually teach:

- *about* computers. Teaching the operation, use, and programming of computers in classroom settings.
- *with* computers. Uses of computers as tools to gather and analyze laboratory data.
- *from* computers. Computers dispense or test information through tutorial and drill-and-practice programs.
- about *thinking with* computers. Using problem-solving programs.
- *managing* learning with computers. Using word processors, school schedulers, and test makers.

As an intelligent adult and a citizen in a technological society, you should become literate about computers. Teachers have always had to incorporate technological changes, such as pencils, printed books, films, filmstrips, radio, and television, into their teaching. You will do the same with computers if you learn the essentials:

1. Knowledge of computer components and terminology.
2. Programming computers to carry out your wishes.
3. Evaluating software and hardware.
4. Teaching/learning the uses of computers in your science teaching.

Using Computers as Objects of Instruction

You and your students *can* learn the basics of computers. You don't have to be an electronic or computer expert to use computers in your science teaching, any more than you need to know how your TV, VCR, or CD player works in order to use it. What you do need to know is (a) what computer parts (hardware components) are necessary, (b) how to select the right programs (software) to run your computer and meet your teaching and your students' learning needs, and (c) how to load programs (diskettes, discs, or tape), turn on, and run the computer. The following are computer basics you should know and teach to your students.

What Are the Major Components of a Computer?[2]

The computer you use in your elementary or middle school will probably have the multimedia technology components like those in Figure 10–1. As you read the text about major components, follow Figure 10–1 to reinforce your learning. In addition, a glossary of necessary computer terms appears at the end of this text.

Computers are made of electronic circuits that receive, store, process, and transmit information. Thousands, or even hundreds of thousands, of these circuits can be put on silicon devices called **chips,** smaller than your fingernail. The most important chip, called the **central processing unit (CPU),** controls all other parts of the computer and can be thought of as its "brain." Other chips perform the following functions:

- **ROM (Read Only Memory).** Computer's special operating instructions that cannot be erased, even when the computer is turned off.
- **RAM (Random Access Memory).** Memory that stores and holds instructions only while the computer is on. This memory is erased when it is turned off. It is designated by the number of characters or individual letters,

called **bytes,** that it can store, e.g. 486K (486,000 bytes. K = 1000 bytes × 486). The higher the number, the more information the computer can store. Many current computers have RAMs with ranges from 8MB to more than 136MB (MB = million bytes, or 1000K; 136MB = 1,000,000 bytes × 136, or 136,000,000).

What Are Hardware and Software? A term used for the physical parts of computers is **hardware.** Keyboards, monitors, disk and disc drives, mouse, modem, speakers, fax, and printers are all hardware.

Another important part of computers is the software. **Software** programs, when loaded into a computer at the disk drive, instruct the computer what to do. These programs are usually on 3½" or 5¼" diskettes, depending on the kind of disk drive. Software is written in a language that the CPU can understand and gives a series of instructions that allow a computer to do a particular task. This is called **programming** the computer. Programs may be written by you and your students, or you may use programs written by others. Probably, you and your students will begin with programs written by others until you are more proficient and feel confident with your software.

Computer hardware and software vary considerably in their capacities to perform tasks; therefore, their prices also vary. Prices will be explored later in this chapter.

Now that you have a rudimentary knowledge of a computer—its hardware and software and how it functions—let's look at how it can be used for science teaching/learning.

HOW CAN MULTIMEDIA COMPUTERS ENRICH SCIENCE TEACHING/LEARNING?

Multimedia computers and other classroom multimedia technology are effective because they speak to today's visually oriented students. It is

6. Speakers

2. Monitor

4. Diskettes

3. Disk and
CD-ROM drive

8. Microcomputer assembled

5. Printer

1. Keyboard

7. Modem connected
to telephone

9. You (the operator)

Microcomputer Component	Function
1. Keyboard	To enter instructions and information into the computer (INPUT); usually has same numbers and letters as standard typewriter plus extra keys
2. TV Screen or Monitor	To view a program or see what is being typed on the keyboard
3. Disk and CD-ROM drive	To detect and "read" information stored on a diskette; may be a cassette recorder and/or a disk drive
4. Diskette	Magnetic disk goes into disk drive and programs can be loaded and stored on them; information source
5. Printer	Makes paper copy of electronic listings in computer (output)
6. Speakers	To add sound to graphics and text
7. Modem/fax	To communicate with other computers through telephone lines
8. Mouse	To enter instructions and information into the computer by "pointing" rather than typing.
9. You	Unless you do something to the microcomputer, nothing happens. They do not run by themselves. So turn it on and learn to use it while using it.

FIGURE 10–1

Multimedia computer components

staggering to consider that the students in your classroom have probably logged about 8,000 hours in front of a TV screen! Many of them also have spent many hours playing computer and video games. They are eager to use multimedia technology in their classrooms as well.[3]

By capitalizing on this high motivation, computers can enrich your science teaching in many ways, especially in these areas:

1. Computing literacy.
2. Computer-assisted instruction (CAI).
3. Computer problem solving.
4. Computer-managed instruction (CMI).

Each of these areas can have a significant impact on your science teaching. However, most elementary or middle school teachers do little computer problem solving or computer-managed instruction. The rest of this discussion will concentrate on the two computer fields that are most readily adapted to the your elementary or middle school science classroom: computing literacy and computer-assisted instruction.

Computing Literacy and Science Teaching/Learning

All of the material just presented to you about computing should also be taught to your students. Here are those computing literacy concepts in the framework of how they fit into your classroom science teaching:

1. Explain what computers are and how they work, and present in writing the basic computer vocabulary or language needed.
2. Give the meaning of and show examples of computer programming.
3. Tie computers to science/technology/society by showing
   a. how computers affect people's lives now and in the future;
   b. how scientists use computers in their work; and
   c. what career opportunities are available for people with computer skills.

4. Present opportunities for students to develop skills by using computers as tools to learn, write and calculate, and then to save, display, and print this information.
5. Help students do simple computer programming.

For an expanded discussion of these points read:

■ Odvard Egil Dyrli and Daniel E. Kinnaman, "What Every Teacher Needs to Know About Technology. Part 3: Teaching Effectively With Technology," *Technology and Learning, 15,* no. 6, March, 1995, 52.

Once your students understand how computers work and can apply some basic computer language, you can move to other aspects of using computers in your science program.

Using Technology as a Delivery Medium for Science Teaching/Learning

Previous chapters have covered a variety of aids to teaching science: hands-on/minds-on activities, books, films, field trips, and other materials. Think of the computer as another aid to enrich the science learning of your students. Computer-assisted instruction (CAI) may be used in five main ways to enrich your science teaching:

1. Drill and practice.
2. Dialog and tutorial.
3. Simulation and modeling.
4. Data gathering/analysis/processing.
5. Teacher and student word processing and record keeping.

Figure 10–2 depicts the interrelationship among these five CAI learning activities and science teaching. The pyramid is founded on four bases: drill and practice, dialog and tutorial, simulating and modeling, and teacher utility. Data gathering/analysis/ processing is the pinnacle of the pyramid because it draws on the other four aspects and requires the highest level of thinking, participation, and learning. In effect,

FIGURE 10–2
Uses of computer-assisted instruction (CAI) in science teaching

this level ties together Bloom's taxonomy of cognitive thinking, types and uses of computer programs, and your science teaching.

CAI Drill and Practice Does Not Have to Be Boring

The most common use of CAI is drill-and-practice activities, although this is a very limited use of computers. If used effectively, CAI drill-and-practice activities are useful for

1. individualizing work for all students so they may progress at their own learning levels and pace;
2. identifying specific weaknesses for students to work on;
3. reteaching vocabulary or scientific terminology;
4. presenting science content usually covered by teachers using workbooks, textbooks, games, and other teaching materials;
5. showing questions, diagrams, or models in color, and even in animation;
6. alerting students immediately as to whether their responses are right or wrong;
7. showing the right answer immediately if incorrect answers are given; and
8. providing immediate positive reinforcement for all right answers.[4]

CAI drill and practice is usually used for repetitive applications of skills (practice and review using newly acquired science vocabulary), not to present new science concepts. Look for CAI drill-and-practice science programs that reinforce what you have taught, that entertain, and that are on a learning level suitable for your particular students.

Uses of CAI Tutorial Software in Your Science Teaching/Learning

Another use of CAI for science teaching is interactive tutorial or dialog. Generally, CAI tutorials involve students in active dialog, which requires them to answer correctly before going to the next step. A topic is introduced, and various concepts are "taught" by presenting principles from Step A, to Step B, to Step C, and so on to the conclusion of the lesson. If students answer questions incorrectly, they are returned to a lower level. A review is given to see if they have mastered the lesson. Some examples of science materials appropriate for CAI tutorial programs are the circulatory system, the names of the organs in the respiratory system of a fish, the parts of a microscope, and star constellation names. These types of computer activities are consistent with constructivist learning and reinforcing prior knowledge. An example of a program that explores human anatomy (basic organization and terminology, bones and body organs, and body systems and how they relate to each other) is *Bodyscope* from MECC, 6160 Summit Drive North, Minneapolis Minnesota 55430–4003; (800) 685–MECC.

Utilizing CAI Simulation and Modeling in Science Teaching/Learning

You would get little argument if you said the best way for elementary or middle school students to learn something was through firsthand experiences. However, this is not always practical, cost-effective, or safe. Simulation and modeling are the next best methods. If the learner is active, not merely a passive observer, the computer activity is called **simulation.** Simulation follows the constructivist idea that learners construct their own unique concepts through active participation.

Simulations have great potential as a CAI teaching tool. The computer can simulate activities that are difficult or impossible to do in your classroom, such as wave properties of oceans, organism population growth, introduction of new organisms into a food chain, and compass directions and measurements. Students enjoy involvement in the graphic animated displays. They are placed in a situation where they control an environment by interacting with the computer. In a CAI simulation, they collect data, correlate results, and learn skills, attitudes, and concepts. Your job is to help your students understand the relationship of the CAI simulation to reality.

In simulations, slower students may type in as many requests for assistance as necessary without embarrassment. A computer never gets angry or impatient; its pace adapts to the student using it. Conversely, advanced students may skip parts of a program that they already understand and proceed at their pace. CAI simulations move students to higher or lower levels as needed.

In CAI simulations, students must constantly be creating ideas to keep the simulation going. They must construct sentences, solve problems, and make decisions. By being active participants in the CAI simulation, students get practice in solving problems in situations with which they can easily identify.

Many good commercial CAI simulation programs are available for your science teaching. A sample of one follows.

Board the Magic School Bus. Kindergarten to sixth grade students are introduced to a meaningful multimedia science adventure with Scholastic's **The Magic School Bus Explores** series. These computer programs are based on the best-selling book series, The *Magic School Bus* books, and the popular PBS television series of the same name.

In the programs, Ms. Fizzle, a high-spirited teacher, takes her class on extraordinary field trips by means of a magical school bus. The bus changes size and shape so students can grasp science topics through original and interesting viewpoints.

The Magic School Bus Explores the Solar System has Ms. Fizzle's class on a trip to the planetarium, when the bus "morphs" into a rocket ship and blasts off into outer space. Then Ms. Fizzle disappears and the class has to find her in the solar system. Students gather information from interactive experiments and reports as part of their search for Ms. Fizzle.

In another program, *The Magic School Bus Explores the Human Body,* the bus shrinks in size. One of the students mistakes the bus for a cheese snack and swallows it. Inside the student's body, the class has to explore 12 body parts before they can escape. Interactive games, experiments, and multimedia reports at each body part make this learning fun. For additional information about *The Magic School Bus* interactive science series contact: Scholastic, Inc., 555 Broadway, New York, NY 10003; (212) 343-6100.

Computer simulations allow students to enjoy a discovery lesson while absorbing valuable science concepts. You must provide closure and analysis and encourage expressions of the concepts learned through such activities as drawing posters and role-playing.

Observational Skills Are Developed in CAI Modeling. Another type of CAI software is called *modeling.* **Modeling** differs from simulation in that the learner is an observer of a phenomenon but not an active participant. CAI modeling programs might investigate the following:

■ Tracing blood flow from the heart to body parts and back to the heart.
■ Observing the germination of seeds and the phototropism of growing plants.

- Following the steps in the working of an automobile or steam engine.
- Following the pathway of electrons in a flashlight circuit.
- Observing the movement of magma underground, through a volcano, up to the eruption of lava.

An excellent example of a multimedia computer modelling program is the easy-to-use *Bird Anatomy,* in which there is detailed study of bird characteristics. Users can zoom in for quality graphics on wing space, head area, beaks, claws, and other features. Bird calls and ecological information are also included. For information on this very inexpensive software ($7 non-members, $4 members) contact: Boston Computer Society (Macintosh Office), 1972 Massachusetts Ave., Cambridge, MA 02140.

You can use CAI simulations and modeling to enrich your hands-on/minds-on science activities and discussions, but do not use them as substitutes for real experiences.

CAI Lab Activities Develop Higher Science Thinking Skills

Students should be taught to use the computer as scientists do—to store and retrieve data, communicate, help with analysis, prepare tables and graphs, and write summary reports.[5]

The highest level of thinking/learning/acting in science teaching is problem solving/decision making. Computer CAI software is available for developing problem-solving/decision-making skills through data gathering/analyzing/processing programs. You should become familiar with "lab programs" for these important reasons:

1. It is easy to neglect data gathering/analyzing/processing skills, because drill and practice are what many elementary teachers know best, feel comfortable with, and do themselves.
2. Lab programs use the computer as a tool to aid discovery, not merely as mechanical flash cards.

3. You should emphasize the most creative and innovative uses of computers, rather than the least imaginative and repetitive uses.

Many lab programs exist. Let's look at the two common types: *computer/sensor* and *computer/ printed text/video.* Reviewing these two types of CAI lab programs will introduce you to the next level of electronic teaching aids.

Simulated Interactive Lab Activities

Simple devices that are easy to add to existing computer systems are readily available. Among these devices, called **peripherals,** are **sensors** or **probes** that allow the computer to monitor experimental variables such as temperature, sound, light, and heart rate, and feed the data into the computer for analysis and processing.[6] User-friendly peripherals allow your students to become active participants in science experiments. This technology need not replace the hands-on/minds-on aspects of your classroom science program; it can enrich and reinforce it.

How Multimedia Computers and Sensors Work Together

A hands-on/minds-on experimental activity that uses a multimedia computer and sensor to gather, process, and display data directly from the environment is called a **microcomputer-based laboratory** or **MBL.**[7] A lot can be done with simple and inexpensive MBL systems. MBLs turn the focus away from trivial mechanical processes to higher and more creative scientific processes, such as analyzing, hypothesizing, and evaluating. With MBLs, data gathering/analyzing/processing is so easy that it motivates explorations and discovery. Students focus on thinking about data, not merely gathering it.[8]

Table 10–1 lists some MBL programs that are available.

CD–ROM—Data Bases in Small Places

A recent electronic development—the CD–ROM or compact disk–read only memory—has enabled

TABLE 10–1
Microcomputer-based laboratory (MBL) software programs

MBL Program Vendor	Sensor/Probes Used	Type Lab Activities
Comp Trol Lab EduTech 303 Lamartine St. Jamaica Plains, MA 02130	photo gate	pendulum and acceleration
Experiments in Science HRM 175 Tompkins Ave. Pleasantville, NY 10570 (800) 431-2050	light, temperature, timer, plugs, and probes	optics, heart rate, evaporation, humidity
Heat, Light, and Sound Experiments Cross Educational Software 1802 N. Trenton St. PO Box 156 Reston, VA 71270	temperature and light sensors and sound intensity meter	thermal radiation, solar, and heat gain
Atarilab Starter Kit Atari PO Box 61657 Sunnyvale, CA 94086	temperature probe	dewpoint, evaporation, melting point, temperature measurement
Quantum Technology, Inc. PO Box 8252 Seary, AR 72143	pH, temperature, light, pressure, magnetism	environmental and weather

computer-based laboratory programs to more fully connect computers and sensors with enormous electronic filing and sorting systems called **data bases.**

CD ROMs are roughly the same size as CD audio discs. They are used to hold written text, pictures, sound, and full-motion video. An *enormous* amount of information can be stored on one CD–ROM. One CD–ROM can store whole encyclopedias (e.g., *Grolier's Electronic Encyclopedia*) or the data from 380 floppy discs. One CD–ROM can hold more than 600 megabytes of data, the equivalent of about 250,000 pages of text or 20,000 images. It is easy to see why libraries are using CD–ROMs for ERIC and other data-based systems. The National Science Foundation and the Carnegie Corporation funded and tested one CD–ROM, called *Helper*

K–8, that contains 1,000 hands-on science lessons that are easily retrievable and that may be freely copied and distributed. This single 5″ disc contains as much information as 250 books! You may receive a demonstration version on two floppy diskettes for use on an IBM–PC or compatible computer from PC-SIG, 1030 East Duane Avenue, Sunnyvale, CA 94086.

CD–ROMs unite with computers and electronic sensors to make science learning enjoyable as well as informative.

Multimedia Learning Combines MBLs, Computers, and CD–ROMs

Innovative MBLs are becoming more available to schools so that print materials may be combined with the latest electronic technology—

Many CD-ROM disks are already available for science education.

television, computer software, CD–ROMs, and probe and sensor devices.

An example of this exciting approach to learning is *Science for Kids,* a hands-on CD-ROM science curriculum program that approaches learning through discovery and inquiry. *Science for Kids* is produced by a collaboration of scientists, educators, psychologists, artists, programmers, engineers, and children. Currently, there are five science CD-ROMs in the series: *"CELL-EBRATION!," Forces and Motion, Simple Machines, The Heart,* and *Adventures with OSLO Tools and Gadgets.* Let's review *Adventures with OSLO Tools and Gadgets.*

Science for Kids: Adventures with OSLO Tools and Gadgets. Producer/Vendor: Science for Kids, 9950 Concord Church Rd., Lewisville, NC 27023; 800-KSCIENCE.

This charming physical science CD is targeted for students in grades K–8 and explores simple machines. The following five programs, combined into one CD-ROM, enable students to have fun while they are unearthing the mystery and magic of simple machines:

- an animated storybook about a llama named Dolly
- a discovery database that graphically defines simple machines,
- an exciting adventure game in which students explore for treasure in Tooltown and in the Valley of Machines,
- a lively arcade-style maze,
- a coloring gallery with musical markers.

All *Science of Kids* programs provide extensive and contemporary full-motion animations, audio and music, graphics, written text, and video, utilizing almost 600 MB on the CD–ROM disc. Some lessons center on classroom activities and discussions, while others use the multimedia computer. Students complete hands-on activities and interact with the multimedia CD–ROM computer program. A science lab kit is available for conducting the hands-on activities. A teacher's guide gives an overview, vocabulary, objectives, lesson plans, and activities. Students keep a journal as part of the program, and all lessons are in English and Spanish.

Students and teachers have responded well to all the *Science for Kids* multimedia computer programs.

WHAT'S THE LATEST MULTI-MEDIA TECHNOLOGY FOR MY SCIENCE CLASSROOM?

The next generation of multimedia technology for the science classroom includes interactive videodiscs, LCD projection systems, and telecommunications.

Interactive Videodiscs Add Challenging Realism

Picture yourself teaching elementary or middle school students about volcanic action. You would love to have them experience the sights, sounds, and other sensory aspects of these dramatic forces of nature. But how? Take them to a volcano? That isn't practical for most of us, and it is potentially dangerous.

But an electronic device called an **interactive videodisc** can give some of these sensory impacts. Videodiscs are 12″ plastic platters that look like silvery phonograph records or large compact discs. They are produced by copying the contents of a master videotape by means of a laser beam. Videodiscs are also called **laser discs,** because they are not only recorded but also play back by a laser beam. This makes them almost indestructible because there is no needle (or anything else) to touch, scratch, or wear down the surface of the disc. A beam of light reads and passes the stored electronic data from the disc to the videodisc player.

One videodisc can hold any combination of 108,000 individual pictures (the equivalent of 1,400 carousel trays of color slides), printed text, diagrams, sound/music, films, and animations on its two sides!

Videodiscs are really catching on in science education. *Windows on Science,* the first videodisc-based science program approved for state adop-tion as a "textbook" is now being used in elementary schools in Texas. For more information, contact *Windows on Science,* Optical Data Corp., 30 Technology Dr., Warren, NJ 07059 or (800) 248-8479.

Using Videodiscs in Your Science Teaching/Learning

Start by getting a videodisc system including a player, a monitor or TV screen, and one of these three means of accessing the images stored on the disc:

1. A hand-held remote control device comes with every videodisc player. You punch in a frame number on the remote and immediately locate the data. Visual and/or sound material is projected onto the TV or monitor screen without fast-forwarding, rewinding, or sorting.
2. A bar-code scanner, like the one that scans food prices at your grocery store, sends commands to the videodisc player when you run it over the barcode directory that comes with the disc. Within seconds, the exact image you want is on the screen.
3. A computer connected to the videodisc player uses software to control what will appear on screen.

Now you, or any student, can instantly call up any specific piece of data on a videodisc inserted into the player, by any of these three means. You/they can play or replay material in any way that suits the learning situation. The videodisc system is very durable, making it ideal for student use.

Videodiscs are especially valuable in science teaching/learning because of the interactive processes they afford. You can use videodiscs (and CD ROMs) in many ways, based on the level of student interaction you want, the hardware and software you have, and the ways you want the interaction to take place. Table 10–2 shows the four levels of interaction, the components that are needed, and a sample of ways they can be used in

TABLE 10–2
Videodisc and CD–ROM levels of interaction for science teaching/learning

Interaction Levels	Type of Interaction	Components Needed
0	**Stored Data Only** (not interactive)—collections of slides, photos, animations, films, printed text	Videodiscs and player monitor
I	**Electronic Index of Stored Data**—each single frame described and categorized with a number for rapid retrieval by punching number into remote control device; example: Questions are raised about volcanoes; teacher brings up appropriate slides, films, photos that enrich discussion.	Same as above, plus remote control device
II	**Electronic Scanning of Stored Data**—students use videodisc's index to find data by: a. *Keywords* (volcano, eruption, Mount Saint Helens) b. *Topical names, chapters, outline headings* (Earth's changing face) c. *Graphics* (maps of active volcanic areas, magma diagrams)	Same as above, plus microprocessor
III	**Higher Thinking Skills Tools**—all of the above functions plus these videodisc tools: a. *Simulations* with audio/visual materials for students to interact, collect, analyze, etc. b. *Tutorials* to teach at child's learning level and select appropriate data mode (slides, films, print materials, etc.) c. *Textbooks* and videodisc materials correlated with science curriculum d. *You* can create lessons using frames and films from videodiscs in any sequence you want (called authoring videodisc system)	Same plus laserdisc player, computer interface software

your science classroom. For further information about videodiscs see:

■ *Explore with Videodiscs: A Special Supplement to Curriculum Product News* (Stamford, CT: Curriculum Products News (CPN, 1994).
■ Richard Alan Smith, "Videodiscs–The Next Temptation," *Computing Teacher* (Conference Issue), (1990–91), 8–9.

To review some of the advantages of videodiscs for teaching/learning science, refer to Table 10–3.

Videodiscs embellish science teaching/learning by dispensing instant individual illustrations and sound for hard-to-grasp material. They invite creativity for teachers and students. And best of all, they are really easy to use. It is little wonder they are one of the most popular teaching/learning technologies.

TABLE 10–3
Advantages of videodiscs and CD–Roms

Any combination of text, diagrams, slides, maps, films, animations, and computer commands

Two sound tracks containing any combination of recorded voice, music, sound effects; can have one track in English and another in Spanish

Store 108,000 frames or one hour of motion video

Play forward and backward at variable speeds and freeze single frames indefinitely without harming disc or player

Random access medium—locate any frame or sequence on disc by keying the frame number

Excellent quality audio and video production and playback

Extremely durable, data stored under protective plastic surface; cleaned by damp cloth and even scratches do not affect reproduction

Small and easy to store

Getting Started With Videodiscs and CD–ROMs. The way you use video/laserdiscs and CD–ROMs in your science teaching will probably depend on these practical considerations.

Budget. Prices of electronic equipment are rapidly dropping, but you will need $500–1,000 for a videodisc player; $400 or more for interactive videodisc or CD–ROM packages that correlate with your school curriculum (including appropriate software and student response books), at least $700 for a computer and color monitor, and about $15 for individual videodiscs and CD–ROMs. Start with basic hardware/software and add more as money becomes available.

Reduce or eliminate start-up costs.[9] If teachers share materials, costs per child can be reduced. Teachers, students, schools, parent–teacher groups, and local business people can raise money for such purposes in a variety of ways. Here are some realistic approaches.

- Your PTA could contact one of the following fundraising organizations to help raise money for technology. Investigate them carefully. Even though they have been used successfully by many schools, this text cannot endorse them.
  A+ America, 5130 Industrial St., Maple Plain, MN 55592, (800)557-2466
  The Computer Learning Foundation, 2431 Park Blvd., Palo Alto, CA 94306
  ITW Hi-Cone, 1140 West Bryn Mawr, Itasca, IL 60043
  Innesbrook Wraps, P.O. Box 16046, Greensboro, NC 27416 (800)334-8461.
  Market Day Food Co-Operative, 555 West Pierce Rd., Ste. 200, Itasca, IL 60043 (800)252-8169.

- Hardware and software can be obtained through donations by individuals or businesses that are upgrading their current systems.

- School sale of scrip, where parents or relatives buy scrip and use it at face value (just like a gift certificate) at supermarkets or retail stores. The school gets a percentage of the face value. Stores get customers and make a contribution to the community.

- Supermarkets and other stores can sponsor programs in which store receipts, product labels, or bar codes may be redeemed for technology products. Students, teachers, relatives, and senior citizen groups can provide and manage the receipts from stores offering these premiums.

- Phone-a-thons raise funds by telephone calls to alumni or parents of alumni. Walk-a-thons consist of students securing pledges of money from relatives, friends, and neighbors for every mile they walk.

- Many corporations (particularly high tech ones) have programs that match dollars contributed by their employees to schools. Exam-ple: if an IBM employee contributes 20% of the price of IBM hardware or software *for education* and files the appropriate form, IBM will provide the remaining 80%. Microsoft Corporation will also match employee contributions for education. Check to see if these or other corporations of your students' parents or relatives participate in such programs.

■ Invite product vendors to demonstrate their multimedia technology during an open house or technology night. Vendors could be charged a booth fee, visitors could pay a small admission fee, and corporate sponsorship by a technology company could also be secured.

■ Donations by local retail stores (gift certificates, free restaurant dinners, weekend getaways from local travel agencies, etc.) could be raffled.

■ Student-produced video yearbook sales are very popular. Everyday school activities are videotaped and edited by students and teachers.

The amount you raise is limited only by your creativity and determination, and the amount of money your friends, relatives, and neighbors are willing to give you.

Become Videodisc and CD–ROM/Computing Literate. Start by talking to any teacher in your school or district who has a videodisc or CD–ROM. Actually work with him on a step-by-step orientation. If no teachers or machines are available, contact commercial publishers of interactive video packages specifically developed for education. Most also sell the hardware components you will need to set up an interactive videodisc system.

Select a video/laserdisc or CD–ROM system that correlates with your science curriculum and/or your science textbook. When you feel more comfortable with commercial videodiscs or CD–ROMs, prepare a videodisc of your own slides, printed text, maps, or films. Organize your own "menu" or indexing system for you and your students to use.

Examples of Using Videodiscs and CD–ROMs.
You can use commercial or self-made video/laserdiscs and CD–ROMs in your science classroom in many ways:

1. Create an almost instant access storage system for volumes of information. Using a computer and an automatic videodisc or CD–ROM changer, you can cross-reference materials from up to 72 separate videodiscs or CD–ROMs and retrieve the required information.

2. Illustrate materials for your science lessons. Your computer, connected to a videodisc player and monitor, combine your lesson plan with appropriate audiovisual aids. You can incorporate bar codes right into your lesson plans and at appropriate places, check on them to display the appropriate material.

3. Present science lessons to small groups of students. For example, to explain the concept of phototropism, select time-lapse shots and slides of plants growing toward the light to make the learning more dramatic and meaningful. You can pause at critical points, show entire sequences in slow motion, and review important concepts quickly and easily.

4. Reinforce hands-on/minds-on science activities. If your students are studying variables that affect seed germination, films and animation of the process on videodisc or CD–ROMs strengthen and clarify students' conceptual development.

5. Help your students research, study, and present reports. Your students can use the materials stored on videodiscs or CD–ROMs just as they would an encyclopedia. When they are ready to present their reports, they can use the indexing menu in conjunction with the remote control device to bring up, sequence, and display pertinent segments of the video/laserdisc. Some teachers have trained a corps of students to be videodisc helpers, assisting others with videodiscs.

6. Develop your own teaching materials, ranging from simple handouts and overhead transparencies to student science labs or workbooks.

7. Supplement your written assessments with video/laserdiscs and CD–ROMs by presenting slides or sequences on the TV screen and asking students to respond to your related questions. This may be most appropriate and practical when showing animation and films

to test your students on items such as microscopic slide identification (onion skin, etc.), plant and animal physiology processes and development, aspects of the outdoor environment (especially in inclement weather), or aspects of Earth as seen from space.[10]

You and Your Students Can Produce Videotapes

Camcorders and VCRs make it easy for you and your students to produce science videotapes. These videocassettes could be used as culminating activities for student projects, challenges for individuals or small groups, or instructional for teacher presentation. Here are some ideas on how you and your students can produce science video challenges.[11]

1. Prepare a script for a 10- to 20-minute videotape that has these elements:
   - *Grab the Audience*. Use a discrepant event, a funny story, an unusual happening, or a natural occurrence to stimulate the viewer to want to participate in the challenge.
   - *Set up the Challenge*. Ask viewers to duplicate what they just saw. A shoe box of science materials is provided for viewers to perform hands-on/minds-on activities relating to the challenge. Viewers are urged to stop the videocassette before they manipulate the science materials.
   - *Try to Solve the Challenge*. Viewers are encouraged to use whatever problem-solving techniques they can (e.g., brainstorming or trial-and-error) to solve the problem presented. They may resume the tape when they have solved the challenge or need additional information.
   - *Assess Findings*. Viewers can check their findings against the demonstration on the videocassette for alternative solutions, scientific principles involved, further information, and everyday scientific/technological applications.

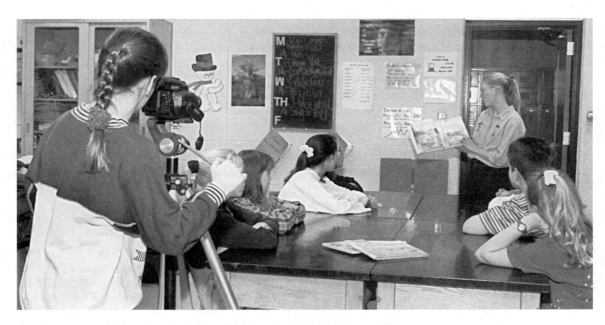

Student-made videotapes can be used in a variety of ways, including practicing for cross-age tutoring as students here are doing.

FIGURE 10–3
Liquid crystal display (LCD) projection system

2. Videotape your challenge, try it out with groups of students or adults, request evaluations from viewers, and modify (re-record) any sections that need it.
3. Solicit ideas for additional videocassette challenges from viewers.

With a camcorder, VCR, some inexpensive videocassettes, and 25 students, you can soon have quite a collection of challenges.

Making Your Science Presentations Bigger and Better With LCDs[12]

If you are lucky enough to have a computer or videodisc in your science classroom, you probably have wrestled with this problem: You want to show your class something from the computer or videodisc player, and you have the students crowd around the single TV monitor. There's usually shoving, other discipline problems, and complaints: "Miss Orkand, I can't see." Until now, the only solution was a $5,000 large-screen video projector. However, a new electronic breakthrough can solve this problem—a liquid crystal display (LCD) projection system that is simple to operate, practically indestructible, and relatively inexpensive ($600 and up).

An LCD projection system is an electronic device that attaches to your computer or videodisc player. It looks like a plastic briefcase (without handles) with a window, and is usually no larger than 12" × 18". Instead of showing your videodisc on your computer monitor, the device projects it on the system's transparent LCD screen. You put the LCD screen on an overhead projector just as you would a transparency. The image is lit up, projected, and enlarged to whatever size is practical on any size white screen. Imagine the impact microbes will have on your students if they are projected on a 9-foot screen, instead of a 15-inch monitor! Any computer or videodisc software can be shown using an LCD projection system, including films, animation, graphics, and printed text. Numbers, graphics, and print text stand out more clearly than when crowded on small TV screens. (See Figure 10–3.)

Optimal Conditions for Using LCD Projection. Although the LCD projection system is simple to operate and relatively inexpensive, these conditions can affect the quality of its use in your science classroom:

1. You must use an overhead projector that has light projection from the base, not the top.
2. Many LCD projection systems are designed to work only with a certain microcomputer model. Any other system may require additional adapters.
3. You can display your computer or videodisc simulations on a TV monitor and LCD projection system at the same time by using a Y adapter or similar electronic coupler that comes with some LCD systems, but some clarity may be sacrificed.
4. Clarity (resolution) of graphics suffers on some LCD screens. Look for high megahertz rates (the time it takes the liquid crystals to fade and reappear on your screen) or fast refresh times for greater clarity.
5. Make sure the LCD projector system has a fan (to remove heat from the overhead projector), a remote control device, and special software for editing and saving.

Before you buy any LCD projector system, test it under your own conditions: light, distance from screen to projector, and overhead projector you will use. Vendors are willing to demonstrate their products in schools.

Large-screen LCD projectors add a wide range of teaching/learning options. But something new is always coming along to make teaching better. The new kid on the block now is *whiteboarding with software*.

Whiteboarding With Software

For as long as there has been teaching, teachers have used writing boards. Two newer technologies that enrich the use of writing boards are Microfield Graphics' *SoftBoard* and Panasonic's *Panaboard*. Here is a description of each.

SoftBoard. (Microfield Graphics, Inc., 9825 SW Sunshine Court, Beaverton, OR 97005, (800) 334-4922). *SoftBoard* combines a real porcelain/steel whiteboard writing surface with the remote benefits of whiteboarding software. You connect the *SoftBoard* to a PC or Mac with the supplied cable, load the *SoftBoard* software, and the unit automatically configures itself. Lasers scan the surface and report any activity from special writing pens to an attached computer. Included Windows or Macintosh software converts your writing and drawings into viewable images. Whatever you create on a SoftBoard appears instantly on your PC or Mac. Once it's there you can save it, print it, cut and paste it, e-mail it, fax it, even network it to multiple sites.

Panaboard. Panasonic Co, One Panasonic Way, Secaucus, NJ 07094 (800) 524-0864. *Panaboard* is a whiteboard that has a built-in printer to print out what you write down. With a touch of a button, *Panaboard* scans and prints out anything you write, draw, or even tape on it. Your students can immediately have letter-sized copies of what you write during your science presentations. Students who can't copy what you write or draw on the writing board are relieved of any handicap. Figure 10–4 shows how the *Panaboard* functions.

Let the World In: Telecommunicating

Another electronic technology technique available to enrich your science teaching/learning is telecommunicating. **Telecommunicating** is communicating with computers in your local area or remote locations over phone lines. To understand telecommunicating or electronic networking, visualize your personal computer not as a computational machine but as a communication device. Just as national and international phone systems have magnified the usefulness of your individual telephone, electronic networks magnify the utility of your computer. Here are a few of the benefits of using telecommunicating in your professional and personal life:[13]

FIGURE 10–4
Panasonic's *Panaboard*

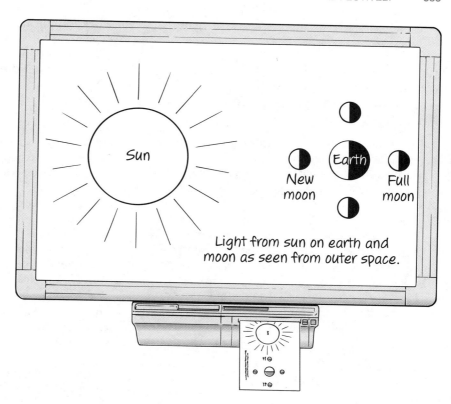

Light from sun on earth and moon as seen from outer space.

1. Resource sharing allows you, your fellow teachers, and your students to share data and peripheral devices and send files and electronic mail. You can also have access to software by connecting to large libraries of audio, visual, and graphical information.

2. Science teaching/learning is enriched by adding vitality and excitement to the classroom. Classes all over the world can communicate on a day-to-day basis on scientific issues, research, or ideas. Example: Elementary school students throughout the United States measure daily precipitation and acidity of collected rainwater samples and share the information with each other via a computer network. As a result, a daily acid rain map is created.

3. Time and money are saved by having the freedom and flexibility to use network services whenever it is convenient for you, whether it's 6 A.M. or midnight.

4. Resources are managed more effectively, because you do not have to store voluminous files of paper and computer disks. A central network server stores and dispenses data so you do not have to have your own backup copies of each program. Networking software improves management of student data, and gives teachers and administrators faster and more accurate access to information with less paperwork.

5. Remote accessibility is possible, because telecommunicating allows laptops and the portable computing devices to connect to networks. Teachers, students, and parents can do their science work, distribute data to other network users, and enjoy all the other advantages of networks while away from the school

building. Telecommunication is a true global access technology.

What Do I Need to Get Started With Networking?

To start networking in your classroom or home, you need a computer and modem, which works this way:

1. A **modem** (electronic device) connects your computer to a standard telephone line. Some modems use a connector wire; others just have the telephone receiver face down on the modem.
2. The modem translates or "modulates" electronic impulses from your computer into audible tones that can be transmitted through the telephone receiver, and also "demodulates" or translates incoming audible signals back into electronic impulses that your computer can interpret. That's how we get the name *modem: Mo*dulate / *Dem*odulate.

Modems cost $50 and up and require special communication computer software, which may or may not come with the modem. You pay for telephone charges used; many phone companies charge only local charges for national communications databases and networks. Some online services charge hourly fees in addition to subscription fees.

With a modem and computer, you have access to the worldwide Internet. But first, you must make two networking decisions:

- Pick your **userid** *(USER ID*entification name), which every network user must have. Yours might be: jill _orkand.
- Decide on a unique **electronic address** that is either your school or home. Yours might be: cowpath.edu

When sending mail over the Internet, the userid and address are separated with an @, so you might log on as:

jill_orkand@cowpath.edu

Now you are ready to use the Internet for your science teaching/learning.

Network Applications for Science Teaching/Learning.

A wealth of applications exist for using networking in your science classroom or home. Consider these:

1. *Messaging* is the electronic exchange of information between individuals or groups. *E-mail* is the most universally used way to send and receive electronic mail. It is used around the world to exchange keypal messages, work on cooperative projects, work with mentors, and request and send information.
2. *Discussion groups* usually supply free memberships, which include automatic copies of every message on their list. Thousands of such groups abound. Most popular for science teachers are *Kidsphere, EDTECH,* and *CONDISC.*
3. *Newsgroups* are like giant bulletin boards. They require special software to read and post messages, and they are not available from every Internet service provider. Unlike discussion groups, you do not subscribe to newsgroups, and posted messages are not sent directly to your mailbox. One widely used newsgroup is USENET, which is organized under more than 8,000 topic-oriented message bases.
4. *Remote log-in* uses the Internet command, *TELNET,* to log in to a distant computer as if you were seated at that machine. Not all on-line services offer remote log-in; if yours does, you can access data posted on *NASA's Spacelink* or *Argonne National Laboratory's* science bulletin board.
5. *File transfer* uses another common Internet command, **FTP** (*F*ile *T*ransfer *P*rotocol), to send and receive files between your computer and others. You need a specific password to get into most computer systems, but many offer *Anonymous FTP;* this means you will be admitted by simply typing the word *anonymous.*

Some other tools that will help you "surf the net" include:

- *ARCHIE* (from *archives*) keeps track of millions of files at anonymous worldwide FTP locations. When you specify a search word to ARCHIE, you can travel to these locations and get the files you want by using the FTP command.

- *GOPHER* is a multilevel menu system that automatically connects you to Internet locations to *go for* the files you select and bring them to your computer automatically.
- *VERONICA* works from within GOPHER to simultaneously search GOPHER locations by topic.
- *WAIS* stands for *W*ide-*A*rea *I*nformation *S*ystem. It searches through many hundreds of on-line databases and locates documents that contain specified key words or phrases.

In summary, your science classroom computer can be used to search through database materials from throughout the United States and other parts of the world. **Databases** (electronically stored information) exist in all curricular areas, including science. For instance, if your students are studying the interrelationships between wind direction, speed, and weather conditions, they can instantly gather information from a variety of geographic locations without leaving your classroom. This not only motivates students and encourages them to use higher thinking processes, but it also helps students learn how to effectively select and secure information, a process that is vital in our information-laden society. Telecomputing allows your students to send and receive electronic mail anywhere in the world. It is a kind of electronic data pen pal for the sharing of computer information.

Local Area Networks Can Save You Money in Telecommunicating. The fundamental channel into the Internet is through a registered host computer. Software from the host computer is shared electronically via LAN (**L**ocal **A**rea **N**etworks). This eliminates the expense of having to buy many software packages or disk drives for each machine. LANs also reduce the illegal copying of software. You will gain substantial dollar savings, as well as teaching advantages, by

participating in a LAN. LANs cost $200 and up per terminal, but they more than pay for themselves in teaching/learning benefits.

To summarize, telecommunicating can enable you and your students to:

- access commercial databases and information services,
- do collaborative research with other teachers and students locally or around the world,
- get up-to-the-minute weather and other science-related data,
- communicate using electronic mail, and
- join discussions on bulletin boards, newsgroups, and computer conferences about science topics.[14]

APPLICATIONS OF MULTIMEDIA TECHNOLOGY TO YOUR CLASSROOM[15]

Here are some classroom-tested suggestions for using computers and other electronic multimedia technology to assist your students in learning science. Let's start with hardware and software.

Take the Plunge and Do It!

Start with your instructional objectives, not hardware or software. First decide what you want to do with multimedia technology; then it is relatively easy to determine how to do it and what hardware and software you'll need. Before buying anything, become familiar with the relatively inexpensive computers and available peripherals and software by asking critical questions of hardware/software representatives:

1. Is science software available and suitable for the particular computer/video in your classroom? (See computer software evaluation later in this chapter.)
2. Is the electronic equipment durable and easily portable?
3. Does the computer have a typewriter-style keyboard?

4. Is there a minimum of 64K+ random access memory (RAM)?

5. Is the electronic equipment vendor reliable? Can the vendor readily supply maintenance and repairs when needed?

6. Will the vendor demonstrate the equipment and let you try it to find out what each system looks like and how the parts work?

Have a vendor and/or computer-using friends and colleagues help you master basic computer vocabulary. You need to be familiar with the names of input devices like *typewriter, joy stick, modem, fax, touch panel, CD–ROMs, video/laser player, graphics tablet;* output devices like *printer, loudspeaker,* and *television screen,* and memory means for storing information electronically like *central processing unit.* Vocabulary is essential. You can't ask a question when you don't even know the words for the things you want to ask about. (See the Computer and Telecommunications Glossary.)

Set up the computer at the vendor's. Follow the wires and examine each connection from keyboard and printer to computer ports. How many plugs are there? What's plugged in and what's not?

Learn the procedure for starting up a computer lesson on some common computers. Remember to turn on the computer/monitor!

Find out what kinds of science lessons are available for your particular science teaching/learning needs.

Gain hands-on experience with a variety of lessons, simulations, and computer games. Always do them first yourself.

Build up a file of articles, books, information sources, and bibliographic resources, starting with sources in this chapter.

Plan and arrange the physical elements of your classroom to make the most efficient use of your computer/multimedia technology.

Arranging and Managing Your Computer/Multimedia-Oriented Classroom

There are at least three ways in which schools arrange for using computer/multimedia technology: centralized computer center or lab, classrooms with one computer/multimedia setup with large video screen, and classrooms with more than one computer/multimedia arrangement. Here is how they might function.

School-Wide Computer/Multimedia Center or Lab. Some elementary and middle schools are setting up computer or technology centers or labs, grouping all their electronic technology equipment in one room. Classes are scheduled into the computer center, and either a computer specialist teacher conducts computer lessons, or individual teachers work with their own classes there. For a detailed plan for setting up a classroom computer system, including every aspect of implementation and possible sources of funding, see:

■ Robert V. Bullough, Sr. and LaMond F. Beatty, *Classroom Applications of Microcomputers,* 2nd ed. (Englewood Cliffs, NJ: Merrill/Prentice Hall, 1991).

One Classroom, One Computer/Multimedia Setup. If you have one computer/multimedia setup, you probably are hooked up to a large-screen monitor or projection system. You, or your students, work at the computer, CD–ROM, or videodisc player, and images are displayed on a screen for the entire class to view. Interaction can take place as students view the screen and discuss what they see.

More Than One Computer/Multimedia Arrangement. It is likely that you have, or will have, more than one computer/multimedia arrangement in your self-contained classroom. Here are some guidelines for setting up and managing a computer (and possibly other electronic technology such as MBL, videodiscs, telecommunication equipment) for a class of 30 to 35 students.

1. A variety of educational technologies should be used to accommodate the range of learning styles and backgrounds of your students (e.g., texts, videos, hands-on/minds-on materials, computers, MBLs,

LCDs, electronic writing boards, telecommunication equipment, and software).
2. Tables should be strategically grouped so students can work in cooperative learning groups.
3. The following learning stations should be set up for groups of five students: listening station, video station, hands-on/minds-on materials station, a word processing station, an MBL station, and a writing station. Figure 10–5 gives a suggested floor plan for a science/technology-oriented classroom incorporating these stations.

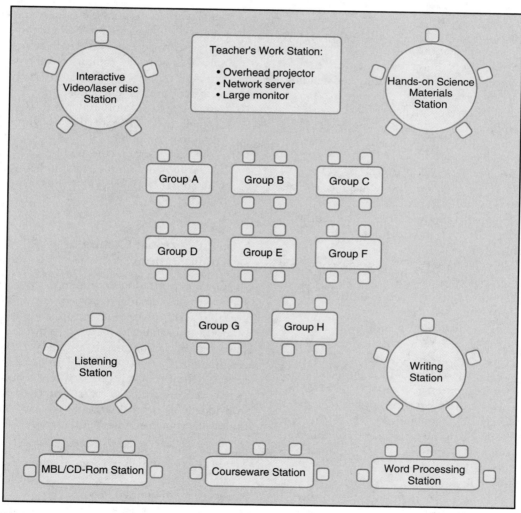

FIGURE 10–5

Multimedia/technology-oriented self-contained science classroom

Source: Designs for Elementary School Science and Health. A Cooperative Project of Biological Science Curriculum Study (BSCS) and International Business Machines (IBM) (Dubuque, IA: Kendall/Hunt, 1989) 50.

4. The teacher's work station should have a computer (to serve as the central server for students' computers and to connect with other computers in school and the Internet), an LCD projection system and large-screen monitor so that everyone in your class can read the words and numbers printed by the computer, an electronic writing board, a printer, and a fax/modem connected to a telephone outlet.

5. Your classroom should contain these types of computer stations:
   - Student computer work station to use Internet for data collection and sending science e-mail and bulletin board/newsgroup correspondence.
   - Microcomputer-based laboratory (MBL) for student-conducted interactive science activities.
   - An interactive videodisc/CD–ROM station for viewing and engaging in the videos and software.

6. To begin a computer literacy program with elementary or middle school students, it is probably best to follow these steps:
   a. Obtain one of the many simple computer textbooks/software programs.
   b. Go through each section of the textbook with the whole class.
   c. For the hands-on sessions, call one student at a time to the keyboard of the computer at the teacher work station. While the student does the activity on the computer, the rest of the class follows in their textbooks and watches what is actually happening on the TV screen. Your job during this phase is to point out what the student at the computer is doing.
   d. After five minutes, call on another student to go to the computer to give as many students as possible hands-on experience. You may need to have pairs or groups of threes doing the hands-on part of the activity.

7. Use normal overhead room lighting but avoid glare on the TV screen from windows. Also avoid setting up the TV screen so that it is silhouetted against a bright window.

8. Arrange to lock the computer when it is not used. Many schools engrave the name of the school on all components and bolt them to tables or portable carts.

9. Arrange your classroom schedule so that students who are responsible can use the computers on a sign-up basis when they have completed their other classroom responsibilities. You will find computers very popular and can positively motivate students to complete assignments. Encourage this.

10. Also encourage your students to share any of their own software that is compatible with your computer.

11. Periodically review the computer content and skills with simple tests and introduce your students to new software as it becomes available.

Student Personal Computer Learning Stations

In addition to locating a computer at your work station for class demonstrations or having it on a portable cart, you should set up student computer learning stations where up to five students can work on learning software and word processing. These would be similar to the learning centers described in Chapter 6, where collections of materials are arranged for students to work on individually or in small groups. You can do the same with your computers in these ways:

1. Place your computer, software, and other pertinent materials in your computer learning station, and locate it so you can see it from any place in your classroom.

2. Instruct your class on the basics of turning on, programming or loading (booting) your computer, and any other necessary simple directions for beginning computer literacy.

3. Select two or three students who know about and have used computers, and train them to be peer computer experts. They will have to know the hardware and software in your room, how to operate the computer, and how to positively help their classmates.

4. Set up a schedule so students can sign up for computer time at the computer station. Include some open or free times. Your schedule should record time spent on the computer by each student, so you can ensure that everyone gets computer time.

Which Software?

Computer programs, generally referred to as *software,* vary greatly in suitability for use with your elementary and middle school students. Software that is designed to supplement or be an integral part of science programs and textbooks, called **courseware,** is becoming available. You may be called on to suggest which software and courseware your school should buy in the coming years. It will take time to develop the skills to do this. Here are some questions to guide you in selecting and evaluating software and courseware for your elementary and middle school science program:

1. Is the program easy to use?
2. Is the program design flexible?
3. Is the menu complete?
4. Is the program content accurate and well designed?
5. Does the program offer a complete learning package, including a teacher's guide?
6. Is the reading level what you need?
7. Are the graphics direct, attractive, and appropriate?
8. Is there a program purchase warranty?
9. Has the software been reviewed or recommended?

Also consider these additional questions designed specifically for you as a science teacher:

1. Is the software and courseware program correlated with science curriculums or textbooks you use?
2. Does the software manual give a list of science vocabulary used in the software?
3. How are the software content or teaching techniques correlated with science content and processes that are your goals?
4. Are follow-up or enrichment science activities or demonstrations offered?

For additional assistance with software and courseware assessment see:

- *Microsoft Courseware Evaluation,* Northwest Regional Evaluation Laboratory, 300 SW 6th Avenue, Portland, OR 97204.
- *PRO/FILES,* EPIE Institute, Box 839, Water Mill, NY 11976.
- *The Educational Software Selector (T.E.S.S.),* Teachers College Press, 1234 Amsterdam Avenue, New York, NY 10027.

Computers and other electronic multimedia technology open many vistas for teaching science in the elementary and middle schools, and you can avail yourself of them now. Consider them another tool in your teaching arsenal. Be curious, but critical. Attend computer workshops, conferences, and exhibitions. Most importantly, find out why students are so enthusiastic about computers and other electronic technology and learn to share their enthusiasm.

I have coined the term *teachnology* to describe the way computers and other electronic multimedia technologies can serve you in your science teaching. Experiment with them to see how you can find effective ways to incorporate them into your own hands-on/minds-on guided discovery-oriented classroom.

SUMMARY

Computers and other electronic multimedia technologies are available to elementary and middle school classrooms and can be as valuable as your other teaching aids in teaching science. You have to become computer literate if you are to use computers effectively. This means learning not only computer language and how to run a computer, but also how to evaluate and select hardware and software.

After you become familiar with the workings of the computer, you can find a variety of ways to use it in your science teaching. You and your students must learn *about, with,* and *from* computers. Five ways of using computer-assisted instruction (CAI) in your science teaching are drill and practice, dialog and tutorial, simulation and modeling, data gathering/analysis/processing, and teacher utility. Samples of each were presented, along with suggestions about how to use them in your science teaching.

A hands-on/minds-on science program can be enriched with computer programs that involve students in interactive science experiences called microcomputer-based laboratories, or MBLs. Other electronic resources available now for developing higher level science thinking in your students are videodiscs, CD–ROMs, liquid crystal display (LCD) projection systems, interactive TV, and telecomputing. The benefits of telecommunication were explored. Practical ways to reduce or eliminate computer and multimedia teachnology setup costs were explored. Directions were given for making videotapes with your students.

Guidelines were suggested for evaluating software for your elementary science computer, along with computer data collection resources, such as computer journals, magazines, and books. Specifics for getting started on local and world-wide networks were detailed. Applications of networking were presented, with practical suggestions for your classroom science teaching.

SELF-ASSESSMENT AND FURTHER STUDY

1. Visit a local computer/multimedia store and ask for a computer demonstration using a tutorial or other computer-assisted instruction program— preferably in science—for elementary and middle school students. Make a simple evaluation sheet to evaluate the program for these items:
   - Program name and grade level(s) applicability.
   - Program description, with necessary computer peripherals and prices.
   - Explanation of the ease of loading and using for students, and how you feel students would react to it.
   - *Your* reaction to using it.
   - How it would fit into your science program.
2. Wherever possible, call 800 numbers or write to vendors for videodisc and CD–ROM catalogs. After reading the catalogs, call for a demonstration of videodiscs or programs that may meet your needs.
3. Draw a floor plan for a technology-oriented science classroom. Use Figure 10–6 as your starting point. Be sure to include stations for teacher work, interactive videos, CD–ROMs, hands-on/minds-on science materials, MBL, word processing, videodiscs, courseware, listening, and writing.
4. Discuss the procedures for starting, selecting, and training a cadre of students to serve as peer computer helpers. How can you avoid and handle the possible elitism problems that could develop?
5. Locate teachers in your school or district who are successfully using a computer with their science teaching. Ask them about hardware, software,

classroom usage, costs, and problems. Evaluate how you could use these ideas in your own classroom.

6. List five science topics that could be enriched by using computer/videodisc/CD–ROM programs. Research vendors to find specific videodiscs and CD–ROMs to meet your teaching/learning needs in these science topics. Then review them (with vendors demonstrating them for possible purchase) in your classroom with your students to see if they are effective.

7. Plan and make a videocassette challenge with a group of your students on a science topic of interest to them. Include a box of simple materials for conducting the hands-on/minds-on activities that accompany the challenge.

8. Investigate which LANs are available to enrich your science teaching/learning. Make a plan of what you need to do to get on-line and how you can integrate telecommunicating in your science program.

9. Preview an interactive videodisc and assess how it might be used in your science program.

10. Using the computer journals and magazines in this chapter as a beginning, read articles and reviews of software. Make a list of software you would use and give reasons why.

NOTES

1. Susan Veccia, "District Connect: The dark side of the Moon," *MultiMedia Schools, 2,* no. 1, Jan./Feb. 1995, 6.

2. For an introduction to computers for beginners, complete with easy-to-follow color diagrams, read Albert G. Holzinger, "The Right Stuff," *Nation's Business, 82,* no. 4, Apr. 1994, 20–28.

3. For an expanded discussion of this topic, see Odvard Egil Dyrli and Daniel E. Kinnaman, "What Every Teacher Needs to Know About Technology. Part 2: Developing a Technology-Powered Curriculum," *Technology and Learning, 14,* no. 5, Feb. 1995, 46–51.

4. For suitable uses for CAI drill and practice activities, see Odvard Egil Dyrli and Daniel E. Kinnaman, "Tapping the Power of Today's Technology, Part 2: Integrating Technology into your Classroom Curriculum," *Technology and Learning, 14,* no. 5, Feb. 1995, 38–43.

5. Sylvia Charp, "Editorial," *Technological Horizons in Education (T.H.E.), 23,* no. 2, Sept. 1995, 4.

6. To visualize how MBL equipment places the computer in the role of lab partner, see these excellent articles: Larry Frick, "Computers in the Sciences: 'Probing' Temperature and Heat," *The Computing Teacher* (Conference Issue), (1990–91): 14–16, and M. C. Linn, "Computer as Lab Partner," *Teaching Thinking and Problem Solving, 18,* no. 3 (Hillsdale, NJ: Lawrence Erlbaum Associates, 1986).

7. This term and many of the ideas on MBLs can be found in: George E. O'Brien, "Computer-Based Laboratory Learning," *Science and Children, 28,* no. 6, Mar. 1991, 40–41; and Tom Lam, "Probing Micro-computer-Based Laboratories," *Hands-On! 8,* no. 1 (Winter 1984–85):1–7.

8. R. Nachmias and M. C. Linn, "Evaluations of Science Laboratory Data: The Role of Computer Presented Information," *Journal of Research in Science Teaching, 24,* no. 5 (1987): 491–506, and C. L. Price, "Microcomputer Applications in Science," *Journal of Science Education, 1,* no. 2 (1989): 30–33.

9. Greater detail is supplied in these authoritative articles: Gregory Jordahl and Ann Orwig, "Getting Equipped and Staying Equipped, Part 2, Finding the Funds," *Technology and Learning, 15,* no. 7, Apr. 1995, 28–38; "Help Your School Get Money to Spend for New Instructional Technology. Creative Fund-Raising on a Small or Large Scale," in *Curriculum Product News, 28,* no. 8, Apr. 1994, 16–19.

10. Greater specification is given in "Ten Uses of Interactive Videodisc Systems in the Educational Environment," in *T.H.E. Journal* (Spring 1990) 6.

11. For greater specifics see Alan J. McCormack, "The Family Channel," *Science and Children. 28,* no. 2 (October 1990): 24–26.

12. For specifics on LCDs, see "A Look at the Big Picture," *EPIEgram, 16,* no 3 (1988): 10–12.

13. For information on telecommunications for teachers see Odvard Egil Dyrli and Daniel E.

Kinnaman, "What Every Teacher Needs to Know About Technology, Part 5: Connecting Classrooms: School Is More Than a Place," *Technology and Learning, 15,* no. 8, May/June 1995, 82–88., and *The Educator's Guide to the Internet,* (Virginia Space Grant Consortium, 2713-D Magruder Blvd., Hampton VA 23666).

14. To see how this technology is being used in schools today, see Therese Mageau, "Teaching and Learning On-Line," *Electronic Learning, 10,* no. 3, Nov./Dec. 1990, 26–30; Peter H. Lewis, "Plugging into the Network," *The New York Times,* (November 3, 1991) Section 4A, 38–41; John Kenderdine, Mary Ann Hull, and Ronald Sirianni, "Your Computer, My Computer, Let's Network. We're All 'EIES,'" *The Science Teacher,* 55, no. 3, Mar. 1988, 40–42.

15. For more ideas on initiating your computer/multimedia layout see Joan Novelli," "How to Finally Get Comfortable With Your Computer," *Instructor,* October 1994, 68–73.

GUIDED DISCOVERY ACTIVITIES

Using Guided Discovery Activities

Students should learn a disciplined way of asking questions, making investigations, and constructing explanations of a scientific and technological nature. The latter can certainly be developed in a personal/societal context. Students should learn that scientific inquiry is a powerful, but not the only, route to progress in our world. Inquiry should not be taught in isolation but as a tool for finding answers to questions about the world in which students live. In addition, science teachers should very clearly and consistently emphasize students' conceptual development of scientific explanations, as opposed to step-by-step methods that too often characterize the nature of scientific inquiry.[1]

This text contains guided discovery hands-on/minds-on resource activities for science and technology programs in nursery or pre-schools, elementary schools (K–5), and middle or junior high schools (6–8). As mentioned in the opening quotation, these resource activities are intended to assist you in guiding your students to

- learn disciplined approaches to asking questions,
- conduct investigations and construct scientific/technological explanations within a personal/societal context, and
- see science as only one tool for finding answers about their world.

They will be helpful to you in incorporating creative problem-solving skills into your existing science curriculum.

An important advantage of the guided discovery approach is that both teachers and students become more interested in science when the learner is able to participate, on his or her own level, in physical and mental activities similar to those of scientists. This type of participation actively engages students in scientific/technological processes.

All of the science/technology activities included here have been tested by teachers and students in preschools, elementary schools, and middle or junior high schools. The teachers did not have any special preparation or training in science. In fact, science had not been part of their curricula until these activities were introduced into their classrooms. Teachers evaluated each activity; the activities were rewritten to incorporate their suggestions, and then these revised activities were retested.

The prime objective of these activities is to have students, as active participants, discover or self-construct the scientific/technological concepts embedded in the activities. Do not tell your class the purpose of an activity or what can be expected to happen. However, before you go

---

[1]George E. DeBoer and Rodger W. Bybee, "Curriculum perspectives: The Goals of Science Curriculum." In Rodger W. Bybee and John D. McInerney, eds., *Redesigning the Science Curriculum: A Report on the Implications of Standards and Benchmarks for Science Education* (Colorado Springs, CO: Biological Sciences Curriculum Studies, 1995), 73.

into your classroom to present a particular activity, read the lesson plan thoroughly and actually do each step hands-on/minds-on. Pay particular attention to the questions (printed in *italic* type), which are meant as guide questions only. Although these activities have been tested in actual classroom situations, no teacher can be certain that a class will respond "according to plan" throughout an activity, so be flexible in your expectations. Also be aware that you do not have to follow the activities exactly. The ideas presented here are intended only as a resource. You must modify these activities to meet the diverse needs, interests, backgrounds, learning styles, and abilities of your individual class.

These guided discovery activities also need not be taught in the order presented since they are meant as sample activities only. It is best to supplement and integrate guided discovery activities with many other curricular activities. After you have had experience with the sample activities, you will gain competence and confidence in designing your own.

USING DIRECT AND IN'DIRECT TEACHING IN THE ACTIVITIES

Direct teaching is used in every hands-on/minds-on guided discovery activity. When it is appropriate for the teacher to demonstrate an activity step, the **T** symbol is clearly marked in the activity. The teacher also uses expository teaching when presenting concepts and leading discussions with small groups or the whole class. Here are several ways direct instruction may be used:

■ *Connecting to prior knowledge.* In introducing students to an activity, you can relate the new science content to content previously introduced. For example, at the beginning of the "Why Does Water Appear to Disappear?" activity, the teacher could lead a discussion of what students know about evaporation by asking:

Where does the rain in a rain puddle go?

Then, after completing the various activity parts:

When we took observations and recorded that the water level in our uncovered aquarium went down, where did we agree the water went?

Let's review and make a list of what we remember about the experiments we did to find out why wet things take longer to dry on wet days.

■ *Using analogies.* Analogies provide additional ways of assisting students to connect new ideas and relationships with things they already know. You can *tell* students or lead them to discovering the analogies by astute questioning. Examples:

If we think of the earth's history as a 24-hour day, then humans have been in existence only for the last minute of that day.[2]

The human circulatory system is similar to a parcel delivery system: Red blood cells work like trucks, carrying needed materials from a central distribution point for delivery throughout the body. Arteries and veins are like roads, acting as access routes through which the various points of delivery are reached. The heart is like the warehouse or the central point in which vehicles are loaded and dispatched, and to which empty vehicles are returned to be reloaded.[3]

■ *Providing an advance organizer.* You can aid your students in organizing and interrelating ideas in a lesson by providing an advance organizer, which depicts the organizational stratagem for the lesson, including major concepts and ideas and how they are connected to each other. Example:

During the next 2 weeks, we will be discussing animals known as **vertebrates**. *Vertebrates are*

---

[2]W. K. Hartmann, R. Miller, and P. Lee, *Out of the Cradle: Exploring the Frontiers Beyond the Earth* (New York: Workman, 1984).

[3]D. A. Stepich and T. J. Newby, "Analogical Instruction Within the Information Paradigm: Effective Means to Facilitate Learning," *Instructional Science* 17 (1988), 129–144.

*all similar in one very important aspect: They have a **backbone**. We will be talking about five phyla of vertebrates: mammals, birds, reptiles, amphibians, and fish. And we will see how animals in each phyla differ from one another: for example, whether they are warm-blooded or cold-blooded, whether they have hair, scales, or feathers, and whether they lay eggs or bear live young.*[4]

As indicated, direct instruction has a specific but limited role in learning. To help your students with more complex learning, such as applying science concepts and principles, planning science investigations, or problem solving, more indirect instruction strategies are required.

Indirect instruction focuses on students engaging in exploration, inquiry, or discovery—processes that are at the core of each guided discovery hands-on/minds-on activity. Indirect instruction is based on these premises:

- Questions and problems precede answers in the learning process.
- Students must process information mentally to achieve meaningful understanding.
- Students must be actively involved in the learning.

Researchers say indirect instruction has a better chance of success when (1) concepts, patterns, and abstractions are primary goals, (2) higher thinking skills are to be developed, (3) it is essential that students participate to achieve the objectives, (4) problem solving is the main goal, and (5) it is necessary for long-term retention.[5]

---

[4]J. E. Ormrod, *Educational Psychology: Principles and Applications* (Englewood Cliffs, NJ: Merrill/Prentice Hall, 1995), 437.

[5]R. E. Mayer, *Educational Psychology: A Cognitive Approach* (Boston: Little, Brown, 1987); J. A. Shymansky, L. V. Hedges, and G. Woodworth, "A Reassessment of the Effects of Inquiry-Based Science Curricula of the '60s on Student Performance," *Journal of Research in Science Teaching* 27, 127–144.

PLANNING AND ORGANIZING ACTIVITIES

A great deal of thoughtful planning and organization is needed to convert a well-designed activity into an enriching science/technology experience.

The following ideas are guidelines for preparing enriching science experiences for students.

1. Decide what you specifically want your students to learn.

2. Select a teaching/learning technique by which you will introduce, orient, and structure your hands-on/minds-on activity.

3. Decide whether or not you should prepare a data collection sheet for students to use.

4. Work out the details of distribution and collection of science equipment and materials. Generally, it is much safer if students stay at their "laboratory" or activity stations (desks pushed together in a non-laboratory room). Take supplies and materials to the stations rather than having students come up for them. Similarly, have designated students go to individual stations to collect materials at the conclusion of the lab activity. This can be done effectively in a cooperative learning group (CLG) arrangement, and appropriate tasks can be assigned to students for these purposes. Expanded discussion of CLGs follows.

5. Decide whether your students will work individually or in cooperative learning groups. The following symbols will be used in the margin of each guided discovery hands-on/minds-on activity to suggest possible grouping arrangements for you to use at various times during the activity. If more than one symbol appears, choose the arrangement you prefer for your class.

T   Teacher directing discussion or demonstration with total class.

I   Student working individually on a task.

G   Students working in groups of two, three, or four members.

6. Perform the lab activity yourself *before* presenting it to your class to see what is involved, to spot any possible difficulties, and to modify it as necessary to suit your particular class.

COOPERATIVE LEARNING: VITAL TO GUIDED DISCOVERY ACTIVITIES

Cooperative learning plays a vital role in guided discovery hands-on/minds-on activities. Glenn T. Seaborg, the 1951 Nobel Prize winner in chemistry and now the principal investigator for Great Explorations in Math and Science (GEMS), a science curriculum project, reminds us that cooperation is the norm in science.

In the case of all great "discoveries" it must be remembered that science is a group process. When we devise experiments and research today, we do so on the basis of an enormous body of knowledge contributed by people from all over the world over thousands of years. . . . The modern research effort is above all a team effort.[6]

Working cooperatively is important for students also. Children have a special way of communicating with one another that enables them to work well together. Researchers have also found that many students learn more effectively in cooperative learning situations.

Cooperative learning usually refers to students working collaboratively in small groups, considering a problem or assignment together, verbalizing what they know, considering the multiple viewpoints of the group members, taking data together, and coming up with group solutions to problems. This is different from *competitive learning*, where students compete for grades, and from *individualized learning*, where students work alone. Cooperative learning has these features:

- Group members are assigned roles (for example, principal investigator, recorder, materials manager, or reporter).
- There is face-to-face interaction among students.
- Students are responsible for their own learning as well as for that of their teammates.
- Teachers help students develop interpersonal small-group skills.
- Teachers interact with the groups as needed.

What are the advantages of having students work in cooperative groups?

Advantages of Cooperative Learning Groups

In the 1960s, Martha Piper developed a cooperative learning group (CLG) model to assist teachers in effectively guiding hands-on/minds-on science activities.[7] She and others (Roger and David Johnson, Robert Jones, and the Biological Science Curriculum Study Group) then built on the original and developed variations that are widely used today.[8]

But what is a CLG model? Basically, a CLG model consists of classroom group techniques for facilitating and guiding hands-on/minds-on science activities. CLGs are especially useful in classrooms where science materials and equipment are limited, cooperative group

---

[6]Glenn T. Seaborg, "Some Thoughts on Discovery," *GEMS Network News* (Lawrence Hall of Science, University of California, Fall/Winter 1991), 5.

[7]Martha K. Piper, "A Science Activity Teaching Plan," *School Science and Mathematics* 80, no. 5 (1980) 390–406.

[8]The author acknowledges these comprehensive descriptions of CLG models and highly recommends you read: David A. Dockterman, *Cooperative Learning and Technology* (Watertown, MA: Tom Snyder Productions, Inc., 1994); Roger T. Johnson, David W. Johnson, and Edythe Johnson Holubec, *Structuring Cooperative Learning: Lesson Plans for Teachers* (Edina, MN: Interaction Book Co., 1987); Robert M. Jones, *Teaming Up! The Inquiry Task Group Management System User's Guide* (LaPorte, TX: ITGROUP, December 1990); *Science for Life and Living: Integrating Science, Technology, and Health: Sneak Preview* (Colorado Springs, CO: Biological Sciences Curriculum Study, 1990); and any edition of *Cooperative Learning* (The Magazine for Cooperation in Education), 136 Liberty Street, Santa Cruz, CA 95060.

processes and skill development are desired, and an orderly and controlled classroom system is necessary.

CLGs offer hands-on/minds-on science teachers many advantages, among which are the following:

1. They very effectively promote problem solving and divergent thinking and can produce greater achievement in many subject areas and in a wide age range.[9]
2. They provide for group sharing of limited science equipment and supplies.
3. There is *positive interdependence*—that is, students concern themselves with the performance and learning of all team members, making students more positive toward their school, teachers, subject areas, and each other (regardless of abilities, special needs, or culturally diverse backgrounds).
4. Students have a vested interest in each other's success, so all students tend to be more successful, creating positive and realistic student expectations about working with each other.
5. Success builds success, and this improves self-confidence.
6. Students develop both cognitive and group participation skills.
7. The teacher is assisted in classroom management by students who
   a. manage science materials,
   b. take responsibility for helping team members with assignments and problems, and
   c. alleviate some teacher stress by maintaining order and keeping students working.
8. Teachers can use CLGs outdoors as well as in classrooms.
9. Students become more positive about contributing in groups.
10. Cooperative learning is fun—students like to work in CLGs.

[9]Robert M. Jones and John E. Steinbrink, "Home Teams: Cooperative Learning in Elementary Science," *School Science and Mathematics* 91, no. 4 (April 1991), 139–143.

To make full use of these advantages, you must learn how to set up CLGs, assign roles to student members, and guide the teams in their activities.

Setting Up CLG Teams

Initially, you should assign students to a team, because they tend to gravitate to friends only. For primary grade students, or older students who have not worked previously in CLGs, it is best to start with two students. As students acquire basic cooperative group skills, combine two groups of two as a working team. Generally, CLG teams of three to five are recommended for hands-on/minds-on science activities. Include both girls and boys with a variety of abilities and cultural diversity. Keep teams together for at least three to six weeks so teammates have time to learn to work with each other. As a team builder, let each team choose its own name. Then, change team membership, so students get to work with other classmates.

Develop a procedure for fairly rotating jobs and post it prominently so all students can see it. *Wherever possible,* all students should have experiences in all CLG jobs to develop the skills involved. What are CLG jobs?

CLG Job Functions and Assignments

A specific job is assigned to each CLG team member. The names and functions are quite similar in all CLGs. The following are from Robert Jones's Inquiry Task Group Management System (ITGMS):[10]

- *Principal Investigator.* In charge of all team operations (that is, checking assignments, communicating activity directions, asking teacher informational questions, assisting group members, conducting group discussions about activity results, and either directing activity or assigning it to other team members).

[10]For a fuller explanation of the CLG job assignments and functions, see Robert M. Jones, *Teaming Up!,* 10–12.

- *Materials Manager.* Gets and distributes materials to each team, sets up and operates any activity equipment, and is usually the only student moving around the room without special permission during an activity.
- *Recorder/Reporter.* Collects, records, and certifies data on team work or lab sheets, reports results to total class orally or in writing on Class Summary Chart posted on chalkboard.
- *Maintenance Director.* Is responsible (with team members he assigns) for clean-up and return of materials and equipment, directs used materials disposal, and is responsible for team members' safety.
- *Technical Advisor.* Moves to teams having difficulties and assists; may prepare activity materials for teacher or inspect equipment. This is a special role for dependable students who work quickly and accurately.

- *Observer* (teacher's administrative assistant.) May use form to record and share team problems.

CLG Job Badges. To supply easy identification of team members' jobs and responsibilities, students should wear **job badges.** These badges might look like those illustrated, which are used by the ITGMS.

Badges help both teachers and team members keep track of job responsibilities and resolve conflict. They also help team members remember what they are supposed to do. If teachers spot a difficulty (or impending problem), they can refer to a team member's badge to guide the person to proper action. This technique provides very positive and effective behavior management.

You can make up badges or allow students to design and make their own. Try to include

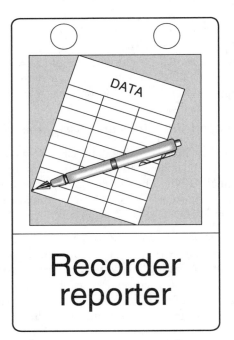

Cooperative Learning Group (CLG) job badge

Cooperative job description card

Source: Reprinted by permission from Robert M. Jones, *Teaming Up! The Inquiry Task Group Management System User's Guide,* LaPorte, TX: ITGROUP, December 1990, 55.

Source: Reprinted by permission from Robert M. Jones, *Teaming Up! The Inquiry Task Group Management System User's Guide,* LaPorte, TX: ITGROUP, December 1990, 43.

pictures for easy job identification, laminate for durability and strength, and punch holes for stringing around the neck. Encourage CLG team members to refer to job descriptions and badge pictures to resolve disputes regarding who does what.

CLG Job Description Cards. Job description cards may be left at each science activity station for students to use while performing their assigned part of the activity. Users have found it is best to write direct "you" statements on each card. The cards spell out—with words or pictures—the job responsibilities and limits. The illustration is a sample of an ITGMS job description card for one member of a four-member team.

Job description cards should be modified according to team size (two, three, four, or five members), students' ages, maturation, learning levels and styles, and any other variables that affect their usage. Often, teachers color code CLG job description cards according to job description.

Using CLGs in the Classroom

So how do you get started using CLGs in your classroom? Although each classroom situation is unique, several CLG models adhere to the following prototype developed by Martha Piper. Initially, you should follow the specific sequence given here, but with time you'll be able to modify the sequence and the steps themselves as you and your students gain experience and confidence with CLG techniques.[11]

Step 1: Introduction. The teacher introduces the hands-on/minds-on guided discovery activity to the whole class by completing these tasks before a small group begins work:

- Arrange (or rearrange) furniture to facilitate hands-on/minds-on activities and to avoid

CLG classroom furniture arrangement

excessive noise, movement, or confusion. Consider the furniture configuration in the illustration.

- Write the activity objective on chalkboard or chart.
- Introduce or review pertinent activity information, safety precautions, vocabulary, and such CLG skills as

   When we begin, move quietly and quickly into your team.

   Stay with your team at all times.

   Speak softly when working and take turns.

   Do only your assigned job.

- Solicit and answer all students' questions now.

Step 2: Distribution of Science Materials. Do not begin distributing materials until all Step 1 items are completed. Then, have the Materials Manager collect science materials from the central materials station and deliver to each team station. *Note: This step can make or break the best planned activity. Make certain that Materials Managers are reliable and know the specifics of their jobs!*

Step 3: Team Investigation. Principal Investigators in each team review directions with team members so that they all understand the procedures to be used. Materials Managers direct

---

[11] A good source for specifics on using CLGs is Scott B. Watson, "Cooperative Methods," *Science and Children* 29, no. 5 (February 1992), 30–31.

materials setup, while the teacher moves from team to team to ensure proper use of materials and to monitor procedures, safety, and results. Principal Investigators may signal the teacher if assistance is needed. Recorders/Reporters collect data on data sheets, check with other team results, and post results on the Class Summary Chart.

Step 4: Discussion of Activity Results. The teacher conducts a discussion of the results posted on the Class Summary Chart, clarifies concepts and skills, discusses the similarities and discrepancies of team data, and may assign follow-up activities involving readings, duplicated worksheets, and other individualized reinforcements.

Step 5: Team Clean-Up. Maintenance Directors (and any assigned team members) make sure work areas are clean, inspect all materials and equipment, and return supplies to designated areas. *Note:* This should be a team effort; the Maintenance Director is not the custodian for the group.

Step 6: Team Member Assessment. The teacher (cooperatively with students) uses a variety of devices to assess team members' demonstrated mastery of CLG processes and skills objectives.

CLGs are valuable techniques for hands-on/minds-on science programs with possibilities for *all* elementary and middle school subject areas. For an excellent step-by-step account of how to set up and use cooperative learning groups in your classroom, read Robert M. Jones, *Teaming Up! The Inquiry Task Group Management System User's Guide* (LaPorte, TX: ITGROUP, December 1990).

ACTIVITY PREPARATION AND SAFETY

1. Make certain you have the necessary science equipment and supplies in sufficient amounts to allow all your students to participate in the lab activity. Whenever possible, have work stations already set up with science materials and equip-

ment before students come into the room or to the work stations.

2. Perform initial steps like boiling water, heating or cooling materials, and double checking supplies *before* an activity begins.

3. If any chemicals are used, even diluted vinegar, make sure washing materials are available for students to use immediately following the activity.

4. Whenever possible, substitute plastics for all glassware. However, be certain when using heat that the plastics are able to withstand the temperatures. Whenever students use plastic bags, make sure the bags are too small to fit over their heads.

5. If an open flame is to be used, have a fire extinguisher available and give specific instruction on its proper use. Review fire safety techniques such as dropping and rolling on the ground if clothing catches fire. Often, it is best for *teachers* to be responsible for using the open flame.

6. Be aware that many elementary schools do not allow the use of open flames, or they limit their use to teacher-conducted activities only. Check your school's policy before using open flames.

7. Avoid completely the use of electrical house current (110 volts) for student activities. Instead, use dry cells when students are handling electrical equipment directly.

8. Assemble glass tubing and stoppers yourself, before class, but try to substitute plastic tubing whenever possible. It is convenient to store the assembled stoppers and tubing for later use, rather than disassembling and reassembling them for each activity. (See the following section for suggestions on using tubing and stoppers.)

CONDUCTING ACTIVITIES AND GUIDING STUDENTS

Carefully planned hands-on/minds-on science/technology activities may end in chaos and frustration on your part and your students' unless the activities are carefully conducted as well. The following are some suggestions to help your activities run smoothly.

1. Help your students see the purpose of the activity.

2. Check to see that all your students understand the procedures to be followed. Write the steps on the chalkboard and/or have students refer to their hands-on/minds-on data collection sheets. If you use CLGs, go over procedures and cooperative job assignments with individual students.

3. Introduce safety precautions *before* students begin any work. Here are some general safety precautions:

   a. Familiarize yourself with federal, state, and local school safety regulations, especially your own school district's policies.

   b. Stress the serious nature of lab work by being a role model who practices safe behavior and uses necessary protective equipment, such as safety goggles.

   c. Instruct students to report all accidents, regardless of how slight, to you and the CLG leader immediately.

   d. Make sure that directions for using chemicals and heat sources are followed *exactly.* If students are not certain about a procedure, they should ask you or the appropriate cooperative group leader.

   e. Instruct students always to cut materials away from them, being careful to stay far enough away from other students to avoid cutting them. You may want to pre-cut materials for those students you judge unable to safely do it themselves.

   f. Do not allow students to insert glass tubing into stoppers. Substitute plastic tubing whenever possible. If you must insert glass tubing or thermometers into stoppers, be sure to follow these safety precautions:

     (1) Use only glass tubing that is fire polished at both ends.

     (2) With glycerine, liberally lubricate the end of the tubing to be inserted in the stopper as well as the stopper hole.

     (3) Wrap a cloth around your hand to give greater protection in case the tubing should snap.

     (4) Start twisting the tubing into the stopper. Hold the tubing close to the end being inserted. This reduces chances of snapping off tubing.

   g. Avoid using strong acids. Whenever possible, use substitutes such as vinegar. If acids come in contact with skin, flush the area liberally with water, use a baking soda solution to counteract the acid or vinegar, and take the student to a nurse or doctor.

   h. Caution students not to smell or taste *anything* unless they know exactly what it is and have been informed by you that it is safe. Tell them to read all labels carefully.

   i. Make provisions for all broken glass, excess chemicals, and other waste materials to be placed in proper containers. Avoid pouring chemicals into sinks.

   j. Check to see that there is adequate ventilation in the room.

   k. When heating a solution in a test tube, always point the test tube away from any individuals.

   l. Tell students never to mix chemicals unless they are specifically instructed to do so. Have students wash their hands and nails immediately after each activity.

m. Keep all aisles clear and wipe all spills immediately so the floors do not get slippery.

n. Purchase only safety goggles marked "Z87" on their faces, since they meet the standards set by the American National Standards Institute. Demonstrate the proper way to wear and sanitize goggles when students use sharp objects (knives), chemicals (vinegar), or materials that could fly into their faces (rubber bands).

o. Constantly be alert to any student allergies or sensitivities to foods, plants, chemicals, or other substances used in the activities.

p. Remind students never to put any objects in their mouths; be alert to the choking hazards of pennies, paper clips, marbles, and other small objects.

See Appendix J for additional information on safety during hands-on/minds-on activities.

4. During hands-on/minds-on activities, supervise students at all times! Move about the room throughout the activity to help, answer questions, spot and prevent possible discipline problems, and guide or demonstrate anything that is needed.

5. Always build in sufficient time at the conclusion of each activity for students to clean up and put materials and equipment in their assigned places.

6. Hold a discussion at the conclusion of every activity. Review what was learned and apply students' findings toward tentative conclusions or toward further study. Develop key concepts through artful questioning. Once these concepts are developed, identify them by name. For example, if students engage in an activity where they observe a chameleon eating crickets, tell students that animals that eat other animals are called *predators* and those that are eaten are called *prey*.

HOW ACTIVITIES ARE ORGANIZED

It would be impossible to design specific science activities that would be useful for all elementary and middle school teachers in extremely varied teaching/learning environments. Therefore, the following guided discovery science/technology activities are presented to you as possible resources only. As resources, they are ready for use or to be drawn upon and modified for your particular classroom teaching/learning needs. They are not intended to be a science curriculum. Grade levels are given in a range, since it is impossible to say categorically, "This is a first grade activity," and because different teachers may use all or part of the activity as presented. Only you can determine which activity will fill your teaching needs. To assist you in making these decisions, guided discovery resource activities are organized in the following way.

Sections 1, 2, and 3

1. Activities in the first three sections are arranged in three general science/technology groups:
   - Physical Sciences and Technology (Section 1)
   - Life Sciences and Technology (Section 2)

- Earth, Ecology, and Environmental Sciences and Technology (Section 3)
2. Within the three general science/technology groups, activities are clustered around subgroups. For example, under physical sciences, the subgroups include Matter and Energy, Thermal Energy, and Air Pressure.
3. Activities are arranged within subgroups by grade levels (i.e., K–2, 3–5, 6–8).
4. Each activity is identified by a question, such as "What Are Water Molecules, and How Do They Affect Each Other?"
5. Each subgroup of science/technology activities begins with several loosely structured Quickie Starters, followed by the more structured guided discovery activities.

In summary, then, throughout Sections 1, 2, and 3, you will follow an overall outline using the following format:

- General science/technology group
- Science/technology subgroup
- Quickie Starters
- Guided discovery activities with suggested grade levels

Sections 4 and 5

Although the activities in Sections 1–3 may be modified for students of varying abilities and to accommodate many teaching styles, those in Sections 4 and 5 are specifically designed as follows:

- Section 4 contains activities for students with special needs, including those with visual impairments, developmental delays, visual perception problems, emotional disabilities, and hearing impairments. The activities are grouped according to the category of disability and, within each category, by grade level.
- For teachers who follow or would like to incorporate a developmental-learning approach in their classrooms, Section 5 groups activities according to Piagetian operations (such as classification, conservation, etc.) and gives suggestions on how to involve students in these processes. The Piagetian operation at work in the activity is identified in the activity title, and an age range, rather than grade-level range, is suggested for each activity.

Like the Quickie Starters, these guided discovery science activities are loosely structured to provide teachers with the flexibility to modify each activity for individual students or groups of students.

GUIDED DISCOVERY HANDS-ON/MINDS-ON ACTIVITIES FORMAT

Each guided discovery lesson plan in Sections 1–3 includes most or all of nine major parts:

1. Problem to be solved
2. Recommended grade level(s)
3. Concepts: *What Concepts Might Students Discover?*
4. Materials: *What Will We Need?*
5. Discussion questions: *What Do Students Know?*
6. Activity steps: *What Will Students Do?*
7. Scientific/technological processes
8. Teacher knowledge: *What Must I Know?*
9. Student application: *How Will Students Use or Apply What They Discover?*

Some of these lesson plan parts, which are described in the following sections, contain information to be used by you, and some contain information to be used by your students. Some parts will be used with the total class, in small cooperative learning groups, or by individual students. Which ones are to be used, when, and how must be determined by you, the teacher. Some teachers—mostly in the upper elementary or middle/junior high school grades—who use the guided discovery activities have duplicated the following parts of the lesson plan for students to use on "lab" or data collection sheets:

- Problem to be solved
- Activity steps: *What Will Students Do?*
- Scientific/technological processes
- Student application: *How Will Students Use or Apply What They Discover?*

If you wish to prepare such data collection sheets, you have permission to reproduce those parts of the guided discovery lesson plans that your students can use directly in your classroom. (*Caution:* The text may not be further distributed or sold.) The other parts of the lesson plans will be useful for your own background. In using discovery activities with students who do not read well, you can read the appropriate sections aloud. Some teachers have found it useful to record the directions on cassette audiotapes for students to use by themselves.

The most important element in these discovery activities is that students can discover and construct their own concepts through actual physical and mental participation in the activities. Do not tell the students beforehand what they should expect to find. This robs them of the joy of discovery.

Here are more details of the guided discovery hands-on/minds-on resource activities format.

Problem to Be Solved. The problem of each guided discovery activity is stated as a divergent question or questions, such as, "What Causes the Seasons?" This helps you quickly select the specific area within one of the three sciences to present to your class.

Recommended Grade Level(s). To help you easily select guided discovery activities that are most appropriate for your group, the activities are organized by grade-level ranges and groups:

- Primary or lower elementary grades (kindergarten to second grade).
- Upper elementary grades (third to fifth grades).
- Middle or junior high school (sixth to eighth grades).

Grade levels are usually written as ranges because many of the guided discovery activities have been tested and found to work reasonably well in several grades. The difficulty level depends on how deeply you want to probe and the level at which your students are working. Some activity lessons have more than one part, and the age levels may differ for parts that are more advanced or complex. Therefore, for instance, Part I may be appropriate for K–2, Part II for 3–5, and Part III for 6–8. One way to determine on which level you should start is to determine your students' prior knowledge and misconceptions. The lesson section "What Do Students Know?" contains sample questions to help you make this determination.

Remember that grade-level ranges are guidelines only. Because of the uniqueness of each class, only you can judge the suitability of any particular guided discovery activity and how it has to be modified to fit your class.

Concepts: What Concepts Might Students Discover? This portion of the lesson identifies the scientific principles and concepts students might discover in doing the guided discovery activities. The list of concepts is not exhaustive, and others may be discovered by your students as a result of their backgrounds, your skill in guiding them, and other factors. Scientific/technological content presented under this heading can also supply information for you to strengthen your own science content background. A general list of scientific/technological content is also presented at the beginning of each of the science areas: physical, life, and earth and environmental science.

Materials: What Will We Need? The science supplies and equipment needed to perform the guided discovery activities are noted. Whenever possible, easily obtainable and nontechnical materials are suggested. For instance, instead of using a beaker (costly) for a nonheating activity, a plastic tumbler may be suggested, or a Pyrex baby nursing bottle may be suggested for a beaker that will be heated. Materials easily found in the immediate environment are stressed for two reasons:

- Most elementary schools do not have extensive science supplies or money to purchase them.
- It is important for students to see that the activities can be done with things easily available; it is hoped that the students will replicate the activities at home. However, please make it very clear that students should *never* use open flame or dangerous or unknown substances without adult supervision!

Enlist your students' help in getting supplies and items needed for your guided discovery activities from their homes or environment. In addition to saving you time, it will provide for greater involvement of the students in their guided discovery science activity. Often a note sent home to parents telling them what will be studied and needed brings excellent results.

Discussion Questions: What Do Students Know? Suggested discussion questions are given for you to ask *before* your students start the guided discovery activities. The purpose of this part of the lesson is to motivate students and set the learning environment. It also helps *you* discover your students' misconceptions about the scientific/technological concepts to be explored so that you can provide the best possible learning activity.

Three types of questions that occur within this part of the lesson, as well as within the activity steps and application parts, are vital in helping your students have real experiences in working and thinking like scientists:

- *How Might We Find Out?* This type of question guides students to design their own investigations to discover answers to their questions.
- *What Do You Think Will Happen?* This type of question asks students to hypothesize—make educated guesses—and predict *before* starting their investigations. You and/or your students should record these hypotheses for comparison with actual results.

- *How Did Your Hypotheses/Predictions and Findings Compare?* In comparing what was predicted and what happened, students get a chance to hone their scientific problem-solving and higher thinking skills.

Activity Steps: What Will Students Do? This question refers to the guided discovery activities or investigations the students actively participate in, leading to their discovery of the concepts and principles listed under "What Concepts Might Students Discover or Construct?"

As mentioned earlier, the letters *T, I,* and *G* appear in the margin next to relevant parts of an activity procedure to indicate whether it is a teacher, individual, or group task.

Scientific/Technological Processes. Scientific processes listed in italic type at the left of each lesson show you the types of mental operations your students will be required to perform in each part of the guided discovery lesson. Hypothesizing, inferring, and comparing are just a few of the scientific processes students will be practicing.

What Must I Know? Along with suggestions for guiding students in their discoveries, this part of the lesson gives you the information you must know to make the discoveries as meaningful as possible. This information includes

- *teaching tips* explaining more complicated or involved parts of the guided discovery activity,
- *science content* (facts, concepts, principles, or theories) relevant to the guided discovery activity, and
- *variables* in the guided discovery activity that can affect its outcome.

In addition to reviewing this information, you should become as knowledgeable as possible about the science/technology content, so that you can respond to your students' questions and guide them in finding answers, but not necessarily "lecture" them on the content. Science/technology content is also presented in "What Concepts Might Students Discover or Construct?" You should supplement the information in this textbook with science/technology content in your classroom science textbook, children's trade books, and libraries. To assist you, this text lists several children's and/or adult science books at the end of the activities in each science/technology topic area.

Student Application: How Will Students Use or Apply What They Discover? Open-ended questions in this last part of each lesson plan suggest to students additional investigations they might do to apply the concepts they have discovered to everyday situations; for example, "On a cold day, why do you feel warm in the sunlight but very cold in the shade?" You should encourage interested students to attempt to answer these questions by asking them. "How Might You Find Out?". Many of the activities suggested by these questions can be done at home and need not take additional class time. These open-ended questions will also help children probe the *values* level of science as well as integrate other curricular subjects such as mathematics, social studies, and language arts.

FORMAT OF THE LESS-STRUCTURED GUIDED DISCOVERY ACTIVITIES

In addition to the detailed guided discovery hands-on/minds-on activities just described, teachers may choose from a variety of less-structured activities.

The Quickie Starters in Sections 1–3 can be used in preschools, primary grades, open classrooms, and other classes to provide enrichment and encourage enjoyment of science.

The activities for special needs students (Section 4) and the Piagetian-guided activities (Section 5) are also less structured.

The Quickie Starters: Open-Ended Activities are meant as simple sample activities that

■ can assist you in discovering students' naive science concepts or misconceptions,
■ can be done informally with minimum planning and materials,
■ motivate and stimulate ideas that can lead to deeper investigations into a problem,
■ give students science/technology enrichment opportunities,
■ provide fun and success in science and technology,
■ supply enthusiasm for "doing more science," and
■ offer a wide range of opportunities for individualizing science/technology for your students.

The less-structured activities contain fewer lesson plan details than do the guided discovery activities in Sections 1–3, and many use this simple format:

■ Materials
■ Opening Questions: *What Do Students Know?*
■ Some Possible Activities

You may want to develop more detailed lesson plans for these less-structured activities using the guided discovery hands-on/minds-on activity format. In doing so, explore other creative ways of using the Quickie Starters, or where appropriate, use guided discovery science activities in the less-structured format.

As with guided discovery science activities, the less-structured activities also start with opening questions to elicit students' interest and motivation in the activity. Less-structured activities are more open-ended, and students are freer to wander and explore. For these reasons, the Quickie Starters are presented before the more structured guided discovery activities, so you may use them as motivators and introductions to the more structured scientific investigations.

Physical Sciences and Technology

Physical, life, and earth and space science express the primary subject matter of science. Science subject matter focuses on those science concepts, principles, and theories that are fundamental for all students to know and be able to use . . . .

As a result of activities in grades K–4, all students should develop an understanding of:

- properties of objects and material,
- position and motion of objects, and
- forms of energy, heat, light, electricity and magnetism.

As a result of activities in grades 5–8, all students should develop an understanding of:

- properties of matter,
- particulate model of matter,
- motions and changes in motions, and
- transformations of energy. (p. 9)[1]

MATTER AND ENERGY

QUICKIE STARTERS: OPEN-ENDED ACTIVITIES

Where Did the Water Go? (K–2)

Materials

Sponges, paintbrushes, dish cloths (This activity should be done on a sunny day, outside the classroom.)

What Do
Students Know?

What will happen to water if you brush it on different things outside?
How can you find out?
From where do you think the water will disappear first? Why?

---

[1]Reprinted with permission from National Science Standards. Copyright 1995 by the National Academy of Sciences. Courtesy of the National Academy Press, Washington, DC.

Some Possible
Activities

Invite students to take a paintbrush, dip it in water, and brush it over several places to see what happens. Have them play a game to see whose water disappears first. Have students feel the places from which the water disappeared rapidly and compare them with places from which the water did not seem to disappear as fast. For example, students could compare the feel of sidewalks in the sun and sidewalks in the shade. Have students repeat the activity, but this time have them use sponges and washcloths instead of brushes. Have them place wet sponges or cloths on different places and determine which ones dry first.

How Can We Dry Clothes Faster? (K–2)

Materials

Paper towels, different pieces of cloth (some that are thin and some that are thick like a towel), sponges, twine, clothespins

What Do Students
Know?

How can we make these things wet?
How can we dry them?
How can we use the twine and clothespins to help them dry?
Where is the best place to put the clothesline? Why?
Which things do you think will dry first?

Some Possible
Activities

I

Have students make a clothesline; then have students dip the various cloths and sponges in water, drain them, and place them on the clothesline with clothespins.

Why Does Water Roll Off Some Things? (K–5)

Materials

Waxed paper, paper towels, napkins, typing paper, plastic wrap, eye droppers, food coloring

What Do Students
Know?

What might happen if you dropped droplets of water on these different kinds of paper and plastic?
How can you find out?
What kind of paper will hold the water the best?
What kinds of paper or plastic will water run off of the easiest?

Some Possible
Activities

G

Have students discover which materials soak up (**absorb**) water the best and which absorb the least. Which materials do not absorb, or **repel,** water droplets? Use red and blue food coloring to make different colored water drops. Have students use the eye droppers to place one red drop and several blue drops of water, at a distance from each other, on wax paper or plastic wrap. Challenge students to maneuver the paper or plastic to try to capture all the blue drops, one at a time, with the red drop.

Paper napkin   Waxed paper   Plastic wrap

Have students play Water Droplet Race. Show them how to make drop slides of the same lengths and inclinations, as shown in the art. Students can vary the material they use for each slide. Have three students compete with each other to see on which slides the drops move down the fastest.

Paper napkin   Waxed paper   Plastic wrap

Applications to Everyday Life	*How might you use the previous information in choosing your clothes for rainy days? For hot days?*

GUIDED DISCOVERY HANDS-ON/MINDS-ON ACTIVITIES

Why Does Water Appear to Disappear? (K–8)

What Concepts Might Students Discover?	A liquid appears to disappear when it changes to an invisible gas when heated. The term to describe this process is **evaporation.**
What Will We Need?	An aquarium, paint jars, and various containers, each filled with water Measuring cup Meter- or yardstick and/or a wire coat hanger Paper clips 3" × 3" × 1" sponge Masking tape and/or marking pens
What Do Students Know?	*Where does the rain in a rain puddle go?* *Why do wet things take longer to dry on wet days?* *How can we measure how much water a sponge holds?* *What are some ways to speed up how fast wet objects dry?*

PROCESSES[2]

Part I (K–2)

What Will Students Do?

G

Measuring

1. Using masking tape or marking pens, mark the beginning water levels of some uncovered water containers, such as an aquarium, a paint jar, a water jar used for plant cuttings, etc.

Observing
Measuring

2. Check the water levels each morning and, using a measuring cup, add enough water to the containers to bring the water levels back up to the original water level marks you made.

[2] *Note:* Processes in all hands-on/minds-on guided discovery activities are identified in italic type in the left-hand column.

Recording   3. Keep a record of how much water was added to your containers each week.

Hypothesizing   *Where did the water go?*
      What caused the water level to change?

Part II (3–8)

What Will Students Do?   1. Using the meterstick or yardstick, wire coat hanger, and paper clips, build either of the balances shown.

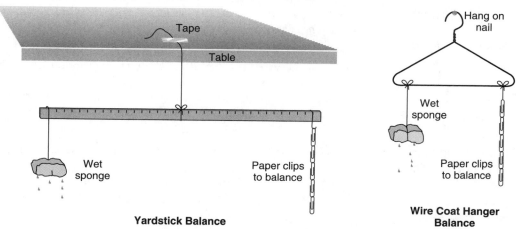

Yardstick Balance

Wire Coat Hanger Balance

2. Soak your piece of sponge until it is dripping water, then hang it with an S-shaped paper clip or string to one end of your balance. Add paper clips to the other end until the balance is level.

Measuring   *How many clips did it take?*

Graph of Evaporation Data

Observing
Hypothesizing

3. Every 15 minutes, check to see if the balance is level.
   What do you see happening after several observations?
   Why do you think the paper clip end of the balance is lower?
   Keep a written record of what happens.

4. At each 15-minute observation, take off and record how many paper clips must be removed to keep the balance level.

Graphing

5. When the sponge is dry, take your written observations and plot a line graph with the data. Set up your graph like the one on page A–21.

Hypothesizing

What are some variables that might affect how quickly the water in the sponge evaporates?

Designing an Investigation

How could you set up an experiment to test these variables?

What Must I Know?

Some of the variables that affect the rate of evaporation are type of liquid, evaporation temperature of the liquid, air temperature, wind velocity, relative humidity, and so on. Guide students in gathering data and in recording and graphing the results in the same way as was done in this activity.

How Will Students Use or Apply What They Discover?

1. *Why does water evaporate faster from your hands when you vigorously rub them together?*
2. *Why does your hair dry faster on a dry day than on a wet one?*
3. *Why will a wet towel dry faster if it is spread out rather than crumpled in a ball?*

What Are Water Molecules, and How Do They Affect Each Other?
(K–8)

What Concepts Might Students Discover?

The deeper the water, the greater the pressure.
A **force** is defined as a push or pull on an object.
Molecules of the same substance tend to "stick to" each other because they are attracted by an invisible force.
Each molecule of the substance pulls other atoms to it.
The force of attraction between molecules of the same kind is called **cohesive force.**
Water has cohesive force.

What Will We Need?

12-inch squares of waxed paper	Pan or bowl
Medicine dropper	Ruler
Water (enough to fill containers as desired)	Pennies, paper clips, or marbles
	Two 1-gallon plastic milk jugs
Pencil or nail	Masking tape
Glass or plastic tumbler	Large basin or tub

What Do Students Know?

Why does a drop of water hold together as it runs down a windowpane?
Why are beads of water hemispherical, especially on a well-waxed automobile?
Why can some bugs walk on the top of water?
Why do you think drops of water from a medicine dropper are hemispherical while falling through the air?

PROCESSES

What Will Students Do?

Observing

Part I (K–2)

1. Obtain a 12-inch square of waxed paper. Using a medicine dropper, place three or four drops of clean tap water on your waxed paper.
   How would you describe the shape of the water droplets?
   What is their color?

Observing

2. Push the drops of water around with a pencil point.
   What happens to the water when you push the pencil point into a water droplet?

Observing
Hypothesizing

   What happens when you push several droplets near each other?
   Why do you think this happens?

Part II (K–2)

What Will Students Do?

Hypothesizing
Designing an Investigation

1. Obtain a glass or plastic tumbler and place it in a bowl or pan. Fill the tumbler completely full of water, until some water overflows.
   Do you think you can add any more water to the tumbler?
   Can you think of how you might test your hypothesis or guess what will happen?

2. Test your hypothesis or try this test. Holding a medicine dropper no more than ½ inch above the water level of the glass, slowly drop water into the tumbler. (See diagram.)

Measuring

How many drops of water can you add until the water runs over the rim of the tumbler?

Observing	*How would you describe the shape of the water above the rim of the tumbler? (Hint: Bend down so that you are on eye-level with the rim of the tumbler.)*
Inferring	*Why does the water rise above the rim of the tumbler?*
Observing	*At what point does the water run over the rim of the tumbler?*
Inferring	*Why do you think the water finally runs over the rim of the tumbler?*
Hypothesizing	*What do you think would happen if you added these things to the glass of water instead of water drops: pennies, paper clips, or marbles? Try it.*

Part III (3–5)

Hypothesizing	*If the side of a plastic milk jug were punctured with very small holes (one above another) and the jug were then filled with water, what do you think would happen to the water?*
	How would the water pour out of the holes?

What Will Students Do?

1. Obtain a clean 1-gallon milk jug.
2. About 1½ inch or 4 centimeters from the bottom of the milk jug, puncture a *very small hole* with a pencil or nail. Puncture three additional small holes ½ inch apart, vertically, above the first hole. Put masking tape over the holes. *Caution:* Do not make the holes too large.
3. Fill the container half full with water. Hold the plastic jug over a sink, large basin, or tub and remove the masking tape as shown.

Observing	*What do you notice about the way the water comes out of the holes?*
Inferring	*Why do you think the water comes out of the holes like this?*
Hypothesizing	*If the jug were filled closer to the top with water, do you think there would be a difference in the way the water comes out?*

4. Tape over the holes, refill the jug until the water is within an inch of the top, and remove the tape.

Observing	*What do you notice about the way the water comes out of the holes?*
Comparing	*What difference did you notice in the way the water came from the holes of the jug when there was less water and when there was more water in it?*
Inferring	*What can you say about how water pressure varies with depth?*

Hypothesizing   *What results do you think you would get if you used a quart, half-gallon, or 2-gallon container?* Try it and record your findings.

Part IV (3–5)

1. About 2 centimeters or ½ inch apart as shown in the diagram, puncture 4 very small holes in a horizontal line about ½ inch from the bottom of the second 1-gallon plastic jug. Put masking tape over the holes. *Caution:* Do not make the holes too large. Also make the holes very close together.

Hypothesizing   *What do you think will happen when water is poured into this container and the masking tape is removed?*

Hypothesizing   *How many jets of water will you get coming out of the holes in the bottom of the plastic jug?*

2. Hold the jug over a sink or large tub, pour water into the jug, and remove the tape.

Observing   *How many jets of water come out?*

Designing an Investigation   *What could you do to the water pouring out of the bottom of the jug, without plugging any holes, to get only one jet of water?*

3. Test your hypothesis.
4. Try this activity using quart or half-gallon milk cartons.

What Must I Know?

Students should pour water into the plastic jug and pinch the jets of water together with their fingers just as though they were going to pinch someone. The jets will form one stream. If the water comes out in one jet, there must be some kind of force holding the water together. The force that holds similar molecules to each other is called **cohesive force.** Each molecule of water has cohesive force that pulls and holds other molecules of water to it. The diagram represents how molecules of water are held together to form a water droplet due to cohesive force. The pinching of the water brings the jets of water in contact, allowing cohesive force to hold them together. This is true because the cohesive force between two substances increases as the distance between them decreases.

Water molecules held together by <u>cohesive</u> forces

How Will Students Use or Apply What They Discover?

1. *Why do you think a dam is built with very thick walls at the bottom and thinner walls at the top?*
2. *Why do your ears sometimes hurt when you dive deep into a swimming pool? What pushes in on your ears as you go deeper?*
3. *Why are the walls of a submarine so thick and strong?*
4. *What would happen to water escaping from two holes of a can if you plugged one hole?*

5. *What will happen to the water coming out of the bottom hole of the can as the water level gets lower in the can?*

6. *Why do many towns have water storage tanks towering high above the city or built on a hill?*

Reference Books—Water
Teacher: Water Matters, Vol. 1, *Water Resources Guide and Poster Set* (Arlington, VA: National Science Teachers Association, 1994).
Students: Barbara Taylor, *Water at Work* (New York: Watts, 1991).

THERMAL ENERGY (HEAT)

QUICKIE STARTERS: OPEN-ENDED ACTIVITIES

What Makes Things Get Hotter? (K–5)

Materials

6-in piece of wire coat hanger, mineral oil, brass button, wool cloth, piece of metal, pencil eraser, notebook paper, ice cubes, newspapers or paper towels, miscellaneous magazines

What Do Students Know?

How do your fingers feel when you bend a wire hanger back and forth? Why do you think this happens?

Some Possible Acitvities

1. Bend a 6-inch piece of wire hanger back and forth 10 times as shown. Quickly touch the wire at the point where you bent it.
   What do you feel? (Heat)
   What do you think will happen if you bend the wire more times, e.g., 20, 25, 30, 35 times? (Each time the wire gets hotter.)

What Must I Know?

Caution: Try this activity out first to find out how many bends will make the wire too hot for students to touch.

2. Rub your hands together very fast and hard.
   What do you feel?
   Try this again but put a few drops of oil or water on your hands first.
   How do you think the second rubbing will feel different from the first rubbing?

Now rub different things together and quickly touch them to your upper lip or the tip of your nose (sensitive parts of your body): brass button on a piece of wool, metal on paper, pencil eraser on paper, and so on.

What Must I Know?

Note: It is recommended that young students go to the bathroom before and after the following activity!

3. Hold an ice cube in your hand over newspapers or paper towels.
   How does your hand feel with the ice cube in it? (Cold)
   What is happening to the ice cube?

Leave an ice cube in a nearby dish and notice the difference between this ice cube and the one in your hand.
Why the difference? (Heat from your hand melts the ice cube faster than heat from the room melts the ice cube in the dish.)

Which became warmer—your hand or the ice cube you held? (Ice cube; heat moved from hand to ice.)
How is this the same as when you pour a warm soft drink over ice cubes? (The warm drink gets cooler as heat moves to the ice.)

G 4. Students in grades 3–5 can go on a "Heat Hunt" in school and at home. Look for places where heat is produced (school or home furnace, oven and stove, toaster, microwave oven, sunshine through windows). List these places in a booklet or chart and illustrate it with magazine pictures. Then, use these three categories to organize your list of heat producers:
- Where did you see it?
- What was heated?
- How was it heated?

What Must I Know?

Caution: Remind students not to touch heat-producing appliances or other hot objects.

GUIDED DISCOVERY HANDS-ON/MINDS-ON ACTIVITIES

What Is Thermal Energy, or Heat? (K–8)

What Concepts Might Students Discover?

When an object is heated, its molecules move faster or vibrate more.
When an object is cooled, its molecules move more slowly.
Heat is the total energy an object has because of the motion of its molecules.

What Will We Need?

Baby-food jar with screw top	Sugar cubes
Sand	Colored cinnamon candies
Thick towel	or jelly beans
Thermometer	Tea bags
12 baby-food jars or clear	Pencils
plastic tumblers	2 Pyrex™ or tin pans

What Must I Know?

Motion (shaking, stirring, rubbing, etc.) can be a source of heat.
The molecules in liquids are in continuous motion. This is called **Brownian motion.**
Scientists use controlled experiments to test their ideas.
Solids break into smaller pieces (**dissolve**) faster in hot water than in cold water.

PROCESSES

Part I (K–5)

Hypothesizing

What do you think will happen to the sand in a baby-food jar if you shake it many times?

What Will Students Do?

1. Fill a baby-food jar three-fourths full of sand, screw the top on the jar, and then wrap it with a thick towel.

G   *Collecting Data*

2. Each person should take a turn doing the following:
   a. Shake the sand vigorously for 5 minutes.

Measuring
   b. Measure the temperature of the sand.

Recording
   c. Write your findings on a record sheet like the one that follows.

Person	Minutes of Shaking	Temperature in °F or °C
1	5	
2	10	
3	15	
4	20	
5	25	

d. Pass the jar to the next person.

Comparing   e. When everyone has had a turn, compare the temperature of the sand
from the first to the last reading.

Analyzing   *How were they different?* (The temperature rose higher after shaking.)

Communicating Results   f. Set up a graph like the one on page A–29, then graph the data from the record sheets. *Note:* May be more applicable for students who have been exposed to graphing.

Part II (6–8)

Hypothesizing   *What caused the molecules to move in Part I?*
Designing an Investigation   *How could we set up an experiment to test the effect of heat on molecule movement in a liquid?*

What Will Students Do?

1. Fill three baby-food jars or plastic drinking glasses with water to within ½ inch (1 cm) of the top and let them stand until the water is room temperature.
2. Slowly lower a sugar cube into one container, a handful of cinnamon candies or jelly beans into the second, and a tea bag into the third. (See diagram.)

CONTROL: Substances dissolving without stirring

Make certain that the containers are in a spot where they will not be moved or jostled.
3. Set up three more jars/tumblers and materials the same as in Steps 1 and 2, but this time stir the water until the materials dissolve, as shown in the diagram.

EXPERIMENT: Substances dissolving with stirring

Hypothesizing   The way this experiment was set up is called a **controlled experiment** in science. *Why do you think it is called this?*
4. Taking observations every ½ hour, record how long it takes for the control containers to look like the experimental containers.
Hypothesizing   *Which materials do you think will dissolve first? Why?*
Inferring   *Would the results be different if hot water were used? If cold water were used? Why?*
Designing an Investigation   *How could we test this?*

Part III (6–8)

<table>
<tr><td>What Will
Students Do?</td><td></td><td>1. Set up two more sets of containers with sugar, cinnamon candies, and tea bags.
2. Place one set of containers in ice-cold water in a pan and the other set in a pan of very hot water.</td></tr>
</table>

Hot water   Cold water

Hypothesizing   *In which containers—in pans of hot or cold water—will the materials dissolve first?*

Inferring   *What does the hot water in the pan do to the molecules in the containers?*

What Must I Know?

This is a review of Brownian motion, the continuous movement of particles suspended in a liquid. This activity also introduces several new concepts. Students will be helped to see that increasing the motion of molecules generates considerable heat. Therefore, matter that displays greater heat has greater movement of its molecules. In addition, the concept of a control is used as a standard against which scientists check their experimental work. If you think your students are ready, you can introduce the concept of variables. For instance, in Part III, the variable being tested is heat and its effect upon dissolving.

How Will Students Use or Apply What They Discover?

1. *Why do you rub a match against the side of a match box?*
2. *Why do matches not catch fire while sitting in a match box?*
3. *When you bend a wire back and forth several times, why does it get warm?*
4. *When you put two pencils together and rub them back and forth several times, what happens to your hands?*
5. *A person tried to strike a match against a piece of glass to light it. The match would not light. Why?*
6. *If you feel the tires of your car before you take a trip and then just after you get out of the car, they will not feel the same. How do you think they will differ? How would you explain the difference?*
7. *A person was chopping wood with an axe. After chopping very hard for about 10 minutes, she felt the axe. How do you think the axe felt and why?*

How Is Heat Transmitted by Radiation, Convection, and Conduction? (3–8)

What Concepts Might Students Discover?

The sun or light bulbs give off radiant heat.
Heat can be transmitted from one body to another by conduction and radiation.

Light objects reflect radiant energy more than do dark objects.
Dark objects absorb more radiant energy than do light objects.
Some objects conduct heat better than others.
Heat can be transmitted within a gas or liquid by convection.

What Will We Need?

3 tin cans of same size	Lamp with 150 to 300 watts
Small can of shiny white paint	Candle
Small can of dull black paint	Matches
2 small paintbrushes	9 thumbtacks
Styrofoam covers for cans	Tripod stand
3 thermometers	Silver or steel knife
4 × 4-in square of aluminum foil	4-in length of copper tubing

What Must I Know?   These activities may be done in groups. For immature or unruly children, the teacher should demonstrate these activities.

PROCESSES   **Part I   Radiation (3–5)**

Hypothesizing   *What do you think will happen to the three thermometers in the three different cans after being in the sun or near light bulbs for a while? (See diagram.)*

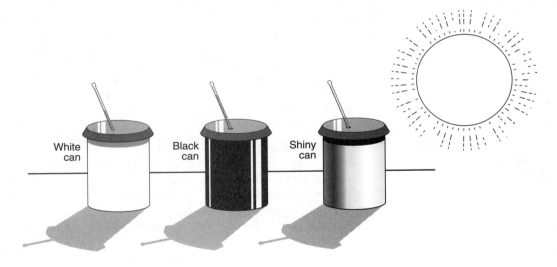

White can   Black can   Shiny can

What Will Students Do?

1. Obtain three identically sized cans and remove all labels. Paint one can dull black and another can shiny white; leave the third can unpainted, shiny metal.
2. Fill each can with regular tap water.
3. Put a styrofoam cover on each can and insert a thermometer through each cover.
4. Set the cans in direct sunlight or at equal distances from a 150- to 300-watt light bulb.

Measuring   5. Prepare a table for data collection and record the temperature of the
Observing   water in each can at 1-minute intervals.

Hypothesizing	*What do you think will happen to the water temperature in the different cans?*
	If there are different temperatures, how would you explain that?
Inferring	*How would you relate the result of the unequal absorption of heat in the tin cans to different land and water surfaces of the earth?*
Inferring	*Knowing what you do about how **radiant** (light) energy reacts on different surfaces, how would you explain the differences in the three thermometers?*
Hypothesizing	*How might this be related to the microclimates of certain geographic areas?*

What Must I Know?

The shiny aluminum of the unpainted can and the shiny white paint of the second can reflect radiant energy, whereas the dull black paint absorbs most of the radiant energy. Dark patches of ground absorb more radiant energy faster than do shiny water surfaces or lighter colored land surfaces.

Part II   Convection (3–5)

Hypothesizing

Where do you think the warmest and coolest spots are in your classroom? Try this activity to see if you can find the answer.

What Will Students Do?

G

1. As far away as possible from the room's source of heat, tape three thermometers to a wall at these places: near the ceiling, halfway up the wall, and one near the floor.

Observation

Communicating

Analyzing

2. Make a chart of the thermometer readings once an hour for one day.
3. Using the data collected, graph the results.
   From your data and graph, answer these questions:
   Which thermometer had the highest temperature? The middle temperature? The lowest temperature?

Inferring

Why do you think the temperatures were different?

What Must I Know?

Convection is the transfer of heat by either a gas (air) or a liquid (water). When the air in the room is heated, it expands and becomes lighter per given volume. It then rises because it is lighter. This rising and falling is called a **convection current.**

How Will Students Use or Apply What They Discover?

When you see "wiggly lines" rising from the blacktop of a parking lot on a sunny day, how is this the same as the convection current in our classroom?
Why does a "cloud" fall down from a freezer that is above a refrigerator when you open the freezer door?
Why does smoke usually rise up a chimney? Under what conditions would smoke come into the house through the fireplace opening?
Why would a pinwheel start to spin if put over a lit light bulb?

Part III Conduction (6–8)

What Must I Know?

Because of the use of open flame, it is recommended that you supervise students closely. You may wish to demonstrate all or part of the activity.

Hypothesizing

What do you think will happen to tacks that have been attached with wax to a strip of aluminum foil, to a silver or steel knife, and to a copper tube when the tips of these metals are heated?

What Will Students and Teacher Do?

1. Obtain a 4 × 4-in square of aluminum foil, a candle, a match, and nine tacks.
2. Roll the aluminum foil tightly.
3. Light the candle. Drip some wax onto three tacks and the aluminum foil rod so the tacks stick to the foil.
4. Obtain a tripod stand, silver knife, and a 4-in length of copper tubing.
5. Stick three tacks each to the knife and to the copper tubing as you did with the foil.
6. Place the foil, knife, and copper tubing on a tripod stand as shown in the diagram. Heat the tips of each of these with a candle flame. Have students observe and record what happens.

Observing

Inferring   *Why did the tacks not all fall at the same time?*

Inferring   *From observing this activity, how do you think the heat affected the three metals?*

How Will Students Use or Apply What They Discover?

1. *When you stand in front of a fireplace and only the front of you is warmed by the fire, how is the heat transferred?*
2. *How does heat or thermal energy come from the sun?*
3. *What colors are more likely to absorb heat?*
4. *Why do people generally wear lighter colored clothes in the summer?*
5. *In the can experiment, what kind of energy did the black surface absorb?*
6. *How was the heat transferred from the black surface to the thermometer?*
7. *Why is it desirable to have a copper-bottomed tea kettle?*
8. *Why would you not want a copper handle on a frying pan?*
9. *What metals conduct heat well?*
10. *What advantage would there be in having a car with a white top rather than a black top?*
11. *Why do many people in warmer climates paint their houses white?*
12. *Why would you prefer to put a hot dog on a stick rather than on a wire to cook the hot dog over a camp fire?*
13. *Why do astronauts wear shiny space suits?*

What Effect Does Heat Have on the States of Matter? (6–8)

What Concepts Might Students Discover?

There are many forms of sugar.
It is possible to obtain carbon from burning sugar.
Sugar may be broken down chemically.

What Will We Need?

Hot plate
Aluminum pie pan
Sugar cube or teaspoon of sugar
Empty, tall glass tumbler
Pot holder or insulated cooking mitt

What Do Students Know?

Hold up a piece of sugar and ask:
What are some of the properties or characteristics of this piece of sugar?

What Must I Know?

Students might say the sugar is white, cubical in shape, small, made up of crystalline material, sweet, and so on. In its present form, sugar is a white solid. There are, however, ways of changing its appearance. One of the easiest ways is simply to crush the cube, producing sugar in a smaller crystal form. These crystals can be crushed further to make a powdered sugar. Another way to change the cube's appearance is to dissolve it in a cup of water. Once the sugar is dissolved, it cannot be seen, yet the solution will taste sweet. This means that sugar is still present, because some of its characteristics are identifiable. In what ways can sugar be changed so it cannot be identified?

Because of the use of heat, you may wish to demonstrate all or part of this activity.

PROCESSES

What Will Students Do?

1. Obtain an aluminum pie pan and place it on top of an electric hot plate. Regulate the burner so the pan is heated slowly.
2. Place 1 teaspoon or cube of sugar in the middle of the pan. (See diagram.)

Hypothesizing	*What do you think will happen to the sugar when it is heated?*
	3. Watch what happens to the sugar.
Observing	*What happens as the sugar begins to melt?*
	4. Hold a tall, empty glass cup upside down over the bubbling sugar. Use a pot holder or cooking mitt to do this.
Hypothesizing	*What do you think will appear on the inside of the glass?*
Observing	5. Observe the inside of the glass very carefully.
	6. Lift the glass, wait 10 seconds, then touch the inside of the glass with your fingers.
Observing	*What do you feel?*
Inferring	*What do you think it is?* (Water vapor)
	7. After the sugar stops bubbling, describe what you see in the pan.
Inferring	*What do you think this material could be?*
Comparing	*What does it look like?*
	Taste this material. (Take this opportunity to remind students that they should *never* taste anything unless you say it is all right.)
Observing	*How does it taste?*
	Does it have the properties of sugar?

What Must I Know? It is probably carbon. Sugar has carbon combined in its molecular structure.

How Will Students Use or Apply What They Discover?

1. *From what you have learned about sugar, can you explain why a marshmallow turns black when roasted over a fire?*
2. *Why does sugar turn brown as it slowly heats up and melts?* (This brown liquid is caramel flavor.)

Reference Books—Thermal Energy (Heat)
Teacher: Brian Knapp, *Fire* (Austin, TX: Steck-Vaughn Co., 1990).
Student: Betsy Maestro, *Temperature and You* (New York: Dutton, 1990).

AIR PRESSURE

QUICKIE STARTERS: OPEN-ENDED ACTIVITIES

What Makes Balloons Grow Bigger and Move Farther? (K–2)

Materials Balloons, metric tape or meterstick

What Do Students Know? *Which team can get their balloons to go the farthest? How?*

Some Possible Activities **G** Go outside and divide the class into groups of five. Students should blow their balloons up as much as they can. Do not tie off the ends. Have one student in each group release his or her balloon. *Caution:* Make sure students do not release balloons into the faces of their classmates. Have the second student in each group go to where the first balloon landed, then have him or her release his or her balloon. This continues until all the students in the team have had a turn. The distance is then measured metrically to determine how far their balloons went from the starting point. The team whose balloons went the greatest distance wins.

What's in Your Baggies? How Do You Know? (K–2)

Materials

Plastic sandwich bags with plastic ties, sand, buttons, water

What Do Students Know?

How do you know if something is real?
What are some properties of matter?
How do you find out about properties of matter?
How is sand different from buttons?
How is water different from sand?
Can things be real that we cannot see?

Some Possible Activities

Take three plastic sandwich bags and half fill them separately with sand, buttons, and water. Twist the top of each bag and tie it with a plastic tie. Take a fourth bag, swish it through the air, quickly close the mouth, twist it tightly, and tie it with a plastic tie. (See diagram on next page.)

Ask students to respond to these questions by looking at and carefully handling the bags. How are the properties of the objects in the bags the *same?* (They occupy space, have weight, exert pressure on the sides of the bags, can support a weight put on them, etc.) We call these things **properties of matter,** and they show us that the things in the bags are all real—even the air that we cannot see.

How are the properties of the objects in the bags *different?* (They do not all weigh the same, some change shape when you squeeze them, some are solid [buttons and sand], one is a liquid [water], and one is a gas [air] that looks invisible.)

You found out about properties of matter by observation.

How could you find out if the objects in your bags could be moved from one bag to another?
How could you find out if the objects have a smell?

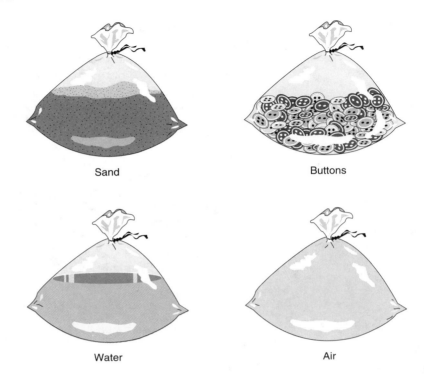

Sand

Buttons

Water

Air

How Can You Make a Kite and Get It to Fly? (K–2)

Materials	Plastic such as that used by dry cleaners, paper to cover the kite, small pieces of wood to form the supports, string, transparent tape or glue, cloth for the tail
What Do Students Know?	*How can we make kites?* *What will we need?* *How should they be constructed?* *What shape should they be? Why?*
Some Possible Activities	Encourage students to plan in small groups how they are going to make their kites before they construct them. Guide them in discussing the properties of air and how it affects kite building and flying. After they have done this, you might bring in some books on kites. Discuss the role of the tail and how it helps to stabilize the kite. Have students experiment with how long the tail should be by flying their kites on windy and calm days. If there is a local kite store, invite students to visit it or invite the owner to your classroom. Discuss some of the dangers of flying kites near power lines. *Caution:* Point out that they should *never* use wire instead of string to fly a kite because of the danger involved if the wire hits a power line. Invite students to make several kinds of kites and find out how different cultures use them; for example, have students find out how the Japanese use kites

to celebrate certain holidays. *Caution:* Warn against putting plastic wrapping over heads or on faces.

GUIDED DISCOVERY HANDS-ON/MINDS-ON ACTIVITIES

What Is Air? (K–2)

What Concepts Might Students Discover?	Air is real. Air is around us all the time. Air is found inside solids and liquids. Air takes up space and has weight. Air exerts pressure.
What Will We Need?	Piece of cardboard Commercial-sized mayonnaise jar or aquarium Drinking glass or plastic tumbler Food coloring
What Do Students Know?	*How do you know something is real?* *What could you do to find out whether air is real?*

PROCESSES

What Will Students Do?

Observing

1. Swing your hands back and forth.
   What can you feel?

Observing
Inferring
Observing

2. Swing a piece of cardboard back and forth.
   What do you feel now?
   What is the cardboard pushing against?
   What do you feel pushing against you when you ride your bicycle down a hill?

Hypothesizing

What do you think will happen to a glass if it is turned upside down and pushed straight down under water?

3. Turn a glass upside down and push it *straight* down in a large jar of water or an aquarium as shown. (Use food coloring to make the water more visible.)

4. Now turn the glass sideways as shown.

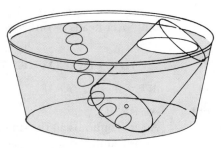

Observing   *What happens to the inside of the glass?*
What are the bubbles that escape from the glass?
Where did the bubbles come from?

**How Will Students Use
or Apply What They
Discover?**

1. *How can you keep water in a straw by closing the top end with your finger
as shown?*

Put straw in   Put finger on   Remove straw   Lift finger from
water   straw   straw

2. *If you fill a paper bag with air and then crush it, what happens and why?*
3. *Why does juice flow better from a tin can if you punch two holes instead of one?*
4. *Can you push a straw through a potato?*
   Try this activity:
   a. Place a potato on a table and ask a partner to hold it. Raise the straw
      about 5 inches above the potato and then quickly and forcibly stick
      the potato, as shown in (a).
      What happened? Why?
   b. Repeat Step 4a but this time hold your thumb over the end of the
      straw as you stick the potato, as shown in (b).
      Why is this different than before?

(a)   (b)

What Must I Know?

The first straw usually bends and only partially penetrates the potato. The second straw does not bend and goes through the potato. Blocking the straw end traps and compresses the air inside the straw, creating greater air pressure. Some of the potato is forced into the straw, further increasing the air pressure.

How Do the Effects of Moving Air Differ From the Effects of Nonmoving Air? (K–5)

What Concepts Might Students Discover?

The pressure of liquids or gases will be low if they are moving quickly and will be high if they are moving slowly. This principle is called **Bernoulli's principle.**

What Will We Need?

3 pieces of notebook paper	Ping-Pong ball
Drinking straw	Thistle tube or funnel
Pop bottle	Cylindrical container (oatmeal, salt)
Pin with a head	Candle
Small index card (3 × 5 in.)	Matches
Thread spool	

What Must I Know?

Before doing this student inquiry activity, potential energy and kinetic energy should be explained.

PROCESSES

What Will Students Do?

Part I (K–2)

1. Obtain a piece of notebook paper.
2. Make a fold 1 inch wide along the long end of the paper. Make another 1-inch fold at the opposite end as indicated in the diagram.
3. Place the paper on a flat surface.

Hypothesizing   *What do you think will happen if you blow under this folded paper?*

4. Using the drinking straw, blow a stream of air under the paper.

Blow through straw under paper

Drinking straw

Observing *What do you notice about the way the paper moves?*
Describe how the air was circulating under the paper before you blew under it.

Comparing *What do you know about the air pressure under the paper—when you blow under the paper—as compared with the air pressure exerted on top of the paper?*

Part II (K–2)

Hypothesizing *What do you think will happen to a wad of paper placed in the opening of a pop bottle if you blow across the bottle opening?*

What Will Students Do?

1. Wad a small piece of paper so it is about the size of a pea (¼-in or ½-cm diameter).
2. Lay the pop bottle on its side.
3. Place the small wad of paper in the opening of the bottle, next to the edge of the opening. (See diagram.)
4. Blow across the opening in front of the bottle. Make sure you bend down so that *you are level with the bottle.*

Blow across opening of bottle

Observing *What happens to the wad of paper?*
Inferring *Why is the wad of paper forced to do that?*

Comparing   *What do you know about the air pressure in the bottle and the air pressure at the opening of the bottle when you blow across it?*

Hypothesizing   *What do you think will happen if you place a wad of paper in the opening of a pop bottle (as before) and blow directly into the bottle?*

5. Blow hard directly into the bottle as shown.

Blow directly into bottle

Observing   6. Record your observations.

Inferring   *What do you conclude from your observations?*

Part III (K–2)

Hypothesizing   *If a pin with a head is inserted through the center of a card and then into a spool, what will happen when you blow through the other end of the spool?*

**What Will
Students Do?**

1. Place the pin in the center of the index card so that the head is under the card. (See diagram.)
2. Put the thread spool over the pin.
3. Hold the card with one hand and the spool with your other hand.
4. While blowing, let go of the card.

What Must I Know?   *Warning:* Instruct students *never to suck in* on the spool.

Blow through here

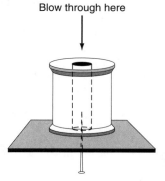

Observing   *What happened to the card while you blew through the spool?*
     What happened when you stopped blowing through the spool?

Inferring   *Why do you think this happened?*

Inferring   *What is holding up the card?*

Inferring   *Why does the air you blow through the hole not make the card fall?*

Inferring   *Why do you need the pin in the middle of the card?*

What Must I Know?

Two variables may affect the outcome: (1) The bottom of the spool must be very smooth (sand it if necessary), and (2) the student must take a deep breath and sustain a long, steady air column down the spool.

Part IV (K–2)

Hypothesizing

What will happen to a Ping-Pong ball if it is placed in the large end of a thistle tube or funnel and you blow through the small end of the thistle tube or funnel?

**What Will
Students Do?**

1. Hold the Ping-Pong ball in the wide, larger opening of the thistle tube or funnel, put your mouth on the other end, and blow with a long, steady breath. (See diagram.) *Hint:* Get a deep breath before you put your mouth on the tube end to blow. *Caution:* After each person blows through the tube, wash the funnel thoroughly with soap and water and an alcohol wipe, if possible.

Blow here

Thistle tube

Ping-Pong ball

2. While blowing hard and steady through the tube end of the funnel, let go of the Ping-Pong ball.

Observing
Inferring

Record your observations.
Why does the ball do what it does?
Why does the ball spin around in the thistle tube or funnel?

Part V (K–2)

Hypothesizing

If you were to hold a piece of paper by each corner and blow across the top of the paper, what would happen to the paper?

**What Will
Students Do?**

1. Hold the lower left corner of a piece of notebook paper with your left hand and the lower right corner with your right hand.
2. Blow hard across the top of the paper. (See diagram.)

Observing
Inferring

What happens to the paper while you are blowing across it?
Why does the paper move in this direction?

**How Will Students Use
or Apply What They
Discover?**

1. *Why is it unwise to stand close to the edge of a platform as a moving train is coming?*

Blow across top of paper

2. *When you rapidly pass by another student's desk that has a sheet of paper on it, what happens to the paper? Why?*
3. *How would this principle of air pressure work when you fly a kite?*
4. *What happens to a girl's skirt if a car speeds close by her?*
5. *What would happen if a plane stopped moving in the air? How could this happen?*

What Must I Know?

If a plane is moving fast enough, the upward pressure on the wings is enough to overcome gravity. The plane must keep moving to stay aloft. If it stopped in midair, it would glide down immediately.

6. *Look at the following drawing of an airplane wing. Is the air moving faster at A or B? Why?*

7. *How do wing slopes vary and why?*

Part VI (3–5)

What Must I Know?

Because of the use of open flame, it is recommended that you supervise students closely. You may wish to demonstrate all or part of the activity.

What Will Students and Teacher Do?

Hypothesizing

1. Position a cylindrical container and candle as shown in the diagram and light the candle.
   What do you think will happen to the candle flame if you blow as shown? Why?

2. Blow a deep breath against the front of the container, keeping your mouth even with the candle.

Observing

What happens to the flame?

Inferring

Why do you think this happens?

What Must I Know?

The tendency of a fluid (a liquid or gas) to follow the wall contour of a curved surface is called the **Coanda effect**. In this case, the air (gas) acts like a fluid and follows the contour of the round container. The airstreams meet on the other side, combine, and blow out the candle.

Reference Books—Air Pressure
Teacher: Mary-Jane Wilkins, *Air, Light, and Water* (New York: Warwick Press, 1991).
Student: Barry Moser, *Fly! A Brief History of Flight Illustrated* (New York: Harper, 1993).

SOUND ENERGY

QUICKIE STARTERS: OPEN-ENDED ACTIVITIES

What Makes a Drum Louder? (K–2)

Materials

Cylindrical oatmeal container, puffed rice or wheat cereal, large balloon or sheet rubber, strong rubber band, pencil with eraser or drumstick.

What Do Students Know?

How can you make a drum sound louder?

Some Possible Activities

Stretch the large balloon or piece of sheet rubber over the open end of the oatmeal container and place a strong rubber band around that end to hold the rubber securely in place. This makes a simple drum. Sprinkle puffed rice or wheat cereal on the drum head. Tap the drum head softly with the drumstick or eraser end of the pencil and observe what happens. Now hit it harder. Ask:

What differences did you notice when you hit the drum softly and when you hit it harder?

Help students to see the patterns formed by the puffed cereal when the drum head is struck softly and how the pattern changes when the drum head is struck harder. Also notice how much higher the cereal moves above the drum head when it is hit harder. Relate more energy (hitting the drum harder) with louder sound from the drum.

How Can You Make Sounds Less Noisy? (K–2)

Materials

Two small battery-operated radios; several different-sized boxes, each of which can fit over one or more of the others and over the radio; cloth; paper; insulating material; cotton balls

What Do Students Know?

How can we deaden the sound of this radio by using these materials?

Some Possible Activities

Invite two groups of students to have a "deadening the sound" race, each using a radio with the same volume level and the listed materials. Give the groups a definite time (30–60 minutes) to brainstorm how they can deaden the sound of the radio, set up an experiment, and collect data. Later, discuss how sound can go through objects and what kinds of things deaden sound well. Then ask:

How can what you found in your "deadening the sound" race help to reduce sound in our classroom and make it more comfortable to our ears?

GUIDED DISCOVERY HANDS-ON/MINDS-ON ACTIVITIES

What Is Sound, and How Is It Produced and Conducted? (K–2)

What Concepts Might Students Discover?

When an object vibrates, sound may be produced.
Sound may be made by vibrating a number of different objects.
Sound may be conducted by a number of different objects.

What Will We Need?

As many of the following things as possible should be placed at work stations for groups of four or more students:

Rubber band	Aluminum foil
Fork and spoon	Cotton
6 empty pop bottles	Bell
Alarm clock	Aluminum pie pan
4 feet of string	Toothpicks

What Do Students Know?

How could you make a sound with a rubber band?

PROCESSES

What Will Students Do?

Designing an Investigation

1. *How could you make a rubber band produce a sound? How is the sound produced?*

What Must I Know?

The students should stretch a rubber band and cause it to vibrate. They should get the idea that the vibration causes the sound. *Caution:* Point out that students must be careful not to let the stretched rubber bands pop off their hands and that they must not try to snap each other with the rubber bands.

Hypothesizing

Can you hear sound by placing your ear against different objects while causing them to make a sound?

2. Try making sounds with the different objects.

Hypothesizing

What can you do to stop the sound once it has started?

3. Test your ideas.

Observing
Comparing

4. Determine which materials are better than others for producing sound.
In what ways are these materials the same or different?

How Will Students Use or Apply What They Discover?

1. *How would you produce a loud sound?*
2. *What would you do to make our classroom less noisy?*
3. *Why do drapes in a room make sounds softer?*

How Does the Length of an Air Column Affect Sound? (K–2)

What Concepts Might Students Discover?

The higher the pitch of a note, the more rapid the vibrations of the producing body.
Pitch can be varied by adjusting the length of an air column.

The higher the water level in a bottle, the shorter the air column, and the higher the pitch (when blowing across the top of the bottle).

What Will We Need?

8 identical pop bottles
Medium-sized beaker
Drinking straws (waxed paper straws work better than plastic)
Scissors

What Do Students Know?

What might happen if you blew across the openings of pop bottles filled with varying amounts of water?
Would a sound be produced?
If sounds were produced, would they all be the same? If not, which would be the highest? The lowest?

PROCESSES

What Will Students Do?
Hypothesizing

Part I

1. Fill eight identical pop bottles with varying amounts of water.
   What might happen if you blow across the lips of the bottles?
2. Blow across the bottles.

Observing   *Do all bottles give off the same sound?*
Observing   *Which bottle gives off the highest note? The lowest note?*
Hypothesizing   *How could you make a musical scale out of the pop bottles?*

3. Arrange the bottles to make a musical scale.
4. After you have made the musical scale, try to make a harmonizing chord.
   If you number the lowest note "1" and the highest note "8," what are the numbers of the bottles you used for your chords?

Inferring   *What conclusions can you draw concerning the length of an air column and the sound produced?*
Hypothesizing   *What is the relationship between the length of an air column and a note produced by an open tube?*

What Must I Know?

Once a scale is achieved, drop oil from a medicine dropper onto the top of the water in each bottle, just enough to cover the top. This will prevent evaporation and a change in pitch.

Part II (K–2)

What Will Students Do?

1. Give each student a drinking straw and a pair of scissors.
2. Have students cut and pinch the straw to form a reed like the one shown.

Pinch here

Side view

Cut a V

Top view

Hypothesizing

Why do we cut and pinch the straw?

3. Have students blow on the "V" cut into the straw. (*Note:* They will need to experiment to get the proper lip vibration.)
4. Now cut the straws into different lengths to get different pitches.

Inferring

What is the relationship between the length of a straw and the sound it produced?

Hypothesizing

How can the drinking straws be used to play songs?

How Will Students Use or Apply What They Discover?

1. *How would the results vary if you put equal amounts of water in bottles of varying sizes?*
2. *Does the thickness of the glass in the pop bottle affect the tone produced?*
3. *Could you produce the same results using test tubes?*
4. *Does the pitch differ when hitting bottles with a spoon or ruler and when blowing over the top of the bottles? Test it.*
5. *How can the drinking straws be used to play songs?* Experiment to get the straws calibrated in lengths in relation to octave. Try to play simple songs like "Mary Had a Little Lamb."

What Must I Know?

Once a scale is achieved, drop oil from a medicine dropper onto the top of the water in each bottle, just enough to cover the top. This will prevent evaporation and a change in pitch.

How Do Solids and Liquids Conduct Sounds? (K–5)

What Concepts Might Students Discover?

Sound can travel through solid substances.
Sound can travel through liquid substances.
Sound can travel through gaseous substances.

What Will We Need?	Meter- or yardstick	20 feet of copper wire
	Pencil	20 feet of steel wire
	2 paper cups	Bucket
	20 feet of strong cord or nylon fishing line	Water
	Buttons	2 rocks

What Do Students Know?

Have you ever heard people talking when you were in one room and they were in another room next to yours?

How do you suppose you could hear them through the wall and the air?

You know that sound travels, but what substances will sound travel through?

PROCESSES

What Will Students Do?

Observing

Part I (K–2)

1. Obtain a meter- or yardstick and a pencil.
2. Hold the meterstick to your ear. Have a partner scratch the other end of the stick with a pencil. What happens?
3. Hold the stick away from your ear and repeat the activity.

Applying

Does sound travel better through a solid or through the air?

Part II (K–2)

What Will Students Do?

I

Hypothesizing
Designing an Investigation

1. With one hand, hold a meter- or yardstick firmly against a desk. With the other hand, pluck the overhanging part of the stick, causing it to vibrate.

   What causes the sound to be produced?
2. Produce a high-pitched sound by vibrating the stick.

   Produce a low-pitched sound by vibrating the stick.

Part III (3–5)

What Will Students Do?

1. Get two paper cups and 20 feet of string or nylon fishing line.
2. With a pencil, punch a very small hole in the bottom of the paper cups just large enough to stick the string through.
3. Stick the ends of the string through each one of the paper cups. Tie a button to the ends of the string ending inside the cups so the string will not be easily pulled from the cups. (See diagram.)

Paper Cup |←————————————— 20 feet —————————————→| Paper Cup

String

Hypothesizing

When you talk into one of the cups, what will happen to the other cup? Why?

4. Talk into one cup while another student holds the other cup to his or her ear and listens.

Designing an Investigation

How can sound best be transferred from one cup to the other? Hint: Make sure the string is stretched very tightly and that nothing is touching the string. *Why?*

Observing

Record what you did to best transmit the sound.

Hypothesizing

5. *How will the sound be conducted if you use copper or steel wire?* Try it.

Observing

What happens when you use copper wire?

Inferring and Comparing

Is the sound carried better through copper wire than through string? Why or why not?

Hypothesizing

Why is it important for the string to be tight and not touching anything?

Part IV (3–5)

Hypothesizing

How is sound carried in liquids?

Designing an Investigation

How would you find out?

What Will Students Do?   Obtain a large bucket full of water. Take two pieces of metal or two rocks and hit them together under water. Now hit them together out of water.

Inferring   *Did you hear a sound when you hit the objects together? Why?*
What is your conclusion about the ability of a liquid to carry sound?
Comparing   *Which sound was louder—in air or water?*

How Will Students Use or Apply What They Discover?

1. *How far do you think sounds would travel between phones using copper wire, string, and steel wire?* Design an experiment to see which conducts sound farther.
2. *How would you use eight rulers to make a musical scale?* Think about what you did to get a low pitch and a high pitch.
3. *What is the purpose of making musical instruments out of wood?*
4. *How well do you think liquids other than water conduct sounds?*

Reference Books—Sound
Teacher: Etta Kaner, *Sound Science* (Reading, MA: Addison-Wesley, 1991).
Student: David J. Darling, *Sounds Interesting: The Science of Acoustics* (New York: Dillon Press, 1991).

SIMPLE MACHINES (MECHANICS)

QUICKIE STARTERS: OPEN-ENDED ACTIVITIES

How Can You Make Balls Roll Faster? (K–2)

Materials   Balls of different sizes, including Ping-Pong, golf, tennis, and larger ones; boards to make inclined planes

What Do Students Know?   *What things can you do with these balls?*

Some Possible Activities

Find out which balls roll easiest across the floor, what happens when they are kicked, and which ones will roll the farthest after rolling down an inclined plane. Find out which balls balance best. Throw the balls against the wall at different angles and find out how they bounce off the wall. For example, how should you throw the ball so it will come back to you? Float the balls in water and find out which ones float and which do not. Also, notice how deep they sink in the water. Line up the balls in a vertical line leading from an inclined plane. Roll a ball down the inclined plane so it hits the end of the line. Then roll two balls down so they hit the line one after another. Place all but one of the balls in a close group. Roll another ball into the group and see how the balls scatter. Play croquet with different balls. Construct a tetherball.

How Do Wheels Help Toys Move? (K–2)

Materials

Rollers, small round wheels, buttons, bottle caps, toy cars, small round rocks, oranges, apples, thimbles, boards to make inclined planes, disks cut from poster board, thumbtacks, matchboxes, coat hanger wire

What Do Students Know?

What can you do with these things?
What kinds of games can you play?
How can you make a toy car using the matchboxes and other things?
Which of the things you see are wheels? Which are not wheels?
How are wheels different from the other things?

Some Possible Activities

The students could try seeing how far different things would roll on the floor after rolling down an inclined plane. They could also make toy cars with the matchboxes by tacking the bottle caps or buttons to the sides. The students may also be invited to make toy cars out of a square, small board where axles are made from clothes hangers. These are stapled to the board and then bent at the ends after the button or bottle cap wheels are attached.

Coat hanger wire

Staples

Wire bent to keep wheel on

MATCHES

MATCHES

GUIDED DISCOVERY HANDS-ON/MINDS-ON ACTIVITIES

What Is an Inclined Plane, and How Can You Use It? (3–8)

What Concepts Might Students Discover?

Inclined planes are used for moving objects that are too heavy to lift directly. The work done by moving an object up an inclined plane is equal to the weight of the object times the height of the plane.

Resistance × height of plane = Effort × length of plane

An **inclined plane** is one example of a **simple machine.**

What Will We Need?

Smooth board 4 ft × 6 inch
Support block 4 × 8 inch
Block with screw eye in one end or a rubber band wrapped around it
Spring scale

What Do Students Know?

What is an inclined plane?
Why use an inclined plane?
Where are there inclined planes on the school grounds?

PROCESSES

What Will Students Do?

Hypothesizing

1. Take the 4-foot board and place the 4 × 8-inch block under one end so that end of the board is raised 4 inches. Place the block with the screw eye in it on the inclined board as shown in the diagram. Slip the hook of the spring scale through the eye of the block.
   What force do you think will be required to pull the block?
   Will it be greater, equal to, or less than the weight of the block? Why?
2. Slowly and evenly pull the scale and block up the board.

Scale

4" support

Measuring
Recording
Measuring

3. Record the amount of force needed to pull the block up the board. Do this several times and record your observations.
   Using the data obtained, determine the average force required to pull the weight.
4. Repeat the activity but this time make the inclined plane steeper by changing the support block so its 8-inch dimension is under the end of the board.

Measuring
Comparing

5. Again, find the average force needed to pull the weight up the board.
   How do the two forces compare?

Applying

6. Lift the block straight up, as shown in the next diagram. Repeat this several times and find the average reading on the scale.

Comparing	*How is the force needed different when lifting the block straight up than when pulling the block up the board?*
Inferring	*Why?*

7. The following formula is used to calculate the force needed to move a weight up an inclined plane:

$$\text{Resistance} \times \text{resistance distance} = \text{Effort} \times \text{effort distance}$$

Inferring	Use this formula to calculate the force that should have been necessary to move the weight up the inclined plane.
Inferring	*Why do the experimental results and the calculated results not agree exactly?*
Hypothesizing	*What can you say about the amount of force required as an inclined plane becomes steeper?*
Hypothesizing	*What is the advantage of having a long inclined plane rather than a short inclined plane if both planes are the same height?*

How Will Students Use or Apply What They Discover?

1. Why do roads not go straight up and down mountains?
2. Which of the following examples is an inclined plane?
   a. ramp   d. stairway
   b. hill   e. wedge
   c. gangplank   f. head of an axe
3. A person moved a 100-pound safe up an inclined plane 20 feet long and 2 feet high.
   How much effort did the person have to use to move the safe?

What Is the Advantage of Using a Wheel and Axle? (3–8)

What Concepts Might Students Discover?

A **wheel** is a simple machine that aids in moving an object.
Every wheel has an axle. The wheel is used to turn the axle, or the axle is used to turn the wheel.
The work obtained from a simple machine is equal to the work put into it minus the work used in overcoming friction.
A small effort applied to a large wheel can be used to overcome a large resistance on a small wheel.
A **wheel and axle** machine usually consists of a large wheel to which a small axle is firmly attached.

The mechanical advantage is equal to the radius of the wheel divided by the radius of the axle.

What Will We Need?

Screw hook
Block of wood
Rubber bands
Ruler
Sheets of coarse sandpaper
5 or 6 round pencils

4 thread spools
1 bicycle per class
1 of the following: pencil sharpener, meat grinder, or can opener
Balance weight

PROCESSES

What Do Students Know?

What Will Students Do?

Measuring

Recording

Recording
Observing

Part I (3–8)

In what way does the wheel help to move objects?

1. Turn the screw hook into the end of a block of wood. Attach a rubber band (or a spring scale) to the hook.
2. With the rubber band on your finger, lift the block into the air and measure the stretch with a ruler, as in (a) in the diagram. Record your measurement.
3. Position the block on a table with the rubber band extended, as in (b) in the diagram, and measure the stretch of the rubber band. Now drag the block on the table and measure the rubber band's stretch once the block begins to move. Record your measurements.
   What change is made in the stretch of the rubber band?
4. Repeat the procedure in Step 3, this time with sandpaper beneath the block, as in (c) in the diagram.
5. Now place two round pencils underneath the block and drag it across the table, as in (d) in the diagram. Measure the stretch of the rubber band just before and after the block begins to move.

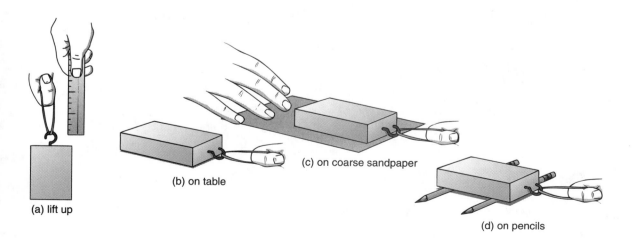

(a) lift up

(b) on table

(c) on coarse sandpaper

(d) on pencils

Observing	*What happens to the stretch of the rubber band this time?*
Comparing	*What difference do the pencils make underneath the wood as you try to move it?*
Comparing	*How does your measurement change?*
Inferring	*What do you suppose is the purpose of measuring the movement of the block of wood?*

6. Try the experiment again, only this time use four spools for the wheels and round pencils for the axles. Place the wood on the axles.

Observing   Observe what happens as you push the block of wood very gently.

Measuring	Measure the stretch of the rubber band as you pull the block of wood.
Comparing	*What difference is there in the stretch of the rubber band this time compared to moving the board without wheels?*

What Must I Know?   Older students can repeat the activity using the spring scale.

Part II (3–8)

What Do Students Know?   *What is a winch?*

What Will Students Do?   1. Obtain a small winch or use a pencil sharpener, meat grinder, or can opener.

Hypothesizing   *What is the advantage of using a winch?*

2. Hook a weight to the axle as shown in the diagram.

Brace or clamp

weight

Hypothesizing   *What do you think will be gained if a large wheel is turned to move a small axle?*

3. Turn the large wheel.

4. Count the number of turns you make to raise the weight 2 inches.

What Must I Know?

A small force applied to a large wheel can be used to move a large resistance attached to the axle. This is done, however, at the expense of distance, since the large wheel has to be moved a great distance to raise the resistance a short way.

Part III (3–8)

What Will Students Do?

Observe a bicycle.

Inferring

Where on a bicycle is friction used to advantage?
How is the bicycle wheel constructed to help reduce friction?

What Must I Know?

The wheel produces less friction because there is less surface area coming in contact with pavement than if a weight such as a person were pulled along a surface.

Observing

Where are the wheels and axles on a bicycle?
When you ride a bicycle, where do you apply the force?

Inferring

Why do you apply the force to the small wheel?

What Must I Know?

The effort is applied to the small wheel to gain speed. Using a great force, you move the small sprocket a short distance, and it, in turn, moves the large wheel a greater distance but with less force. Look at the diagrams of the following objects and decide whether they increase the ability to move heavier objects or increase the speed.

Wheel & axle   Pencil sharpener   Meat grinder   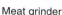 Winch

How Will Students Use or Apply What They Discover?

1. Pulling an object across the table produced a force.
   How can you tell which required a greater amount of force to pull: the board without pencils under it or the board that had the pencils as axles?

What Must I Know?

A spring scale can be substituted for the rubber band. If you have a balance, you can determine how many pounds of force you need to pull the board across the table. If you use a rubber band, you must calculate how far the rubber band stretches. The rubber band will not stretch as much the first time.

2. *How are roller bearings and ball bearings used?*
3. You want to move a heavy desk drawer across your room to another shelf.
   How can you go about doing this with the least amount of effort and the greatest amount of speed?

What Is a Screw, and How Is It Used? (3–8)

What Concepts Might Students Discover?

A **screw** is an inclined plane wrapped around a rod.
As with an inclined plane, force is gained at the expense of distance.
A large weight can be moved by a small force if the smaller force is applied over a greater distance.

What Will We Need?

Triangular pieces of paper
Colored pencil or crayon
Pencil
Colored string
Several large screws

Tape measure
Pieces of soft wood
Screwdriver
C-clamp

What Do Students Know?

Show the class several examples of screws and ask the following questions:
What are these called?
What purpose do they serve?
Where are they in the classroom?
What advantage do they have over nails?
What type of machine studied thus far resembles a screw?

What Must I Know?

A screw is a circular, inclined plane.

PROCESSES

What Will Students Do?

Part I (3–8)

1. Obtain a small piece of paper and cut it in the shape of a triangle as shown in the diagram.

2. Color the edge of the paper so you can see it and then wind the paper around the pencil.

Paper

Pencil

Paper wrapped around pencil

Observing

What kind of machine did the paper represent before you rolled it around the pencil?

What Do Students Know?

Part II (3–8)

What is this called? (See diagram) *What is it used for?*

Effort force

Threads

String

Resistance force

What Will Students Do?
Hypothesizing
Measuring
Comparing
Hypothesizing

1. *If you wrap a piece of string around the threads of this screw, which will be longer: the length of the screw or the length of the string? Why?*
Try it and measure and compare.

2. *How can you fasten two pieces of wood together using a screw and a screw-driver?*
Do it.
Measuring — *How far did the screw go into the wood?*
Observing — *How many turns of the screw did it take?*
Inferring — *Why?*
In what direction did the screw turn?
In what direction did the screw move into the wood?

What Must I Know?
Screw threads change screwdriver force into downward force. Less effort is needed to screw into wood, although it takes many turns.

How Will Students Use or Apply What They Discover?
What are examples of screws in your daily life?
How do these work?

What Must I Know?
Some examples of screws used in daily life include a bolt, lightbulb, and screw top. As these objects are turned, their threads tighten into the nut, light socket, and bottle, respectively.

Part III (3–8)

How Is a Screw Used in a Jack?

What Do Students Know?
What kind of machine did the paper in Part I represent after you rolled it around the pencil?
How are the screw and the inclined plane related?

What Will Students Do?
1. Obtain a C-clamp and insert a pencil as shown in the diagram.

Hypothesizing	*What do you think will happen to the pencil when you move the screw inward?*
Hypothesizing	*How much effort will have to be applied to break the pencil?*

2. Look at the diagram of the jack.

Jack

Communicating	Describe how the jack works.
Comparing	*How is the jack similar to a screw?*
Inferring	*What is the purpose of using a jack on a car?*
Inferring	*How is it possible for a person who weighs 150 pounds to lift a car weighing 3,000 pounds by using a jack?*

How Will Students Use or Apply What They Discover?

1. *When were jacks used in old barber shops?*
2. *Where else are jacks used?*
3. *How many seconds would a person have to exert a force to raise a car a small distance?*
4. *What machine is involved in a spiral notebook?*
5. *If you were asked to push a heavy rock to the top of a hill, how would you move it up the hill?*

What Must I Know?

Involve the custodian of your school to show your students examples of simple machines.

What Is a Movable Pulley, and How Can You Use It? (3–8)

What Concepts Might Students Discover?

Pulleys that move with the resistance are called **movable pulleys.**
Movable pulley systems have a mechanical advantage greater than 1.
The mechanical advantage of a movable pulley system is equal to the number of stands holding up the resistance.

What Will We Need?

Ring stand and clamp for attaching pulleys
2 single pulleys
String or nylon fishing line for the pulley
Spring scale

100-gram weight
50-gram weight
Yard- or meterstick

PROCESSES

What Will Students Do?

1. Obtain a ring stand and a clamp for attaching a pulley, a single pulley, some string or nylon fishing line, a spring scale, and a 100-gram weight. Assemble your equipment as shown in the diagram.

Force approximately
equal to weight

Hypothesizing   *How much do you think you will have to pull on the scale to raise the 100-gram weight?*

2. Pull on the scale and raise the weight.

Observing   *How is the scale affected when you raise the weight?*

Measuring   3. Repeat this activity several times and record each measurement.

Hypothesizing   *What do you think will happen when you use two pulleys to raise the 100-gram weight?*

4. In addition to the equipment you have, obtain a second pulley and a 50-gram weight. Assemble your equipment as shown in the diagram.

Observing   5. Pull the 50-gram weight and record your observations.

50-gram weight

100-gram weight

6. Remove the 50-gram weight and attach the spring scale to the free end of the fishing line, as shown in the following diagram.

Hypothesizing   *How will the scale be affected when you raise the 100-gram weight?*

7. Raise the weight by pulling on the scale.

Observing   *What happens to the scale when you raise the weight?*

Measuring   8. Repeat the activity several times and record each measurement.

      Why is there an advantage in using this type of pulley system?

9. Remove the scale and once again attach the 50-gram weight.

Hypothesizing   *How far do you think the 50-gram weight will move when it raises the 100-gram weight?*

Hypothesizing   *How far do you think the 100-gram weight will move when it is raised by the 50-gram weight?*

100 grams

10. Obtain a yard- or meterstick.

Measuring 11. Move the 50-gram weight and measure how far both the weights move.

Recording 12. Repeat this part of the activity several times and record your measurements.

Summarizing *What can you say about pulleys from the measurements you just recorded?*

13. Look at the measurements you recorded when one pulley was used and those you recorded when two pulleys were used.
What does the information tell you about pulleys?

How Will Students Use or Apply What They Discover?

What kind of pulley system would be needed to raise a piano weighing 300 pounds?
Draw a sketch of that pulley system.

What Is a Lever and How Can You Use It? (3–8)

What Concepts Might Students Discover?

A **lever** is a simple machine.
A lever cannot work alone.
A lever consists of a bar that is free to turn on a pivot called the **fulcrum.** By using a first-class lever, it is possible to increase a person's ability to lift heavier objects. This is called the **mechanical advantage.** The mechanical advantage of a lever is determined by the formula

$$\text{Mechanical advantage} = \frac{\text{Effort arm}}{\text{Resistance arm}}$$

The weight times the distance on one side of the fulcrum must equal the weight times the distance on the other side if the lever is balanced.
A first-class lever has the fulcrum between the resistance and the effort.

What Will We Need?

Roll of heavy string or nylon fishing line
Meter- or yardstick
100-gram weight
20-gram weight
Platform with an arm or ring stand and clamp for suspending objects
Assorted weights of various sizes

What Must I Know?

Define *resistance, force,* and *fulcrum* before beginning the activity.

PROCESSES

What Will Students and Teacher Do?

1. Using some heavy string, a yardstick, a 100-gram weight, a 20-gram weight, and a ring stand and clamp, assemble the apparatus as shown in the diagram.

Hypothesizing   *Where do you think you should attach the 100-gram weight and the 20-gram weight so the yardstick will balance?*

2. Attach the weights so the yardstick is balanced.

Observing   *How far is the 100-gram weight from the end of the yardstick?*

Observing   *How far is the 20-gram weight from the end of the yardstick?*

3. Look at these three things: the string, which is suspending the yardstick; the 20-gram weight; and the 100-gram weight.

Inferring   *What is the relationship between the weight and distance on each side of the fulcrum?*

Inferring   *What are the advantages of using a first-class lever of this type?*

4. Use the following formula to calculate the mechanical advantage (M.A.) of the lever.

$$\text{M.A.} = \frac{\text{Effort arm}}{\text{Resistance arm}}$$

What Must I Know?

At the completion of the activity, explain to the class that a **first-class lever** consists of a bar that is free to turn on a pivot point called the **fulcrum.** The weight moved is called the **resistance.** The force exerted on the other end of the lever is called the **effort.** Draw the preceding diagram on the board to illustrate this point. State that in a first-class lever, the fulcrum is always between the resistance and the effort. Repeat this activity using assorted weights and calculate the M.A. using the formula given in Step 4. Use metric measurements, if possible.

How Will Students Use or Apply What They Discover?

1. *How is the M.A. affected when different weights are used?*
2. *What does an M.A. of 4 mean?*
3. *Where are first-class levers used?*

Reference Books—Simple Machines
Teacher: Barbara Taylor, *Machines and Movement* (New York: Warwick Press, 1990).
Students: Christopher Lampton, *Seesaws, Nutcrackers, and Brooms* (Brookfield, CT: Millbrook Press, 1991).

MAGNETIC AND ELECTRICAL ENERGIES AND INTERACTIONS

QUICKIE STARTERS: OPEN-ENDED ACTIVITIES

What Can Magnets Do? (K–2)

Materials

Several strong magnets, steel ball

What Do Students Know?

What might happen if you bring a magnet next to a steel ball or another magnet?

Some Possible Activities

Put a magnet on a table and hold a steel ball 1 inch (2–3 cm) away from the magnet's end.
What happens when you let go of the steel ball?
Try it again.
Why do you think this happens?

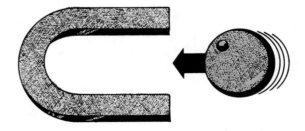

Now try the same thing using two magnets.
What happens to the magnets?

A

B

Try the same thing again, but turn one magnet around so its opposite end faces the first magnet.

What happens now? Why do you think this happens?
What other things might you be able to move with magnets?
How could you find out?

What Are the Shapes and Names of Magnets? (K–2)

Materials

Large assortment of magnets of different sizes, shapes, colors, and materials (lodestone, bar, U-shaped, horseshoe, cylindrical, disk, doughnut-shaped); variety of items attracted to magnets (paper clips, iron or steel washers, and nails); variety of objects not attracted to magnets (rubber bands, paper, plastic chips, bits of wood); 2 shoeboxes, one labeled "Magnets Pick Up" and one labeled "Magnets Do Not Pick Up."

Bar   V-shaped   U-shaped   Horseshoe   Cylindrical   Lodestone   Doughnut-shaped

What Do Students Know?

How are all these things [magnets] the same?
What are they called?

Some Possible Activities

Touch one magnet at a time to the piles of paper clips, iron or steel washers, and nails.
What happens to the paper clips and other things?
Try the same thing with the other objects.
What happens? Why do you think the paper clips, the iron or steel washers, and the nails were pulled to and stuck to the magnets?
Put those objects that were picked up by the magnets into the box marked "Magnets Pick Up" and those objects that were not picked up by the magnets into the box marked "Magnets Do Not Pick Up." Objects that pull and hold iron and steel things are called **magnets,** and their exact names are descriptive of their shapes, such as lodestone, bar magnet, U-shaped magnet, cylindrical magnet, and doughnut-shaped magnet.
What other shapes might magnets have?
Bring in magnets you have at home.
Where are the magnets used?

Magnets pick up

Magnets do *not* pick up

GUIDED DISCOVERY HANDS-ON/MINDS-ON ACTIVITIES

What Is a Magnet? (K–5)

What Concepts Might Students Discover?

The place on the magnet where it picks up iron or steel objects is called the **pole.** A magnet has two poles, one called the north, and the other called the south.

The same or like poles push apart, or **repel**. Different or unlike poles pull together, or **attract**.

Around every magnet is an area called the **magnetic field,** which is made up of invisible magnetic lines of force.

What Will We Need?

2 cylindrical bar magnets
2 rectangular bar magnets
String
Wooden meterstick without a metal edge
1 large and 1 small bar magnet
Paper clip
Steel washer

Steel BB
Transparent tape
Steel needle
Glass or plastic pan
Water
⅛-in. slice of cork

What Must I Know?

The materials listed are for a group of two or three students. Set up stations and equip each group with a set of materials.

What Do Students Know?

Display a cylindrical bar magnet for the class.
What is this called?
What is it made of?
How can it be used?
What are the properties or characteristics of a magnet?
What things can a magnet do?

What do you think would happen if two cylindrical bar magnets were placed side by side?
How could you find out?

PROCESSES

What Will Students Do?

I **G**

Observing
Observing

Part I (K–2)

1. Place one cylindrical bar magnet on the table and bring the second magnet near it.
   Observe what happens.
2. Reverse one of the magnets. Observe what happens.
   What happens when you put the second magnet beside the first one?
   What happens when you turn one magnet around?

Why do you think one magnet rolls when the other comes near it?
What did you notice when the magnets pulled together?
What did you notice when the magnets pushed apart?

Inferring   *How do you know from this activity that both ends of the magnet are not the same?*

Inferring   *What did you do to make the magnets push apart?*
Inferring   *What did you do to make the magnets pull together?*

Part II (K–2)

What Do Students Know?

What are the parts of a magnet?

What Will Students Do?

Hypothesizing

Inferring

Hypothesizing
Observing

Inferring

Inferring

1. Using two rectangular or cylindrical bar magnets, tie a string around the middle of one of the magnets as shown in the diagram (next page).
2. By holding the string, suspend the magnet in the air.
   What do you think will happen when another magnet is brought near the suspended one?
3. Bring another magnet near the suspended one.
   Why do you think the magnet moves?
   What do you think will happen when you reverse the magnet in your hand?
4. Reverse the magnet and bring it near the suspended one.
   Why does the suspended magnet react differently when you approach it with the other end of the magnet?
   What causes the magnet to react in different ways?

Inferring
Explaining

How do you know there is a force present even though it cannot be seen? What is a force?

What Must I Know?

Point out that a **force** is a push or pull. This can be shown by pushing or pulling a child who is seated in a chair.

Part III (3–5)

What Do Students Know?

How can you measure the force of attraction between certain objects and magnets?

What Will Students Do?

1. Get a wooden meterstick *without a metal edge*, a large and a small bar magnet, a paper clip, a steel washer, a steel BB, and transparent tape.
2. Tape the meterstick to your desktop so it will not move. Put a paper clip at the end of the meterstick and place the large bar magnet at the 6-cm line (as shown in the diagram).

3. *Very slowly* move the magnet along the meterstick's edge toward the paper clip. Stop exactly when the paper clip starts to move toward the magnet!

Observing

How many centimeters away was the magnet when the paper clip started to move?

Record your findings on a chart like the following:

Object	Distance from Object to Magnet
Paper clip	

4. Repeat Step 3 two more times and then average the three findings.

Hypothesizing   *Why average three observations?*

5. Do the same tests using the steel BB and the washer.

Inferring   *If the distances the objects moved were different, why do you think this is so?*

6. Repeat the tests using the small magnet with each object, three times each. Average the findings and record the data on your chart.

Comparing   *Which of the two magnets was the stronger?*

Inferring   *How do you know from your findings?*

Inferring   *Why do you think the distances between the magnet and the paper clip, the BB, and the washer were different?*

Inferring   *What do these tests tell you about the strength of magnets and how different objects are affected?*

Communicating   Using the data from your charts, graph the results of these tests.

Part IV (3–5)

What Will Students Do?   1. Obtain a steel needle, a magnet, and a pan with an inch or two of water in it.

Hypothesizing   *What can you find out about the needle and the magnet?*

Bar magnet

Needle

2. Make a magnet of the needle (magnetize it) by holding a magnet in one hand and stroking a needle *in one direction only* 25 or more times, as in diagram (a). Lay the needle on the cork so the needle is in a horizontal position. Float the cork in the pan of water, as shown in diagram (b). (*Hint:* Adding one drop of liquid dishwashing detergent to the water will enable the floating cork to turn much more easily as the needle responds to the magnet.)

(a)   (b)

3. Bring a magnet near the needle on the cork.

Inferring   *Why do the cork and the needle move when you bring a magnet near them?*
Inferring   *What happens to the needle when it is stroked with the magnet?*
Summarizing   *What caused the cork and needle to move?*

How Will Students Use or Apply What They Discover?

1. *How does a compass work?*
2. *How could you use a magnet to make a compass?*

What Is Static Electricity? (K–8)

What Concepts Might Students Discover?

All bodies are capable of producing electrical charges.
Conductors allow electrons to move, but **insulators** do not allow electrons to move easily.
Like charges repel; unlike charges attract.

What Will We Need?

Carpet square	Transparent tape
Lucite or resin rod or a hard rubber comb	Balloons
	String
Wool cloth	Wire coat hanger
Flour	Glass rod
Small pieces of paper	Piece of silk about the size
Tap water	of a small handkerchief

What Do Students Know?

What can you state about how poles of magnets react toward one another?
What is the energy that we use to produce light and to operate many machines and household appliances?
What things can produce electricity?
How can you find out if all charges of electricity are the same?

PROCESSES

Part I (K–2)

What Do Students Know?

What happens sometimes when you walk over carpet and touch a doorknob or slide across a car seat and touch a metal car door?

What Will Students Do?

Hypothesizing
Observing

1. Stand next to a doorknob and shuffle your feet *briskly* on a carpet square at least 20 times.
   What do you think will happen if you touch the doorknob with one finger?
2. Touch the doorknob with one finger and observe what happens.
   What did you see?
   What did you feel?
   What did you hear?

How Will Students Use or Apply What They Discover?

Where in nature does this happen?

What Must I Know?

Friction between the carpet and the student's feet causes electric charges to build up on the student. These charges, called **static electricity,** may be slowly discharged into air or rapidly discharged when the student touches a metal object such as the doorknob. Lightning is the discharge of huge amounts of electrical charges.

Part II (K–2)

What Will Students Do?

Hypothesizing

1. Obtain the following materials: a lucite or resin rod or a hard rubber comb, wool, flour, small pieces of paper, and a source of tap water.
2. Take the resin rod (or hard rubber comb) and rub it with the wool cloth.
   What do you think will happen when the rod is touched to the flour?
3. Touch the rod to some flour.

Resin rod or
hard rubber comb

Flour

Observing
Hypothesizing

What happens to the flour?
Why do you think the flour is affected by the rod?

Observing

4. Clean the rod, rub it again, and touch it to the small pieces of paper.
   What does the rod do to the paper?
5. Rub the rod briskly with the wool cloth.
6. Turn on a water tap so a very slow stream of water comes out.

Hypothesizing

   What do you think will happen to the stream of water when the rod is moved close to it?
7. Move the rod close to the stream.

Static
electric field

Observing   *What happens as the rod comes near?*
Inferring   *Why does the water react as it does?*
Inferring   *Why do you think it reacts as it does without being touched?*

What Must I Know?

The students should note how close they have to bring the rod before it affects the stream of water. Develop the concept that there is an invisible field of electrical force around the rod that either pushes or attracts the water. This force cannot be seen, but it must be there because it affects the stream of water. Define *force* as a push or pull. In this case, the water is pushed or pulled, without being touched, by moving the rod toward and away from the water.

Designing an Investigation   *How can you find out if rubbing the cloth on the rod causes the electrical force?*
8. Rub the rod again with the cloth.
9. Now rub your hand over the rod.

Hypothesizing

   What do you think will happen to the stream of water?
10. Repeat the procedure by approaching the slow stream of water with the rod.

Observing   *What effect does the rod have on the water this time?*
Inferring   *Why does the rod not have the same effect?*
Inferring   *What happened to the charge that the wool cloth induced in the rod?*
Inferring   *Why do you think the charge failed to last?*

What Must I Know?

When the resin rod is rubbed with wool, **electrons** are rubbed off these materials onto the rod. The rod, however, is an insulator, so the electron movement is slight. The rod becomes negatively charged because each electron produces a small amount of negative charge. When a hand is rubbed over the rod, the rod becomes discharged because the electrons leave the rod and enter the hand. The rod is then neutral. Explain the difference between a conductor and an insulator.

Part III (K–2)

What Do Students Know?

After your discussion concerning conductors and insulators, would you say the rod is a conductor or an insulator?
Why do you think so?

What Will Students Do?

Observing
Inferring

1. Tear off two 12-inch strips of sticky transparent tape, making sure they don't stick to each other by keeping the sticky side on the outside.
2. Holding one strip of tape in one hand, slowly bring the second strip toward the other.
   What happens?
   Why?

Part IV (3–5)

What Will Students Do?

1. Obtain two balloons.
2. Inflate the balloons.
3. Tie a string to each balloon and suspend them from a bar or a coat hanger as shown in the diagram.

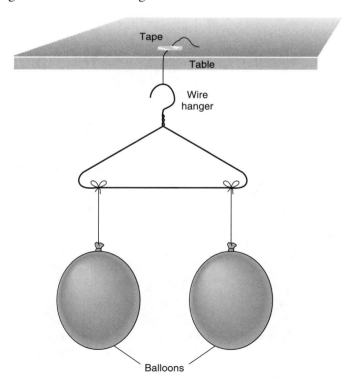

4. Rub each balloon with the wool cloth.

Observing   *What do the balloons do?*

Inferring   *Why do they repel each other?*

Summarizing   *Do you think the balloons are conductors or insulators?*

Hypothesizing   *What do you think will happen if a charged resin rod is brought near the balloons?*

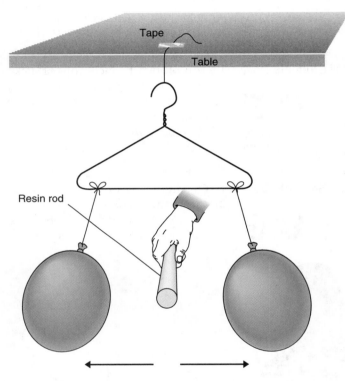

5. Rub the resin rod with wool and place it near the balloons.

Observing   *In which direction do the balloons move?*

Inferring   *Why do you think they were repelled by the rod?*

Assuming   *Do you think the balloons have a like or unlike charge? Why?*

Hypothesizing   *What do you think will happen to the balloons if you touch them with a glass rod?*

What Must I Know?   These balloons were charged in the same way; therefore, each must have the same charge. When they do have the same charge, they repel each other because like charges repel.

6. Rub the glass rod with the piece of silk.
7. Place it near the balloons.

Observing   *What happens as it comes near the balloons?*

Comparing   *How does the glass rod affect the balloons in comparison to the resin rod?*

Comparing   *What can you say about the charge on the resin rod compared to the glass rod?*

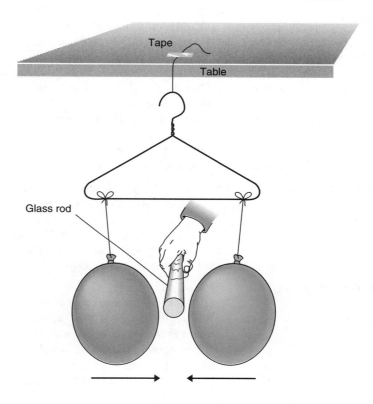

Tape

Table

Glass rod

What Must I Know?   The glass rod will have a positive charge since electrons were rubbed off
                          the rod onto the silk. It will attract the balloons because they were neg-
                          atively charged by the resin rod, and unlike charges attract.

Part V (6–8)

What Will Students Do?   1. Vigorously rub an inflated balloon against a piece of wool.
                             2. Place the balloon on a wall. (See diagram.)

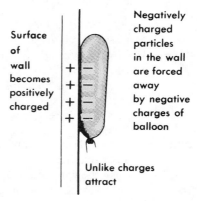

Surface
of
wall
becomes
positively
charged

Negatively
charged
particles
in the wall
are forced
away
by negative
charges of
balloon

Unlike charges
attract

Hypothesizing	*What do you think will happen to the balloon?*
Inferring	*Why does the balloon not fall?*
Inferring	*Is the force that pulls the balloon to the wall greater or less than the gravitational force pulling the balloon down to earth?*
Inferring	*What happened to the negatively charged particles in the wall when the balloon came near?*
Summarizing	*After following the previous steps, what can you say about charging matter?*
Summarizing	*What is a conductor?*
Summarizing	*What is an insulator?*

What Must I Know?

When you rub the balloon with wool, it becomes negatively charged, because it got an excess of electrons from the wool. When the balloon is placed next to the wall, the balloon's negative charge forces the electrons in the wall away from the surface, leaving the surface positively charged. The balloon sticks because the unlike charges attract. The balloon is negative and the wall surface is positive, as is indicated in the diagram.

How Will Students Use or Apply What They Discover?

1. *What is electricity?*
2. *How can you use a magnet to make electricity?*
3. *Why might you get a shock after walking across a wool carpet and then touching a metal doorknob?*
4. *Why does your hair get attracted to your comb? Why is this most noticeable on very dry days?*
5. *Why do clothes stick together after being dried in a clothes dryer?*

How Can You Make Electricity by Using Magnetism? (6–8)

What Concepts Might Students Discover?

Around a magnet there are magnetic lines of force.
If you break the magnetic lines of force, you can make electricity.
A *force* is defined as a push or a pull.

What Will We Need?

Insulated copper wire (about 3 yards)
Bar magnet
Magnetic compass

What Do Students Know?

How is electricity used?
How does electricity get to your home for you to use?
What is the area of force around a magnet called?
What is a force?
How can you use a magnet to produce electricity?

PROCESSES

What Will Students and Teacher Do?

1. With a partner, obtain a length of insulated copper wire (about 3 yards), a bar magnet, and a magnetic compass.
2. Take the wire and wrap it 20 to 30 times around the magnetic compass as indicated in the diagram.

3. Loop the other end of the wire into a coil as shown in the diagram.

Inferring   *What happens when electricity goes through a wire?*
Inferring   *What do you think the area around the wire could be called?*
Inferring   *What has the electricity produced?*
Designing an Investigation   *How do you think magnetism could be used to produce electricity?*
Observing   4. Take the bar magnet and plunge it back and forth through the coil of wire. Instruct your partner to watch what happens to the compass.
Observing   *What happens to the compass?*
Inferring   *Why do you think the compass needle does what it does?*
Applying   *What attracts the compass needle?*
Hypothesizing   *What do you think causes the needle to be deflected?*
Hypothesizing   *Where do you think the magnetism was produced to cause the compass needle to move?*
Inferring or Interpreting   *If there is magnetism produced in the wire around the compass, what do you think the plunging of the magnet through the coil of wire has to do with it?*
Inferring or Interpreting   *When is electricity produced in the wire?*
Summarizing   *What is the force of a magnet called?*
Summarizing   *What does a magnet do to a magnetizable object?*
Summarizing   *What does a magnet do to a nonmagnetizable object?*
Summarizing   *Explain how magnetism can be used to produce an electrical current.*

What Must I Know?

Around every magnet there is an area that can push or pull susceptible objects such as iron filings. This area is thought to consist of lines of force. When these lines of force are broken by plunging the magnet back and forth through a coil of wire, electricity is made in the wire. **Electricity** is defined as a flow of electrons along the wire, producing an electrical current. Whenever there is an electrical current produced, there will be a magnetic field around the wire. This magnetic field causes the magnet (compass needle) in this activity to move. Using magnets to produce electricity is the principle involved in making electricity in a dynamo. Make certain that the compass is far enough away from the magnet to avoid direct magnetic influence.

How Will Students Use or Apply What They Discover?

How can you use electricity to make a magnet?

How Can You Make a Temporary (Electro) Magnet? (6–8)

What Concepts Might Students Discover?

When electricity passes along a wire, it produces a magnetic field around the wire that acts like a magnet.

A magnetic field can make iron temporarily magnetic.

The more electric current flows through a wire in a unit of time, the more magnetism is generated around the wire.

If a circuit is broken, electricity will not flow.

What Will We Need?

Insulated copper wire   Teaspoon of iron filings
Iron nail   Paper clip
Dry cell battery

What Must I Know?

The supplies listed are for two to four students.

What Do Students Know?

How is magnetism made by electricity?
By using a wire that is carrying a current, how could you make a large magnetic field?
If you wanted to magnetize a nail, how would you do it?

PROCESSES

What Will Students and Teacher Do?

1. Obtain a dry cell battery, an iron nail, a piece of insulated copper wire, some iron filings, and a paper clip.
2. Wrap the wire around the nail several times as shown in the diagram.
3. Scrape the insulation off two ends of the wire. Connect only *one* end of the wire to one terminal of the dry cell.

Electromagnet

Iron filings
& paper clip

CAUTION: DO NOT HOLD WIRE TO TERMINAL
FOR MORE THAN 3 SECONDS!

4. Holding the other end of the wire along the insulated portion, touch the bare end of the wire to the other terminal of the dry cell for only a few seconds. *Caution:* Do not let the wire and terminal remain in contact for more than a few seconds because intense heat builds up, and you could get a burn through the insulation.

Hypothesizing   *What do you think will happen to some iron filings if you place them near the nail and then touch the loose end of the wire to the terminal?*

5. Do this carefully, releasing one end of wire from the terminal after a few seconds.

6. Place a paper clip on the nail and repeat.

Observing   *What happens to the filings and paper clip while the loose end of the wire is touching the terminal?*

Inferring   *Why do the iron filings temporarily stay on the nail?*

Inferring   *What is temporarily produced around the wire when both ends of the wire are touching both terminals?*

Inferring   *What did the nail temporarily become?*

Observing   *What happened to the iron filings and nail when you removed the loose wire so that it no longer touched the terminal?*

Inferring   *Why do they fall when you disconnect the wire?*

Applying   *What must you do with the circuit to produce electricity?*

Summarizing   *What can you say about the production of magnetism around a wire when electricity goes through it?*

Summarizing   *What would you call the temporary magnet you made by passing electricity through a conductor?* **(electromagnet)**

Designing an Investigation   *How do you think you could increase the strength of the magnetism in the nail?*

Hypothesizing   *What do you think would happen if you wrapped more wire around the nail?*

Hypothesizing   *Will the magnetism increase or decrease? Why?*

Assuming   *Is the magnet you produced a temporary or a permanent magnet? Why?*

Inferring   *How do you know?*

How Will Students Use or Apply What They Discover?
T

1. Try an experiment where you test whether more turns of wire affect how many paper clips your electromagnet picks up. Collect data and set up a graph like the one shown on the next page.

By what other means could the magnetic field around the nail be increased? What do you think might happen if you used a bigger dry cell or more dry cells connected together?

How Are Parallel and Series Circuits the Same and Different? (6–8)

What Concepts Might Students Discover?

For the electrons to move in a circuit, there must be a path that is unbroken to and from the source of electrical energy.

If one lamp burns out in a **series circuit**, the circuit is broken.

In a **parallel circuit**, one lamp can burn out, but the rest of the circuit will still function.

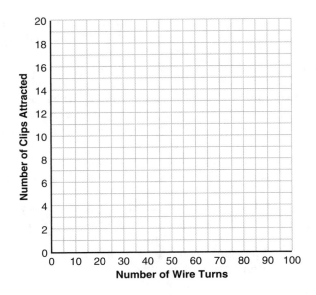

What Will We Need?

2 dry cells   4 sockets
4 small lamps   Connecting wires
2 switches

What Do Students Know?

In what different ways can you use a dry cell and wire to make a circuit?
How could you make a parallel or series circuit?
What would happen if one light on a string of Christmas tree lights were unscrewed?
What would you do to find out?
Why is it that strings of Christmas tree lights do not all behave the same?

PROCESSES

What Will Students Do?

1. Connect a dry cell, two small lamps, a switch, two sockets, and connecting wires so the light works.

Hypothesizing

What do you need to do to make the lights work?

What Must I Know?

The following diagram of the series circuit is for your information. It should not be shown to the students until they have completed the activity.

SERIES CIRCUIT

Small lamp and socket

Switch

Hypothesizing   *What purpose does the switch serve?*
Hypothesizing   *What do you think will happen when you unscrew one of the lights?*
    2. Unscrew one of the lights.
Inferring   *Why did the other light go out?*
Hypothesizing   *What can you do to make the lights go on again?*
    3. Using the same equipment, rearrange the circuit so that if one light goes out, the other will still burn.

What Must I Know?

The following diagram of a parallel circuit is available for your information. It should not be shown to the students until after they finish this activity.

PARALLEL CIRCUIT

Switch

Small lamp
and socket

    4. Unscrew one of the lights. If you wired it differently than the first time, one of the lights should still burn even though you unscrewed the other.
Inferring   *Why?*
Comparing   *What is the difference between the two types of circuits you have constructed?*

What Must I Know?

In a parallel circuit, there may be more than two paths for the current to take to complete its circuit. If one of the circuits is broken, the current can still use the other circuit, as indicated in the preceding diagram.

How Will Students Use or Apply What They Discover?

    1. *What kind of circuits do you have in your home?*
    2. *How could you find out what kind of circuit a string of Christmas tree lights is?*
    3. Examine a flashlight.
      What kind of a circuit does it have?

Reference Books—Magnetic and Electrical Energies and Interactions
Teacher: Neil Ardley, *The Science Book of Magnets* (New York: Harcourt Brace Jovanovich, 1991).
Student: Terry J. Jennings, *Magnets* (New York: Gloucester Press, 1990).

LIGHT ENERGY, SHADOWS, LENSES, AND COLOR

QUICKIE STARTERS: OPEN-ENDED ACTIVITIES

How Does Light Move and Pass Through Some Things? (K–2)

Materials

Flashlights, transparent materials (clear plastic food wrap, sandwich bags, and cups); translucent materials (waxed paper, cloudy plastic); opaque materials (oaktag or construction paper, thin pieces of wood and metal); printed page of directions

What Do Students Know?

Give each student a flashlight. Darken the room and write this statement on the chalkboard, "We cannot see without light." Ask: *Can you tell what I wrote on the chalkboard? Why not? How can you use your flashlights to find out what I wrote?* Turn the lights on and discuss why light is needed for us to see things. (*Hint:* Take the flashlights away before the discussion.) Ask: *Does light move through all materials?*

Some Possible Activities

G

Give each group of four students some samples of the transparent, translucent, and opaque materials, along with a page with print on it. Ask the students to place one kind of material at a time over the printed page you gave them. For each material, have students fill in a chart with one of these choices: (1) can see through it easily, (2) can see through it, but it is very cloudy, (3) cannot see through it.

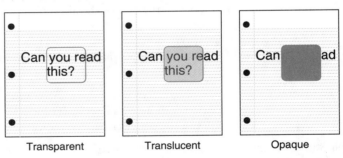

Transparent   Translucent   Opaque

How Will Students Use or Apply What They Discover?

1. Make a chart like this for light sources in your apartment or house:

Room	Light source	Artificial or natural light

2. *Why is natural light needed?*
3. *Why is artificial light needed?*

How Can You Make a Shadow Theater? (K–2)

Materials

Flashlight or filmstrip projector, waxed or rice paper, heavy cardboard or thin wood, puppets made from cardboard

What Do Students Know?

How are shadows made?
How can we use this information to make a Shadow Theater?

Some Possible Activities

Have students stand in front of a source of light (e.g., a flashlight or filmstrip projector). Turn off the classroom lights and turn on the flashlight. The students will see their shadows. Explain that the students are opaque and light cannot pass through them. Shadows, then, are the result of blocked light by opaque materials. Have students make puppets from cardboard. Make a screen out of a heavy cardboard or wood frame which holds waxed paper or rice paper. Shine a flashlight on the puppet that is between the flashlight and the screen, as shown in the diagram.

Flashlight

Puppet

Waxed paper screen

How can the size of the shadows be changed?
How can you make the shadows darker or lighter?
How else can the shadows be changed?

GUIDED DISCOVERY HANDS-ON/MINDS-ON ACTIVITIES

What Does a Prism Do to White Light? (K–2)

What Concepts Might Students Discover?	White light, when passed through a prism, disperses to form a continuous **spectrum,** or a rainbow. White light is a mixture of many colors of light. Each color in the spectrum has a different wavelength.
What Will We Need?	Prism, light source (direct sunlight, flashlight, or filmstrip projector)
What Do Students Know?	*What is a prism?* *What does a prism do?*
What Must I Know?	This activity should be done in groups of two or more students.

PROCESSES

Part I

What Will Students and Teacher Do?

1. Obtain a prism.

Hypothesizing

What do you think will happen to the light rays after they pass through the prism?

T I G

2. Place the prism in the path of a strong beam of light as indicated in the diagram.

Observing   *What happens to the light rays when they pass through the prism?*
Observing   *What colors do you see?*
Observing   *Which color seems to have bent the most?*
Observing   *Which color seems to have bent the least?*
Inferring   *What do you know about the way the different colors of light are refracted (bent) by the prism?*
Inferring   *What is white light made of?*

What Must I Know?   The students should see that white light is produced by the combination of several wavelengths of light. Draw a prism on the board and have the students show how the spectrum is formed. Their drawing should be something like the previous diagram.*

Part II (K–2)

Hypothesizing   *What do you think will happen if you look through the prism at your partner?*

What Will Students Do?   1. Look at your partner through the AB side of the prism (see diagram).

Note: Scientists previously labeled spectrum colors as red, orange, yellow, green, blue, indigo, and violet. The latest evidence eliminates indigo as a spectrum color.

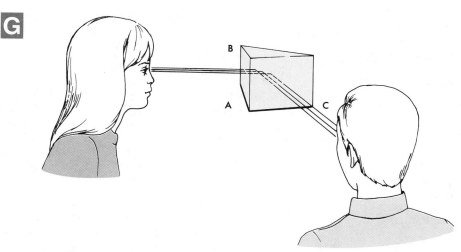

2. Record your observations.

Inferring   *Why is it possible to see your partner without looking directly at him or her?*

Inferring   *What happens to the light entering the prism that makes it possible for you to see your partner?*

Inferring   *What does the prism do to the light rays?*

Comparing   *What is the difference between a prism and a mirror in the way that each affects light?*

What Must I Know?

Prisms are used in expensive optical equipment instead of mirrors because prisms absorb less light. At the conclusion of this activity, place a diagram of a prism on the board and have the students draw how light passes through it. If they do not understand how a prism can be used in a periscope, draw and discuss the following diagram.

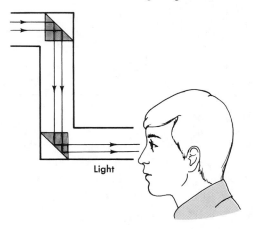

Light

How Will Students Use or Apply What They Discover?

1. *What happens to X-rays when they pass through a prism?*
2. *What would happen if you passed light through two prisms?*
3. *Why are prisms used instead of mirrors in expensive optical equipment?*

How Does Light Appear to Travel? (3–8)

What Concepts Might Students Discover?

To our eyes, light *appears* to travel in a straight line.

What Will We Need?

4 index cards (5 × 8 in.)	Round (oatmeal) box
Hole puncher or pointed object (pencil)	Waxed paper
Modeling clay	Rubber band
Flashlight	Candle
White paper	Matches
Comb	Pie tin

What Do Students Know?

How does light appear to your eyes to travel?

What Must I Know?

You may conduct these simple activities, or students may do them by themselves, to assist them in seeing that light *appears* to our eyes to travel in a straight line. Because light appears to travel in a straight line, images appear upside down (inverted) in a camera. Focusing—moving objects back and forth—is also a result of light appearing to travel in a straight line.

PROCESSES

What Will Students and Teacher Do?

T **G**

Hypothesizing

Part I (3–8)

1. Holding all the index cards together, use a hole puncher or pointed object to punch a ¼-inch (7-mm) hole in the center of each card. Push each card into a lump of modeling clay and space the cards about 1 foot (30 cm) apart, making sure to line up the center holes as shown.
   What do you think will happen if you shine the light through the first card?
2. Shine a light using the flashlight through the first card's hole.

Observing
Hypothesizing

What do you notice about the path of the light?
What will happen if you move the first card 1 inch (25 mm) to one side?

3. Move the first card 1 inch to the left or right.

Observing
Comparing
Inferring

What happens now?
How is this different from what you observed in Step 2?
What does this tell you about how light appears to travel?

Part II (3–8)

What Will Students Do?

G

1. Lay the flashlight flat on a piece of white paper. Stand the comb, teeth down, in front of the light.
2. Darken the room and turn on the flashlight.

Observing	*What happens to the light?*
Inferring	*Why?*
	3. Trace the light rays onto the paper.
Describing	*How would you describe the rays?*

What Must I Know?   The rays should appear as straight lines.

Part III (3–8)

What Must I Know?   You should demonstrate this activity for immature or unruly students. Due to the open flame, students should be carefully supervised. For older students, this activity should be done in groups of two. One student will perform the activity while the other observes and vice versa.

What Do Students Know?

How does a camera use light?
What does it mean to focus a camera?

What Will Students and Teacher Do?

T **G**

1. Obtain a round oatmeal box, waxed paper, rubber band, candle, and matches. Puncture a very small hole in the end of the box with your pencil. Cover the open end of the box with waxed paper and secure the paper with a rubber band.
2. Place the candle (attached to the pie tin with melted wax) in front of the pinhole end of the box and light the candle. Darken the room.
3. Move the small-holed end back and forth in front of the candle while your partner watches the waxed-papered end.

Rubber band

End of tube

Observing	*What appears on the waxed-papered end of the box?*
Observing	*What is different about the image on the waxed paper?*
Inferring	*Why do you think the image appears this way?*
Hypothesizing	*Why did you move the punctured end of the box back and forth?*
Inferring	*From this activity, what would you conclude about how light appears to travel?*
Inferring	*How do you think a picture of an object appears on the film in the back of a camera?*

How Will Students Use or Apply What They Discover?

1. *What would happen to the image on the waxed paper if you moved the box 3 feet (or a meter) from the candle?*
2. *What would happen to the image if you blew the candle flame out? Why?*

What Must I Know?

After students have completed the previous activity, place the previous diagram on the board and have students draw the image of the candle. They should draw an inverted flame. Discuss how the light travels through the hole, as indicated by the second diagram, and results in an inverted image on the waxed-papered end.

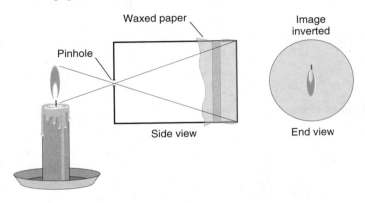

Waxed paper

Image inverted

Pinhole

Side view

End view

Reference Books—Light Energy, Shadows, Lenses, and Color

Teacher: Bernie Zubrowski, *Mirrors Finding Out About the Properties of Light* (New York: Morrow, 1992).

Student: Clyde Robert Bulla, *What Makes a Shadow?* (New York: HarperCollins, 1992).

Life Sciences and Technology

As a result of their activities in grades K–4, all students should develop an understanding of:

- characteristics of organisms,
- life cycles of organisms, and
- organisms and environments.

As a result of their activities in grades 5–8, all students should develop an understanding of:

- structure and function in living systems,
- reproduction and heredity,
- populations and ecosystems, and
- diversity and adaptations of organisms. (p. 10)[1]

PLANT ANATOMY AND PHYSIOLOGY

QUICKIE STARTERS: OPEN-ENDED ACTIVITIES

What Kinds of Things Can We Do With Plants?

Materials

Magazines, newspapers, colored paper, paintbrushes, poster paint

Some Possible Activities

1. *Hug and feel a tree.* Have students hug a tree trunk, feel its surface, and describe how it feels. Encourage students to smell the bark. Have them draw and give a name to their favorite tree or cut pictures of trees out of magazines.

2. *Press plants.* Invite students to collect parts of plants, such as leaves and flowers. *Caution:* Stress collecting fallen plant parts only. Do not allow students to pick from living things. Also, make sure students do not collect any parts from poisonous plants such as poison ivy. Have students press the plant parts between newspapers. Place some books or something heavy on the newspapers. After several days, remove the weights and newspapers. Discuss how drying helps to preserve the plants.

[1]Reprinted with permission from National Science Standards. Copyright 1995 by the National Academy of Sciences. Courtesy of the National Academy Press, Washington, DC.

3. *Make splatter pictures of leaves.* Have students collect different types of leaves and bring them to class. Tell students to place the leaves on colored paper. Then show students how to dip brushes in poster paint and splatter paint over the leaves to make a picture outline. Have students compare the different types of leaves and what methods they had to use to make good splatter pictures. For example, ask how the thickness of the paint affected the quality of the picture.

How Can Some Plants Grow Without Seeds? (K–2)

Materials	Small tumblers (preferably clear plastic); small sweet potatoes, white potatoes, and carrot tops (with some root); toothpicks; cuttings from coleus, philodendron, ivy, and other houseplants
What Do Students Know?	*How can we get new plants to grow without planting seeds?* *What is needed for new plants to grow?* *How can we take good care of our new plants?*

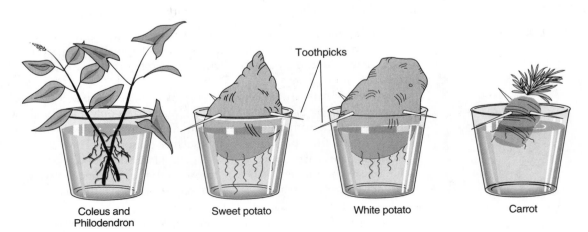

Coleus and Philodendron   Sweet potato   Toothpicks   White potato   Carrot

Some Possible Activities

Put three toothpicks each in a sweet potato, white potato, and carrot, as shown in the diagram. Place the plants in small tumblers of water. Take cuttings of houseplants and place them in small tumblers of water. Put all the tumblers in a well-lit place and make sure the water levels are maintained so that the water always touches the plants. Have students observe and measure the changes in the plants, such as root development, height, number of leaves, and so on.

GUIDED DISCOVERY HANDS-ON/MINDS-ON ACTIVITIES

What Is Variation? (K–2)

What Concepts Might Students Discover?

There is tremendous variation in nature.

What Will We Need?

A variety of fallen leaves collected
   from home or school
Ruler

Large bag of pea pods
Paper plates

What Do Students Know?

How are leaves the same and different?
How could you find out?

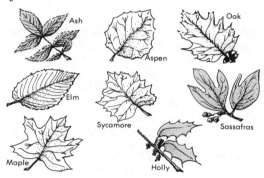

PROCESSES

What Will Students Do?

Comparing
Inferring

Classifying

Inferring

Part I   How Are Leaves Alike and Different? (K–2)

1. Collect different kinds of leaves and obtain a ruler.
2. Place the leaves on your desk and compare them.
   What can you say about the shapes of the leaves? How do they differ in size?
3. Place the leaves in groups according to properties, such as color, size, kind (maple, oak, etc.), number of points, and arrangement of veins.
   How many groups did you get?
   Why do you think leaves vary in size, shape, color, number of points, and other characteristics?

What Must I Know?

Leaves may vary because of inheritance, or because of the environment in which they live. For example, the leaves of a particular species may be large if the environment in which the plant grows richly supplies the things needed by the plant.

Summarizing

4. Summarize how your leaves vary.

Part II   How Do Seed Pods Vary? (K–2)

What Will Students and Teacher Do?

Students: Get two pea pods, open each pod, count the number of peas in each pod, and put peas and pods on your paper plate.

Teacher: Ask who found the most peas in their pods and record this number on the chalkboard. Do the same for the least number of peas. Draw a horizontal line between the extreme numbers and divide the remaining space into equal spaces. For example, if the range is 2 to 10, mark the spaces 2, 3, 4, 5, 6, 7, 8, 9, 10.

How Will Students Use or Apply What They Discover?

Have students come to the chalkboard and place an X above the number that corresponds to the number of peas in their pods. This will provide a histogram or line plot like the one shown.

Recording

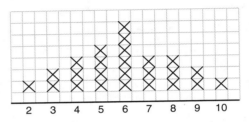

Hypothesizing
Inferring

If you open another pea pod, what might be the most likely number of peas in it? Is there a relationship between the number of peas in the pod and the pod's length?

What Must I Know?

You can substitute other vegetables and fruits—string beans, melons, apples—for counting and making histograms or line plots. You can guide your students to observe that seeds from plants in the same family produce identical numerical seed patterns.

How Will Students Use or Apply What They Discover?

1. *What other things in nature vary?*
2. *How do dogs vary?*
3. *How do humans vary?*

What Are Seeds, and How Do They Grow? (K–5)

What Concepts Might Students Discover?

Soaked bean seeds are different from dried beans.

A seed has different parts: the **embryo** (tiny plant), the **cotyledon(s)** (stored food), and a **seed coat** (skin). Each part is needed for the germination and growth of the plant.

Part I   What Are the Parts of a Seed? (K–2)

What Will We Need?

1 lima bean seed soaked overnight
1 unsoaked lima bean seed
Piece of waxed paper
Hand lens

What Do Students Know?

What is a seed and what parts does it have?
How can we find out?

PROCESSES

What Will Students and Teacher Do?

Comparing
Labeling

Give each student the materials listed. Ask students to respond to the following questions, using their seeds as their sources of observation. List the responses on the board.

How are soaked seeds different from dried seeds?
What do you think you will see when you open your seeds?
1. Open your soaked seed.
   Demonstrate for students how to open a seed.
   How does what you see compare with your hypotheses (guesses)?
2. Draw and label a picture of your open seed.

Inferring
Inferring
Inferring
Designing an Investigation

Which part of the seed do you think might grow into a plant?
What do you think might happen to the other parts of the seed?
Which parts do you think are needed for the plant to grow?
How could you set up an experiment to test your ideas about what seed parts are needed for the plant to grow?

What Must I Know?

This activity is an important introduction to what a seed is, what its parts are, and the functions of those parts in producing a new plant. Activities that follow will investigate variables that affect seed germination.

Part II   Which Parts of a Seed Are Needed for It to Grow Into a Plant?[2] (K–5)

What Will We Need?

Plastic bag   5 soaked lima beans
Paper towel   Stapler

What Do Students Know?

Designing an Investigation

What parts of a seed are needed for it to grow into a plant?

How can we test to see which seed parts are needed and which are not?
Which parts of a soaked bean can you remove to see if they are needed for growth?

PROCESSES

What Will Students Do?

1. Make a "germination bag" by lining a plastic bag with a moist paper towel and stapling the bag across its center, as shown in the diagram.
2. Prepare five soaked lima beans as follows: (1) a complete bean, (2) a bean with the seed coat removed, (3) a bean with one cotyledon removed, (4) one cotyledon only, and (5) the embryo only. Put the beans into the germination bag and number them 1–5 on the outside of the bag.

[2]For greater details and expanded directions, see "From Seed to Plant," *Elementary Science Supplement to the Syllabus, Level I* (Albany, NY: The State University of New York, The State Education Department, 1986), 39–54.

3. Put water in the germination bag as shown, close the bag, and attach it to a bulletin board, wall, or chalkboard.

4. Observe your germination bag for several days. *Note:* Open the bag daily for 15 minutes to prevent mold formation and add just enough water to keep the paper towel slightly moist.

Hypothesizing	*Which of the five seeds, if any, started to grow?*
Inferring	*Why do you think that is so?*
Observing	*How were all seeds in your germination bag treated the same?*
Observing	*Which seed or seed part grew best?*
Observing	*Which parts did not grow at all?*
Inferring	*Why do you think they did not grow?*
Observing	*Which seed parts are needed in order for a seed to grow?*
Observing	*From observing your germination bag, which seed part(s) do you think can be removed without stopping the seeds from growing?*
Inferring	*Why do you think this is so?*
Inferring	*Do all whole seeds grow? Why or why not?*

How Will Students Use or Apply What They Discover?

1. *Why might seeds die after they have sprouted if they are not planted in soil?*
2. *How long might sprouts live if not planted in soil?*
3. *Why do some kinds of sprouts live longer than others?*
4. *What might happen to seeds if they remain wet for a long time?*
5. *Why do seeds not germinate if the embryos are removed?*
6. *Why will seeds die if the cotyledons are removed?*

Part III   How Does Temperature Affect the Sprouting, or Germination, of Seeds? (K–5)

What Will We Need?

8 lima bean seeds   2 paper towels
8 radish seeds   Stapler
2 clear self-sealing plastic bags

PROCESSES

What Will Students Do?

1. Place four lima bean seeds and four radish seeds in two separate plastic germination bags, adding a paper towel and water to each bag, as in Part II.

I G

Refrigerator

Dark cabinet

2. Put one germination bag in a cool, dark place (e.g., the refrigerator in the teachers' room or cafeteria) and one in a warm, dark place (e.g., inside a cabinet). See diagram.

Hypothesizing   *How do you think the difference in temperature will affect the germination of the seeds? Why were both environments kept dark?*

Collecting and   3. Set up a chart like the example that follows. Observe your germination
Recording Data   bags each day for 2 weeks and record your observations.

Note: Open the bags daily for 15 minutes to prevent the formation of mold and keep the paper towels just slightly moist.

Seed name and amount	Date planted	Germination date		Germination conditions	Number of seeds germinated
		Predicted	Actual		

4. At the end of the two weeks, compare the seeds in the two germination bags.

Comparing   *What differences do you notice?*
Inferring   *Why do you think these differences occurred?*

What Are Plant Growth Stages and Parts? (K–5)

What Concepts Might   Plants grow from seeds to full growth in stages.
Students Discover?   Plants have leaves, roots, stems, and flowers.
Not all plants have all four parts.
Leaves are able to make food.
The stems carry minerals and water from the roots to the leaves and flowers.
Flowers make seeds that can produce more of the same type of plant.
Some roots store food.

Part I   What Are the Stages of Growth in Plants? (K–5)

What Will We Need?   Seeds germinated in germination bags from previous activities

What Do Students Know?   *How did our seeds grow into plants? Was there a pattern from seeds to plants?*

What Must I Know?   Duplicate the following diagram. Cut and scramble the four segments for students to arrange in sequence.

PROCESSES

What Will Students Do?   Review seed germination by arranging the diagrams provided by your teacher into the proper sequence. Mark "A" for the first stage, "B" for the second, and so on.

What Must I Know?   The progression from seed to plant *usually* follows this sequence:

A. Seed swells from moisture, coat softens and splits, and tiny root and stem emerge.
B. Upper stem breaks soil surface, and cotyledons are lifted out of seed cover.
C. Cotyledons and tiny leaves unfold. Roots deepen and spread out.
D. More extensive root system cotyledons get smaller and shrivel, and more and larger leaves develop and make food through photosynthesis.

Part II   How Do Roots Grow? (K–5)

What Concepts Might Students Discover?   Roots grow around objects in the soil.
Seeds need water to grow.
Roots grow downward.

What Will We Need?   4 germinated bean seeds
Paper towels
2 pieces of glass or thick clear plastic to place seeds between

4 small pebbles
2 tongue depressors or applicator sticks
Tape

What Do Students Know?   *What do you think might happen to roots if they were planted facing up instead of down, or if something were in their way?*

What Must I Know?

In the primary grades, this activity might have to be done as a demonstration because of the difficulty young children might have in manipulating the equipment. For older students, this activity should be done in groups of two to four students.

What Will Students and Teacher Do?

1. Place four bean seeds (that have already been germinated) between two moist paper towels. Put the paper towels with the seedlings between two pieces of glass or rigid clear plastic. Put small pebbles under each root, place the applicator sticks or tongue depressors between the pieces of glass or clear plastic, and tape as shown in the diagram.

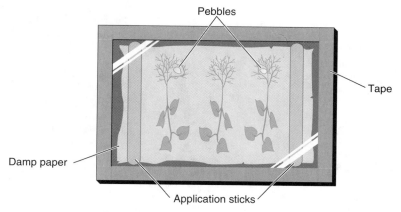

Pebbles

Tape

Damp paper

Application sticks

Hypothesizing

What is the reason for putting the tongue depressors between the pieces of glass or plastic? Why tape the sides?

2. Stand the glass so the roots point up and the stems point down.

Hypothesizing

What do you think might happen to the growth of the stems and roots?

Observing and Recording
Inferring
Designing an Investigation

3. Observe the plant growth for several days and record your observations. *Was your hypothesis true or false? Does it need to be modified?*

If you were going to do this activity again, how would you change it to make it better or more interesting?

How Will Students Use or Apply What They Discover?

1. *How might the roots react if objects like cotton, a piece of wood, or a rock were placed in their way?*
2. *What would happen to the roots if the glass were rotated 90° in the same direction every day?* Try it and keep records of your observations.

Part III   How Does Water Get Into a Plant? (K–5)

What Concepts Might Students Discover?

Roots absorb water through small root hairs.
Root hairs are damaged when a plant is transplanted or pulled.

What Will We Need?

Radish seeds	Clear self-sealing plastic bags
Paper towel	Stapler
Water	Hand lens

What Do Students Know?

What could you do to determine what a root does for a plant (its function)?

What Will Students Do?

1. Obtain a paper towel, several radish seeds, and a self-sealing plastic bag. Soak the towel so it drips with water. Place the towel in the bag to make germination bag as shown on p. 97.
2. Staple the bag across its center, insert several radish seeds, and add water. Seal and attach your germination bag upright to a bulletin board, wall, or chalkboard.
3. Observe for several days and record your observations. Use a hand lens.

Observing/Recording   *What do you notice about the roots?*

Observing   *What are the small fuzzlike projections coming from each root called?*

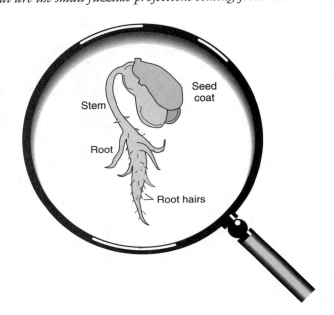

Inferring   *Why do you think the root has root hairs?*

Hypothesizing   *What could happen to the roots and root hairs of a plant when the plant is transplanted?*

Hypothesizing   *Why is some transplanting unsuccessful?*

Designing an Investigation   *What would you do to determine what the function is of roots and root hairs?*

Hypothesizing   *What do you think might happen if you removed the root hairs from the root?*

Hypothesizing   *What do you think might happen if you exposed the root hairs to air and sun?*

How Will Students Use or Apply What They Discover?

1. *Why are roots different shapes?*
2. *Why are some roots comparatively shallow and others deep?*
3. *How do people use the roots of plants?*
4. *What are the functions of the root, other than to absorb food materials?*

Part IV   How Are Roots Useful? (K–5)

What Will We Need?

2 small, healthy coleus, geranium, or petunia plants
Potting soil
2 empty, clean milk cartons

What Will Students Do?

1. Obtain two similar petunia, coleus, or geranium plants and remove all the roots from one plant. Obtain some soil and fill the bottom half of two milk cartons. Place the petunia without roots with its stem down, on top of the soil.

Observing
Inferring

What do you notice about the plant when you let go?
How do you think roots might have helped this plant?

2. Push the bottom part of the stem to a depth of almost 2 inches into the soil. Water the plant daily. Allow it to remain undisturbed for four or five days. As a control, plant the other petunia with roots as shown.

Hypothesizing
Observing
Summarizing

What do you think will happen to the plant without roots?

3. After 4 or 5 days, record what happens.

From your observations, how do you think roots might have helped the plant?

Petunia
with
roots

Petunia
without
roots

What Must I Know?

Some plants might develop new roots in this situation. If they do, remove the plant and discuss the function of the newly developed roots.

Part V   What Are the Purposes of a Stem? (K–5)

What Concepts Might Students Discover?

Water must move from the roots to the leaves if a plant is to make food and live.

One of the main purposes of the stem of a plant is to carry water from the roots to the leaves.

There are small tubes, called **capillaries,** inside the stem that carry water to the leaves.

Water moves up the stem.

What Will We Need?

Geranium, coleus, or celery stem
Red food coloring or ink
Drinking glass or clear plastic cup

Paper towel
Water

What Do Students Know?

How does water get from the roots of a plant to the leaves?
How do you think a florist produces blue carnations?
If you wanted to change a white carnation into a blue carnation, what would you do?
How could you find out if your idea was correct?

What Will Students Do?

1. Fill a cup with water, tint with food coloring, and add a rolled paper towel, as in diagram (a).

Observing   What do you see happening between the water and the paper towel? What is this interaction?

Inferring   Why do you think this happens?
How does this scientific principle work in plants?

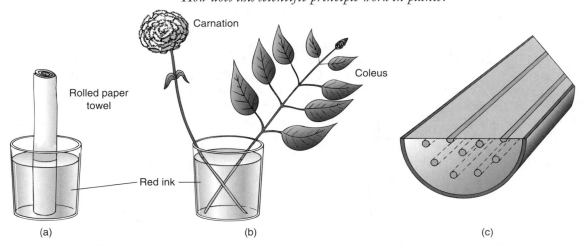

Coleus

Carnation

Rolled paper towel

Red ink

(a)   (b)   (c)

2. Obtain a geranium, celery, or coleus stem with leaves on it, some food coloring or red ink, some water, and a drinking glass. Put some water in the drinking glass and color it with the food coloring or ink.
   Important: A white flower (carnation) can be added to this activity as well. See diagram (b).

Hypothesizing   Why do you think you added coloring to the water?

3. Cut a small slice off the bottom of the stalk of your stem and set the stem into the glass of colored water. Allow it to sit in a sunny area for two hours.

4. At the end of this period, cut open the stem. See diagram (c).

Observing   What has happened to some of the colored water?

Observing   What parts of the stem appear to contain the colored water? How do you know?

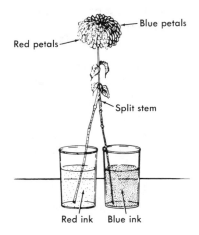

Blue petals

Red petals

Split stem

Red ink   Blue ink

Describe these parts.

Inferring *From this activity, what can you conclude about how a stem functions?*

How Will Students Use or Apply What They Discover?

1. *What effects might different temperatures have on how rapidly a solution moves up a stem?*
2. *What do you think might happen if you put half of a split stem in one color of water and the other half in another color of water?*
3. *What happens to the upward movement of water in a stem when the plant is in the dark or out of sunlight? How could you find out?*

Part VI   Why Do Some Parts of Plants Grow Upward? (3–5)

What Concepts Might Students Discover?

Light and gravity play a role in determining how plants grow.
Roots respond to gravity.
Stems are affected by light.

What Will We Need?

Germinated bean seeds between glass (from Part II activity)
Sunny window or light source
Ruler
Germinated bean seeds
Potting soil
Clean milk carton
Shoebox with cover

What Do Students Know?

What do you think might happen to a plant if its light source is very limited?
What do you think might happen to the stem of a plant if it is inverted (turned upside down)?
What effect does light have on the way a plant grows?
What might happen to the way a plant grows if it were placed near a window?
What effect does gravity have on the parts of sprouting seeds?
What could you do to find out?

What Must I Know?

The students should suggest arranging the sprouting seeds and apparatus as shown.

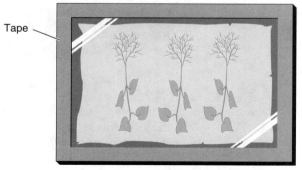

Tape

Seeds on soaked paper covered by glass
or plastic wrap.

What do you think might happen to the stems if you rotate the seedlings every few days?

What Will Students Do?

Observing and Recording

1. Place the germinated bean seeds encased in taped glass or clear plastic sheets in bright light, but not in direct sunlight.

2. Keep a 1-week record of your observation of how the stems and roots grow as you rotate the glass sheets 90° each day.

What Must I Know?

The roots will grow down (toward the earth), and the stems will grow up (away from the earth). The plant responses that cause this are called **tropisms. Geotropism** forces roots down as auxins (plant hormones) are concentrated by gravity along the bottom cells of stems and root tips. The bottom cells in the stem are stimulated by the hormones to grow faster than cells higher up; they get longer and curl upward. Root cells are more sensitive to these hormones than are stem cells, so the root cells inhibit cell growth. Root top cells elongate faster, and root tips curve downward.

Communivating
Inferring
Inferring
Hypothesizing

Hypothesizing

3. Graph your findings or present them in another pictorial or visual way.
   Hint: How could you use your ruler in your observations?
   What can you conclude from your data?
   What would you expect other plants and seeds to do under similar conditions?
   What results would you expect if you used different or limited light sources?
   Try this.

4. Plant four germinated bean seeds ¾-inch to 1-inch (2 cm) deep in moist soil in a clean milk carton.

5. Place the milk carton in a shoebox that has only a single, 1-inch hole cut in the middle of one end, cover the box, and turn the opening toward bright sunlight or a strong lamp, as shown in the diagram.

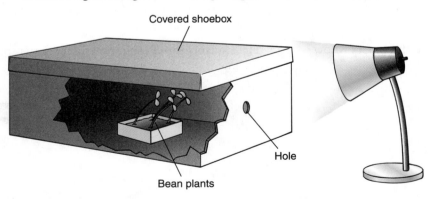

Covered shoebox

Hole

Bean plants

Observing

6. Lift the cover every 2 days and see how the beans are growing. Add water as needed.

Inferring

What is happening to the stems and leaves?
Why do you think they are growing as they are?

Hypothesizing

What do you think might happen if you turned the milk carton with the seeds completely around?

Try it and observe what happens in 2 days. Repeat this procedure.

What Must I Know?

Students should see that the beans grow toward the opening in the shoebox, and when turned around, they reverse their direction of growth toward the opening again. Green plants need sunlight and are forced toward the light by **phototropism,** which causes the cells on one side of leaves to grow faster than the other. This causes the turning effect of the leaves toward the sunlight.

How Will Students Use or Apply What They Discover?

1. *Of what value is this experiment to you?*
2. *What other living things are affected by light and gravity?*
3. *What are some other factors that affect the growth of plants?*
4. *Design an experiment to test some of these factors.*
5. *Knowing what you do about phototropism, why is it necessary to turn your plants at the windowsill every few days? What might happen if you do not turn them?*

How Is Sunlight Used by Growing Plants? (K–5)

What Concepts Might Students Discover?

Green plants have a green substance called **chlorophyll.**
Leaves produce gases and water vapor during photosynthesis.
Gas will expand when heated.
Because gases are lighter than water, they will go through water and escape.
Water vapor from leaves condenses on plastic film.
Leaves have little openings (called **stomata**) through which air enters or leaves the leaf.

What Will We Need?

Double boiler pot	Clear plastic cup	Lamp or sunlight
Water	Healthy plant	Wooden splint
Assorted green leaves	growing in pot	Matches
Alcohol	3M Post-it® foil stars	2 clear plastic bags
Hot plate	Elodea water plants	2 small, identical
Rock	1-gal wide-mouthed jar	geranium plants
1" × 4" strip of filter	Glass or plastic funnel	Plastic ties
paper or white	Test tube	Hand lenses
coffee filter		

Part I   What Makes Most Leaves Green? (K–2)

What Do Students Know?

What color are most leaves? Why do you think this is so?

PROCESSES

What Will Teacher Do?

Caution: Because there will be boiling of water, the teacher should physically perform this activity.

Observing

1. With water in bottom and green leaves and alcohol in top, set up double boiler pot on hot plate.
   What color are the leaves as we put them in the alcohol?

2. Heat the double boiler so that water boils for 10 minutes. Review parts of plants and discuss leaves while the water boils.

3. Remove leaves from pot and observe.

Inferring   *Why are the leaves no longer green?*

Observing   *What color is the alcohol now? Why?*

What do we call the "green stuff" in leaves? This is called chlorophyll.

What Must I Know?   Another method to find "hidden" colors in plant leaves uses the following technique, which students can perform independently or in groups.

What Will Students Do?   1. Use a rock to rub a leaf impression about 1 inch up on a 1" × 4" strip

 of filter paper or *white* coffee filter, as in diagram (a).

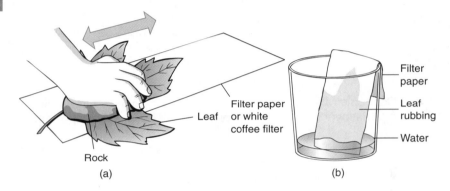

Leaf   Filter paper or white coffee filter   Rock   (a)

Filter paper   Leaf rubbing   Water   (b)

2. Place enough water to cover the bottom of a clear plastic cup and fold the paper so it hangs from the cup, just touching the bottom. See diagram (b).

Hypothesizing   *What do you think will happen? Why?*

Observing   3. Observe the changes.

What happened?

Inferring   *Why?*

What colors were revealed?

Try this activity with different leaves.

What Must I Know?   As the water slowly rises, it hits the plant leaf "stain" and separates out some of the pigments in the leaf. This reveals the "hidden" colors of the leaf. *Note:* Using acetone (nail polish remover) in place of the water will produce better results by separating more pigments more effectively. If you use acetone, place in a closed glass jar instead of an open plastic cup. *Warning:* Acetone fumes are potentially harmful.

Part II   How Does Light Affect Chlorophyll? (K–2)

What Do Students Know?   *How do you think chlorophyll is made?*

What role does light play in this process?

What Will Students Do?   1. Select a healthy outdoor or indoor plant. Peel and stick a few foil stars

 on one or two leaves, while the plant is in the pot or ground and in growing conditions (has water, sun, etc.).

2. Leave stars on for 1 week.
3. Remove stars from leaves.

Observing   *What do you see?*
Inferring   *Why do you think this happened?*
Hypothesizing *What do you think will happen to the spots that were under the stars if the plant is put back in the sun for 1 week?*

4. Do it, observe, and record your data.

What Must I Know?

Plants are green because of chlorophyll. It absorbs light energy from the sun and helps plants make food. Without sunlight, plants use up the chlorophyll, the leaf starts to turn white, and the plant eventually dies.

Part III   What Comes Out of Leaves in Sunlight? (3–5)

What Do Students Know?

What happens when your head is under water and you let some air out of your mouth? What do you see?
What do you think might happen to a leaf if it were placed under water in sunlight?

What Will Students Do?

1. Put a water plant such as elodea in a 1-gallon wide-mouthed jar.
2. Invert a glass or plastic funnel over the elodea and place a test tube completely full of water over the stem of the funnel, as shown in the diagram.
3. Place the jar in direct sunlight for 3 days.

Observing   *What do you see coming up from the elodea plant?*
                 What happened to the level of water in the test tube?
Hypothesizing *What do you think might be in the test tube?*
Designing an Experiment *How might you set up an experiment to find out what is in the test tube?*

What Must I Know?

Note: The teacher or a responsible student should perform the following steps if students are too young.

4. When most of the water in the test tube has been displaced, quickly remove the test tube and insert a glowing splint or lit match into the test tube, as shown in the diagram.

| Observing | *What do you see happening to the wooden splint or lit match?* |
| Inferring | *Why do you think this happened?* |

What Must I Know?

If students do not infer from this activity that the splint burned brightly because of oxygen given off from the elodea plant in sunlight, you can tell them. Students can be guided to see that oxygen is given off by plants during photosynthesis.

Leaves have small pores called stomata through which air enters and gases escape (see drawings).

Have students use hand lenses to view stomata.

Part IV   What Else Comes Out of Leaves in Sunlight? (3–5)

What Will Students Do?

1. Place a clear plastic bag over one geranium and tie the bag around the stem, just above the soil level.
2. Wave a second plastic bag through the air and tie it as well, as illustrated in the diagram.
3. Put both plastic bags in direct sunlight for at least 3 hours.

Observing	*After 3 hours, what do you see forming on the top of the plant in the plastic bag?*
Inferring	*What do you think they are?*
Inferring	*Where do you think they came from?*
Hypothesizing	*Why do you think the plastic was tied off above the soil line?*
Observing	*How is the plastic bag without the plant different after 3 hours?*
Inferring	*Why do you think this happened?*
Hypothesizing	*Why do you think the empty plastic bag was used in this activity?*
	What is this called in an experiment? (Control)

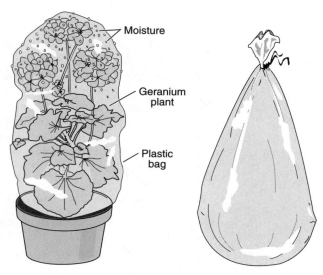

Moisture

Geranium plant

Plastic bag

What Must I Know?

Moisture is formed in the plastic bag with the plant as a by-product of photosynthesis in the leaves. The purpose of tying off the bag at the stem was to prevent moisture evaporating from the soil from entering the bag. The "empty" clear plastic bag is the control.

References—Plant Anatomy and Physiology
Teacher: DyAnne DiSalvo-Ryan, *City Green* (New York: Morrow Junior Books, 1994).
Student: Linda Martin, *Watch Them Grow* (New York: Dorling Kindersley, 1994).

ANIMAL ANATOMY AND PHYSIOLOGY

QUICKIE STARTERS: OPEN-ENDED ACTIVITIES

What Do Fish Need to Live? (K–2)

Materials

Gallon (4-liter) glass or clear plastic container (such as commercial-sized mayonnaise jar, obtainable from fast-food restaurant), seasoned water (tap water left to stand overnight to remove chlorine), gravel or sand, aquatic plants, 2 or 3 goldfish or guppies, dip net, live or dried fish food

What Do Students Know?

What things do fish need to live?
How can we learn to take care of our fish?
What must we do to keep the fish healthy?

Some Possible Activities

Refer to the index in this text to find the instructions for setting up and maintaining a freshwater aquarium, using the materials listed here. Help students set up the aquarium and establish routines for feeding, cleaning, and changing the water when it becomes smelly or cloudy. Point out that guppies and goldfish can be raised at normal classroom temperatures. Discuss why the following elements are needed for the fish to live: water, plants, food, and light. Carefully remove any pregnant fish (usually identified by a swollen abdomen with a dark spot) with the dip net and place them in a separate aquarium. For older students, discuss the relationships among variables, parts of the aquarium, and the effects upon the lives of fish. For example: *How does the amount of light affect the algae in water? What is the number of fish 1 gallon of water will support, as observed by fish gulping at the top of the water? How do overfeeding and pollution of the water affect the fish?* *Note:* See "How Does a Lack of Oxygen Affect Animals?" (page A–118).

What Are the Stages That Insects Go Through? (K–5)

Materials

Jars with covers (clear plastic, if possible), mealworms (from pet shop), bran or other cereal flakes, hand lenses, spoons, pictures of people and insects at different growing stages

What Do Students Know?

What are the stages insects, such as moths, butterflies, and mealworms, go through in their life cycles?
What are the stages people go through as they grow?
How are the stages alike and different?

Some Possible Activities

Using pictures of people and insects at different stages of growth, discuss how these living things grow. Introduce the mealworms and challenge students to hypothesize how the mealworms will grow and change in several stages. Using spoons, you or the students can transfer several mealworms and some bran or cereal flakes into a jar with a lid. Provide a jar for each student or group of two or three students. Punch several small holes in the lids for air. Have students observe the mealworms twice a week and record on a chart or log any observed changes in appearance (color, length, stage, etc.) or behavior. At the end of observations, help students make a chart comparing the stages of insects' lives with humans', like the one shown.[3]

STAGES	
People	Insects
Child	Larva
Teenager	Pupa
Adult	Adult

---

[3]For additional information on insect stages and record keeping, you are urged to read *Elementary Science Supplement to the Syllabus, Level I* (Albany, NY: The University of the State of New York, The State Education Department, 1988): 62–64.

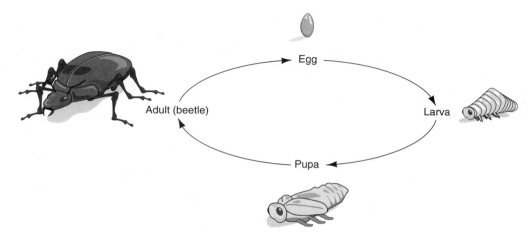

In addition, make a diagram with students, similar to the one shown, and include photos or drawings to visualize the stages of mealworm (and other insect) metamorphosis.

Make the same kind of diagram for stages of human life (infant, child, teenager, and adult).

GUIDED DISCOVERY HANDS-ON/MINDS-ON ACTIVITIES

How Do Ants Live? (K–2)

What Concepts Might Students Discover?

Ants are social insects.
All insects have three body parts: the head, thorax, and abdomen.
All insects have six legs.
Ants are beneficial because they help keep the forests and fields clean.
There are different kinds of ants in a colony.
These different ants do different kinds of work in the colony.

What Will We Need?

Large-mouth glass jar (commercial mayonnaise or pickle jar)
    with screw top punctured with very small holes
Empty washed soup can
Soil to fill the jar two-thirds full
Small sponge
Pan large enough to hold the large-mouth glass jar
Sheet of black construction paper
Crumbs and bits of food: bread, cake, sugar, seeds
Colony of ants

What Do Students Know?

What do the different kinds of ants look like?
In what ways are the ants different?
How does the body of a worker ant compare to that of a queen ant?
How many pairs of legs do ants have?
What are the antennae on the head used for?
What does the egg of an ant look like?

Where do ants make their homes?
How do ants move?
How could you keep ants from leaving a jar?

What Must I Know?

You should become familiar with the life cycle and body parts of ants, such as shown in the diagram.

Ant eggs

Mature ant

PROCESSES

What Will Students Do?

G

Designing an Investigation
Hypothesizing

1. Obtain a large-mouth glass jar with a screw cover, a clean empty soup can, soil to fill the jar two-thirds full, a sponge, a large pan, a sheet of black construction paper, crumbs and bits of food (bread, cake, sugar, and seeds), and water.
How could you arrange these materials to make a home for ants?
What effect will a sheet of black paper placed around the jar have on the ants? (This simulates the dark underground so ants will tunnel close to the sides of the glass jar.)

Hypothesizing	*Why place the soup can in the center of the jar with soil around it to the sides of the jar?* (So ants will not burrow into the center but will tunnel out to the jar's sides and be more visible)
	Where might you get ants? (Pet shop or home or school grounds)
	What is the purpose of placing the jar in a pan of water? (So the ants cannot escape)
	2. Construct the ant home and add some ants.
Observing/Recording	3. Observe and record what the ants do.
Observing	*How do the ants connect their homes in the jar?*
Hypothesizing	*What might happen to the ants if they did not carry soil to the surface?*
Hypothesizing	*What do you think might happen if there were no queen in the ant colony?*
Comparing	*What changes have been made by the ants since they were first placed in the jar?*

How Will Students Use or Apply What They Discover?

1. *In what ways are ants useful to people?*
2. *What are some other insects that live and work together?*
3. *What are some living things that are sometimes mistaken for insects?*
4. *What might happen if the ant colony were placed in a light, warm place?*
5. *How are ants different from spiders?*
6. *What would be a good description of social insects?*

What Do You Know About the Birds Around You? (K–5)[4]

What Concepts Might Students Discover?

Birds vary in color and size.
Birds sing different songs.
Birds make different kinds of nests.
Birds eat different kinds of food.
The male bird may have a more colorful plumage than the female.
Some birds migrate.
Some birds change color with the season.
Birds care for their young.
Some birds prey on other birds.
Some birds dominate the eating of food.
Birds need trees and shrubs for protection from predators.

What Will We Need?

Bird food (bread, popcorn, commercial birdseed)	Small pieces of cloth
	Water trays
Bird feeders (commercial or made in class)	Bird book (showing local birds)
	Pictures of birds
Plastic cups	

[4]For more specifics on bird behavior, food preferences, and relevant observational activities, see *Outdoor Biology Instructional Strategies: For the Birds Folio* (Berkeley, CA: The Regents of the University of California, 1980), published by Delta Education, Inc., P.O. Box 915, Hudson, NH 03051–0915; to take part in a seed preference test, contact: Cornell Lab of Ornithology, 159 Sapsucker Woods Rd., Ithaca, NY 14850–1999.

What Do Students Know?	Carefully record on the board the responses of students to the following questions: *How might we attract birds to our school grounds so we can observe them?* *What kinds of birds might we attract in our neighborhood?* *How are birds alike and different?* *Where do some birds go during the winter?* *What kinds of homes do birds live in?* *What are some behaviors that are unique to birds?* *What kinds of foods do birds eat?* *Where would be the best place to set up a bird feeding/observation station on our school grounds?* *What are the names of some local birds?* *What do these birds look like?*
What Must I Know?	If the natural environment lends itself to feeding and observing birds, have students observe birds on the way to and from school, or take a class field trip to a local area, park, or zoo. In a city, you will probably see sparrows or pigeons, jays in picnic areas, ducks in ponds, geese on golf courses, and seagulls at the seashore. In addition, you may want to provide pictures of different birds, nests, and eggs for students to handle, observe, and discuss

PROCESSES

What Will Students Do?

Hypothesizing	*As a result of our discussion, what would make a good bird feeding/observing area?* (Tree and shrub shelter that is free from predators and visible from the classroom) *How could we find out?*
	1. Survey your school grounds and pick the best spot. 2. Find out what kinds of birds are common in your area, what their food preferences are, how they eat (on the ground or from feeders), and any other information that will make your feeding/observing most useful for birds. 3. Put up bird feeder(s) and a water tray.
Designing an Experiment	4. Design an experiment or follow the suggestions provided to answer one or more of the following questions about birds. Try it.
	A. What kinds of foods do different birds prefer?
Comparing	Try offering small equal amounts of two kinds of food (e.g., bread and birdseed) to the birds at the same time. *Caution:* Do *not* feed birds directly from your hand; instead, place food on the ground.
Observing	*Which food do they prefer?*
	B. How can you get birds to come as close to you as possible? (Offer food; be quiet and motionless) **C. Where do birds prefer their food to be put?** Put some food in such places as a birdfeeder on a tree limb or a pole, on the ground, in a plastic cup, under a piece of cloth, and so on.
Observing	*Did different birds like different places?* *What was the most popular feeding spot?*

D. Does one individual bird or kind of bird get the most food?

Observing   Try to find one bird or kind of bird that seems to get most of the food.
How does he do it?

What happens when you try to give food to the other birds?

Hypothesizing   *Why do you think this happens?*

E. Do loud noises or sudden movements affect birds more?

While birds are gathered, make a really loud noise, but make sure to remain perfectly still.

Observing   *What happens to the birds?*

Now make a sudden dramatic movement, but be very quiet.

Observing   *What happens now?*

Comparing   *Did the loud noise or the sudden movement scare the birds more? How do you know?*

Hypothesizing   *Why do you think this is so?*

How Will Students Use or Apply What They Discover?

1. *How can you find out more about birds?*
2. *Why is it so important to continue feeding birds and supplying water once we begin?*
3. *Why is it so much fun to feed and observe birds?*
4. *How are these "wild birds" the same and different from domestic (pet) birds like parrots and canaries?*
5. *How do birds help people?*
6. *How might birds harm people?*
7. *What are some different ways birds in our neighborhood build their nests?*

What Must I Know?

The following types of questions can be asked about any of the local birds. These questions may have to be modified, however, depending on the kinds of birds that are found in your region.

Redheaded Woodpecker. (1) *Where does the woodpecker build its nest?* (2) *How does it build its nest?* (3) *What kind of food does the woodpecker eat?* (4) *How does the woodpecker benefit and harm our environment?*

Hummingbird. (1) *How does the male hummingbird differ in color from the female?* (2) *Where do hummingbirds get their food?* (3) *Are hummingbirds as big as a cardinal or sparrow?* (4) *Why do you have difficulty finding their nests?* (5) *How do hummingbirds help in the pollination of plants?*

Starling. (1) *Why do many other birds prefer not to live near starlings?* (2) *What color is the starling?* (3) *How does the starling vary in color compared*

to the hummingbird and woodpecker? (4) Why do farmers dislike starlings during fruit harvesting season?

How Do Birds Differ From Mammals? (3–8)

What Concepts Might Students Discover?

Birds are the only animals that have feathers.
Both mammals and birds are warm-blooded.
Birds have two legs and two wings.
The female mammal has glands for nourishing her young with milk.
Mammals are more or less covered with hair.
Birds do not vary as much in structure as do mammals.
The bones of birds are somewhat hollow and light in weight.
Mammal bones are not hollow and are proportionately heavier.
Birds tend to eat approximately the amount of their weight in food each day.
Mammals do not eat as much per body weight as do birds.
Birds use considerable energy in flying and therefore need a great amount of food.
Female birds lay eggs.
Almost all female mammals give birth to live babies.
Only a few mammals, such as the platypus, lay eggs.

What Will We Need?

Live or stuffed specimens of birds and mammals or pictures of them.
Beef and chicken bones (one of each for every two students). If possible, these should be cut in half.
Wing bones of chickens (or any other bird).

What Do Students Know?

Give as many common characteristics of birds as you can.
Give as many common characteristics of mammals as you can.
In what ways do birds differ from mammals?
What could you do to compare more closely the differences between birds and mammals?

What Must I Know?

Record on the board students' responses to the previous questions. Or allow students to divide into groups and discuss the questions. Each group could report its ideas to the class.

PROCESSES

What Will Students Do?

Do this activity in groups of two or more students. Encourage students to bring specimens, alive or stuffed, to school. Perhaps a pet day or an animal show might be arranged to make the most of this activity. Allow students to help furnish any of the other activity materials, such as beef and chicken bones. Encourage students to bring pictures of animals to class; place these on a bulletin board.

1. Obtain a cut chicken bone, a cut beef bone, and a wing bone of a chicken.

Classifying

How did you know which bone was from a chicken and which was from a steer?

Observing and Comparing   Examine the centers of the two bones and record how the structure of the beef bone differs from that of the chicken bone.

2. Look at the chicken wing bone.

Comparing   *How does its structure compare with the arm bones of a person?*

Summarizing   3. Make a list of the characteristic ways birds and mammals differ.

Comparing   4. Compare your list with those made by other members of your class. Make any corrections or additions to your list that you think should be made, perhaps including the items that follow.

Birds

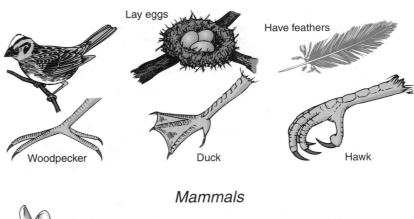

Lay eggs   Have feathers

Woodpecker   Duck   Hawk

Mammals

Are warm-blooded

Have hair   Are born alive

Other mammals: man, whales, bears, deer, etc.

How Will Students Use or Apply What They Discover?

1. *What are the main structural differences between birds and mammals?*
2. *How does the structure of a feather help a bird to fly?*
3. *How does the structure of a feather help keep birds warm in winter?*
4. *What do birds do to their feathers to make themselves warmer?*

How Does a Lack of Oxygen Affect Animals? (3–5)

What Concepts Might Students Discover?

Animals need oxygen to live.
Oxygen dissolves in water. Some animals need dissolved oxygen in water.
A gas will dissolve better in a cool liquid than in a hot liquid.
Fish breathe through gills.

What Will We Need?

2 pint-sized jars with caps
2 goldfish or other small freshwater fish in a small bottle
Electric hot plate on which to boil water
Matches
Pan large enough to boil a pint of water

**What Do Students
Know?**

What happens to the air dissolved in water when you boil water?
What do you think might happen to fish if they were placed in water that had been boiled and then cooled?
What would you do to find out?

PROCESSES

**What Will Students and
Teacher Do?**

Designing an Experiment

The teacher may choose to boil the water ahead of time for younger students.

1. Obtain a bottle with two fish, two pint-sized jars with caps, an electric hot plate, and a large pan.
2. Heat the water to boiling and let it boil for several minutes.
3. While the water is being heated, label one jar "Boiled Water" and the other "Tap Water."
4. After the water has boiled, turn off the heat.
5. Carefully pour the boiled water into the jar labeled "Boiled Water," cap the jar, and allow the water to cool to room temperature.

Hypothesizing

What might happen if you place a fish in tap water?

6. Fill the second jar with tap water, put in one fish, and cap the jar.

Observing
Hypothesizing

Observe the fish's movements.
What might happen if you place a fish in the cooled boiled water and cap the jar?

7. Place the other fish in the jar of cooled boiled water and cap the jar.

Observing

Observe the fish's movements. (*Caution:* If the fish turns on its side, take it out of the jar immediately, gently shake it in the air by the tail for a second, and place it into a jar of regular tap water.)

Comparing
Inferring

How did the movements of the two fish vary?
Why did the fish in the cooled boiled water seem to vary in its movements compared to the other fish?

Tap water
A

Cooled boiled water
B

What Must I Know?

When water is boiled, the air molecules dissolved in it move more rapidly and escape into the air. The water lacks air as a result. Fish get the oxygen they need from air dissolved in water. When the air passes over the gills, the oxygen is absorbed by the blood passing through the gills. Fish are not able to survive in the cooled boiled water because it contains little oxygen for the gills to absorb.

Inferring

Why did you first heat the water and then cool it?
Why was the lid put quickly over the heated water?

8. If you have not already done so, take the fish out of the jar of boiled water, gently shake it for a second or two by the tail, and place it in a jar of plain water.

Inferring

Why is it necessary to shake the fish in the air for a few seconds?

What Must I Know?

Shaking the fish causes air to pass over the gills so the fish gets oxygen from the air; the shaking also stimulates the circulation of the blood in the fish.

Inferring

What do animals in the sea need to live?

Inferring

How do they get the oxygen they need?

What Must I Know?

Explain to the class that air is composed of a mixture of gases and that it is the oxygen in the air that animals need to breathe.

How Will Students Use or Apply What They Discover?

1. *What experiment would you do to determine whether other animals require air (oxygen) to live?*
2. *How could you use the gill movement of fish to show that the boiled water does not contain oxygen?*
3. *Why might it be more difficult for fish to get oxygen from water containing a lot of algae than from clear water?*
4. *How might water pollution, like large amounts of detergents, affect fish breathing?*

References—Animal Anatomy and Physiology
Teacher or older students: Carol Hampton, Carolyn Hampton, and David Kramer, *Classroom Creature Culture: Algae to Anoles* (Arlington, VA: National Science Teachers Association, 1994); P. M. Hickman, *Habitats* (Menlo Park, CA: Addison-Wesley, 1993).
Younger Students: D. Silver, *One Small Square Backyard* (New York: W. H. Freeman, 1993); N. Luenn, *Squish! A Wetland Walk* (New York: Atheneum/Simon and Schuster, 1994).

HUMAN ANATOMY, PHYSIOLOGY, NUTRITION, AND HEALTH

QUICKIE STARTERS: OPEN-ENDED ACTIVITIES

How Does Your Body Cool Itself? (K–5)

Materials

2 old socks (wool or cotton are best) for each student, electric fan

What Do Students Know?

Why do you feel cool on a hot summer day when you come out of the water after swimming?
What parts of your body are at work to cool you down when you come out of the water?
Why does a fan cool us even on a hot day?

Some Possible Activities

Have students remove their shoes and socks and put a dry sock on one foot and wet sock on the other foot. Ask:
Which one feels cooler? Why?
To improve the cooling effect, use a fan to blow air over the students' feet.
Hint: Suggest to students that they go to the bathroom before doing this activity.

Wet sock   Dry sock

How Big Are Your Lungs? (3–5)

Materials

Dishpan, 2 ft (60 cm) of rubber or plastic tubing, ruler, measuring cup, water, gallon jug

What Do Students Know?

How much air do your lungs hold?
Do boys have bigger lungs than do girls?
Do smokers have more lung capacity than nonsmokers?
Do joggers' lungs hold more air than the lungs of people who do not jog?

Some Possible Activities

Fill the dishpan about one-quarter full of water. Fill the jug to the very top with water. Put your hand tightly over the mouth of the jug and invert it in the dishpan, making sure not to let any air get into the jug. Put one end of the tubing in your mouth and slip the other end into the mouth of the jug. With one continuous breath, keep blowing until you are completely out of air, as shown in diagram (a). *Important:* Make sure the mouth of the jug remains below water level.

When you cannot blow any more water out of the jug, slide your hand over the jug's mouth and turn it right side up. To measure how much air you exhaled, do this:

1. Pour measuring cups filled with water into the jug until you have refilled the jug, as shown in diagram (b).
2. The amount of water you use to refill the jug is the amount of air you exhaled.

(a)   (b)

Caution: For hygienic reasons, use separate plastic tubing for each student. It is inexpensive when purchased from pet or aquarium shops.

GUIDED DISCOVERY HANDS-ON/MINDS-ON ACTIVITIES

How Do Humans Breathe? (K–8)

What Concepts Might Students Discover?

When a person exercises, breathing rate increases.
Breathing increases because more carbon dioxide is produced.
Carbon dioxide causes the diaphragm to involuntarily work more rapidly.
When the diaphragm moves up the rib cage, it forces air out of the lungs.
When the diaphragm moves down, air is pulled into the lungs.
Lung capacity varies from person to person and can be increased by aerobic training.
Gases and water vapor are exhaled from the lungs.

What Will We Need?

Mirror (preferably metal)
Tape measure
3 plastic cups
Turkey baster
Plastic drinking straws
½ c or 100 cc of limewater
    or calcium hydroxide (obtain
    from a drugstore)

Water
Stopwatch
Plastic sandwich bag
Rubber bands
Small balloons
Scissors
Model or chart of the chest cavity

Part I What Comes Out When You Breathe? (K–2)

What Do Students Know?

What do you see when you breathe outside on a very cold day?
Why do you think that happens?
How might we find out?

PROCESSES

What Will Students Do?

Hypothesizing

1. Obtain a mirror.
   When you breathe, what leaves your mouth?
   How might you find out?
2. Hold a mirror near your nose and mouth and exhale on it.

Mirror

Exhale on mirror

Observing
Inferring
Assuming
Hypothesizing

What do you see on the mirror?
Why does moisture collect on the mirror?
Where does the moisture come from?
What kinds of gases do you think you exhale?

What Must I Know?

Explain that exhaled air contains about 80 percent nitrogen, 17 percent oxygen, 0.03 percent carbon dioxide, and small percentages of other gases.

How Will Students Use or Apply What They Discover?

1. *What happens to the nitrogen you inhale?*
2. *What gas in the air do you need?*
3. *What gas do you exhale more of than you inhale?*
4. *How might we find out?*

Part II Does Breathing Change Your Chest Size? (K–2)

Designing an Investigation

How does the size of your chest vary when you breathe?
How might you find out?

What Will Students Do?

1. With a tape measure, check and record these measurements.

	Top of Chest	Lower Diaphragm
Inhale		
Exhale		

2. Construct a class graph to illustrate variations in measurement among students.

Interpreting

Is there any observable correlation between inhale and exhale and chest measurements between boys and girls, tall and short, and so on?

Part III   How Can We Test Our Breath? (3–5)

What Will Students Do?

Observing/Communicating

1. Obtain two clear plastic cups, a turkey baster, a straw, and 100 cc of limewater (or some calcium hydroxide). Mix half the limewater with regular water in each cup. Let the water settle.
2. Put a straw in one cup and the turkey baster in the other.
   Describe how the limewater in the cups looks.
3. One of you blow through a straw into the limewater while the other pumps the bulb of the turkey baster into the limewater.

A. Breath in limewater   B. Baster in limewater

Observing   *What happens to the limewater as you blow (exhale) through the straw into the water?*

What do you notice at the bottom of the cup after a minute or two of blowing through the straw?

Inferring   *Why does the water get "cloudy"?*

What do you think is on the bottom of the cup?

Observing   *What happens to the limewater when you squeeze the turkey baster into it?*

Inferring   *Why do you think the limewater did not change?*

Hypothesizing   *Why do you think the turkey baster part of the activity is important?*

Inferring   *What would the turkey baster part of the activity be called in an experiment?*

What Must I Know?

When carbon dioxide is added to limewater, the water changes to a milky color because the carbon dioxide combines with calcium hydroxide to form a white precipitate. You can test the white powder that falls to the bottom by adding some vinegar; vinegar will cause calcium or carbonate to foam. The turkey baster was used to pump air into the limewater to show that air does not affect the limewater. This is our control. The variable being tested is carbon dioxide in breath.

How Will Students Use or Apply What They Discover?

1. *Why would an increase in carbon dioxide in the blood cause the heart to beat faster?*
2. *What does the following hypothesis mean: "A person needing oxygen naturally breathes faster"?*
3. *What other things would make you breathe faster? How could we find out?*

Part IV   What Makes You Breathe Faster? (3–8)

What Do Students Know?

How many times a minute do you breathe?
How do you know?
How would you go about finding out?

What Must I Know?

This activity should be done in groups of three students: One does the activity, one is the timekeeper, and one is the recorder. At the completion of each activity, the students should rotate in their tasks until all have completed the activity. For exercise, students may run in place. For students unfamiliar with how to use a stopwatch, show them how it is used. Also explain that one breath is the exhale phase as a cloud forms on the mirror, and not both the exhale and inhale phases.

What Will Students Do?

1. Do the following with two other students: Using a stopwatch, one of you counts the number of times a second student normally breathes. Do this by counting the breaths on a mirror. Let the third student record the number of times the second student breathes. Do this three times, 1 minute apart.
2. Have the student being tested run in place for 1 minute and then repeat Step 1.
3. Use this chart for recording your data.

Time	At Rest	After Exercise
1 minute		
2 minutes		
3 minutes		

4. When you finish three "At Rest" and three "After Exercise" data collections, rotate the jobs until all three of you have breathed, counted breaths, and recorded data.

Comparing
Hypothesizing
What is the average number of times per minute a person breathes at rest?
How would you figure that?

Comparing
What is the average number of times per minute a person breathes after exercise?

Communicating 5. Graph your rest and exercise record on a diagram like the one shown.

Hypothesizing	*What makes a person breathe faster?*
Inferring	*Why did you count the number of times a person breathes in three minutes rather than in just one?*
Hypothesizing	*What gas do you need from the air?*
Hypothesizing	*What do you breathe out or exhale?*
Designing an Investigation	*How can you prove that you exhale water? (Hint: See the activity in Part I.)*
Hypothesizing	*What gas do you breathe from the air that your body does not use?*

Part V How Can We Make a Model of Lungs? (3–8)

What Must I Know?

You may wish to punch a hole in the plastic cups (see Step **3**) before students begin this activity. The heated tip of an ice pick will pierce the plastic easily.

What Will Students Do?

1. Obtain a plastic drinking straw, a small plastic bag, 2 rubber bands, a clear plastic cup, a small balloon, and scissors.
2. Cut the straw in half.
3. In the bottom of the cup, punch a hole the same width as the straw.
4. Stretch and blow up the balloon a few times.
5. Using a tightly wound rubber band, attach the balloon to the straw. Be sure the balloon does not come off when you blow into the straw.

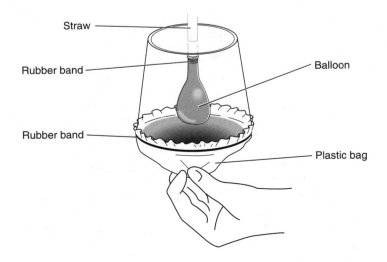

Straw

Rubber band

Balloon

Rubber band

Plastic bag

6. Push the free end of the straw through the cup's hole and pull until the balloon is in the middle of the cup.

7. Place the open end of the cup into the small plastic bag and fold the bag around the cup, securing it tightly with a rubber band or masking tape if necessary. The plastic bag should be loose, not stretched taut, across the cup's opening.

Hypothesizing

What do you think might happen to the balloon if you pull down on the plastic bag at the bottom of the cup?

Observing and Recording

8. Pull down on the plastic bag. Record your observation.

Hypothesizing

What do you think might happen if you push up on the plastic bag?

Observing and Recording

9. Push up on the plastic bag. Record your observation.

Inferring

Why do you see these changes?

Inferring

Where in your body do you have something that works like this?

What Must I Know?

Introduce the word **diaphragm.** Use a model or a chart of the chest cavity for reference.

Observing

Where do the diaphragm, lungs, and chest lie in relation to one another in the chest cavity?

10. Diagram and label the parts of the body used in breathing, as shown in the diagram.

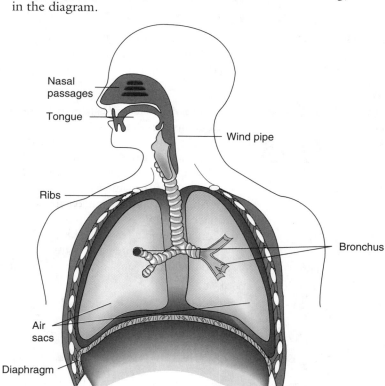

Respiratory system

How Does Our Skin Protect Us? (3–8)

What Concepts Might Students Discover?

The skin protects us from microorganisms that cause disease.
A cut or wound in the skin can let microorganisms enter the body.
Microorganisms sometimes cause infection and disease.
A cut or wound in the skin should be properly treated immediately to prevent microorganisms from causing infection.
Antiseptics kill microorganisms; thus, they can be used for the treatment of cuts or wounds.
Heat can kill microorganisms.

What Will We Need?

4 unblemished apples
3 sewing needles
Book of matches
Candle on a pie tin

Rotten apple
Small sample of soil
5 small pieces of cardboard for labels
Alcohol

What Do Students Know?

How is the covering of an apple or an orange like your skin?
What are the advantages of the covering on apples, oranges, and other types of fruit?
How does the covering of your body, the skin, protect you?
What does it mean when a person says he or she wants to sterilize something?
In what ways might you sterilize something?

What Must I Know?

If open flame is not permitted in your school, or if you feel your students cannot handle it, you should sterilize the needles over open flame yourself. Otherwise, demonstrate to students how to safely do this.

PROCESSES

What Will Students and Teacher Do?

T G

1. Obtain five pieces of cardboard for labels, a candle in a pie tin, a match, three needles, and one rotten and four unblemished apples.
2. Put the labels (a), (b), (c), and (d) on the four unblemished apples.
3. Sterilize three needles by heating them in the flame of a candle.
4. With a sterile needle, puncture apple (a) in three places. Apply alcohol over two of the punctures.
5. Push the second sterilized needle into the soil and then into three places in apple (b).
6. Puncture apple (c) with the third sterile needle, but do not apply any alcohol to the three punctures.
7. Do nothing to apple (d) or to the rotten apple.

alcohol

(a) Three punctures with sterile needle; alcohol applied on two punctures

(b) Puncture with needle stuck in soil

(c) Puncture with needle but no alcohol

(d) Control (no holes)

Rotten

8. Place all four labeled apples in a warm place for several days.
   Why was apple (d) not punctured?

What Must I Know?

If necessary, point out that apple (d) is the control in the experiment. Be sure students understand the term *control*.

Hypothesizing · *What do you think might happen if the apples stand for a few days?*

Comparing · *In what ways do you think they will look alike?*

Comparing · *How will they be different? Why?*

9. Observe the apples daily. Every other day make a diagram or illustration of the changes taking place. Discuss these with your lab group.

Observing · *What has happened to some of the apples?*

Comparing · *How are the apples alike?*

Comparing · *How are they different?*

Inferring · *What do you think might have caused some of these changes?*

Comparing · *Which spots on the apples seem to be the most prominent? Why?*

Comparing · *Which other apple does apple (c) resemble most?*

Observing · *What has happened to apple (d)?*

Inferring · *What was apple (d) in your experiment?*

10. Cut all five apples in half. *Caution:* Do not eat the apples because the alcohol is poisonous.

Comparing · *Which apples seem to look most like the rotten apple?*

Inferring · *Why do you think so?*

Inferring · *Why did you apply alcohol over only two punctures in apple (a)?*

Observing · *What effect did the alcohol have? What about the third puncture?*

What Must I Know?

Alcohol is an antiseptic. The alcohol destroyed most microorganisms present in the wound.

Inferring · *What happened to all the microorganisms on the needles after they had been heated?*

Comparing · *The skin of an apple is similar to what part of your body?*

Inferring · *Why did the rotten spots seem to grow a little larger each day?*

What Must I Know?

Microorganisms have a fantastic growth rate. As long as there is a substantial amount of food present and space enough for growth, they will continue to reproduce.

Inferring · *What do you think might happen if your skin were punctured?*

Hypothesizing · *What might a person do to a wound or puncture if he or she did not want to get an infection?*

What Must I Know?

The wound should be cleaned, an antiseptic applied, and the wound covered with a sterile bandage.

How Will Students Use or Apply What They Discover?

1. *How might you set up the previous experiment using oranges instead of apples? What do you think would happen?*
2. Conduct the same experiment, but this time place the apples in a cool place.
   What effect does temperature have on decay?
3. *In what other ways does your skin protect you?*

Why Does Your Body Need Food for Growth and Health? (3–8)

What Concepts Might Students Discover?	Our bodies grow at different rates during different times in our lives. Students are constantly changing in height, weight, length of hair and nails, and so on. Food is needed for growth. Food is needed for energy to do things in our everyday lives. Foods contain nutrients necessary for energy, growth, and good health. There are simple tests for identifying nutrients in foods.

What Will We Need?

Students' pictures of themselves	Ringstand
Pictures of malnourished children	Water
Tape measures	Measuring cup
Scales for weighing students	Saucepan or Pyrex flask
Whole shelled walnuts	Celsius thermometer
Needle	Matches
Cork	

Part I   Why Is Food Needed for Growth? (3–8)

What Must I Know?
Before 3 years of age, human growth is very rapid and then slows a bit. When a girl is 10 or 11, her cells begin to rapidly grow again. Boys at 13 do the same. Our bodies grow by making new cells, and these cells need food, water, and oxygen.

What Do Students Know?
Have you always been the size you are now?
Are you growing now? How do you know?
What helps you grow?
What could prevent you from growing?

PROCESSES

What Will Students Do?

1. Using information from your parents, fill in the chart on the next page. Attach photos of you at each year to make a timeline that shows how you have grown.
2. Look at the pictures of malnourished or starving children provided by your teacher.

Comparing   *What differences do you see between these children and your pictures?*
Inferring   *Why do you think these children are so thin and sickly looking?*

Measuring and Recording   3. Keep a weekly record of your current growth. Include your height and weight and any other characteristic you want.

4. Make a list of some of the activities you engage in each day, such as running, bike riding, and so on.

Hypothesizing   *How does food help you do these things?*
Inferring   *How might you find out?*

Part II   How Does Food Give Us Energy? (3–8)

What Must I Know?
Since this activity uses open flame, use your discretion as to whether you do it or allow students to do it. Guide your students to see that the unit for measuring heat is the calorie, just as the unit for measuring tempera-

Recording

Age in Years	Height in Inches	Weight in Pounds	Photo
Birth			
1			
2			
3			
4			
5			
6			
7			
8			
9			
10			

ture is the degree. The **calorie** is the amount of heat needed to raise 1 gram (about half a thimbleful or 1 M&M candy) of water 1 degree Celsius. *Note:* This calorie is known as the "small" calorie. The large Calorie in food calories is equal to 1000 small calories, and is spelled with a capital "C."

What Will Students and Teacher Do?

1. Put a whole, unshelled walnut on the point of a needle and push the other end of the needle into a cork. Put the cork and walnut on the base of a ringstand with the walnut pointing up.
2. Put 1 liter of water into the saucepan and place the pan on the ringstand so that it is 1 inch above the walnut, as shown in the diagram (p. A–132).

Measuring
3. Measure and record, in Celsius degrees, the temperature of the water.
4. With the match, light the walnut until the walnut is burning well.

Measuring and Recording
5. As soon as the walnut stops burning, check and then record the temperature of the water.

Comparing
6. Subtract the water temperature before burning from the water temperature after the burning stopped.

Comparing
What is the difference in temperatures?

What Must I Know?

You can introduce the concept that the difference in temperatures indicates the amount of energy (calories) released by the walnut when burned.

How Will Students Use or Apply What They Discover?

1. *Which of the following foods, in equal quantities, do you think will give more energy?*

    bread   celery   olive oil   sugar   apple

    How might you find out?
2. *How many Calories do you think your body "burns up" each day in activities? How might you find out?*

3. *If you eat more food Calories than you "burn up," what might happen to you?*
4. *If you eat fewer food Calories than you "burn up," what might happen to you?*
5. *Who probably "burns up" more food Calories: a professional basketball player or a "couch potato"? Why do you think so?*
6. *What other things does food give you besides energy? How can you find out?*

What Else Do We Need From Food, and How Can We Test for It? (3–8)

What Concepts Might Students Discover?

Water is essential for life.

Water and these types of nutrients are needed to keep our bodies healthy and growing properly: carbohydrates (starch and sugar), fats, proteins, minerals, and vitamins.

We can test foods to see which nutrients and how much water they contain.

Because we are all different, we need different amounts of nutrients.

People who study nutrients (called **nutritionists**) suggest average amounts of nutrients. These amounts are called the Recommended Daily Allowances, or RDA.

Sometimes nutritionists recommend selecting foods from the basic food groups, such as meats, fruits, vegetables, breads and cereals, and dairy products. However, there are people (called **vegetarians**) who are very healthy and yet never eat meat or dairy products. They get their needed nutrients from other foods.

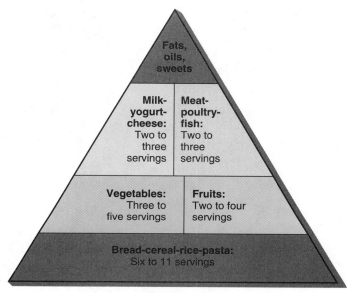

U.S.D.A Food-group pyramid

Part I   How Much Water Is in Our Foods? (3–8)

What Must I Know?

Although water is not one of the basic nutrients, you must have it every day. You could not live without it. Besides getting water from the tap, here are some common foods and the percentages of water we get when we eat them.

lettuce 95%	carrots 90%
yogurt 90%	apple 85%
pizza 50%	bread 35%

What Will We Need?

Blunt plastic knives	Paper plates
Weighing scale or wire hanger balance	Small paper cups
Box of paper clips	Thick white bread
Apples, lettuce, tomatoes	Bread toaster
Hand juicer	

What Do Students Know?

How could we find out how much water is in certain foods?

PROCESSES

What Will Students Do?

1. Using a weighing scale or the wire hanger balance shown in the diagram, weigh all foods and record their weights in the "Before" column of the chart.

Measuring and Recording

Measuring and Recording

2. Spread the lettuce leaves out on paper plates to dry overnight.

3. The next day, weigh and record the weight of the lettuce leaves left out overnight. Record your measurements in the "After" column of the chart.

I **G**

Water Content Chart		
	Weight (in grams or paper clips)	
Food	Before	After
Lettuce		
Tomato		
Oranges		
Apples		
Bread		

Comparing
Inferring

Did the leaves weigh more or less than before?
Why do you think this happened?

Measuring   4. Weigh a tomato and record its weight in the "Before" column.

5. Using a hand juicer, squeeze out all the tomato juice.

Measuring and Recording   6. Weigh the tomato pulp (without the juice) and record this number in the "After" column.

Measuring   7. Using the orange and the apple, repeat steps 4, 5, and 6.

Measuring and Recording   8. Weigh the piece of thick white bread and record the weight in the "Before" column.

Recording   9. Toast the bread in the toaster, weigh it, and record the number in the "After" column.

How Will Students Use or Apply What They Discover?

1. *What foods can you think of that are eaten in both fresh and dried forms?* (Grapes/raisins, apricots, plums/prunes, etc.)

2. *How does the shape of cut fruit pieces change when they dry out (shrink)?*
How might we find out? (Cut up fruit pieces, trace their shapes with a
marking pen, and compare the shapes when they dry.)

Part II   What Is Starch, and How Do You Test for It? (3–8)

**What Concepts Might
Students Discover?**

Starch forms a large proportion of the nourishing parts of wheat, oats,
corn, rye, potatoes, and rice.

Starch is part of a group of substances called **carbohydrates,** which all contain the same chemical elements: carbon, hydrogen, and oxygen.

All ordinary plants are carbohydrates.

Starch turns blue-black in the presence of an iodine solution.

What Will We Need?

Paper plates	Cracker
Medicine dropper	Cornstarch
Thin slices of banana, apple, potato, white	Iodine solution
bread, cheese, egg white, butter	Granulated sugar

**What Do Students
  Know?**

Which of these foods contains starch?
How might we find out?

What Must I Know?

Iodine is used to test for starch. When iodine comes in contact with starch,
the starch turns blue-black. *Caution:* Iodine solution is poisonous, may
cause burns if it is too strong, and can stain clothing. It must not be eaten.
For this reason, you may opt to dispense the iodine drops yourself if your
students are too immature to safely do so themselves. In either case, point
out the dangers to your students.

**What Will Students and
Teacher Do?**

1. On a paper plate, arrange and label each food sample as shown.

Observing

2. Look at the colors of each food and record them on a chart.
3. Either the teacher or a student should place a drop of iodine solution on each sample of food.

Observing
Comparing
Classifying
Inferring

4. Look at the color of each food where the iodine drop touched it.
   How have some of the food colors changed?
   Which foods have something in common after getting an iodine drop?
   If starch turns blue-black in iodine, which of your sample foods would you say contain starch?
   Which do not have starch?
   Important reminder: Because iodine is poisonous, do *not* eat any of the tested foods or give them to pets. Dispose of them properly.

Part III   What Are Fats, and How Do We Test for Them? (3–8)

What Concepts Might Students Discover?

Some foods have a lot of fat, and others have little or no fat.

Fats that are thick (solid) at room temperature usually come from animals like cows, pigs, and sheep. These fats are called **saturated fats.**

Fats that are soft (semisolid) at room temperature usually are made from animals (e.g., lard and butter) or are manufactured (e.g., margarine).

Fats that are liquid at room temperature usually come from plants (e.g., peanut oil, olive oil, corn oil).

Fats are needed by our bodies, but too much fat can cause stomach and heart diseases.

Fats supply more than twice as much fuel and energy for the body as the same amount of starch, sugar, or protein.

Fats leave greasy spots, which is a simple test for identifying them.

What Will We Need?

Paper plates
Water
Butter
Vegetable oil
Samples of common snack foods: peanuts, bread, margarine, celery, carrots, mayonnaise, lettuce, bacon, corn and/or potato chips, pretzels, cheese, cookies, cake, apple, whole milk, yogurt, chocolate
Brown paper bags or brown paper towels cut into 2-in squares (provide enough squares so that there is one for each food sample)
Source of light: sunlight or lamp
Medicine dropper

What Do Students Know?

Why is it important to know which foods contain fats?
How much fat should we have in a healthy diet?
How are fats alike and different?
Are some fats "better" for the body than others?
What is cholesterol and what are the latest scientific findings about it and health?
How can we test some of our foods to see whether or not they contain fats?
What are some variables that we must control in our experiments?

What Will Students and Teacher Do?

Gather the class and ask:
How do you think we might test to see if foods contain fat?
List all suggestions, and then introduce this one if it was not suggested:

T I G

1. Put several drops of water on one square of brown paper, as in diagram (A). On a second square, put drops of oil (B).

A. Water   **B.** Oil

Observing *How did the oil feel?*

What Must I Know?

Another test for fats is that they feel "slippery" when rubbed between the fingers.

Observing *Describe how the stains look.*
Predicting *What do you think will happen to the two stains after 10 minutes?*
Write your guesses on the chalkboard.

Comparing 2. After 10 minutes, return to the paper and check.
What happened to each stain?
Where did the water drop go?
Why are oil drops still shiny?

What Must I Know?

The water evaporated, but the oil stains remained shiny. This is the spot test for fats. Have groups of two to four students conduct their own spot tests using the samples of snack foods.

G

3. Get a paper plate containing samples of snack foods, 17 squares of brown paper, and a copy of the Fat Spot Test Lab Sheet shown in the diagram.

Predicting 4. Mark an X in the "Predicted Fat" column for foods you think contain fat.

FAT SPOT TEST LAB SHEET		
Food Samples	Predicted Fat	Contains Fat
Peanuts		
Bread		
Margarine		
Celery		
Carrots		
Mayonnaise		
Lettuce		
Bacon		
Corn/Potato chips		
Pretzels		
Cheese		
Cookies		
Cake		
Apple		
Whole milk		
Yogurt		
Chocolate		

5. Firmly rub each food sample 10 times on a separate square of brown paper, and label the paper with the food's name.
6. After 10 minutes, hold each paper square up to a source of light.
7. Mark an X in the "Contains Fat" column of your chart for each food that left a greasy spot.

Comparing   *How did your predictions compare with your findings?*
Summarizing   *How would you summarize your test findings as to which foods contained the most fat?*

What Must I Know?   Bring the following information to students' attention: Many scientists recommend that every day we should get no more than 30% of our Calories from fat, with no more than 10% of these Calories coming from saturated (animal) fat, and no more than 300 mg of cholesterol. Discuss how students might select foods with less fat and the importance of reading food labels for ingredients.

How Will Students Use or Apply What They Discover?

1. *What might happen to people if they eat too much fat, especially saturated or animal fats?*
2. *How could we have a party, serving good-tasting foods, and still cut down on the amount of fat we eat?*
3. *Why might it be healthier to eat such foods as skim milk, lowfat cottage cheese, and nonfat ice cream?*

Part IV   What Is Protein, and How Do We Test for It? (3–8)

What Concepts Might Students Discover?

Protein is one group of food nutrients that the body uses for building tissues and repairing broken down cells.

Proteins are very vital for children's proper physical and mental growth and development.

Proteins are made up of many **amino acids.**

Some amino acids are synthesized in the body's cells, but others, the **essential amino acids,** must be supplied through the diet.

Amino acids are found in egg whites, milk curd, wheat gluten, the muscle fiber of meat, and beans and other vegetables.

Those foods that contain all the essential amino acids are called **complete proteins**; those with only some of the essential amino acids are **incomplete proteins.**

Protein cannot be made by, or stored in, the body and must be eaten regularly to promote the repair of used body cells.

What Must I Know?

Tests for protein may be dangerous for some students, since they usually involve open flame or acids. Therefore, avoid the use of certain tests, do the tests as a teacher demonstration, or have more mature students (i.e., middle schoolers) do them after careful instruction and under close supervision.

What Will We Need?

Matches	Copper sulphate
Candle in pie tin	Cup with 2 tbsp water
Water or fire extinguisher	Paper plate
Feather	Two medicine droppers
Sample foods: granulated sugar or cube; 1-inch-thin slices of cooked egg white, white bread, white turkey meat, cheese, mashed soybeans; flour (for second test)	Limewater

What Do Students Know?

What is protein?
Why does our body need protein?
Which foods contain protein?
How can we test for protein?

What Will Students and Teacher Do?

1. Light the candle in the pie tin. Using a clothespin to hold a feather, put the feather in the flame. *Caution:* If students are immature, the teacher should perform this step. Check your school policy on using an open flame. Have water and/or fire extinguisher handy.

Observing   *How would you describe the smell of the burning feather?*
That smell is the same as the one produced when protein is burned.

Designing an Experiment   *How might we find out if burning proteins smell like burning feathers?*
2. Using the clothespin as a holder, try burning bits of the sample foods.

Observing   *Which foods smell like burned feathers?*
Inferring   *What do you think these foods are made of?*
How else might we test for protein?

Here is another test for protein:

1. Dissolve as much copper sulfate as you can in 2 tablespoons of water in a cup. (*Caution:* Copper sulfate is a poison, so do not taste or eat.)

2. Arrange food samples on a paper plate as shown.
3. Put a clean medicine dropper in the limewater and another one in the copper sulfate solution. *Caution:* After each use, make sure each medicine dropper is replaced in the proper solution. Do not mix the solutions.
4. For each food sample, do the following:
   a. Squeeze two drops of limewater on the sample.
   b. Squeeze two drops of copper sulfate solution in the same spot as the limewater on each food sample.

Observing   *What color do you see on some food samples?*

What Must I Know? If the mixture of the limewater and the copper sulfate solution turns violet, the food contains protein. The darker the violet color, the greater the protein content.

Inferring   *Why do you think some of the foods turned violet?*
Inferring   *Why were some foods darker violet than others?*
Inferring   *Why did some foods not turn violet?*

How Will Students Use or Apply What They Discover?

1. Make a list of high-protein foods that you and your family eat.
2. *What do you think might happen to the quality of an incomplete protein if you mixed it with another incomplete protein, such as in dishes like macaroni and cheese, rice and beans, or bread and peanut butter? What other combinations might be tried?*
3. *Why do scientists caution us to eliminate, or drastically cut back on, animal proteins, even though they are complete proteins?*

Part V   What Are Minerals, and How Do We Test for Them? (3–8)

What Concepts Might Students Discover?

Minerals make up a large part of our bones and teeth, which is why minerals are so important for children.

Although we need small amounts of many minerals (called *trace elements*), calcium is needed in larger quantities for bone and teeth formation.

Calcium is found in large quantities in milk and milk products and in smaller quantities in green leafy vegetables and oranges.

Vinegar (acetic acid) reacts with calcium and can be used as a test.

What Will We Need?

2 chicken leg bones stripped of all meat
2 covered jars large enough to hold the chicken bones
Soap
Water
Paper towels

What Do Students Know?

What do bones do for our bodies?
Why must bones be strong and hard?
What might make bones strong and hard?
What might cause bones to get soft and weak?
How might we test for calcium?

What Must I Know? Vinegar indicates the presence of calcium or a carbonate by fizzing and bubbling. Because vinegar is a mild acid, you and your students should wash their hands with soap and water after conducting the activity. After a few days, the chicken leg bone left in vinegar will get rubbery and very soft.

What Will Students and Teacher Do?

Observing

T **G**

1. Pass both chicken leg bones around the classroom.

   How do the bones feel? Are they hard or soft?
2. Place a chicken bone in each jar.
3. Pour vinegar in one jar only and water in the other, cover both jars, and let stand for several days.
4. Remove the bone from the jar of vinegar, rinse it thoroughly with water, and dry it well with a paper towel. Remove the other bone from its jar of water.
5. Pass both bones around the classroom and ask:

Observing
Comparing
Inferring

   Do both bones feel the same?
   If not, how are they different?
   Why do you think the bone that was in vinegar is soft and rubbery?

How Will Students Use or Apply What They Discover?

1. *Why do you think it is so important for students to eat a lot of milk products?*
2. *What might happen if you did not eat enough milk products?*
3. *Why would it be healthier to eat lowfat or nonfat milk products?*

Part VI   What Are Vitamins, and How Do We Test for Them? (3–8)

What Concepts Might Students Discover?

Scientists have discovered more than 25 vitamins our bodies need, but they believe there are many more.

The lack of one vitamin could result in a vitamin deficiency disease such as rickets, scurvy, or pellagra.

Vitamin C is probably the best-known vitamin and is found in citrus fruits, tomatoes, raw cabbage, strawberries, and cantaloupe.

We can easily test for the presence of vitamin C.

What Will We Need?

Teaspoon	Empty plastic gallon jug
Cornstarch	Iodine
Measuring cup	Ruler
Water	6 clean baby food jars
Pan	Variety of juices that are canned, frozen, or
Hot plate	fresh: orange, apple, grape, pineapple, etc.
Medicine droppers	6 wooden stirrers

What Must I Know?

A simple, easy-to-make vitamin C indicator liquid can be made ahead of time and will keep for several days. You will know when it is time to dispose of it, because it will lighten from its optimum color of royal blue to a very pale blue. To make 1 gallon of vitamin C indicator:

1. Boil 1½ teaspoons (6 mL) of cornstarch in 1 cup (250 mL) of water for 2 minutes.
2. Put 10 full droppers of the cornstarch mixture into a gallon jug of water, use a clean dropper to add 1 dropper full of iodine, cover the jug, and shake it until you have a uniform blue color.

When using the vitamin C indicator liquid, explain that the fewer drops of juice needed to make the blue color disappear, the more vitamin C that juice contains.

What Will Students Do?

1. Using your ruler to measure, pour 1 centimeter (½ in) of vitamin C indicator liquid into each of the six clean baby food jars. Label each jar with the name of the juice you will test for vitamin C.

Measuring and Recording

2. Using a clean medicine dropper for each juice, add one kind of juice to each jar of indicator liquid, one drop at a time, and record the number of drops. (See the diagram.) Stir the liquid indicator with a clean wooden stirrer as you add drops.

| Canned orange juice | Fresh orange juice | Canned apple juice | Fresh apple juice | Canned grape juice | Frozen grape juice |

Observing
Comparing

3. When the indicator is no longer blue, the test is finished.
   Which juice(s) caused the blue color to disappear with the least number of drops?

Comparing
Summarizing

   Which juice(s) caused the blue color to disappear with the most drops?
   From these tests, which juice(s) had the most vitamin C?

How Will Students Use or Apply What They Discover?

1. *How do you think the following conditions could affect the vitamin C content of foods: heat, sunlight, air, age of food, and so on? How could you design experiments to test these variables?*
2. *Which do you think is better for you—vitamins eaten in foods or vitamins taken in pills or supplements? How could you find out?*
3. *What might happen if you got too much of a vitamin?*

Part VII   What Are Sugars, and How Do You Test for Them? (3–8)

What Concepts Might Students Discover?

Sugars are sweet substances made by green plants and are used mainly by humans for energy.

Sugars belong to a larger family of substances called saccharides or carbohydrates. These substances all contain carbon, hydrogen, and oxygen.

The chemical names of all saccharides ends in *-ose*. Fructose (found in ripe fruits) is called a simple sugar, or monosaccharide; *mono-* means it is made up of one sugar molecule. If two sugar molecules combine, they form a disaccharide; *di-* means two. Sucrose, or table sugar, is a disaccharide of glucose and fructose and is usually made from sugar cane or sugar beets.

An indicator for monosaccharides, or simple sugars, is TES-Tape™, used by diabetics to test for the presence of glucose in their urine.

The change in the yellow TES-Tape™ to a dark green characterizes a positive test for simple sugar.

Some common simple sugars are found in milk, honey, and ripe fruits, especially bananas. Starches broken down by chewing will also test positive for simple sugars.

What Must I Know?

Common table sugar will give a negative result on TES-Tape™, because sucrose is *not* a simple sugar. Other tests, such as ones using Benedict's solution or Fantastic™ cleaning solution, can test other sugars, but the teacher should demonstrate these because they require heat and the chemicals involved are poisonous. With proper instruction and careful supervision, responsible middle-school students could conduct these tests. Use your discretion.[5]

[5]For ideas on how to perform other tests for sugars, see Robert C. Mebane and Thomas R. Rybott, *Adventures with Atoms and Molecules Book II: Chemistry Experiments for Young People and Adventures with Atoms* (Hillsdale, NJ: Enslow Publishers, 1987); Mebane and Rybott, *Molecules Book III: Chemistry Experiments for Young People* (Hillsdale, NJ: Enslow Publishers, 1991); and Jean Stangl, *The Tools of Science: Ideas and Activities for Guiding Young Scientists* (New York: Dodd, Mead and Co., 1987).

What Will We Need?   TES-Tape™ (get in drugstore)   Oranges
Bananas (fairly ripe)   Maple syrup
Milk   Honey
Different kinds of apples   Paper plates
  (MacIntosh, Delicious, Rome)   Small paper cups
Table sugar, moistened with water

What Will Students Do?   *Note:* For efficiency in distribution, the teacher and/or designated students should prepare the following beforehand for each group of two to four students: paper plate containing cut samples of foods and small cups with very small samples of honey, milk, and maple syrup; 1-inch TES-Tape™ strip for each food to be tested; data collection sheet.

Organizing

1. Get a paper plate that contains food samples, TES-Tape™ strips, and a data collection sheet.
2. Assign one group member to each of the following tasks: tester, observer, and recorder.
3. *Tester:* Number each food, then write the numerals 1 through 10 on separate TES-Tape™ strips.
   Using the appropriately numbered strip that corresponds to the food being tested, touch ½ inch of the TES-Tape™ to each food separately, until the strip is wet.
   Now hand the TES-Tape™ to the observer.

Observing

Communicating

Communicating

4. *Observer:* Look at the wet end of the TES-Tape™. *What color is the wet end?*

Give the following information to your recorder:
a. the number of the sample TES-Tape™ strip,
b. the name of the food sample, and
c. the color of the wet end of the TES-Tape™ strip.
Repeat the preceding procedures with all of the food samples.

5. *Recorder:* As each food is tested, record on the TES-Tape™ data collection sheet the data that the observer gives you. Attach each TES-Tape™ strip in the appropriate place on the chart.

TES-Tape™ SUGAR TEST DATA COLLECTION SHEET		
Food Samples	Tape Color After Test	Tape Strip
Orange		
Banana, ripe		
Banana, green		
Maple syrup		
Milk		
Honey		
Mac apple		
Yellow Delicious		
Rome apple		
Table sugar		

Inferring

Inferring

Comparing

Observing

Inferring

From the data collected, which foods contain simple sugar?
What evidence do you have to support this?
From the changes in the TES-Tape™ color, which foods appear to have the most simple sugar? The least?
Which foods, if any, did not change the color of the TES-Tape™?
Why do you think this happened?

How Will Students Use or Apply What They Discover?

1. Bring in labels from food packages, read the ingredients lists, and list all the forms of sugar each food contains, such as honey, brown sugar syrup, sweeteners, corn sugar, corn sweeteners, molasses, invert sugar, sucrose, fructose, dextrose, maltose, lactose, and so on.

2. *What are some of the health problems that might develop if you eat too much sugar?*

3. Find out the amounts of sugar (both labeled and "hidden") in the common foods you eat, such as soft drinks—which can contain about 8 tea-

spoons per 12 ounces—or breakfast cereals—which contain about 2½ teaspoons (10 g) of sugar plus 3 teaspoons (13 g) of other carbohydrates for a total of 5½ teaspoons (23 g) per 1-ounce serving.

4. *What do you think might happen if you tested artificial sweeteners (saccharin, Aspartame, etc.) with TES-Tape™?*
5. *Why would it be healthier to eat fresh fruit as a snack rather than cakes, candy, and soft drinks, even though all of these contain sugar?*

How Can You See Which Soda Has More Sugar? (3–8)

What Concepts Might Students Discover?

Diet sodas are lighter than regular sodas because of the large quantity of sugar in regular sodas (as much as 8 teaspoons or more per can!).
Sugar is heavier than water.

What Will We Need?

3 pairs of 12-oz cans of soda, unopened, assorted flavors and brands; each
    pair should contain 1 diet and 1 regular of same flavor and brand
Aquarium filled with water
Scale

What Do Students Know?

Which cans will float, and which will sink?
Are the sodas the same?
Which is heavier, sugar or water?
How do you know?
How might we test this?

PROCESSES

What Will Students Do?
Observing
Inferring

1. Place the six unopened sodas in the aquarium filled with water.
    Do you see any difference between the cans in the water?
    Why? Do you see any pattern?
2. Weigh each can and record your data in a chart like the one shown.

Pair	Brand	Flavor	Diet Weight	Regular Weight	Weight Difference
1.					
2.					
3.					

Inferring
Comparing
Comparing

What does your data show? What accounts for the weight differences?
How do the weights of the diet sodas compare?
How do the weights of the nondiet sodas compare?
Check the list of ingredients on soda cans to see the order of abundance.

What Must I Know?

The mass of a diet soda is usually about 10–15 grams less than the mass of a nondiet soda. The difference is usually sugar or corn syrup.

How Does Your Body Change and Use Starch in the Foods You Eat? (K–8)

What Concepts Might Students Discover?

Large food particles must be broken down into smaller molecules before they can be absorbed into the body.

The breaking down of food by chemical means is called **digestion.**

Food must be dissolved before it can be used by the body.

Starch is a nutrient.

Starch must be changed to dissolved sugar for it to pass through the lining of the small intestine.

What Will We Need?

2 jars with covers	Iodine (a small bottle with an eye dropper)
4 cubes of sugar	Crackers
Water	Funnel
Teaspoon	Paper towels
Cornstarch	Medicine droppers
3 clear plastic cups	TES-Tape™
Sugar	4-in squares of waxed paper
Wooden stirrers	

What Must I Know?

Caution: Iodine is poisonous; do not allow students to handle it unsupervised. Also, iodine may stain skin, clothing, and other materials.

What Do Students Know?

How will a cracker be used by your body when you eat it?
What is going to happen to the cracker?
When will the cracker be ready to be used by your cells?
How will your body prepare this cracker for use?
If your body does not use every bit of the cracker, what is going to happen to that which is not used?
Where will your body digest this cracker?
What substances does your body contain to break down the cracker into usable substances?

PROCESSES

What Will Students Do?

Part I   How Can Large Molecules Be Broken Down? (K–2)

1. Pour equal amounts of cold water into two jars. Place two cubes of sugar into each jar and screw the covers on tightly. Place one jar aside and let it stand still. Shake the other jar vigorously.

Observing   2. Compare the results occurring in the two jars.

No shaking   Shaking

Inferring   *Why did the sugar cubes break down and dissolve faster in one jar?*
Applying   *What does this activity tell us about chewing food before swallowing it?*

What Must I Know?   The more students chew their food, the more enzymes will be able to mix with the food to break it down chemically. Chewing also helps to break the food down into smaller particles so more of it comes in contact with the enzymes.

Part II   How Is a Starch Solution Different From a Sugar Solution? (3–8)

What Will Students Do?

1. Obtain a teaspoon of cornstarch, two clear plastic cups ¾ full of water, and a teaspoon of sugar. Put the cornstarch into one cup of water and the sugar into the other. Stir each glass with a separate wooden stirrer.

Observing   *How does the starch solution appear?*
Observing   *How does the sugar solution appear?*

Water and sugar   Water and cornstarch

Inferring   *Which has dissolved? How do you know?*
Hypothesizing   *What do you think might happen if you let both glasses stand for a day?*
Inferring   *How would the results of this experiment help to explain why starch has to be changed so your body can use it?*

2. Stir the starch and water again until the starch is mixed with the water. Take a teaspoon of the starch and water mixture and put a drop of iodine into it to dilute the mixture to a straw color, as in diagram (a).

What Must I Know?   As pointed out in previous activities, iodine is used to test for starch. Starch in the presence of iodine turns blue-black.

Observing   *What color does the mixture turn?*

(a) Water and cornstarch   (b) Water and sugar   (c) Cracker

3. Rinse the spoon thoroughly and repeat Step 2, substituting sugar water for the starch and water mixture (b).

Comparing   *How does the result differ?*

4. Put a drop of iodine on a cracker (c).

Observing   *What is the result?*

Comparing   *How does the color of the iodine on the cracker compare with the iodine in the starch and water solution?*

What Must I Know?   The water-sugar and water-cornstarch solutions should be saved for use in Part III.

Part III   How Does Molecule Size Affect the Ability to Pass Through a Filter? (3–8)

1. Line a funnel with a piece of paper towel and set the funnel in an empty clear plastic cup. Stir the starch solution (from Part II) again. Slowly

pour some of the starch water into the funnel. After the water has run through the funnel, look at the inside of the paper.

Observing   *Is there any powder left inside the funnel?*

Hypothesizing   *How could you test to see if it is starch?*

Hypothesizing   *How could you test to see if there is any starch left in the water that passed through the filter?*

2. Perform the test for starch in water shown in the diagram.

Observing   *What color did the mixture turn?*

Inferring   *Is there starch present?*

Hypothesizing   *What do you think will happen if sugar water is poured through filter paper?*

Hypothesizing   *How could you tell if there was sugar in the water before and after you poured it through the funnel?*

Inferring   *Which do you think could go through the wall of your intestine better—starch or sugar? Why?*

Part IV   How Does Saliva Affect the Digestion of Starch?

Hypothesizing   *How can we verify that saliva begins the process of digestion by changing starch to sugar?*

1. Test one cracker for starch by putting a few drops of iodine on it.

Observing   *What color does the spot of iodine turn?*

2. Now test the same cracker for sugar by placing a few drops of water on it and then testing it with TES-Tape™.

3. Get another cracker, place it in your mouth, and chew it slowly for 1 to 2 minutes. Put a small amount of chewed cracker on a piece of waxed paper in two places.

4. Test one chewed cracker sample for starch using the iodine test.

Observing   *What do you observe?*

Iodine turns black.

TES-Tape™ does not change color on water drop.

iodine dropper

chewed cracker and iodine

waxed paper

chewed cracker and TES-Tape™ (darker edge showing sugar present)

Observing
Inferring

5. Test the other chewed cracker sample for sugar using the TES-Tape™.
   What change do you observe?
   How has the saliva in your mouth changed the starch in the cracker?
   Caution: Dispose of waxed paper and chewed cracker samples immediately. Do not touch other chewed cracker samples.

How Will Students Use or Apply What They Discover?

1. *How does saliva affect other foods such as poultry, fruits, and vegetables?*
2. *Why should diabetics control the amount of starchy foods they eat?*
3. Test other foods for starch content.
4. *How might heat affect the digestion of starch?*

What Must I Know?

Note: At the conclusion of your study of nutrients and health, a summary chart could be made using the mnemonic *Cats Wait For Mice Very Patiently*, as shown here.

The Nutrient Chart

	Nutrient	Bodily Function	Food Source
CATS	Carbohydrates (starch and sugar)	Energy	Grains; fruits; vegetables
WAIT	Water	Maintenance: carries nutrients in blood; maintains temperature	All
FOR	Fats	Energy/maintenance; carry some vitamins	All
MICE	Minerals	Maintenance: regulate and maintain body functions	Fruits/vegetables, dairy products
VERY	Vitamins	Maintenance: regulate and maintain body functions	Fruits/vegetables
PATIENTLY	Protein	Growth; tissue building/repair	Meats, legumes, dairy products

References—Human Anatomy and Physiology
Teacher or older students: Human Physiology Block V (Arlington, VA: National Science Teachers Association, 1993); Sarah Stein, *The Body Book* (Arlington, VA: National Science Teachers Association, 1993); Ruth Westheimer, *Dr. Ruth Talks to Kids: Where You Came From, How Your Body Changes, and What Sex Is All About* (New York: Macmillan, 1993). *Students:* Margaret Miller, *My Five Senses* (New York, Simon and Schuster, 1994); Dorothy Hinshaw, *Nutrition: What's in the Food We Eat* (New York, Holiday House, 1992).

SECTION 3

Earth, Ecology, and Environmental Sciences and Technology

As a result of their activities in grades K–4, all students should develop an understanding of:

- properties of earth materials, and
- objects in the sky.

As a result of their activities in grades 5–8, all students should develop an understanding of:

- the structure of the Earth system,
- Earth's history, and
- Earth in the Solar System. (p. 10)[1]

ASTRONOMY (EARTH IN SPACE)

QUICKIE STARTERS: OPEN-ENDED ACTIVITIES

What Causes Shadows, and How Can They Be Changed? (K–2)

Materials

Flashlight, 2 pieces of white paper, scissors, paste, funnel, pencil or crayon

What Do Students Know?

What are shadows, and how are they formed?
How can you make shadows larger or smaller?
What are some of the things (variables) that affect the size of shadows?
Why do shadows change shape and size during the day?

Some Possible Activities

Work with a partner. Put a funnel on a large sheet of white paper. One of you should shine the flashlight on the funnel while the other one traces and cuts the shadow out with scissors, in this sequence.

1. First, while holding the flashlight low, trace and cut out the shadow of the funnel.

[1]Reprinted with permission from National Science Standards. Copyright 1995 by the National Academy of Sciences. Courtesy of the National Academy Press, Washington, DC.

2. Next, put a new piece of white paper under the funnel, hold the flash-light high, and then trace and cut out the shadow of the funnel.
3. Compare the size and shape of the two cut-out shadows.

Why do you think the shadow was longer when the flashlight was held low?
During what part(s) of the day do shadows look this way outdoors?

How Can Shadows Help You Tell Time? (K–2)

Materials

For each student or group of 2 to 4 students: Long nail, hammer, 8½" × 11" pieces of white paper, square board big enough to hold the paper, pencil

What Do Students Know?

Do you think that shadows outdoors change during the day? How might we find out?
If shadows change, at what time will they be the shortest? The longest? Why do you think so?

Some Possible Activities

Put a piece of paper in the middle of the board and drive the nail into the board and paper as shown, making sure the nail will not easily come out of the board.

Place the board where it will get sunlight all day. Every hour, draw an X at the tip of the shadow cast by the nail. Write down the time you marked the X as well. Repeat this activity with a new piece of paper every school day for 1 week, keeping the board in exactly the same spot. At the end of the week, assist students in answering these questions:
At what times during the day were the shadows the longest? The shortest? Were these times the same each day?

An instrument that is used to tell time by the position of the sun and its resulting shadows is called a **sundial.**

GUIDED DISCOVERY HANDS-ON/MINDS-ON ACTIVITIES

Why Is There Day and Night? (K–2)

What Concepts Might Students Discover?

The earth **rotates,** or turns around.

The earth rotates from west to east.

It takes 24 hours for the earth to make one complete turn or rotation. The rotation of the earth explains why part of the 24-hour period is night and part is day.

The sun is always shining, even when it is night and you cannot see the sun.

What Will We Need?

Clay or styrofoam ball   Strong flashlight or filmstrip projector
Knitting needle   Pin

What Do Students Know?

When it is daytime here, where is it night?
When it is night here, where is it day?
What could you do to find out about daytime and nighttime on the earth?

PROCESSES

What Will Students Do?

1. Make a clay ball as large as a baseball; use it as a model of the earth. A styrofoam ball may be used.
   In what way do you think the ball is like the earth?
2. Push the knitting needle through the clay or styrofoam globe. Darken the room. Let the flashlight or filmstrip projector, which represents the sun, shine on the ball.

Inferring   *What side of the earth (ball) do you think is having night?*
Inferring   *What side of the globe do you think is having day?*
Inferring   *What tells you that the sun is always shining somewhere on the earth?*

Clay or styrofoam ball   East
Day   Sun
Night   West
Earth   Move the earth counterclockwise

3. Stick a pin in the ball to represent the place where you live. Turn the ball slowly in a counterclockwise motion.

Hypothesizing   *Using the clay or styrofoam ball, how could you make night come to the place where you live?*

What Must I Know?

The ball, representing the earth, is turned slowly counterclockwise to show where night would begin to fall and where it would be midnight and sunrise.

Inferring   *What time of day is it when your pin is on the same side as the sun?*
Inferring   *When your pin is away from the sun, what time of day would it be?*

How Will Students Use or Apply What They Discover?	1. *What would happen if the earth did not turn?* 2. *If the earth did not turn, which side would you rather be on? Why?* 3. *Why is it inaccurate to say the sun "rises" in the east and "sets" in the west?* 4. *If it is 9 A.M. in New York City, what time will it be in San Francisco?*

Why Does the Moon Shine? (3–5)

What Concepts Might Students Discover?	Objects are seen when they give off their own light or when they reflect light from another source. The moon does not give off its own light. Its light is reflected light from the sun.
What Will We Need?	Large ball 1"-diameter ball of foil, with attached string Masking tape Box with tight-fitting lid (shoebox) lined with dull black paper Flashlight 2"-diameter styrofoam ball, with attached string
What Do Students Know?	Darken the room, place a ball on the table, and ask: *What is on the table?* *What do you need to be able to see the object?* Turn on the lights. *Why do you see the ball now?* *Do you see it because it is giving off its own light or because it is reflecting light from some other source?* Look at the ceiling lights. *Why is it possible for you to see the lights? How is this light different from the light you see when you look at the ball?* Darken the room. *What are two reasons why you may not see any lights in the room?*

PROCESSES

What Will Students Do?

Hypothesizing	*How do you think the moon shines?*
Inferring	*What is reflected light?*

1. Suspend the foil ball on a 1-inch string from inside the box lid lined with dull black paper, as shown in the diagram. Insert the flashlight in the end of the box and seal any space around it with masking tape. Make a small eyehole under the flashlight.

Eye hole

2. Put on the lid and seal the edges around the lid with tape.

Observing and Inferring   *What do you see when you look through the eyehole? Why?*

3. Turn on the flashlight.

Observing and Inferring   *What do you see when you look through the eyehole? Why?*

Inferring   *Do you see the ball because it reflects light or because it gives off its own light?*

Classifying   *What two kinds of light do you see?*

Inferring   *What is the source of each kind of light?*

4. Look out the window.

Inferring   *Why are you able to see some objects?*

Inferring   *What is the source of light?*

Inferring   *Do the objects seen outside the window give off reflected light or light of their own?*

Inferring   *What does the sun give off?*

Inferring   *Why does the moon shine?*

5. Obtain a styrofoam ball that has an attached string. Use your box, flashlight, and suspended foil ball but add the larger styrofoam ball, suspending it 2 inches from the top, as shown in the diagram. Seal the edges of the box again. Then seal the old eyehole and make a new eyehole in the side of the box, as indicated in the drawing.

Formulating a Model   *If the small ball is the moon, what does the flashlight represent?*

6. Turn on the flashlight and look through the new eyehole in the side of the box.

Inferring   *What does the large ball represent?*

7. Look at the ball representing the earth and tell which side is day and which side is night.

Inferring   *On which side would you be if you could see the moon?*

Inferring   *How is it possible for you to see the moon if you are on the dark side of the earth?*

Summarizing   *Why does the moon shine?*

How Will Students Use or Apply What They Discover?

1. *If you lived on another planet, would you be able to see earth?*
2. *What are the positions of the sun, moon, and earth (a) when it is night for you and (b) when it is day for you, as shown in the diagram?*

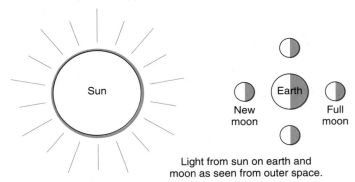

Light from sun on earth and moon as seen from outer space.

Why Does It Appear That There Are Phases of the Moon? (3–5)

What Concepts Might Students Discover?

Sometimes the moon appears fully round, appears to our eyes to change shape, or may appear to get smaller and smaller, or even larger and larger.

What Will We Need?

Black construction paper   Small ball
Globe   Flashlight or filmstrip projector
Basketball   Straight pin
Soft white chalk

What Must I Know?

Before the activity, consult the local newspaper to see when the moon's quarter will be visible.

What Will Students Do?

1. Take home a large sheet of black construction paper and some white chalk and observe the moon for the next 5 days. Draw the shape of the moon as you see it each night. *Note:* Should the skies be overcast, making it impossible to observe the moon, use the local newspaper to get the information.

Observing

In what ways does the moon's shape seem to change?

2. Arrange a globe, small ball, and a flashlight or filmstrip projector as shown in the diagram.
3. Place a pin on the night side of the earth as indicated in the diagram. The pin represents you.

Inferring

Draw how much of a moon you would see if you were where the pin is.

4. Move the moon around the earth to the day side.

Inferring

On which side of the earth is the moon when you cannot see it?
Where is the moon when it is full?

5. Make diagrams to help you explain your answers to these questions.

6. Look at the following diagram, which shows some positions of the moon in relation to the earth and the sun.

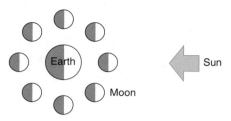

G 7. Choose two partners to help you. Using a basketball and flashlight, have one partner hold the flashlight and shine it on the basketball being held by your second partner, as he or she walks in a circle around you. See the diagram for how to do this.

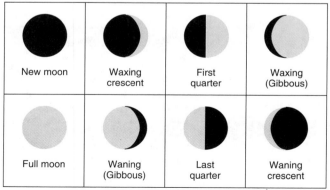

Inferring 8. As you observe the light on the ball in various positions, match the following moon phases with the appropriate eight moon positions shown in the diagram accompanying Step 6. What you see is what would be observed from the earth.

Phases of the Moon as Seen from the Earth

Inferring	*In what position is the basketball when it is covered by the shadow?*
Inferring	*Where would the moon have to be when it is covered by a shadow?*
Inferring	*When the basketball shows no shadow, what phase of the moon would this represent?*
Summarizing	9. Draw how the full moon looks from earth.
Summarizing	*What causes the phases of the moon?*

How Will Students Use or Apply What They Discover?

1. *If the moon is not out at night, on what side of the earth must it be located?*
2. *If the moon could remain motionless in the sky, how would it look every night?*
3. An additional activity for the whole class is to set up a Moonwatch Bulletin Board,[2] as follows:
   a. Each night, have three students draw the shape of the moon on Moon Watch Cards (see diagram) by filling in the "lighted" part of the circle. (Look up phase of the moon in the newspaper if clouds prevent actual viewing.)

3" x 5" index card — / Date: / **Moon Watch Card**

   b. Have the three students compare their drawings and arrive at one drawing.
   c. Post the drawing on a bulletin board like this:

	1	2	3	4	5	6	7	8	9	10	11	12	13	14	15	16	17	18	19	20	21	22
February	)	)	)	●	●	●																
March																						
April																						
May																						
June																						

   d. As a pattern develops, have the class try to predict the next day's moon shape.

References—Astronomy (Earth in Space)

Teacher or older students: D. Louis and Mary Jane Finsand, *North Polar Constellations* (Arlington, VA: National Science Teachers Association, 1991); Fred Schaaf, *Seeing the Sky* (Arlington, VA: National Science Teachers Association, 1990); Debra Sutton et al., *Moons of Jupiter—Teacher's Guide* (Berkeley, CA: Great Explorations in Math and Science [GEMS], 1993). *Students:* R. Mike Mullane, *Liftoff! An Astronaut's Dream* (New York: Silver Burdett, 1994); *The Visual Dictionary of the Universe* (Eyewitness Visual Dictionaries) (New York: Dorling Kindersley, 1993); Steve Parker, *The Space Atlas* (New York: Dorling Kindersley, 1993); Seymour Simon, *Our Solar System* (New York: Morrow, 1992); Sally Ride and Tam O'Shaughnessy, *Voyager: An Adventure to the Edge of the Solar System* (New York: Crown, 1992).

[2]For additional details on moon watches, see: G. Robert Moore, "Revisiting Science Concepts," *Science and Children* 32, no. 3, November/December 1994, 31–32, 60.

METEOROLOGY (WEATHER)

QUICKIE STARTERS: OPEN-ENDED ACTIVITIES (K–2)

How Are Clouds and Fog Formed?

Materials

Ice cubes; 2 clear, narrow-mouthed bottles; hot and cold water

What Do Students Know?

What is a cloud and how is it formed?
What is fog and how is it formed?

Some Possible Activities

Fill a bottle with very hot water and let it sit for a few minutes. Now pour out most of the water, leaving about 2 centimeters ($\frac{3}{4}$ to 1 inch) of water in the bottom of the bottle. For a control, set up an identical bottle with an equal amount of cold water. Place an ice cube in each bottle as shown in the diagram. As your students observe the two bottles, ask:
What do you see happening in each bottle?
What do we call what you see in the hot-water bottle?'

Ice cube — Ice cube

Fog does not form — Fog forms

Cold water — Hot water

Why do you think clouds or fog formed in the bottle with hot water and not in the bottle with cold water?
How do clouds and fog form in nature?

What Is the Greenhouse Effect? (K–2)

Materials

Large-mouthed jar with cover, 2 identical thermometers, 2 large cards, 2 rubber bands

What Do Students Know?

How does a greenhouse (where plants are grown) get so warm, even on a cold winter day?
During the summer, why is it hotter in an automobile when all the windows are shut tight rather than open?
What is meant by "solar heating"?

Some Possible Activities

Get two thermometers that have identical readings and use rubber bands to attach them to large cards. Place one thermometer and card in a large-mouthed jar and screw on the cover. Set up a "heat trap" in a sunny window, as shown, to illustrate the principle of the greenhouse, cold frame, or solar house. Make sure each thermometer is shaded from the direct sunlight by the cards.

Sunny window

Control

Cards to shade
the thermometers

Take readings every half hour.
What differences do you observe on the two thermometers?
Why do you think the temperature in the jar is higher?
How is this knowledge used by architects and builders to make solar-heated houses?

GUIDED DISCOVERY HANDS-ON/MINDS-ON ACTIVITIES

How Can You Measure Temperature Changes?/What Is a Thermometer? (K–2)

What Concepts Might Students Discover?

Thermal energy (heat) gives increased energy to molecules, causing them to exert more pressure or expand.
Warm temperatures make things expand more than do cold temperatures. An instrument that measures changes in temperature is called a **thermometer** (*thermo*—heat, and *meter*—to measure).

What Will We Need?

Clear, narrow plastic drinking straw
Scissors
Cold water or rubbing alcohol
Red food coloring

Small vial or medicine bottle
Modeling clay
3" × 5" index card
Tape

What Do Students Know?

Where in this classroom might be the warmest places?
Where in this classroom might be the coolest places?

How could we find out the answers to these two questions?
What instrument(s) might we use in our investigation?

What Must I Know

This activity can be done individually or in groups of two to four students. Thermometers measure the temperature of matter, or how hot or cold something is. Mercury or colored alcohol is usually the liquid used in thermometers. When heated, the liquid expands and moves up the tube. We say the temperature goes up. Conversely, when cooled, the liquid contracts and moves down the tube. We say the temperature goes down. Thermometers are used in many scientific, as well as personal, aspects of life, such as in taking body temperatures, in measuring air or water temperatures, in cooking, and so on.

PROCESSES

What Will Students Do?

Measuring

1. Put 2.5 centimeters (1 inch) of cold water into the small vial or medicine bottle and add several drops of red food coloring. (*Note:* Rubbing alcohol responds more quickly to temperature changes and can be used instead of water, depending on the ages and maturity of your students.)

2. With scissors, cut the end of the drinking straw at a slight angle. (*Note:* Your results will be best if you use the narrowest straw you can. Also, changes in air pressure and evaporation may affect your thermometer. To prevent this, after setting up the thermometers, put a few drops of oil into the top of the drinking straw, or seal the straw with modeling clay.)

3. Put the straw into the vial and completely seal the top of the vial with modeling clay, making sure it is airtight.

4. Tape a 3 × 5-inch index card to the drinking straw. As shown in the diagram, mark the level of the colored water in the straw.

Hypothesizing

What do you think might happen to the colored water in the drinking straw if you put your thermometer in a warmer spot?

Observing

5. Put your thermometer in a warmer spot or in a pan of warm water and observe what happens. On the card, mark the new height of the liquid in your drinking straw.

Recording Data	Draw a picture of what happened to the colored water in the drinking straw.
Inferring	*Why do you think the colored water moved up the drinking straw?*
Hypothesizing	*What do you think might happen now if you put your thermometer in a cooler spot?*

6. Put your thermometer in a cooler spot or in a pan of cold water.

Recording Data	Draw a picture of what happened to the colored water in the drinking straw.
Inferring	*Why do you think the colored water moved down the drinking straw?*

What Must I Know?

Check each student's drawing to see if he or she observed that as the temperature went up, so did the colored water in the straw. The colored-water level went down when the temperature went down. Discuss the interrelationship between expansion and contraction of molecules and temperature, or the amount of molecular motion.

How Will Students Use or Apply What They Discover?

1. Each day for a week, have students observe and record where the level of the liquid is in their thermometers at the opening, lunch, and closing time of school. Then have students answer these questions:

Comparing

Of your three thermometer readings each day, which one was the highest and which one was the lowest?

Extrapolating
Hypothesizing

During a week, which was the warmest morning, lunch, and afternoon?
Where do you predict tomorrow's levels will be for your three thermometer readings?

Measuring/Comparing

2. Take thermometer readings and compare where the level of the colored water is in the coolest and warmest spots in your classroom.

Measuring

3. Using a commercial thermometer, measure the air temperature. Have students use this temperature to mark their drinking-straw cards with actual numerical readings. Have students take their daily readings on their thermometers for a week, with you giving them the actual numerical reading each time.

Predicting

4. After 1 week, ask your students to predict what the actual numerical temperature will be for the three daily readings.

Describing

5. Make a list of various jobs where people use thermometers. Describe how thermometers are used in each job.

How Can Solar Energy Be Used? (3–5)

What Concepts Might Students Discover?

Water in a saline solution absorbs the sun's energy and evaporates, leaving the salt behind. When cooled, water vapor condenses and changes into water droplets.

What Will We Need?

Salt	Large clear plastic bowl
Water	Plastic wrap
Tablespoon	Large rubber band
Small weight (rock)	Small glass custard cup
Large sheet of black construction paper	

What Do Students Know?

In what ways can you make the sun do work for you?

What Must I Know?

This activity may be done individually or in groups of two to four.

PROCESSES
What Will Students Do?

Part I   How Can You Make a Solar Still? (3–5)

1. Pour 3 tablespoons of salt into the larger clear plastic bowl, add 1 inch (2.5 cm) of water, and stir until all the salt is dissolved.
2. Place the small glass custard cup in the water in the center of the bowl.
3. Cover the large bowl with plastic wrap and fasten the wrap with a large rubber band.
4. Place a weight (small pebble) on top of the plastic wrap directly above the custard dish, as shown in the diagram.
   Caution: Make certain that the plastic wrap sticks tightly to the sides of the bowl and that the large rubber band keeps it sealed when the pebble is placed on the wrap.

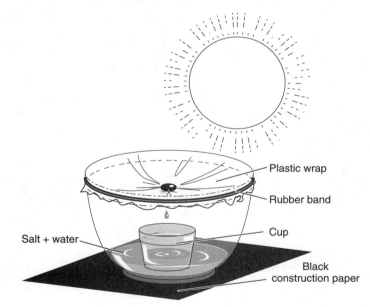

5. Carefully place the bowls in direct sunlight on a sheet of black construction paper, making sure the custard cup is directly under the weight pushing down on the plastic wrap.

Hypothesizing   *What do you think might happen to the salt water?*

Hypothesizing   *Why do you think you were told to cover the salt water with plastic wrap?*

Hypothesizing   *Why do you think you were told to put the bowl on black construction paper?*

Observing   6. Record your observations every day.

What Must I Know?

When there is only salt remaining in the large bowl and all the water is in the custard cup, Part II should be done by the group.

Part II What Is Desalinated Water? (3–5)

What Will Students Do?

Comparing
Inferring
Inferring
Inferring
Inferring
Observing

1. Take off the plastic wrap and taste the water in the custard cup.
   How does the water taste?
   Where did the water in this dish come from?
   What happened to your salt solution?
   Where did the water go?
   Why did the water "disappear"?
   What is left in the bottom of the large bowl?
2. Pour the contents of the large bowl onto a piece of black construction paper.

Inferring

   What is this substance?

How Will Students Use or Apply What They Discover?

1. *How does the sun's energy (solar energy) benefit people?*
2. *How could this procedure be helpful to people who live near the ocean but do not have enough drinking water?*
3. *What are some other uses for this method of obtaining drinking water?*
4. *What are some other ways in which the sun's energy (solar energy) can be used to help people?*
5. *How does the pictured solar water heater work?*

How Can You Measure Wind Direction and Speed? (3–8)

What Concepts Might Students Discover?

Wind, or moving air, brings about changing weather conditions.
A **wind vane** is an instrument that shows the direction from which the wind is blowing.
Winds are named for the direction from which they blow. For example, a north wind is blowing from the north to the south.
An **anemometer** is an instrument that shows wind speed.

What Will We Need?

Scissors	Magnetic compass
Construction Paper	Small mirror
Drinking straw	Long sewing needle
Glue	12" (30 cm) monofilament nylon line
Pencil with eraser	Ping-Pong ball
Straight pin	Protractor
Glass bead	Bubble level (hardware store)
Empty thread spool	Red marking pen
Two 1-sq-ft (1000-sq-cm) pieces of corrugated cardboard	Tongue depressor

What Do Students Know?

How can you tell the direction the wind is blowing?
How does knowing wind direction help us understand weather and weather prediction?
What instruments can be used to find wind direction and speed?
How can we make and use these instruments?

PROCESSES

Part I   What Is a Wind Vane, and How Do We Make One? (3–5)

What Will Students Do?

1. Cut, from construction paper, an arrow-shaped point and tail fin, as shown in the diagram.
2. Attach the point and tail fin to the straw by cutting notches in both ends of the straw and gluing the cut-outs in place.
3. Attach the straw to a pencil by sticking the straight pin through the middle of the straw, through a glass bead, and into the pencil eraser. Make sure the straw can swing easily in all directions and is balanced. *Note:* Move pin in straw until it balances with arrow and tail attached.
4. Glue the empty thread spool to the center of the corrugated cardboard and mark North, South, East, and West on the cardboard as shown in the diagram.

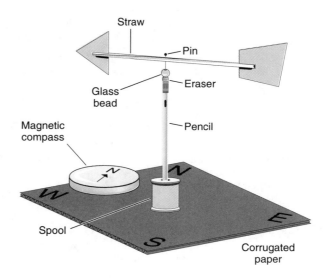

5. When the glue has dried, push the pencil into the hole of the spool and check to see that the straw moves easily. You now have a wind vane.

6. Carefully take your wind vane outdoors and line up the north label on your wind vane with the north on a magnetic compass. If wind is strong, tape the cardboard to concrete.

Observing   *What do you see happening to the arrow?*

Observing   *From which direction is the wind blowing? How do you know?*

Applying   *How would you name this wind?*

What Must I Know?

The arrow will swing around until the point faces the direction from which the wind is blowing. This direction then becomes the wind's name.

How Will Students Use or Apply What They Discover?

1. *Does the wind always blow from the same direction? How could we find out?*

2. Keep a record of wind observations three times a day for 1 week. Make sure to record the data on a chart:

	Monday			Wednesday			Friday		
Date	10/7								
Location	playground								
Observation time	9:30	11:30	1:30						
Wind direction	E	E	SE						
Any changes	yes; leaves blew to side of building								

3. *After 1 week, do you see*
   a. *any pattern of winds during the day?*
   b. *any pattern of winds from day to day?*
   c. *any prevailing or consistent direction from which the wind blows?*
   d. *any correlation between wind direction and weather conditions, such as temperatures, humidity, clouds, and so on?*

4. Check local TV weather and newspapers for wind direction.

Part II   How Can You Detect Winds in the Sky? (3–5)

What Do Students Know?

Are winds in the sky always the same as down here on the earth's surface? How do you know?
How might we find out?
Why is it important for pilots to know the speed and direction of winds up high?

What Must I Know?

You may have noticed that high clouds sometimes move in different directions from middle or low clouds. High cloud movement may also differ from surface winds. Students may work with a partner for this activity.

What Will Students Do?

1. Set up a small mirror in the center of a cardboard square and mark North, South, East, and West, as in the diagram.

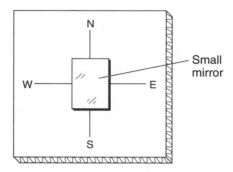

2. Place this cardboard and the wind vane from Part I next to each other in the same outdoor area. Make sure the points marked North line up with North on the magnetic compass.
3. Look into the mirror to see the clouds' reflection.

Observing   *In which direction are the clouds moving?*
This indicates wind direction at cloud level.

Observing   *In what direction is the wind on the ground moving?*

4. Use the wind vane to determine the direction of the wind on the ground.

Comparing   *How do cloud movement direction and ground wind direction compare?*

Record Keeping   5. Keep a log of cloud movement directions three times a day for 1 week as you did with wind vane observations.

Observing/Comparing   Notice any changes during the day and any patterns over the week.
Comparing   Compare the data with your weather vane data.

Part III   How Can You Measure How Fast the Wind Blows?[3] (3–8)

What Will Students Do?

1. Thread a sewing needle with a 12-inch monofilament line, push the needle through the Ping-Pong ball, and knot and glue the end of the line to the Ping-Pong ball. Glue the other end of the line to the center of a protractor. With the marking pen, color the line red.
2. Glue a bubble level to the protractor as shown in the diagram.
3. Glue a tongue depressor to the protractor as a handle. You now have an anemometer to measure wind speed.
4. When the glue is dry, carefully take your anemometer outside to test it in the wind.

[3]The author highly recommends the following packet of activities for making and using weather instruments: *Science Activities in Energy*, DOE/CA–0006 (P.O. Box 117, Oak Ridge, TN 37830: American Museum of Science and Energy/Oak Ridge Associated Universities).

5. To take readings of the wind's speed, follow these directions:
   a. In the wind, hold the protractor level using the tongue depressor handle.
   b. Keep the protractor level by making sure the bubble is centered in the bubble level.
   c. Observe any swing of the Ping-Pong ball and string and see what angle the string makes on the protractor. For instance, in the diagram the string moved to approximately 65 degrees.

How Will Students Use or Apply What They Discover?

1. Use your anemometer in various spots on your school grounds, and then refer to the following chart to find the wind speed.

Protractor Anemometer Wind Speeds

String Angle	Wind Speed (Miles Per Hour)	String Angle	Wind Speed (Miles Per Hour)
90	0	50	18.0
85	5.8	45	19.6
80	8.2	40	21.9
75	10.1	35	23.4
70	11.8	30	25.8
65	13.4	25	28.7
60	14.9	20	32.5
55	16.4		

2. After you have tested the wind speed in different places on your school grounds, record the data on a chart like this one:

Date						
Time						
Protractor angle						
Wind speed						
Wind direction						

Where does the wind blow the fastest on your school grounds?
Does wind blow faster at ground level or at higher levels?
Is there a place where wind blows faster, such as between two buildings or at a corner of two wings of a building? Why?

How Can You Measure Air Pressure Changes? (3–8)

Part I   What Is a Barometer? (3–8)

What Concepts Might Students Discover?

Air exerts pressure.
Air pressure changes.
Air pressure may indicate the type of weather.
Low air pressure usually indicates rainy or cloudy weather.
High air pressure usually indicates fair weather.

What Will We Need?

Balloons
Can with plastic snap top (e.g., coffee can) or top made of large balloon and rubber band
Straw
Glue
Straight pin
Index card

What Do Students Know?

Have each student blow up a balloon. Ask:
What is in the balloon?
How do you know there is pressure exerted in the balloon?
How can you discover whether or not air has the same pressure at all times and in all places?
What is a barometer?
What is it used for?
How might location affect the readings of a barometer?

What Must I Know?

Room temperature will affect the barometer students make in this activity. This barometer does not, therefore, measure only air pressure differences. You may want to have some students keep their barometers outside class and then compare the readings from the different locations.

PROCESSES

What Will Students Do?

I G

1. Obtain a can that has a plastic snap top, a straw, glue, a straight pin, and a card.
2. Cover the can with the plastic snap top, making certain the can is sealed completely. *Caution:* Often the plastic snap top will not sufficiently seal

the can. Using a piece of a large balloon and a tight rubber band to seal the can is a good alternative.

3. Place a small amount of glue in the center of the lid and attach a straw, as shown in the diagram. Place another drop of glue on the other end of the straw and attach the pin.

4. Mark an index card with lines that are the same distance apart. Tape the card on the wall as shown in the diagram.

Hypothesizing   *What might happen to the plastic snap top or balloon if the air pressure on it increases?*

Hypothesizing   *What might happen to the plastic snap top or balloon if the air pressure decreases?*

Coffee can with plastic snap top or large balloon and rubber band

Straw

Pin

Wednesday
Tuesday
Monday
Thursday
Friday

Daily average

What Must I Know?   When air pressure increases, it pushes down on the plastic lid or balloon, causing the straw to give a high reading. When the air pressure is low, the opposite will happen. A falling barometer may indicate that a storm is approaching.

5. Record the readings of the barometer three times a day for a week.

Comparing   *How do the readings of the barometer differ during the day?*

Comparing   *How do the readings differ from day to day?*

Inferring   *What might cause the readings to vary?*

6. Record the type of weather that exists at the time of each barometer reading.

Inferring   *What kind of air pressure generally existed during your fair-weather readings?*

Inferring   *What kind of air pressure generally existed during your stormy-weather readings?*

7. Compare the readings of barometers in different locations.

Inferring   *What reasons can you give for your barometer readings?*

How Will Students Use or Apply What They Discover?

1. By using the readings of your barometer, predict what the weather will be.

2. *Does air travel from an area of high pressure to an area of lower pressure, or from an area of lower pressure to an area of higher pressure? Why?*

3. *What could you do to improve your barometer?*
4. *What other materials could you use to make a barometer?*

Part II   How Can We Make Another Barometer? (3–8)

What Will We Need?

Empty 2-liter soda bottle	Food coloring
Glass measuring cup	Marking pen
Water	Transparent sticky tape

What Do Students Know?

How can we make another barometer?
Which barometer do you think will show air pressure changes better?

What Will Students Do?

1. On a *stormy or rainy day,* invert an empty 2-liter soda bottle into a glass measuring cup that has just enough colored water to go into the neck of the bottle (see diagram).
2. While holding the glass measuring cup, push down carefully on the bottle until it is very snug inside the cup.
3. While holding the cup and pushing the bottle down firmly, have your partner seal the bottle where it sits in the cup with transparent sticky tape.

2-liter soda bottle

Water level

Sealed with tape

Glass measuring cup

4. Mark a line on the measuring cup to show where the water level is inside the bottle.
5. Check the water level each day, especially on sunny days.

Hypothesizing *Why do you think a glass, not plastic, cup was used?*
Observing *When is the water level the highest? Lowest? Why?*
Inferring *How does this barometer compare to the one made in Part I?*

What Must I Know?

The amount of air *inside* the bottle remains constant (at the atmospheric pressure on the rainy day when you sealed the bottle). The air pressure outside the bottle varies and pushes on the plastic bottle. On drier days, air pressure increases, forcing the water to rise.

How Can You Measure Humidity Changes?/What Is a Hygrometer? (3–8)

What Concepts Might Students Discover?

Air contains moisture.
Pressure and temperature affect the amount of moisture air can hold at any given time.
Relative humidity is the amount of water vapor actually contained in the atmosphere divided by the amount that could be contained in the same atmosphere.
Relative humidity can be measured.

What Will We Need?

2 thermometers   Wide cotton shoelace
Small bottle or dish of water   Empty milk carton
Thread   Piece of cardboard

What Do Students Know?

What instrument is used to measure the amount of water, or humidity, in the atmosphere?
How can this instrument be made, and how does it work?

PROCESSES

What Will Students Do?

1. Obtain an empty milk carton, two identical thermometers, a cotton shoelace, and some thread.
2. Cut a 4-inch section from the cotton shoelace and slip the section over the bulb of one of the thermometers. Tie the shoelace section with thread above and below the bulb to hold the shoelace in place. Thread the other end of the 4-inch section through a hole in the milk carton and allow it to rest in a small bottle or dish of water inside the milk carton.

Shoelace

Inside water level

Wet bulb   Dry bulb

3. Attach both thermometers to the milk carton as shown in the diagram. You now have a **hygrometer**—an instrument that measures the relative humidity in the atmosphere. *Caution:* The two thermometers should register the same temperature before the shoelace is placed over one of them; otherwise, the difference in readings must be considered a constant that is part of all computations.

4. When the shoelace is wet, fan it with a piece of cardboard for 1 minute.

Hypothesizing   *What do you think might happen to the thermometer with the wet shoelace? Why do you think so?*

Observing   5. Check the temperature readings of the two thermometers.

Hypothesizing   *How do you account for the difference in readings between the thermometer with the shoelace (called the "wet bulb") and the one without the shoelace (called the "dry bulb")?*

FINDING RELATIVE HUMIDITY IN PERCENT

Difference in Degrees between Wet-Bulb and Dry-Bulb Thermometers

	1	2	3	4	5	6	7	8	9	10	11	12	13	14	15	16	17	18	19	20	21	22	23	24	25	26	27	28	29	30
30°	89	78	68	57	47	37	27	17	8																					
32°	90	79	69	60	50	41	31	22	13	4																				
34°	90	81	72	62	53	44	35	27	18	9	1																			
36°	91	82	73	65	56	48	39	31	23	14	6																			
38°	91	83	75	67	59	51	43	35	27	19	12	4																		
40°	92	84	76	68	61	53	46	38	31	23	16	9	2																	
42°	92	85	77	70	62	55	48	41	34	28	21	14	7																	
44°	93	85	78	71	64	57	51	44	37	31	24	18	12	5																
46°	93	86	79	72	65	59	53	46	40	34	28	22	16	10	4															
48°	93	87	80	73	67	60	54	48	42	36	31	25	19	14	8	3														
50°	93	87	81	74	68	62	56	50	44	39	33	28	22	17	12	7	2													
52°	94	88	81	75	69	63	58	52	46	41	36	30	25	20	15	10	6													
54°	94	88	82	76	70	65	59	54	48	43	38	33	28	23	18	14	9	5												
56°	94	88	82	77	71	66	61	55	50	45	40	35	31	26	21	17	12	8	4											
58°	94	89	83	77	72	67	62	57	52	47	42	38	33	28	24	20	15	11	7	3										
60°	94	89	84	78	73	68	63	58	53	49	44	40	35	31	27	22	18	14	10	6	2									
62°	94	89	84	79	74	69	64	60	55	50	46	41	37	33	29	25	21	17	13	9	6	2								
64°	95	90	85	79	75	70	66	61	56	52	48	43	39	35	31	27	23	20	16	12	9	5	2							
66°	95	90	85	80	76	71	66	62	58	53	49	45	41	37	33	29	26	22	18	15	11	8	5	1						
68°	95	90	85	81	76	72	67	63	59	55	51	47	43	39	35	31	28	24	21	17	14	11	8	4	1					
70°	95	90	86	81	77	72	68	64	60	56	52	48	44	40	37	33	30	26	23	20	17	13	10	7	4	1				
72°	95	91	86	82	78	73	69	65	61	57	53	49	46	42	39	35	32	28	25	22	19	16	13	10	7	4	1			
74°	95	91	86	82	78	74	70	66	62	58	54	51	47	44	40	37	34	30	27	24	21	18	15	12	9	7	4	1		
76°	96	91	87	83	78	74	70	67	63	59	55	52	48	45	42	38	35	32	29	26	23	20	17	14	12	9	6	4	1	
78°	96	91	87	83	79	75	71	67	64	60	57	53	50	46	43	40	37	34	31	28	25	22	19	16	14	11	9	6	4	1
80°	96	91	87	83	79	76	72	68	64	61	57	54	51	47	44	41	38	35	32	29	27	24	21	18	16	13	11	8	6	4
82°	96	91	87	83	79	76	72	69	65	62	58	55	52	49	46	43	40	37	34	31	28	25	23	20	18	15	13	10	8	6
84°	96	92	88	84	80	77	73	70	66	63	59	56	53	50	47	44	41	38	35	32	30	27	25	22	20	17	15	12	10	8
86°	96	92	88	84	80	77	73	70	66	63	60	57	54	51	48	45	42	39	37	34	31	29	26	24	21	19	17	14	12	10
88°	96	92	88	85	81	78	74	71	67	64	61	58	55	52	49	46	43	41	38	35	33	30	28	25	23	21	18	16	14	12
90°	96	92	88	85	81	78	74	71	68	64	61	58	56	53	50	47	44	42	39	37	34	32	29	27	24	22	20	18	16	14

Air Temperature (Reading of Dry-Bulb Thermometer) in Degrees Fahrenheit

Example:
Temperature of dry-bulb thermometer 76°
Temperature of wet-bulb thermometer 68°
The difference is 8°

Find 76° in the dry-bulb column and 8° in the difference column. Where these two columns meet, you read the relative humidity. In this case, it is 67 percent.

What Must I Know?

When the shoelace is wet, the evaporation of the water results in a cooling of the wet-bulb thermometer, whereas the dry-bulb thermometer will continue to read the temperature of the air around it. *Note:* This is the same phenomenon that occurred in a previous activity in Section 2, where students wore one dry wool or cotton sock and one wet wool or cotton sock to show the cooling effect of evaporation.

6. Look at the relative humidity table provided. To locate the relative humidity on the table, find temperature of the dry-bulb thermometer on the y-axis (vertical axis) and the difference between the readings of the two thermometers on the x-axis (horizontal axis). The example below the table shows a dry-bulb temperature of 76° F, a difference of 8° F (wet-bulb, 68° F), and a relative humidity of 67 percent.

7. Take readings on your hygrometer every day for 2 weeks and record your findings. Also try readings in different places.

Inferring

What reasons can you give for different readings?

How Will Students Use or Apply What They Discover?

1. *Using your hygrometer, can you predict which days are better for drying clothes outside?*
2. *What other instruments can you find that will indicate or measure relative humidity?*
3. *How is relative humidity used by weather forecasters to predict weather?*
4. *Why were you asked to fan the wet-bulb thermometer?*
5. *How does relative humidity explain why you feel more uncomfortable on a humid 90-degree day than on a dry 90-degree day?*
6. *Why might you feel more comfortable in winter in a room that is 70 degrees with 65 percent relative humidity, than in a room that is 70 degrees but with only 30 percent relative humidity?*

References—Meteorology (Weather)
Teacher or older students: Jack Williams, *The Weather Book: An Easy-to-Understand Guide to USA's Weather* (Arlington, VA: National Science Teachers Association, 1992); *Project Earth Science: Meteorology* (Arlington, VA: National Science Teachers Association, 1994); H. Michael Mogil and Barbara G. Levine, *The Amateur Meteorologist: Explorations and Investigations* (Arlington, VA: National Science Teachers Association, 1993).
Students: Seymour Simon, *Winter Across America* (New York: Hyperion, 1994); Nathaniel Tripp, *Thunderstorm!* (New York: Dial Books for Young Readers, 1994); Bruce Hiscock, *The Big Storm* (New York: Atheneum, 1993).

GEOLOGY (EARTH'S CHANGING SURFACE)

How Are Rocks Broken Up? (K–2)

Materials

2 plastic vials or medicine bottles with snap lids, dry bean seeds, water

What Do Students Know?

How can seeds break up rocks and soil?
How can we set up an experiment to test if seeds can break up rocks and soil?

**Some Possible
Activities**

Fill both vials or medicine bottles with as many dry beans as will fit. Add as much water as you can to one vial of beans. Snap the lids on both vials.

A Water   **B** No water

Ask students what they think might happen to the two vials. Observe both vials the next day. In the one with the water, the beans will have expanded and lifted the lid off. In the vial without water (called the control), there will be no observable change. Help students infer that swelling and growing plants change the land by breaking up rocks and soil just as the swelling beans lifted the vial's lid off. Ask students to find places on your playground or on concrete walks where plants grow through and crack rocks like this:

QUICKIE STARTERS: OPEN-ENDED ACTIVITIES (K–5)

How Can You Build Stalactites and Stalagmites?

Materials

Paper towel, Epsom salts, water, spoon, 30 cm (1 ft) of thick string, large tin can, 2 small jars or clear plastic cups, 2 heavy washers

**What Do Students
Know?**

*How are some rocks formed in caves?
What is a stalactite, and how is it formed?*

What is a stalagmite, and how is it formed?
Where else are stalactites and stalagmites formed?

Some Possible Activities

Fill the large tin can about three-quarters full of water. Add Epsom salts, one spoonful at a time, stirring vigorously after each addition, until no more Epsom salts will dissolve. (*Note:* Epsom salt crystals will fall to the bottom of the can when no more will dissolve.) Fill the two small jars or plastic cups with the Epsom salt solution and place the containers 5 centimeters (2 inches) apart on the paper towel. Tie a heavy washer to each end of the string. Place one washer in each of the small jars or paper cups. *Note:* Arrange the string in the cups so that you have at least 5 centimeters (2 inches) between the string and the paper towel.

After several days, mineral deposits will form on the paper towel and string as shown.

Note: Help students learn the difference between stalactites and stalagmites. Point out that the deposits that hang down are called **stalactites** (*C* for ceiling), while those that point up are called **stalagmites** (*G* for ground).

GUIDED DISCOVERY HANDS-ON/MINDS-ON ACTIVITIES

How Are Rocks Alike and Different, and How Do We Use Rocks? (K–5)

What Concepts Might Students Discover?

Rocks exhibit eight major properties or characteristics that are used to identify and classify them: hardness, texture, color, streak, cleavage, density, chemical, and luster. Simple tests can help us identify and classify rocks by their properties. Rocks are used in many forms in our everyday lives.

What Will We Need?

Large steel nail	Penny
Glass baby food jar	Newspaper
Hammer	Cloth sack
Magnifying glass	Rock samples
Safety goggles	

What Do Students Know?

Where could you find different kinds of rocks on our school grounds, at home, or on the way to school?

How are rocks the same and different?
When you feel rocks, how might they differ?
How might we test rocks to see if they are hard or soft, heavy or light, dark or light, and so on?

What Must I Know?

This activity should be done in groups of two to four students. *Cautions:* (1) In hardness tests, the use of a knife is recommended, but a steel nail is substituted here for safety reasons. (2) *Always* put rocks in a cloth sack and use safety goggles when hammering rocks.

You and designated students should assemble the following items in a cloth sack before the activity begins: a large steel nail, a penny, a glass baby food jar, a newspaper, a hammer, a magnifying glass, and six samples of different rocks.

PROCESSES

What Will Students Do?

G

Observing
Comparing
Comparing
Comparing

Comparing
Inferring
Inferring
Classifying
Communicating

Designing an Investigation

1. Open your cloth sack and place your materials on the newspaper.
2. Observe the rocks closely.
   In what ways are the rocks alike?
   In what ways do the rocks look different?
   When you feel the rocks, how do they differ?
   Compare two rocks of the same size.
   How does their weight compare? Is one heavier than the other?
   Why do you think some rocks are rough and jagged?
   What do you think has happened to the rocks that are smooth and rounded?
3. Place your rocks in groups (classifying them by properties).
   How did you group your rocks? In what other ways might you group your rocks?
   How do you think you could tell the hardness or softness of a rock?
   (Scratch with steel nail, penny, fingernail, and so on.)

What Must I Know?

The Mohs hardness scale ranks rocks from 1 to 10, with talc being softest at 1 and diamond hardest at 10. Here are some common materials that students can test and approximate their hardness.[4]

---

[4]For an expanded Scale of Hardness chart with excellent color samples of each type of rock, see *Science Interactions—Course 2* (Westerville, OH: Glencoe Division of Macmillan-McGraw-Hill Publishing Co., 1995), 310–311.

Hardness Number	Common Materials	How to Test Hardness
1	Soft lead pencil	Greasy flakes on fingers
2	Chalk	Scratched by fingernail
3	Marble	Scratched by copper penny
4	Yellow brass	Scratched by nail
5	Glass bottle	Scratched by nail
6	Window glass	Scratched by file
7	Sandpaper	Scratches glass easily

Note: Materials above 8 are extremely hard and are not easy to test.

4. Try some of your ideas for testing other properties of rocks.

Hypothesizing — *If two rocks were the same size, how could you find out which rock was heavier (denser)?*

Designing an Investigation — *How could you tell whether a rock looked the same on the inside as it did on the outside?* (Place a rock in a cloth sack and cover the sack with newspaper. Wear safety goggles and hit the rock with a hammer.)

Designing an Investigation — *How would you find out how rocks become smooth and rounded?* (Place rocks in a plastic jar of water and shake the jar vigorously.)

Inferring — *Why are some rocks made of many smaller rocks or pieces?*

Observing — *Are the pieces of the rock rounded or jagged?*

Observing — *Are the pieces dull or shiny in the rock?*

Hypothesizing — *Why do you think they are like that?*

What Must I Know? The following is a simple test to find density.

1. Weigh the rock in air and record its weight.
2. Immerse the rock in water, weigh the rock, and record its weight.

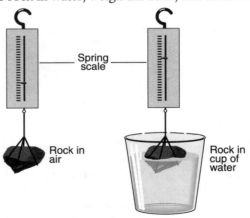

3. Subtract the difference in the weights.
4. Divide the "air weight" by the difference to get the specific gravity of the rock.

Note: Another way to show students that two objects with the same volume can be different weights due to their specific gravities involves the following activity.

1. Put a can of diet cola in a bowl of water and a same-size can of regular cola in another bowl of water.
2. The can of diet cola will float (because it is lighter in weight for its volume), while the regular cola will sink (because the sugar in it makes it heavier for the same volume).

Diet cola floats   Regular cola sinks

What Must I Know?

Densities *under* 1.00 will *float* because water density is 1.00 (examples: cork = 0.24, fish = 1.00). Densities *over* 1.00 will sink (example: clay = 1.63).

How Will Students Use or Apply What They Discover?

1. *In what ways are soft rocks used?*
2. *In what ways are hard rocks used?*
3. Survey your school, home, and community and make a chart of where rocks or rock materials are used daily. Use the following chart as an example.[5]

Everyday Object	Product Made From Rock	Rock or Mineral
Window	Glass	Sand
Wire or old penny	Copper	Copper ore
Fishing weights	Lead	Galena
Toothpaste	Fluoride	Fluoride crystal
Pretzel	Table salt	Salt crystal
Tooth filling	Gold	Gold nugget
Food can or foil	Aluminum	Bauxite ore

4. *What is concrete, how is it made, and how is it used?*

What Is a Fault, and How Does It Change the Earth's Surface? (K–5)

What Concepts Might Students Discover?

Some land has been formed by sedimentation, causing layering.
When too much force is applied to the earth's layers, they crack.

[5]For an expanded chart, see Richard David Barnes, *Popcorn Rock—An Experiment in Crystal Science* (Bountiful, UT: PR NEWS, 1989), 15.

The line where the earth's crust cracks and moves is called a fault.
A normal fault is where the earth's crust drops.
A thrust fault is where the earth's crust rises over an adjacent part of the earth.
Earthquakes may be caused by the earth's crust sliding along a fault.

What Will We Need?

1 quart jar
Sand
Humus or peat moss
Several types of soil—loamy, sandy, and clay
2 cigar-box molds filled with layers of colored plaster of paris
2 clear plastic cups
Soda straw
Straight pin
Staples
Tape
Paper clips
Water
2 × 4 × 6-inch piece of wood cut in half along a sloping line
1 *layered* cupcake per student (see instructions in Part IV)
Small paper plates
Clear plastic straws cut slightly larger than cupcake's height (5 per student)
Plastic knives
Drawing paper
Colored pencils or markers

What Do Students Know?

If great force is applied to a rock or parts of the earth's structure, what will happen to the rock or the structure?
What is an earthquake?
What causes an earthquake?

What Must I Know?

This activity should be done in groups of two to four students. The molds should be made ahead of time, by you and/or designated students, by mixing two or three *separate* pints of plaster of paris with different colors of food coloring. The wet plaster of paris should be layered in the cigar boxes and allowed to partially dry before cutting it as indicated in the following steps. *Caution:* Do not let the plaster of paris become too dry or it will be too hard to cut.

PROCESSES

What Will Students Do?

I **G**

Observing
Hypothesizing

Part I   How Does the Earth's Surface Form Layers? (K–2)

1. Obtain a quart jar, some sand, humus or peat moss, and several types of soil. Half fill the quart jar with water. Add sand to the jar until the sand is 1 inch thick in the bottom of the jar.
   What happens to the sand?
   What will happen if you pour soil and humus or peat moss onto part of the sand?
2. Try it. Add several other types of soil and humus or peat moss to the jar and observe.

Comparing   *How do the materials in the jar resemble parts of our earth?*

Inferring   Explain how you think parts of our earth have become layered.

Hypothesizing   *What do you think might happen if you shake the jar of water, sand, humus, and soils?*

Hypothesizing   *What might happen if you let the jar stand for several days?*

Observing and Recording   Try it and record what you see in a few days.

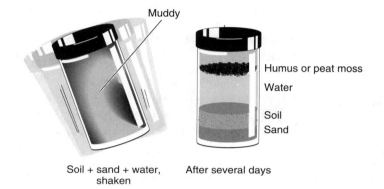

Soil + sand + water,
shaken

After several days

Part II How Is a Fault Caused by Water Evaporating? (K–5)

What Will Students Do?   1. Set up a simple balance as shown in the diagram. Fill one cup with water.

Hypothesizing   *In what ways can you balance the sand and water?*

Add enough sand to balance the water cup.

G

2. Use one of your methods to balance the sand and water.

Hypothesizing   *Now that these are balanced, what might happen if you take some sand from one side of the balance and place it on the other side?*

Observing   3. Do this and observe.

Inferring   *How is what you did with the balance similar to some of the things that happen in the earth's crust?* (Materials shift on the surface of the earth.)

What Must I Know?   The land surface of the continents is always being worn away. The particles formed from this wearing away (**erosion**) often flow into streams and are carried to the sea. When the material gets to the ocean floor, it causes that part of the floor to become heavier and may cause the crust of the earth and the layers to bend. If they bend far enough, faults may appear. This is an explanation for one type of fault, although it is a rare type.

4. Rebalance the sand and water and let it stand undisturbed for several days.

Inferring   *Why does the sand side go down?*

Part III   How Do Normal and Thrust Faults Change the Earth's Surface? (3–5)

What Will Students Do?   1. Obtain a cigar box mold from your teacher and remove the plaster

block. Your teacher has cut the block in two. Raise one of these blocks above the other as indicated in the diagram.
A **fault** is a place where the earth's crust and layers have broken similar to the layers in your model.

Comparing   *How is the appearance of the block similar to the appearance of the earth in some places you have seen?*

Summarizing   Explain how you think a rock structure could reach a condition similar to the one you have arranged in your model.

What Must I Know?   The rock structure could have formed a fault owing to stresses within the earth that drew the sections of rock apart. This stress could have caused one section to fall. This kind of fault is called a **normal fault** and is represented in the diagram.

Normal fault

2. Obtain a 2 × 4 × 6-inch piece of wood that has been cut in two along a sloping line.

Comparing   *How is this model fault different from the normal fault? What would you call this type of fault?*

What Must I Know?   Explain that this type of fault is called a thrust fault. The **thrust fault** occurs when compression pushes sections of rock closer together, forcing one section of rock to move or slide up, as shown in the diagram.

Thrust fault

Inferring   *How could this structure have been formed in nature?*
Summarizing   *How would you define a thrust fault and explain how it works?*

What Must I Know?   Other faults, such as the one that caused the San Francisco earthquake of 1989, may be caused mainly by horizontal movement of the earth. The San Andreas fault in California is of this type.

Hypothesizing   *What connection is there between an earthquake and a fault?*

Part IV   How Can We See Layers in Earth? (K–5)

What Must I Know?   **Geologists** study the earth and use many devices to discover what is under the surface.

Core sampling is done by putting hollow drilling tubes into the ground and extracting a sample of what the tubes went through.

What Must I Know?   Layered cupcakes may be made by teacher or parent volunteer as follows:

1. Use either different flavors and/or white batter mixed with food coloring.
2. Put batter in four layers in foil or paper cups.
3. Bake and frost cupcakes.

What Do Students Know?   *What do you think is inside the cupcake?*
How do scientists learn what's underground?

What Will Students Do?

1. Obtain one cupcake on a paper plate, five cut clear straws, plastic knife, drawing paper, and markers.
2. Do *not* remove foil or paper cup from cupcake.

Hypothesizing   3. Draw what you think is inside the cupcake.

What Must I Know?   Point out that the cupcake represents the earth and explain how geologists use core sampling. Explain how to take side "core samples" (see next step).

Core samples of
cupcake

(a)   (b)   (c)

4. Take two side "core samples" of your cupcake:
   a. Carefully insert a straw into the side of the cupcake (diagram a), rotate slightly, remove, and place sample on paper plate.
   b. Repeat with another straw.

Inferring

Can you determine what the entire cupcake looks like with these two core samples?
If not, what must you do?

5. Take three samples by inserting the straw straight *down* into the cupcake, as in diagram (b).
6. Compare these samples with those taken from the side (c).

Comparing

How are they different?

7. Make a drawing of what you now think the inside of the cupcake looks like.
8. Use your knife to cut down and separate the cupcake into halves.
   How does this compare to your drawings?

What Must I Know?

For more information on this type of activity, see the Cupcake Geology activity in the Mesa Public Schools Curriculum Unit "Earthquakes" by JoAnne Vasquez Wolf.

How Are Crystals Formed? (3–5)

What Concepts Might Students Discover?

Crystals are nonliving substances that form into rocklike bodies of various shapes.

Crystals grow in size when more layers of the same substance are added on; the same basic crystal shape, however, remains the same.

Crystal size is determined by differences in the rate of crystallization.

If crystals are disturbed in the forming process, they will break apart into hundreds of microscopic pieces.

True solids are crystalline in form.

Crystalline form is important in determining some of the properties of substances.

What Will We Need?

Tablespoon	Pyrex beaker or heatproof baby bottle
Salt	Alum
3 jar lids	Insulated cooking mitt
2 small glasses	Washer
Water	Pencil
2 pieces of string	Popcorn Rock™6
Magnifying glass or hand lens	Clear glass bowl
Sugar	White distilled vinegar
Hot plate	Food coloring

[6]Inexpensive materials and directions for growing "Popcorn Rock" can be obtained from your local Popcorn Rock dealer or from R. D. Barnes, 389 West 100 South, Bountiful, UT 84010, (801)295-5762.

What Do Students Know?

What are crystals?
How could you "grow" a crystal?
What happens when a crystal is "growing"?
Why is a study of crystals important?

What Must I Know?

These activities can be done by individual students or by groups of two to four people.

PROCESSES

Part I   Growing Salt Crystals by Evaporation (3–5)

What Will Students Do?

Observing

1. Obtain a tablespoon of salt, a jar lid, and a small glass of water. Mix the salt into the glass of water. Stir the water well. Let the solution stand for a few minutes until it becomes clear.
   What happens to the salt?

2. Very gently pour some of the salt solution into the jar lid. Put a piece of string in the solution, letting one end hang out, as in diagram (a). Let the solution stand for several days where the lid will not be disturbed.

Hypothesizing

   What do you think might happen to the salt solution?

3. After several days have passed, use your magnifying glass to look at the materials in the lid and lift the string out of the jar lid.

Communicating

4. Describe what you see with the hand lens (b).

Salt solution   Salt crystals

Salt crystals

(a)   (b)

Comparing

How are the materials in the lid different from your original salt solution?

Inferring

Why do you now have a solid when you started out with a liquid?

Hypothesizing

What name could you give to the formations in the lid?

What Must I Know

The salt dissolved in the water. When the salt water stood for several days, the water evaporated, leaving behind salt crystals. Crystals are nonliving substances that are found in various geometrical shapes.

Part II   Growing Sugar Crystals by Evaporation (3–5)

What Will Students Do?

1. Obtain a tablespoon of sugar, a jar lid, and a small glass of water. Be sure the tablespoon is clean. Mix a tablespoon of sugar into the glass of water. Stir the water well. Let the solution stand for a few minutes until it becomes clear.

Observing   *What happens to the sugar?*
Comparing   *How is the sugar solution similar in appearance to the salt solution?*

2. Very gently pour some of the sugar solution into the lid and let the solution stand undisturbed for several days.

Hypothesizing   *What do you think might happen to the sugar solution?*
Observing

3. After several days have passed, use your magnifying glass to look at the materials in your lid.

Sugar crystals

Communicating   4. Describe what you see.
Comparing   *How are the materials in this lid different from the salt crystals? How are they alike?*
Inferring   *What happened to the sugar solution?*

What Must I Know?

When the sugar water stood for several days, the water evaporated, leaving behind sugar crystals.

Part III   How Does the Rate of Evaporation Affect Crystal Size Formation? (3–5)

What Do Students Know?

Where are crystals found in nature?
How do crystals form?

What Must I Know?

The teacher or a very responsible student should set up materials for younger or less mature students.

What Will Students and Teacher Do?

1. Heat 200 mL of water in a Pyrex beaker or baby bottle. Add 3 tablespoons of alum. Heat and stir the mixture until the alum fully dissolves, as in diagram (a).

T I G

2. Using an insulated cooking mitt, remove the bottle and put it on a solid surface where it cannot be moved or struck.
3. Carefully pour a small amount of the alum solution into a clean jar lid (b). Place the lid in a secure, dry place *away from* radiators or direct sunshine.
4. Tie a sanded washer to one end of a piece of string. Wind and tie the other end to a pencil so that when the pencil is suspended across the bottle top, the washer hangs down about ½ inch from the bottom of the bottle (c). Place bottle in the secure, dry place next to the jar.

(a)   (b)   (c)

Observing   5. Observe the bottle and lid every day, but do not shake or move the containers.

Recording   6. Record your observations and use your data to answer these questions:
Where did the first crystals form: bottom of bottle, sides of bottle, or string?

Comparing   *How does the size of crystals in the bottle compare to that in the jar lid?*
Classifying   *Why is crystalline form important in determining the properties of a substance?*

Hypothesizing   *Why do some rocks have large crystals and some have small crystals?*

What Must I Know?   True solids are crystalline in form. Crystalline form is important in determining some of the properties of substances. Differences in the rate of crystallization determine differences in crystal size. Crystals in the jar lid are smaller than those in the bottle due to the differences in cooling times. Slower cooling (bottle) produces larger crystals, whereas faster cooling (lid) produces smaller crystals.

How Will Students Use or Apply What They Discover?

1. *How are crystals used in industry?*
2. *If there were no crystals on earth, how would people's way of living be affected?*
3. *How might you "grow" very large crystals?*

Part IV   How Can You Make "Popcorn Rock" Stalagmites? (3–5)

What Must I Know?

Popcorn Rock is the trade name for a naturally occurring mineral found in the western United States. It is called Popcorn Rock because popcornlike aragonite crystals (calcium carbonate) can form on the rock, in the same way that limestone formations are occurring in Carlsbad Caverns National Park, New Mexico.[7]

It is recommended that the Popcorn Rock experiment begin on Thursday, as early in the morning as possible. Then allow seven days for the Popcorn Rock crystals to form, be observed, and discussed.

What Will Students Do?

Day 1 (Thursday).   Place the Popcorn Rock in a clear glass bowl and add just enough white distilled vinegar to cover the rock completely. Place the bowl in a place where it will not be disturbed.

Popcorn Rock   +   Vinegar   +   Time   =   Popcorn crystals

Hypothesizing   *What might happen to the rock in the vinegar?*
Observing and Recording   Observe your rock three times a day and record any changes you see.
Observing   *Day 2 (Friday).   What do you see forming on the highest ridges of the rock late in the afternoon?*
Let the Popcorn Rock remain undisturbed over the weekend.
Observing   *Day 5 (Monday).   What do you see about ¼ inch above the evaporating white vinegar?*
Comparing   *What do the crystals look like?*
Inferring   *What do you think those crystals are?*
Hypothesizing   *Day 6 (Tuesday).   Do you think the Popcorn Rock "grows" from the bottom (like hair) or does it "grow" from the tips of the crystals (like tree branches)?*

What Must I Know?

Bleached-blonde hair has new, dark-colored hair below the older, light-colored hair. Names carved in tree bark remain at the same level, even as the tree grows taller.

Devising an Experiment   *How might we devise experiments to resolve this?*

---

[7]The author is indebted to the following publication for excellent lessons using Popcorn Rock. The publication is available from its author: Richard David Barnes, *Popcorn Rock—An Experiment in Crystal Science* (Bountiful, UT: PR NEWS, 1989).

Hypothesizing   *Day 7 (Wednesday).   How might putting a very small amount of food coloring in the vinegar help us resolve whether Popcorn Rock "grows" from the bottom or from the tips of the crystals?*
Try it.

What Must I Know?   Capillary action, similar to osmosis in trees, pulls the vinegar, calcium carbonate, and food coloring up from the bottom. If the aragonite crystals are "growing" from the bottom, the food coloring will remain in the lower crystals, formed after the vinegar was added. Popcorn Rock "grows" from the bottom, making it a stalagmite. Let the Popcorn Rock crystals form until all the vinegar has evaporated. If crystals get broken, put the rock back in the vinegar and start over.

How Will Students Use or Apply What They Discover?

1. Some students may have noticed that bubbles formed in the vinegar. *What caused the bubbles, and how might we find out what the bubbles are?*
2. *What might happen if you allowed your Popcorn Rock crystals to form in a sealed plastic bag?*
3. *Why do you think vinegar was used to form the Popcorn Rock crystals? Would the same thing happen if a different liquid were used? Which liquid(s) would you suggest?*
4. *How might we test your hypotheses?*

References—Geology (Earth's Changing Surface)

Teacher and older students: All of the following are from The National Science Teachers Association, Arlington, VA: *How to Teach with Topographic Maps,* 1994; Kathryn Sheehan and Mary Waidner, *Earth Child,* rev. ed. 1994; *Earth Caretakers: Native American Lessons,* 1993; Dougal Dixon, *The Practical Geologist,* 1992.
Students: Seymour Simon, *Mountains* (New York: Morrow, 1994); Penni Rubin and Eleanora I. Robbins, *What's Under Your Feet,* 2nd ed. (Golden, CO: Colorado School of Mines, 1993).

ECOLOGY AND THE ENVIRONMENT

QUICKIE STARTERS: OPEN-ENDED ACTIVITIES

How Clean Is the Air You Breathe?

Materials   For each group of two to four students: four 10-cm square pieces of waxed paper, four 12-cm square pieces of wood, petroleum jelly, 16 thumbtacks, hand lens

What do Students Know?   *How can we find out if air in some areas has more particles in it than air in other areas?*
Where do you think we might find these areas?
What might account for air in some areas having more particles in it than does air in other areas?
Where could the particles in the air have come from?
What effect could dirty air have on your health?

Some Possible Activities

With thumbtacks, attach squares of waxed paper to wood blocks and coat the waxed paper with a thin coating of petroleum jelly, as shown in the diagram.

Put the wood blocks—"Particle Collectors"—outside in places where you think the air is "dirty," such as where there is a lot of bus and car travel, near airports, next to factories, and so on. Also, put some in wooded areas, such as parks, and some indoors at home or at school. Make sure no one disturbs your collectors. Write down the place you put each collector and the date.

After 4 or 5 days, bring the collectors back to class, making sure you do not touch the sticky side of each collector. Look at the waxed paper with a hand lens.

Which collectors (places) had the most particles? Why?
Which collectors (places) had the fewest particles? Why?

Which Materials Break Down (Decompose) Easily? (K–5)

Materials

For each group of two to four students, supply a self-sealing plastic storage bag that is about 10½ × 11 inches (27 cm × 28 cm), garden soil (*not* packaged fertilized potting soil), solid wastes, water, and earthworms.[8]

What Do Students Know?

What happens to our garbage after it is picked up by the garbage collectors?
Where is it taken?
Do some things break down (decompose) better than others?
What are they made of?
Do some things resist decomposing?
What are they made of?

[8]If you cannot get earthworms from local gardens or pet shops, send for *red worms* from Flowerfield Enterprises, 10332 Shaver Road, Kalamazoo, MI 49002 (616)327-0108; B & P, Box 398, Olathe, CO 81425 (303)323-6550; or the Cape Cod Worm Farm, 30 Center Avenue, Buzzards Bay, MA 02532 (508)759-5664. Information on composting with worms can be gotten from this activities guide: *Worms Eat Our Garbage: Classroom Activities for a Better Environment,* Flower Press, 10332 Shaver Rd, Kalamazoo, MI 49002.

Some Possible Activities

Put about 5 inches (12 cm) of garden soil in the bottom of the plastic bag. (Do *not* use packaged, sterilized soil, since you want bacteria and insects if possible.) Add ½ inch (1 cm) of thin pieces of solid wastes from the garbage or from the environment, such as leafy vegetables, fruits, aluminum foil, rubber bands, wooden toothpicks, different kinds of cloth and paper, styrofoam, and other plastic items. *Caution:* Do not put meat scraps or fats into your bag. Slightly moisten the soil, add three or four earthworms, seal the bag securely, and leave it at room temperature or near a radiator or heat source. Gently shake the bag daily.

Observe and record what you see each week for 4 to 6 weeks, then go back and answer the questions in the preceding section.

GUIDED DISCOVERY HANDS-ON/MINDS-ON ACTIVITIES

How Does the Environment Affect Living Things? (3–5)

What Concepts Might Students Discover?

All living things have certain requirements that must be met by their environments.

A **habitat** is a place where an animal or plant naturally lives or grows.

An **environment** includes all the conditions (i.e., food, water, air, temperature, etc.) which an organism (plant or animal) needs to live.

Certain environmental factors determine community types. Different environments are needed to sustain different types of life.

A **community** is a collection of living organisms that have mutual relationships among themselves and with their environment. Some types of communities are on land and some are in water.

Land communities can be subdivided into forests, bogs, swamps, deserts, and others.

Regions with similar geography, climate, vegetation, and animal life are called **biomes.**

Ecology is a branch of science that investigates the interrelationships of organisms and their environments and looks at how all living things are connected to each other and to their environments.

Natural phenomena can change an environment, but humans are some of the most powerful change agents.

What Will We Need?

3 large, wide-mouthed, commercial-sized mayonnaise jars with lids in good condition (try fast-food restaurants)

4 cups of washed beach sand

5 small aquatic plants (approximately 3 to 4 in. or 10 cm in height)

Freshwater fantailed guppy

2 water snails

5-in or 12-cm square of fine-mesh screening material

Nail

Hammer

Soda bottle cap

1 small cactus plant (approximately 3 or 4 in. or 10 cm in height)

2 small dried twigs (no longer than ¾ of the length of the mayonnaise jars)

Chameleon, lizard, skink, horned toad, or colored lizard

4 pencils

Tape

Live mealworms

Cup of coarse-grained gravel

Several small ferns, mosses, lichens, or liverworts

Small water turtle or frog

Live insects or turtle food

What Do Students Know?

What does environment mean to you?
What are some things that live around you?
What are some environments that you know about?
What is ecology, and why is it important for us to know about it?
What is an aquarium?
What is a terrarium?

What Must I Know?

All environments contain geological features, weather, climate, and living things (plants and animals), and all interrelate and affect each other. This is what the study of ecology is all about.

Students should learn how to set up and closely observe an aquarium—a water home for plants and animals—and different kinds of terrariums—land homes for plants and animals.

The following activities help students set up and observe closely three habitats for an extended period of time and allow them to study the ecology of each environment.

PROCESSES

Part I What Are the Parts of a Water Habitat (Aquarium), and How Do They Interrelate? (3–5)

What Will Students Do?

This activity is to be done in groups of four students. Each group might be responsible for only one habitat.

1. Obtain the materials listed. *Note:* The materials listed are for all three parts of this activity.
2. Clean one mayonnaise jar thoroughly with soap and water and rinse it well.

3. Wash 2 cups of sand to be placed in the jar. Spread this over the bottom of the jar.
4. Fill the jar with water and let it stand for several days before adding plants and fish.
5. Place the five aquatic plants as suggested by the pet shop owner.
6. Place the guppy and two snails in the jar.
7. Now cover the jar with the screening material.

Food jar aquarium   Soda bottle aquarium

What Must I Know?   A simpler soda bottle aquarium[9] can be made as an alternative. This type of aquarium is also pictured in the diagram.

Inferring   *Why do you think it is necessary to clean the jar before using it?*
Inferring   *Why should the sand be washed before putting it in the jar?*
Inferring   *What would dirty water do to the gills of the fish?*
Inferring   *Why must the gills of the fish be kept clean?*
Inferring   *How do fish breathe?*
Hypothesizing   *How could you find out?*
Inferring   *Why do you think the water was allowed to stand for several days before the fish were placed in the aquarium?*
Inferring   *What does our health department add to water that might be injurious to fish?*
Inferring   *Why were the snails added to the water?*

What Must I Know?   The snails will eat the small green algae (the slimy plants that collect on the sides of the tank).

[9]For free excellent directions on how to make simple aquariums and terrariums from empty soda bottles, send your request to Bottle Biology Project, University of Wisconsin—Madison, 1630 Linden Drive, Madison, WI 53706 (608)263-5645.

Hypothesizing	*Why were plants added to the aquarium?*
Inferring	*What would the fish eat in nature?*
	Would your guppy live if it did not feed on anything? Why?
Inferring	*What do plants make that the fish can use?*
Inferring	*What does the fish make that the plants can use?*

What Must I Know?

Plants make oxygen and food, and the fish produce carbon dioxide and waste products. The aquarium is not perfectly balanced, so food must be added from time to time for the fish.

Part II   What Are the Parts of a Dryland Habitat (Desert Terrarium), and How Do They Interrelate? (3–5)

What Will Students Do?

G

1. Obtain one of the large, commercial-sized mayonnaise jars.
2. Clean the mayonnaise jar and lid with soap and water and rinse them well.
3. Dry off the jar and screw the lid on.
4. With the jar on the floor, make holes in the lid by hammering the point of a nail through the lid.
5. Place the jar on its side and tape two pencils to the sides of the terrarium, as shown in the diagram, to keep the jar from rolling.
6. Spread the remaining 2 cups of sand onto the bottom of the jar.
7. Place the small bottle cap filled with water, the cactus, and one twig into the jar.
8. Place a lizard, skink, chameleon, or horned toad in the jar.
9. Cover the jar with the punctured lid.
10. Water the terrarium once every 2 to 3 weeks only if dry. Place the jar so that it receives direct sun every day. A simple terrarium can also be made from an empty soda bottle, as shown in the diagram.

Food jar terrarium   Soda bottle desert terrarium

11. Feed the animals live mealworms (see Appendix E for feeding requirements). These can be obtained from a local pet shop.
12. Keep the bottle cap filled with water.

Hypothesizing   *Why do dryland animals have such leathery skin?*
Hypothesizing   *Why must the terrarium be placed in direct sunlight?*
Inferring   *Why do you think ferns or mosses would not survive in this habitat?*
Hypothesizing   *Would frogs or turtles be able to live in this habitat? Why or why not?*

Part III   What Are the Parts of a Wetland (Bog) Terrarium, and How Do They Interrelate? (3–5)

What Will Students Do?

1. Clean one of the mayonnaise jars and its lid with soap and water and rinse them well.
2. Dry off the jar and screw the lid on.
3. With the jar on the floor, make holes in the lid by hammering the point of a nail through the lid.
4. Place the jar on its side and tape pencils or wood strips to the bottom to keep the jar from rolling.

Lid

Gravel

Tape wood strips

Bog terrarium

5. Spread the gravel out on the bottom of the jar so it will be concentrated toward the back of the jar, as shown in the diagram.
6. Place the ferns, mosses, lichens, and liverworts over the gravel.
7. Pour some water in the jar. (Do not put in so much that it covers the back portion of the arrangement.)
8. Place a dried twig in the jar.
9. Place a small water turtle or frog in the jar.
10. Cover the jar with the punctured lid.
11. Feed the turtle or frog insects or turtle food every other day (see Appendix E).
12. Place the terrarium in an area where light is weak.

Comparing and Observing   *How does the life found in the aquarium differ from that found in the desert and/or bog terrariums?*

Observing   *What kinds of conditions do the fish, turtle, frog, or lizard have to have to survive in their particular habitats?*

Observing   *What kinds of conditions do the bog plants require to grow well?*

Observing
Hypothesizing

What kinds of food do the fish, the lizards, or the turtle eat?
What do you think would happen to the turtle if you left it in the desert habitat or to the lizard if you put it in the bog habitat?

How Will Students Use or Apply What They Discover?

1. *What other kinds of environments or habitats could you make through the use of mayonnaise jars or soda bottles?*[10]
2. *What does the "environment" have to do with the kinds of organisms found in it?*
3. *What are some organisms that are able to live in many different environments?*
4. *What might happen to a fern plant if it were transplanted to a desert region?*
5. *What might happen to a penguin if it were taken to live in a desert?*
6. *What might happen to a human being if he or she were suddenly moved into an arctic region?*
7. *What statements can you make about the effect of environment on a living thing?*
8. Complete the following chart for the aquarium or terrarium habitat you constructed, describing the food, water, shelter, and other conditions you provided for the organisms living there.

NAME OF HABITAT:	
Habitat Living Conditions	Description
Food	
Shelter	
Air	
Temperature	
Climate	
Water	
Others	

How Do Animals and Humans Affect Their Water Environments? (Water Pollution) (3–8)

What Concepts Might Students Discover?

All living things need water, and a steady supply of clean water is vital. People make their water impure or unclean (polluted) by adding such human and factory wastes as human sewage, nitrates from overuse of chemical fertilizers, pesticides and herbicides, phosphates from detergents, and so on.

Because of the interrelationship of all parts of a habitat or environment, water pollution affects all living things.

[10]For more information on building simple habitats, see: *Bottle Biology,* Kendall/Hunt, 4050 Westmark Dr., Dubuque, IA 52004-1840, 1(800)228-0810.

What Will We Need?   See each individual activity for needed materials. *Note:* Some items may be used from previous activities.

Part I   What Are Some Effects of Water Pollution? (3–8)

What Must I Know?   Humans often do things, sometimes unknowingly, that result in water pollution. This water pollution can affect water environments in ways that are extremely detrimental to the organisms that inhabit the water.

You can do this activity as a teacher demonstration or group activity. For each group of four students, four jars should be set up, by you and/or by designated student helpers, 2 weeks in advance of conducting this activity.

1. Fill four containers (see "What Will We Need" that follows) one-third full with aged tap water, ½ inch (4 cm) full of pond soil or aquarium gravel, and then fill the rest of the jar with pond water and algae.
2. Add 1 teaspoon of plant fertilizer to each jar, stir well, and loosely screw on the jar covers.
3. Put the jars near the window in good, indirect light, or under a strong artificial light.
4. Label the jars, *A, B, C, D.*

What Will We Need?

4 quart-sized or 2-liter clear containers (plastic soda bottles, food jars with covers, etc.)	Measuring cup and spoon Plant fertilizer Hand lens
Tap water aged for 3 to 4 days	Liquid laundry detergent (not green)
Soil and/or gravel from an aquarium or pond	Motor oil
Water with algae and other aquatic microorganisms from a freshwater aquarium or a pond	Vinegar

PROCESSES

What Will Students and Teacher Do?

1. Each group has four jars that were set up 2 weeks ago. They contain pond water, algae, pond soil or aquarium gravel, and fertilizer.

Observing and Recording   On your recording sheet, describe how each jar looks. Make sure to use your hand lens.

RECORDING OBSERVATIONS		
Date _____ Observers'/Recorders' Names _____		
Jar	Observation Before Additive	Observation After Additive
A		
B		
C		
D		

Hypothesizing   *Why do you think pond water, pond soil, and fertilizer were put into the jars?*
Hypothesizing   *Why do you think the jars were given a lot of indirect light?*

2. Add 2 tablespoons of detergent to jar A; enough motor oil to cover the surface of jar B; and ¼ to ½ cup (250 mL) of vinegar to jar C. Jar D will not have any additive and will be the control. See the diagram.

Detergent   Motor   Vinegar   Control
                   oil

3. Loosely cover the jars and return them to the light as before.
Hypothesizing   *What do you think might happen in each of the jars?*
Observing and Recording   4. Observe and record your observations two to three times a week.
Summarizing   After 4 weeks, summarize your observations.
Inferring   *Why do you think jars A, B, and C went through such changes?*

How Will Students Use or Apply What They Discover?

1. *How might you set up activities to try to reverse the effects of the pollutants used in jars A, B, and C?*
2. *Where in everyday life do we see the effects of water pollution like that in jars A, B, and C?*
3. *How could these effects be prevented?*

Part II   How Can We Try to Reverse the Effects of an Oil Spill? (3–8)

What Will We Need?

Aluminum pan   Dishwashing liquid
Water   4 hard-boiled eggs
Motor oil   Paper plate
Feathers   Very large rubber band
Paper towels   Turkey baster

What Do Students Know?

How difficult do you think it is to clean up an oil spill?
How do you think it could be done?
What is the most effective way to clean up an oil spill?
What devastating effects does an oil spill have on the environment?

What Must I Know?

Oil spills adversely affect land and water plants and animals directly by coating them with oil, often leading to their deaths. In addition, an oil spill affects future plant and animal life by destroying eggs and interfering with plant reproduction.

Sometimes, the procedures used to reverse oil spills can interfere with environmental interrelationships, especially when chemicals are used.

What Will Students Do?   Fill an aluminum pan half full of water, cover the water surface with motor oil, and use it for the following parts of the activity.

Feathers in Oil/Water

1. Leave feathers in the oil-water mix for several minutes.
2. Remove the feathers.

Hypothesizing   *How do you think we might remove oil from the feathers?*
Try wiping the feathers with paper towels.

Observing   *Did wiping with paper towels remove all the oil?*
Try cleaning the feathers with dishwashing liquid.

Comparing   *Which method of cleaning the oil off the feathers was better?*
Designing an Investigation   *What other ways might we try to remove the oil from feathers?* Try them.

Eggs in Oil/Water

1. Put four hard-boiled eggs (with shells on) into the oil-water mix and then remove one egg at a time after each of these intervals: 15 minutes, 30 minutes, 60 minutes, 120 minutes.

Observing   *What happens to the eggs?*

2. Try removing the oil from the eggs with the methods you used for the feathers.
3. After cleaning the oil off the eggs, crack and remove the shells.

Observing   *Did the oil get inside the egg that was in the oil for 15 minutes? The one for 30 minutes? The one for 60 minutes? The one for 120 minutes?*

Recording   Record your findings.
If oil did get into the egg, can it be removed?

Removing or Containing Oil

Hypothesizing   *Using the following materials, how might you remove or keep the oil from spreading: paper towel, dishwashing liquid, turkey baster, large rubber band?*

1. Lay a paper towel on the surface of the oil and let it stay for 3 minutes. Remove the paper towel and put it on the paper plate.

Observing   *What do you see happening to the paper towel and oil?*

2. Add more motor oil, if needed, and spread a very large rubber band on the top of the oil.

Observing   *What happens to the oil?*

3. Using the turkey baster, try to suck up the oil.

Observing   *What happens to the oil?*

4. Squeeze the oil back into the pan of water. Add several drops of dishwashing liquid.

Observing   *What happens to the oil?*
Inferring   *Which method was best for removing the oil?*
Inferring   *Which method was best for keeping the oil together in one place?*

A Paper towel soaking up oil

B Rubber band containing oil

C Turkey baster removing oil

D Dishwasher liquid breaking up oil

How Will Students Use or Apply What They Discover?

1. *What possible problems and adverse effects might result when chemicals are used to remove oil from animals in a real oil spill?*
2. *How might an oil spill up in Alaska affect people in the continental United States?*
3. Sometimes oil spills are purposely set on fire. *What adverse effects might this have on the environment?*

Part III   How Might We Reverse the Effects of Water Pollution by Phosphates? (3–8)

What Concepts Might Students Discover?

Phosphates, from fertilizers and certain detergents, run off the land and pollute water ecosystems.

What Must I Know?

Phosphates can cause an overgrowth of algae, which may kill other living things by depleting the amount of oxygen in the water and adding too much carbon dioxide.

These phosphate pollutants can be cleaned using calcium.

What Will We Need?

Jar A from Part I containing pond water, algae, fertilizer, and dishwashing detergent.

2 clear jars
Teaspoon
Lime (from plant nursery)

What Do Students Know?

Remind students how the pond water with algae was altered by adding fertilizer and dishwashing liquid. The chemicals overstimulated algae growth. Now ask:
How do the adverse effects of too much fertilizer and detergent affect water environments?
Can phosphate pollution of water be reversed?
How might we do this?

What Will Students Do?

Observing
Hypothesizing

1. Divide the pond water from jar A equally into two jars marked *1* and *2*.
2. In jar 1, add 1 teaspoon of lime, stir well, and mark it *1—Lime Added.* Mark the other jar *2—Control* and do nothing to it.
   What change do you see in either jar?
   What do you think the white substance might be on the bottom of jar 1?

How Will Students Use or Apply What They Discover?

1. *If overfertilization can cause phosphate pollution, how can we safely fertilize our lawns and gardens?*
2. *How might composting food and organic scraps (like grass clippings and leaves) help with both waste and fertilizing problems?*
3. *How might we wisely use detergents to prevent phosphate pollution?*

What Is Air Pollution, What Causes It, How Does It Affect the Environment, and How Might It Be Prevented and Reversed? (K–8)

What Concepts Might Students Discover?

Fuels made from things that were once living (wood, coal, oil, etc.) are called **fossil fuels.**

When fossil fuels burn, they give off a sooty material called carbon, as well as several invisible chemicals.

Particles and chemicals in the air are called **pollutants,** and they can cause health and other environmental problems.

When smoke particles and the moisture in the air are trapped near the earth's surface, they combine to form **smog** (*sm*oke + f*og*).

Statues, monuments, buildings, and other things in our outdoor environment are slowly being destroyed by pollution in our atmosphere.

We can sample our air to find air pollutants.

Cigarette and cigar smoking are dangerous for the smoker and pollute the air for others.

Gas wastes from automobiles and factories react with water in the air to form acids. These acids fall to earth in some form of precipitation (snow, rain, hail, sleet, mist, or fog) and in this form are called **acid rain.**

Acid rain is harmful to plants, animals, physical features of the environment, and people.

There are things that can be done to prevent and reverse air pollution.

What Will We Need?

See each individual activity for needed materials. *Note:* Some items may be used from previous activities.

Part I   What Are Air Pollutants, and How Are They Formed? (K–8)

What Will We Need?

Paraffin candle
Aluminum foil pan
Matches
Clothespin
Masking tape

What Must I Know?

If students are too young or not yet responsible enough to use open flame, you should perform this activity.

PROCESSES

What Will Students and Teacher Do?

Hypothesizing
Observing

1. Light a candle. Tell students you are going to use a clothespin to hold the pan over the candle for 20 seconds.
   What do you think might happen to the pan?
   What do you see on the underside of the pan?
2. Rub the black substance with the sticky side of a piece of masking tape.

Inferring
Comparing

What do you think the black substance is?
Where have you seen material like this before?
Where might we find evidences of burned materials in our environment?

Part II   How Might Pollutants in the Air Affect the Growth of Plants? (K–8)

What Will We Need?

Clean milk cartons   2 spray bottles
Soil   Water
Bean seedlings   Vinegar

What Must I Know?

Either use bean seedlings from previous activities or plant new ones a week or two before this activity.

Bean seedlings

Water   Vinegar

What Will Students Do?

1. Get two clean milk cartons, punch small holes in the bottom, fill the cartons with potting soil, and put four to six bean seedlings in each carton.
2. Label one milk carton *Water* and the other one *Vinegar*.
3. Fill one spray bottle with water and label it *Water*. Fill the other bottle with vinegar and label it *Vinegar*.
4. Put both milk cartons in direct sunlight. Spray the Water milk carton with water and the Vinegar milk carton with vinegar, as shown in the diagram.
5. Repeat Step 4 daily for 1 week, making sure to spray each milk carton with its corresponding sprayer.

Observing   *What happened to the bean seedlings in the milk carton sprayed with water?*
Observing   *What happened to the bean seedlings in the milk carton sprayed with vinegar?*
Hypothesizing   *From your experiences with previous activities, how could you find out the pH of the soils?*
Inferring   *How is this activity related to the effects of acid rain on plants?*

Part III   How Can We Find Air Pollutants in Our Environment? (3–5)

What Will We Need?

Funnels	Jars
White filter paper	Hand lens
Litmus or hydrion paper	

What Must I Know?   This activity works best on a rainy day.

What Will Students Do?

1. Put a funnel in a jar and line the funnel with white filter paper.
2. On a rainy day, place several jars with funnels in different spots on your school grounds.
3. When the rain stops, collect the jars and remove the filter papers.
4. Open the filter papers and allow them to dry.
5. While the filter papers dry, test the rainwater in each jar with litmus or hydrion paper.

Hypothesizing   *Why do you think we are going to test the water with litmus or hydrion paper? What do you think we are looking for?*
Inferring   *If the pH of the rainwater tested is above 7, what might that mean?*
Communicating   6. Make a list of all the other pH values obtained by other members of the class.
Comparing   Compare the findings.

pH

Magnifying glass

Dried filter paper

Inferring   If differences are found, how might they be explained?
Hypothesizing   How might findings differ if samples were gathered from different places
                   in your community such as bus stops, an airport, or factories?

7. Now that the filter paper has dried, use a hand lens to look at it.

Observing   What do you see on the filter paper?
Inferring   Where do you think the residue came from?
Hypothesizing   If you repeat this activity on a dry day, do you think you might collect more
                   or fewer particles than on a rainy day? Why?
                   Try it and compare.

Part IV   How Can We Find Out if Vehicles Pollute the Air? (3–8)

What Must I Know?   Safety is a prime factor in this activity. You, a parent, and/or your school custodian should work together with students to conduct this activity. When doing the actual data collection, have the driver start the vehicle with the car in park and with the hand brake on. A second adult should stay with students to make sure they are away from the vehicle at all times!

What Will We Need?

Index cards	Yard- or meterstick
Jar of petroleum jelly	Cars, school buses
Thumbtacks	Hand lens

What Will Students and Adults Do?

1. Make a chart on the back of each index card that contains the following information:

Date of testing	
Vehicle manufacturer	
Model	
Year of vehicle	
Last tune-up date	
Name of tester	

2. Fill in this information *before* testing each vehicle.
3. Then lightly smear petroleum jelly on each card to be used.
4. With thumbtacks, attach the card, petroleum jelly side up, to a yard- or meterstick.
5. Go outside, accompanied by adults, to a parking lot. While one adult starts a vehicle, you and a second adult hold the yardstick 6 inches (15 cm) from the vehicle's exhaust pipe for 1 minute. *Caution:* Stay as far away from the vehicle as possible while still holding the card 6 inches from the exhaust.
6. Return to the classroom and use a hand lens to examine the index cards.

Observing   What kinds of solid particles did you find?
Inferring   Do you think there might be pollutants you cannot see?

Hypothesizing	*How might a Vehicle Inspection Station give you additional information about vehicle pollutants?*
Hypothesizing	*Which vehicles might give off more pollutants than others?*
Hypothesizing	*Why is it important to have vehicles inspected and tuned-up regularly?*
Inferring	After you and your classmates have tested several buses and cars, try to answer these questions:

Does the age of the car affect the amount of pollutants it emits?
Does the size of the car and engine make any difference?
Does the kind of gasoline used (regular unleaded, high-test unleaded, diesel, etc.) affect the amount of pollutants?
Does the brand of gasoline make any difference?

Part V   What Is Smog and How Is It Formed? (3–8)

What Must I Know?	Because of the use of matches and open flame, decide if you or your students will conduct the following activity.
What Will We Need?	Warm water Large clear glass jar or bowl Matches Rope Aluminum foil 5 to 6 ice cubes
What Will Students and Teacher Do? 	1. Put some warm water in a jar or bowl, swish it around, and pour it out, but leave some water droplets inside to make the air moist in the bowl. 2. With a match, light a piece of rope and drop it into the jar or bowl. 3. *Quickly* cover the top of the bowl tightly with aluminum foil. 4. Place ice cubes on top of the foil as shown in the diagram.

Observing	*What happens to the air inside the bowl when the temperature drops because of the ice cubes?*
Observing	*How do you know?* (Smoke rises.)
Inferring	*Why is this phenomenon called* smog? (*smoke* + *fog*)
Inferring	*In real life, what things that contribute to atmospheric smog are like the burning rope* (vehicle and factory emissions), *ice cubes* (cold air inversion), *and warm water* (water vapor in the air)?

Part VI   How Does Cigarette and Cigar Smoking Add to Our Pollution? (3–8)

What Must I Know?   This activity should be conducted by you, and preferably done *outdoors*.

What Will We Need?
Cotton	Glass turkey baster
Cigarette	Matches

What Will the Teacher Do?

1. Put a piece of cotton into the glass part of the turkey baster.
2. Light an unfiltered cigarette and insert the unlit end into the baster's spout, as shown in the diagram.
3. Compress and release the rubber bulb until the cigarette is completely finished smoking.

Observing   *What did you notice coming out of the cigarette?*

4. Remove the cotton from the baster.

Observing   *What do you see on the cotton?*

Cotton

Stained cotton

Hypothesizing   *If we did this activity with a filtered cigarette, would the results be any different?*

Designing an Investigation   *How would you go about testing your ideas?*
How would you test to see if pollutants go into the air as well as into the cotton?

Inferring   *Do smokers pollute the air as well as harm themselves?*

Part VII   How Do Smokers Pollute the Air? (3–8)

What Will We Need?
3 index cards	Petroleum jelly
Stapler	Hand lens
Twine	

What Will Students Do?

1. Give each index card a label: *Frequent, Rare,* or *Never.*
2. Staple a long piece of twine to each card.
3. Cover each card with a thin layer of petroleum jelly.
4. Following the labels you used in Step 1, hang each card from the ceiling in a room where:
   a. people *frequently* smoke cigarettes,
   b. people *rarely* smoke cigarettes, or
   c. people *never* smoke cigarettes.
5. After 1 week, collect all the cards and bring them back to the classroom. Examine with a hand lens.

Observing	*Using a hand lens, what do you see on each card?*
Comparing	*What differences do you see between cards from smoking and nonsmoking rooms?*
Inferring	*What do you think might cause the difference?*
Inferring	*What does this activity tell you about how smoking cigarettes might affect others as well as smokers themselves?*

Part VIII   How Does Air Pollution Affect the Physical Things in an Environment? (3–8)

What Will We Need?

Small squares of wood
Various colors and types of paint (water-based, oil-based, acrylic, etc.)
2 plastic garbage bags

What Must I Know?

After the garbage bags are filled full of painted squares, ask one of the school bus drivers to fill the bags with bus exhaust.

What Will Students and Bus Driver Do?

1. Paint the small wooden squares with a variety of paints and colors.
2. After the squares are dry, on the back of each square record the colors and types of paint used.
3. Place half of the squares of wood inside one large plastic garbage bag and half in a second garbage bag.
4. Have the school bus driver fill the garbage bags with bus exhaust and fasten the bags quickly and tightly to retain the fumes.
5. At the end of 1 week, check the pieces of wood in one garbage bag.

Observing   *What changes, if any, do you see?*

6. At the end of 2 weeks, check the pieces of wood in the other garbage bag.

Observing   *What changes, if any, do you see?*

Comparing   *How do the pieces of wood that were in the bag for 1 week compare to those that were in for 2 weeks?*
What were the changes?

Inferring   *What caused this to happen?*

How Will Students Use or Apply What They Discover?

Based on your observations in this activity, why do you think we have to paint our buildings so often?

Part IX   What Are Some Ways to Clean Polluted Air? (3–8)

What Will We Need?

Disposable vacuum bag full of dust
Large metal bucket
Plant sprayer with water

What Must I Know?

Discuss how some industries have soot and dust rising from them all the time. Some industries burn garbage too. They must use pollution-control devices to clean the air in their smokestacks. One of these devices is the **scrubber,** which removes dirt particles and most of the poisonous sulfur and nitrogen oxides from the soot. A scrubber sprays a liquid on the pollutants, trapping them, then carries the pollutants away before they can go out of the smokestack. The liquid and pollutants form a thick liquid or paste known as **sludge.** This sludge is then treated with a chemical and made into nonpolluting cakes. Researchers are trying to turn these cakes into building materials to recycle them.

Do this activity yourself, outdoors, and make sure students are upwind to avoid the dust.

What Will the Teacher Do?

1. Go out to a spot on the playground that is far away from the school building.
2. Slowly pour dust from the vacuum bag into the bucket. As the dust falls, squirt it gently with water from the plant sprayer. Do not use a hard, fast water jet.

Observing   *What happens to the dust?*

Inferring   *How is the wet dust, called sludge, now less polluting than when it was dry?*

Hypothesizing *How do you think this process is used to keep soot and dust from escaping from factory smokestacks?*

Hypothesizing *What do you think can be done with the dried sludge?*

Part X   What Can We Do to Control Air Pollution in Our Environment? (3–8)

What Will We Need?

Low-level-light houseplants: spider plants, golden pothos, azaleas, mums, Dracaenas, bamboo, ficus

What Must I Know?

NASA and other scientific groups have found that houseplants are excellent filters of indoor pollution because they take in pollutants and trap them in the soil. The plants listed above are especially suited for this purpose and are ideal for school. They tolerate low light conditions, dryness, and periods of neglect, such as vacation periods. For a free fact sheet about plants that have proved to be effective air cleaners, send a self-addressed, stamped envelope to the Foliage for Clean Air Council, 4405 N. Washington St., Falls Church, VA 22046.

What Do Students Know?

What are some ways we could clean the air in our classroom?
Discuss ways of cutting indoor air pollution and recommend growing plants if students do not suggest it.
How can we find out which plants are best for cleaning indoor air and how to care for these plants?

What Will Students Do?

1. Make a list of the most desirable air-cleaning plants and collect as many as you can by buying them, bringing in plants from home, asking local plant nurseries to donate plants and/or cuttings, and so on.
2. Find the best places in the classroom for each particular plant.

How Will Students Use or Apply What They Discover?

1. *If a minimum of one 12-inch-tall plant is recommended for every 100 square feet of floor surface, how many air-cleaning plants should we have in our classroom?*
2. *What other kinds of air-cleaning plants might we consider for our classroom?*

3. *Why would mixing fish-tank-filter charcoal with the soil in our air-cleaning plants help filter out air pollutants?*
4. *Why is NASA so interested in researching plants that filter air pollutants?*

References—Ecology and Environment
Teacher and older students: Philip Neal, *Acid Rain—Considering Conservation* (London: B. T. Batsford, 1991, distributed by Trafalgar Square, North Pomfret, VT 05053); Kathleen Hogan, *Eco-Inquiry: A Guide to Ecological Learning Experiences for the Upper Elementary/Middle Grades* (Dubuque, IA: Kendall-Hunt, 1994); Richard J. Wilke, ed., *Environmental Education Teachers Resource Handbook* (Arlington, VA: National Science Teachers Association, 1994); David Bones, ed., *Getting Started: A Guide to Bringing Environmental Education Into the Classroom* (Ann Arbor, MI: National Consortium for Environmental Education and Training, 1994).
Students: Laurence Pringle, *Oil Spills: Damage, Recovery, and Prevention* (New York: Morrow, 1993); Vicki McVey, *The Sierra Club Kid's Guide to Planet Care and Repair* (San Francisco: Sierra Club, 1993); *The Visual Dictionary of the Earth* (New York: Dorling Kindersley, 1993); Ann Downer, *Spring Pool: A Guide to the Ecology of Temporary Ponds* (New York: Watts, 1992).

Guided Discovery Science Activities for Students With Special Needs

Labels often get in the way of looking at individuals. "Special" individuals differ significantly in what they need to succeed in the world. They have "special needs," a phrase that is becoming more and more popular as a description of these members of our society.[1]

The activities in this section are designed for students with special needs. You either have, or soon will have, such students in your classroom. There are over 8 million youngsters in schools today (1 in 10) with some form of special need. Public Law 94-142, now called the Individuals with Disabilities Education Act (**IDEA**), directs that all students have a right to a full free public education within the *least restrictive environment*. Further, the Americans With Disabilities Act (ADA), a civil rights law, prohibits discrimination because of disability. The current trend influenced by these two laws is the integration of students with special needs into the regular classroom for most or all of the school day. This is called **inclusion.** Therefore, whether the special need is a sensory, mental, emotional, or social one, it is important for you to educate yourself about the disability and to find ways to adapt your teaching for the special needs student in your classroom.

Guided discovery science activities can provide a sense of achievement to special needs students who may seldom enjoy such success in school. It is not easy to accomplish the task of providing individualized science activities; however, by becoming aware of your students' individual strengths and weaknesses and the possible ways of helping each student best function, you will begin to individualize your science program.

Guided discovery science activities are presented for students with the following special needs:

1. Blindness or visual impairments
2. Developmental delays (previously referred to as educable mentally handicapped)

[1]From Ann P. Turnbull et al., *Exceptional Lives: Special Education in Today's Schools* (Englewood Cliffs, NJ: Merrill/Prentice-Hall, 1995).

3. Visual perception problems (as may be present in students with specific learning disabilities)
4. Emotional special needs
5. Deafness or hearing impairments

Although other special needs and disabilities are prevalent and important, the activities in this section are limited to these five categories of students because they are the most frequently encountered by classroom teachers.

These activities are not meant to be exhaustive but are suggestions of ways to meet the special needs of your students in science. As you practice using the activities, you will get to know your students better and will be able to find more ways to provide successful science learning activities for them. You can modify the guided discovery science activities in Section 5 for this purpose, as well. Learning to be more sensitive to students with special needs will help you respond more sensitively to all of your students. The unexpected gain to you of focusing upon "special needs" students will be to see all your students as individuals.

The format used in this section is the Quickie Starter: Open-Ended Activities format used in Sections 1 through 3. This less-formal format was selected because, in general, students with special needs respond well to activities that are hands-on, concrete, and more open-ended. This format also allows the teacher more flexibility in modifying the activities for individual students. As you become more confident with science activities for students with special needs, you will be able to modify some of the activities in Sections 1 through 3, as well.

STUDENTS WITH BLINDNESS OR VISUAL IMPAIRMENTS

Learning About Magnets (K–8)

Materials

Assorted magnets, common objects attracted and not attracted by magnets (paper clips, rubber bands, plastic and metal zippers, pencils, paper, wire, etc.), 2 shallow boxes, sandpaper
(*Note:* Avoid sharp or pointed objects.)

What Do Students Know?

What are magnets?
What things do they pick up?

Box with sandpaper sides

Box with smooth sides

Some Possible Activities

Have students handle the magnets and describe their shapes (bar, disc-shaped, horseshoe, U-shaped, cylindrical, etc.). Ask:

How will you know if a magnet picks up (attracts) an object?

Students will readily discern by touching the magnet that something was attracted to it if an object "sticks" to the magnet. Ask students to name the objects on the table and then test to find out which objects are attracted by the magnet. They can sort objects tested by the magnet into two shallow boxes. One box with smooth sides can be for objects attracted by magnets. Sandpaper glued to another box for objects not attracted by magnets can facilitate tactile sorting. Once students understand the sorting system, they can verify the contents of both boxes by themselves and even test new objects.

Identifying Objects in the Environment (K–8)

Materials

Masks to cover eyes, pairs of noisemakers (rattles, party horns, "clickers," etc.)

What Do Students Know?

Can you find your partner if you cannot see him or her? How?

Some Possible Activities

Take a group of sighted and blind or visually impaired students outside your classroom to a relatively open (free of trees, shrubs, or other obstacles) lawn area. Have other students or adults keep students from moving outside the area as they engage in this activity. Play a game in which students assume the roles of limited-vision animals. Have students pair up. Instruct sighted students to wear masks over their eyes. Have one student in each pair be a predator; the other, prey. Give each prey one of a variety of noisemakers (clickers, party horns, and so on). At a signal from you, prey try to find the other prey who have the same noisemakers. Predators, in the meantime, try to capture the noisy prey.

After the game, have students all sit quietly and listen to the environmental sounds. Ask:

Which sounds can you identify?
Which sounds are made by the same source?
In which direction do you hear the various sounds?
Which sound do you like the best? Why?
Which sound do you like the least? Why?
How do you think a particular sound was made?

For more information about this and other life science activities for students who are visually impaired, see Jane E. Cappiello, "Hands-on Science for Blind Students," *Science Scope* 15, no. 4 (January 1992) 44–45; and Larry Malone and Linda DeLucchi, "Life Science for Visually Impaired Students," *Science and Children* 16, no. 5 (February 1979): 29–31.

Finding Out About Body Position and Heart Rate (K–8)

Materials	Stethoscopes, braille-faced clocks
What Do Students Know?	*Does your heart beat faster when you lie down, stand up, or run?*
Some Possible Activities	After raising the question with students who are blind or visually impaired, give simple instructions on how to use the equipment and carry out the activity. Introduce the term **variable** and explain that the variable they will investigate is body position and how it affects their heart rate. Have students learn to use the stethoscope to listen to their heartbeats while counting the beats per minute on the braille-faced clock. An adult or older student can help younger students with the numbers. After students have taken and recorded their heart rates in lying, standing, and running situations, discuss the results. Help them to see the effect of body position on heart rate. You can extend the activity by asking additional questions. Ask: *What other variables could be investigated in this activity?* *What effect would the following things have on heart rate: age, amount of movement, time of day, drinking soda pop, smoking, and so on?*\
\
Encourage students to explore the variables without giving them specific directions on how to do it.

"Seeing" and Comparing Polluted Water Samples (3–8)

Materials	4 jars of water containing different pollutants, light sensor (available on Federal Quota from the American Printing House for the Blind, P.O. Box 6085, Louisville, KY 40206), light source (sunlight or filmstrip projector)
What Do Students Know?	*How can you use your sense of hearing to find out which jars contain the most polluted water?*
Some Possible Activities	Prepare four jars of water with varying amounts of pollutants (soil, debris, egg shells, etc.). Introduce and demonstrate to the students the light sensor device. This device produces an auditory signal of varying pitch and volume as a result of its exposure to different intensities of light. Set up the four jars of various pollutants with a light source behind them, as shown in the diagram.

Light sensor   Light source

At close range, have students point the light sensor directly at each jar, as shown in the diagram. A beeping sound will be emitted; the greater the amount of light coming into the sensor, the higher and more frequent the beeping. Students will discover that the fewer pollutants there are in each jar, the greater the amount of light coming through the jar, and, therefore, the more shrill and rapid the beep from the sensor. More pollutants result in much less light coming through the jar to the sensor, and thus a slower and lower pitched beep occurs. *Note:* For an excellent expanded description of using the light sensor with students who are blind, see Frank L. Franks and LaRhea Sanford, "Using the Light Sensor to Introduce Laboratory Science," *Science and Children* 13, no. 6 (March 1976): 48–49.

STUDENTS WITH DEVELOPMENTAL DELAYS

Developing a Thermic Sense (Sense of Temperature) (K–8)

Materials	Several metal bowls, water of varying temperatures
What Do Students Know?	*How do hot things feel?* *How do cold things feel?*
Some Possible Activities	Fill several metal bowls with varying temperatures of water, from ice cold to very warm. *Caution:* Do not use water hot enough to scald or injure any student. Let the water sit in the bowls for a few minutes, then have the students feel the *outside* of the bowls. Ask:

Which bowl feels cold?
Which one feels warm?
Which one feels hot?

If a student does not know the difference, try the following procedure. Say:
This bowl feels *cold*.
Does it make your hand cold?
This bowl is *hot*.
Is your hand hot?

Hot

Cold

Where else have you felt hot and cold things?
Relate this activity to everyday experiences by comparing it to holding a glass of iced drink, a cup of hot soup, and so on.
Point out the dangers of hot and cold. Ask:
Why should we use a potholder if we are holding something hot from the oven or stove?
Why should you wear a coat and gloves when it is very cold outside?
Where are very hot things in our homes and school?
Have pictures of ovens, stoves, radiators, and so on. Ask:
Which things are very cold in our school?
Take students to the cafeteria and have them show you (or you show them) the refrigerator or freezer.

Learning the Concept of Weight (K-8)

Materials

Small blocks of wood of the same size, but made of different kinds of woods, such as balsa (model airplane wood), oak, pine, or mahogany

What Do Students Know?

Which of these blocks do you think would be the heaviest? Lightest?

Some Possible Activities

Ask students to explain what it means when people say something is heavy. Have them use whatever words will help them to develop the concept, as long as the words do not connote misconceptions. They might say, "It's harder to lift." If they have difficulty with the concept of heavy and light, help them to develop it. Now give them the blocks. Ask:
Do you think they all weigh the same?
Which one seems the heaviest? Lightest?

Have students feel the blocks and place them in order from heaviest to lightest. Label the heaviest block with an H and use an L for the lightest one. Ask students what things in the classroom are heavy and light. Place an H or L on the objects selected. (Some examples of heavy might be: desks, cabinets, people; examples of light: paper, pencils, paper clips; and so on.) Explain why it is dangerous to lift very heavy things.

Discriminating Among Tastes (K–8)

Materials	Box of cotton swabs; bottles of solutions of common liquids that are salty, sweet, sour, bitter, acid, and neutral
What Do Students Know?	*How many of you would like to play a game?* *Are you a good detective?*
Some Possible Activities	Tell students they are going to play a detective game to try to find out what is in the bottles you have. *Caution:* Tell them *never* to taste anything they do not know about. Ask why they should not do this and explain the dangers of poisons. Tell students that none of the things in the bottles is poisonous and that they are things they taste every day.

Give each student his or her own swab and explain why this is necessary (to prevent spreading germs, colds, other diseases, etc.). Give all students a sample of something sweet, such as syrup. Ask:
What kind of taste is this?
Have them agree that it is sweet and, if possible, have them identify the source. Throw the cotton swabs away and give each student a second one. This time use a sour solution. Repeat the identification procedure and orally introduce the word *sour*; if appropriate for the group, write the word on the chalkboard. Repeat this procedure for all of the solutions.

Ask students what kinds of foods they eat that are salty, sweet, sour, bitter, acid, or neutral. Have them cut out pictures from magazines for each category. Discuss their lunch in school and visit the cafeteria to observe some foods. Have students note which category each food is in.

Note: For older or less developmentally delayed students, you can show them that different places on the tongue react more strongly to certain tastes. Touch solutions to these four sensation areas of the tongue.

Recognizing Common Odors (K–8)

Materials	Common strong-smelling substances in jars, such as onion, perfume, alcohol, pepper, cinnamon, peppermint, and so on
What Do Students Know?	*Who can tell us what this odor (smell) is?*

**Some Possible
Activities**

Have students smell a familiar substance (peppermint) by holding the appropriate jar at least 1 foot from their noses and fanning the odor towards them. (This avoids overwhelming the student with the odor and teaches him or her a safe way to smell unknown substances that might injure the student's sensitive nose.) *Note:* At first, to help students learn to recognize various odors, present the smell in the appropriately labeled jar, allowing students to see the material. Then ask students to discriminate among various odors while blindfolded.

For students who are more advanced, wait to label the jars until after students identify the odors. Use both oral and written words for the names of odors, as appropriate. Have students identify odors in their homes, school, and outdoors. Have them cut pictures from magazines of common strong-smelling substances and label them, such as gasoline, flowers, paint, smoke, and so on. Have students identify odors they like and dislike. Stress that some odors are dangerous, such as gas and smoke.

STUDENTS WITH VISUAL PERCEPTION PROBLEMS[2]

Observing Properties of Leaves (K–2)

Materials

Variety of leaves (maple, oak, elm, birch, etc.)

**What Do Students
Know?**

What do you notice about the shape of this leaf?

**Some Possible
Activities**

Have each student look at a maple leaf. Ask:
What is this?
Where do you think it came from?
How many points does it have?
What color is it?
How many large lines (veins) are there coming from the stem?

[2]The author is indebted to the following article and others in the *Science and Children* issue devoted to Science for the Handicapped: Marlene Thier, "Utilizing Science Experiences for Developing Perception Skills," *Science and Children* 13, no. 6 (March 1976): 39–40.

Let the student experience the leaf through sensory activities, that is, feeling it with the hand, rubbing it against the cheek, smelling it, and crushing it.

What does the smell make you think of?

How else would you describe the leaf?

Ask students to think of other properties. Introduce the word *property* for students to use when referring to the leaf's attributes. Introduce other species of leaves. Ask:

How are the leaves alike? Different?

What properties are the same?

What properties are different?

Comparing Properties of Shells or Buttons and Classifying Them (K–2)

Materials	Assortment of shells or buttons
Some Possible Activities	Give each student a handful of shells or buttons. Ask: *How are these things alike?* *How are they different?* Group them together by the same property. *Which properties might you use?*

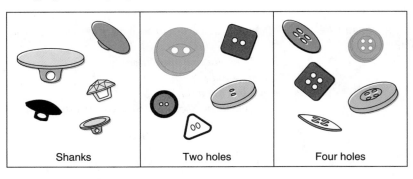

Allow students to group the objects. Ask:
How can you group the buttons according to a different property?
Note: In this activity, students not only make visual discriminations but also act upon them.

Using Plants to Teach Visual Sequencing (K–2)

Materials

Milk cartons, soil, pea seeds, chart paper, gummed paper

Some Possible Activities

Have each student plant a pea seed in a milk carton. Make certain students keep the soil moist and that they have a certain time each day for observing the plant and recording their observations. As soon as germination takes place and plants break through the soil, set up a chart for students to use to record the growth of each plant. Have them mark on the chart each day any changes that take place. They can measure plant height with strips of gummed paper, which can then be put on the chart to show the various stages of growth over a 6-week period, as shown in the diagram.

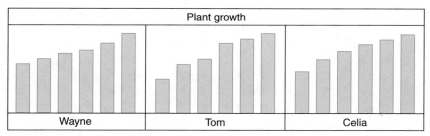

When working with younger children, plant an additional seed each week so students can see plants ranging in growth from 1 to 6 weeks. This will help them with visual sequencing. They begin by observing a natural phenomenon, then learn to record small changes over a period of time and in a sequenced progression—something they need to know.

Learning Relative Position and Motion (K–5)

Materials

Mr. O[3] for each student, white pipe cleaners, gummed white dots, blocks

Some Possible Activities

Students with perceptual problems usually have poor directionality concepts. "Mr. O," from the SCIS Relative Position and Motion unit, can help these students learn position in space, relative position in the environment, directionality, and figure-ground relationships.

Show students Mr. O. Tell them that he sees things only from his point of view. Cut out a Mr. O for each student. For younger children, after introducing Mr. O, play a game to familiarize them with his parts and to introduce words for directions in relation to him, as shown on the diagram.

[3]For a detailed description of Mr. O, see Robert Karplus et al., *Relative Position and Motion* (Level 4), Teacher's Guide SCIS, 3 (Hudson, NH: Delta Education, 1992), pp. 29–39.

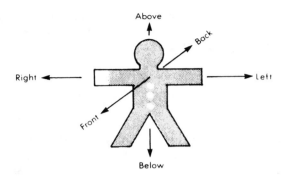

Younger children can also hang Mr. O around their necks while you point out the following things:

Mr. O's right hand is white.

Put a white pipe cleaner around your right hand.

Mr. O has three white buttons on the front of him.

Put three white gummed paper dots on the front of you.

Now ask the students to place a block to the right of Mr. O. Ask:

Where is the block in relation to Mr. O?

Where is the block in relation to you?

Is it near or far?

Do the same with the left side, in front of, in back of, above, and below, using only one variable at a time. Gradually build to more than one variable.

Once the student begins to understand this use of Mr. O, take Mr. O from around the child's neck and turn Mr. O to face him or her. Ask:

Where is Mr. O's hand now in relation to yours?

Place the block to the right, left, front, and back of Mr. O and ask the student to report the position, relative first to Mr. O, and them to himself or herself.

Note: Students become aware of needed changes in describing directionality from a non-ego-centered frame. They begin to develop direction-giving capabilities through awareness of relative position in space and figure-ground relationships. Students with visual perception problems have great difficulty with this task and need the systematic help shown here.

Developing Visual Scrutiny and Analysis in an Outside-the-Classroom Walk (K–5)

Materials

Small envelopes or plastic bags, paper, pencils

Some Possible Activities

Select a site outside your classroom where you and your students can take a walk. Before going, instruct students to observe, record, or collect the following:

- Task cards (3" × 5" index cards can be used to write down what the students will look for)
- Samples of five different-colored natural objects that have fallen to the ground (caution students not to pick anything from living organisms)

- Places (to be listed on their recording sheets) where they saw
  a. three different colors on the same plant,
  b. five different shades of any one color (green, for instance) along the path,
  c. six different textures on living organisms, and
  d. as many different colors as they can find
- Samples of evidence that animals have inhabited the environment
- Samples of dead insects
- Samples of evidence that people have been in the area
- Samples of different kinds of seeds in the area
- Other samples that are applicable to your outdoor site

Have the students place their samples in small envelopes, plastic bags, or other suitable containers. With younger children or children who have severe visual perception problems, it is best to use one of the activities at a time, so they focus on one variable in their environment and filter out distractions. The activities are also progressive, moving from observing many different plants (looking at plants and finding colors) to finding the same variable on only one plant (how many different colors on one plant). Later, in the classroom discussions, help students describe their samples and share them with their classmates. Further activities in pasting samples on paper, writing descriptive words for each object, and talking about their findings aid students who have visual perception problems in developing needed skills for further exploration of their environments and for reading, writing, and spelling.

STUDENTS WITH EMOTIONAL DISABILITIES

Learning About the Environment by Touching (K–5)

Materials   Paper, crayons, chalk, soft pencils, aluminum foil

What Do Students Know?   *How can our fingertips give us different kinds of information than can our eyes?*

Some Possible Activities

Direct contact with and the understanding and mastery of everyday living experiences under a sensitive teacher's guidance can produce an extensive and exciting learning environment for the child with an emotional disability. One such activity can be a tactile experience. Take your students (with assistance from parents) on a walk around the school. Have students select surfaces and use the suggested materials to do rubbings of those surfaces. In urban areas, they can do rubbings of sidewalks, sewer covers, grates, signs, and fences. The rubbings can be used to create texture panels and are also effective when they are individually matted and mounted. You might also attempt to get your students to talk about how the objects felt, whether they were rough, smooth, soft, hard, wet, or dry.

You can find many more activities for children with emotional disabilities in the following practical book: *An Outdoor Education Guide for Urban Teachers of the Emotionally Handicapped,* proceedings presented by the State University of New York State Education Department Division for Handicapped Children, and the Division of Health, Physical Education and Recreation, in cosponsorship with State University College of Arts and Science at Plattsburgh and Clinton, Essex, Warren, and Washington Counties BOCES, Special Study Institute, funded through PL 91–230 (June 1991).

Learning About the Environment by Listening and Moving (K–5)

Materials

A walking trip in the community

What Do Students Know?

What people-made sights and sounds can you identify?
How can you use your body to reproduce these sights and sounds?

Some Possible Activities

Sitting or working in a confined space (a desk and chair, for instance) for long periods of time creates static learning experiences. This is especially true for children who are emotionally disabled. They need to stretch and expand their bodies and minds, probably more than other children. These students can also begin to feel the same freedom of movement outside as they would experience in a gymnasium. Take students into the community and ask them to identify the following people-made sights and sounds.

Taxi cabs	Construction machines	Helicopters
Fire alarms	Motorcycles	Fire engines
Airplanes	Cars	Trucks
Ambulances	Buses	Air hammers

Ask:
What are the sounds of each vehicle?
How can you use your body to show the intensity and rhythm of each vehicle?
How is the fire engine sound different from the ambulance sound?
Show the differences with your movements.
Would you move in a fast, slow, or jerky way if you sounded like an airplane?
A dump truck?
How are car horn sounds different? Make the sounds.
How do various sounds make you feel? Happy? Sad?
Show how you feel by your movements.
Imitate with your body a vehicle starting and stopping.

STUDENTS WITH DEAFNESS OR HEARING IMPAIRMENTS

Students with hearing impairments can gain valuable experience in the regular classroom; however, there must be an attempt to individualize instruction.

All of the guided discovery science activities described for other special needs students are applicable for those who are deaf or hearing impaired, as are the guided discovery activities in Sections 1 through 3, when you use the following minimal adaptations of your regular classroom procedure.[4]

1. Seat students where they can see your lip movements easily. Avoid having them face bright lights or windows.

2. Speak naturally, in complete, grammatical sentences. Do not overemphasize lip movements or slow your rate of speech. Do not speak too loudly, especially if the student is wearing a hearing aid.

3. Avoid visual distractions such as excessive make-up, jewelry, or clothes that might draw attention away from your lips.

4. Do not stand with your back to a window or bright light source. This shadows your face and makes speech reading difficult.

[4]Adapted from Norris G. Haring and Linda McCormick, eds. *Exceptional Children and Youth,* 6th ed. (Englewood Cliffs, NJ: Merrill/Prentice Hall, 1994), 1.

5. Try not to move around the room while speaking, or to talk while writing on the board. If possible, use an overhead projector, which allows you to speak and write while still maintaining eye contact with students.

6. During class discussions, encourage students with hearing impairments to face the speaker. Allow them to move around the room, if necessary, to get a better view.

7. In some cases, a sign-language interpreter might be assigned to a student. Allow the interpreter and student to select the most favorable seating arrangement. The interpreter should interpret everything said in the classroom as precisely as possible. The interpreter may also be asked to interpret the student's oral or signed responses to the teacher and class. Interpreters are not tutors or classroom aides but rather professional personnel who facilitate classroom communication.

8. When possible, write assignments and directions on the chalkboard or distribute photocopied directions to the class. If assignments are given orally, you might ask a hearing student to take notes for a deaf or hearing impaired student.

9. Ask students who are deaf or hearing impaired to repeat or explain class material to make sure they have understood it. If embarrassed by their special needs, these students might learn to nod affirmatively when asked if they understood, even though they may not have understood the instructions at all.

10. If a student has a hearing aid, familiarize yourself with its operation and ask the student or the student's special class teacher to demonstrate it to the class. The student should assume responsibility for the care of the aid.

11. Maintain close contact with the other professional personnel who have responsibility for the student's education. If possible, regularly exchange visits with the special class teacher or therapist to observe the student in other educational settings.

SECTION 5

Piagetian Types of Guided Discovery Activities

Outlined in this section are a few special Piagetian types of activities to help you see how Piaget's theory may be applied to different elementary-school levels. These activities are given headings of specific operational cognitive abilities, such as classification and conservation, to show you how to take an operation and devise activities to involve students in these processes. Many of the other activities in this section are also Piagetian in design but are not organized around specific operations as are these Piagetian activities.

In conducting these activities, you should realize that perhaps one-half or more of your students may not perform the tasks correctly. If this happens, the students who did not achieve these specified goals need further involvement with similar experiences. By no means should these students be told that they failed. Piaget stated that the students themselves will know when they perform the tasks correctly. He believed, for example, that appropriate reinforcements for physical knowledge can come only from the objects themselves.

These activities are not included specifically to teach a particular operation but to demonstrate how students might be involved in physical experiences relative to their approximate development. Each student will get out of the activity what he or she is cognitively ready to assimilate. The activity questions are provided to illustrate how you might interact with students to determine what they are focusing on and how they reason. Practice in the use of these activities should sensitize you to students because you will be listening closely to them and learning how to intervene with questions to cause them to think about what they are doing. Learning this style of teaching should help you better develop students' thinking processes and science knowledge.

Note that some of these activities are teacher-conducted to try to discover students' prior knowledge, misconceptions, naive theories, or incomplete science concept development.

Class Inclusion: Do Children Know That Subclasses Are Included in a Major Class? (Ages 6–7)

1. Show several pictures of plants and animals. Ask:
   How many plants are there?
   How many animals are there?
   Are there more animals than plants?
   Are there more living things than just the animals?
2. Invite students to collect pictures of animals that move fast and slow, for example, a fly or a rabbit and a turtle or a snail. Try to get more examples of fast animals than of slow ones. Place the pictures of the animals on the tackboard. Ask:

Which moves faster?

   What are all the pictures of?
   How many slow animals are there?
   Are there more fast animals than slow animals?

Discussion
Class inclusion is a very important operational ability. It is a good indicator that a student is developing representational thought, which is essential in using such symbols as letters of the alphabet. A student who has difficulty with class inclusion probably has problems with reading.

Spatial Relations (Ages 6–7)

1. Give students pieces of straw and ask them to construct a diamond shape as best they can. Their construction should be accurate, with the points at the top and bottom.

2. Ask students to duplicate the following designs:

Discussion

If students cannot duplicate the correct shape or size of an object, they do not have good geometrical spatial conceptualization.

Try having students read words with letter combinations (words) such as *park, bath, dad, quick, man,* and *woman.* If students do not perform well on the spatial tasks and the letter discrimination, involve them with activities found in the Elementary Science unit: Attribute Games and Problems, Webster Division, McGraw-Hill, 1974, or Material Objects unit: SCIS II, Rand McNally, 1976. Both of these units contain activities to help students discriminate better and develop spatial relations concepts.

One-to-One Correspondence (Ages 6–8)

1. Obtain five each of bottle caps, buttons, and straws (other types of markers may be substituted). Have students line up the buttons in a row, then ask them to line up the bottle caps directly across from the buttons. Ask:
   Are there more, fewer, or the same number of buttons as bottle caps?
2. Move the buttons so they are spread out but do not move the bottle caps. Ask:
   Are there now more, fewer, or the same number of buttons as bottle caps? Why?
   If students think there are more buttons than bottle caps, ask:
   Please count them. Now what do you think?
   If they still do not realize that each button corresponds with each bottle cap, have them connect each pair by placing a straw between them.

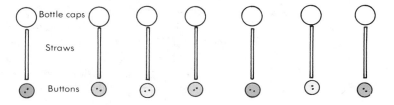

Ask:
Are there more, fewer, or the same number of buttons as bottle caps now?

Discussion

If students still cannot conceptualize one-to-one correspondence, have them place the materials in a box to be collected. Repeat this activity several times, using different markers, until the students do correspond.

Coordinating Systems—Horizontal and Vertical (Ages 6–12)

This is an exercise in reproducing and estimating the length of a line.

1. Give students a meterstick, compass, string, small right-angle triangle (see diagram), rulers, and paper strips. Ask:
   What is the length of each line?

2. Now ask:
   Can you draw a picture just like this one?'
   Remove the picture from students' vision. Tell them that they may refer to it again if necessary.

Discussion

Development progresses as follows:

Children of ages 6 to 7 usually use no measurement.

Ages 7 to 8 measure the length of the lines.

Ages 9 to 10 superimpose the right-angle triangle to measure angle.

Ages 10 to 12 begin to use measurement to accurately reproduce the angle.

Students unable to coordinate the horizontal and vertical as presented here may have problems in geometry and in understanding certain science concepts, particularly in geology and astronomy.

Conservation by Length (Ages 7–8)

1. Take two strips of paper of the same length. Ask:
   Is this strip just as long as the other?
2. Cut up one of the strips and combine the pieces as shown on the right side of the diagram. Tell the students that you have a rabbit that is going to move along the two paper paths. Ask:
   Would the rabbit make just as many hops on each path, or would it make more or less hops on one of the paths?
   Why do you think so?

Discussion

If students think the uncut paper is longer, they do not conserve length and will have difficulty understanding units and measurement.

Conservation of Length (Ages 7–8)

1. Draw the following diagrams of the snakes. Ask:

What do you notice about the lengths of the snakes on the left?
In the diagram on the right, is the coiled snake longer, shorter, or the same length as the other snake?

2. Take a rope and lay it out flat. Then coil it. Ask:

Is the rope now longer, shorter, or the same length as when it was straight?

Discussion

Ask students to measure the rope. Even if students measure the rope, however, if they do not conserve length, they will still think the curled rope is shorter.

Conservation of Area (Ages 7–8)

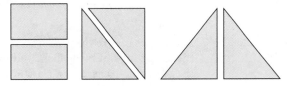

1. Cut a full piece of paper into two rectangles (A). Ask:
   Do these two pieces of paper cover the same amount of table?
2. Cut another full piece of paper diagonally, as shown in B, and arrange the pieces as shown in C. Ask:
   Do the cut pieces of paper in C cover as much area as the paper in A?
   Why do you think your answer is correct?
   How could you prove your answer is right?

Discussion

If students suggest that C covers as much as A, this indicates they conserve area. They should then suggest that if the two pieces of paper in C were combined together as in A, they would be the same. This indicates that students are capable of reversing and establishing logical necessity. This also means that they reason; since nothing has been taken away, the paper covers as much. Reversibility and logical necessity are intrinsically involved in conservation tasks.

Ascending a Class Hierarchy (Ages 7–8)

1. Prepare 10 pictures of animals. Include some birds, fish, and mammals.

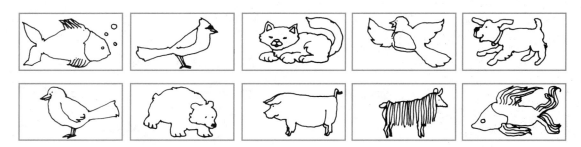

Tell students:
Please group these animals any way you want.
Ask:
How did you group them? Why did you group them that way?
Which of these groups were fish?
Which of these groups were birds?
Which of these groups were mammals?
Is there some way we can place all of the pictures in one group?
What would the group be? Why?
Are birds animals?
Are fish animals?
Are hairy animals (mammals) animals?

Discussion
If students realize on their own that all of these things are animals, and that the subgroups of birds, fish, and mammals can be grouped under animals, they are able to ascend a classification hierarchy.

Spatial Relations (Ages 7–8)

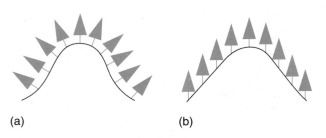

(a)   (b)

Ask students to draw a mountain and place trees on it.

Discussion
If they have good spatial relations, students will draw the trees perpendicular to the mountain as shown in diagram (b).

Constructing a Set Containing a Single Element (Ages 7–9)

Show six triangles. Let five triangles be all red and the sixth one yellow. On the back of the yellow one, make an X. Show the students both sides of the triangles. Then place all of the triangles color side up with no markings. Ask:

Which one of these objects is entirely different from the others?
What makes it different?
How could we group all of these objects?

Discussion

If students can identify the triangle with the X on the back as being different, they are able to establish a set as having a single element.

Ordering by Weight (Ages 9–10)

1. Obtain several (six or more) different metal containers of the same volume, or use medicine vials or empty 35-mm film containers of the same volume, and fill them with different kinds of materials, such as salt, sand, soil, water, baking soda, rice, flour, and so on.

Soil   Salt   Sand   Water   Baking soda   Rice   Flour

Tell students:
Please place these things in order by weight.

2. Ask students to weigh the containers and order them. Ask:
How good were your estimations?

Discussion

Students may have difficulty ordering by weight for as long as 2 years after they are able to order by length or height.

Descending a Classification Hierarchy (Ages 9–11)

1. Ensure that students know the characteristics of mammals. Prepare 10 pictures of mammals, birds, and other animals. Include several dogs, as well as other mammals, and ducks, as well as other birds.

Tell students:
Please group these animals any way you like.

Ask:
What groups did you form?
How many mammals did you get?
How many birds did you get?
Is there any way you can divide your mammal group? How?
Is there any way you can change your bird group?
What group of animals do dogs belong to?
What group of animals do ducks belong to?
What group do mammals belong to?
What group do birds belong to?

2. Ask the students to mix together all of the pictures again, make a few groups, and then use these groups to make some subgroups. Ask:
How did you group your animals?
Why did you group them that way?

Discussion

If students go from animals, to mammals and birds, and then to dogs and ducks, they have indicated that they can descend a classification hierarchy.

Conservation of Weight (Ages 9–12)

1. Obtain some clay. Have students prepare two round balls that weigh the same. They can check the weight of the balls by using a balance. Tell students:
Please make one of your clay balls into a hamburger shape.
Ask:
Will this piece of clay now weigh more, less, or the same amount as before? How can you tell?

2. Have students weigh the clay and find out. Ask:
What did you find out?
Why do you think it weighs the same?
Is there some rule you can give about changing the shapes of things and what happens to their weight?

Discussion

If students state that spreading things out changes the thickness but also increases the area covered, and that there is no loss in weight, they are giving a compensation type of justification. This means that the weight of the increased area compensates for the loss in weight in the thick area. If they state that when you roll the ball up again, it will weigh the same, they are demonstrating reversibility. This means they can reverse their thought processes. Both reversibility and compensatory reasoning characterize concrete-operational thought.

Conservation of Displacement Volume (Ages 11 and Older)

1. Obtain a graduated cylinder or use a jar. Fill it three-fourths full of water. Take a cube of clay and wrap a string around it so it can be low-

ered into the water. Have students place a rubber band around the container to estimate where the water level will be when the clay is lowered into it. Lower the clay very slowly.

Ask:

How good was your estimate?

2. Move the rubber band so the top of it marks where the water level is. Now take the clay out of the water. Cut the clay in half. Tie each half with string. Have students estimate where they think the water level will be now when you lower these two halves into the water. Use a marking pencil to mark where they think it will be. Do not move the rubber band. Slowly lower the two pieces of clay into the water. Ask:

What did you discover?

Can you give a rule for what you discovered?

Discussion

If students explain that the volume of the two halves of clay is the same as the volume of the whole piece and that they displace the same amount of water, they are conserving displacement volume. Here it is the volume, and what it displaces, that is important, not the weight.

LIST OF APPENDIXES

Appendix A   Fifty-Five Years of Elementary-School Science: A Guided Tour

Appendix B   Science Supplies, Equipment, and Materials Obtainable From Community Sources

Appendix C   Selected Sources of Scientific Supplies, Models, Living Things, Kits, Computers, and Collections

Appendix D   Noncommercial Sources and Containers for Living Things

Appendix E   Food Requirements for Various Animals

Appendix F   Planning a Learning Center

Appendix G   Selected Professional References for the Teacher or School Library

Appendix H   Professional Societies for Science Teachers and Supervisors

Appendix I   Model for Problem Solving (Sample)

Appendix J   Safety Suggestions for Hands-on/Minds-on Activities

Appendix K   Constructing Storage Areas for Supplies and Houses for Living Things

FIFTY-FIVE YEARS OF ELEMENTARY-SCHOOL SCIENCE: A GUIDED TOUR

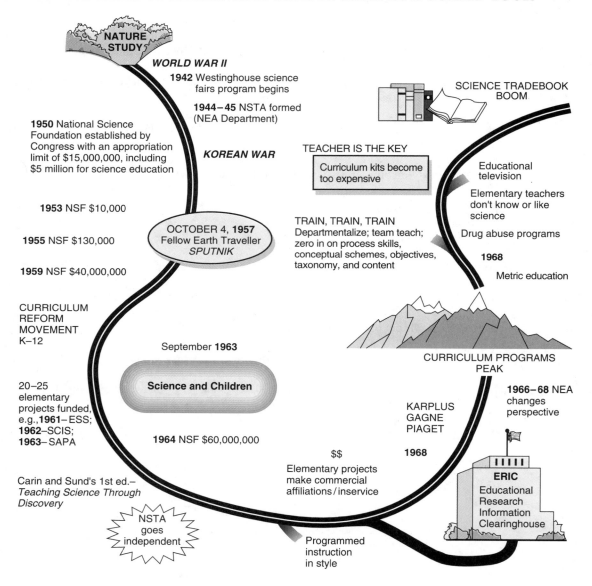

By Phyllis R. Marcuccio

Source: Modified from Phyllis R. Marcuccio, "Forty-Five Years of Elementary School Science: A Guided Tour." Reproduced with permission from *Science and Children* 24, no. 4 (January 1987): 12–14. Copyright 1987 by the National Science Teachers Association, 1840 Wilson Blvd., Arlington, VA 22201.

1970 NSF $50,700,000
1972 NSF $35,200,000

More than 20 elementary school science series available by **1972**

DO IT YOURSELF CURRICULUM

CURRICULUM PROGRAMS BEYOND THE TEXTBOOK

MAN ON THE MOON!

Did it work?

CULTS IN VOGUE
VIETNAM WAR ENDS

1969

National Assessment of Educational Progress

Outdoor and environmental education Open classrooms

1976
BICENTENNIAL
1976–77
NAEP 2

NSF $7,500,000 Funds for elementary school science almost disappear

MIDDLE SCHOOLS

MEDIA CENTERS

Gifted and talented movement

Accountability

Mainstreaming

NSF STUDIES SHOW HANDS-ON WORKS

1980
NSF $17,000,000

Energy education

1982
NSF $3,800,000

SLUMPING ECONOMY

1983–84
NSF $52,500,000

TEST IT! AND WE'LL KEEP IT!

1986 NSF $46,000,000

NAEP 3 (limited science)

REJUVENATION! Science is fundamental

NAEP 4

THE CHALLENGER DISASTER

1984
NEW ISSUES
Merit pay, quality teachers, standards for teacher training

BACK TO BASICS
TEXTBOOKS AGAIN

1985 NSF 42,460,000

A New Beginning

A Nation at Risk Science for the 21st Century Carnegie Report

Teachers need inservice

1989 AAAS issues Project 2061 Report–Scientific Literacy

SEARCH FOR EXCELLENCE IN SCIENCE EDUCATION

Cooperative Group Learning

1990 NSTA adopts 2 major goals of science education:
(1) scientific literacy for all
(2) ensure an adequate supply of future engineers and scientists

National Education Goals set by President and State Governors

1991
NSTA–SS&C

Constructivism

Multicultural Education

Information Age and the Internet

Proficiency Tests

1995 National Science Education Standards

20 years of NAEP Assessment

Performance Assessment

Women/minorities in science

1993 BSCS 35th Anniversary

Professional Development

NOTES ON THE GUIDED TOUR

Notable Achievements

- Elementary-school science now has a niche in elementary schools: It is accepted as important for all students, it is integrated with other subjects in the curriculum, and it is supported by principals and other administrators.
- There is a new breed of elementary science specialists.
- Hands-on teaching is giving rise to new ideas and techniques and is fostering creativity, intuition, and problem-solving skills. (Hands-on teachers are "guides" rather than "tellers.") The popularity of hands-on teaching is also creating a need for more inservice training and for more science centers and labs.
- Nonschool settings, such as outdoor education centers and museums, have increased their support, often introducing subject matter that includes issues of social concern like pollution, ecology, and energy education.
- Teaching tools—books, software, television, and other audiovisual equipment—have become better in a number of ways: They are more accurate, attractive in format, and sensitive to social issues like affirmative action.
- Up-to-date research in science education is readily available through ERIC (Educational Research Information Clearinghouse).
- Recent and projected certification programs subject teachers to more rigorous standards.
- Studies and testing, forums and conferences exist to deal specifically with the concerns of elementary science.
- Teacher education institutions now train for junior high certification, and they have redesigned the way in which preservice teachers are taught to teach elementary science.
- The business and industry communities, concerned about the interrelationships of science, technology, and society, have sought a role in science education. Organizations like the American Chemical Society, the National Academy of Science, and the American Association for the Advancement of Science have also cooperated to forward the cause of science education.
- SI metric measure has been generally adopted.
- A teamwork approach to curriculum building now exists among teachers, scientists, administrators, community, and government.
- There are established pockets of commitment to science, and programs have been developed to point out excellent science teaching throughout the country.

Familiar Road Signs

- Surges in National Science Foundation funding
- Efforts following crisis situations
- The continuing presence of textbooks
- National Assessment of Educational Progress reports
- Calls for new curricula
- Calls for inservice programs

Some Remaining Problems

- Teachers continue to be educated in the same way.
- No comprehensive, agreed-upon scope and sequence has been established.
- Progress depends on funds from the National Science Foundation.
- The pool of students interested in science is shrinking—nearly half the current ninth-grade class in urban high schools will not even graduate, let alone seek science-related careers.
- Despite millions of dollars spent on curriculum studies, teachers still depend on textbooks.
- The United States continues to lag behind other countries in the amount of science being taught to children.
- The best science students are not attracted to science teaching careers.
- Average Americans care more for pseudoscience than science.
- Teachers do not apply educational research.

SCIENCE SUPPLIES, EQUIPMENT, AND MATERIALS OBTAINABLE FROM COMMUNITY SOURCES

This is only a partial list of places in the community that are possible sources of items for a science program in elementary and middle schools. Other sources that should not be overlooked include local factories, the janitor or custodian of the school, the school cafeteria, radio and television repair shops, florists' shops, other teachers in the school, junior and senior high school science teachers, and so on. The materials are there; it just takes a little looking.

There are times, though, when in spite of the most careful searching, certain pieces of equipment or supplies are not obtainable from local sources; there are also many things that schools should buy from scientific supply houses. A partial list of some selected, reliable scientific supply houses is given in Appendix C.

Dime Store or Department Store

balloons
balls
candles
compasses (magnetic)
cotton (absorbent)
flashlights
food coloring
glues and paste
inks
magnifying glasses
marbles
mechanical toys
mirrors
mousetraps
paperbook matches
scissors
sponges
thermometers

Drugstore

adhesive tape
alcohol (rubbing)
bottles
cigar boxes
cold cream
corks
cotton
dilute acids, preferably 1–5%
dilute H_2O_2 (1½%)
forceps
heat-resistant nursing bottles
limewater
medicine droppers
pipe cleaners
rubber stoppers
soda bicarbonate
spatulas

straws
sulfur
TES-Tape™
tincture of iodine, diluted to straw color

Electrical Appliance Shop

bell wire
burned-out fuses and light bulbs
dry cells
electric fans
electric hot plates
flashlight bulbs
flashlights
friction tape
magnets (from old appliances)
soldering iron

Fabric Shop

cardboard tubes
cheesecloth
flannel
knitting needles
leather
needles
netting
scraps of different kinds of fabrics
silk thread
spools

Farm or Dairy

birds' nests
bottles
clay
containers
gravel

hay or straw
humus
insects
leaves
loam
lodestone
rocks
sand
seeds

Fire Department

samples of materials used to extinguish various types of fires
water pumping equipment

Garden Supply Store

bulbs (tulips, etc.)
fertilizers
flowerpots
garden hose
garden twine
growing plants
labels
lime
seed catalogs
seeds
spray guns
sprinkling cans
trowels and other garden tools

Gas Station

ball bearings
cans
copper tubing
gears
gear transmissions
grease

inner tubes
jacks
maps
pulleys
tools
valves from tires
wheels

Grocery Store

aluminum foil
ammonia
baking soda
borax
candles
cellophane
clothespins
cornstarch
corrugated cardboard boxes
fruits
paper bags
paraffin
plastic wrap
salt
sponges
sugar
vegetables
vinegar
wax
waxed paper

Hardware Store

brace and bits
cement
chisels
clocks
dry-cell batteries
electric push buttons, lamps, and
    sockets
extension cords
files
flashlights
fruit jars
glass cutters
glass friction rods
glass funnels
glass tubing

hammers
hard rubber rods
insulated copper wire
lamp chimneys
metal and metal scraps
nails
nuts and bolts
paints and varnishes
plaster of paris
pulleys
sandpaper
saws
scales
scrap lumber
screening
screwdrivers
screws
steel wool
thermometers (indoor and
    outdoor)
3–6 volt toy electric motors
tin snips
turpentine
wheelbarrow
window glass (broken pieces
    will do)
wire
yardsticks

Machine Shop

ball bearings
iron filings
iron rods
magnets
nuts and bolts
scrap metals
screws
wire

Medical and Dental Offices and Hospitals

corks
flasks
funnels
glass tubing
hard lenses

litmus paper
microscopes
models, such as teeth
rubber sheeting
rubber stoppers
rubber tubing
test tube holders
test tubes
thermometers
tongue depressors

Music Shop

broken string and drum heads
musical instruments
pitch pipes
tuning forks

Pet Shop

air pumps
animal cages
ant houses
aquariums
cages
fish
insects
nets (butterfly, fish, etc.)
plastic tubing
strainers
terrariums

Restaurant, Diner, or Fast-Food Outlet

beverage stirrers
bones (chicken, etc.)
bottles
cans (coffee, 5-gallon size)
drums (ice cream)
five-gallon cans (oil)
food coloring
gallon jars (wide-mouthed, pickles,
    mayonnaise, etc.)
gallon jugs (vinegar)
pie tins
plastic spoons
plastic trays
soda straws

For additional sources of common, easily obtained supplies and apparatus suitable for your elementary- or middle-school science program, see *NSTA Directory of Science Education Suppliers* (Arlington, VA: National Science Teachers Association, published annually).

APPENDIX C

SELECTED SOURCES OF SCIENTIFIC SUPPLIES, MODELS, LIVING THINGS, KITS, COMPUTERS, AND COLLECTIONS[1]

Accent Science
P.O. Box 1444
Saginaw, MI 48605
(517) 799-8103

American Geological Institute
4220 King St.
Alexandria, VA 22302
(703) 379-2480

American Science and Surplus
601 Linden Pl.
Evanston, IL 60202
(708) 475-8440

Apple Computer, Inc.
20525 Mariani Ave.
Cupertino, CA 95014
(408) 996-1010

Bausch & Lomb
42 East Ave.
Rochester, NY 14603
(716) 338-6000

Bel-Art Products
6 Industrial Rd.
Pequannock, NJ 07440
(201) 694-0500

Carolina Biological Supply Co.
2700 York Road
Burlington, NC 27215
(919) 584-0381

Center for Multisensory Learning
Lawrence Hall of Science
University of California
Berkeley, CA 94720
(415) 642-8941

Central Scientific Co. (CENCO)
11222 Melrose Ave.
Franklin Park, IL 60131
(800) 262-3626

Chem Scientific, Inc.
67 Chapel St.
Newton, MA 02158
(617) 527-6626

Connecticut Valley Biological Supply Co., Inc.
82 Valley Rd.
P.O. Box 326
Southampton, MA 01073
(800) 628-7748

Delta Education, Inc.
P.O Box 915
Hudson, NH 03051-0915
(800) 258-1302

Edmund Scientific Co.
101 E. Gloucester Pike
Barrington, NJ 08007
(609) 573-6240

Educational Activities, Inc.
P.O Box 392
Freeport, NY 11520
(800) 645-3739

Education Development Center
55 Chapel St.
Newton, MA 02160
(617) 969-7100

Fisher Scientific Co., Educ. Div.
485 S. Frontage Rd.
Burr Ridge, IL 60521
(800) 955-1177

Frey Scientific Co.
905 Hickory Lane
Mansfield, OH 44905
(419) 589-1900

Hubbard Scientific, Inc.
3101 Iris Ave., Ste. 215
Boulder, CO 80301
(800) 446-8767

Ideal School Supply Co.
11000 S. Lavergne Avenue
Oak Lawn, IL 60453
(800) 323-5131

Lab-Aids, Inc.
17 Colt Ct.
Ronkonkoma, NY 11779
(516) 737-1133

LaPine Scientific Co.
13636 Western Ave.
Blue Island, IL 60406
(708) 388-4030

McKilligan Supply Corporation
435 Main Street
Johnson City, NJ 13790
(607) 798-9335

NASCO
901 Janesville Avenue
Fort Atkinson, WI 53538
(414) 563-2446

Nasco West Inc.
P.O Box 3837
Modesto, CA 95352
(209) 529-6957

Sargent-Welch Scientific Co.
P.O Box 1026
Skokie, IL 60077
(800) SARGENT

---

[1]For an extensive compilation of sources for science equipment/supplies, computer software, educational services, media producers, and publishers, see Phyllis Marcuccio, compiler, *Science Education Suppliers* (Arlington, VA: National Science Teachers Association, published annually).

**Science Kit and Boreal
Laboratories**
777 E. Park Drive
Tonawanda, NY 14150
(800) 828-7777

**Ward's Natural Science
Establishment, Inc.**
5100 West Henrietta Rd.
P.O Box 92912
Rochester, NY 14692-9012
(800) 962-2660

Wilkens-Anderson Co.
4525 W. Division St.
Chicago, IL 60651
(312) 384-4433

APPENDIX D

NONCOMMERCIAL SOURCES AND CONTAINERS FOR LIVING THINGS

Organisms	Noncommercial Source	Culture Containers
POND SNAILS	Freshwater ponds, creeks	Aquaria, large battery jars, gallon glass jars
LAND SNAILS	Mature hardwood forests: on rocks, fallen logs, damp foliage	Terraria, large battery jars
DAPHNIA	Freshwater ponds: at water's edge, and associated with algae	Gallon glass or plastic jars
ISOPODS AND CRICKETS	Under rocks, bricks, and boards that have lain on the ground for some time; between grass and base of brick buildings	Glass or plastic terraria, plastic sweater boxes (Provide vents in cover.)
MEALWORM BEETLES	Corn cribs, around granaries	Gallon glass jars with cheese cloth
FRUIT FLIES	Trap with bananas or apple slices. (Place fruit in a jar with a funnel for a top.)	Tall baby food jars, plastic vials (Punch hole in jar lids, cover with masking tape, and then prick tiny holes in tape with a pin.)
WINGLESS PEA APHIDS*	Search on garden vegetables, e.g., English peas	On pea plants potted in plastic pots, milk cartons (Keep aphids in a large terrarium so they cannot wander to other plants in the school.)
GUPPIES	Obtain free from persons who raise guppies as a hobby. (They are usually glad to reduce the population when they clean tanks.)	Aquaria, large battery jars
CHAMELEONS*	Dense foliage along river banks or railroad tracks (Catch with net or large tea strainer.)	Prepare a cage using a broken aquarium. (Broken glass can be replaced by taping cloth screening along sides.)
FROGS*	Along edges of ponds, ditches, creeks (Catch with large scoop net.)	Large plastic ice chest (Set near a sink so a constant water supply can be provided.)

Source: Carolyn H. Hampton and Carol D. Hampton, "The Establishment of a Life Science Center." Reproduced with permission by *Science and Children* 15, no. 7 (April 1978): 9. Copyright 1978 by The National Science Teachers Association, 1840 Wilson Blvd., Arlington, VA 22201-3000.

*These species are difficult to obtain from their natural habitats. Unless you have a convenient source, it is better to buy them commercially. Try a local aquarium or pet shop.

Note: For additional excellent articles on raising and using living things in elementary-school classrooms, see Carol Hampton, Carolyn H. Hampton, and David Kramer, *Classroom Creature Culture: Algae to Anoles,* rev. ed. (Arlington, VA: National Science Teachers Association, 1994).

Organisms	Noncommercial Source	Culture Containers
CHLAMYDOMONAS AND EUGLENA	Freshwater pond	Gallon glass jars, aquaria, battery jars
ELODEA (ANARCHARIS)*	Ponds, creeks: usually along edge or in shallows	Aquaria, large battery jars
EELGRASS*	Wading zone or brackish water	Aquaria, large battery jars
DUCKWEED	Edge of ponds or freshwater swamps	Aquaria, large battery jars
COLEUS AND GERANIUM	Persons who raise them (Start by rooting cuttings in 1 part sand, 1 part vermiculite, in plastic bags;	Clay pots, milk cartons, tin cans

*These species are difficult to obtain from their natural habitats. Unless you have a convenient source, it is better to buy them commercially. Try a local aquarium or pet shop.

APPENDIX E

FOOD REQUIREMENTS FOR VARIOUS ANIMALS

Food and Water	Rabbits	Guinea Pigs	Hamsters	Mice	Rats
Daily					
pellets or grain	rabbit pellets: keep dish half full	corn, wheat, or oats	large dog pellets: 1 or 2		canary seeds or oats
green or leafy vegetables, lettuce, cabbage, and celery tops or	keep dish half full 4–5 leaves	2 leaves	1½ tablespoon 1 leaf	2 teaspoons ⅛–¼ leaf	3–4 teaspoons ¼ leaf
grass, plantain, lambs' quarters, clover, alfalfa or	2 handfuls	1 handful	½ handful	—	—
hay, if water is also given					
carrots	2 medium	1 medium			
Twice a week					
apple (medium)	½ apple or salt block	¼ apple	⅛ apple	½ core and seeds	1 core
iodized salt (if not contained in pellets)		sprinkle over lettuce or greens			
corn, canned or fresh, once or twice a week	½ ear	¼ ear	1 tablespoon or ⅓ ear	¼ tablespoon or end of ear	½ tablespoon or end of ear
water	should always be available		necessary only if lettuce or greens are not provided		

APPENDIX E, *continued*

FOOD REQUIREMENTS FOR VARIOUS ANIMALS

Food and Water	Water Turtles	Land Turtles	Small Turtles
Daily			
worms or night crawlers	1 or 2	1 or 2	¼ inch of tiny earthworm
or			
tubifex or blood worms and/or			enough to cover half the area of a dime
raw chopped beef or meat and fish-flavored dog or cat food	½ teaspoon	½ teaspoon	
fresh fruit and vegetables		¼ leaf lettuce or 6–10 berries or 1–2 slices peach, apple, tomato, melon or 1 tablespoon corn, peas, beans	
dry ant eggs, insects or other commercial turtle food			1 small pinch
water	¾ of container	always available at room temperature; should be ample for swimming and submersion large enough for shell	half to ¾ of container

Food and Water Plants (for Fish)	Goldfish	Guppies
Daily dry commercial food adults;	1 small pinch	1 very small pinch; medium-size food for adults; fine-size food for babies
Twice a week shrimp—dry—or another kind of dry fish food	4 shrimp pellets or 1 small pinch	dry shrimp food or other dry food: 1 very small pinch
Two or three times a week tubifex worms add enough "conditioned" water to keep tank at required level	enough to cover ½ area of a dime allow one gallon per inch of fish; add water of same temperature as that in tank —at least 65°F	enough to cover ⅛ area of a dime allow ¼ –½ gallon per adult fish; add water of same temperature as that in tank —70° to 80° F
Plants: cabomba, anacharis, etc.	should always be available	

Food and Water	Newts	Frogs
Daily small earthworms or mealworms or tubifex worms	1–2 worms	2–3 worms
	enough to cover ½ area of a dime	enough to cover ¾ area of a dime
or raw chopped beef	enough to cover a dime	enough to cover a dime
water	should always be available at same temperature as that in tank or at room temperature	

Source: Grace K. Pratt, *How to . . . Care for Living Things in the Classroom* (Arlington, VA: National Science Teachers Association, 1978), 11.

Note: See also: *Using Live Insects in Elementary Classrooms for Early Lessons in Life,* available from Center for Insect Science, Education Outreach, 800 E. University Blvd., Suite 300, Tucson, AZ 85721.

APPENDIX F

PLANNING A LEARNING CENTER

State Purpose

The purpose of a learning center should be clear, both to the teacher and the students, and should be stated as a part of the center; for example, "At this center you will examine some seeds. You will compare sizes, weights, volumes, and shapes of the seeds."

Consider Student Levels

The center must be appropriate for the students who will be using it. The backgrounds and experiences, cognitive levels of operation, socioeconomic levels, maturity levels and levels of independence, and psychomotor levels of students must be defined and used as the basis for planning the activities and expected learning outcomes of the center.

Define Concepts and Skills to Be Developed

A clear statement of the concepts, subconcepts, and skills to be developed by the students using the center is necessary if the center is to be a true teaching/learning situation. Fulfilling this criterion is the point where many centers break down into "busy work."

Outline Expected Learning Outcomes

These statements can be in the form of performance—or behavioral—objectives. Here, a concise statement of what the student is expected to learn as a result of using the center can also serve as a guideline for evaluating student success.

Select Appropriate Activities and Methods

These must be carefully selected to harmonize with the criteria previously mentioned. The activities must serve the purpose of the center and be appropriate to the students using it. They must be designed to assist students in reaching the expected goals. The directions must be clearly within the abilities of students and presented so that students can follow them independently. The materials must be readily available.

Do Evaluations

Use the objectives for the center as a base to determine whether the student has attained the expected learnings, concepts, and skills stated. The center and its materials may need periodic servicing.

Implement Change as Needed

Student performance will provide insight into how each center can be improved or changed to meet the needs of the students it serves, the curriculum, and the objectives and goals stated for the center.

APPENDIX G

SELECTED PROFESSIONAL REFERENCES FOR THE TEACHER OR SCHOOL LIBRARY

Professional Books in Elementary-School Science

Abruscato, Joseph. *Teaching Children Science.* Englewood Cliffs, NJ: Allyn & Bacon, 1992.

Blough, Glenn O., and Schwartz, Julius. *Elementary School Science and How to Teach It,* 7th ed. New York: Holt, Rinehart & Winston, 1990.

Cain, Sandra E. *Sciencing: An Involvement Approach to Elementary Science Methods,* 3rd ed. New York: Merrill/Macmillan, 1990.

Esler, William K., and Esler, Mary K. *Teaching Elementary Science,* 5th ed. Belmont, CA: Wadsworth, 1989.

Friedl, Alfred E. *Teaching Science to Children: An Integrated Approach.* Westminster, MD: Random House, 1986.

Gabel, Dorothy. *Introductory Science Skills.* Prospect Heights, IL: Waveland Press, 1984.

Gega, Peter C. *Science in Elementary Education,* 7th ed. Englewood Cliffs, NJ: Merrill/Prentice Hall, 1994.

Harlan, Jean, and Rivkin, M. S. *Science Experiences for the Early Childhood Years,* 6th ed. Englewood Cliffs, NJ: Merrill/Prentice Hall, 1996.

Harlen, Wynne. *Teaching and Learning Primary Science.* New York: Teachers College Press, 1985.

———, ed. *Primary Science: Taking the Plunge.* London: Heinemann Educational Books, 1986.

Henson, Kenneth T., and Janke, Delmar. *Elementary Science Methods.* New York: McGraw-Hill, 1984.

Jacobson, Willard J., and Begman, Abby Barry. *Science for Children,* 2nd ed. Englewood Cliffs, NJ: Prentice-Hall, 1991.

Lerner, Marjorie E. *Readings in Science Education for the Elementary School.* New York: Macmillan, 1985.

Lorbeer, George C., and Nelson, Leslie W. *Science Activities for Children,* 9th ed. Dubuque, IA: Wm. C. Brown Publishers, 1992.

Lowery, Lawrence, and Verbeeck, Carol. *Explorations in Physical Science.* Belmont, CA: D. S. Lake Publishers, 1987.

McIntyre, Margaret. *Early Childhood and Science.* Arlington, VA: National Science Teachers Association, 1984.

Peterson, Rita; Bowyer, Hane; Butts, David; and Bybee, Rodger. *Science and Society: A Sourcebook for Elementary and Junior High School Teachers.* New York: Merrill/Macmillan, 1984.

Renner, John W., and Marek, Edmund A. *The Learning Cycle and Elementary Science Teaching.* Portsmouth, NH: Heinemann, 1988.

Sprung, Barbara, et al. *What Will Happen If . . . Young Children and the Scientific Mind.* New York: Educational Equity Concepts, 1986.

Tolman, Marvin N., and Morton, James O. *Science Curriculum Activities Library Series: Physical Science Activities for Grades 2–8, Earth Science Activities for Grades 2–8, Life Science Activities for Grades 2–8.* West Nyack, NY: Parker Publishing Co., 1992.

Victor, Edward, and Richard D. Kellough. *Science for the Elementary School,* 7th ed. Englewood Cliffs, NJ: Merrill/Prentice Hall, 1993.

Wasserman, Selma, and Ivany, J. W. George. *Teaching Elementary Science: Who's Afraid of Spiders?* New York: Harper and Row, 1988.

Wolfinger, Donna M. *Teaching Science in the Elementary School.* Boston: Little, Brown, 1984.

Zeitler, William R., and Barufaldi, James P. *Elementary School Science: A Perspective for Teachers.* New York: Longman, 1988.

Science Education Periodicals for Teachers and Children

Children and teachers can keep abreast of the rapid development in science research and science education by referring to the following periodicals. They provide the most information and are an invaluable supplement to science textbooks.

(T) teacher oriented
(C) child oriented

American Biology Teacher. The National Association of Biology Teachers, 11250 Roger Bacon Dr., Reston, VA 22090 (Monthly) (T)

Audubon Magazine. The National Audubon Society, 613 Riversville Rd., Greenwich, CT 06830 (Bimonthly) (C & T)

Biology & General Science Digest. W. M. Welch Co., 1515 Sedgwick St., Chicago, IL 60610 (Free) (T)

Cornell Rural School Leaflets. New York State College of Agriculture, Ithaca, NY 14850 (Quarterly) (T)

Current Science and Aviation. American Education Publications, Discover, Time Inc., 3435 Wilshire Blvd., Los Angeles, CA 90010 (C & T)

Grade Teacher. Educational Publishing Co., Darien, CT 06820 (Monthly Sept.–June) (T)

Journal of Research in Science Teaching. John Wiley & Sons, 605 Third Ave., New York, NY 10016 (T)

Junior Astronomer. Benjamin Adelman, 4211 Colie Dr., Silver Springs, MD 20906 (C & T)

Junior Natural History. American Museum of Natural History, New York, NY 10024 (Monthly) (C & T)

Monthly Evening Sky Map. Box 213, Clayton, MO 63105 (Monthly) (C & T)

My Weekly Reader. American Education Publications, Education Center, Columbus, OH 43216 (Weekly during the school year) (C)

National Geographic. National Geographic Society, 17th and M Sts. N.W., Washington, DC 20036 (Monthly) (C & T)

Natural History. American Museum of Natural History, 79th St. and Central Park West, New York, NY 10024 (Monthly) (C & T)

Nature Magazine. American Nature Association, 1214 15th St. N.W., Washington, DC (Monthly Oct. to May and bimonthly June to Sept.) (C & T)

Our Dumb Animals. Massachusetts Society for the Prevention of Cruelty to Animals, Boston, MA 02115 (Monthly) (C & T)

Outdoors Illustrated. National Audubon Society, 1000 Fifth Ave., New York, NY 10028 (Monthly) (C & T)

Popular Science Monthly. Popular Science Publishing Co., 335 Lexington Ave., New York, NY 10016 (Monthly) (C & T)

Readers Guide to Oceanography. Woods Hole Oceanographic Institute, Woods Hole, MA 02543 (Monthly) (T)

School Science and Mathematics. Central Association Science and Mathematics Teachers, P.O. Box 48, Oak Park, IL 60305 (Monthly 9 times a year) (T)

Science. American Association for the Advancement of Science, 1515 Massachusetts Ave. N.W., Washington, DC 20025 (T)

Science and Children. National Science Teachers Association, Arlington, VA 22201 (Monthly 8 times a year) (C & T)

Science Digest. 959 8th Ave., New York, NY 10019 (Monthly) (T)

Science Education. Science Education Inc., C. M. Pruitt, University of Tampa, Tampa, FL 33606 (5 times yearly) (T)

Scienceland, 501 Fifth Ave., New York, NY 10017 (Monthly) (C)

Science Newsletter. Science Service, Inc., 1719 N. Street, N.W., Washington, DC 20036 (Weekly) (T)

Science Teacher. National Science Teachers Association, National Education Association, 1840 Wilson Blvd., Arlington, VA 22201 (Monthly Sept. to May) (T)

Science World. Scholastic Magazines, Inc., 50 W. 44 St., New York, NY 10036 (T & C)

Scientific American. 415 Madison Ave., New York, NY 10017 (Monthly) (T)

APPENDIX H

PROFESSIONAL SOCIETIES FOR SCIENCE TEACHERS AND SUPERVISORS

American Association for the Advancement of Science
1333 H St. NW
Washington, DC 20005

American Association of Physics Teachers
5112 Berwyn Rd.
College Park, MD 20740

American Chemical Society
Chemical Education Division
1155 Sixteenth St. NW
Washington, DC 20036

Association for Supervision and Curriculum Development
1250 North Pitt St.
Alexandria, VA 22314

Council for Elementary Science International
1840 Wilson Blvd.
Arlington, VA 22201

National Association of Biology Teachers
11250 Roger Bacon Dr., No. 19
Reston, VA 22090

National Association for Research in Science Teaching
(No permanent headquarters.)

National Association of Geology Teachers
(No permanent headquarters.
Current officers listed in *Journal of Geological Education*.)

National Science Teachers Association
1840 Wilson Blvd.
Arlington, VA 22201

MODEL FOR PROBLEM SOLVING (SAMPLE)

Steps	Focus Questions/Question Stems

Planning	1. What is the problem?
	2. What background information do I already have?
	   • What do I already know about . . . ?
	3. What new information do I need?
	4. What procedure or sequence of actions do I need to follow?
	   • How can I find what I need to know about . . . ?
	5. How will I know when I have solved the problem?

Obtaining Data	What information is needed? ▓ What are the properties of . . . ? ▓ What are the names of . . . ? ▓ What kinds of . . . ? ▓ How long, wide, big . . . is it? ▓ How much does it weight? ▓ What color is it? ▓ How hot is . . . ?
Organizing Data	In what useful way(s) can the information be organized? ▓ Which ones belong to this group? ▓ In what order do these . . . belong? ▓ What categories are there? ▓ How can this be graphed? ▓ What is the result of this . . . calculation?
Analyzing Data	What useful analyses can be made of the organized information? ▓ In what ways does . . . compare/contrast with . . . ? ▓ What seemed to be the effect of . . . ? ▓ What seemed to cause . . . ? ▓ What must have been the pattern (sequence) of events? ▓ What factors (variables) are involved? ▓ What assumptions were made?
Generalizing and/or Synthesizing from Data	What can be drawn from the analyses of information? ▓ How can I explain . . . ? ▓ How can I show I need to . . . ? ▓ What is the principle of . . . ? ▓ If this continues, then what is likely to happen? ▓ What can I predict? ▓ What might happen if I . . . ? ▓ What model shows what we know about . . . ? ▓ What new problems does this suggest? ▓ How does . . . apply to . . . ?
Decision Making	1. What decision needs to be made? 2. What are the alternative choices and the reasons for each? 3. What are the consequences of each alternative? 4. Who will be affected by each possible choice and in what way? 5. What values are directly related to each choice, and how do they relate to it? 6. Which choice is the best choice?

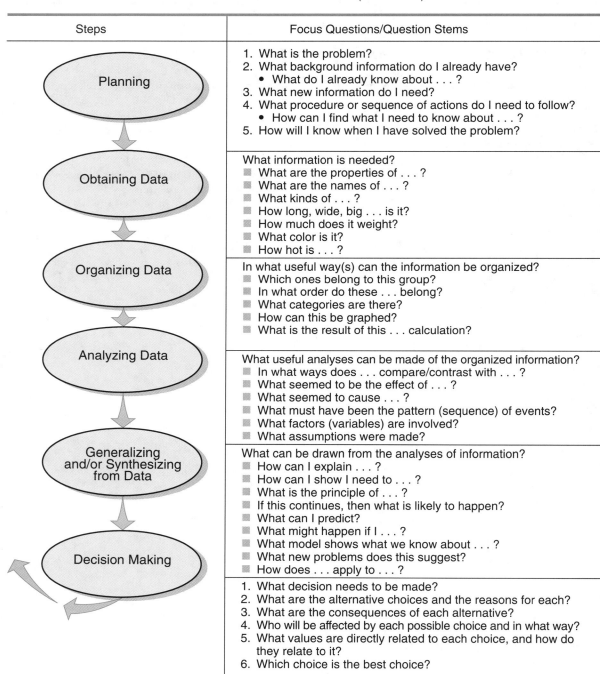

Source: Elementary Science Syllabus, 18–19. Reproduced with permission by The University of the State of New York. Copyright 1985 by The University of the State of New York, The State Education Department, Division of Program Development, Albany, NY 12234.

Skills	Products
■ Communicating information ■ Creating models ■ Formulating hypotheses ■ Manipulating ideas ■ Predicting ■ Questioning ■ Recording data ■ Using cues	1. A statement of the problem 2. List of facts (background information) 3. List of questions (related to later steps in the process) 4. Sequential plan (a list of tasks, student assignments, and times for completion) 5. Sketch or description of the expected (predicted) final product
■ Acquiring information ■ Developing vocabulary ■ Manipulating materials ■ Measuring ■ Observing ■ Recording data ■ Using cues ■ Using numbers	■ Collections ■ Counts ■ Definitions ■ Lists ■ Photographs ■ Sketches ■ Tape recordings
■ Classifying ■ Communicating information ■ Creating models ■ Manipulating ideas ■ Manipulating materials ■ Replicating ■ Using numbers	■ Calculations or computations ■ Charts, tables ■ Diagrams, scale drawings ■ Graphs ■ Groups, categories of information ■ Outline ■ Sorted objects
■ Identifying variables ■ Inferring ■ Interpreting data ■ Manipulating ideas ■ Using cues	■ Description of a pattern or sequence ■ List of variables ■ Statements of cause and effect relationships ■ Statements of similarities and differences ■ Summary
■ Acquiring information ■ Communicating information ■ Creating models ■ Formulating hypotheses ■ Generalizing ■ Manipulating ideas ■ Predicting ■ Questioning	■ A model or simulation ■ A new hypothesis ■ A new prediction, problem, theory ■ Applications to new situations ■ Statements of principles ■ Statements which accept or reject hypotheses ■ Statements which confirm or do not confirm predictions ■ Written report
■ Acquiring information ■ Communicating information ■ Making decisions ■ Manipulating ideas ■ Questioning	1. Statement of the decision to be made 2. List of alternative choices, supported by reasons 3. List of consequences of each alternative 4. List of persons directly affected by each choice and the way each is affected 5. List of values related to each choice supported by statements of how the values relate 6. A personal choice, supported by defendable reasons for the choice

APPENDIX J

SAFETY SUGGESTIONS FOR HANDS-ON/MINDS-ON ACTIVITIES

1. Do not permit students to handle science supplies, chemicals, or equipment in the classroom until they have been given specific instructions in their use.

2. Instruct students to report immediately to the teacher
   - any equipment in the classroom that appears to be in an unusual or improper condition,
   - any chemical reactions that appear to be proceeding in an abnormal fashion,
   - any personal injury or damage to clothing caused by a science activity, no matter how trivial it may appear.

3. Prevent loose clothing and hair from coming into contact with any science supplies, chemicals, equipment, or sources of heat or flame.

4. Do not allow science materials, such as chemicals, to be transported through hallways by unsupervised students or during a time when other students are moving through the hallways.

5. Instruct students in the proper use of sharp instruments, such as pins, knives, and scissors, before they use such objects.

6. Instruct students never to touch, taste, or inhale unknown chemicals.

7. Instruct students never to pour chemicals (reagents) back into stock bottles, and never to exchange stoppers or caps on bottles.

8. Warn students of the dangers in handling hot glassware or other equipment. Be sure proper devices for handling hot objects are available.

9. Check electrical wiring on science equipment for frayed insulation, exposed wires, and loose connections.

10. Instruct students in the proper use of eye-protection devices before they do activities in which there is a potential risk to eye safety.

11. Give appropriate, specific safety instructions prior to conducting any activity in which there is a potential risk to student safety, and provide appropriate reminders during the activity.

12. Instruct students in the location and use of specialized safety equipment, such as fire extinguishers, fire blankets, or eye baths, when that equipment might be required by the science activity.

13. Instruct students in the proper care and handling of classroom pets, fish, plants, or other live organisms used as part of science activities.

14. Have sufficient lighting to ensure that activities can be conducted safely.

15. For students with handicapping conditions or special needs, ensure safe access to the facility, equipment, and materials. Consider:
    - access to laboratories and equipment, placement of chemicals, distances required for reaching, and height and arrangement of tables.
    - physical accessibility to equipment needed in cases of emergency.

16. Provide practice sessions for safety procedures.

Source: Elementary Science Syllabus, 49. Reproduced with permission by The University of the State of New York. Copyright 1985 by The University of the State of New York, The State Education Department, Division of Program Development, Albany, NY 12234.

Note: Additional information may be found in *Preventing Child Exposures to Environmental Hazards: Research and Policy Issues—Symposium Summary,* National Symposium of the Children's Environmental Health Network (5900 Hollis St., Suite E, Emeryville, CA 94608), March 18–19, 1994, Washington, DC.

APPENDIX K

CONSTRUCTING STORAGE AREAS FOR SUPPLIES AND HOUSES FOR LIVING THINGS

Your classroom has unused space that can be used for storage, such as spaces below window ledges, countertops, sinks, above and around heating units (radiators), and even under student desks.

You can purchase excellent commercially made cabinets that fit any of these spaces, or your students and/or your custodian and you can construct them. With some creativity, you and your students can arrange these cabinets in a variety of ways.

Small Items Storage

With a guided discovery activities science program, you will constantly need to store many small items. Shoe, corrugated cardboard, cigar, and other small boxes provide space for collecting, organizing, and storing small, readily available materials for particular science areas. The following diagrams illustrate how to

construct and store shoe boxes for small science items. Cardboard or clear plastic shoe boxes may be used. You may also use large cardboard boxes for storage, placing them in easily obtained wood or steel shelving units especially designed for this purpose. Your custodian can help with this.

SHOE BOX COLLECTION

STORAGE OF SHOE BOX COLLECTIONS

a. Insect cage with wire screening   b. Insect containers with windows

Living Things Storage

Encourage your students to bring small animals (including insects) and plants into your classroom. To be well prepared, have the following kinds of containers available:

- Insect cages
- Small animal cages
- Aquariums
- Terrariums

Insect Cages.[3] Use small cake pans, coffee can lids, or covers from ice cream cartons for the cage cover and base. Roll wire screening into a cylinder to fit the base and then lace the screening together with a strand of wire.

You can cut windows in a paper coffee container, oatmeal box, or another suitable cardboard or styrofoam container. Cut out the window and glue clear plastic wrap, cellophane, silk, a nylon stocking, or some other thin fabric over the opening as shown.

Another home for insects such as ants that live in the soil can be made by filling a wide-mouthed quart or gallon pickle or mayonnaise jar with soil up to 2 inches from the top. Cover the jar with a nylon stock-ing and place it in a pan of water. Put the insects in and cover the jar with black construction paper to simulate the darkness of being underground.

Small Animal Cages. You can also use some of the insect cages for other small animals. Larger animals can be housed in cages that you and your students construct from window screening. Cut and fold the screening as shown in the diagram. Use nylon screening or be very careful of the sharp edges of wire screening. Tack or staple three sides of the screening to a wooden base and hook the other side for a door.

For housing *nongnawing* animals, you will need a wooden box and sleeping materials such as wood shavings. *Gnawing* animals need a wire cage. A bottle with a one-hole stopper and tubing hung on the side of the cage will supply water. Before proceeding, consult publications such as *Science and Children* and read some of the articles on the care and maintenance of various animals.

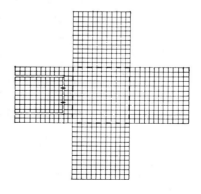

---

[3]For additional information about insects in the classroom, see: Laurel D. Hansen, Roger D. Akre, and Elizabeth A. Myhre, "Homes Away From Home: Observe Insects Indoors With These Creature Containers," *Science and Children* 31, no. 1 (September 1993), 28–31; Rebecca Olien, "Worm Your Way Into Science—Experiments With These Familiar Creatures Promote a Better Understanding of the Natural World," *Science and Children* 31, no. 1 (September 1993), 25–27.

Terrariums. The word *terrarium* means "little world." In setting up a terrarium for any animal, you should try to duplicate in miniature the environment in which the animal originally lived. You can make a terrarium with five pieces of glass (four sides and bottom) taped together. The top should be made of glass as well, but should have a section cut out to allow for access to the terrarium. Place the finished glass terrarium in a large cookie or cake pan. Commercially made terrariums are also available.

Another simple terrarium can be made from a two-liter, plastic soda pop bottle, charcoal, pebbles, topsoil, small plants, and scissors (see the diagram).

Suggestions for caring for plants and animals and for setting up different kinds of terrariums can be obtained from

- Biological Supply House, Inc., 8200 South Hoyne Avenue, Chicago, IL 60620. Free by writing on school stationary for Turtox Service Leaflets, especially: No. 10—*The School Terrarium* and No. 25—*Feeding Aquarium and Terrarium Animals.*
- NSTA Publications, 1840 Wilson Blvd., Arlington, VA 22201. Send $1.50 for How to Do It Pamphlets, especially: *How to Care for Living Things in the Classroom,* by Grace K. Pratt (Stock No. PB 38/4).

Soak the bottle in warm water to remove labels and glue. Carefully pry the bottom (a) from the bottle (b) so the bottom remains intact. Turn the bottle on its side. Rub your hand over it to find the ridge. With scissors, make a slit about 1.5 cm above the ridge. Cut all the way around the bottle at that level, staying above the ridge. Discard the top of the bottle and the cap.

Put layers of charcoal, pebbles, and topsoil into part a. Select and arrange the plants in the soil. You can add moss, bark, or small ornaments to your terrarium. Moisten, but do not saturate, the soil. Invert bottle (b) upside down into a. Push down gently to seal. Your terrarium is ready!

Constucting a soda pop bottle terrarium

Source: Virginia Gilmore, "Helpful Hints—Coca-Cola® Bottle Terrarium." Reproduced with permission by *Science and Children* 16, no. 7 (April 1979): 47. Copyright 1979 by the National Science Teachers Association, 1840 Wilson Blvd., Arlington, VA 22201.

Computer and Multimedia Telecommunications Glossary

For those with little or no experience with computers or telecommunications, here is a beginner's list of common terms and definitions.

address   A number or name that tells where to find a place in a computer's memory.

authoring language   A computer program that helps a person write lessons or other programs for a computer.

backup   A copy of important computer data. The reason for backing up your data is so that you can retrieve important information in case something goes awry with your machine, like a hard drive failure or a virus attack.

BASIC   Stands for *B*eginners *A*ll-Purpose *S*ymbolic *I*nstruction *C*ode, which is an easily learned language that all microcomputers use.

baud rate   The speed at which telecommunicated data are transmitted, measured in bits per second. Common baud rates are 300 and 1200.

binary code   A code for writing information for a computer using 1s and 0s to stand for numbers and letters.

bit   Stands for *bi*nary digi*t*, the basic unit for computer memory. Each bit has a value of 0 or 1, or "off" or "on."

boot   The start-up program used when the computer is turned on and referred to in the phrase "boot the disk."

bug   A mistake in a computer program or a problem with the hardware. To get rid of a "bug," you "debug" the program.

bulletin board system   A computerized system on which messages are left for others to read; BBS for short.

byte   A group of bits: one bye is eight bits. It takes one byte to store each unit of information. For instance, the word *love* requires four bytes.

CAI   Teaching by computer, or *c*omputer-*a*ssisted (aided) *i*nstruction.

cathode ray tube (CRT)   A technical name for the computer's monitor, the screen that visually shows its stored electronic data.

CD–ROM   Stands for *c*ompact *d*isk–*r*ead *o*nly *mem*ory. A disk with information recorded on its surface. You can read or copy the information, but you can't change or erase it.

central processing unit (CPU)   The heart of the computer dealing with information.

chip   A very tiny piece of silicon that carries many electrical signals.

COBOL   Stands for *CO*mmon *B*usiness *O*riented *L*anguage and is a computer language used mostly for business applications.

communication satellite   A satellite used to facilitate telecommunications.

CPU   Stands for *c*entral *p*rocessing *u*nit. The "computing" part of the computer responsible for the control and execution of instructions and the performance of mathematical operations and comparisons.

cyberspace   The "place" you feel you are in when you enter, communicate through, and travel over computer networks.

dedicated phone line   A telephone line used only for modern telecommunications in order to eliminate the possibility of interruption, which can garble the transmission.

diskette Also called a floppy diskette, this is a removable method of storing computer data. Diskettes are thin, square-shaped objects that come in two sizes—5.25-inch and 3.5-inch. The 5.25-inch diskettes are flexible. The 3.5-inch diskettes are rigid.

download To transfer information (files) from one computer to another.

electronic mail Personal messages sent electronically and called E-mail for short. To send or receive a message requires an I.D. number and password.

hard disk drive A data storage device for PCs that consists of a rigid platter that is fixed inside a sealed casing. A hard disk can store more information and retrieve data faster than a diskette.

hardware Physical equipment that makes up a computer system.

icon A picture on the display screen that represents a disk, a document, a software program, or a computer function. Selecting the pictures replaces the need to type a command. For example, to start or change a document, the user can select the picture representing the document instead of typing the command.

information utility A company from which you can access information via computer. Examples are CompuServe and THE SOURCE.

Internet A loosely knit, international network of computers (*Inter* from international, *net* from network).

K An abbreviation for kilo, which means 1,000, and is the unit of computer memory. 64K of memory equals 64,000 bytes. The larger the K your computer has, the more memory or amount of data it can store.

keyboard Similar to a typewriter keyboard and used to type information into a computer.

log-in To sign in on a computer.

LOGO A computer language used widely in education. It includes a graphic system called "turtle graphics." LOGO is a very interactive language.

MB An abbreviation for megabyte, a unit of measurement of computer memory or storage equivalent to approximately one million (1,048,576) bytes.

menu A display shown on the monitor or TV screen that gives a list of options—like a table of contents in a book.

menu-driven software Software that is used in a GUI (graphical user interface) environment. Menu-driven software gives you a menu with commands that you can select by highlighting using a mouse or the arrow keys.

MHz An abbreviation for megahertz, a unit used to measure a computer system's speed. One megahertz is equivalent to one million cycles per second. If two computers have the same central processing unit, but different megahertz, the one with the higher megahertz will run faster.

microprocessor An integrated circuit containing all the central processing functions of a computer; also called a CPU.

modem Stands for *mo*dulator-*dem*odulator. This is a hardware unit that allows a computer to transmit or receive data over a telephone line. The modem may be external or internal to the computer.

monitor A display screen used to view what is being typed into the computer, such as a document or a series of commands.

motherboard The printed circuit board that is the foundation of a PC system. This board contains the computer's CPU (central processing unit), RAM (random-access memory) chips, and expansion slots that enable you to add more functions to your PC.

MPC Stands for *m*ultimedia *PC*. A specification developed by Tandy and Microsoft for the minimum platform capable of running multimedia software. PCs carrying the MPC logo (the rainbow-colored letters MPC on a black background) are able to run any software also carrying the logo.

multimedia The presentation of information on a computer using a combination of sound, graphics, animation, and video.

network A group of computers and associated devices that are connected by communications facilities. Small or large, a computer network exists to provide computer users with a means of communicating and transferring data electronically.

on-line Being electronically connected to another computer.

output The information a computer sends out. To see this information, an output device is needed, such as a monitor or printer.

PASCAL A high-level computer language named for the French mathematician Blaise Pascal.

PCMCIA Stands for *P*ersonal *C*omputer *M*emory *C*ard *I*nternational *A*ssociation, a nonprofit trade organization with more than 200 members, including Intel, Microsoft, and Toshiba. The members set standards for removable credit-card-sized storage media (PCMCIA cards) that have one or more integrated circuits.

peripheral Any piece of equipment connected to a computer, such as a monitor, modem, or printer.

PILOT Stands for *P*rogrammed *I*nquiry *L*earning *O*n *T*eaching and is an easy language used primarily by educators to create CAI programs.

PIM Stands for *p*ersonal *i*nformation *m*anager. This is software that keeps track of personal information like names, phone numbers, addresses, to-do lists, and notes. Most PIMs have several search methods to make finding data easier.

printout A paper copy of electronically stored information from a computer produced by a computer-connected printer. Often called "hard copy."

program A set of instructions that tells the computer what to do and how to do it. See the many programming languages listed in this glossary.

RAM Stands for *r*andom *a*ccess *m*emory. While the computer is on, it stores information for a short period of time.

ROM Stands for *r*ead *o*nly *m*emory. This information can be "read" only by the computer, cannot be changed, and is not erased when the machine is turned off.

software The programs and data used to control the computer. Programmers write software for microcomputers.

telecommunications The transmission of signals from one computer to another over long distances using telephone lines, microwaves, and/or satellites.

teleconferencing A number of computer users can link up and hold a conversation, just like a "conference call" by telephone.

upload To transfer information (files) from your computer to another.

VGA Stands for *v*ideo *g*raphics *a*rray. Refers to a monitor with high-resolution capabilities, allowing it to display a clearer picture on the screen.

word processing A way of making written communication more creative by allowing the user to change words, rearrange paragraphs, correct spelling and grammar, and perform other editing functions. When writing is completed electronically, hard copies are secured from the computer-attached printer.

Piagetian Glossary

abstraction Mental activity or feedback involving the performing of operations.

accommodation The modification or fabrication of schemata (mental structures that adapt and change with cognitive development). The application of an existing structure to a new situation in the environment.

adaptation A cognitive, continuous process consisting of assimilation and accommodation.

affectivity Behavior involving feelings, interest, values, attitudes, maturation.

assimilation The process of integrating new perceptual stimuli into behavioral patterns or schemata.

associativity The process of putting together elements in different ways to get the same result, or the process of reaching the same goal by different paths.

centration The tendency of an organism to focus only on one part of a stimulus; for example, on the length of a candy bar rather than the length and width together.

cognitive process Mental process, involving reasoning, perceiving, memorizing, imagining, abstracting, and so on.

concrete operation A stage of mental development involving the individual's performing such logical operations as adding, subtracting, seriating, classifying, numbering, and reversing.

conservation The realization that changing an object physically—for example, by shape, length, direction, or position—does not alter the amount present.

egocentricity The tendency of an individual to perceive others as though they have his identical schemata or believe that the way he sees something is the only way it can be interpreted.

epistemology The branch of philosophy concerned with the nature of knowledge. To Piaget, it was open to psychological investigation; he asked, What knowledge or mental operations are learned before others, or What is the sequence of mental abilities?

equilibration The regulating process by which the individual continuously changes and develops.

formal operation A stage of mental development involving an individual's performing hypothetical, propositional, and reflexive thinking.

identity The operation of comparing, contrasting, or giving an example of a concept. The mind compares two sets (one-to-one correspondence) to see if they are equal.

intelligence All the mental processes and coordinations of these that structure the behavior of the individual. To Piaget, intelligence was not fixed; it grew.

internalization The process of making symbols, language, memories, and images a part of the mind.

intuitive A tendency to make judgments without using the mind to reason about them.

knowledge All that has been perceived and grasped by the mind.

learning The process of assimilating or accommodating.

measurement The ability to number, order, or perform seriation.

memory The act of using mental images to reconstitute the past through recognition, evocation, etc. It differs from perception by not being dependent upon the present and from intelligence by not being concerned with solving problems.

object permanence The realization that an object continues to exist when not present in the perceptual field.

operation A mental action such as multiplying, combining, classifying, and so on. It can be reversible.

ordering, or seriating Placing objects in order in a series.

perception The process of being aware of something through the senses.

preoperational A stage after the sensorimotor, but prior to the concrete-operational period, in which children learn symbols, names, and language but cannot yet perform operations.

reversibility The process of reversing a mental operation.

sensorimotor The first stage of mental development in which the knowledge the child learns is related to sensory inputs and her motor or muscular responses.

stages A period of development or intelligence characterized by certain general mental structures.

structure Mental organization or coordination in systematizing information. It may involve the interrelating parts or schemata.

transformation The process of something constantly changing in appearance.

transitivity The process of being able to perform the following type of mental operation: A>B, B>C, therefore A>C.

INDEX

AAAS (American Association for the Advancement of Science), 22, 27, 54, 194

AAAS Project 2061, 27, 54

AAMD (American Association on Mental Deficiency), 297

A+ America, 328

Abstract learning, 51–52

Accommodation process, 42–43

Accretion process, 42

Activities for Integrating Math and Science Project (AIMS), 211

Activity cards, 282–283

ADA (Americans with Disabilities Act), 284

Advance mental organizers, 69

Advance organizers, 47, 67–68, 69

Ag in the Classroom, 205

AIMS (Activities for Integrating Math and Science Project), 211

Aims for classroom planning, 171–172

Allen, T. E., 79

Alphabet books, 252, 253

Alternative assessment, 122–123. *See also* Authentic assessment

Ambiguity, accepting, 14

American Association for the Advancement of Science (AAAS), 22, 27, 54, 194

American Association on Mental Deficiency (AAMD), 297

American Printing House for the Blind, 291

Americans with Disabilities Act (ADA), 284

Amidon, Edmund, 79

Analytic scoring, 156

Analytic skills, 20, 31

Anderson, Bill, 3

Anderson, Charles, 44, 181

Anecdotal records, 153

Animals in classroom, 190–191

Anonymous FTP, 334

Antarctic Mystery, An (Verne), 236

Anthropomorphic responses, 20–21

ARCHIE (Internet tool), 334–335

Architectural barriers, 295

Art
  for authentic assessment, 149–150
  integrating with science, 257–258

Asimov, Isaac, 127, 138, 236

Assessment, 54–55, 121–122. *See also* Authentic assessment
  alternative approaches, 122–123
  assessment data for communication with public, 127
  broad approaches, 125
  defined, 124
  diagnostic assessment, 125, 126–127
  versus evaluation, 124–125
  formative assessment, 125
  versus measurement, 124–125
  performance assessment, 123
  process, 122–127
  purpose, 122
  Q/L strategies, 100–104
  special needs students, 274
  summative assessment, 125

Assimilation process, 42

At-risk students, 307–308. *See also* Culturally diverse students; Special needs students

Attention skills, 47

Auditory learning, 51, 63

Ausubel, David, 47, 52, 53, 63, 67–68

Authentic assessment, 123–124. *See also* Rubrics
  anecdotal records, 153
  applications, 161–162
  artwork, 149–150
  checklists, 140–141, 154
  communication assessment, 147
  concept mapping, 132–133
  constructivist learning cycle and, 128–129
  cooperative group performance, 152–153
  creative drama, 148–149

data capture assessment, 133

demonstrations by students, 150

discovery/interpretation stage, 141–145

discrepant events, 130–131

essay tests, 141–144

explanations/solutions stage, 145–147

exploration stage, 133–141

graphing from data, 144–145

guidelines, 127

hands-on practical assessment, 133–137

invitation stage, 129–133

materials for students, 131–132

model building, 150

multiple-choice tests, 145–146

observation checklist for scientific processes, 140–141

observation journals, 137–140

pictorial interpretations, 141

planning skills, assessing, 146–147

portfolios, 151–152

principles, 128

product creation, 149

story applications, 148

Autonomy, encouraging, 185–187

Baker, Linda, 48

Bar graphs, 264–265

Barman, Charles R., 72

Basketball pattern discussions, 99

Behavioral disorders, 303–304

Behaviorism, 39–41

Behavior modification, 305–306

Benchmarks for Science Literacy, 22

Biographies of scientists, 281

Biological Sciences Curriculum Study (BSCS), 209, 211, 297–298

Biological Supply House, 190

Bird Anatomy, 323

Blind students, 287–292

Bloom, Benjamin, 52, 69–70, 321

Bodyscope program, 321

Books
  alphabet books, 252, 253
  children's literature, 249–250
  fiction tradebooks, 250–252
  minibooks, 252
  student-written tradebooks, 252–253
  teacher/student made science books, 252
  textbooks, 245–248
Boyle, R. A., 45
Braille, 290
Brandi, Rosemary, 3
Brandwein, Paul W., 26
Britain, L., 46, 97
Bruner, Jerome, 53, 76, 77
BSCS (Biological Sciences Curriculum Study), 209, 211, 297–298
Bulletin boards, 245, 280–281
Bybee, Rodger W., 207

CAI. *See* Computer-assisted instruction
California Learning Assessment System (CLAS), 121
California State Department of Education, 54
Cargo for Conservation, 205
Carson, Rachel, 97
CD–ROMs, 323–324, 328–330
Center for Multisensory Learning, 290
Central processing unit (CPU), 318
Cerebral learning modality, 51
Chaille, C., 46, 97
Challenge cards, 275–276
Champagne, Audrey B., 41
Charney, Ruth S., 82
Charts and graphs, 264–267
Checklists, for authentic assessment, 140–141, 154
Children's literature, integrating with science, 249–250
Chips, in computers, 318
Cider Mill School, 256
CLAS (California Learning Assessment System), 121
Classification skills, 10
Classroom management, 169–170, 187, 194–197
  for computers, 336–338
  discipline problems, 196–197, 199
  first-aid approaches, 196–197
  long-term approaches, 197
  preventing problems, 195–196
  reinforcement techniques, 199

techniques for, 197–199
  work rules and directions, 199
Classroom organization, 187–194
  animals in classroom, 190–191
  for computers, 336–338
  learning centers, 191–193
  learning environment, 188–194
  outdoors science learning, 193–194
  plants in classroom, 190
  scheduling science time, 187–188
  science activity area, 188–189
  special needs students, 304–305
  storage area, 190
Classroom planning
  aims for, 171–172
  constructivist levels of, 170–180
  goals, 172–180
  interdisciplinary thematic units, 172–180
  objectives, 177–179
CLM (Constructivist Learning Model), 73–74
Closed questions, 101, 102, 111–114
Cloze procedure, 246
Cognitivism, 17, 38, 39–41
  developing skills with math/science education, 261
  indirect instruction and, 71–72
  research on classroom applications, 50–57
  stages of development, 39, 40
Cole, Joanna, 235
Commercial science programs, 209–215
Communication assessment, 147
Community surveys, student-conducted, 276
Comparative organizers, 69
Computer-assisted instruction (CAI), 320–323
Computer Learning Foundation, 328
Computer literacy, 317, 320, 329
Computer programming, 318
Computers, 316–317. *See also* Computer-assisted instruction (CAI)
  central processing unit (CPU), 318
  chips, 318
  classroom arrangement/management, 336–338
  components, 318
  courseware, 339
  getting started, 335–336
  hardware, 318, 335–336

laptops, 317
  learning stations, 338–339
  mainframes, 316
  microcomputer-based laboratory, 323
  microcomputers, 316–317
  minicomputers, 316
  as objects of instruction, 318
  programming, 318
  RAM (random access memory), 318
  ROM (read only memory), 318
  science teaching/learning and, 318–326
  software, 318, 339
Concept application, 73
Concept introduction, 73
Concept mapping, 47, 132–133
Concepts, scientific, 18
Concept webs, 47, 132–133
Concrete-to-abstract thinking, 51–52
Conduct disorders, 304, 305–307
Conservation of energy law, 19
Constructivism, 17, 46, 53
  classroom planning and, 170–180
  developmentally appropriate science activities, 49–50
  indirect learning models, 73–74
  learning cycle and authentic assessment, 128–129
Constructivist Learning Model (CLM), 73–74
Constructivist-Oriented Instructional Model to Guide Learning, 73–74
Content Core, The, 22
Controlled experiments, 13–14
Controlled variables, 13
Convergent questions, 101, 102, 111–114, 131
Converse, Ronald E., 190
Cooperation, 14, 16
Cooperative group performance, 152–153
Cooperative learning, 16, 109
Council for Exceptional Children, 287
Courseware, 339
CPU (central processing unit), 318
Creative drama, 148–149
Creative writing, integrating with science, 253–254
Creativity, defined, 253
Cross, Burnett, 16
Cross-age tutoring, 278

Culturally diverse students, 307–310.
    See also Special needs students
    adapting science teaching, 310
    at-risk students, 307–308
    benefits of hands-on/minds-on
        science, 308
    limited-English-proficient (LEP)
        students, 308–310
    NSTA multicultural position
        paper, 307
    Q/L strategies, 108, 112–113, 114
Curcio, Frances, 266
Curiosity, 14, 15, 21, 24
Curriculum, integrating science. *See*
    Integration

Dance, 258–259
Data
    analyzing, 31
    gathering, 31
    generalizing, 31
    interpretation skills, 11
    organizing, 31
    qualified, 154
    quantified, 154
    recording skills, 10
    synthesizing, 31
Databases, 335
Data capture assessment, 133
Deaf students, 292–294
DeBono, Edward, 253
Decision-making skills, 11, 27, 323
Declarative knowledge, 46
Demonstrations by students, 150
Dependent variables, 13
Descriptions, 20
Descriptive, Empirical-Inductive, and
    Hypothetical-Deductive
    Models, 73
Developmentally appropriate science
    activities, 49–50
Developmentally handicapped (DH)
    students. *See* Special needs
    students
Developmental stages, 39, 40
Dewey, John, 50, 77
DH (developmentally handicapped)
    students. *See* Special needs
    students
Diagnostic assessment, 125, 126–127
Dictionaries, 137–138
Directed discovery learning
    centers, 191
Direct instruction, 40, 63–70
    advance organizers, 67–68, 69

benefits, 70
components, 68–69
effective use of, 65–67
mastery learning, 69–70
principles, 66, 69
teaching functions, 68–69
Directories of Federal Resources,
    205–206
Discipline problems, 196–197, 199.
    See also Conduct disorders
Discovery, 73, 77–78
Discrepant events, 130–131
Discrimination process, 43
Discussion groups, electronic, 334
Discussions
    improving with cooperative
        learning, 109
    panel discussions, 281
    Q/L strategies, 98–99
Disequilization, 41–42
Divergent questions, 101, 102–104,
    111–114, 131, 183–184
Domains of sciencing, 24, 25
Dommers, John J., 190
Drama, 148–149
Drill-and-practice activities, 321
Dunn, Kenneth, 51
Dunn, Rita, 51

Edison, Thomas Alva, 16
Ehrlich, Paul, 16
Einstein, Albert, 19
Eisenhower National Clearinghouse
    for Mathematics and Science
    Education (ENC), 205, 316
Electronic address, 334
Electronic networking, 332–335
Elementary Science Study (ESS),
    211, 298
E-mail, 334
Emotional/behavioral disorders,
    303–304
Empirical process, 8
ENC (Eisenhower National
    Clearinghouse for
    Mathematics and Science
    Education), 205, 316
Encoding process, 48
Energy conservation, law of, 19
Enrichment centers, 275–276
Equilibration, 39
ERIC Clearinghouse on Disabilities
    and Gifted Education, 287
ESS (Elementary Science Study),
    211, 298

Essay tests, 141–144
Evaluation, versus assessment,
    124–125
Evidence, 14
Exceptionally talented students. *See*
    Gifted/talented students
Experience charts, 138–139
Explicit teaching. *See* Direct
    instruction
Exploration, 73. *See also* Indirect
    instruction
Exposition. *See* Direct instruction
Expository organizers, 69

Facilitating teaching style, 55–57
Facts, from tested observation, 17–18
Failure, positive approach to, 14–17
Fantastic Voyage (Asimov), 236
Felt boards, 244–245
Fiction tradebooks, 250–252
File transfer protocol (FTP), 334
Fish and Wildlife Service, U. S., 194
Flanders, Ned A., 79
Flannel boards, 244–245
Formative assessment, 125
FOSS (Full Option Science
    System), 212
Freado, Monica, 273
Fred Keller Plan, 69
Free discovery. *See* Indirect instruction
Frensch, P. A., 78
FTP (File Transfer Protocol), 334
Full Option Science System
    (FOSS), 212
Fundraising, 328–329
Funk, Wilfred John, 138

Gagné, Robert, 50, 51, 52, 53, 63
Gardner, Howard, 44
GEMS (Great Explorations in Math
    and Science), 212
Gender bias, in teaching science,
    61–62, 83
Generalizations, 13
Generalization skills, 11
General Learning Cycle Reference, 73
Gifted/talented students, 298–303
    broadening perspectives of, 300
    challenges for, 300
    defining, 299
    inclusion of, 301–302
    leadership qualities of, 301
    learning from and with, 299–300
    out-of-classroom opportunities, 302
    parents' roles, 300–301

resources for ideas, 303
teaching methods for, 302–303
Glaser, Robert, 77
Glass, Lynn W., 26
GLOBE Program, 205
Goals. *See also* Objectives
altering ready-made lessons,
179–180
for classroom planning, 172–180
organizing into interdisciplinary
thematic units, 173–176
for sciencing, 24
use in teaching, 172–173
GOALS (Group-Oriented Adapted
Levels System), 306
Goals 2000: Educate America Act, 23
Goodlad, John, 187
GOPHER (Internet tool), 335
Graphing assessment data, 144–145
Graphs, 264–267
Great Bay Living Lab, 206
Great Explorations in Math and
Science (GEMS), 212
Great Lakes Environmental Research
Laboratory, 206
Great Solar System Rescue, The, 315
Group cooperation, 14, 16
Group-Oriented Adapted Levels
System (GOALS), 306
Guided discovery. *See also* Hands-
on/minds-on approach; Indirect
instruction
encouraging autonomy, 185–187
less-structured activities, 184–187
open-ended questions and,
183–184
sample lesson, 180–182
science lessons, 180–184
writing lesson plans, 182–183

Halt-time, 108
Handicapped students. *See* Special
needs students
Hands-on/minds-on approach,
52–53, 63, 74–80. *See also*
Guided discovery
advantages, 76–78
applications for teaching, 80–83
benefits for culturally diverse
students, 308
facilitating teaching style, 55–57
heuristics of discovery, 77–78
importance of, 83–87
information processing, 47–49, 78
intellectual potency, 76–77

intrinsic motivation, 77
language learning, compared with,
238–241
lesson format, 84
less-structured activities, 85–87
lifelong learning, 78–80
metacognition, 48–49, 77–78
research on effectiveness, 79–80
special needs students, 284–287
textbooks for, 245–248
Hands-on practical assessment,
133–137
Hands-on Universe, 205
Hanley, Peg, 206
Hardware, 318, 335–336
Health education, integrating with
science, 260–261
Hearing impairments, 292–294
Heck, Karen, 273–274
Helper K–8, 324
Heritage Education Program, 206
Heuristics of discovery, 77–78
Histograms, 264
Holistic scoring, 156
Hornig, Leopold E., 41
Humane Society, 190
Humphrey, Hubert H., 230–231
Hunter, Madeline, 69
Hypotheses, 11, 13–14

IBM Corporation, 328
IDEA (Individuals with Disabilities
Education Act), 284–285
IEA (International Association for the
Evaluation of Educational
Achievement), 134
ILS (Integrated Learning System), 294
Improving Urban Elementary Science
(IUES), 212
Inclusion, 284. *See also* Special needs
students
effect on science teaching, 285
of gifted/talented students,
301–302
Independent variables, 13
Indiana Dunes National Lakeshore, 206
Indirect instruction, 63, 70–74
cognitive research and, 71–72
constructivist models, 73–74
learning cycles, 71–72
SCIS learning cycle, 72–73
STS and, 71–72
Individuals with Disabilities Education
Act (IDEA) (PL 94-142),
284–285

Inference, 9–12
Information processing, 47–49, 78
attention, 47
encoding, 48
metacognition, 48–49, 77–78
Innesbrook Wraps, 328
Inquiry skills. *See* Indirect instruction;
Processing skills
Instructional Theory into Practice
(ITIP), 69
Integrated Learning System (ILS),
294
Integration, 235–236
art and science, 257–258
creative writing and science,
253–254
defined, 236
hands-on/minds-on approach
compared with language
learning, 238–241
health and science, 260–261
listening skills and science,
238–240
mathematics and science, 261–267
music and science, 259–260
non-textbook science printed
matter, 248–254
nutrition and science, 260–261
physical activities and science,
258–259
reading and science, 240–245
social studies and science, 254–256
STS themes and, 236–238
textbook use, 245–248
Intellectual potency, 76–77
Interactive videodiscs, 326–330
Interdisciplinary science, defined, 236
Interdisciplinary thematic units,
172–180
International Association for the
Evaluation of Educational
Achievement (IEA), 134
International Science Fair, 205
International System of Measurement
(SI), 262–264
Internet, 332–335
Intrinsic motivation, 77
Invented words, 82, 242–245
Invention, 73
Investigation, 24
questions, 19–21
variables, 12–14
ITIP (Instructional Theory into
Practice), 69
ITW Hi-Cone, 328

IUES (Improving Urban Elementary Science), 212

Johnson, Rita, 69
Johnson, Stuart, 69
Jones, Ron, 169–170
Jordan, I. K., 292–293
Journals, 137–140
Jurassic Park, 236

Kaloko-Honokohau National Historical Park, 206
Karplus, Robert, 72–73
Keller, Fred, 69
Kellough, Richard, 69, 179, 245
Kelly, E. B., 247
Kenzie, Marie, 273–274
Kinesthetic learning, 63
Knowledge, 24, 46–49. *See also* Prior knowledge; Products of science
    acquiring new knowledge, 47–49
    concept mapping, 47, 132–133
    declarative knowledge, 46
    information processing, 47–49, 78
    logical-mathematical knowledge, 46
    meaningful verbal learning, 47, 53
    physical knowledge, 46
    procedural knowledge, 46
    social arbitrary knowledge, 46
    social knowledge, 63, 65–66
Krishnamurti, 110
Kunc, N., 287

Lab activities, in computer-assisted instruction, 323
LAN (local area network), 335
Language learning, compared with hands-on/minds-on approach, 238–241
Laptop computers, 317
Laser discs, 326–330
Lateral thinking, 253
Law of conservation of energy, 19
Lawrence Livermore National Laboratory, 206
Laws, 19
LCD projection systems, 331–332
Leadership qualities of gifted/talented students, 301
Learning
    abstract learning, 51–52
    auditory learning, 51, 63
    hierarchy of, 50, 51
    kinesthetic learning, 63
    lifelong learning, 6–8, 78–80

modalities of, 50–51
    Piaget, impact of, 38–39
    pseudolearning, 80
    reception learning, 47
    styles of, 51
    verbal learning, 47, 53
    visual learning, 51, 63
Learning centers, 191–193
Learning cycles, 71–72
    SCIS learning cycle, 72–73
Learning disabilities, 296–297
Learning environment, 188–194
Learning impairments, 297–298
Learning stations, 338–339
LEP (limited-English-proficient) students, 308–310
Lesson plans, 182–183, 187. *See also* Science lessons
Levels system for conduct disorders, 306
Lifelong learning, 6–8, 78–80
Limited-English-proficient (LEP) students, 308–310
Line plots, 264
Line-segment graphs, 265–266
Listening skills, 109–110. *See also* Questioning/listening (Q/L) strategies
    integrating with science, 238–240
Literature, integrating with science, 249–250
Local area network (LAN), 335
Local projects, 21–24
Logical-mathematical knowledge, 46
Logs, 139–140

Macmillan/McGraw-Hill science series, 221–227
Madrazo, Gerry M., Jr., 190
Magazines, student-created, 254
Magic School Bus Explores, The (Cole), 235–236, 322
Mahr, Karen, 110
Mainframe computers, 316
Mainstreaming. *See* Special needs students
Mallan, John T., 71
Manipulated variables, 13
Market Day Food Co-Operative, 328
Martin, Margery, 7, 19–20, 37
Marx, R. W., 45
Maslow, Abraham, 109
Mastery learning, 69–70
Materials manipulation skills, 10

Mathematics, integrating with science, 261–267
    cognitive skills development, 261
    examples, 267
    graphs, 264–267
    metric system, 262–264
    problem solving skills, 261–262
    research on, 261
MBL (microcomputer-based laboratory), 323
McCormack, Alan, 24, 275
McGlathery, Glenn, 254
Meaningful verbal learning, 47, 53
Measurable performance, 179
Measurement, versus assessment, 124–125
Measurement skills, 10
Mechling, Kenneth R., 7
Mental readiness, 74–75
Mental retardation, defined, 297. *See also* Special needs students
Messaging, 334
Metacognition, 48–49, 77–78
Metacomponential skills and processes, 78
Metric system, 262–264
Microcomputer-based laboratory (MBL), 323
Microcomputers, 316–317. *See also* Computers
Microsoft Corporation, 328
Minibooks, 252
Minicomputers, 316
Minority students. *See* Culturally diverse students
Model building skills, 150
Model creation skills, 11
Modeling, 322–323
Modems, 334
Moltz, LaMoine L., 190
Motivation, 77, 276
Multimedia technology, 315–316
    CD–ROMs, 323–324, 328–330
    classroom applications, 335–339
    combining resources, 324–326
    computers, 316–317
    defined, 316
    as delivery medium for science teaching/learning, 320–321
    interactive videodiscs, 326–330
    LCD projection systems, 331–332
    producing videotapes, 330–331
    telecommuting, 332–335
    whiteboarding with software, 332
Multiple-choice tests, 145–146

Music instruction, integrating with science, 259–260

NAEP (National Assessment of Educational Progress), 27
Naive theories and misconceptions, 37–38
  challenging, 45–46
  effects on teaching/learning, 44–46
  examples from children, 44–45
  versus scientific explanations, 44
NASA Educational Workshops for Elementary School Teachers, 205
National Academy of Sciences, 23
National Assessment of Educational Progress (NAEP), 27
National Center for Improving Science Education, 21, 54
National Center on Education and the Economy, 23
National Council for the Social Studies (NCSS), 255
National Diffusion Network (NDN), 205, 228–229
National Geographic Kids Network (NGKN), 212
National projects, 21–24
National Research Council of the National Academy of Sciences, 23
National Science Education Standards Project, 23, 171
National Science Teachers Association (NSTA), 22, 26, 54, 127, 206
  Position Statement on Multicultural Science Education, 307
  Scope, Sequence, and Coordination (SSC) Project, 54
NCSS (National Council for the Social Studies), 255
NDN (National Diffusion Network), 205, 228–229
Neale, Daniel, 181
Negative wait-time, 108
Networking, 332–335
Neurologically Oriented Model, 73
Newsgroups, 334
New Standards Project, 23
NGKN (National Geographic Kids Network), 212
Nonverbal questions, 97–98
Northwest Women in Science, 206
NSTA. *See* National Science Teachers Association
Number skills, 10

Nutrition education, integrating with science, 260–261

OBIS (Outdoor Biology Instructional Strategies), 210
Objectives. *See also* Goals
  behavioral/performance objectives for lessons, 179
  for classroom planning, 177–179
Observation, 8–9, 10
  building skills with CAI, 322–323
  checklist for scientific processes, 140–141
  components, 12
  facts resulting from, 17–18
Observation journals, 137–140
  record pages, 139
  science dictionaries, 137–138
  science experience charts, 138–139
  science logs, 139–140
Office of Educational Research and Improvement, 23
Olfactoral learning modality, 51
Oliver, Donna L., 7
Open-ended questions, 101, 102–104, 111–114, 131, 183–184
Open inquiry, 53
Open learning centers, 191
Operational definitions, 82–83, 243–245
Orthopedic impairments, 295–296
Outdoor Biology Instructional Strategies (OBIS), 210
Outdoors science learning, 193–194
Outstandingly talented students. *See* Gifted/talented students

Panaboard software, 332
Panel discussions, 281
Paraphrasing, 113
Parents, role with gifted/talented students, 300–301
Paulu, Nancy, 7, 19–20, 37
Performance assessment, 123
Peripherals, 323
Perkins, David, 78
Personal computers. *See* Computers; Microcomputers
Personal Construct Model, 73
Personalized System of Instruction (PSI), 69
PET (Program for Effective Teaching), 69
Philips, William C., 37
Phillips, Darrell, 83

Physical activities, integrating with science, 258–259
Physical knowledge, 46
Piaget, Jean, 6, 17, 38–39, 41–43, 53, 77, 80, 82
Piagetian theories, 38–39, 49–50
Pictorial interpretations, 141
Pictorial riddles, 282
Ping-pong pattern discussions, 98–99
Pintrich, P. R., 45
Planning. *See* Classroom planning
Planning skills, 31
  assessing, 146–147
Plants in classroom, 190
PL 94-142 (Individuals with Disabilities Education Act), 284–285
Plots, line, 264
Portfolio assessment, 151–152
Position Statement on Multicultural Science Education, 307
Positive approach to failure, 14–17
PQRST technique for studying, 247–248
Pratt, Grace K., 190
Predictions, 11, 37
Principles, 18
Prior knowledge, 12, 27
  expanding knowledge base, 42
  importance of, 41–44
  schemata, 9–12, 41–44
Probes, 106–107, 323
Problem-solving skills
  computer-assisted instruction and, 323
  math/science education and, 261–262
  model for, 27–28
  Q/L strategies, 104–107
Procedural knowledge, 46
Processing skills, 6–14
  inference, 9–12
  learning centers, 191
  lifelong learning skills, 6–8, 78–80
  observation checklist, 140–141
  questioning strategies, 104–106
  role of variables, 12–14
  scientific observation, 8–9
  table of skills, 10–11
Product creation, 149
Products of science, 17–19
  laws, 19
  scientific concepts, 18
  scientific facts, 17–18
  scientific principles, 18
  scientific theories, 18–19

Program for Effective Teaching
    (PET), 69
Programming computers, 318
Project RESEED (Retirees Enhancing
    Science Education through
    Experiments and
    Demonstrations), 3–4
Project 2061, 27, 54
Project WILD, 205
Proportional reasoning, 43
Pseudolearning, 80
PSI (Personalized System of
    Instruction), 69
Public Law 94-142, 284–285

Q/L strategies. See
    Questioning/listening strategies
Qualified data, 154
Qualitative questions, 183–184
Quality Circles (QCs), 16
Quantified data, 154
Quantitative metrical questions, 184
Questioning/listening (Q/L)
    strategies, 95–97
  assessing knowledge, 100–104
  basketball pattern, 99
  classroom applications, 110–114
  cooperative learning techniques, 109
  cultural differences, 108,
    112–113, 114
  discussions and, 98–99
  encouraging student questions, 100
  halt-time, 108
  improving teacher skills, 107–110
  for increasing students'
    interest, 107
  levels of questioning, 100–104
  listening skills, 109–110
  negative wait-time, 108
  nonverbal questions, 97–98
  nonverbal signals, 113
  paraphrasing, 113
  ping-pong pattern, 98–99
  probes, 106–107
  for problem-solving skills, 104–107
  processing skills and, 104–106
  purposes, 97–104
  recognizing achievement, 109
  returning questions to students, 98
  rewards, 108–109
  summarizing, 111–112
  teacher silent-time, 113
  teaching strategies, 100
  translation wait-time, 108
  wait-time, 107–108

Questions, 19–21
  closed questions, 101, 102,
    111–114
  convergent questions, 101, 102,
    111–114, 131
  divergent questions, 101, 102–104,
    111–114, 131, 183–184
  for investigation, 19–21
  levels of questioning, 100–104
  nonscientific answers, 20–21
  nonverbal questions, 97–98
  open-ended questions, 101,
    102–104, 111–114, 131,
    183–184
  qualitative questions, 183–184
  quantitative metrical questions, 184
  types, 20
Quickie Starters, 85–86

Rabi, Isidor I., 19–20
RAM (random access memory), 318
Rauch, Kristin, 252
Reading, integrating with science,
    240–245. See also Textbooks
Read only memory (ROM), 318
Reception learning, 47
Reform projects, 22–23, 210–212
  benefits, 218–220
  classroom applications, 228–231
  developed commercial programs,
    209–215
  Macmillan/McGraw-Hill science
    series, 221–227
  new generation science textbook
    series/packages, 220–227
  sample lesson, 215–218
  Science for Life and Living project,
    209–215
  science reforms, 207
  STS and, 218–220
  trends in, 207–209
Regular Education Initiative (REI),
    274–283
Reid, H. Kay, 254
Reif, Richard J., 252
Reinforcement techniques, 199
Reisman, David, 77
Remote log-in, 334
Renner, John, 261
Replication skills, 10
Research
  classroom applications of
    cognitivism, 50–57
  effectiveness of hands-on/minds-
    on approach, 79–80

indirect instruction and
    cognitivism, 71–72
  math/science integration, 261
Resources, 205–207, 278–279, 303
Responding variables, 13
Restructuring, 43
Rewards, 108–109
Riddles, pictorial, 282
Rogers, Howard, 16
ROM (read only memory), 318
Rosenshine, Barak, 52, 65, 68–69
Roth, Kathleen, 44–45
Rowe, Mary Budd, 80, 107–108, 261
Rubrics, 154–161
  authentic assessment categories, 156
  data storage and retrieval, 160–161
  defined, 154–155
  purpose, 156
  scoring performance levels,
    156–159
  standards for, 156
  writing rubrics, 155
Rutherford, James, 83

Salomon, Gavriel, 78
SAPA (Science—A Process Approach),
    50, 210
Sapelo Island National Estuarine
    Research Reserve, 206
SAVI/SELPH (Science Activities
    for the Visually Impaired/
    Science Enrichment Learning
    for the Physically
    Handicapped), 210, 290
Schemata, 9–12, 41–44
Science. See also Sciencing; STS
  defining, 4–5
  nature of, 24
  processes of, 6–14
  standards, 5
Science, Technology, and Health
    Model, 73
Science and Technology for Children
    (STC), 210
Science—A Process Approach (SAPA),
    50, 210
Science books, teacher/student
    made, 252
Science boxes, 279–280
Science Curriculum Improvement
    Study (SCIS), 210, 261
  learning cycle, 72–73
Science dictionaries, 137–138
Science education
  domains of, 24, 25

gender bias, 61–62, 83
local projects, 21–24
national projects, 21–24
state projects, 21–24
Science Education Programs That Work, 228–229
Science experience charts, 138–139
Science fair, 205
Science for All Americans, 22
Science for Children: Resources for Teachers, 228
Science for Kids, 325–326
Science for Life and Living project, 209–215
Science kits, 279
Science lessons, 180–184
  behavioral/performance objectives, 179
  format, 84
  lesson plans, 180, 182–183
  open-ended questions in, 183–184
  sample lesson, 180–182
  writing lesson plans, 182–183
Science Linkages in the Community (SLIC) Institute, 194
Science logs, 139–140
Science magazines, student-created, 254
Science processes. *See* Processing skills
Science reforms. *See* Reform projects
Sciencing, 5–6. *See also* Science
  aspirations for elementary/middle grades, 21
  attitudes toward, 14–17
  cycle of, 6–7
  domains of, 24, 25
  elements of, 6
  emphasis on STS, 24–32
  goals, 24
  values and, 14–17
Scientific concepts, 18
Scientific facts, 17–18. *See also* Naive theories and misconceptions
Scientific knowledge. *See* Products of science
Scientific literacy, 4–5
Scientific models, 18–19
Scientific observation, 8–9. *See also* Observation
Scientific principles, 18
Scientific products. *See* Products of science
Scientific theories, 18–19
SCIS. *See* Science Curriculum Improvement Study

Scope, Sequence, and Coordination (SSC) Project, 22, 54
Scoring guides. *See* Rubrics
"Search, Solve, Create, Share, and Act" model, 27–28
Second International Science Study (SISS), 134
Seed germination experiment, 13
Self-Instructional Package (SIP), 69
Semantic webs, 47, 132–133
Sensors, 323
Sex discrimination, in teaching science, 61–62, 83
Sheltered instruction, 309
Shuell, Thomas J., 42–43
SI (International System of Measurement), 262–264
Siegler, Robert S., 48
Simulation, 321–322
SIP (Self-Instructional Package), 69
SISS (Second International Science Study), 134
Skepticism, 14
SLIC (Science Linkages in the Community) Institute, 194
Small-group learning, 16, 109
Smith, Edward, 44
Social arbitrary knowledge, 46
Social knowledge, 63, 65–66
Social studies
  integrating with science, 254–256
  STS themes, 255–256
Society, nature of, 24. *See also* STS
SoftBoard software, 332
Software, 318, 339
  courseware, 339
  Panaboard, 332
  SoftBoard, 332
  for special needs students, 283
  tutorial software, 321
  whiteboarding with, 332
Special needs students, 273–274. *See also* Culturally diverse students; Gifted/talented students
  Americans with Disabilities Act (ADA), 284
  assessment, 274
  behavior management, 273–274
  categories of, 286
  classroom design, 304–305
  cognitive differences, 296–297
  community resources, 278–279
  conduct disorders, 304, 305–307
  cross-age tutoring, 278

emotional/behavioral disorders, 303–304
  friendships, importance of, 287
  general learning impairments, 297–298
  hands-on/minds-on approach for, 284–287
  hearing impairments, 292–294
  individualization, 274–275
  learning disabilities, 296–297
  modifying science learning, 287
  motivating students, 276
  organizing volunteers, 276–277
  orthopedic impairments, 295–296
  practical techniques for, 286–287
  Public Law 94-142, 284–285
  regular education initiative (REI), 274–283
  software for, 283
  teacher values and, 285
  teaching concepts to, 273
  television shows for, 279
  visual impairments, 287–292
  volunteers for, 276–277
SSC (Scope, Sequence, and Coordination) Project, 22, 54
State projects, 21–24
STC (Science and Technology for Children), 210
Sternberg, R. J., 78
Story applications, 148
Story-dances, 258–259
Strafford, Donald, 261
STS (science/technology/society), 24–32
  decision-making skills, 27
  emphasizing relevant problems, 26–27
  indirect learning and, 71–72
  integrating problem solving in content areas, 27–29
  integration and, 236–238
  problem solving/decision making/action taking sequence, 29–32
  problem-solving model, 27–28
  reform projects and, 218–220
  "Search, Solve, Create, Share, and Act" model, 27–28
  social studies themes, 255–256
  STS club and magazine, 283
Students
  collections and hobbies, 281–282
  learning styles, 51
  misconceptions of, 37–38

Summarizing strategy, 111–112
Summative assessment, 125
Surprise science boxes, 279–280

Tactical learning modality, 51
Talented students. *See* Gifted/talented students
Task cards, 282–283
Taxonomy, 24, 63, 64
Teacher dominance, 63
Teaching
    adapting for different needs, 287, 310
    applications for hands-on/minds-on approach, 80–83
    computers as delivery medium, 320–321
    direct instruction functions, 68–69
    encouraging students to discover science, 83
    gender bias and, 61–62, 83
    goals and, 172–173
    guided discovery, 80–82
    inclusion and, 285
    naive theories and, 44–46
    pace of instruction, 80
    Piaget, impact of, 38–39
    selecting topics for study, 53–54
    styles of, 55–57
    variation in activities, 52
Teaching methods, 62–63
    direct versus indirect, 62
    examples, 63
    gifted/talented students, 302–303
    taxonomy of, 63, 64
    teacher as coach, 62
    teacher dominance, 63
Technological literacy, 4–5

Technology. *See also* STS
    defining, 4–5
    nature of, 24
Telecommuting, 332–335
Teleological responses, 20–21
Teletypewriter (TTY), 294
TELNET command, 334
Terminal behavior, 179
Textbooks, 245–248
    classroom arrangement for science reading, 246
    determining reading level, 246
    individualizing assignments, 247–248
    PQRST technique for studying, 247–248
    reform projects, 220–227
Thematic studies, 236–238
Thematic units, interdisciplinary, 172–180
Theories, 18–19
Thier, Herbert, 72–73
Token economy system, 306–307
Tradebooks, 250–253
Traditional teaching style, 55–57
Transfer of training, 78
Translation wait-time, 108
Trust, Jerry, 193–194
TTY (teletypewriter), 294
Tuning, 42–43
Turtox Service Leaflets, 190
Tutorial software, 321
Tutoring, cross-age, 278

Userid, 334
USMES (Unified Sciences and Mathematics for Elementary School), 211

Values, and sciencing, 14–17
Van der Klift, E., 287
Variables, 12–14, 183
Variables identification skills, 11
Verbal learning, 47, 53
Verne, Jules, 236
VERONICA (Internet tool), 335
Videodiscs, 326–330
Videotapes, producing, 330–331
Visual displays, 243–245
    bulletin boards, 245, 280–281
    felt boards, 244–245
    flannel boards, 244–245
    writing boards, 244
Visual impairments, 287–292
Visual learning, 51, 63
Volunteers, organizing, 276–277
Vygotsky, Lev, 53

WAIS (Wide-Area Information System), 335
Wait-time, 107–108
Waves on the Great Lakes, 206
Welton, David A., 71
Whiteboarding with software, 332
Wide-Area Information System (WAIS), 335
Windows on Science, 211, 326
Wisnawski, Bill, 3
Wright, William C., 190
Writing boards, 244

Yager, Robert, 24, 87

Zahopoulos, Christos, 3–4